The Nazi Hydra in America

— • —

Suppressed History of a Century

Wall Street and the Rise of the Fourth Reich

by Glen Yeadon, with John Hawkins

Prog RESS ive

2008

The Nazi Hydra in America

Suppressed History of a Century

Wall Street and the Rise of the Fourth Reich

Published by Progressive Press,
P.O. Box 126, Joshua Tree, Calif. 92252,
www.ProgressivePress.com

Digital Advance Review Edition
Revision of August, 2008.
Printed by Lightning Source Inc. in USA
ISBN: 0-930852-44-3   EAN: 978-0-930852-44-3
Regular Offset Edition: ISBN 0-930852-43-5, EAN 978-0-930852-43-6

Library of Congress CIP Data applied for
Length: 300,000 words
First Printing: 2008

Classification: Nonfiction, Politics, History

Distribution, North America:
Baker & Taylor, Ingram, Disticor – Canada.
Overseas:
Gazelle – UK, New Horizons – South Africa, Woodslane – Australia.

Topic: Fascism in the United States and Germany –
a counter-revolution by the plutocracy
against constitutional democracy.

Prog*RESS*ive

Table of Contents

Introduction

"When fascism comes to America, it will come wrapped in an American flag," Huey Long, an assassinated American maverick politician of the 1930's, famously foretold. It arrived ceremoniously on the morning of September 11, 2001, when anonymous terrorists crashed four jetliners into New York's World Trade Center Towers, the Pentagon and a field in Pennsylvania. Three thousand perished in the flames as the nation watched the tragedy unfold in shock and horror. Predictably, Americans rallied around the flag and the Bush administration. America's new century had a new Pearl Harbor, and the media beat the war drums to the thunderous applause of flag-waving armchair patriots.

Within 45 days of the atrocity, Congress passed the ill-named Patriotic Act – without a single congressman reading the bill; the printing of the bill had been deliberately delayed by the Bush administration to ensure passage. Written largely by Attorney General John Ashcroft, it was a full-scale assault on our rights and freedoms. This act eliminated our rights to unwarranted searches, the right to legal counsel, the right to a trial. It greatly expanded the government's ability to spy on citizens without a warrant.

With the continued assault on our freedoms under the Bush administration, some authors have begun to point out the fascist character of this regime, and even the Bush family's past ties to the Nazis. It is true that Bush's grandfather Prescott was Hitler's American banker. Yet the United States was well along the path to fascism before the younger Bush was appointed president. The confusion stems as much from misplaced American pride in its freedoms as from ignorance about the nature of fascism.

Fascism is a marriage between corporations and the government. Upton Sinclair defined it as capitalism plus murder, an appropriate definition in light of the Bush war for oil in Iraq. Most people associate fascism with the rabid virulent police state of the Nazis and the accompanying Holocaust, and forget the less dramatic, more fundamental aspect, of how corporations control the government in a fascist state.

Since fascism is a top down revolution by a society's elite to gain total control over a capitalistic society, it doesn't require a revolution the streets – unlike socialism which is driven from the bottom up as the masses seek to eliminate the elite and regain control over their lives. Moreover, the virulent police state never comes first. Hitler, like Bush, was appointed to office. It took Adolf Hitler six years to consolidate his power before he could unleash his Panzer forces against Poland. Since 9/11, Bush has also had six years to consolidate his power, and is maneuvering to unleash America's military might against Iran.

For decades, the U.S. government has been edging towards fascism by placing the interests of corporations above the interest of the people. The second Bush regime accelerated this trend, and put in place the framework and machinery needed for a virulent police state. The three marks of a police state are already on display.

Federal and state police spy on and intimidate citizens.
Federal and state police serve the central government instead of serving the citizens.
Federal and state police enforce the policies of the central government instead of responding primarily to criminal misdeeds.

Evidence of each is abundant. In the first case, we even have Bush's word that he'll continue to spy on citizens without a court order, if the courts rule against him. Those counting on the Democratic majority in congress to moderate the virulence of the Bush regime need to look elsewhere for help; this congress just voted to expand Bush's illegal and unconstitutional spying on Americans.

The outing of Valerie Plame as a CIA agent demonstrates the vindictiveness of the Bush and his administration towards those who differ with him, as well as callous disregard for the law. Bush's candid remark that the constitution is just a damn piece of paper demonstrates a fascistic contempt for liberty and freedom. His verbal attack on the constitution is confirmed by his attempts to rule by decree, using unconstitutional "signing statements" to amend newly passed laws.

During his first term Bush issued over 100 such statements, raising over 500 constitutional challenges. Since these statements have no constitutional basis, they would likely be ruled unconstitutional; but leaving them to stand unchallenged lets them become law *de facto*. Instead of the eloquent prose of Thomas Jefferson or the witty remarks of Ben Franklin, we have the blithering ramblings of a draft-dodging dry drunk passing for law, bypassing the system of checks and balances the founding fathers wisely devised.

The Bush clique incessantly demands that Congress grant him the power to declare martial law, and inserts a $385 billion contract in the budget, for a Halliburton subsidiary to expand and update concentration camps, raising the specter of an imminent and apocalyptic threat to our freedoms. Can America avoid the headlong rush into a virulent fascist police state, or has the Bush regime pushed the country too far to avoid it?

In September 2006 Congress did pass the Defense Authorization Act, which allows the president to declare martial law with little or no reason. It is clear that the Bush administration and the Republican party goals are to criminalize any dissent. This is evident in various bills the Republicans have introduced in congress and state legislators that would hold protestors liable for any delay that may cause a corporation or individual. It is evident in the Bush administration vendetta against journalists that report the truth and their confidential sources. It is readily evident in the US fall from 17th to 53rd place in freedom of the press, as ranked by Journalists Without Borders.

Bush consolidated his power further on May 9, 2007 with the issuance of "National Security Presidential Directive/NSPD 51" and "Homeland Security Presidential Directive/HSPD-20." These orders outline Bush's plan for dealing with catastrophic emergencies. Bush grants himself the responsibility for ensuring "constitutional" government – the sole authority for the entire federal government, and not just the executive branch! The directives define a catastrophic emergency as any incident, regardless of location, that results in extraordinary levels of mass casualties, damage, or disruption severely affecting the U.S. population, infrastructure, environment, economy, or government function. With such a broad definition, another 9/11 style attack, a hurricane, an earthquake, a large wild fire, or a stock market crash could be classified as a catastrophic emergency and trigger martial law.

I've been sounding the warning about creeping fascism for over a decade now, often as the lone voice in the wilderness. Recent events make the warning more urgent. The construction of prison camps is accompanied by the Army's issuance of a new manual for using prison labor. Most serious are the warnings by figures like Paul Craig Roberts, a Assistant Secretary of the Treasury under President Reagan, that the Bush regime is up to another false flag operation. Roberts believes the Bush regime will concoct another 9/11-like domestic terrorist act as an excuse to invade Iran and declare martial law. This is indeed a very serious warning coming from a conservative Republican insider.

News reports have revealed that the Department of Homeland Security is training members of the clergy to urge their flock to obediently turn over their guns to the government, in line with Romans 13. Most recently, FBI translator and whistleblower Sibel Edmonds broke a federal gag order to report a neocon plot to leak materials for a nuclear device. This would lead to a nuclear 9/11 or Reichstag fire on American soil, to be blamed on Islamic countries, along the plot lines of the novel *The Shell Game*. All these reports indicate that the planning for a Hitlerian dictatorship has reached an advanced phase.

Shortly you may be faced with the hardest decision you ever make, will you try to defend yourself or will you quietly march off to the camps like the Jews. Hopefully you will not have to make that decision. Many things could intervene and render the plans for martial law obsolete. But one should be prepared for the worst.

Like the Nazis, the Bush regime has taken pains to pass laws permitting their criminal behavior. These laws are against all principles of justice, civilization, and morality. To debase the rule of law is a criminal act in itself.

The Nazi Hydra in America is a penetrating, provocative and controversial study of the roots of American fascism. From the days of the robber barons and the Reichstag fire to the 9/11 atrocity and the present tyranny of the George W. Bush regime, the *Nazi Hydra* outlines the footprint of global fascism cloaked in the banner of free trade.

While Eisenhower's troops defeated the Third Reich on the battlefields of Europe, the war against fascism was lost on the home front, to the same cadre of American elitists who built Adolf Hitler's war machine. At the center of this close-knit confederacy, two firms stand out: Brown Brothers Harriman, and Sullivan & Cromwell.

Starting after World War I and through post-World War II, *Hydra* systematically explores the intricate connections among the Nazis, corporate America and Wall Street — a confederation of traitors that armed Hitler, sabotaged America's war effort, avoided prosecution and triggered the Cold War.

Many readers will find the book disturbing. America's Right Wing will try to discredit it in an attempt to distance itself from its past support of the Nazis. Some will try dismissing the *Nazi Hydra* by labeling it a "conspiracy theory." However, the names, dates, places and events examined in this book are indisputable. The conspiracy fact is how American fascists, with the complicity of the media, have kept this secret history hidden from the public.

For instance, most Americans are unaware of the coup attempt to remove President Franklin D. Roosevelt, and the opposition he faced from Nazi supporters in Congress and other branches of government. Following the failed coup led by the duPonts, Morgans and other leading American industrialists, the native fascists began to work inside the political system, just as Hitler did after the Beer Hall Putsch. The Republican Party and its close association with big money capitalized on the Nazi ideology of corporatism. In its reelection campaigns, the Republican Party employed known Nazis and paid for Nazi broadcasts to attract German-American voters.

Few Americans know that three days before the Japanese bombed Pearl Harbor, the McCormick papers published the top secret Rainbow 5 battle plan, prepared in the event that the U.S. was forced into the war in Europe. Sen. Burton Wheeler, a fascist and a member of the America First pro-Nazi group, released the top secret plan in an attempt to brand Roosevelt as a warmonger. In his declaration of war against the United States, Hitler cited the plans as the final straw.

By 1943, top Nazi officials realized they had lost the war and began preparing for their future by sending overseas gold, other assets, and additional agents. Their plan relied on the irrational fear America held for communism, as well as support from Nazi supporters in other countries, especially the U.S. The Nazis must have been very pleased with the help they received from America's Right Wing and the Republican Party. In fact, every Republican president after Dwight Eisenhower, or their families, had connections with the Nazis and provided them aid.

The extent of corporate America's involvement with the Nazis may never be fully known. Many of the files remain classified, and others undoubtedly have been purged. However, the list of American corporations that knowingly and willingly continued to trade with the Nazis during the war exceeds 300. It includes Ford, General Motors, General Electric, ITT, Standard Oil of New Jersey, Chase, and the bluest of the blue chips, IBM.

The scope of the Nazi intrigue in the United States is generally underestimated, and assumed to be confined to a few noisy street agitators like William Pelly and Elizabeth Dilling, and a few corporations, such as Ford and General Motors. In reality, Nazi influence has been pervasive. After the war, for instance, John Rogge, the prosecuting attorney for the Sedition Trial, received a tip from U.S. Army Capt. Sam Harris, a member of the prosecuting team at Nuremberg, concerning indisputable evidence linking the former Nazi government and certain leading U.S. citizens.

Rogge traveled to Germany with four aides to interview Hermann Goering, Joachim von Ribbentrop and other top Nazis. Rogge's findings were definitive and explosive:

Our investigation showed us that we had completely underestimated the scope and scale of Nazi activities in the United States. When I went to Germany I felt that the biggest threat to American democracy emanated from the machinations of persons like the defendants in the sedition trial (i.e. the little fascist crackpots). I found that a far more dangerous threat lay in the inner-connection between German and American industrialists, and that some of the best-known names in America were involved in Nazi intrigue.

As Rogge prepared his final report, an aide for Attorney General Tom Clark asked that all the names of American politicians and businessmen be omitted. Rogge refused and submitted his report, which the Department of Justice never released. Rogge was fired after he lectured on fascism at Swarthmore College, naming several prominent Americans who reportedly conspired with the Nazis to bring about the defeat of Roosevelt in the 1940 election — John L. Lewis, William Rhodes Davis, Sen. Wheeler, former Vice President James Garner, former Postmaster General James Farley, and former President Herbert Hoover.

It's true that some degree of fascism — the merger of government and corporate power — is present in every capitalist-based economy. However, if such a growing capitalist society fails to check the power of corporations, eventually they become wealthy enough to begin to control the government. Founding fathers like Thomas Jefferson were already aware of the danger posed by corporations:

I hope we shall take warning from the example of England and crush in its birth the aristocracy of our moneyed corporations, which dare already to challenge our Government to trial and bid defiance to the laws of our country.

Today, American democracy is under siege as never before by an elitist group of the military-industrial-petroleum corporate interests. That's why it's so important that everyone concerned with the hijacking of America joins efforts to remove these men from power.

We hope that this book will help educate readers about the true economic history of the past and present, which is essential to understanding how the the body politic and the fascist state are used to cloak the corporate agenda. With this book, we hope to shine a cleansing light on the dividends of war reaped by the ruling classes in America.

To be victorious against an enemy, citizens must know that enemy almost better than they know themselves. The enemy of American democracy knows no borders; it can even arise here if the propaganda is repeated steadily and loudly. "See, in my line of work you got to keep repeating things over and over and over again for the truth to sink in, to kind of catapult the propaganda." (George W. Bush, speaking at the Athena Performing Arts Center, Greece Athena Middle and High School, Rochester, N.Y., May 24, 2005.)

History is repeating itself, and this time the American citizenry is at fault for not recognizing the symptoms of the fascist disease. Americans don't know the real history beyond the propaganda of "freedom and democracy" that has now replaced the threat of weapons of mass destruction in this cabal's lexicon as the rationale for war. It is wise for each person who values freedom and democracy to understand the ploy of repetitive propaganda.

Hitler's Nazi regime mastered the use of propaganda to create outward enemies while the foundation of Germany's freedom was steadily destroyed. A perfect example was Pastor Martin Niemöller. Under orders from Hitler, Niemöller was imprisoned and finally transferred to the infamous Dachau concentration camp until the war ended in 1945. He emerged from his years of detention as a towering symbol of the Church's struggle. During his trips to America, he addressed more than 200 audiences, sometimes with the now-famous concluding words:

> Not many Germans lost much sleep over the arrests of a few thousand pastors and priests.

> First, they came for the socialists, and I did not speak out because I was not a socialist. Then they came for the trade unionists, and I did not speak out because I was not a trade unionist. Then they came for the Jews, and I did not speak out because I was not a Jew. Then they came for me, and there was no one left to speak for me.

It is our hope that this book will serve as a call to arms. At some point in our lives, we all, as dutiful citizens, have taken an oath of allegiance to serve and protect this nation from all enemies, foreign and domestic. That task cannot be accomplished if we are ignorant of the forces of history that operate in the dark.

We as citizens have a powerful weapon. It is known as truth. But it has little power unless we are willing to "speak truth to power," to gain an understanding of the corporate beast and its insatiable appetite, as viewed through the lens of history.

In 1943, a group of students and a professor in Munich formed the White Rose Society, distributing leaflets in opposition to the Nazi regime. When the members were caught, they were beheaded for treason. Yet their words live on, as fitting today as they were in Nazi Germany.

> "Nothing is so unworthy of a civilized nation as allowing itself to be governed without opposition by an irresponsible clique that has yielded to base instinct. Who among us has any conception of the dimensions of shame that will befall us and our children when one day the veil has fallen from our eyes and the most horrible of crimes — crimes that infinitely out-distance every human measure — reach the light of day?"

Let this book stand as a vanguard warning about what Americans' futures will be if this regime remains unopposed. In the very near future, you will be faced with a single choice — live in fear or live free.

Preface:
George W. Bush, the Neocons & the Nazis: Ties that Bind

(From the Streets of Little Beirut)

Numerous writers have compared the Bush tactics with those used by Hitler, while others have documented the connection between Prescott Bush and the Nazis. However, there is much more behind the Bush regime's transformation of the United States into a fascist police state. Few people realize the Republican Party paid for Nazi broadcasts in the 1930s, or that the GOP employed Nazis in election campaigns. Fewer are aware that Herbert Hoover conspired with top Nazi officials in Berlin to unseat Roosevelt in the 1940 election. Others have forgotten that as chairman of the Republican Party, George H. W. Bush senior set up the ethnic heritage groups of the party as havens for former Nazis, or that he employed known Nazi war criminals on his campaign staff.

Moreover, as the New York Republican convention nears, it is increasingly obvious that protestors will be dealt with brutally. New weapons such as a sound blaster developed for the military are already in place in New York, blurring the lines between the military and civilian affairs. Over fifty protestors are being tightly watched and tailed, while their only crime is their opposition to Bush. The Republican governor has suggested that free speech is not a right but a privilege that can be revoked. Additionally a massive operation is going on in Florida and other states to deny Blacks their right to vote. Finally, the Bush administration is using terror alerts to frighten voters and to condition them to the possibility of a canceled election. These and similar tactics are no different from those that Hitler's Brown Shirts employed.

The fascist philosophy underlying the present Bush administration.
(Diagram on p. 18.)

There are numerous connections between the Bush family and the Nazis, and the philosophy of the neocons within the Bush administration has already been linked to fascism. Here we will begin to outline those links between the Bush 43 regime and the Nazis, using a two-pronged approach.

Several authors have noted the link between senior members of the Bush administration and the fascist Leo Strauss. Exploring further, we see those philosophical roots lead back to the robber barons and the empire of J.P Morgan. Due to the natural congeniality between then and the corporate state of fascism, most of America's leading industrialists became the main supporters of fascism in the US. Indeed, they were responsible for bringing Hitler to power, and for building Hitler's war machine.

Strauss is usually portrayed as a Jewish refugee from Nazi Germany. However, he wasn't the hapless Jewish refugee generally depicted. Strauss adopted Zionism at the age of 17, and there is a close and sinister association between Zionism and the Nazis. Many Zionists supported Hitler and the Nazis; in fact, they concluded a transfer agreement with the Nazis. The Zionists were attempting to leave Europe's Jews with only two choices: emigrate to Palestine, or perish in the Holocaust.

As a student, Strauss began studying the philosophers who provided the bases for fascism: Nietzsche, Heidegger, and Schmitt. He became their devoted lifelong follower. Strauss's philosophy and views became increasingly fascist as his studies progressed. Their hallmark was his belief in totalitarian government. He rejected all principles of natural law, and believed in keeping the masses ignorant and in general servitude.

Strauss left Nazi Germany with the warm commendation of the Nazi jurist and philosopher Carl Schmitt, legal engineer of Nazi rule and the toppling of the Weimar Republic. Schmitt was personally responsible, in 1934, for arranging a Rockefeller Foundation scholarship for Strauss, which enabled him to leave Germany, to study first in France and then England. He arrived in the United States from Britain in the fall of 1937. Briefly appointed Research Fellow in the Department of History of Columbia University, he then became a member of the graduate faculty at the New School for Social Research in 1938.

The New School of Social Research was founded in 1919, a year after Willard Straight's death from influenza. Straight had been a partner of J.P. Morgan. He believed that America's security depended upon the British fleet and that it was in the United States' own interest to enter the war. At the same time, he saw the war as an opportunity for American bankers and industrialists to make substantial gains internationally at the expense of Britain. Morgan was an anglophile and also supported U.S. entry of the U.S. in the war. In 1915, Straight left the Morgan empire for a position with the American International Corporation, itself affiliated with the National City Bank.

In 1914, Straight and his wife Dorothy (née Dorothy Payne Whitney) invited Herbert Croly to edit the first edition of the New Republic, a new liberal magazine funded by Straight. During WWI, J.P. Morgan was obsessed with the media and endeavored to control it. Providing backing for the New Republic had a threefold purpose for Morgan. Firstly, it would keep him abreast of the thinking in left-wing circles. He even had an inside man in the communist press. Secondly, Morgan believed a magazine like the New Republic allowed the left to blow off steam, thus acting as a safety valve. Finally, he also believed it would give him a power of veto on any actions originated by the left, in case they ever went radical.

Morgan's efforts to control the media didn't stop with the New Republic. In 1915, he got together twelve leading men within the newspaper business and commissioned them to determine how one could control the national press. They agreed that it would be sufficient to control 25 of the most influential papers. Morgan immediately sent emissaries to purchase the editorial policy of the 25 selected papers. He also used his money to form the American Legion and to craft it into a union-busting and redbaiting group of hired thugs. that ran amok during the 1919 Red Scare terrorizing and murdering countless union leaders and leftists.

The Council on Foreign Relations (CFR) was another Morgan front group aimed at controlling the American people. The CFR evolved out of the Rhodes Roundtable group during WWI. Most of the early members were Morgan employees who had met their English counterparts during the Paris Peace Conference. The CFR was a bridging group between the Morgans and the Rockefellers, and the Rockefellers provided much of the financial support. As the Rockefeller fortune came to outgrow the Morgan's, the CFR became more dominated by the Rockefellers. Percy Rockefeller, a Skull and Bones member who served on the board of the Morgan Guaranty Trust, further strengthened the bridge between the Morgan and Rockefeller dynasties.

The New Republic certainly fits the blueprint of Morgan's efforts to control the media. Initially, all outside contributions had to be unanimously approved by its editorial board. The New School for Social Research followed in the footsteps of the New Republic. Straight's widow and the wife of another J.P. Morgan partner, Mrs. Thomas Lamont, were instrumental in establishing the New School. Alvin Johnson, the assistant editor of the New Republic was named Director of the New School two years later, in 1921.

Strauss remained at the Morgan-connected New School for Social Research for ten years. In 1948, he accepted a position at the Rockefeller-founded University of Chicago. Not only was Strauss a promoter of fascist ideology, but his entry into the United States and his work there through most of his life was supported financially by two of the most powerful American fascist families. While the dealings of the Rockefeller-owned Standard Oil Company with the Nazis during the war allowed the family the thin pretense that they were not personally involved, other actions by the Rockefeller family confirm their fascist ideology. It was the Rockefeller Foundation that provided funding for much of the Nazi research into eugenics, including the twin research conducted in the concentration camps by Mengele.

Strauss's connections to the neo-cons within the Bush administration are well-known at this point. Numerous other neo-cons serving in the Bush administration or the American Enterprise Organization, who funded the Project for the New American Century (PNAC), were students and followers of Strauss. This can be seen in their dictatorial approach and in their strong pro-Israeli views. An interesting aspect of Strauss's tenure at the University of Chicago is that it is was during this time that both David Rockefeller and John Ashcroft received their degrees from the University of Chicago.

The Rockefeller family played a key role not only in funding Strauss but also in destroying the economies of Third World nations. The Rockefellers have used the University of Chicago and their various family foundations to promote an economic policy of ruin. The laissez-faire economics promoted by the Chicago school has failed numerous times in the past and was one of the leading causes of the 1929 stock market crash and resulting Great Depression. Such economic policies only lead to global fascism and corporate rule, which are the prime goal of the Rockefeller family.

This is evident in David Rockefeller's support of free trade agreements, the World Trade Organization and the World Bank. These trade organizations and agreements have impoverished much of the Southern Hemisphere with their draconian demands for privatization and cuts in social spending. Moreover, these trade agreements effectively reduce the government's role to that of an enforcer of corporate policies. All of these free trade agreements contain a clause setting up a tribunal comprised of corporations to settle all disputes, including claims against the government. The clause effectively bypasses the court systems in signatory countries. In effect, these clauses confer supreme sovereignty to multinational corporations who answer to no one. Under these clauses, corporations are free to claim environmental laws, labor laws and other laws are harmful to the company and cause it financial loss, which results in massive settlements against the government and in the overturning of needed laws.

One of the chief advocates of these free trade agreements is Dick Cheney, who has promised David Rockefeller that he would deliver a hemisphere trade agreement before the end of the current Bush administration.

These unconstitutional free trade agreements have become commonplace as a result of the Rockefellers' ability to control and direct economic thought in the United States. In essence, the Rockefellers maintain a monopoly on economic theory. To understand how they gained such control tales us back to the 1920s, when two economists rose to prominence: Ludwig von Mises and Friedrich A. Hayek. Both were helped by Rockefeller money. Von Mises toured the United States in 1926. The tour of American Universities was sponsored by the Laura Spelman Rockefeller Foundation and was greatly successful in promoting the views of the Austrian School of Economics. Hayek personally tutored David Rockefeller in economics.

In 1950, von Hayek was brought to the United States to teach at the University of Chicago, but he didn't teach economics, he was actually made a professor on the Committee on Social Thought. This was an exceptionally dangerous position for a man that held the views von Hayek did. In 1945, von Hayek's The Road to Serfdom was published. This poorly written book was an attack on the concept of the nation-state. In it, von Hayek argued that the nation-state was a hindrance to peace, and socialism led to totalitarian systems, which treated their citizens as serfs. In place of the nation-state, von Hayek proposed a supra-national authority or world federation consisting of the financial elite.

This elite would then be free to rule the world according to their own interest. In 1947, von Hayek created the Mount Pelerin Society, made up of the financial elite of Europe, as a first step toward his supranational authority. In the years since, the Mount Pelerin Society has been influential in creating numerous "conservative" think tanks, which promote free market economic policies for the Establishment. The society has expanded to include the following think tanks: the Heritage Foundation in 1973, the Fraser Institute in 1974, the Manhattan Institute in 1977, and the Pacific Institute for Public Policy Research in 1978.

The influence of the Chicago University on modern economics is unprecedented. Since 1969, most of the Nobel prizes in economics have been awarded to the free traders, despite the spectacular failures of laissez-faire economies.

Economists who dare publish articles opposing the thought of the Chicago University are quickly ridiculed, their works dismissed, and their careers wrecked, in testimony to the power of the Rockefeller family and its control over economy and free thought.

The connection between the University of Chicago and fascism was renewed in the 1960s under Gen. Pinochet in Chile. It was the "boys from Chicago", students of Milton Friedman, who destroyed the economy and reduced the citizens to serfdom in Pinochet's fascist Chile, where dissent was eliminated by right-wing death squads.

According to von Hayek's prescription, corporations are given the status of sovereign nations while the nation-states are reduced to mere quislings of the corporate state and enforcer of their laws. This is the same agenda as that of the World Trade Organization, the International Monetary fund and the many so-called "free trade agreements." Many of the Bush neocons are further linked with von Hayek by their beliefs in Mandeville. Von Hayek rejected the idea that man was created in the image of god and traced his philosophical ancestry to the early eighteenth century Satanist, Bernard Mandeville.

Thus, the Bush administration's philosophy is clearly rooted in fascist ideology and in the fascist dogma of the corporate state. That these roots come from two of America's richest families confirms fascism as a top-down revolution by the elite to maintain their control and power. The fascist roots of the Bush regime are manifested in the operative side of its philosophy, through the Psychological Strategy Board under Nelson Rockefeller. C D Jackson served in the Eisenhower administration; he was in charge of the psychological warfare. Both Bruce and Howell Jackson were part of the PNAC project, the blueprint for the Bush regime.

The operative route: how the fascists manifested themselves. (Diagram on p. 18.)

The partners of J.P Morgan provide the operative connection between the Bush administration and fascism. Thomas Lamont was a prominent figure in the 1934 fascist plot to remove Roosevelt from office. The plot called for retired Marine General Smedley Butler to lead the force – much of it consisting of American Legionnaires – to take over the White House. Roosevelt would be given a chance to step down and to cooperate with the plotters. If herefused to let the business leaders seize power, then the plotters would kill him.

However, Butler was an honorable man, and he leaked the information concerning the plot to Roosevelt. Roosevelt knew he could not simply dismiss it when it was connected with several leading industrialists and bankers. To foil the plot, Roosevelt leaked information about it to the press. The resulting commotion in the front pages of the country's newspapers undermined any efforts by the plotters to proceed. Butler described his military career as follows.

"War is just a racket. A racket is best described, I believe, as something that is not what it seems to the majority of people. Only a small inside group knows what it is about. It is conducted for the benefit of the very few at the expense of the masses…. I helped make Mexico, especially Tampico, safe for American oil interests in 1914. I helped make Haiti and Cuba a decent place for the National City Bank boys to collect revenues in. I helped in the raping of half a dozen Central American republics for the benefits of Wall Street. The record of racketeering is long. I helped purify Nicaragua for the international banking house of Brown Brothers in 1909-1912 (where have I heard that name before?). I brought light to the Dominican Republic for American sugar interests in 1916. In China I helped to see to it that Standard Oil went its way unmolested."

A third partner of J. P. Morgan, Henry Davison, financed the Yale Aviation Club, of which his son Trubee was a member. Many of the Aviation Club members were also members of the Skull and Bones secret society at Yale. The club gained fame during WWI. Robert Lovett led the unit during the war. Artemus Gates was another member.

The most interesting aspect of this group of college aviation buffs is how many of them later served in WWII on the targeting selection committee. Henry Simpson, Secretary of War and a former Bonesman, appointed John McCloy as his Assistant Secretary of War in charge of intelligence. Robert Lovett was appointed Assistant Secretary of War for air. Directly under Lovett was Trubee Davison, assistant chief of staff at A-1. Artemus Gates served as Assistant Secretary of the Navy for air. James Stillman Rockefeller served with the Airborne Command and Airborne Center as assistant chief of staff.

Clearly the Department of War, and particularly the air command had an unusually high number of members from the Yale Aviation Unit and the Skull and Bones. These individuals all had extensive ties to Wall Street firms, which had a history of doing business with the Nazis. They were well positioned to influence the target selection in the air campaign against Germany.

Lovett was a lifelong advocate of what amounts to terror bombing, the bombing of civilian centers. The air campaign against Germany left eighty percent of the homes destroyed. Factory production was only reduced by twenty percent . Even then, much of the reduction came about not by damage to the factories, but from delays and shortages of parts caused by the disruption of the transportation system by bombing. For example, Cologne was a city targeted for massive bombing attacks. While the city lay in ruins, the Ford and I.G. Farben plants escaped all but minor bomb damage. In Berlin, a city that had been reduced to rubble from the bombing campaign, the Allies chose the I.G. Farben building for their headquarters. It had escaped all but minor damage from the bombs.

Robert Lovett and Prescott Bush were both Bonesmen employed by Brown Brothers Harriman. In fact, many of the top directors and partners of Brown Brothers & Harriman were Bonesmen. It was one of the main firms on Wall Street to have extensive dealings with the Nazis.

The deals with the Nazis were so extensive at Brown Brothers Harriman that Prescott Bush had 23 firms seized from him for trading with the enemy. Five firms were seized from Bush in 1942, another 18 firms shortly after the war. The 18 firms had been allowed to operate during the war only because seizing them had been judged detrimental to the war effort and their continued operation posed little risk to the Allies.

Before the firms were seized, Prescott Bush hired the Dulles brothers to conceal the Nazi ownership in these firms. This deliberate act closed any window of deniability; it was treason by both Bush and the Dulles brothers. It confirms that both parties knew that the continued operation of these companies was in violation of U.S. policy and of the Trading with the Enemy Act, and that both parties freely chose to aid the Nazis when the U.S. was at war with Nazi Germany.

The Wall Street law firm of Sullivan and Cromwell employed both John Foster and Allan Dulles. Throughout the 1930s and the early 1940s, the Dulles brothers were busy cloaking Nazi ownership of numerous corporations and their cartel arrangements with I.G. Farben. Not only was their work treasonous in and of itself, it also delayed the production of war materials and munitions.

Aside from his 23 corporations seized for violating the Trading with the Enemy Act, Prescott Bush was a leader in the American eugenics movement, which succeeded in the passage of sterilization laws in many states for anyone judged unfit. These laws served as the basis of the Nuremberg Laws passed by the Nazis. Much of the Nazi eugenics research was funded, even during the war, with money from the Rockefeller Foundation and the Carnegie Foundation. The Harrimans were also major financial backers of the movement.

After the war, John Foster Dulles, with the aid of Rockefeller money, led a world tour of third-world nations stressing the danger of population expansion of non-Aryan races. George H. W. Bush, Prescott's son, has followed in his father's footsteps in setting up population control in third-world nations through the UN. In his first political race, George H. W. Bush campaigned against the Civil Rights Act of 1964, and as a member of Congress he warned of the danger of too many Black babies. While population control may be a laudable goal, in the hands of the Bush family it becomes another eugenic tool aimed at eliminating non-Aryan races.

Cold Springs Harbor, the center of eugenics research in the 1920s and 1930s, is still operating. It is currently a leader of the human genome project. While the genome project will undoubtedly provide many future medical benefits, Cold Springs remains firmly under the control of the same families involved in the American eugenics movement. Current directors William Gerry and Allen Dulles Jebsen are the grandsons of Harriman and Allan Dulles respectively.

The genome project provides the ideal cover to develop a gene-specific bioweapon, a weapon with the sole purpose of committing genocide on a massive scale. Such a weapon has been described by the PNAC as a politically useful tool. The PNAC is the road map George W. Bush is following as a "War President."

This is not the only link between the Rockefeller Foundation and questionable programs. In 1931, with funding from the Rockefeller Foundation, Dr. Cornelius Rhoads infected human subjects with cancer cells. Rhoads later established the U.S. Army Biological Warfare facilities in Maryland, Utah, and Panama. It was named the U.S. Atomic Energy Commission. While there, he began a series of radiation exposure experiments on American soldiers and civilian hospital patients.

Following the war, Allan Dulles faced an investigation for treason. While Dulles was crafty enough to escape the charges, one of those aiding him in covering up his crimes was Richard Nixon. While still serving in the navy, Nixon was given some captured documents to review. The contents would have revealed Allan Dulles as a traitor. In exchange for burying the documents, Dulles agreed to fund Nixon's first political campaign. Nixon's campaign also benefited from large contributions from a large New York bank connected with Brown Brothers and Harriman.

Captured Nazi documents reveal they had a comeback plan. Their plan to regain power after the war revolved around using their friends and fascist sympathizers in other countries – particularly in the United States – to do their bidding while rebuilding Germany. The documents note that, as late as 1944, the Nazis were hoping for a Republican victory in the presidential election because they would get an easier peace. The second part of their plan aimed at provoking a war between the U.S. and the Soviet Union, which would allow the Nazis to retake power in Germany without U.S. intervention.

Eisenhower was politically naïve. When John Foster Dulles approached him in Europe to run for election in 1948, Eisenhower had no foreign policy concept formulated. He was easily swayed by Dulles' idea of massive nuclear retaliation, which led to the appointment of Dulles as secretary of state. While Eisenhower was no Nazi and expressed his hatred of Nazis and Germans in his letters to his wife, he allowed American Nazis like the Dulles brothers to gain a great deal of control over his administration. Eisenhower appointed Allan Dulles as CIA Director, and Prescott Bush and John Lovett were Eisenhower's close golfing buddies. Prescott Bush was also the driving force in selecting Richard Nixon as Eisenhower's running mate. Nelson Rockefeller was appointed to head the Psychological Strategy Board. Numerous employees of Sullivan and Cromwell, the two Wall Street firms most involved with the Nazis, held important positions within the administration.

John McCloy and General Draper, both from the former Control Council of Germany, fulfilled important roles in the Eisenhower administration. Nothing was left to chance in the rebirth of the Nazis. In postwar Germany, the three most powerful figures: John McCloy head of the Control Council, Lewis Douglas, the head of the Finance Division of the Control Council, and German Chancellor Konrad Adenauer, were all brothers-in-law. They all had wed daughters of John Zinsser, a partner of JP Morgan.

While the American Nazis succeeded in gaining partial control of the Eisenhower administration and were able to stoke the fires of the Cold War, they failed to secure total control. Although these American Nazis managed to dupe the tired old general, they never succeeded in completely tricking him. Even after suffering a debilitating heart attack, the old general refused to turn over the reins of power to Nixon, a man he loathed. Before leaving office, Eisenhower realized he had been duped and left us his rather cryptic warning about the military-industrial complex, suggesting the dangers of corporate rule.

Since 1960, Eisenhower's warning has gone largely unheeded. Beginning with the rise of fascism and the elitism within the Reagan administration, the military keeps taking up a bigger portion of the budget, and social welfare has been largely eliminated, much as in Nazi Germany. Today, under the regime of George W. Bush, it is clear that the corporations within the military-industrial complex are in control of the country. Dick Cheney can pad his retirement account at Halliburton with millions of dollars of overcharges for services not delivered in the Iraq War. Meanwhile, many soldiers are sent into combat without body armor.

A recently disclosed top-secret document from the NSC reveals that staff were instructed to cooperate fully with Dick Cheney's Energy Task Force as it considered the "melding" of two seemingly unrelated areas of policy: "the review of operational policies towards rogue states," such as Iraq, and "actions regarding the capture of new and existing oil and gas fields." The document suggests that Cheney's Energy Task Force was actually a discussion for geostrategic plans for oil, putting the issue of war in the context of the captains of the oil industry sitting down with Cheney and laying grand, global plans. This would confirm Bush's plans for regime change in 60 countries, and his support for rebel forces opposing the democratic government of Venezuela, as well as the increasing hostility of the Bush administration towards Iran.

Too many people still believe that fascism can't happen here. It is happening here today. The Gestapo is firmly in place in the form of Ashcroft's justice department. The FBI no longer serves to protect the citizens; instead it is being used to protect this regime, by such means as the gagging of Sibel Edmonds, for instance. The FBI is no longer primarily charged with criminal investigation; instead, it's being used to enforce this regime's policies. The FBI, other federal law enforcement agencies and the military are illegally spying on anyone opposed to this regime. Moreover, Representative Porter Goss, Bush's choice to head the CIA, has introduced legislation that would allow the CIA to conduct operations inside the United States, including arbitrary arrests of American citizens.

Ike's military-industrial complex, the PNAC document, the World Trade Organization, free trade agreements, and the George W. Bush regime are all parts of the many-headed Nazi Hydra in America.

If George W. Bush declares a red alert or martial law or manages to steal another election, will you be one of the first sent to the concentration camps? Will you go quietly like a lamb? Will you allow the Gestapo to haul away your neighbor, your wife, your son or daughter? Will you live next to the crematories with your head in the sand as the Germans did? Or will you oppose the regime and help reestablish the constitutional republic?

The time to decide is now – tomorrow may be too late. The corporate state of fascism has risen from the ashes of 9/11 like a giant phoenix. It will consume all that opposes it. The Fourth Reich has risen. Be aware. Your life and freedoms depend on it.

Glen Yeadon

Aug. 21, 2004,
Portland, Ore.

The Bush Regime and the Nazi Family Tree

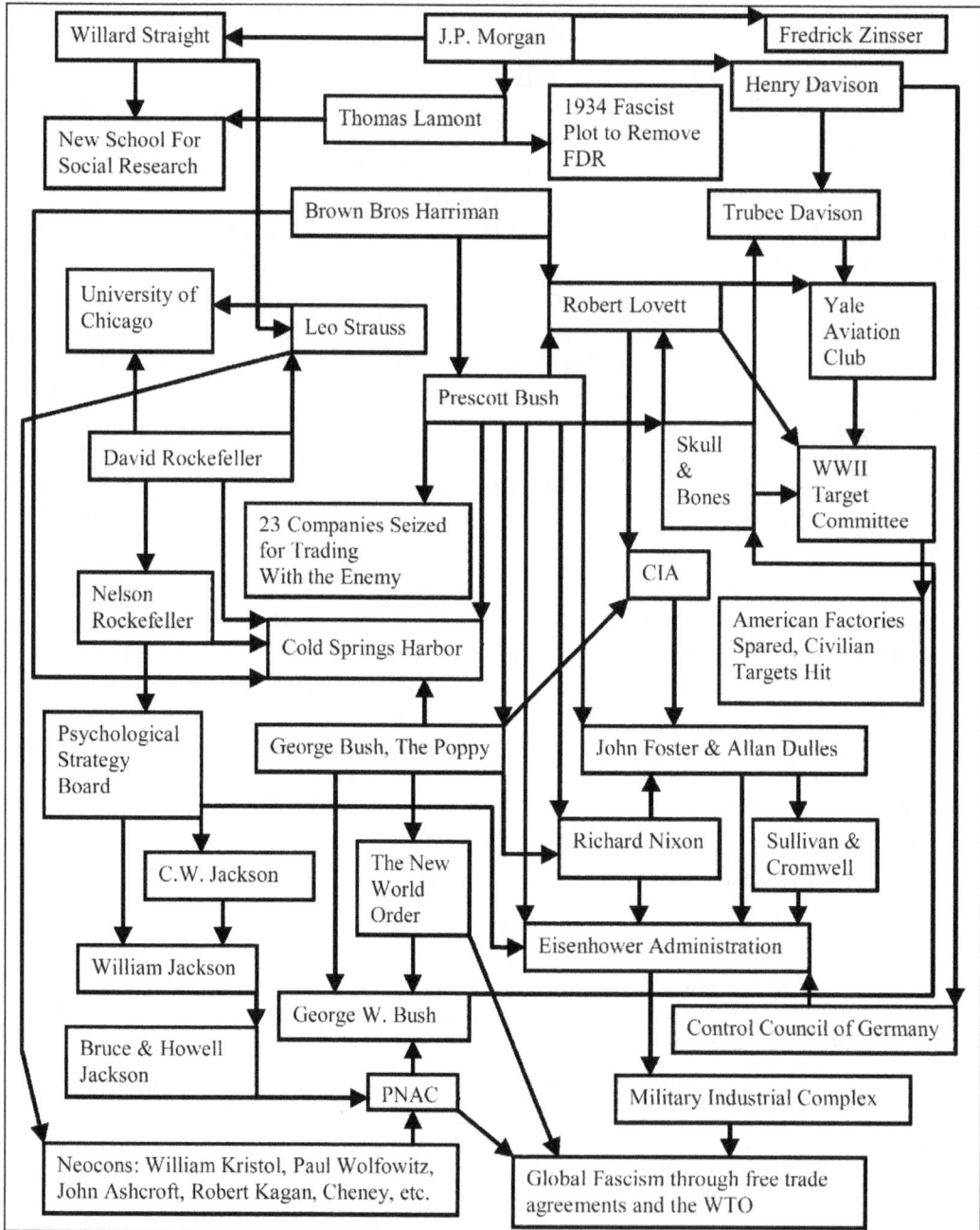

Chapter 1,
What Fascism Is

Definitions of Fascism

Few words cause more confusion and heated debate than fascism. It is often used in the sense of extreme repression. Often the understanding of fascism is limited to the Nazis dictatorship. The term has been applied to many individuals, such as Joseph McCarthy, J. Edgar Hoover and others. It is frequently — often wrongly — used to describe police and law enforcement, and government and its policies.

What then is fascism exactly? *Webster's Dictionary* defines it as: "A government system marked by a centralized dictatorship, stringent socioeconomic controls and belligerent nationalism."

Benito Mussolini, the world's first fascist dictator, said: "Fascism should rightly be called Corporatism, as it is a merge of state and corporate power."[1] The word fascism stems from the Italian word *fascio*, a union or league, and the Latin word *fasces*, an ancient Roman symbol of authority consisting of an executioner's ax bound in a bundle of rods. Under ancient Roman law, it originally symbolized the power to kill mercifully with the ax or mercilessly by beating the condemned to death with the rods. It is also interpreted as "Strength Through Unity," the fascist motto in V for Vendetta; in other words, corporatism. The reverse side of the Mercury dime depicts a fasces.

Upton Sinclair defined fascism simply as "capitalism plus murder."[2]

According to Franklin Roosevelt:

The liberty of a democracy is not safe if the people tolerate the growth of private power to a point where it becomes stronger than their democratic state itself. That, in its essence, is fascism − ownership of government by an individual, by a group, or any controlling private power.[3]

Another good definition of fascism comes from Heywood Broun, a noted American columnist in the 1930s:

Fascism is a dictatorship from the extreme right, or to put it a little more closely into our local idiom, a government which is run by a small group of large industrialists and financial lords... I think it is not unfair to say that any businessman in America, or public leader, who goes out to break unions is laying the foundations for fascism.[4]

A lengthy description of fascism often credited to Mussolini is in the 1932 *Italian Encyclopedia* edited by Giovanni Gentile. Excerpts from that description are given in Appendix 1.[5]

Overall, these definitions are vague and abstract. Roosevelt's definition comes closest to the true essence, but even his is incapable of taking into account all forms of fascism. Like democracy, fascism comes in many forms. Further, no fascist state has ever first appeared full-blown. Even the Nazis and Mussolini took several years to consolidate their power. It's that gradual transition that makes fascism so insidious.

The lack of a clear definition of fascism led the War Department to develop a training program to teach new inductees what they were fighting. The War Department released Program 64 on March 24, 1945. An excerpt from that program alludes to the difficulty in precisely defining a fascist.

Three Ways to Spot U.S. Fascists.

Fascists in America may differ slightly from fascists in other countries, but there are a number of attitudes and practices that they have in common. Following are three. Every person who has one of them is not necessarily a fascist. But he is in a mental state that lends itself to the acceptance of fascist aims.

1. Pitting religion, racial, and economic groups against one another in order to break down the national unity is a device of the divide and conquer technique used by Hitler to gain power in Germany and in

other countries. With slight variations, to suit local conditions, fascists everywhere have used this Hitler method. In many countries, anti-Semitism is a dominant device of fascism. In the United States native fascists have often been anti-Catholic, anti-Jew, anti-Negro, anti-Labor and anti-foreign born. In South America native fascists use the same scapegoats except that they substitute anti-Protestantism for anti-Catholicism.

Interwoven with the master race theory of fascism is a well-planned hate campaign against minority races, religions, and other groups. To suit their particular needs and aims, fascists will use any one or a combination of such groups as a convenient scapegoat.

2. Fascism cannot tolerate such religious and ethical concepts as the brotherhood of man. Fascists deny the need for international cooperation. These ideas contradict the fascist theory of the master race. International cooperation, as expressed in the Dumbarton Oaks proposals, run counter to the fascist program of war and world domination. Right now our native fascists are spreading anti-British, anti-Soviet, anti-French and anti-United Nations propaganda.

3. It is accurate to call a member of a communist party a communist. For short, he is often called a Red. Indiscriminate pinning of the label Red on people and proposals which one opposes is a common political device. It is a favorite trick of native as well as foreign fascists.

Many fascists make the spurious claim that the world has but two choices — either fascism or communism — and they label as communist everyone who refuses to support them. By attacking our free enterprise, capitalist democracy, and by denying the effectiveness of our way of life, they hope to trap many people.[6]

Program 64 set off a major firestorm of criticism in Congress. Led by pro-fascist members, the controversy raged until the War Department gave up the program.

Characteristics of Fascism

This book defines fascism as follows, with one condition. *Fascism is a repressive totalitarian regime in which a small elite controls and uses the government for their benefit. Any action by a government that places the rights of a corporation or a group of elites above the rights of the people is a step toward fascism.* However, even this definition fails to delineate the transformation from a capitalist democracy to a fascist state. For instance, when did Germany become a fascist state? Did it occur with Hitler's appointment as chancellor? Or was it before or after the appointment?

While the March 1933 election was not free, nevertheless, the Nazi Party failed to gain a majority in the Reichstag. Thus it can be argued that the transformation occurred after that election. However, Germany was well along the road to a full fascist state before Hitler's appointment.

The lack of a clear line marking the transformation to a fascist state points again to the movement's insidious nature, and the impossibility of relying on simplistic definitions. Since there is no all-encompassing definition, it is best to look at the traits that explore the degree of fascism. While many of the traits of fascism are almost universally included on such lists, some are hotly contested. Political scientist Lawrence Britt listed the following:

1. Powerful and Continuing Nationalism: Fascist regimes tend to make constant use of patriotic mottos, slogans, symbols, songs and other paraphernalia. Flags are seen everywhere, as are flag symbols on clothing and in public displays.

2. Disdain for the Recognition of Human Rights: Because of fear of enemies and the need for security, the people in fascist regimes are persuaded that human rights can be ignored in certain cases because of "need." The people tend to look the other way or even approve of torture, summary executions, assassinations, long incarcerations of prisoners, etc.

3. Identification of Enemies/Scapegoats as a Unifying Cause: The people are rallied into a unifying patriotic frenzy over the need to eliminate a perceived common threat or foe: racial, ethnic or religious minorities; liberals; communists; socialists, terrorists, etc.

4. Supremacy of the Military: Even when there are widespread domestic problems, the military is given a disproportionate amount of government funding, and the domestic agenda is neglected. Soldiers and military service are glamorized.

5. Rampant Sexism: The governments of fascist nations tend to be almost exclusively male dominated. Under fascist regimes, traditional gender roles are made more rigid. Opposition to abortion is high, as is homophobia and anti-gay legislation and national policy.

6. Controlled Mass Media: Sometimes media are directly controlled by the government, but in other cases, the media are indirectly controlled by government regulation, or sympathetic media spokespeople and executives. Censorship, especially in wartime, is very common.

7. Obsession with National Security: Fear is used as a motivational tool by the government over the masses.

8. Religion and Government are Intertwined: Governments in fascist nations tend to use the most common religion in the nation as a tool to manipulate public opinion. Government leaders frequently use religious rhetoric, even when the major tenets of the religion are diametrically opposed to the government's policies or actions.

9. Corporate Power is Protected: The industrial and business aristocracy of a fascist nation often puts government leaders into power, creating a mutually beneficial business-government relationship and power elite.

10. Labor Power is Suppressed: Because the organizing power of labor is the only real threat to a fascist government, labor unions are either eliminated entirely or are severely suppressed.

11. Disdain for Intellectuals and the Arts: Fascist nations tend to promote and tolerate open hostility to higher education and academia. It is not uncommon for professors and other academics to be censored or even arrested. Free expression in the arts is openly attacked, and governments often refuse to fund the arts.

12. Obsession with Crime and Punishment: Under fascist regimes, the police are given almost limitless power to enforce laws. The people are often willing to overlook police abuses and even forego civil liberties in the name of patriotism. There is often a national police force with virtually unlimited power.

13. Rampant Cronyism and Corruption: Fascist regimes are almost always governed by groups of friends and associates who appoint each other to government positions, and then use governmental power and authority to protect their friends from accountability. It is not uncommon in fascist regimes for national resources and even treasures to be appropriated or even outright stolen by government leaders.

14. Fraudulent Elections: Sometimes elections in fascist nations are a complete sham. Other times, elections are manipulated by smear campaigns against or even assassination of opposition candidates, use of legislation to control voting numbers or political district boundaries, and manipulation of the media. Fascist nations also typically use their judiciaries to manipulate or control elections.[7]

Some additional, more definitive traits of fascism, roughly in order of their importance, are:

Top-Down Revolution or Movement: Fascism is a rebellion or revolt by the elite to preserve their social economic status. This is the primary reason fascism begins during periods of economic turmoil. While the large number of followers of fascism such as Hitler's Brown Shirts came from the middle and lower classes, the elite of German society controlled the party. It was only after Hitler assured the prominent business leaders of his opposition to socialism and unions that he gained power.

Unbridled Corporatism: The corporate leaders direct government policy for their own benefit. Fascism reduces controls on business and suppresses or bans unions.

Extreme Anti-communism, Anti-socialism and Anti-Liberal Views: Fascists regard the state as supreme and the individual as subordinate to the state. Fascism cancels or forces deep cuts in social programs.

Extreme Exploitation: Fascist regimes reduce people to objects of the state without human rights. Citizenship may be revoked from groups of people to exploit them and seize their property. (See also No. 2 on Britt's list.)

Totalitarian: Fascism does not tolerate dissent. Dissenters face imprisonment or execution. Fascism packs the courts with party ideologues, leaving no recourse for grievances.

Extreme Nationalism: Excessive display of nationalism with flags, mottoes, slogans and other national symbolism is common to all fascist regimes. Fascist governments glorify the military and divert most of the government spending to the military and defense items. Often this extreme nationalism results in the expanding the country's borders through wars. (Common to both lists.)

Destructive Divisiveness: All politicians in a democracy use divisions to win elections. However, under fascism, the divisiveness is uniquely destructive and often takes the form of racism, class warfare or even genocide. (Similarity with No. 3 on Britt's list.)

Opportunistic Ideology: Fascists often adopt popular stances on issues to gain and hold power, but once fully in control, they reverse themselves in favor of reactionary positions. Hitler borrowed from socialism to gain power only. Once he gained power, he repudiated these ideas, and socialists were some of the first prisoners in the concentration camps.

Violence and Terror: Fascist regimes use violence and terror to gain and preserve power. Hitler had his Brown Shirts intimidate voters and opposition leaders by starting street brawls and even murdering the opposition. Once in power, he used the Gestapo, the secret state police, to root out and remove any opposition.

Expounding of Mysticism or Religious Beliefs: Hitler often spoke of the declining moral values in Germany, and used the church to manipulate public opinion. The Nazis modeled the SS after both religious and pagan customs. (Common to both lists.)

Cult-like Figurehead: A popular figurehead surrounded by a small cadre of cult-like followers has headed every fascist regime to date.

Censorship: The press and media are tightly controlled under fascism, and reduced to the role of the party's mouthpiece. (Common to both lists.)

It must be emphasized that not all of these traits need be present in a fascist state. For instance, Nazi Germany was the only fascist state to show extreme racism. There is scant evidence of it in Franco's Spain, Peron's Argentina and Pinochet's Chile. Even in Italy, racism was minor before the Nazis took control.

Strictly speaking, fascist states to are totalitarian and place the rights of corporations above the rights of their citizens. However, there is a wide gray area in defining when a government becomes totalitarian, or at what point protecting corporations becomes fascist.

Understanding this gray area is essential to recognizing how fascist regimes arise. It points to the inherent danger in all societies based on a free market economy. Once an elite class gains enough wealth to control and run the government, it ceases to exist in its own right. Not all free market economies end in fascism; many have ended in right-wing dictatorships. The various coups in Central and South America provide plenty of examples. A few may end in a Marxist revolution, as in Cuba, and others may become democracies. The turn to fascism is the extreme case.

Once again, this gray area makes fascism dangerous and hard to recognize. Unlike communism, fascism does not need a revolution to emerge, although fascist putschists will often use mobs to underpin their coups. Considering the enormous impact the Nazis had on the world, Germany greeted Hitler's appointment as chancellor with indifference. His appointment followed a long list of short-lived German governments and chancellors. A newsreel shown widely throughout movie theaters in Germany placed Hitler's appointment last in the six events covered, behind reports on a horse race, a horse show and a ski jump. Similarly, reaction outside Germany was largely indifferent and restrained.[8]

The great indifference to Hitler's appointment indicates how easy it is for a democracy to slide into fascism. In *The End of America*, published in July 2007, Naomi Klein outlines ten steps to a fascist takeover:

"Invoke an internal and external threat; establish secret prisons; develop a paramilitary force; surveil ordinary citizens; infiltrate citizens'groups; arbitrarily detain and release citizens; target key individuals; restrict the press; cast criticism as 'espionage' and dissent as 'treason;' and subvert the rule of law."

Klein then gives current, Bushist examples of each. She also notes how many of the steps were followed in the Thai military coup of September 2006, "as if they had a shopping list… Thailand was a police state within a matter of days." The scenario in the U.S. is more gradual, more banal, but just as overwhelmingly thorough.

Any objective assessment of the George W. Bush administration after the reports of torture at the Iraqi Abu Ghraib prison in May 2004 would find most of the traits from all three lists. Undoubtedly, this government has been one of the most repressive in U.S. history. By spring 2004, some journalists were already describing it as fascist.

The Philosophy of Fascism

Further insights into fascism can be gained by looking at its roots in modern philosophy. March 23, 1919 in Milan, Italy, Mussolini formed the *Fasci di Combattiment,* fighting leagues or bands. Some writers suggest there was already a well-developed theory of fascism dating back to Karl Marx, but this is part of the futile yet concerted effort by the Right Wing to link fascism with communism and the Left.

Much of their argument stems from the fact that several of the philosophers of fascism, including Mussolini, Sergio Panunzio and George Sorrell, had once been members of the Socialist Party or associated with the Left in other ways. The Socialist Party had expelled Mussolini for his support for the war, and both he and Giovanni Gentile grew to despise socialism. To argue that fascism is a leftist ideology is like claiming that President Reagan was a liberal because he had once been a member of the Democratic Party.

The earliest efforts to define the fascist philosophy came with the printing of the *Fascist Doctrine,* written by Gentile and often credited to Mussolini. Gentile served as minister of education in Mussolini's first cabinet, and organized a purge of liberals and democrats in Italian universities. He believed future revolutions would occur in backward countries where people needed to focus their strength on restoring the nation. (This is the opposite of Marx's theory that revolutions would be a struggle by the working class to gain power in industrialized countries.)

Gentile hated the socialists for their support of continuous strikes and work stoppages in Italy during the chaos immediately following World War I. He sensed the Italian nation was beginning to crumble. Gentile also believed that humans have no purpose, outside the nation and all must make sacrifices for it – whereas Marx looked forward to a withering away of the state.

Other themes in the *Fascist Doctrine* originate with more traditional influences. Corporatism and its theories of class collaboration, and economic and social relations can be traced to the model laid out by Pope Leo XII's 1892 encyclical *Rerum Novarum.*[10] There is great similarity between the fascist and encyclical versions of corporatism. The encyclical addressed politics and the way in which the Industrial Revolution transformed society. It sharply criticized socialism and its theory of class struggle, while also citing capitalism for exploiting the masses. Seeking a principle to replace the Marxist doctrine of class struggle, the encyclical urged social solidarity between the upper and lower classes, and approved nationalism as a way of preserving traditional morality, customs and folkways. Pope Leo XII proposed a kind of corporatism, organizing political societies along industrial lines, much like medieval guilds. The pope went so far as to reject the democratic ideal of "one person, one vote" in favor of representation by interest groups.

Italian fascism as a political and economic system combined parts of corporatism, totalitarianism, nationalism and anti-communism. In many regards, it may be considered an ideology of negation: anti-liberal, anti-communist and antidemocratic. It was a reactionary ideology in that it promoted whatever views would be useful to further exploit the people. It was also a reaction against the French Revolution, that landmark event that launched a major shift in European culture and governments, whose motto of "Liberty, Equality, Fraternity" the European nobility hated the most.

The concept of liberty from repressive regimes in the daily lives of the citizenry incensed the early philosophers of fascism. Freedom from forced religious values, the right to vote, majority rule in which the minority still held a set of inalienable rights – these were radical ideas in a time of debtor's prisons, indentured servants and vassal states. Such ideas directly threatened kings, nobles, and the Church.

Equality in the eyes of the law was unspeakable. How could a mere peasant have the same rights under the law as kings, nobles and merchants? There had been a time when the king's word was the law. The social standing of one's birth determined one's rights. The only rights a person had were those the king was willing to extend — and which he could withdraw at any moment. Fraternity, in the sense that all men and women shared humanity, was considered heresy. Society had treated slaves as animals and women as property, not part of a greater humanity. All three terms meant a loss of control by those in power, and the 19th century saw a flourishing counter-revolution of obscurantist philosophy.

Some writers look for signs that 19th century German thinkers like Schopenhauer,[11] Hegel,[12] or Weber[13] foreshadowed Nazism, but with little basis. The 19th century precursor to the fascist ideology was Social Darwinism, an English manufacture, as will be seen in Ch. 3. Germany contributed the mad nihilist Fredrich Nietzsche (1844–1900), known for his *Thus Spake Zarathustra* and *The Will to Power*. Hitler liked to be photographed staring at a bust of Nietzsche, the *enfant terrible* who theorized two sets of morals for the ruling and slave classes. He believed that ancient empires grew out of the ruling class and that religions – which denigrate the rich, the powerful, rationalism and sexuality – arose from the slave classes. "The unhealthy must at all costs be eliminated, lest the whole fall to pieces." He developed the idea of an *Übermensch*, or overman, a superhuman, symbolizing man at his most creative and highest intellectual development. "A daring and ruler race is building itself up... to become the 'lords of the earth.'"[14]

> ... a secret circular went out from the Reich Interior Ministry which marked the beginning of a programme of euthanasia for mentally ill or deformed children up to 3 years old. Doctors would be required to report all such cases to the health authority on special forms; the forms would then be forwarded to a panel of three medical assessors who would adjudicate over life or death by appending "-" or "+." Should all three place a "+," a euthanasia warrant would be issued, signed by the Reichsleiter Philipp Bouhler of the Fuhrer's Chancellery or SS Oberfuhrer Dr Viktor Brack, head of the Chancellery's Euthanasia Department II. And so it happened: infants marked for death were transferred to what were referred to as Children's Special Departments in politically reliable clinics, there to be given a "mercy death" by injection, or in one institution at Eglfing-Haar simply starved by a progressive reduction of diet.[15]

This superman or perfected man was mirrored in the racialist Nazi concept of "Aryan," as contrasted to the "Semitic" Jewish minority, as shown in this lurid passage from Hitler's *Mein Kampf*:

> With satanic joy in his face, the black haired Jewish youth lurks in wait for the unsuspecting girl whom he defiles with his blood, thus stealing her from her people. With every means he tries to destroy the racial foundations of the people he has set out to subjugate. Just as he himself systematically ruins women and girls, he does not shrink back from pulling down the blood barriers for others, even on a large scale. It was and it is Jews who bring Negroes into the Rhineland, always with the same secret thought and clear aim of ruining the hated white race by necessarily resulting bastardization, throwing it down

from its culture and political height, and himself rising to be master. [16]

While the Civil Rights Act of 1964 has eliminated much of the racial hate in the United States, a good deal remains just below the surface. In late 1998, Sen. Majority Leader Trent Lott of Mississippi and Rep. Bob Barr of Georgia were exposed as members of the Council of Conservative Citizens. The group's Web site, cofcc.org, still continues to bash blacks in a primitive fashion, and calls itself the No Longer Silent Majority.

The Rise of the Third Reich

Two factors were largely responsible for shaping global policies of the 1920s: the Treaty of Versailles and the rise of Bolshevism. Both figure prominently in Hitler's rise.

The Versailles Treaty placed severe limits on Germany and demanded harsh reparations. The French delegate Clemenceau demanded even harsher terms than approved by the treaty, hoping to permanently weaken Germany and ensure that France would be the sole continental power. Most historians regard the treaty as the primary cause of the rise of the Nazis, but the Bolshevik Revolution also played a part. It was the bogeyman that most aroused demagogues on the right. Communism, socialism, worker revolutions and unionism threatened the existing social order. In the United States, the Red Scare of 1919 led to extreme anti-unionism. [17] Fascist regimes offered big business owners and rightist leaders protection against communism and worker class movements.

The war was partially responsible for the global rebirth of the hard Right. From their service on the frontlines, many soldiers developed a strict sense of order and harsh justice compatible with right-wing beliefs. J.P. Morgan formed the American Legion to protect business interests and to act as a union-busting group of thugs. The Freikorps in Germany served the same purpose; Hitler himself was a member.

During the 1920s and 1930s fascism came to be viewed as a bulwark against Bolshevism. The Harding, Coolidge and Hoover administrations actively sought to strengthen Mussolini's hold on Italy to prevent the rise of socialism or communism there.

The end of World War I brought an end to the German Empire and monarchy. A series of weak center-right coalition governments governed the short-lived Weimar Republic (1919–33). Financial problems and internal turmoil rocked the ill-fated republic. The only period of stability was a short span of six years, 1923–29. Fourteen chancellors and 19 cabinets governed before Hitler's appointment as chancellor. The last year of the republic was especially chaotic with the failure of three governments (Heinrich Brüning, Franz von Papen and Kurt von Schleicher). The rapid changes contributed to the instability and increasing polarization in Germany.

During the 14 years of the Weimar Republic, the government repressed communists and socialists through violence, often assassination. Early on, it used the Freikorps to put down communist uprisings. Gen. Franz Epp, a leader of the Freikorps, led 30,000 soldiers to crush the Bavarian Socialist Republic, killing more than 600 communists and socialists. The Freikorps officially disbanded in 1921, but suppression of the Left continued, often resulting in street battles between the Right and Left. [18]

In 1926, the German army formed an Economic High Command to rearm and prepare for a new war. The Weimar government did nothing to suppress these actions. Instead, it conducted hundreds of treason trials in secret against any worker or journalist who revealed the truth. [19]

Hitler was a member of the List Regiment in Munich. During the attempted socialist takeover of Bavaria, historians believe that Hitler personally executed as many as 10 men. After the uprising was put down, Hitler was promoted in 1919 to a position as a *Vertrauens–mann* or undercover agent by Capt. Karl Mayr, who was in charge of Section I b/P of army intelligence, a bureau organized to investigate subversive political activities among the troop. Hitler remained an undercover agent until his discharge in late March 1920.

Hitler's first foray into politics came on Sept. 12, 1919, when his superior officers ordered him to investigate the German Workers' Party. Hitler attended a mid-September meeting in a little beer hall named Sterneckerbrau to gather information for his report. The fledging party had aroused the attention of the military, which was suspicious of all workers' groups. Anton Drexler had founded the party on March 7, 1918 under the name "Free Labor Committee for a Good Peace." The party consisted of roughly 50 railroad men and Drexler friends. After the war, Drexler changed the name, but the same members and chairman remained.

Hitler attended the meeting dressed in civilian clothes. Originally, Dietrich Eckart was slated as the main speaker, but canceled due to illness at the last moment, and Gottfried Feder took his place. Feder was an economic hack, and Hitler was glad when he finished his speech. After an attack on his views, Feder replied with a spirited defense. If the meeting had closed at this point, history might have taken a very different path. However, someone from the audience demanded Bavaria separate from Prussia and unite with Austria. Hitler had pronounced views on German unity and demanded the floor, delivering a rousing speech. It was the first time Hitler spoke before a political party, and the look of astonishment in the eyes of his audience pleased him. Hitler had no high opinion of the members of the tiny party, and had no intention of returning. However, before leaving the meeting, Drexler shoved a pamphlet into Hitler's hands.

The pamphlet outlined Drexler's views. While sketching out a "new world order" based on National Socialism, the pamphlet was largely an anti-Semitic tract. A portion follows:

There is a race — or perhaps we should call it a nation — which for over two thousand years has not possessed a state of its own, but has nevertheless spread over the entire earth. They are the Jews. They are not peasants, farmers or factory workers; they do not work in the coalmines or in the building trade. They are the secret "givers of bread" behind every limited liability company; they are the ones who barter everything fashioned by the intellectual and manual skill of mankind. They quickly conquered the money market, although they began in poverty, and were thereby made all the richer in vice, vermin and pestilence. All this they accomplished in the various countries they penetrated, and thus they became the indispensable bankers in all civilized countries and the economic leaders, exerting power over princes and rulers.

Only one per cent of the total population is Jewish but for thousands of years the Jews, from the highest to the lowest, have grimly pursued the thought that this tiny people should never serve rulers but always govern them. Yet they are unable to form a state of their own. Consequently in every country they strive to monopolize the money market, the economy, politics, literature, the press, and this race has almost made themselves the masters of the world.[20]

Hitler recorded his first impression of the party in *Mein Kampf* as follows:

My impression was neither good nor bad; a new organization like so many others. This was the time in which anyone who was not satisfied with developments and no longer had confidence in the existing parties felt called upon to found a new party. Everywhere these organizations sprang from the ground, only to vanish silently after a time. The founders for the most part had no idea what it means to make a party — let alone a movement — out of a club. And so these organizations nearly always stifle automatically in their absurd philistinism.[21]

Sept. 16, 1919, Hitler received a postcard saying the party accepted his membership and inviting him to attend a special meeting of the executive committee. Although he considered the postcard presumptuous, Hitler decided to go. He soon met Dietrich Eckart, a member of the Thule Society. Behind the front of a literary club studying Nordic culture, the Society was a hard-right political group devoted to anti-Semitism and aristocratic rule. Its agents had penetrated the government and were adept forgers with powerful ties to the Freikorps.

Eckart began tutoring Hitler by giving him books to read, teaching him to dress properly, introducing him to prominent people, and giving him money — funding that most likely came from other wealthy Eckart acquaintances. The introductions to prominent individuals arranged by Eckart paid large dividends in advancing Hitler and the party.

One of the first such introductions was to Frau Helene Bechstein, wife of the piano manufacturer Carl Bechstein. Hitler intrigued Helene. She soon gave him sizable contributions and began urging her friends to do the same. Her patronage eased the way for Hitler's acceptance in the highest social circles in Germany.[22]

Hitler recognized that for the party to continue to grow, Karl Harrer, the chairperson and another Thule Society member, had to be replaced. By Feb. 6, 1920 Drexler and Hitler had finished writing the party program, the infamous 25 points (see Appendix 2). Hitler's speeches had already contributed to the party's growth.

At this time, the party changed its name to National Socialist German Workers Party. Hitler also insisted on a party flag that could outdo the communist banner. A dentist from Stamberg suggested the design. The swastika has a long history dating back centuries and is found in various cultures, including American Indians. It had long been a symbol of the Teutonic Knights, and was used by the Thule Society and several Freikorp units.

By all accounts, Hitler lived frugally during this time, saving money for the party's needs and expansion. Since his discharge from the regiment in March 1920, he had no regular source of income. Hitler and the party were compensated from members' monthly dues and admission charged at meetings and rallies. However, party membership was still fewer than 3,000 by the end of the year. While Hitler was attracting crowds of around 6,000, the party spent much of the income on the welfare of party members, many of who were unemployed.

Before the end of 1920, Hitler insisted on one luxury item, a car, that he believed would dignify the party leadership. A second-hand Selve was purchased from funds raised mysteriously by a party member.[23]

Hitler also wanted a larger forum. He told Eckart that the *Volkischer Beobachter* newspaper was in financial difficulties and could be bought for 180,000 marks. At 8 a.m., Drexler and Eckart set off to raise the funds. By noon, they had secured 60,000 marks from Gen. von Epp and another 30,000 marks from others. At 4 p.m., the purchase of the paper was properly registered.[24] Hitler named Eckart as the editor of the newly acquired paper.

Shortly after buying the paper, Hitler hired his former sergeant major, Max Amann, as the party's business manager. Amann was a Thule Society member and could arrange for short-term credit for the party.

In July 1921, Hitler went to Berlin for six weeks to confer with north German right-wing leaders. A former electric company executive and Eckart friend, Dr. Emil Gansser, arranged for Hitler to speak at the prestigious National Club of Berlin. The speech impressed Adm. Ludwig von Schroeder, former commander of the German Marine Corps. The admiral proved to be a great help in winning over the support of the Prussian upper class to the Nazi cause.

While Hitler was in Berlin, a factional revolt directed against him broke out in the party. On his return to Munich, Hitler threatened to resign unless given dictatorial powers over it. The ruse worked and Hitler solidified his position.

In the late summer of 1921, the party's defense squads of volunteer brawlers reorganized under paramilitary lines. On Oct. 5, 1921 the party officially named them *Sturmabteilung* or Storm Troopers (SA). It cost a great deal to equip the SA. Shelter and food had to be provided, uniforms, flags and weapons had to be purchased, and there was the cost of transporting them to and from rallies. The money came from the High Command of the Bavarian Army, the Reichswehr. According to author James Pool, the aid was given on the initiative of Capt. Ernst Roehm without the knowledge of his superiors in the Bavarian army, but there is reason to doubt this.[25] Officially in charge of the press and propaganda for the Bavarian Reichswehr, Roehm had much more influence than his rank of captain suggested. Unofficially, the generals took his advice on political matters. He organized many of the Freikorp units and was responsible for hiding arms from the Allied Control Commission. Roehm also was the leader of the SA.

By November 1922, the Nazi Party had moved into larger headquarters and employed 13 full-time staff. A central file system and archive also were developed. Nov. 22, 1922, Ernst (Putzi) Hanfstaengl attended one of Hitler's speeches on a suggestion from Capt. Truman Smith, the assistant military attaché of the U.S. Embassy. Hanfstaengl was an anti-communist, and his mother, who was from a wealthy American family, owned an art business in Munich. Impressed by Hitler's speech, he joined the Nazi Party. Soon after, he loaned $1,000 to the party to buy a couple printing presses to convert the *Volkischer Beobachter* from a weekly to a daily paper.[26]

By the end of 1922, the German mark fell to 400 against the U.S. dollar. Hyperinflation continued through 1923. During the hyperinflation, Max Erwin von Scheubner-Richter was the most important fund-raiser for the Nazi Party. The wealthy Scheubner-Richter approached aristocrats, big business leaders and leaders of heavy industry for contributions. Scheubner-Richter was a close friend of Gen. Erich Ludendorff, who channeled money to him from industrialists. Ludendorff was a prominent World War I general who fled to Sweden claiming left-wing politicians had stabbed the German army in the back. In 1924, he became one of the first Nazis to be seated in the Reichstag.

Scheubner-Richter also was close to White Russian émigrés, and worked to bring about close cooperation between right-wing Russian émigrés and the Nazi Party. Through him, Hitler received the unqualified support of Gen. Vasili Biskupsky. In 1922, Biskupsky declared his support for Grand Duke Cyril, a pretender to the Russian throne. As a first cousin to Czar Nicholas II, he was a rightful heir to the crown. Both the Grand Duke and his wife, the Grand Duchess Victoria, took up the Nazi cause and gave generously.[27]

There also are credible reports that Hitler traveled to Switzerland to raise funds during the hyperinflation. Even trifling sums in foreign currency were worth enormous sums in German marks.

In October 1923, Gen. Eric Ludendorff suggested to Fritz Thyssen that he attend a speech by Hitler. Thyssen, whose family owned one of Germany's largest steel firms, was immediately struck by Hitler's views, and began contributing money to the Nazi Party. In October he gave Ludendorff 100,000 gold marks (not the inflated paper German marks) to divide between the Nazis and the Oberland Freikorps.

Here lies the controversy and the need for a close look at Hitler's rise to power. There has been a concerted effort in recent years to distance big business from support for the Nazis. Writers and historians try to downplay this connection and resort to deception. They base their argument on the size of Germany's industries, saying that only a few qualified as big businesses. This is as absurd as defining big business in the United States today to be only the 30 companies in the Dow-Jones Industrial index. Some writers have defined big business in Germany so that less than 10 qualify.

The same writers, including Pool,[29] try to minimize Thyssen's contribution by noting it was divided between the Nazis and the Freikorps. This argument is weak and misleading. Today in the United States, it's almost standard practice for a businessman or a corporation to contribute money to both parties to cover all possible outcomes, although the donations are seldom equal, and this practice is common across time and national boundaries. In fact, at the time of the Beer Hall Putsch in Germany, giving to multiple parties was especially prudent, since Germany's proportional parliamentary system awarded seats in the Reichstag on total votes received, rather than a winner-take-all system. Thus, even minor parties won a voice in the Reichstag.

Moreover, the Freikorps helped fund the Nazis. A close look at Hitler's trial reveals a close association between the two. Also, the Freikorps was a militia and not a political party. It did not fund other political candidates.

While the Nazis and Hitler were well known around Munich, they were unknown elsewhere. The Nazis had yet to seat their first representative in the Reichstag. Thyssen must have had an extraordinary degree of faith in the Nazis to make such a generous donation at a time of economic strife. The table below gives the composition of the Reichstag seats throughout the Weimar Republic.

Date	Jan 1919	Jun '20	May '24	Dec '24	May '28	Sept '30	July '32	Nov '32	Mar 1933
Total	423	459	472	493	491	577	608	584	647
SPD	165	102	100	131	153	143	133	121	120
USPD	22	84							
KPD		4	62	45	54	77	89	100	81
Centre Party	91	64	65	69	62	68	75	70	74
BVP		21	16	19	16	19	22	20	18
DDP	75	39	28	32	25	20	4	2	5
DVP	19	65	45	51	45	30	7	11	2
Wirt-schafts Partei	4	4	10	17	23	23	2	1	
DNVP	44	71	95	103	73	41	37	52	52
NSDAP			32	14	12	107	230	196	288
Others	3	5	19	12	28	49	9	11	7

SPD: Social Democrats; USPD: Independent Socialists; KPD: Communists; Centre Party: Catholics; BVP: Bavarian Peoples Party; DDP: Democrats; DVP: Peoples Party; Wirtschafts Partei: Economy Party; DNVP: Nationalists; NSDAP: Nazis[28]

After the Nazis' November 1923 attempt at an armed coup d'état, the Beer Hall Putsch, the Bavarian government only halfheartedly tried to round up and arrest members of the Nazi Party. Anton Drexler and Dietrich Eckart were arrested, but Eckart was released after 10 days because of sickness and died a month later. Franz Guertner, the minister of justice, worked feverishly behind the scenes to ensure Hitler received a light sentence. Of more than 100 people for taking part in the putsch, Guertner decided to prosecute only 10: Hitler, Ludendorff, Ernst Pochner, Wilhelm Frick, Ernst Roehm, Friedrich Weber, Herman Kriebel and three storm troopers — Brueckner, Wagner and Pernet, who were merely spear-carriers.

Frick had been Hitler's secret agent inside the police department. Weber was the commander of the Oberland Bund. Kriebel commanded the Kampfbund, an amalgam of the Reich War Flag, the Oberland Bund and Nazi storm troopers. The Oberland Freikorps was the parent organization of the Oberland Bund, a participant in the putsch. There was extensive cross-membership between the Nazis and the Oberland Bund. Further, the Thule Society helped fund the Oberland Freikorps.[30]

In essence, the Oberland Bund helped to provide Hitler with manpower for the Beer Hall Putsch. Looking at this evidence, the ridiculous claims by Pool and other writers that Thyssen's donation to the Nazis is overrated are obvious. Thyssen's donation went exclusively to Hitler and his thugs.

Hitler's trial provides more evidence of his funding sources. Feb. 7, 1924, Herr Auer, vice president of the Bavarian Diet, testified:

The Bavarian Diet has long had information that the Hitler movement was partly financed by an

American anti-Semitic chief, who is Henry Ford. Mr. Ford's interests in the Bavarian anti-Semitic movement began a year ago when one of Mr. Ford's agents, seeking to sell tractors, came in contact with Diedrich Eichart the notorious Pan-German. Shortly after, Herr Eichart asked Mr. Ford's agent for financial aid. The agent returned to America and immediately Mr. Ford's money began coming to Munich.

Herr Hitler openly boasts of Mr. Ford's support and praises Mr. Ford as a great individualist and a great anti-Semite. A photograph of Mr. Ford hangs in Herr Hitler's quarters, which is the center of the monarchist movement.[31]

Shortly after Auer's testimony, W.C. Anderson resigned and Ford experienced severe difficulties in doing business in Germany. Ford's donation came amid Germany's hyperinflation period, when foreign currency was especially valuable. The extent of the donation is unknown.

Further confirmation of Ford's funding comes from an interview Hitler gave seven months before the Beer Hall Putsch to Raymond Fendick, a foreign correspondent for the *Chicago Tribune*. Fendick wrote:

We look on Heinrich Ford as the leader of the growing fascisti movement in America. We admire particularly the anti-Jewish policy, which is the Bavarian Fascisti platform. We have just had his anti-Jewish articles translated and published. It is being circulated to millions throughout Germany.[32]

In 1924, Kurt Luedecke traveled to America to get more funding from Ford. Luedecke insists he was sent on the direct orders from Hitler. Luedecke had glowing remarks for Ford's editor of the *Dearborn Independent*, William Cameron.

Further confirmation of Ford's support for Hitler comes from newspaper articles. The *Berliner Tageblatt* made an appeal to the American ambassador to investigate the report of Ford's financing of the Nazis, noting that Hitler had money to spend during the hyperinflation period when marks were worthless. The *Manchester Guardian* reported Hitler received more than moral support from two American millionaires.[33]

While there is no direct proof, it can be surmised that the *Guardian* was referring to either the duPont family or W. Averell Harriman. Irénée duPont, heir apparent of the duPont family, was a Hitler admirer who followed his career closely. The duPonts quickly reestablished their cartel agreements with IG Farben as soon as World War I ended. Harriman traveled to Berlin in 1922 to set up the Berlin branch of W.A. Harriman & Co. George Herbert Walker was a director of the company; he was the father-in-law of Prescott Bush. Harriman and Thyssen had agreed to set up an American bank for Thyssen before 1924. The resulting bank, Union Bank, was seized from Prescott Bush in 1942 under the Trading With the Enemy Act.

The perplexing question of why American big businessmen would support Hitler at this early date has never been addressed. Before the Beer Hall Putsch, Hitler was largely unknown outside Munich and even within Germany. Given Ford's character as a miser who hated making donations to charities and organizations, why would he back a political party that had so far failed to seat a single representative in the Reichstag, at a time when the country was on the brink of a financial collapse? Only two explanations seem reasonable: Hitler's strong anti-communist stance or his extreme anti-Semitism. Both Harriman and Irénée duPont were anti-Semitic, although not fanatics like Ford. Throughout the 1920s, both U.S. foreign policy and trade policy show that American investors were sympathetic with Mussolini because of his anti-communist stance.

Hitler's trial revealed he received $20,000 from Nuremberg industrialists. The most significant contributor was Emil Kirdorf. In a Jan. 3, 1937 article in the *Preussiche Zeitung*, Kirdorf hints at his early support for Hitler: "In 1923 I came into contact for the first time with the Nationalist Socialist movement ... I first heard the Fuehrer in the Essen Exhibition Hall. His clear exposition completely convinced me."[34]

More evidence of Hitler's early financiers comes from the records of the Kilgore Committee.

By 1919 Krupp was already giving financial aid to one of the reactionary political groups which sowed the seed of the present Nazi ideology. Hugo Stinnes was an early contributor to the Nazi Party. By 1924 other prominent industrialists and financiers, among them Fritz Thyssen, Albert Voegler, Adolph Kirdorf and Kurt von Schroeder were secretly giving substantial sums to the Nazis.[35]

Except for Schroeder, all the people named above came from the large steel and coal trusts. Stinnes met with Hitler and Ludendorff on Oct. 25, 1923. Although no direct evidence is available, it appears Stinnes funneled money to Hitler through Ludendorff, one of the large industrialists who benefited from the hyperinflation. Indeed, many large industrialists in Germany benefited handsomely from the hyperinflation, lending creditability to the theory of an organized plot to relieve them of their millions in wartime debt, which they paid off with worthless, inflated marks. After Stinnes died in 1924, his son continued to support the Nazis.

The Nazi Party formed a bridge between the upper and the lower classes. While lower- and middle-class people filled the ranks of the SA, the upper class controlled and guided the policies of the party. Fascism as represented by the Nazis was a top-down movement by the elite to preserve their status.

More proof of Hitler's powerful connections comes from the extremely lenient sentence he received. Article 81 of the German Penal Code declares: "whosoever attempts to alter by force the Constitution of the German Reich or of any German state shall be punished by lifelong imprisonment."[36] Ludendorff was found innocent for taking part in the coup attempt. Hitler received only five years in prison and was released six months after the trial, serving only a year from the time of his arrest. Minister of Justice Franz Guertner secured an early release for Hitler and legalized the Nazi Party, which the trial judge had banned.[37] Guertner later served as minister of justice in the cabinets of Franz von Papen and Kurt von Schleicher. Hitler kept Guertner in that position, even though he was not a party member and protested the Nazi perversion of justice. He died in 1941.

Less lenient sentences were handed out to others in secret trials conducted by the Weimar Republic during the 1920s. For instance, Walter Bullerjahn was sent to prison for 15 years for treason. The Allies had discovered that the arms maker Paul von Gontard had secretly cached an arsenal contrary to the Treaty of Versailles. Gontard disliked Bullerjahn and charged him with revealing to the Allies the fact he was secretly arming Germany. No evidence of any connection between Bullerjahn and the Allies was ever presented in court. Bullerjahn was one of hundreds of victims who received more severe sentences for far less serious crimes than an armed rebellion and coup attempt.[38]

In jail, Hitler wrote *Mein Kampf,* first published July 18, 1925. By the end of the year, the first run of 10,000 was nearly sold out and a second printing was ordered. However, in the following year, sales dropped sharply, reviving only after Hitler seized power.[39]

On Dec. 20, 1924, when Hitler was released from prison, he found the party in disarray and his leadership challenged. The court had seized his car and the party newspaper. He was banned from speaking in Bavaria and in most of Germany. The party had made good inroads into the Reichstag in the May 1924 election, gaining 32 seats, but it suffered stunning losses in the December election that year, losing more than half of the seats gained in the summer. The only good news for Hitler was that Guertner had quashed an effort to deport him.

By spring 1925, Hitler bought a new supercharged Mercedes-Benz for 28,000 marks.[40] His only source of income after his release from prison was an occasional fee for newspaper articles he wrote. He also required a chauffeur who needed to be paid regularly. During the summer, Hitler spent much time at Obersalzberg in the Alps, traveling by car regularly from Munich. During this time, he came into more contact with the feudal princes. The Bavarian aristocrats were equally divided; half of them supported Hitler while the other half detested him. The divorced wife of the Duke of Sachsen-Anhalt began giving Hitler 1,500 marks a month from her alimony.[41] Thanks to his increasing contacts with the princes and their generosity to the party, Hitler changed his program and came out in favor of restoring expropriated lands and property. This change caused a major split in the party. Even Joseph Goebbels denounced the idea, but by the end of the summer, Hitler was in full control.

After his release from prison, Hitler realized that his only path to power was through the ballot box, so he decided to work within the system. However, 1925–29 marked a period of slow growth for the party. Inflation was under control and the communist threat had subsided. Without these two threats, voters turned away from the radical Nazi Party. Nazi records show the number of dues-paying members steadily increased from 27,000 in 1925 to 108,000 in 1928, but the party records are suspect and the real figures may be only half those reported.

Hitler and Big Business

Authors such as James Pool and Henry Ashby Turner, who minimize and distort the support of big business for the Nazi Party, suggest that Hitler's financing from 1925–29 came mainly from dues and speaking fees. Yet the number of dues-paying members was inadequate, and Hitler was banned from speaking in much of Germany.[42] On the other hand, author Carroll Quigley lists the following industrialists as supporters of Hitler during this time: Carl Bechstein, August Borsig, Emil Kirdorf, Fritz Thyssen and Albert Vogler.[43]

There is much evidence to support Quigley's position. Even Turner is forced to acknowledge that Hitler started courting big business support. On June 20, 1926, the Essen newspaper *Rheinisch-Westfalische Zeitung* reported that two days before, Hitler spoke to a closed-door meeting of invited business leaders. Hitler closed the meeting to get around the Prussian state's ban on public speeches. In the subsequent 18 months, he addressed three other such meetings.[44] Hitler was softening his approach to big business thanks to past financial donations. By all reports, after these meetings the business leaders were in favor of Hitler's views. The meetings grew in size from 40 for the first meeting to a high of 800 for the last one.

Turner tries to minimize big business participation in these meetings by claiming that no record of attendance has ever been found in the files of the big businessmen, and that some records would have survived. However, many of these big business leaders supported Hitler in secret, and the need for secrecy was mutual. Hitler had to avoid losing a large number of party members who opposed big business. The big business leaders had to maintain secrecy to avoid consumer boycotts. Ford's business suffered badly after his support of Hitler became known, and the lesson was not lost on these savvy executives. In 1926, even the Bechstein piano firm dismissed Edwin Bechstein after reports surfaced in the press of his fraternization with Hitler.

Turner claims that an obscure man named Arnold, who held a managerial job at a midsize smelting firm, organized the first meeting. Then he assumes only people in similar positions were invited.[45] It is unlikely that a group of midlevel managers from small to midsize firms meeting with Hitler would have attracted the attention of local newspapers. It also is unlikely Hitler would have traveled to Essen to speak at the request of midlevel business managers unless some prominent names were present.

Turner also tries to distance big business from the Nazis by suggesting that company donations were made by junior or middle-level management. While such an argument sounds reasonable, it is patently false. Almost no business even today allows such decisions by middle-level managers; such daring decisions would likely lead to the employee's dismissal. As an example, Ludwig Grauert, the managing director of the Arbeitnordwest, the iron and steel industry association in the Ruhr, made a $100,000 loan to the Nazis after receiving permission from Ernst Borbet, another director of United Steel. After his boss returned and discovered the loan, Grauert was nearly fired. If Thyssen had not replaced the funds, Grauert would have been dismissed.[46]

In 1927, Elsa Bruckmann, a Munich socialite, arranged a meeting between Hitler and Emil Kirdorf. Kirdorf was a fanatical nationalist and supporter of radical right-wing causes. During the four-hour meeting, Hitler downplayed his anti-Semitism and said the Nazi Party's 25 points would not be implemented. Hitler rarely spoke of the 25-point program and, in later years, only spoke of it derisively. He presented himself as a defender of private enterprise and a supporter of an economy based on Darwinian principles that only the strong survive. Kirdorf suggested Hitler write down his thoughts in a pamphlet to spread secretly among business leaders. Hitler complied and Kirdorf printed the pamphlet, *The Road to Resurgence,* listing Hitler as the author. In October, Kirdorf offered Hitler further aid by inviting him to his home to meet with 14 of his friends.[47]

It is unknown how many pamphlets of *The Road to Resurgence* were printed, but the circulation was extremely limited. Only one of the pamphlets has survived. It was found in the library of a major Ruhr industrial firm. In his shamefully apologetic diatribe to big business, Turner uses this fact to suggest the pamphlet was largely unread.[48] However, as it was found in the library of a large industrial firm, it suggests that whoever received the pamphlet placed it there so others could read it. Further, it is equally probable that these industrialists passed the pamphlet within their own circle of friends. It is more likely these industrialists read the pamphlet eagerly, since they were intrigued by Hitler's ability to rally the workers, along with his anti-socialist and anti-union views .

Hitler continued to meet with business leaders, often in secret, until his appointment as chancellor. Many times, these meetings were so secret that they would take place in a lonely forest glade on the side of an isolated road.[49]

A complete list of Hitler's financial backers may never be known. However, Walter Funk named many business leaders and industries as financial supporters of Hitler during his Nuremberg testimony: Georg von Schnitzler, a leading director of IG Farben; August Rosterg and August Diehn of the potash industry; Wilhelm Cuno of the Hamburg-Amerika Line, the shipping company seized from Prescott Bush for trading with the enemy; Otto Wolf, a powerful Cologne industrialist; and Kurt von Schroeder, a radical Nazi and Cologne banker. Also implicated were Deutsche Bank, Commerz Bank, Dresdner Bank, Deutsche Kredit Gesellschaft and Allianz, Germany's largest insurer.[50]

Many businesses chose to align with and support the Nazis after they gained power. Krupp and IG Farben were both executors of Goering's Four-Year Plan to make Germany militarily self-sufficient by 1940. In April 1933, Gustav Krupp sought a private meeting with Hitler. Krupp agreed to become Hitler's chief fund-raiser and chairman of the Adolf Hitler Fund. In return, Hitler promised to appoint Krupp as the *Fuehrer* of Germany industry. Through the years, Krupp contributed more than 6 million marks of his own money to the Nazis, and his correspondence shows that he enjoyed his job as chairman.[51] It is common knowledge that after Hitler's appointment as chancellor, Krupp greeted people cheerfully with the *Heil Hitler* salutation.

In 1932, Kurt von Schroeder and Wilhelm Keppler formed the group known as "The Fraternity." Members agreed to contribute an average of 1 million marks a year to Heinrich Himmler's personally marked "S" account and the transferable, secret "R" account of the Gestapo.[52]

While Hitler continued to meet with the industrialists, he allowed Gregor Strasser, Goebbels and Gottfried Feder to continue to beguile the masses with socialist views. Hitler never expressed any solid economic views of his own. He would tailor his speech to the audience. Speaking in front of industrialists, he would soften his anti-Semitism and denounce the Nazi 25-point program. In fact, Hitler never did support the 25-point program and referred to it only once in *Mein Kampf,* and then in a derogatory manner. Hitler continued to evolve the party away from socialism and was successful in convincing Goebbels to desert the socialist faction of the Nazi Party led by Strasser. This softening of the Nazi position on capitalism and private property is clearly seen in an *Erklärung*, a clarification of the party position issued April 13, 1928.

Since the NSDAP admits the principle of private property, it is self-evident that the expression "confiscation without compensation" merely refers to the possible legal powers to confiscate, if necessary, land illegally acquired, or administered in accordance with the national welfare. It is directed in the first instance against Jewish companies which speculate in land.[53]

Besides receiving aid from German business leaders and the upper class of German society, Hitler and the Nazis received important support from corporate America, as shown in this excerpt from an interview with the American ambassador to Germany, William Dodd.

Certain American industrialists had a great deal to do with bringing fascist regimes into being in both Germany and Italy. They extended aid to help fascists occupy the seat of power, and they are helping to keep it there …

Propagandists for fascist groups try to dismiss the fascist scare. We should be aware of the symptoms. When industrialists ignore laws designed for social and economic progress, they will seek recourse to a fascist state when the institutions of our government compel them to comply with the provisions.[54]

Dodd did not name any of the industrialists in the interview, but most historians believe he was referring to Henry Ford. Other foreign sources of support for Hitler came from Sir Henri Deterding, the founder of Royal Dutch Petroleum. Deterding was strongly opposed to communism and, as early as 1921, was a Hitler admirer. Deterding was interested in discovering those forces that would remove once and for all the dangers of social or colonial revolutions. At the inquiry into the Reichstag fire, Johannes Steel, a former agent of the German Economic Intelligence Service, testified to Deterding's financial support for the Nazis.[55] The Dutch press reported that Deterding had given Hitler about 4 million guilders. By the 1930s, Deterding began secret negotiations with the German military to provide a year's supply of oil on credit. In 1931, Deterding made a 20 million pound loan to Hitler, allegedly for a promise of a petroleum monopoly once the Nazis were in power. In May 1933, Alfred Rosenberg, Hitler's representative, met with Deterding, confirming the close link between big oil and the Nazis. In 1936, the board of directors forced Deterding to resign over his Nazi sympathies.

Despite Hitler's successful effort in courting support from big business and industrialists, the Nazis remained a minor party until after the 1929 stock market crash. Owing to its huge burden of debt, Germany suffered more than other countries. In the 1930 election, the Nazis won 107 seats in the Reichstag, making it the second largest party. It became the largest party in the Reichstag in the July 1932 election, but still fell short of a clear majority. The depression brought about three short-lived governments, amid political intrigue and backroom deals. However, Hitler's only visible gains from the 1930 election were meetings with the chancellor and the president.

Early in 1932, Hitler decided to run for president against Paul von Hindenburg. Two other candidates were on the ballot: Theodor Duesterberg, a nationalist, and Ernst Thaelmann, a communist. Hitler lost badly to Hindenburg, receiving just 30 percent of the vote to Hindenburg's 49.6 percent. Hitler campaigned on the slogan "Freedom and Bread." Since Hindenburg did not receive a majority of the vote, a runoff was held a month later. In it, Hitler received 37 percent of the vote to Hindenburg's commanding 53 percent.

The final year of the republic was marked by the failure of three separate governments: Bruening, von Papen and Schleicher. The last government of Schleicher lasted only 57 days. Party leaders became embroiled in political plots, forming transient alliances. Von Papen, who like Schleicher was heavily involved in political intrigue, later played a prominent role in Hitler's appointment as chancellor.

The intrigues also involved big business leaders and other prominent industrialists. On Jan. 26, 1932, Hitler spoke to 650 industrialists at the Düsseldorf Industry Club to gain their trust and support. While the Nazi Party was the largest party in the Reichstag after the July 1932 election, Hitler was still denied the office of Chancellor.

Business viewed von Papen's government favorably because it allowed the unilateral breaking of union contracts and lower wages. Estate owners received subsidies, and land reform was stopped. Businesses received tax rebates, but workers received no tax relief.

Politically, the von Papen administration existed only because of the secret support of the Nazis. In return, von Papen granted three Nazi demands. He dissolved parliament, which triggered the July 1932 election; he reinstated the SA and SS, which had been banned; and he disposed of the Prussian government, removing the last obstacle for the Nazis.[56] After the July election, negotiations between von Papen and Hitler broke down, as both sought the office of chancellor.

As early as September 1932, leading Ruhr industrialists told Gregor Strasser that they had suggested to the highest offices in Berlin that Hitler be appointed chancellor. By November, business leaders took a more active role in securing a Hitler government by sending a petition seeking his appointment as chancellor. The petition originated with members of the Keppler Circle and was signed by Kurt von Schroeder, Vogler, Thyssen and others.[57] The petition was less than successful in the business community, as the Nazis became more radical in their demands throughout the summer, into the fall and through the November election.

The radicalism cost Hitler and the Nazi Party dearly. They lost 34 seats in the Reichstag and their source of funding from business leaders was severely cut. Nevertheless, Hindenburg asked Hitler to form a government under two conditions. Hitler refused the offer, resulting in Schleicher's appointment as chancellor. But business leaders soon opposed Schleicher, who restored the inviolability of union contracts and launched a large-scale public works policy to reduce unemployment.

With the arrival of a new year, the Nazi Party's future looked dim. Hopes were dashed by the November election, and the party experienced severe financial difficulties. However, business leaders turned against the new Schleicher government and arranged a meeting between Hitler and von Papen. The objective of the meeting at the Cologne home of Kurt von Schroeder was to form a new government led by Hitler and von Papen.

Baron von Schroeder was a member of the most influential group in Germany, the *Herrenklub*, as well as the Thule Society. He later held several high positions in the Nazi government and directed ITT's Germany subsidiaries. Moreover, von Schroeder had extensive financial contacts in New York and London. He was a co-director of the Thyssen foundry with Johann Groeninger, Prescott Bush's New York bank partner. Schroeder also was vice president and director of Prescott Bush's Hamburg-Amerika Line.

The meeting took place in utmost secrecy on Jan. 4, 1933 with two Americans present: John Foster Dulles and Allen Dulles. The Dulles brothers were there representing their client, Kuhn, Loeb & Co., which had extended large, short-term credits to Germany and needed assurance of repayment from Hitler before committing to support him. Goebbels recorded the success of the meeting in his diary on Jan. 5, 1933: "If this coup succeeds, we are not far from power ... Our finances have suddenly improved."[58]

Hitler now had the backing of both von Papen and the business leaders. Facing pressure from these quarters, Hindenburg relented and appointed Hitler as chancellor on Jan. 30, 1933. Von Papen assumed the vice-chancellor position.

Herein lies the danger of creeping fascism. Hitler was appointed chancellor thanks to a backroom deal, with the blessing of international bankers. He rose to power by electoral rather than revolutionary means. However, Hitler's appointment as chancellor was not due solely to support from big business and from political intrigue. A flaw in the German constitution, which did not account for a stalemated parliament, aided his rise to power. Power in Germany was concentrated in the office of the president, headed by Hindenburg, who had the authority to appoint cabinets and chancellors. Beginning in 1930, Hindenburg began appointing chancellors who were not beholden to parliament, and circumvented it by granting them the emergency powers given to the president by the constitution. Presidential decrees enacted almost all national laws, including the power to tax, because parliament was hopelessly deadlocked in petty political bickering.

Americans should take special note of the concentration of power in Germany in the president's office. US presidents increasingly are relying on executive orders. These executive orders bypass Congress and are most likely unconstitutional, since they usurp the power to rule by presidential decree. Most alarming are the series of executive orders concerning a state of emergency. They give the US president the right to seize the media, farms, private transportation, airlines, medical facilities and housing, and even to conscript citizens into organized work battalions.

In Germany, the Hitler-von Papen government was a coalition between the NSDP and the DNVP, plus big business and landowners, since it was their support of the Nazis that persuaded Hindenburg to appoint Hitler.

The membership of the Nazi Party came mostly from the lower and middle classes: 7% upper class, 7% peasants, 35% workers, and 51% middle class. The largest single occupational group was the elementary school teachers. These percentages reflect the structure of German society. Germany had a large middle class before Hitler assumed power, although the real wealth of the country was concentrated in a few hands.

In 1925, Professor Theodor Geiger conducted an extensive study of the class distribution in Germany. He divided German society into five classes.

Class	Percentage of the population in 1925[59]
Capitalist	00.92
Old Middle Class	17.77
New Middle Class	17.95
Quasi-proletarian	12.65
Proletarian	50.71

While there is no direct comparison between Geiger's study and later breakdowns of party membership by class, the figures indicate the Nazi party had a widespread appeal in the upper class. The small percentage of capitalists indicates the stratification of Germany society, with wealth concentrated in just a few families. Although the middle class membership numbers suggest widespread support for the Nazis, the reality is many of the professions, such as schoolteachers, were required to join the party. Figures for the 1925 class structure and the party membership point to fascism being a top-down movement.

Hitler became chancellor only after he eased the fears of big business leaders and assured them of his support. Fascism is generally a desperate reaction by the elite to preserve their power and wealth in periods of economic crisis and political strife. The resurgence of fascism since the 1980s may be linked to the stresses of shifting from an industrial to an information-based economy. This is especially troubling in the United States, where U.S. supremacy is threatened by increasing dependence on imported oil and manufactures. The fortunes of the American elite depend on an oil-driven economy and the ability of the U.S. to project power with a navy, army and air force running largely on oil.

Politicians and political speeches promise everything; however, the real character of any regime can only be determined by its actual policies. Hitler and the Nazis were no different. They used socialist rhetoric to attract followers, but soon turned on them. Hitler's Nazi economic policies up to the invasion of Poland revealed the true character of fascism without distortion by the fog of war.

The Nazi Government and Big Business

Within his first month as chancellor, Hitler faced a crisis. He proposed to dissolve parliament and hold new elections. Hugenberg, the leader of the DNVP party and a member of Hitler's cabinet, rejected the idea of a new election. Big business backed Hitler, but only after a Berlin meeting between the Nazis and the Reich Association of German Industry. The industrialists gave their support only after Hitler assured them of the need for a fundamental cleavage between democracy and private capital. Private ownership of the means of production could only be ensured once democracy was destroyed. The elderly Krupp welcomed Hitler's remarks and looked forward to a strong, independent state and business prosperity. Once Hitler gained the industrialists' support, Goering appealed to the group for financing for the new election. Three million marks were required; the Ruhr industrialists supplied 1 million.

By choosing to finance the March 1933 election for the Nazis, big business became a full partner of the Third Reich. The support came at a crucial time for Hitler. If business leaders had withheld their support, Hitler's government would have failed.

After a week in office, Hitler got a new decree from Hindenburg to remove the Prussian ministers. Their powers were conferred on von Papen; Goering received the police authority. The Nazis already controlled the national police through the Interior Department, headed by Wilhelm Frick. By Feb. 7, 1933, Hitler had secured control of the national and Prussian police. He then launched a violent, two-pronged attack against the opposition. Goering and Frick, under a cloak of legality, worked from above, while Capt. Ernst Roehm, head of the storm troopers, worked from below, with no pretext of legality. Goering and Frick removed all noncooperative police officials and replaced them with Nazis, usually storm troopers. On Feb. 4, 1933, Hindenburg signed an emergency decree, giving Hitler the right to ban meetings and the press.[60]

The opposition was attacked from below in violent assaults, often leaving one or more people dead. Despite the violence inflicted by storm troopers, it was obvious the week before the election that the Nazis faced strong opposition. Under these circumstances, a plot was hatched to burn the Reichstag and blame the communists. The Nazis fingered a mentally incompetent Dutchman, Van der Lubbe, who was left wandering about the Reichstag after the fire. The following day, Feb. 28, 1933, Hindenburg signed an emergency decree suspending all civil liberties. The Nazis arrested all communist members of the Reichstag and thousands of others. Communist and social democrat newspapers were suspended for two weeks.

The regular German courts acquitted the four communists charged with setting the blaze and convicted poor Van der Lubbe. Several people knew the truth, including Ernst Oberfohren, a Nationalist Reichstag member, but they were murdered in March and April. Goering had most of the Nazis involved in the plot killed during the blood purge of June 30, 1934.[61]

Despite the Nazis' drastic measures, the March 5, 1933 election failed because they succeeded in drawing only 43.9 percent of the vote. The new Reichstag convened March 23 at the Kroll Opera House. To achieve a majority, the Nazis excluded all the communists and 30 socialists from the session. The remaining members were then asked to pass an enabling act giving the government the right to rule by decree for four years. Since the act required a two-thirds majority, it could have been defeated if only a small group of Center Party members voted against it. But the measure passed 441-94, with the social democrats forming a solid minority.

Next, the Nazis issued a series of revolutionary decrees ordering the diets of all German states be reconstituted in proportion to the national election, excluding all communists. A similar measure followed in local governments. An April 7, 1933 decree gave the Hitler government the right to name a new governor for each German state. The governors were empowered to dismiss state governments, including judges. The law was used to seat Nazi governors and judges.[62]

Hitler declared May 1 to be a national holiday and gave a speech on the dignity of labor. The next day, the SA seized all union buildings and offices, arrested all labor leaders and sent most of them to concentration camps, betraying the duplicity of the Nazi character. In July, Hess promised to break up the great department stores, but no action was ever taken.

By July 1933, all political parties except the Nazis were banned. Wholesale and retail trade associations were consolidated into the Reich Corporation of German Trade, under the direction of Nazi Party member Adrian von Renteln. Von Renteln became president of the German Industrial and Trade Committee, a union of all branches of the chamber of commerce. Previously, the chamber of commerce had been a semipublic corporation.

Labor was coordinated without opposition, except from the communists. However, by the spring of 1934, the SA was becoming an acute problem. It was calling for a second revolution and economic reforms favorable to labor and damaging to the heart of the Nazi support — big business. Further, the SA was calling for incorporation into the Reichswehr, with each officer holding the same rank as he had in the SA.

On June 21, 1934, Hindenburg ordered General Werner von Blomberg to use the army to restore order if necessary. Hitler quickly arranged a deal with the top military leaders to destroy the SA in return for his appointment as president, once Hindenburg died. Hitler's previous support from a faction within the military should not be overlooked in this deal. On June 30, 1934, Hitler arranged a meeting of SA leaders in Bad Wiessee. The SS under Hitler's command arrested and shot most of the leaders at the meeting in the middle of the night. Goering did the same to SA leaders in Berlin and murdered most of his personal enemies. In all, the Nazis killed several thousands in the blood purge.

The threat from the army to restore order had been serious, but not overwhelming, since the SA outnumbered the Reichswehr 10 to 1. The choice facing Hitler was clear: support the "second revolution" and socialism, or destroy it. His decision to decapitate the SA and with it any hope for social reforms shows how fascism served big business. Any supporters of a second revolution lucky enough to survive were driven underground.

The close association of the Nazis with big business, and more generally of fascism with the merger of corporations and the state, can be seen in the shift of power in Germany. Carroll Quigley divides the ruling groups of Germany into the five classes in three historical periods:

The Empire	Weimar Republic	The Third Reich[63]
Emperor		Top Nazi Officials
Army	Army	Industry
Landlords	Bureaucracy	Army
Bureaucracy	Industry	Bureaucracy
Industry	Landlords	Landlords

The table above shows big business drastically gaining in power under the Nazi state, which was organized so that everything was subject to the benefit of capitalism, with two limiting clauses: the Nazis controlled the state, and war could force curtailment of capitalistic benefits. In short, the Nazi system was dictatorial capitalism and aptly described as economic Darwinism.

Chief Economic Adviser Wilhelm Keppler stopped efforts to coordinate industry and privatized many of the companies the government had acquired. The previous German governments had a policy of not letting firms fail. If a firm filed bankruptcy, the government would buy all or part of it to keep it solvent. The Nazis privatized several large concerns. In 1932, the government bought Gelsenkirchen (a part of United Steel) and through a complicated series of mergers, the Nazis practically gave the company back to business. In 1936, the Nazis returned the last of the stock to United Steel for 100 million marks. In 1931, the old government had bought several large banks. By the end of 1937, the Nazis had returned the Dresdner, Commerz and Deutsche banks to private hands. In 1936, the Nazis also returned most of the stock in the Deutscher Schiff und Maschinenbau Steamship Co. In September 1936, the Nazis ceded the government's 8 million marks of capital in Hamburg Sud-Amerika. The shipping concern only had a capitalization of 10 million marks. The Nazi government suffered large losses in privatizing the firms.[64]

The Nazis vigorously opposed municipally owned enterprises. In particular, utility companies had remained profitable during the depression, and big business prized them. The day Hitler appointed Hjalmar Schacht to the Ministry of Economy, he issued orders to hasten liquidation of municipal enterprises.

In Italy, Mussolini privatized the Consortium of Match Manufacturers, the state-owned life insurance industry and municipal enterprises. The support of big business and the elite is obvious from the fascist tax code. A June 1, 1933 law allowed industrialists to deduct the costs of new equipment immediately from their taxable income. Supplemented by the law passed on Oct. 16, 1934, businesses were reimbursed partially for any expenses in repairing houses, factories or stores. Tax delinquents had balances reduced by half. Families employing a maid were allowed to claim a dependent and reap the tax benefit. In April 1934, the Nazis granted nearly 500 million marks in tax cuts to businesses. In Italy, the fascists abandoned the inheritance tax, and halved the taxes of managers and directors of corporations. The Italian Minister of Finance boasted: "We have broken with the practice of persecuting capital."[65]

In an economy based on capitalism or free enterprise, businessmen hate and fear competition. Before the Nazi takeover, big business had three different types of organizations to limit competition: cartels, trade associations and employers' associations.

The cartels regulated prices, production and the markets. Trade associations were political groups organized like chambers of commerce. Employers' associations sought to control labor.

Nazi policy left existing cartels relatively unaffected, while cartelizing various new industry groups. The Nazis merged the employers' associations into the Labor Front, and the Ministry of Economics gained control over the trade associations. All of this took place with the blessing of big business.

While big business lost direct control over the three groups, it got what it wanted. Under the Labor Front, big business gained control over labor, wages and working conditions. The Nazis restricted employers from hiring workers who quit or were discharged from another firm unless the previous employer signed a workbook, releasing the employee to seek work elsewhere. By refusing to sign the workbook, employers were able to exert absolute control over employees, holding them as virtual slaves.

Trade associations were reduced essentially to social and propaganda organizations, headed by prominent business leaders. Of 173 of these heads throughout Germany, 108 were businessmen, only 11 were Nazi Party members.[66] Cartels were extended, removing almost all forms of market competition. Only the largest German firms controlled the cartels. The Nazis allowed big business to force all firms into cartels, sparking mergers and destroying small businesses.

The July 15, 1933 law gave the minister of the economy the right to make membership in certain cartels mandatory. The law also allowed the minister to regulate the capacity of enterprises and to ban the establishment of new firms. The Nazis issued hundreds of decrees under this law. On the same day, the ban against boycotts by cartels was lifted. Big business could now refuse to supply smaller firms.

The 1937 corporation law eased the way for big business to buy smaller firms through mergers. The law required a minimum of 500,000 marks in capital for new incorporations and a nominal value of at least 1,000 marks for all shares. The Nazis ordered all firms with less than 100,000 marks capital dissolved. This provision condemned 20 percent of all corporations. At the same time, the law sharply limited shareholder rights.[67]

Legally, supervising cartels was a role of the government and the cartel courts. Under the November 1936 decree, cartels held the sole right to fix prices and regulate the markets. The decree mandated the use of uniform accounting. While this provision didn't affect big business, small firms lost their right to keep their books and count their costs as they wished.

Many people mistakenly believe that the Nazis were totalitarians and exerted full control over the economy and big business. While this was partially true in the later years of the war, even then it was common for big business to ignore decrees. The formation of the Hermann Goering Works is a good example of the degree of independence enjoyed by big business. In preparation for war, Goering first tried to persuade German mining and smelting concerns to use low-grade domestic ore instead of importing the high-grade ore from Sweden, which was draining precious foreign currency, and could be unreliable because of the long shipping route vulnerable to attack and blockade. In fact, the Nazis invaded Denmark and Norway to protect the shipping lanes for Swedish ore. The industrialists politely refused Goering's request — even under threats of arrest for sabotage. Continued resistance to Germany's low-grade ore led Goering to form his own company.[68]

The close relationship between big business and the Nazis was further cemented by Hitler's drive to make Germany self-sufficient. IG Farben, the giant chemical cartel, always preserved a close association with the German military. Initially, the company had several Jews among its directors and was attacked by the Nazis. Once the Jews were replaced and a few rabid Nazis rose to director positions, the company ideology merged with that of the party. One of the critical materials IG Farben supplied to the Nazis was gasoline derived from coal. By the end of the war, IG Farben was using a series of slave labor camps, including Auschwitz. Another product IG Farben supplied was Zyklon-B.

The reorganization of cartels and the laws passed from 1933-38 were fully approved first by big business. Krupp von Bohlen was one of the industrialists who played a key role in the reorganization, often forcing the Nazis to compromise on an issue. The true character of fascism — the merger of big business with the government — is readily obvious in the policies imposed by the Nazis before the Polish invasion. Once in power, Hitler dismissed numerous officials opposed by big business. Thousands more were eliminated in the blood purge. For instance, after the blood purge, Kurt Schmitt was removed as director of the Ministry of Economics on the insistence of big business. Schmitt had fallen into disfavor when he restructured the business organizations.[69]

The primary architect of the Nazi economy was Hjalmar Schacht, the banker who masterminded the stabilization of the currency in 1923. Like Hitler, Schacht detested democracy and parliamentary government. In March 1933, he became president of the Reichsbank and in 1934, minister of the economy, a post he held until he resigned over policy disputes in 1937. His first official act was creating Metall-Forschungsgesellschaft A.G. (Mefo), a dummy corporation of four armament firms. Mefo issued bills similar to promissory notes to government contractors, which could be extended up to five years. Schacht's Mefo bills allowed Hitler unlimited credit to rearm Germany on a large scale. By 1936, Schacht was worried that the continued pace of rearmament would renew inflation. He was acquitted of war crimes at Nuremberg.[70]

While the Nazi economy was good for big business, labor suffered. In the first three years after the Nazis seized power, the net profits of big business rose nearly 500 percent, while wages remained static. Under the Nazis, workers gained no benefit, other than a decrease in unemployment.

Year[71]	Net profit in million marks	Hourly wages in Pfennigs (1929=100)
1932	-390	69.7
1933	120	37.6
1934	370	67.5
1935	460	67.5
1936	520	67.5

What little gains made by labor came with increasing work hours in the required 48-hour workweek. Not only did the Nazis want to suppress union activity, they also wanted to dominate all the workers' time. The Labor Front required workers to join various party organizations, seeking to indoctrinate them with Nazi ideology. The only recourse for labor grievances was through the shop cell, headed by the choice of the factory owner.

In late 1937, armament industries made enormous profits, but the plight of labor was so bad that cries were renewed for the second revolution. In January 1938, industrialists fearing nationalization met with Hitler. Top Nazi officials assured them there would be no nationalization of any industry.

In essence, the Nazis reorganized the economy by abolishing four principles. The principle that all businesses should enjoy equal economic rights was largely eliminated. Free competition was almost abolished, as was the freedom of business enterprise. The principle that business leaders should be free to form voluntary associations was largely abandoned. Reorganization took place only with the approval of big business as a means to remove competition. New associations, such as the Keppler Circle, ensured big business leaders that they had the ear of Hitler and the Nazi Party. The changes made it easy for big business to decide economic policy under the Nazis.[72]

An alliance of big business, army generals and the Nazi Party altered the economy in six significant ways following the reorganization:

1. Suppression of trade unions, supremacy of employers' managerial prerogative in industrial relations.

2. Acceptance of the principle of compulsion in private organizations for market control, whether for expelling outsiders, or forcing small business to join cartels and submit to big business.

3. Inducements by which governmental agencies, using direct controls, could channel favors to particular business groups and institutions of capitalism.

4. Compulsory groupings replaced voluntary trade associations.

5. Expansion of the noncapitalistic institution of public investment for purposes of rearmament.

6. Specific direct controls in a few markets using funds and essential raw materials for rearmament, with allocation by government decisions.[73]

Big business demanded the first three changes. The last three changes resulted from the military goals of the Nazi regime. While favored by both big business and the Nazi Party, the generals were the more precise formulators and the loudest supporters of the last three changes.

Only after the cost of rearmament became burdensome did the Nazis raise taxes on corporations. In 1936, at the peak of the rearmament boom, the Nazis raised the corporate tax rate by 5 percent. However, the fiscal policy of the Nazis shifted the tax burden away from business and onto the consumer.[74]

The Nazi economy was based on capitalism, with a strong taste of social Darwinism. Big business could maximize profits and privatize assets, while shifting costs onto workers and society. Wages were reduced and fixed by big business through a puppet government organization.

The Nazis took the burdening of workers to an extreme in the slave labor camps. It was big business that first proposed to use the prisoners. The Nazis at first dismissed the idea, but after big businesses suggested they would be willing to pay the SS a nominal fee for slaves, the Nazis relented. Most of the slave labor camps of big business were much more brutal than the concentration camps run by the SS (as noted by William Manchester in *The Arms of Krupp*, p. 477). In effect, the slave labor camps saved the employer the cost of adequately feeding workers, who usually starved to death within six months.

Although right-wing elements persist in labeling Nazism as socialism by citing public works projects, the table below of public works spending dispels any notion of socialism in the Third Reich.

Sector	Total Spent in 1,000s of marks[75]
Repair of private houses	900
New houses	170
Agricultural resettlement	300
Regulation of rivers	160
Street construction	210
Underground projects	216
Modernization of railroads	1,055
Highway construction	2,000
Miscellaneous	439
Total	5,450

Except for the housing projects, almost all the categories the Nazis spent money on had a military application. From the moment the Nazis seized power, their plans were to start another war. From his experiences in World War I, Hitler certainly was well aware of the need for modern transportation systems in a military conflict. Thus, modernizing the railroads and construction of the autobahn figured prominently in the Nazis' plans. Much of the money spent on regulating rivers also had a military application in supporting barge traffic. Likewise, Hitler had firsthand experience with the food shortage caused by the British blockade during World War I, so investment in agriculture also had an underlying military objective. The table above also includes figures for public works projects started by the previous government. Thus, the total amount the Nazis spent on public works projects totaled less than 2 billion marks. At the same time, the government receipts from 1934–38 totaled nearly 135 billion marks. The amount the Nazis earmarked for non-military public works projects was minuscule — less than 2 percent — of the government's revenue. Even if all the money listed in the table was to be considered for public works, it still represents only 5 percent of the government's revenue.

With the recent rise of fascism globally, accompanied by free trade agreements, the hard Right is desperately repainting the Nazis in an attempt to distance itself from its past. Their false claims, by spokesmen like Rush Limbaugh, extend to everything the hard Right opposes: allegedly the Nazis were environmentalists, homosexuals and even pagans:

The most notorious environmentalists in history were the German Nazis. The Nazis ordered soldiers to plant more trees. They were the first Europeans to establish nature reserves and order the protection of hedgerows and other wildlife habitats. And they were horrified at the idea of hydroelectric dams on the Rhine. Adolf Hitler and other leading Nazis were vegetarian and they passed numerous laws on animal rights.[76]

The above quote comes from the transcript of a British Channel 4 documentary, *Against Nature*, whose political direction came from Frank Furedi's libertarian magazine. It was extracted from Ron Arnold's Center in Defense of Free Enterprise Web page, where the transcript is featured as a "guest editorial."

The quote is full of half-truths and lies. Nature worship in Germany dates from the origins of modern romanticism. The Nazis were fearful of dams on the Rhine, but not because they were nature worshippers or ecologists. Dams on the Rhine would have required locks to allow for barge traffic. The Nazis wanted the Rhine free of dams so barges could transport armaments and men as quickly as possible.

Hitler was the only leading Nazi who was a vegetarian, and his diet was due to his digestive problems. Sausages gave Hitler extreme stomach cramps. He also avoided alcohol because of his poor digestion.

The Nazis also passed animal rights or cruelty laws, but again not out of any conviction for animal welfare. The penalty for injuring a guard dog at any concentration camp was death. On the Eastern Front, the Nazis depended on horses and mules for much of their transportation needs, especially during the long Russian winter.

The Nazis planted trees to help make Germany self-sufficient. Population growth in the 19th century had made Germany dependent on imports of food, fibers and other materials needed to wage war. Chemistry labs played pivotal roles in reducing imports, including the Haber process in World War I that resulted in the production of explosives from nitrogen in the air, freeing Germany from its dependence on Chilean nitrates.

In World War I, Dr. Hugo Schweitzer was president of the Bayer Co. in the United States. He also headed the German espionage service in America. At the time of his death, U.S. government agents searched his apartment and found a remarkable, unpublished document, *The Chemists War*. In that document, Schweitzer described how the Haber process freed Germany, which faced starvation because of the British blockade. The portion of the document about planting trees follows:

All these endeavors to substitute cotton may appear ridiculous to us who have been brought up with the idea that Cotton is King and that we have been destined by fate to supply this fiber to the civilized world. The farmers who cultivated the madder root and the planters who raised indigo were also inclined to jest when they were appraised of the fact that German chemists had succeeded in reproducing in the laboratories the dyes which their crops furnished, but when the manufactured materials drove the natural products from the markets and left the farmers and planters without a job, hilarity ceased. History may repeat itself and willow bark and nettle, or some other substitute raised on German soil may, in the near future, depose King Cotton. The German chemist has a duty to perform, and with his perseverance and application he does not shrink from any problem however difficult it might appear to outsiders.[77]

Many on the right also claim the Nazis were all homosexuals. Under Rohm, the SA did have a homosexual leaning, but he and most of the homosexuals with him in the SA were eliminated in the Night of the Long Knives. Homosexuals were also some of the first sent to the concentration camps. Hitler was heterosexual. He had a mistress, Geli, before marrying Eva Braun. The rest of the top Nazis were all married.

The Nazis and Religion

Nazis are often categorized as pagans by elements of the Right Wing today, with claims that some of the top party officials engaged in blood rituals and other pagan ceremonies. There is some evidence the

Nazis were interested in Eastern religions and mysticism. However, there is no direct evidence that any of the Nazi officials were devoted to any particular form of mysticism, paganism or religion. Some evidence exists that Himmler may have modeled certain SS ceremonies after pagan rituals, but others say he copied the Jesuits.

For instance, it is claimed that the Nazis used Zyklon-B in the gas chambers because they believed it killed not only the body, but also the soul, making it the supreme final solution. Such a belief stems from philosopher Rudolf Steiner. In the later years of his life, Steiner developed anthroposophy or what he termed the complete science of the spirit. Otto Ohlendorf, a high-ranking Nazi official, was a regular participant in anthroposophic conferences on biodynamic farming or medicinal eurhythmics, and was instrumental in saving the Waldorf Schools as long as possible. The Waldorf Schools were based on Steiner's anthroposophy, and many members were enthusiastic followers of the Nazis. The Nazis closed the Waldorf Schools nonetheless. Reinhard Heydrich, who was Himmler's second in command in the SS, viewed anthroposophy as an "Oriental soiling of the clear Germanic mind," and banned the Anthroposophic Society in 1935.[78]

Attempting to assign a particular religious belief system to the Nazis is foolish. The religious philosophy of the party was as diverse as that of the German culture.

If religious beliefs can be discerned by policy, then the Nazis were Christians, as evidenced by their version of The Lord's Prayer, which was mandated for recitation at the beginning of the day in all schools.

Almighty God, dear heavenly Father. In Thy name let us now, in pious spirit, begin our instruction. Enlighten us, teach us all truth, strengthen us in all that is good, lead us not into temptation, deliver us from all evil in order that, as good human beings, we may faithfully perform our duties and thereby, in time and eternity, be made truly happy. Amen.[79]

None of the top Nazis were devoted to any particular religious beliefs, Christian or otherwise. Both Hitler and Himmler died as members of the Catholic Church, but were not devoted followers. The Nazis were opportunists who used religion in the same way they used socialism to attract followers. *Mein Kampf* is sprinkled with religious references and moralizing by Hitler.

The sword will become our plow, and from the tears of war the daily bread of future generations will grow.
The more the linguistic Babel corroded and disorganized parliament, the closer drew the inevitable hour of the disintegration of this Babylonian Empire and with it the hour of freedom for my German-Austria people.
The Lord's grace smiled on his ungrateful children.
... they speak of this whole field as if it were a great sin, and above all express their profound indignation against every sinner caught in the act, then close their eyes in pious horror to this godless plague and pray God to let sulfur and brimstone preferably after their own death rain down on this Sodom and Gomorrah, thus once making an instructive example of this shameless humanity.[80]

In the quote, Hitler is referring to syphilis.

Today Christians ... stand at the head of Germany .... I pledge that I never will tie myself to parties who want to destroy Christianity .... We want to fill our culture again with the Christian spirit ... We want to burn out all the recent immoral developments in literature, in the theater, and in the press — in short, we want to burn out the poison of immorality which has entered into our whole life and culture as a result of liberal excess during the past ... few years.[81]

There was a complex relationship between the Nazis and the Vatican. In 1929, Archbishop Eugenio Pacelli (later Pope Pius XII) gave Hitler a large cache of church money, allegedly because of Hitler's strong opposition to communism. Sister Pascalina witnessed the transfer of money.[82]

There is other evidence of a conspiracy between Hitler and Rome. One of Hitler's first acts after gaining power was to sign the Concordat, an agreement with the Vatican, which gave the new Nazi regime international prestige. Moreover, the Catholic Church played a prominent propagandist role in softening up European countries in preparation for a Nazi invasion by fomenting dissent and in some countries a Nazi underground. Catholics were prominent in all the countries which adopted fascism: Italy, Spain, Portugal, Germany, Austria and Hungary. And the Vatican was the primary sponsor of the ratlines that allowed Nazi war criminals to escape from Europe and justice after the war.

Hitler and the American Influence

Much of the misinformation and lies about the Nazis comes from a resurgence of the Right Wing since 1980, which has also disseminated a deliberately false definition of socialism. The primary duty of any government is to protect its citizens. Failing that, the government has no legitimate right to exist and is usually quickly removed in a revolution. This government protection extends to protecting the citizens from environmental degradation, labor laws and other social issues.

Today, America's Right Wing has twisted this protection of citizens to only include protection from foreign powers. It knowingly misleads people in classifying environmental protection, the minimum wage, Social Security and a host of other social welfare programs as socialism. Our founders viewed corporations and moneyed interest as a threat equivalent to the dangers of a foreign power, as the words of Thomas Jefferson suggest: "I hope we shall take warning from the example of England and crush in its birth the aristocracy of our moneyed corporations which dare already to challenge our Government to trial, and bid defiance to the laws of our country."[83]

A survey of early state constitutions confirms the seriousness with which the founders viewed the threat from corporations. In an effort to cover up their past support for fascism and to install global fascism through what is falsely termed free trade agreements, America's Right Wing is engaged in a desperate effort to label the Nazis as socialists and to attribute to them any trait they find distasteful.

Hitler modeled the Nazis after Mussolini's fascist Italy. In Italy, fascism grew out of two movements: nationalism and syndicalism, or trade unionism. In syndicalism, it is believed that as equal owners, the members in an organization should share the rewards or profits equally. The principle of private ownership is still recognized. At the same time, Italy had a growing communist movement. Mussolini was a syndicalist who turned nationalist after World War I.

From 1922–25, Mussolini followed a laissez-faire economic policy under Finance Minister Alberto De Stefani. De Stefani reduced taxes, laws and trade controls, but his opposition to protectionism and business subsidies alienated some industrial leaders, which led to his removal. From 1925 on, Mussolini began the cartelization of the Italian economy and the formation of the corporate state. The economic powers were consolidated into the Institute for Industrial Reconstruction, in which big business was the real force in making policy.

America's Right Wing regarded Mussolini as a bastion against communism. Their high regard is obvious in the foreign policies and trade agreements throughout the 1920s, and in the three Republican administrations of Harding, Coolidge and Hoover. In the 1930s, the Right still respected Mussolini for revitalizing the Italian economy. However, by 1939, the Italian economy had only expanded by 15 percent from 1929 levels. The economic well-being of the workers had fallen; private consumption had dropped below 1929 levels. The primary reason was the same as in Germany: War preparations took precedence over a consumer economy.

Yet America's right-wing support for fascism extended far beyond favorable foreign policies and trade agreements with Mussolini. Henry Ford's anti-Jewish views had a major impact on Germany and Hitler. Ford owned the *Dearborn Independent* newspaper, which published anti-Jewish articles that were later reprinted in four volumes known as *The International Jew*. In Germany, the latter appeared in a translated version, *The Eternal Jew*, which soon became the Bible for the Nazis. Theodore Fritsch published six printings of *The Eternal Jew* between 1920–22. By 1933, he had published 29. Once Hitler gained power, it became a stock item of Nazi propaganda. Some passages in *Mein Kampf* appear to have been copied directly from Ford.

The impact of *The International Jew* on Germany should not be underestimated. At that time, many people worldwide worshipped the great industrialist Henry Ford, especially in Germany with its economy in chaos. At the Nuremberg War Crimes Trial, Baldur von Schirach, the leader of the Hitler Youth, testified that he became an anti-Semite after reading *The International Jew*. Ford's book led many Germans to the Nazi Party.

Of course, Ford is not entirely to blame for the extreme Nazi hatred of the Jews. The growing American eugenics movement was equally responsible. The Nuremberg Laws were modeled after eugenics laws passed by various states in the 1920s. In addition, the Rockefeller Foundation financed much of the eugenics research in Germany.

Anti-Semitism in Germany was deeply rooted and dates back as far as Luther's time:

This is a good month to reflect on the toxicity of words meant to kill. Nov. 9 marks the 60th anniversary of Kristallnacht, the 1938 "Night of Shattered Glass" unleashed by the Nazis to terrorize Germany's Jews. The date was chosen specially by Josef Goebbels, Hitler's propagandist, to honor the birthday of Martin Luther, the 16th century monk who was a father of the Protestant Reformation and the founder of what became the Lutheran church.

Hitler greatly admired Luther: "He saw the Jew as we are only beginning to see him today." Indeed, Luther saw the Jews as "hopeless, wicked, venomous, and devilish ... our pest, torment, and misfortune."

Initially, certain that his version of Christianity would appeal to Jews, he expected large numbers of them to covert. When that failed to happen, he turned violently against them. In 1543, Luther Published *On the Jews and Their Lies,* a work that would become known throughout Germany, perhaps the most widely disseminated work of anti-Semitism by a German until the rise of the Nazis 400 years later.

"What then shall we Christians do with this damned, rejected race of Jews?" Luther asked.

"First, their synagogues should be set on fire, and whatever does not burn up should be covered or spread over with dirt, so that no one may ever be able to see a cinder or stone of it... "

"Secondly, their homes should likewise be broken down and destroyed... "

"Thirdly, they should be deprived of their prayer books and Talmuds, in which such idolatry, lies, cursing, and blasphemy are taught."

"Fourthly, their rabbis must be forbidden under threat of death to teach any more... "

"Fifthly, passports and traveling privileges should be absolutely forbidden to the Jews... "

"Sixthly, I advise that ... all cash and treasure of silver and gold be taken from them... "

"Burn down their synagogues, forbid all that I enumerated earlier, force them to work, and deal harshly with them... If this does not help we must drive them out like mad dogs, so we do not become partakers of their abominable blasphemy and all their other vices. I have done my duty. Now let everyone see to his."

This is hate speech.

Sixty years ago next Monday on the night of Luther's birthday, Nazi gangs rampaged across Germany. In every Jewish neighborhood, windows were smashed and buildings were torched. All told, 101 synagogues were destroyed, and nearly 7,500 Jewish-owned businesses were demolished. On that night, 91 Jews were murdered; 26,000 were rounded up and sent to concentration camps. It was the greatest pogrom in history. And it was nothing compared with what was to come.[84]

The yellow star the Nazis forced Jews to wear had originated in earlier centuries. The Vatican confined Jews to ghettos that were locked at night. During the day, the Jews could go about the cities to conduct business, but only if they wore a badge.

But it was the financial and commercial rather than moral support from America that was the key. As time goes by, more reports surface, suggesting US corporate involvement was much greater than previously believed.

Bernd Greiner said 26 of the top 100 U.S. companies in the 1930s collaborated to some degree with the Nazis before, and in some cases after, Hitler declared war on the United States in December 1941. Company headquarters in the U.S. have denied they knew what was going on in Germany, but there is evidence to suggest they knew their German subsidiaries used slave labor, tolerated it and in some cases were actively involved, Greiner said.

Greiner confirmed a report in the newspaper *Die Zeit*, based on his findings of U.S. corporate involvement in Nazi Germany. The findings went beyond allegations of U.S. lawyers and historians last year that automakers General Motors and Ford collaborated with the Nazi regime.[85]

The impact of American industrialists' investments in Germany during the 1920s and 1930s was immense and immeasurable. Besides direct financial aid to Hitler, American industrialists began building factories inside Germany in the 1920s. When the Nazis seized power, these American factories were allowed to continue operation, manufacturing war material. Sewing machine factories owned by Singer were converted to manufacture machine guns.

The greatest benefits the Nazis reaped from these factories was the transfer of technology. Before Ford and GM built factories in Germany, automobiles were largely assembled one at a time there. Ford's introduction of the assembly line streamlined German manufacturing. It allowed the Nazis to rapidly produce large numbers of tanks, airplanes, trucks and even the V2 rockets.

Prescott Bush and the Nazis

The two Wall Street firms that aided the Nazis the most were Sullivan & Cromwell, and Brown Brothers Harriman. Sullivan & Cromwell was the Wall Street law firm that employed Allen and John Foster Dulles. Brown Brothers Harriman was the Wall Street investment firm that employed George Herbert "Bert" Walker and his son-in-law, Prescott Bush. In one three-year period, Brown Brothers Harriman sold American investors more than $50 million of German bonds.

Harriman's firm did not merge with Brown Brothers until after the 1929 stock market crash. Their first success in investing in Germany came in 1920 when Averell Harriman announced that he would restart Germany's Hamburg-Amerika Line. After many months of scheming and political intrigue, the United States had confiscated Hamburg-Amerika's commercial steamships after World War I. By some arrangements with the U.S. authorities that were never made public, these ships then became the property of the Harriman enterprise.

George Walker, Prescott Bush's father-in-law, arranged the credits Harriman needed to take control of the Hamburg-Amerika Line. Walker and Averell Harriman gained control of the steamship company in 1920 through negotiations with its post-World War I chief executive, Wilhelm Cuno, and with the line's bankers, M. M. Warburg. Walker organized the American Ship and Commerce Corp. as a unit of W. A. Harriman & Co., with contractual power over Hamburg-Amerika's affairs. The Harriman 15 Corp., run by Prescott Bush and George Walker, held the Harriman-Bush shares in American Ship and Commerce Corp.

Albert Voegler served on the board of Hamburg-Amerika Line and as a director of the Thyssen-controlled Bank voor Handel en Scheepvaart. Voegler also was the chief executive of Thyssen-Flick German Steel Trust, for which Bush's Union Bank was the New York office. Voegler, Thyssen and

Cuno all contributed heavily to the Nazis from 1930–32. Baron Rudolph von Schroeder was vice president and director of the Hamburg-Amerika Line.

One of the great merchants of death, Samuel Pryor, was included in the deal from the beginning. Pryor, then chairman of the executive committee of Remington Arms, helped arrange it. Walker served on the board of Harriman's shipping front organization, the American Ship & Commerce Co.

Samuel P. Bush, Prescott's father, became chief of the Ordinance, Small Arms and Ammunition Section of the War Industries Board, which was headed by Wall Street speculator and advisor to President Wilson, Bernard Baruch. Samuel Bush took national responsibility for government assistance to and relations with Remington and other weapons companies. This was an unusual appointment for a railroad person. Previously, Bush owned a company that supplied parts for railroad lines that transported Rockefeller oil. In the arrangement with Rockefeller, the railroad lines had to buy their parts from Bush's foundry. Most of Samuel Bush's arms-related records and correspondence in government archives have been burned. However, Samuel Bush's appointment placed him close to Pryor.

The Schroeder family of bankers was a linchpin for the Nazi activities of Harriman and Prescott Bush. Closely associated with the Schroeders were John Foster and Allen Dulles. Baron Kurt von Schroeder was co-director of the massive Thyssen-Hütte foundry, along with Johann Groeninger, Prescott Bush's New York bank partner. A rabid Nazi, he also was the treasurer of the support organization for the Nazi Party's private armies. As previously noted, both John Foster and Allen Dulles were present at the pivotal meeting between von Papen and Hitler. While representing their client Kuhn, Loeb & Co. and seeking assurances from Hitler, their principal contribution was in hiding Nazi ownership and involvement in American firms through a maze of paperwork.

Direct actions taken by the Harriman-Bush shipping line in 1932 and by the Dulles brothers in January 1933 are the two gravest actions ever taken against the United States and humanity in the 20th century. Those actions led directly to the seizure of power by the Nazis, placing the burden for the resulting Holocaust and widespread destruction of Europe squarely on the shoulders of Harriman, Bush and the Dulles brothers.

In 1932, the German government took steps to defend the republic and national freedom by ordering the disbanding of Nazi private armies. The U.S. embassy in Berlin reported the high costs of election campaigns and of keeping a private army of up to 400,000 men had raised questions about the Nazis' financial backers. The Nazi Brown Shirts had intimidated or shot thousands of Germans who opposed Hitler.

After Remington Arms signed a cartel agreement with IG Farben, the U.S. Senate conducted an investigation that found that German political associations like the Nazis and others were nearly all equipped with American guns. The arms were shipped across the Atlantic aboard the Harriman-Bush Hamburg-Amerika Line. Before reaching Antwerp, the weapons were transferred to river barges, which allowed them to be smuggled through Holland without inspection. Besides revolvers, the principal arms were Thompson submachine guns.

On March 7, 1933, Prescott Bush's American Ship and Commerce Corp., notified Max Warburg that he was to be the corporation's official representative on the board of Hamburg-Amerika. Kuhn, Loeb was directly connected with the Warburgs through marriage. Paul Moritz Warburg and Felix Moritz Warburg married Nina Jenny Loeb, Solomon's youngest, and Frieda Schiff, Jacob's only daughter, respectively. Both Warburgs became partners of Kuhn, Loeb & Co.

On March 29, 1933, Max Warburg's son Erich sent a cable to his cousin Frederick Warburg, a director of the Harriman railroad system. The cable directed Frederick Warburg to use all of his influence to stop all anti-Nazi activity in America. On March 31, 1933, the American-Jewish Committee, controlled by the Warburgs, and B'nai B'rith issued a formal, official joint statement, which counseled that no American boycott against Germany be encouraged and advised that no further mass meetings be held or similar forms of agitation be employed. The American Jewish Committee and B'nai B'rith continued with a no-attack-on-Hitler policy all through the 1930s.

On Sept. 5, 1933, the executive board of the Hamburg-Amerika Line (Hapag) met jointly with the North German Lloyd Co. board in Hamburg and merged under Nazi supervision. Prescott Bush's American Ship and Commerce Corp. installed Christian Beck, a longtime Harriman executive, as manager of freight and operations in North America for the new joint Nazi shipping line.

In 1934, testimony before Congress proved that a supervisor from the Nazi Labor Front was aboard every ship of the Harriman-Bush line. The Bush-controlled shipping lines subsidized Nazi propaganda in the United States and functioned as a den of spies for the Nazis until the government seized Hamburg-Amerika in 1942 for violating the Trading with the Enemy Act. Below is an extract from Vesting Order No. 126.[86]

> Seizure of all the assets of the Hamburg-American Line and of the North German Lloyd and of all the American branches jointly operated by them. Prescott Bush, George Herbert Walker and others operated the U.S. arm of Hamburg-American Line, seized herewith. Among other things, the company offered a cash reward to any American who would travel to Germany on a one-way ticket and proselytize for Hitler. The line also smuggled Nazi spies into the U.S., even after America had entered the war.
>
> President Roosevelt felt this constituted treason.

Hamburg-Amerika was one of two companies pivotal to the Harriman-Bush dealings with the Nazis. The other was Union Bank.

In 1922, Averell Harriman traveled to Germany to set up a branch of W. A. Harriman in Berlin, and hired George Herbert Walker to run both the New York and Berlin offices. During his stay in Germany, Harriman met the Thyssen family and agreed to help them set up an American bank.

Early in 1924, Hendrick Kouwenhoven, managing director of Bank voor Handel en Scheepvaart, traveled to New York. Meeting with Walker and the Harriman brothers, they founded the Union Banking Corp. Two of the directors of Union Bank, Groninger and Kouwenhoven, were Nazi directors of the Bank voor Handel en Scheepvaart, formerly the von Heydt Bank. Von Heydt, also a Nazi, was identified as the intermediary between the Guaranty Trust and Hitler. Both Groninger and Kouwenhoven contributed lavishly to Himmler's Circle of Friends.

In 1926, August Thyssen died. The eldest son, Fritz, expanded the Thyssen empire by creating United Steel Works (Vereinigte Stahlwerke AG). Thyssen also brought Friedrich Flick on board. The Thyssen-Flick union was designed to suppress the union movement. With the merger, George Walker hired his son-in-law, Prescott Bush, to manage the United Steel Works account. One division of United Steel Works consisted of the Consolidated Silesian Steel Corp. and the Upper Silesian Coal and Steel Co., both located in the mineral-rich Silesian area of Poland. Until the Depression started in 1929, the arrangement was extremely profitable for all four men — Thyssen, Flick, Walker and Bush. Congressional investigations after the war showed that United Steel had supplied more than 50 percent of the pig iron in Nazi Germany and also was a major supplier of all other ferrous metal products needed by Hitler's war machine.

Due to the Depression, Harriman merged with Brown to form the Brown Brothers Harriman firm. Internally, the Harriman 15 Corp., formed by Harriman and Bush, held Flick's two-thirds share of the stock of Consolidated Silesian Steel Co. Having lost property after WWI, Thyssen and Flick were nervous about Hitler's invasions of Europe, and they sold Consolidated Silesian to Union Bank. Under the complete control of Harriman and Bush, the company became Silesian American Corp., part of UBC and Harriman's portfolio of 15 corporations.[87]

The stock market crash of 1929 and the resulting Depression also bankrupted the Wall Street-backed German Steel Trust. When the German government took over the Trust's stock shares, interests associated with Konrad Adenauer and the anti-Nazi Catholic Center Party tried to buy the shares.

However, Harriman-Bush Union Bank, working in concert with Montagu Norman, the vocal supporter of Hitler and fascism from the Bank of England, made sure that Thyssen regained control over the trust shares.

In May 1933, after the Nazis consolidated power, an agreement was reached in Berlin coordinating all Nazi commerce with the United States. Under the agreement, Harriman International, headed by Oliver Harriman, first cousin to Averell, would lead a syndicate of 150 firms and individuals to conduct all exports from Germany to the United States.

By 1934, with Hitler in solid control of Germany, the profits from the Thyssen-Flick union soared to more than 100 million. Both Union Bank and the Bank voor Handel en Scheepvaart were overflowing with money. Prescott Bush became managing director of Union Bank and took over the day-to-day operations of the German plan.

Instead of divesting himself of Nazi money and activities, Prescott Bush hired Allen Dulles to hide the Nazi assets. Dulles' client list from Sullivan & Cromwell shows his first assignment at Brown Brothers Harriman as June 18, 1936. The entry listed his work at Brown Brothers Harriman as "Disposal of Standard Oil Investing Stock."

Standard Oil was another of Dulles' clients who hired him to cloak agreements with IG Farben. By January 1937, all of Standard Oil's Nazi activities were in one account, "Brown Brothers Harriman-Schroeder Rock." Schroeder was the Nazi bank in which Dulles served as a director. The Rock referred to the Rockefellers.[88] In May 1939, Dulles handled another problem for Brown Brothers Harriman listed as "Securities Custodian Accounts."

In 1939, the Nazis invaded Poland, ending a dispute over taxes between Consolidated and the Polish government. The original Nazi plan was to replace the workers in Polish factories with Soviet prisoners, but that portion of the plan was never implemented. Consolidated Silesian Steel Corp. was located near the Polish town of Oswiecim. When the plan to use Soviet prisoners as forced labor fell through, the Nazis began shipping Jews, communists, gypsies and other minority populations to the camp. This was the beginning of Auschwitz. IG Farben soon built a plant near Auschwitz to take advantage not only of the nearby coal deposits, but also of slave labor. According to a Dutch intelligence agent, Prescott Bush even managed a portion of the slave labor force in Poland; what's clear is that he profited handsomely from it.

July 31, 1941, New York *Herald-Tribune* ran a bold headline "Hitler's Angel Has $3 Million in U.S. Bank." The article described Thyssen as that angel and reported the money actually belonged to "Nazi bigwigs," including Goebbels, Hermann Goering, Heinrich Himmler or even Hitler himself.[89] The account was deposited in Union Bank.

Shortly after the bombing of Pearl Harbor, leaks from Washington suggested Prescott Bush was under investigation for aiding the Nazis in time of war. Once again, rather than divesting himself of the Nazi accounts and his pro-Nazi activities, Prescott Bush wrapped himself in the flag. He became the national chairman of the United Service Organization's annual fund campaign. However, his subterfuge didn't work; the government's investigation continued.[90]

How the government was able to unravel all the cloaking activities of Allen Dulles and deception by Bush and other ranking officers of Union Bank was typical of Roosevelt. Roosevelt was well aware of Americans aiding the Nazis. As a means to counter these traitors, Roosevelt employed numerous private spies. In the case of Brown Brothers Harriman, the spy was an employee of Bert Walker named Dan Harkins. Harkins kept up his pretense of being an ardent Nazi sympathizer while he blew the whistle on Brown Brothers Harriman's spy apparatus to Congress, and continued to report to Naval Intelligence.[91]

Oct. 20, 1942, under authority of the Trading with the Enemy Act, the U.S. Congress seized UBC and liquidated its assets. The seizure is confirmed by Vesting Order No. 248 in the U.S. Office of the

Alien Property Custodian and signed by U.S. Alien Property Custodian Leo Crowley (see Appendix 4 for the complete vesting order). The order listed the following stockholders: E. Roland Harriman – 3,991 shares, Cornelis Lievense – 4 shares, Harold D. Pennington – 1 share, Ray Morris – 1 share, Prescott Bush – 1 share, H.J. Kouwenhoven – 1 share, Johann G. Groeninger – 1 share. All those listed were directors of Union Bank. Groeninger was a Nazi industrial executive.

Government documents show that Union Bank was a clearinghouse for several Thyssen-controlled enterprises and assets, including as many as a dozen individual businesses. They show Union Bank shipped valuable U.S. assets, including gold, coal, steel, and U.S. Treasury and war bonds to their foreign clients overseas as Hitler geared up for his 1939 invasion of Poland.[92]

Moreover, the records show that Bush and Harriman not only hid their Nazi activities from the government, but also continued dealing with the Nazis unabated. These activities included financial dealing with the city of Hanover and several industrial firms while Averell Harriman was serving as President Roosevelt's personal emissary to the United Kingdom.

The documents reveal that all UBC assets and its related businesses belonged to Thyssen-controlled enterprises, including his Bank voor Handel en Scheepvaart in Rotterdam. Nevertheless, Cornelius Livense, president of UBC, claimed to have no knowledge of such a relationship. The documents note that: "Strangely enough, claims he does not know the actual ownership of the company." Livense repeatedly tried to mislead authorities. H. D. Pennington, manager of Brown Brothers Harriman and a UBC director, also lied to them.

Despite the organized efforts to mislead, investigators were able to show that a careful examination of UBC's general ledger, cash books and journals from 1919 onward clearly established the principal, and practically the only source of funds, had been Bank voor Handel en Scheepvaart.

After the war, Fritz Thyssen managed to retain his vast financial holdings, despite four years of interrogation by British and American officials, from 1945–49. They knew he was lying, but underestimated the crafty Thyssen. After losing part of his financial empire following World War I, August Thyssen, Fritz's father, established three banks in the 1920s: the August Thyssen Bank in Berlin, the Bank voor Handel en Scheepvaart in Rotterdam, and the Union Banking Corp., in New York City. To protect his financial empire, all his sons had to do was transfer corporate paperwork from one bank to the other.

Under this scheme, it was not necessary to move physical assets, such as gold and currency, between banks. For example, when Thyssen sold the Holland-American Trading Co., for a tax loss, the Union Banking Corp., in New York bought the stock. Prescott Bush then invested the disguised Nazi profits in American steel and manufacturing corporations that became part of the secret Thyssen empire.

The elder Thyssen took additional steps to protect his empire as World War II approached. His son Fritz, became a member of the Nazi Party in 1923. The other son married into Hungarian nobility and changed his name to Baron Thyssen-Bornemisza, claiming dual citizenship in both Holland and Hungary. Publicly, he detested his elder brother's Nazi views. Privately, they met in secret board meetings in Germany to coordinate their operation.

In 1929, the Bank voor Handel en Scheepvaart held the shares of the August Thyssen Bank, and also American subsidiaries and the Union Banking Corp., New York. At the beginning of World War II, the bank served as the holding company for the vast Thyssen empire and had only one shareholder, a Hungarian citizen.

After the Nazis invaded Holland, they investigated the Bank voor Handel en Scheepvaart. The Nazi auditors had long suspected Fritz Thyssen of being a tax fraud and of smuggling his profits. They were right, but the bank vaults were empty of clues. The assets had been secretly transferred back to the August Thyssen Bank in Berlin under the friendly supervision of Baron Kurt Von Schroeder. Thyssen spent the rest of the war under VIP arrest.

Fritz Thyssen continued the ruse after the war, claiming no ownership of foreign corporations and detesting his relatives who, with help from Allied investigators, were quietly reassembling his financial empire. Under the laws of the occupation of Germany, any property of citizens of a neutral nation seized by the Nazis had to be returned upon proof of ownership. There was a flood of neutral parties from Holland claiming ownership of various parts of the Thyssen empire.

While the Allied investigators focused on the Bank voor Handel en Scheepvaart and the large number of transactions conducted with the Nazis, they were unable to discover where the money had gone. They did not know was that Allen Dulles was secretly the lawyer for the Bank voor Handel en Scheepvaart and Thyssen. Baron Kurt Von Schroeder was the Nazi trustee for the Thyssen companies, which now claimed to be owned by the Dutch.

The Dutch bank was the key to Dulles' *Tarnung* or cloaking scheme. Moreover, it was his most successful effort at *Tarnung*. It has taken investigators more than 50 years to untangle the intricacies of Dulles' web. Despite one small problem, Thyssen's empire would remain intact. Once Germany fell to the Allies, it was time to ship the documents back to Holland so that the "neutral" bank could claim ownership under the friendly supervision of Allen Dulles, who, as the OSS intelligence chief in 1945 Berlin, was in a position to handle any troublesome investigations. Thyssen had hedged his bets with positions on both sides and the middle.

However, the August Thyssen Bank had been bombed during the war, and the documents were buried in the underground vaults beneath the rubble. Even more perplexing was that the August Thyssen Bank was located in the Soviet sector of Berlin. Under the pretext of recovering the crown jewels stolen by the Nazis, Prince Bernhard commanded a unit of Dutch intelligence in Operation Juliana. The Russians gave the prince permission to recover the jewels. Bernhard was a Nazi SS officer and successfully recovered the corporate papers to keep the Thyssen empire intact.

The treachery of Allen Dulles, Prescott Bush and the Rockefellers can only be measured in the enormity of this pipeline to launder Nazi assets. Brown Brothers Harriman was the conduit to invest money into Nazi Germany, Union Bank was the return pipe for the profits.

In 1970, the Bank voor Handel en Scheepvaart, which also served as the group's holding company, merged with Nederlandse Credietbank N.V. After the merger, the resulting holding firm was named Thyssen-Bornemisza Group. Chase Manhattan, the Rockefeller bank, holds 31 percent of the new company. The Thyssen-Bornemisza group is now one of the wealthiest corporations in the world, with a net worth of more than $50 billion. It is so rich it even bought the Krupp family's arms business.

After the war, the Dutch government began an investigation into the location of some more jewelry stolen from the royal family by the Nazis, and started looking at the books of the Bank voor Handel en Scheepvaart. After discovering transaction papers of the Silesian American Corp., they questioned the bank manager, H.J. Kouwenhoven. Shocked at being discovered, he soon traveled to New York to tell Prescott Bush. According to the Dutch, this meeting between Bush and Kouwenhoven took place shortly after Dec. 25, 1947. Two weeks later, the otherwise healthy Kouwenhoven died of a heart attack. The Gehlen network of former Nazis had perfected a means to induce a heart attack without detection.[93]

In August 1942, under the same authority, Congress seized the first of the Bush-Harriman-managed Thyssen entities, Hamburg-Amerika Line, under Vesting Order No. 126, also signed by Crowley. Eight days after the seizure of UBC, Congress invoked the Trading with the Enemy Act again to take control of two more Bush-Harriman-Thyssen businesses — Holland-American Trading Corp. (Vesting Order No. 261) and Seamless Steel Equipment Corp (Vesting Order No. 259). In November, Congress seized the Nazi interests in Silesian-American Corp., which allegedly profited from slave labor at Auschwitz via a partnership with IG Farben, Hitler's third major industrial patron and partner in the infrastructure of the Third Reich.

After the war, the U.S. government seized another 18 companies related to the Harriman-Bush Union Bank for violations of the Trading with the Enemy Act. Several companies seized had continued the Thyssen relationship after takeover of Union Bank in 1942.

In October 1950, the government conducted one of the last seizures of Nazi assets under the Trading with the Enemy Act. The seizure concerned the U.S. assets of a Nazi baroness named Theresia Maria Ida Benedikta Huberta Stanislava Martina von Schwarzenberg. Brown Brothers Harriman continued with the subterfuge, claiming the baroness was a victim of Nazi persecution. However, government investigators concluded she was a member of the Nazi Party.[94]

Meanwhile, in 1951, after the death of Fritz Thyssen, the Alien Property Custodian released the assets of the Union Banking Corp., to Brown Brothers Harriman. Prescott Bush received $1.5 million for his share in Union Bank's blood money, and filed for his 1952 Senate race.

Further examination of the documents show that Bush and Harriman conducted business after the war with related concerns, moving assets into Switzerland, Panama, Argentina and Brazil, which were critical destinations for Nazi war criminals and flight capital.[95]

Additional vesting orders linking Brown Brothers Harriman to Nazi interests are listed in Appendix 3.

Evidence of a continuing conspiracy between Wall Street and former Nazis also comes from the holdings of the Rockefellers. By 1972, the Rockefeller-controlled Chase Manhattan bank in New York secretly owned 38 percent of Thyssen's company. The Thyssen-Krupp Corp. is now the wealthiest conglomerate in Europe.

In the 1970s, Brown Brothers Harriman convinced the docile New York State Banking Commission to issue an order allowing it to shred all records from the Nazi period.[96]

It has been more than 60 years since the government seized Union Bank from Bush and Harriman, and yet most people are unaware that the current president's grandfather was guilty of treason and aided the Nazis. The lack of knowledge about this cover-up is due in a large part to the current corporate media. When John Buchanan broke his 2004 story of the seizures of 18 additional companies from Bush and Harriman, the mainstream media ignored the story. The only paper to print it was *The New Hampshire Gazette.*

Moreover, the seizure of Union Bank was never announced or widely published at the time. Some suspect the hush-up was due to the Roosevelt-Harriman connection, but Roosevelt believed that widespread exposure of American traitors would cause a public scandal, which would affect public morale, cause strikes and provoke military mutinies.[97] Besides, he had plans to deal with the American traitors such as Bush and Harriman after the war. Unfortunately, he died before the end of the war and his plan died with him.

It was not illegal for industrialists to invest in Germany during the 1920s and 1930s, but once the Nazis seized power, the judgment of these industrialists is a concern. Their continued support of the Nazis after 1941 was clearly treason.

American corporations that supported the Nazis have successfully hidden for more than six decades by claiming that the Nazis seized control of their German subsidiaries. Usually, this is false. Almost all subsidiaries in Nazi Germany collaborated with the Nazis with the full knowledge of their American home offices. They went to extraordinary means to keep communication and control. For instance, when the GIs landed on Normandy, IBM CEO Thomas Watson still knew the exact location of every IBM machine in Europe. Even though the Nazis had seized them from other governments and put them to use in such places as the concentration camps, IBM's European subsidiary continued to service them and to convey their locations back to New York.

Unequivocally, John Foster Dulles, Allen Dulles, Prescott Bush and Averill Harriman were the most flagrant in aiding for the Nazis. Not only did they help Hitler seize power, their actions also facilitated other American aid to the Nazis. Bush and Harriman acted as Hitler's American bankers, operating a company that was at the center of the Nazis' espionage ring in the United States. Once it was clear that war was imminent, the Dulles brothers attempted to cloak the Nazi investments of their clients.

Many people and some authors attempt to dismiss Prescott's dealings with the Nazi by claiming it wasn't illegal to invest in Germany before the war and by saying there is no evidence that he was a Nazi. They try to describe Prescott as just a good, ruthless businessman. However, ruthless business practices are nothing more than another expression of fascism and are precisely what Upton Sinclair had in mind when he said, "fascism is capitalism plus murder."

Other Bush apologists try to deflect blame from Prescott by claiming Joseph Kennedy owned stock in Nazi Germany companies, which is true. Kennedy bought his stock from Prescott Bush through Brown Brothers Harriman. But unlike Prescott Bush, Kennedy never served as the Nazis' American banker and never managed a company that was at the heart of Nazi espionage in North America.

The universal claim from the Bush supporters is that there is no evidence to suggest Prescott Bush was a Nazi or fascist. Such a claim is false. Prescott Bush came from America's elite that almost universally supported fascism. He was the president of Connecticut's eugenic society, an organization that advocated eliminating the inferior. Bush was guilty of treason the moment he hired the Dulles brothers to hide the Nazi ownership in his companies. He chose to stand with the Nazis and to defy his own country. He was well aware that he was violating the law — and aware of his guilt.

Prescott Bush didn't need jackboots and a swastika armband, when he controlled the Nazi purse strings in North America.

Chapter 2,
Corporate Law: A History

Part 1: Constitutional Law

Let's begin this chapter with a few stories that made the news. Another 29 deaths were attributed to Firestone tires — tires not included in the first recall after the government received assurances and pressure from corporate management. In other news, California experienced an electricity shortage following the deregulation of its power companies — a shortage, it turns out, that was at least partially self-made by the utilities.

In the early 1990s, the local media in Portland, Ore., carried several stories about a poor lad with leukemia who needed a life-saving bone marrow transplant. When health insurance refused to pay for the transplant, family and friends raised money by holding community car washes and bake sales. But once they had the amount quoted by a Seattle hospital to cover the cost of the transplant, the family members were told that the price had since doubled. The local media picked up the story as a cause célèbre. The community was outraged and within two weeks, the Seattle hospital relented and agreed to do the transplant for the original price. The hospital was basing the cost of the transplant on the highest dollar figure it could extract from that family.

In another case of price gouging in the mid-1990s, it was reported that manufacturers were hoarding interferon supplies in an attempt to drive up the price.

After the Exxon Valdez ran aground, all the oil companies raised their prices by a third, claiming a shortage of crude.

In Kentucky, an explosion killed seven miners. The mining corporation was cited for gross violations of safety regulations; no fans to draw out methane gas were even present. Many of the women left widowed by this explosion ended up on welfare. Annually, more than 6,000 people — roughly 17 a day — are killed on the job, yet we never hear of a corporate operating officer being brought to trial for murder or manslaughter. That number omits the thousands who have died as a direct result of exposure to toxic substances or disease-causing agents in the workplace.

It is now common to hear news of managers altering employees' time cards, requiring them to work after punching out. Or to hear of yet another sweatshop in operation, not in a Third World banana republic, but in our own large cities, where employees are virtual slaves.

By the mid-1990's corporate welfare totaled more than $167 billion a year. For the average taxpayer, that meant paying thousands annually in taxes to support corporations. Meanwhile, social welfare costs are less than one-third of the cost of corporate welfare.

By 1990, just 10 corporations accounted for 22 percent of all profits in the United States. Only 400 corporations controlled 80 percent of all capital assets in the non-Socialist world. Forty-nine American banks hold a controlling interest in 500 of the largest corporations. According to *The New Media Monopoly*, five or six corporations control most of the media of all types in the U.S., including the three largest television networks.

Were the crimes of corporate America just another product of the greed and immorality of the Reagan administration and its agenda of "free enterprise"? Or are these symptoms of a much deeper problem? Fascism is a top-down, elite revolution. Large industrialists brought Hitler to power in a backroom deal. In 2000, special interest money was behind the candidacy of George W. Bush.

The danger posed by corporations and the inherent fascism that accompanies a capitalistic economy pose the greatest threats to our liberty and freedoms. However, most Americans understand little about how corporations became so powerful. They are largely unaware of earlier restrictions on corporations that served the nation in good stead. A brief look at past state constitutions and court cases provides an understanding of how corporations were kept in check in the 1800s. It wasn't until after the Civil War that they became prominent and powerful. Indeed, corporate law evolved in conjunction with the emergence of a wealthy, elite class.

Today, almost everyone has experienced changes corporations have made without permission to personal insurance policies, bank accounts and mutual funds. Corporations control almost every aspect of life today, including the news.

Senior citizens are forced to make monthly pilgrimages to Canada to refill their prescription drugs at lower prices. Maine even adopted a law requiring that future drug prices be competitive with those in Canada. A Web site exists to help seniors obtain mail-order prescriptions from Canada. But because American drug companies were losing millions in these cross-border sales, the George W. Bush administration banned such sales.

So what is the difference between Canadian and American healthcare systems? The extreme Right and the Republican Party scream that Canada's healthcare system is socialistic. This is nonsense. The same corporations make the prescription drugs, yet Americans are being gouged. If those corporations were owned and run by the government, then it would be a socialistic system. So, why the lie? It's simple. Canada chooses to regulate its corporations. In America, we have the same choice, but the right-wing politicians are shills bought and paid for by the corporations they are supposed to be regulating. It is simply a diversion and scare tactic perfected by the Republicans to scream communism or socialism whenever anything threatens their meal ticket.

A good example was the Republican response to President Clinton's proposal to expand Medicare. The Republicans chose Sen. Bill Frist of Tennessee to deliver their response. Frist pretended to be just an old country doctor overwhelmed by regulations, a performance truly deserving of an Academy Award: "You know, my father was a family doctor for 55 years. As a young boy making house calls with him, I remember his stethoscope, his doctor's bag, and best of all his wonderful and compassionate heart."

However, the facts from *Roll Call* reveal a different picture.[1] While Frist is indeed a physician, he is hardly a simple country doctor. In 1968, Frist's father and brother helped launch the Hospital Corporation of America. Frist's wealth comes from his stockholdings in this giant healthcare unit. In 1996, Frist disclosed a minimum of $13.7 million in assets; $8 million of which was in Hospital Corporation of America. Of course, the senator failed to mention his holdings in this healthcare giant in his response. He also forgot that Hospital Corporation of America faced a Justice Department probe on charges of widespread fraudulent Medicare billing schemes. In other words, the corporations themselves are the ones writing the laws and regulations.

Here we have the crux of the problem: regulation. Regulation of corporations is not socialism. When done to promote the common good, it is liberalism in its finest hour. As paper entities, corporations have no natural rights, only people do. Corporations only have conditional debts to fulfill for the society that created them. George Soros stated the problem by noting that one cannot have a global economy without first having a global society. By "society" he meant a government or other regulatory mechanism.[2] The same applies in a nation. This neither implies that corporations are necessarily bad nor evil; they are just tools for any society to better itself. However, left unregulated, corporations can and do gain absolute power, which leads directly to the fascist state of corporate rule.

First it is important to understand how corporate law and regulations evolved. This will dispel many myths about the founding fathers commonly held by the hard Right today. The founders were indeed liberals and did believe in a capitalistic economy. However, they also believed strongly in regulating trade. Indeed, one of the enumerated powers in the constitution granted the federal government power to regulate interstate commerce. It is false to assume that this only applied to tariffs between the 13 colonies, or that the founders supported corporations.

Corporations first arose in England in the mid-1600s when the Crown authorized certain commercial groups. The royal charters regulated the trading companies or corporations, since only the Crown had the right to govern trade. The right of the Crown to regulate or control corporations went largely unused, allowing much abuse and monopolistic power. Some royal charters like the East India Company had their own governors and armies.

In fact, it was the East India Company that sparked the Boston Tea Party. At the time, the colonies were boycotting British tea controlled by the East India Company, and smuggling their own. To rescue the East India Company, Parliament exempted tea from British taxes, thus undercutting the American smugglers. Led on by John Hancock and Samuel Adams, they organized a mob to raid the English tea ships in the harbor. While the story of the Boston Tea Party as a classic protest over rising taxes and tax without representation makes for great patriotic propaganda, it is patently false and has taken on mythical proportions.

There were other abuses the colonies suffered at the hands of English corporations. For instance, American colonial settlements often were patents granted to English corporations by the Crown. The southern and northern portions of Virginia were two such patents held by the London Company and the Plymouth Company, respectively. Their labor supply was indentured slaves. Typically, after seven years of labor, the indentured slave was given 100 acres. Astoundingly, two-thirds of the colonists at the time of the revolution were estimated to have been indentured slaves. Virginia, Maryland and Pennsylvania all began as commercial enterprises run by chartered corporations.

Perhaps the eloquent words of Thomas Jefferson best sum up the founding fathers' outlook on corporations: "I hope we shall take warning from the example of England and crush in its birth the aristocracy of our moneyed corporations which dare already to challenge our Government to trial, and bid defiance to the laws of our country."

The present view of a corporate charter being a property right only came about through judicial and state legislative activism. Before the Civil War, a corporate charter was viewed as a privilege.

The concept of corporate charters as a privilege was clear in the Articles of Confederation. It continued at the Constitutional Convention of 1787, when James Madison twice proposed that Congress be given the power to grant charters. Both proposals failed, although no formal vote was ever taken. Various members opposed such proposals as unnecessary or feared that they would lead to monopolies. Jefferson opposed federal charters out of fear of a national bank, and lost out when Congress granted a federal charter to the Bank of North America in 1791. Since there were fewer than 40 corporations in 1787, the delegates saw little need to regulate corporations, but by 1800, there were already 334.

The Constitution of the United States was left with only two clauses to regulate corporations: the commerce clause in Article I, Section VIII, and the obligation of contract clause in Article I, Section X. The regulation and granting of corporate charters was left to the various states, which continued to treat them as privileges granted only under special acts of their legislators. However, the process of hearings and petitioning the state legislators was plagued with delays, favoritism and outright corruption.

On Dec. 20, 1787, Jefferson wrote to James Madison about his concerns regarding the Constitution. He listed what he didn't like:

First, the omission of a bill of rights, providing clearly, and without the aid of sophism, for freedom of religion, freedom of the press, protection against standing armies, restriction of monopolies, the eternal and unremitting force of the habeas corpus laws, and trials by jury in all matters of fact triable by the laws of the land, and not by the laws of nations.

Besides citing the many freedoms of the Bill of Rights, Jefferson also noted the lack of restriction on monopolies. Many of the 1776 revolutionaries believed any institution made by and of humans, from governments to churches to corporations, must be subordinate to individual people in terms of the rights and powers. Perhaps Thomas Paine stated it best in *The Rights of Man*:

> … that government is a compact between those who govern and those who are governed; but this cannot be true, because it is putting the effect before the cause; for as man must have existed before governments existed, there necessarily was a time when governments did not exist, and consequently there could originally exist no governors to form such a compact with. The fact therefore must be that the individuals themselves, each in his own personal and sovereign right, entered into a compact with each other to produce a government: and this is the only mode in which governments have a right to arise, and the only principle on which they have a right to exist.

Jefferson received a good response in 10 of the measures comprising the original Bill of Rights. The two issues of banning a standing army and blocking corporations from gaining monopolistic control of industries met with resistance and failed to pass. The Federalists were in power, a group Jefferson referred to as "the rich and the well born." The following quote from James Madison confirms the distrust of corporations held by many of the founding fathers:

> There is an evil, which ought to be guarded against in the indefinite accumulation of property from the capacity of holding it in perpetuity by … corporations. The power of all corporations ought to be limited in this respect. The growing wealth acquired by them never fails to be a source of abuses.

As the pace of incorporations increased, there was a movement to grant general charters to relieve the problems with hearings and petitions. This was the first opening to corporate power. In 1795, North Carolina became the first state to pass a general incorporation law, followed in 1799 by Massachusetts, New York in 1811, and Connecticut in 1837.[3] Still, some states required more than a simple majority of the legislature to grant, renew or alter a corporate charter. In the 1840s, citizens in New York, Delaware, Michigan and Florida required a two-thirds vote of their state legislatures to do so. In Wisconsin and four other states, every bank charter had to be approved by the voters, then recommended by legislatures.

Even under a general incorporation law, states still treated the corporate charters as privileges and restricted the activities of corporations. The following are some of the common limitations that were placed on corporations by various states.

Limited Duration: Charters were granted only for a period of 10, 20 or 30 years after which the corporation had to be liquidated and the earnings distributed among the shareholders.

Limited Land Holdings: Many states imposed limits on the extent of land a corporation could own. Most often, this was limited to the needs of the factory or mill site.

Limited Capital Holdings: Once again, many states limited the amount of money or financial assets a corporation could have. Some states banned corporations from owning other corporations or stock in them. Once a corporation exceeded the limit, it had to be either dissolved or split.

Specific Purpose Charters: This was perhaps the most common of all restrictions in the early years of this country. Corporations were chartered only for a specific purpose such as building a canal or road. Once the stated purpose was completed, the corporation dissolved. Today charters are issued that enable a corporation to engage in any type of business.

No Limitations on Liability: Directors, managers and shareholders were held to be fully liable for any debts or damages. Sometimes the lender or injured party was entitled to double or triple the damages. Other states imposed extremely high interest rates until the debt was fully paid.

Restrictive Shareholder Rights: The internal governance of corporations was much more restrictive than it is today. Shareholders had more rights. In case of mergers, some states required a unanimous vote of shareholders.

Restrictions on Pricing: Some states kept the right to set prices on corporate products. Wisconsin, for one, gave the state legislature the power to set prices on products after reviewing the corporations' expenses.

Revocable Charters: States kept the right to revoke or change a charter at the will of the legislature. Almost all the states adopted this clause after 1820.

Before continuing to look at various state constitutions of the early 1800s, a brief review of a couple early Supreme Court cases is needed. One led to most states including a clause for the modification or annulment of any charters the state granted. Chief Justice John Marshall, appointed by John Adams in 1801, shaped the Supreme Court into a third branch of government and strengthened the federal system.

Marshall presided over several landmark cases that weakened the power of states over corporations. Four cases are notable. In *Fletcher v. Peck,* the sanctity of a written contract was upheld. In *Gibbons v. Ogden,* the court established the power of Congress to regulate interstate commerce to avoid a monopoly. In *McCullough v. Maryland,* the court ruled that the state had no right to tax the federal bank. However, it was *Dartmouth v. Woodward* that exerted the most influence in later years. The state legislature had passed a law making Dartmouth a state university. Alumnus Daniel Webster argued the case for Dartmouth College and implied the right to own property was given in its corporate charter.

The U.S. Supreme Court found that a corporate charter

is a contract within the meaning of that clause of the Constitution of the United States, art. 1, s. 10, which declares that no state shall make any law impairing the obligation of contracts.

Marshall's opinion opened the door to later judicial activism, which would obtain the rights of a person and the right to hold property for corporations:

A corporation is an artificial being... it possesses only those properties which the charter of its creation confers upon it... such as are supposed best calculated to effect the object for which it was created. Among the most important are immortality, and, if the expression may be allowed, individuality — properties by which a perpetual succession of many persons are considered as the same, and may act as a single individual. They enable a corporation to manage its own affairs and to hold property without the perplexing intricacies, the hazardous and endless necessity, of perpetual conveyances for the purpose of transmitting it from hand to hand... But this being does not share in the civil government of the country, unless that be the purpose for which it was created.[4]

In state constitutions of the 1800s we find further examples of the corporate charter seen as a privilege. Pennsylvania's 1838 Constitution contains the clause for revocation and establishes a time limit of 20 years for all corporate charters, in Article I, Section 25:

No corporate body shall be hereafter created, renewed, or extended, with banking or discounting privileges, without six months' previous public notice of the intended application for the same in such manner as shall be prescribed by law. Nor shall any charter for the purposes aforesaid be granted for a longer time than twenty years; and every such charter shall contain a clause reserving to the legislature the power to alter, revoke, or annul the same, whenever in their opinion it may be injurious to the citizens of the commonwealth, in such manner, however, that no injustice shall be done to the corporators. No law hereafter enacted shall create, renew, or extend the charter of more than one corporation.[5]

Maryland legislators restricted manufacturing charters to 40 years, mining charters to 50, and most others to 30 years. Several other states, including Louisiana and Michigan, included time limits in corporate charters.

The revocation clause was initially written into the Pennsylvania Constitution in 1784. Clauses of revocation were first commonly found in insurance and banking charters. Further, the revocation clause was broadened and strengthened from 1784–1857 after the legislature was required to revoke charters whenever corporate activities were deemed harmful to the community. Notice the specific mention of corporations engaged in banking. The Indiana and Illinois Constitutions banned private banking corporations in 1816 and 1818. Throughout the early 1800s, Ohio, Pennsylvania and Mississippi revoked charters of banks that engaged in activities that would leave them insolvent or in a financially unsound condition. Limitations on railroads were another common feature in many state constitutions. New York, Ohio, Michigan and Nebraska successfully revoked charters from a wide range of businesses, including oil, matches, sugar and whiskey. By 1870, 19 states included a revocation clause (presently 49 of the 50 states have one). In 1857, Pennsylvania amended its constitution with the following clause in Article XI, Section 6:

> The commonwealth shall not assume the debt, or any part thereof, of any county, city, borough, or township, or of any corporation or association, unless such debt shall have been contracted to enable the State to repel invasion, suppress domestic insurrection, defend itself in time of war or to assist the State in the discharge of any portion of its present indebtedness.

The Alabama Constitution of 1875 exemplifies two common restrictions, in Article XIV Sections 5 and 9, respectively:

> No corporation shall engage in any business other than that expressly authorized in its charter.
> No corporation shall issue preferred stock without the consent of the owners of two-thirds of the stock of said corporation.[6]

The Wyoming Constitution of 1889 best illustrated the concept of a corporate charter as a privilege. Although the Wyoming Constitution allows for creating corporations under general law, it contains many restrictions:

> The legislature shall provide for the organization of corporations by general law. All laws relating to corporations may be altered, amended or repealed by the legislature at any time when necessary for the public good and general welfare, and all corporations doing business in this state may as to such business be regulated, limited or restrained by law not in conflict with the constitution of the United States.

> All powers and franchises of corporations are derived from the people and are granted by their agent, the government, for the public good and general welfare, and the right and duty of the state to control and regulate them for these purposes is hereby declared. The power, rights and privileges of any and all corporations may be forfeited by willful neglect or abuse thereof. The police power of the state is supreme over all corporations as well as individuals.[7]

The second paragraph clearly states that a corporation's powers come only from the people, and that it is subservient to the people for the public good and general welfare. Wyoming's Constitution also is the source of strong antitrust language:

> There shall be no consolidation or combination of corporations of any kind whatever to prevent competition, to control or influence productions or prices thereof, or in any other manner to interfere with the public good and general welfare.

With 24 sections, California's Constitution of 1849 as amended by Article XII in 1879 had perhaps the longest listing of restrictions on corporations.[8] Sadly, 20 of the 24 sections have already been repealed. In Section 3, the state holds all shareholders responsible for the debts of the corporation. Once again, another myth — the myth of limited liability — is destroyed. Notice in the Section 3 text that follows, the shareholder need not be a present owner, but only a shareholder at the time the debt was incurred. In Ohio, Missouri and Arkansas, stockholders were liable over and above the stock they actually owned. In the 1870s, seven state constitutions made bank shareholders doubly liable for any debts:

> Each stockholder of a corporation or joint stock association, shall be individually and personally liable for such proportion of all its debts and liabilities contracted or incurred, during the time he was a stockholder, as the amount of stock or shares owned by him bears to the whole of the subscribed capital stock, or shares of the corporation or association. The directors or trustees of corporations and joint-stock associations shall be jointly and severally liable to the creditors and stockholders for all moneys embezzled or misappropriated by the officers of such corporation or joint stock association during the term of office of such director or trustee.

Section 8 forbids corporations from infringing on the rights of individuals:

The exercise of the right of eminent domain shall never be so abridged or construed as to prevent the Legislature from taking the property and franchises of incorporated companies and subjecting them to public use the same as the property of individuals, and the exercise of the police power of the State shall never be so abridged or construed as to permit corporations to conduct their business in such manner as to infringe the rights of individuals or the general well-being of the State.

Section 9 limits the activities of corporations to those that are defined in their charters:

No corporation shall engage in any business other than that expressly authorized in its charter, or the law under which it may have been or may hereafter be organized; nor shall it hold for a longer period than five years any real estate except such as may be necessary for carrying on its business.

The extent of corporation regulation would require a review of all state laws — a daunting task and beyond the scope of even a single book. However, one can glean a glimpse of it from a list of the more important Supreme Court cases.

The first important case following the Marshall court came in 1839 in *Bank of Augusta v. Earle.*[9] The court ruled that corporations were "persons" in the state of their charter, but were free to do business in other states.

As more and more corporations were chartered, their power increased through judicial activism. With the increase in corporate power, wealth became concentrated in the hands of a few. As president, Lincoln lamented:

I see in the near future a crisis approaching that unnerves me and causes me to tremble for the safety of my country... Corporations have been enthroned and an era of corruption in high places will follow, and the money of the country will endeavor to prolong its reign by working upon the prejudices of the people until all wealth is aggregated in a few hands and the Republic is destroyed.

Part 2: Supreme Court Cases

The three decades following the Civil War saw further increases in the number of corporations and a more rapid pace in favorable court rulings. Part of the increase in corporations no doubt came from the great giveaway of public lands to some 61 railroad companies. However, even with the huge land grants, the railroads could not abide by the conditions set forth by the grants and more than one-third of the land, 190 million acres, was forfeited. Even today, the terms of those grants are disputed in court, most notably in the clear cutting of timber and shipping the raw logs to Asia.

In 1868, the Supreme Court ruled that corporations were not citizens within the context of Article IV, Section 2 of the Constitution, "The citizens of each state shall be entitled to all privileges and immunities of citizens in the several states." The court defined citizens as natural persons, members of the body politic, owing allegiance to the state. Corporations only had the properties conferred by the legislature.

In 1876, the Supreme Court ruled in *Munn v. Illinois* that corporations with a public interest (in this case, the rate grain elevators charged farmers for shipping) were subject to state regulation. The court further ruled that what constituted a reasonable rate was a legislative and not a judicial question. This case is similar to one settled before the Wisconsin Supreme Court. In *Attorney General v. Northwestern Railroad*, the court ruled the state could set maximum fares on classes of rail transportation.[10]

It is important to note here that the dissenting opinion came from Justice Stephen Field, appointed by Lincoln in 1863, whose opinions were often at odds with the majority. He had three concepts of government. He felt it was not a function of the government to protect individual liberty; that government should be limited, in line with his laissez-faire economic views; and that only the U.S. government should have the right to interact with foreign governments. In the Munn case, Field first expressed the view that the Fourteenth Amendment protected private businesses from government regulation.

In 1879, Judge Lorenzo Sawyer of the Ninth Circuit Court ruled in the Orton case that the federal government had control over the railroad land grants. However, he further restricted state regulation in controlling *ultra vires* acts of corporations, that is, acts beyond the powers actually granted to corporations. The ruling led directly to the forcible eviction of settlers in the Mussel Slough Battle of 1880, in which five were killed. Sawyer is best described as a flatterer of Field, who also was involved in this case.

In 1882, Sawyer ruled in the San Mateo Railroad case that corporations were persons. It is a matter of record that Sawyer owned stock in the Central Pacific Railroad. Both Sawyer and Field were close friends of Leland Stanford and other parties involved in the rail cases. Sawyer was uniquely positioned to expand the powers of corporations, using unorthodox interpretations of statutes and judicial review.

In 1886, the high point of pro-business judicial activism, the Illinois Supreme Court struck down state Granger laws regulating railroad rates in *Wabash v. Illinois.* In this year alone, the U.S. Supreme court struck down 230 state laws passed to regulate corporations. This also was the year of the most grievous act of all in furthering corporate power: the court handed down the ruling in *Santa Clara County v. Southern Pacific Railroad,* declaring that corporations were persons under the Fourteenth Amendment. At the outset of the case, Chief Justice Morrison Waite stated:

> The Court does not wish to hear argument on the question whether the provision in the Four–teenth Amendment to the Constitution, which forbids a state to deny to any person the equal protection of the laws, applies to these corporations. We are all of the opinion that it does.

This outrageous ruling has done more to damage our liberty and freedom than any other in the history of the country. In effect, it gave corporations the same rights as persons, but with none of the obligations or social responsibility. It paved the way to rendering people subservient to corporations. It is important to note when year this ruling came down: at the height of the robber barons.

A look at the judges on this Supreme Court shows it was the most antagonistic toward individual freedom and liberty in U.S. history, with the possible exception of the Rehnquist court. Much as the Rehnquist court voided the results of the 2000 election and appointed George W. Bush president, Associate Justice Joseph Bradley cast the deciding vote giving Rutherford B. Hayes the presidency.

This was the same court that rendered the Civil Rights Act of 1875 invalid in *Plessy v. Ferguson.* In essence, the court threw out the Fourteenth Amendment in its ruling. Even more telling of the court's abusive nature on civil rights, of all the Fourteenth Amendment cases between 1890–1910, only 19 dealt with blacks, while 288 dealt with corporations.

This court was not any more friendly to women's suffrage. In *Bradwell v. Illinois,* it upheld an Illinois ruling that denied women a license to practice law. In 1886, the Supreme Court Justices were Samuel F. Miller, Stephen J. Field, Joseph P. Bradley, John M. Harlan, Stanley Matthews, William B. Woods, Samuel Blatchford, Horace Gray, and Chief Justice Morrison R. Waite. Chief Justice Waite, who shared similar views with Field, believed the first 10 amendments applied only to the federal government and were not intended to limit the powers of the various states. In 1874, Samuel Miller declared that any taxation was robbery.

Subsequent Supreme Court justices ridiculed the invoking of the Fourteenth Amendment in the Santa Clara case. Among these were William Douglas, and Justice Hugo Black, who 70 years later in *Connecticut General Life Insurance Company v. Johnson* wrote:

> Certainly when the Fourteenth Amendment was submitted for approval, the people were not told that ratifying an amendment granting new and revolutionary rights to corporations... was intended to remove corporations in any fashion from the control of the state governments. The fourteenth followed the freedom of a race from slavery... Corporations have neither race nor color.

In 1890, the Sherman Antitrust Act was passed outlawing cartels, combinations, trusts or conspiracies that restrained or monopolized trade. As an alternative means of limiting competition, the largest wave of corporate mergers yet then swept across the country. This act also defined corporations as persons.

In 1890, in *Chicago, Milwaukee & St. Paul Railway v. Minnesota,* the court began retreating from its *Munn* ruling (that legislatures could set rail rates), and made rates subject to judicial review and due process if set by a commission. In *Smythe v. Ames* in 1898, the court went further to allow judicial review, even if the rates were set by legislature. This favored railroads and corporations.

In 1890, New Jersey intensified the race to the bottom by relaxing its general corporate laws, permitting corporate charters for holding companies, allowing corporations to trade stock of other corporations, and to issue their own shares as payment. In 1892, New Jersey went further by repealing its antitrust law. In 1896, New Jersey allowed charters to be granted for any legal purpose and removed any restrictions on mergers. Likewise, the 50-year limit on corporate life was removed and, for the first time, New Jersey granted charters to corporations operating outside its borders.

Shareholders' rights also received a blow. Under the new laws of the state, directors were allowed to amend bylaws without shareholder approval, and could now rely on proxy voting, with all shareholder meetings held in New Jersey. The new laws were so popular that between 1897 and 1904, corporations chartered in New Jersey with a net worth of $20 million or more increased to 104, up from a mere 15 in 1896. Enough revenue from the filing fees and franchise taxes was generated to allow the state to abolish property taxes.

In 1899, Delaware passed a General Corporation Law that allowed corporations themselves to write provisions creating, defining, limiting and regulating their power. This change in Delaware law figures prominently as the reason the duPonts reincorporated in Delaware.

In 1893, the court issued perhaps its first anti-union ruling in *U.S. v. Workingmen's Amalgamated Council.* The court upheld an injunction against a union on the grounds that the Interstate Commerce Act required carriers to accept freight without discrimination. Also in 1893, corporations were first given the protection of the Bill of Rights in *Noble v. Union River Logging Railroad* with the ruling that the railroad was denied its Fifth Amendment protection when the Department of Interior attempted to revoke a right-of-way on federal lands.

From 1894–1905, the court issued a host of anti-labor rulings. Before this, it was common under state law to limit the number of hours a person worked. In 1894, the court struck down the eight-hour shift for mechanics and laborers in *Low v. Rees Printing.* Colorado eliminated its eight-hour day for mining and manufacturing with House Bill 203. In 1895, in *Ritchie v. People,* the eight-hour day was removed for female garment workers. *Lochner v. New York* eliminated the 10-hour day for bakers in New York in 1905. In 1895, the court ruled that the Sherman Antitrust Act could be used against interstate labor strikes because they restrained trade.

In 1895, the court upheld a monopoly of 98 percent of the country's sugar production in *U.S. v. E.C. Knight Co.,* ruling that the Sherman Antitrust Act applied only to commerce. In a dissenting opinion, Justice Harlan wrote the ruling placed the Constitution in "a condition of helplessness ... while capital combines ... to destroy competition."

In *Hale v. Henkel,* the court ruled against the corporation's attempt to use the Fifth Amendment, but ruled that excessively broad subpoenas for corporate documents could be a violation of the Fourth Amendment.

In 1911, the court broke Standard Oil into 33 corporations in *Standard Oil of New Jersey v. United States.* This case ended a short period of generally fair rulings against monopolies and trusts. For the most part, it was the climax of the antitrust sentiment started by the muckrakers and Teddy Roosevelt. The Clayton Act of 1914 legislated price discrimination within the same industry and further stipulated that labor unions were not trusts.

In 1917, Idaho became the first state to pass criminal syndicalism laws; 23 other states soon followed. The laws were used to suppress labor organizers, political activists and foreigners.

In 1918, the Supreme Court struck down the Keating-Owen Child Labor Act. It ruled that goods produced by child labor did not fall under the Sherman Anti-Trust Act, again because it only applied to commerce.

Between 1920–24, the court granted corporations protection under the Fourth Amendment, ruling that government officers seizing corporate documents violated the provisions against unreasonable searches in *Silverthorne Lumber v. U.S* and *FTC v. American Tobacco.* This decision came just as investigations were heating up into profiteering by arms makers during WWI. Likewise, the decision provided protection for those corporations that signed cartel agreements with IG Farben and other German corporations during WWII.

In 1937, the court ruled that Congress could protect interstate commerce from labor organizing in *National Labor Relations Board v. Jones & Laughlin Steel Corp.*

In 1938, in Subcommittee on Federal Licensing of Corporations hearings, Sen. Joseph O'Mahoney of Wyoming argued that "a corporation has no rights; it has only privileges."

In 1947, the anti-union Taft-Hartley Act was passed over the veto of President Truman. The act declared the closed shop to be illegal, outlawed secondary strikes and boycotts, allowed employers to exempt themselves from bargaining with unions, restricted union contributions to political campaigns, and required unions and their officers to confirm that they were not supporters of the Communist Party.

The Celler-Kefauver Act of 1950 amended the Clayton Antitrust Act to close the loophole of buying physical assets to achieve the goal of a merger.

In 1969, the Newspaper Preservation Act was passed, exempting newspapers from antitrust laws. Wholesale consolidation of newspapers followed until only a handful of corporations owned all the major papers.

In 1976, the court granted the second most grievous extension to corporate power when, in *Buckley v. Valeo,* corporations were granted freedom of speech. That meant corporations were free to contribute unlimited funds to federal election campaigns, in effect buying the candidate of their choice.

The year 1976 marked the beginning of another long period of pro-corporate rulings, as Republicans were once again able to stack the court with extremely conservative justices.

That year in *U.S. v. Martin Linen Supply Co.*, the court ruled that corporations could use the Fifth Amendment to protect themselves from double jeopardy and avoid retrial in antitrust suits. In addition, the court ruled that advertising was free speech in *Virginia Board of Pharmacy v. Virginia Citizens Consumer Council.* In 1977 in *Marshall v. Barlow*, the court allowed corporations protection under the Fourth Amendment to thwart the efforts of OSHA inspectors. Also that year, the court overturned state restrictions on corporate spending on political referendums in *First National Bank v. Bellotti,* ruling again that money was free speech under First Amendment protections.

Most states, through general law, had restricted the activities of corporations by limiting the amount of wealth or land they could accumulate. It was liberalism at its finest hour protecting the rights of the common man against the plutocrats.

Judicial activism and corruption, and some state legislatures themselves eroded most of the laws governing corporations in the 19th century. This erosion accompanied the rise of a rich elite and the corporatization of America. Before the Civil War, most corporations consisted of railroads or banks. It was only after the Civil War that corporations began significant expansion into other businesses. This is the primary reason so many of the early court decisions and clauses in state constitutions were specific to banks and railroads, as other types of corporations were simply insignificant.

It should be clear that the rich elite as a class did not begin to emerge until after the Civil War, which was concurrent with the court's pro-business rulings that reached a climax with the robber barons of the 1880s. By the end of the 1880s, the Waite court granted the rights of personhood to corporations.

When the judicial system conferred citizenship on corporations without any of the obligations and responsibilities, it left this country in the precarious position of capital — the almighty dollar — having more rights than the owner of the capital.

A case in point: In World War II, the U.S. experienced a shortage of supplies. Moreover, munitions and armaments were slow to come. Corporations refused to produce war munitions instead of consumer goods. In effect, they engaged in a sit-down strike until they had gained outrageously beneficial terms. America faced corporations that openly violated the law, that blackmailed the government with threats of an interruption in the gasoline supply, and that conspired to fix prices. Yet no corporation ever faced charges of price fixing, war profiteering and treason, and more than 300 corporations did business with the Third Reich during the war.

Certainly, the legacy of the Waite court with its many antagonistic rulings against the civil rights of individuals and their liberties, and its extremely pro-business agenda spanning almost 30 years, should be reviewed today. All too often, justices have been chosen for their political ideology rather than their judicial abilities.

The erosion of protections from corporations built into the various state constitutions has led to the present problems we face. Our government is for sale to the highest bidder. The calamitous decision of the court in 1976 equating corruption with free speech has left us citizens with unequal rights. A citizen's voice is not equal to that of a multinational corporation with unlimited financial resources. The court has allowed corporations to grow to gargantuan proportions, precisely the fear Jefferson expressed in his opposition to national charters.

In 1996, 51 of the world's largest economies were corporations, with General Motors larger than Denmark, and Wal-Mart, the 12th largest corporation, larger than 161 countries. The combined sales of these top 200 corporations are larger than all but the world's nine largest countries, equivalent to 28.3 percent of the world's GDP. These top 200 corporations employ 18.8 million people — less than one-third of 1 percent of the world's population — a percentage 100 times smaller. The world's top five employers are General Motors, Wal-Mart, PepsiCo, Ford and Siemens.

The wealthiest 1 percent in America own 40 percent of all U.S. assets. The corporate share of income taxes has fallen from roughly 40 percent in the 1940s to less than 15 percent today. While corporate profits rose by an astounding 130 percent from 1980–1995, the average family saw a net decrease in its real wages. The problem was first detailed in *America: What Went Wrong?* by Barlett and Steele.

The above overview of court rulings and acts of Congress ends with 1987. Thereafter began an era of deregulation and a supine legislature, as an era of extreme conservatism gripped the nation. Jimmy Carter started deregulating a few industries to prop up a sagging economy that was feeling the aftereffects of the OPEC oil shock. In the 1980 presidential race, Ronald Reagan ran on a platform of deregulation. If Carter began limited deregulation, the Reagan administration threw open the floodgates. The last dying gasp in favor of regulation of corporations came in 1984 when the judge ordered AT&T broken into eight Regional Bells in an ongoing monopoly case.

With corporations free to buy the politicians of their choice came a host of new bills passed by Congress granting corporations more corporate welfare, fewer regulations, more power and more rights. With the top tax rates reduced to a mere 31 percent, corporate executives soon reaped exorbitant salaries and benefits at the expense of employees. Employees became expendable and a new industry was born overnight: the temporary employment firms. Meanwhile, CEOs of corporations sought control of corporate boards, further increasing their empire and concentrating their power.

The result of the deregulation in the 1980s–1990s is literally punctuated with dismal failures. The era is marked in the beginning by a multibillion-dollar taxpayer bailout of the savings and loan industry. For much of the 1980s, the savings and loan bailout was a black hole for taxpayers' hard-earned dollars. The deregulated industry had gambled on high-interest junk bonds and foreign loans. When the junk bond market collapsed with the foreign loans, the industry was devastated. Fallout from the resulting carnage led to the Keating Five scandal and Michael Milken trials. Keating had lobbied Congress heavily for deregulation of the savings and loan, but in the end his Lincoln Savings and Loan went bankrupt, as did the reputation of the five congressmen most heavily involved with him. Milken, the junk bond king, faced a 98-count indictment.

The result of the scandals went far beyond the taxpayer bailout. Further concentrating power in fewer hands, the junk bonds were used to finance leveraged buyouts. Many investors in junk bonds found themselves with worthless paper or, if they were lucky, perhaps saw their investment reduced to 15 cents on each dollar invested. In the end, none of the perpetrators of the failed savings and loans faced serious sentencing. Milken was fined heavily and sentenced to a short prison term. His fortune was somewhat reduced, but he was still a multimillionaire.

Evidence exists that in 1988, presidential candidate George H. W. Bush was implicated in delaying the closure of Silverado Savings and Loan until after the election, because his son Neil was on the board.[11]

Perhaps the most damaging aspect of the junk bond fiasco was the spawning of a mania of mergers. Even more than a decade later, mergers continue unabated. The huge corporations that received tax bonanzas from the Reagan administration under the ruse that lower taxes would spur growth did not invest their newfound wealth in research; instead they bought out smaller corporations. Moreover, with each new merger and buyout, power and wealth concentrated. For the employees, it meant massive layoffs. Congress and the Justice Department have both been comfortably asleep at the wheel, allowing corporations to remerge, as in the case of Exxon and Mobil and a couple of the regional "Baby Bell" phone companies.

Among the first industries to be deregulated were the airlines. Fares did come down, but at the high price of safety. Delays are more likely than on-time departures and arrivals. Luggage is lost or damaged all too often. It is now commonplace to hear of an airline crash with possibly 100 or more deaths resulting. Yet, studies reveal that most deaths are not the result of the impact, but of excessively weak seats. On impact, the seats tear loose and passengers are propelled forward at 120 mph. The luckier ones may indeed be those killed when they are thrown against the bulkhead. More often than not, limbs or spines are shattered and, unable to move, passengers perish in the flames or from the toxic fumes. The FAA has known for years of the weak seat design. Car seats can resist the strain of 20-G forces; airline seats, only 9-Gs.[12]

However, from the beginning the FAA was hobbled with a dual mandate from Congress to regulate and promote the industry. Congress acted only after the fatal crash of ValuJet flight 592 following in the wake of a spate of serious safety problems. Nor is it proper to blame the FAA alone for air safety problems. The real problem lies with Congress that creates a toothless agency to placate the public. Why does the agency need a Congressional bill to require stronger seats? A regulatory agency should be allowed to implement reasonable controls over its charges. However, time and again in response to a problem, Congress creates an agency with little or no authority to complete its mission.

Two other examples are the EPA and OSHA, where, in recent years, Congress has blocked planned implementation of stronger new standards, on fine particulates in the case of the EPA, and repetitive motion with OSHA. In short, Republicans have used these two agencies as political footballs. Richard Nixon used both against his political enemies. The Reagan administration made a mockery of the EPA, as well as the Department of Interior headed by James Watt, by appointing a former associate of the radical right-wing Coors family.

The Reagan transition team in 1980 went far beyond the normal bounds of corruption. Reagan turned a blind eye on ethics and a free rein on his transition team, the largest by far of any president. Many members had obvious conflicts of interests. Carter appointees refused to turn over lists of prospective enforcement cases to one member of the transition team (who just happened to be an independent oil producer) and his deputy (whose firm represented Standard Oil of California). At the Labor Department, Reagan's deputy team leader filed a friend of the court brief with the Supreme Court challenging the enforcement of OSHA laws. Such confrontations were visible in every department. In short, Reagan's transition team was given a license to loot on behalf of corporate benefactors.[13]

Since the scandalous Supreme Court decision to equate money with free speech, politicians have been placed in the pocket of corporate America. Campaign finance was an issue in the 2000 elections and remains an issue in Congress, despite the best efforts of George W. Bush and the leaders of the Republican Party to kill campaign finance reform. The Bush administration is rabidly pro-business, as evident in his appointment of Gale Norton to head of the Interior Department. Norton was a protégé of none other than James Watt. Bush also showed his allegiance to corporate America during the California electrical power shortage and Enron scandal.

This leaves American citizens as pawns. While the corporate media blare report after report of crime in the streets, the real crime story of corporate fraud goes unreported. In 1998, the FBI estimated the annual cost of robberies and burglaries at $3.8 billion. The annual cost of corporate or white-collar fraud has been placed in the $100 billion range, although the FBI does not estimate corporate or white-collar fraud — it does not really even have a white-collar fraud unit. Estimates of healthcare fraud alone were between $100 billion and $400 billion. Securities fraud is in the minor leagues at only $15 billion.[14] The two figures point to one glaring and unmistakable fact: regulation works. The securities market is tightly regulated, while the healthcare field is wide open. What little healthcare regulation does exist is primarily on state and local levels. The Savings and Loan scandal alone cost U.S. taxpayers between $300 billion–$500 billion.

The FBI also reported in 1998 that 19,000 Americans were murdered. In contrast, 56,000 Americans died of job-related diseases, such as black lung. No estimate is even available for the number of Americans whose lives were cut short from cancer because of environmental pollution or workplace exposure. Federal contractors routinely violate the Wagner Act on National Labor Relations and other laws, but are still allowed to continue to provide government services.

However, Americans (and indeed all the world's people) face an even greater threat to their freedoms. The threat comes from the drive to take fascism worldwide through the WTO and so-called free-trade agreements. Free trade between nations is beneficial to all. However, free trade means only one thing: a cut in or elimination of tariffs. Any trade agreement that goes beyond those boundaries is just another step toward global fascism and corporate rule.

In free countries, people or their representatives determine laws; they are not set by corporate fiat. This is overturned by recent trade agreements, such as GATT, NAFTA, the now-defeated MAI, or the present negotiations on GATS. All of these so-called trade agreements contain provisions that either overwrite existing labor and environmental laws or mandate payment to any corporation that perceives itself to be injured by public policy, the laws of a sovereign nation or both. Further, these so-called free-trade treaties set up corporate tribunals as the final arbitrator in any dispute, rendering the judicial court system and national sovereignty mute. In essence, these so-called free-trade agreements confer global sovereign status onto corporations.

For instance under GATT, the United States was forced to accept shrimp imports from Thailand. The imports had been banned under U.S. law because Thai law did not require shrimpers to use protective nets for sea turtles.

Presently, the United States is bound by NAFTA to begin allowing Mexican tractor-trailer rigs into the country unrestricted. At best, the only protection ensuring these rigs are up to U.S. safety standards comes from state highway patrols.

However, under these so-called free trade agreements, Canada and Mexico have both suffered more grievous blows. Under NAFTA, Canada was forced to pay a multimillion-dollar ransom to U.S.-based Ethyl Corp. In 1997, Ethyl sued Canada under the provisions in Chapter 11 of NAFTA. Canada had the foresight to ban the hazardous and toxic MMT gasoline additive. Ethyl claimed that such a ban on MMT constituted an expropriation of its assets and sought $250 million in damages. In 1998, the Canadian government, under extreme pressure, removed the ban on MMT and settled the suit with Ethyl for $13 million.[15]

In 1996, Mexico suffered a similar indignity. The Mexican state of San Luis Potosi refused to give U.S.-based Metalclad Corp. a permit to reopen its waste disposal site. The state governor ordered the site to be closed after a geological survey showed it would contaminate the local water supply. Then the governor declared the area part of a 600,000-acre ecological zone. Metalclad sued under Chapter 11 of NAFTA, seeking $90 million in compensation. Eventually, the case was settled with an award to Metalclad for $17 million. Under GATS, Mexico would have faced additional trade sanctions.

Awards against Canada and Mexico were granted under a tribunal set up under NAFTA. The tribunal is, of course, beholden only to the multinational corporations. Canadian or Mexican courts and laws were voided in both cases.

Incredibly, under the rules of the current talks on GATS, injustices such as these would increase. GATS could prevent Canada from expanding its Medicare program to include a national drug or homecare program.[16] Such expansion of Canada's healthcare system could trigger suits similar to those filed by Ethyl or Metalclad. GATS defines services very broadly:

> business services, communication services, construction services, distribution services, financial services, recreation, tourism and travel, transport services, education, health services, water supply, electricity supply, waste disposal[17]

Under GATS, any expansion of the National Park System could trigger a lawsuit forcing the taxpayer to pay millions to some multinational corporation. Likewise, any expansion of a city's public water supply or waste disposal would trigger lawsuits, as would cities that chose to implement a light rail system to ease traffic congestion. Further, under the current rules of GATS, any increase in funding or expansion of additional programs in our public schools would trigger lawsuits. All such suits would be brought before a tribunal established by GATS, without regard to the U.S. court system.

Present trade agreements have little to do with increasing trade and more to do with eliminating any capital risk by requiring compensation for any government actions to protect the public.

The proposed MAI treaty was killed and is effectively dead for now. However, the WTO is still active and MAI has now been replaced with a treaty that is just as dangerous, GATS. Calling such treaties free-trade agreements is a feel-good euphemism keyed to generating support and cloaking the real danger. The erosion of laws governing corporations and the new rounds of trade talks have placed the people of the United States and the entire world in jeopardy of losing their freedoms to global fascism.

There is only one sure method of ensuring that such agreements are eliminated: a constitutional amendment that restricts the activities of all corporations (see Appendix 6 for such a proposed amendment). Under our present constitution, Congress has been given the sole authority in regulating interstate commerce. Such authority could be used to require any corporation to obtain a charter limited by the proposed amendment.

Franklin Roosevelt described fascism best when he said:

The liberty of a democracy is not safe if the people tolerate the growth of private power to a point where it becomes stronger than their democratic State itself. That, in its essence, is Fascism — ownership of government by an individual, by a group or by any controlling private power.

Chapter 3,
The Roaring '20s and
the Roots of American Fascism

IG Farben

Most Americans view the Roaring '20s as a decade of speakeasies, bootleg liquor, flappers and the Charleston. But without a doubt, the 1920s were the most repressive decade of the century, beginning with the Palmer Raids of 1919 and ending with the massacre of the Bonus Marchers in the midst of the Great Depression. As a society, Americans fail to recall the brutal repression unleashed on the labor movement or the many race riots of the decade.

America's collective "apple pie" view of the 1950s, another decade of repression, is similar, consisting of images of "Leave It to Beaver" and "Ozzie and Harriet." Few recall the madness of McCarthyism or images of the developing Cold War.

As a society, Americans are led to overlook great threats to our freedoms that took place during repressive times. If the Palmer Raids or McCarthyism had taken place in any country behind the Iron Curtain, Americans would have been quick to condemn the actions as massive purges of dissidents.

The 1920s held a bountiful promise of progress at the end of WWI. The United States could have seized the chance to become a world power and leader. Instead, the nation retreated into itself and rejected President Wilson's League of Nations in favor of isolationism. New technologies and industries were breaking down doors. Autos were replacing the horse and buggy. Telephones were replacing telegraphs. Electric lights were replacing the kerosene lamp. Air travel became a reality.

It was a decade that did not live up to its promise, that ended in a spectacular failure of laissez-faire economics — the stock market crash of 1929. The resulting Depression was so severe that it left a lasting mark on those who lived through it.

A repressive period has followed every major war this country has fought. The aftermath of the Civil War fits the pattern. McCarthyism followed WWII and coincided with the Korean War. Even with the Vietnam War, repression increased, during the war with the exposure of COINTELPRO and Project Chaos, and afterward in the 1980s, with the Reagan administration.

The infamous Palmer Raids followed on the heels of WWI. The subsequent repression was directed at the perceived threats of the time, the four prime targets of the head of the Army Intelligence Network, Lt. Col. Ralph Van Deman: the International Workers of the World (the IWW union), opponents of the draft, socialists and blacks. These groups were brutally repressed throughout the 1920s. In 1917, even before the war's end, Van Deman had already opened a file on Martin Luther King Jr.'s maternal grandfather.[1]

Van Deman was an anti-Semite credited with establishing military intelligence as a part of the modern army. Most officers within the Military Intelligence Division (MID) at that time also were virulently anti-Semitic. MID officers promoted every anti-Jewish publication, including the *Protocols of the Elders of Zion*. It was commonly accepted in MID that communists and Jews were one and the same. Military officers were greatly influenced by the teaching of eugenics and anti-Semitism at West Point.

The almost universal anti-Semitism and racism of military officers allowed them to overlook the pogroms of the 1920s in Poland and other countries. It lasted until well after WWII, and factored into the failure of the United States to offer sanctuary to Jewish refugees in the late 1930s. It also contributed to the poor treatment of Jewish survivors of Nazi concentration camps. Such beliefs also contributed to the passage of the 1924 bill that restricted immigration of "undesirables."

During WWI, fearing that Germans would exploit black unrest, Van Deman preoccupied himself with black churches as suspected centers of sedition.

The most sinister aspect of Van Deman's network was military encroachment into civilian affairs. During the 1920s, federal troops were activated several times to intercede in civilian events. For example, the Seattle mayor used federal troops to break the Seattle strike. As late as 1947, military intelligence was still directed at the same targets listed by Van Deman, as shown by the inclusion of Martin Luther King Jr., in the 111th Military Intelligence Group's files.

These postwar periods of repression are the times our freedoms are most at risk. As demobilized troops return home, they seek work in an economy that is shifting from war to peace. Unemployment usually rises because many of the former soldiers have little or no peacetime skills. After WWI, inflation ravaged the nation as wartime controls were lifted, adding to the economic woes of returning veterans.

However, the real danger comes from troops formerly engaged in intelligence. These former spies seek to ply their trade in the government or private sector. For instance, following the Civil War, many Union spies went to work for private detective agencies as union busters. After WWI, big business used the newly formed American Legion for union busting and, even more sinister, for destroying political dissent and anyone left of center. The end of WWII ushered in the McCarthy era of wild witch hunts for suspected communists.

After the United States entered the Great War, German agents actively engaged in sabotage in America. The Kingsland fire of Jan. 11, 1917 was traced to a German agent, Fiodore Wozniak, the "Firebug." In that one act of sabotage, Wozniak destroyed 275,000 artillery shells, huge stores of TNT and other munitions valued at more than $17 million.[2]

Although the sabotage hindered the war effort, these acts paled in comparison to the economic sabotage by the corporate warlords of IG Farben. The cartel agreements between American corporations and IG Farben maintained a stranglehold on munitions production, as well as many consumer items.

Often, rather obscure events control future world peace and war. Discoveries in chemistry labs have played enormous roles leading up to both world wars.

Densely populated with limited arable land and a short growing season, Germany has at times been a net food importer. Although it has ample supplies of coal, it lacks high-grade iron ore and other minerals. These factors played a dominant role in Hitler's search for "living space" in the East.

Moreover, WWI pointed up Germany's vulnerability to blockades. Germany's only access to the world's oceans is through the North Sea. England, the lord and master of the high seas, could easily blockade this route. Any factor that decreased Germany's dependence on imports increased its ability to wage war and to challenge England's dominance over Europe.

Germany's chemical industry developed in the 19th century. English chemists were the first to discover that pigments could be produced from coal tar. However, they failed to recognize the significance of the discovery. German industry was quick to capitalize on the development and soon dominated the world's pigment production. The work of German chemists on coal tar launched a new branch of chemistry — organic chemistry. A host of new products came gushing forth: the first sulfa drugs, then plastics and, by the beginning of WWII, synthetic rubber.

One of the developments that had a direct impact on WWI was the Haber process of producing nitrates. Before perfecting this method, Germany was dependent on Chile's nitrate deposits. With the Haber process, nitrates could be produced from the nitrogen in the atmosphere. Germany's war machine was no longer dependent on shipments from Chile, which the British Navy could blockade. Also out of the new chemistry came the development of poison gas.

WWI was the first conflict in which technology overpowered the frontline soldier. Chemistry labs played a pivotal role in Germany's ability to wage war on its neighbors. These labs would play an even larger role in WWII with development of gasoline and synthetic rubber from coal.

At the center of the chemical arms production was IG Farben, Interessen-Gemeinschaft Farbenindustrie AG, or "syndicate of dyestuff corporations." IG Farben was a product of the cartelization of six dye companies: Badische Anilin & Soda Fabrik (BASF), Farbenfabriken vorm (Bayer), Farbwerke vorm (Hoechst), Aktiengesellschaft fur Anilinfabrikaten, Leopold Cassela, and Kalle & Co. The big six merged into IG Farben in 1916.[3]

Carl Duisberg first proposed merging the big six after returning from a trip to the United States. Duisberg traveled to the U.S. to lay the cornerstone for the Bayer factory in Rensselaer, N.Y. During his trip, he became aware of the trust movement in the United States. The Rockefeller Standard Oil Trust fascinated Duisberg, who used it as a model for merging Germany's big six chemical companies into IG Farben.[4]

In the decade preceding WWI, IG Farben relentlessly followed a path that strengthened Germany's capacity to wage war. When WWI broke out, IG Farben controlled the new worldwide chemical industry with cartel agreements and patents. Germany aggressively sought patents in foreign countries, particularly through IG Farben, then refused to grant licenses to corporations in those countries. This shifted all control of the industry to the German homeland.

Because of recent court decisions allowing corporations to patent genes and the resulting genetically engineered food crops, it would be a worthwhile effort to study how Germany used patents to gain worldwide control over the fledgling organic chemical industry.

Joseph Chamberlain summed up England's loss of the coal tar industry in 1883:

It has been pointed out especially in an interesting memorial presented on behalf of the chemical industry that under the present law it would have been possible, for instance, for the German inventor of the hot blast furnace, if he had chosen to refuse a license in England, to have destroyed almost the whole iron industry of this country and to carry the business bodily over to Germany. Although that did not happen in the case of the hot blast industry, it had actually happened in the manufacture of artificial colors connected with the coal products, and the whole of that had gone to Germany because the patentees would not grant license in this country.[5]

Lloyd George reiterated Chamberlain's view in 1907:

Big foreign syndicates have one very effective way of destroying British industry. They first of all apply for patents on a very considerable scale. They suggest every possible combination, for instance, in chemicals, which human ingenuity can possibly think of. These combinations the syndicates have not tried themselves. They are not in operation, say, in Germany or elsewhere, but the syndicates put them in their patents in obscure and vague terms so as to cover any possible invention that may be discovered afterward in this country.[6]

These comments leave no doubt about the effect of the cartel agreements and the patents sought by IG Farben on England, and the U.S. During WWI, the U.S. government seized numerous IG Farben front corporations under the 1917 Trading with the Enemy Act. Cartel agreements between American corporations and IG Farben created monopolies and spheres of influence, cutting out any competition. In effect, the cartel agreements were a second wave of robber barons. However, this time the robber barons resided in Germany and structured the agreements to keep control over American corporations, even to the extent of limiting production of war materiel. The cartel agreements overrode the rule of government.

Recent trade agreements such as NAFTA, GATT, the failed MAI, and GATS (proposed under the banner of free trade agreements) have again placed the rights of corporations above and beyond the reach of the government. All these agreements contain clauses that set up tribunals as the final arbitrator in disputes, bypassing the court systems of the signatory countries, allowing corporations to establish law by decree. The inherent danger of allowing corporations to rule will be readily obvious.

Even before the Nazis came to power, cartel agreements formed a vital part of Germany's plan to wage war and extract revenge for the Treaty of Versailles. The willingness of corporate America's leaders to reestablish cartel agreements with IG Farben during the 1920s, and their subsequent support for fascist groups in the 1930s, were signs of the strength of indigenous fascism in the United States.

Although there were literally dozens of companies seized during WWI for trading with the enemy, the focus is on the ease and speed with which IG Farben was able to reform its cartels, aided by the laissez-faire economic policies of Harding, Coolidge and Hoover.

During the war, corporations reaped fat profits. In 1919, the Wilson administration lifted wartime controls, freeing businesses to raise their prices. Business leaders at that time craved a chance to get back to normal. Before the war, Teddy Roosevelt had followed a policy of breaking up monopolies; during the war, the government had frozen prices. The only threat to reestablishing their monopolies and dominating the economy came from the new labor movement and communism. In the aftermath of the Red Scare of 1919, the pro-business candidate, Warren Harding, won the presidential election, setting the stage for rebuilding the cartels.

WWI should have taught the Allied nations that Germany used international cartels as its spearhead of aggression. The German military mind had long understood the concept of total war. The father of modern German militarism, Karl von Clausewitz, best summarized the idea:

> War is no independent thing, the main lineaments of all strategic plans are of a political nature, the more so the more they include the totality of War and State. Disarm your enemy in peace by diplomacy and trade if you would conquer him more readily on the field of battle.[7]

This philosophy of war and peace became a cornerstone of Germany's political and economic interactions with other nations. The history of IG Farben in the 20th century is one of support for German military adventurism. It consistently advanced German military plans and subordinated its own financial interests to German nationalistic aims.

With the ink hardly dry on the armistice agreement, the *New York Times* received a dispatch from its Berlin correspondent on Dec. 1, 1919: "The firms composing the German dye trust have decided to increase their capital to the extent without parallel, I believe, in the history of German industry. The trust which consists of three great and four minor concerns in the industry, valued at, roughly, 15,000,000,000 marks, is extending for two reasons: It is determined to reassert German supremacy in the dye industry; in the second place, there is the question of nitrate, so important for the agricultural life in the country. The trust is aiming at making the fatherland independent of foreign supplies and to increase production so it will be able to export large quantities."[8]

From 1919 on, IG Farben reestablished dominance using the same methods it had in the first war, as well as newer forms of the cartel. Several IG Farben developments in the interwar period figured prominently in WWII: production of Buna rubber, gasoline from coal, and aluminum and tungsten carbide.

Bayer 205 best illustrates the mind-set of IG Farben, including its use of patents and cartels to establish a German empire. In 1920, IG Farben claimed that Bayer 205, or Germanin, was a cure for sleeping sickness. Through indirect channels, IG Farben made an offer to the British government: the secret of Germanin in exchange for the return of German colonies in Africa lost in WWI. The British government declined the offer. However, a British medical journal in 1922 preserved the resourcefulness of IG Farben:

> A curious illustration of German desire, not unnatural in itself, to regain the tropical colonies lost by the folly of the rulers of the German Empire, is afforded by a discussion which took place at a meeting of the German Association of Tropical Medicine at Hamburg. The *Times* correspondent in Hamburg reports that

one of the speakers said that Bayer 205 is the key to tropical Africa, and consequently the key to all the colonies. The German government must, therefore, be required to safeguard this discovery for Germany. Its value is such that any privilege of a share in it granted to other nations must be made conditional upon the restoration to Germany of her colonial empire.[9]

The intent of IG Farben and Germany could hardly be masked by such a report. An even more ominous warning appeared in 1925:

In open violation of the Treaty of Versailles the Germans shipped munitions to the Argentines. Rottweil (IG's wholly owned subsidiary) still makes and sells excellent military powders, and German factories for munitions have been built or openly offered to build in Spain, Argentina, Mexico, etc.[10]

Article 170 of the treaty specifically forbade German export or import of armaments or munitions. Both the British and American state departments were aware of the violation. British Imperial Chemical Industries avoided lodging any protest because it was locked into a cartel agreement with IG Farben. America, locked in the grip of isolationism, simply ignored the violation.

In 1926, the German army formed the Economic High Command. Robert Strausz-Hupe summed up its express purpose as follows:

Studying the deficiencies of German economy and laying plans for transforming it into *Wehrwirtschaft* [a military economy]. Rapid conquests alone could provide new resources before Germany's reserves, accumulated by barter, ruthless rationing, and synthetic chemistry, had been exhausted in the initial war effort.

These new resources could then be poured into the war machine, rolling on to ever larger territorial conquests, and as long as it kept on rolling, the economy of greater space need never fear a crisis.[11]

IG Farben had direct and indirect communication channels with the Economic High Command. IG Farben adjusted its policies to accommodate the High Command's plans. In 1932, Col. Taylor of duPont reported:

One of the motives back of the French proposal, that all countries should establish a conscription, is to upset the present German system of handling their Reichswehr. The Reichswehr is limited to 100,000 men of 12 year enlistment, and it would appear reasonable to suppose that there should be at present a number of soldiers around the age of 33 or 34; the fact is that when one meets a soldier of the Reichswehr he is a young man in the early twenties, and it is pretty well accepted that there are several men available under the same name and hence training a much larger number of men than permitted.[12]

During the 1920s, there were more than 100 secret treason trials in Germany of journalists and others who revealed the truth. Quoting Dr. H.C. Englebrecht and F.C. Hanighen:

It would seem then that despite the Versailles treaty that Germany is again a manufacturer and exporter of arms. This interference is confirmed by various incidents from the past ten years. There was the Bullerjahn case of 1925. On December 11, 1925 Walter Bullerjahn was sentenced to 15 years in prison for treason. The trial was held in secret and the public was excluded. Both the crime with which the condemned was charged and the name of the accuser were kept deep and dark secrets. After years of agitation by Dr. Paul Levi and the League for Human Rights, the facts were finally disclosed. The accuser was Paul von Gontard, general director of the Berlin-Karlsruhe Industriewerke, the same man who used the French press in 1907 in order to increase his machine gun business. Gontard had been establishing secret arsenals, contrary to treaty provisions, and the Allies discovered this fact. Gontard disliked Bullerjahn and had serious disagreements with him. In order to get rid of him he charged him with revealing to the Allies the fact that Gontard was secretly arming Germany. This was termed treason by the court and Bullerjahn was condemned, although not a shred of evidence was ever produced to show his connection with the Allies. The exposure of the facts in the case finally brought the release of Bullerjahn.

A little later, Carl von Ossietzky, the courageous editor of the *Weltbühne*, was convicted of treason by a German court because he had revealed military secrets in his journal. The secrets he had published were closely related to the secret rearming of Germany contrary to treaty provisions.

There is also some evidence that Germany is importing arms and munitions from other countries. In a confidential report of the exports of Skoda for 1930 and 1931, classified by countries, Germany appears as importer of comparatively large amounts of rifles, portable firearms, aero engines, nitrocellulose, dynamite and other explosives.[13]

Time has blurred one simple fact: Hitler had the support of the ruling class as early as 1923. He entered politics on the order of his commanding officer to attend a meeting of what evolved into the Nazi Party.

In the Beer Hall Putsch, Hitler was guilty of a far more serious crime, armed rebellion, but received a much lighter sentence than Bullerjahn. Hitler served less than two years in prison, and his accommodations were more like a hotel with room service.

The Nazis were only a minor party at the time, and the putsch failed because Hitler lacked popular support. There were hundreds of treason trials in which the defendants received harsh sentences. Early releases from prison were possible with the special support of world opinion, but in 1923, few people outside Germany had ever heard of Hitler.

From the files of J. K. Jenny of du Pont's Foreign Relations Department, a memo dated March 22, 1932 — a full year before Hitler assumed power — reveals that IG and other German industrialists financed Hitler:

It is a matter of common gossip in Germany that IG is financing Hitler. Other German firms who are also supposed to be doing so are Krupp and Thyssen. How much truth there is in the gossip we are unable to state, but there seems to be no doubt whatever that Dr. Schmitz (director-general of IG) is at least a large contributor to the Nazi Party.[14]

The foregoing quotes clearly establish the complacency of the three American administrations of the 1920s toward German violations of the Treaty of Versailles. They detail the ever-increasing role of IG Farben as an agent of the German government, culminating with support of the Nazis, and leave no doubt that the Republican administrations of the 1920s were aware of the violations, as well as of IG Farben's efforts to reestablish its supremacy.

Isolationist policies of the 1920s Republican administrations were clearly a dismal failure that provided a fertile environment for rebuilding Germany's war machine. IG Farben had a long history of supporting German nationalism. Perhaps most alarming was IG Farben's increasing boldness and aggressiveness in violating the treaty. By the mid 1920s, there were clear signs that Germany was preparing for another war.

Even more grievous was the complacency of Republicans to the rebuilding of IG Farben's domestic cartels. To grasp the full extent of this, a brief look at the economic environment following WWI is needed.

Despite the best efforts of an ailing President Wilson to bring the United States into the League of Nations, the war's end saw a U.S. pullback into Fortress America and a strict right-wing isolationist policy. The United States had the opportunity to seize a leadership role in the world, but instead retreated.

Compared to the European countries, the war for the United States was short and without the staggering number of casualties, so U.S. isolationism can not be explained solely by war losses. Although it was in accord with the viewpoint of nativist and patriot groups, it had broad appeal beyond these fringes. Perhaps it was a mass revulsion to imperialist adventurism that was fostered by corporate media manipulation.

From 1900 until the end of the war in 1918, big business took several blows. First and foremost during this time was the trust-busting administration of Teddy Roosevelt. Second, price controls passed during the war restricted corporate profits. Senate investigations into war profiteering extended into the

1930s. Finally, big business believed unionism was a threat and portrayed it as either communism or the product of dirty foreigners.

To the business leaders of that time, getting back to normal meant nothing more than returning to the days of robber barons, trusts and cartels free from government intrusion and unionism. Corporate America was gratified by the laissez-faire economics of the three 1920s Republican administrations.

The cartel agreements with IG Farben were anticompetitive and used to set up monopolies. In essence, anticompetitive agreements increased the profits of larger firms at the expense of smaller companies and consumers. Such agreements were the reverse of Roosevelt's trust-busting days and a free enterprise system.

However, to the business leaders of the 1920s, "competition" was a foul word. Competition, like unionism, had to be avoided. In the view of leading industrialists of that time, competition was destructive. Thus, the empire builders of the 1920s were eager to sign such agreements, and the policies of successive Republican administrations willingly turned a blind eye toward anticompetitive practices.

Economic Warfare and Traitors in High Places

The full extent of IG Farben's ability to disrupt the U.S. war effort can be seen from the number of patents seized by the U.S. in WWII. After the United States entered WWII, the Roosevelt administration established the Alien Property Custodian (APC) and seized 12,300 patents — 5,000 of which covered chemicals, pharmaceuticals and munitions. This situation was allowed to occur for the second time even though the APC and the Trading With the Enemy Act date from 1917.

The most crucial supply problem facing the United States during WWI was its dependence on Chile for nitrates. Nitrates are essential for manufacturing TNT, picric acid and other explosives. The 1915 annual report of the Chief of Ordnance detailed the dependence on a limited supply of Chilean nitrates. Not only were the shipments vulnerable to German submarine attacks, but German interests controlled many of the Chilean companies.

The Germans eliminated their dependence on Chilean nitrates with the development of the Haber process, which produces nitrates from atmospheric nitrogen. By 1913, Germany had a 10,000-ton capacity plant at Oppau. In 1916, Congress made an appropriation to build four large synthetic nitrate plants. At the time, there were 250 patents on synthetic nitrogen, all German-owned. These patents became subject to license under wartime legislation. A $13 million nitrate plant constructed at Sheffield, Ala., had an annual projected capacity of 9,000 tons of ammonia and 14,000 tons of nitric acid. The plant proved useless because the German patents did not contain the composition and preparation of the catalyst.[15]

The importance of nitrate production during WWI is comparable to synthetic rubber production during WWII. In both cases, the Germans controlled the patents and cartel agreements. Perhaps one of the clearest examples of how IG Farben hindered the WWI effort is the case of Dr. Hugo Schweitzer. An American citizen and head of Bayer Co., he conducted an effective industrial espionage campaign. Known in Berlin as No. 963,192,637, he led German espionage in America. The words of his superior, Dr. Albert, sum up Schweitzer's efforts:

The breadth of high-mindedness with which you at that time immediately entered into the plan has borne fruit as follows: One and a half million pounds of carbolic acid have been kept from the Allies. Out of this one and a half million pounds of carbolic acid, four and one-half million pounds of picric acid can be produced. This tremendous quantity of explosive stuffs has been withheld from the Allies by your contract. In order to give one an idea of this enormous quantity the following figures are of interest:

Four million five hundred thousand pounds equals 2,250 tons of explosives. A railroad freight car is loaded with 20 tons of explosives. The 2,250 tons would, therefore, fill 112 railway cars. A freight train with explosives consists chiefly of 40 freight cars, so that 4,500,000 pounds of explosives would fill three railroad trains with 40 cars each.

Of still greater and more beneficial effect is the support which you have afforded to the purchase of bromine. We have a well-founded hope that, with the exclusion of perhaps small quantities, we shall be in a position to buy up the total production of the country. Bromine, together with chloral, is used in making nitric gases, which are of such great importance in trench warfare. Without bromine these nitric gases are of slight effect; in connection with bromine, they are of terrible effect. Bromine is only produced in the United States and Germany. While therefore, the material is on hand in satisfactory quantities for the Germans, the Allies are entirely dependent upon importation from America.[16]

Schweitzer's work not only shows how IG Farben was an integral part of the German war machine, but also illustrates the role of German immigrants. While the vast majority were citizens loyal to their adopted country, during both wars, German espionage relied heavily on German-Americans. The German spies apprehended landing on Long Island during WWII had all previously lived in the United States. Immigrants like Schweitzer who chose to remain loyal to their fatherland had a considerable impact hindering the war effort.

On Schweitzer's death, government agents searching his apartment found an unpublished document, *The Chemists' War.* It detailed Germany's plan for self-sufficiency and foretold of the strategic value of its scientific advances for the next war. Excerpts from the article show that Schweitzer was fully aware of the importance of Germany's scientific advances to its empire building.

Next to steel and iron, aluminum and magnesium play a prominent part as substitutes for copper. It has been found that an aluminum-magnesium alloy possesses great advantage over the latter as an electrical conductor. Magnesium is said to be useful for many purposes for which aluminum is being employed today. This is a very important discovery, because Germany has enormous supplies of magnesium chloride, a by-product of the potash industry, which has been worthless up to now.

That this new scientific achievement will prove of momentous importance appears from the fact that the great chemical works which supply the world with dyestuffs, synthetic remedies, photographic developments, artificial perfume, etc., have entered the field and have become important factors in the artificial fertilizer industry of Germany. The peace negotiations will undoubtedly culminate in the conclusion of commercial treaties between nations.

What enormous power will be exercised by that nation, when possessing such a universal fertilizer and practically world-wide monopoly of potash salts, it will have something to sell that every farmer in the civilized world absolutely requires.[17]

The close association of IG Farben with Germany's war machine is clear, as is the intention of IG Farben to use Germany's monopoly of the emerging organic chemistry field for world domination. Shortages during the first war created by various cartel agreements involved other companies too. Zeiss and its American partner, Bausch and Lomb, controlled production of military optics through a cartel agreement. German firms owned by Krupp often controlled the production of ordnance.

Before U.S. entry into WWI, Bosch practices delayed American aircraft production for the Allies. It was not until the United States entered the war that any action could be taken against Bosch. The same tactics were common before the United States entered WWII.

Domestically, cartel agreements created acute shortages in the medical field. Before WWI, more than 80 percent of surgical instruments were imported from Germany. Germany held patents on medicines like salvarsan, luminal and Novocain. Salvarsan was used at that time to treat syphilis; luminal was used to prevent epileptic seizures. Without substitutes for these drugs, patients went untreated. The shortage of Novocain forced American surgeons to revert to operating without anesthesia.

No better summation of the dangers cartel agreements posed to the United States exists than in the State of the Union address by President Wilson on May 20, 1919:

Nevertheless, there are parts of our tariff system which need prompt attention. The experiences of the war have made it plain in some cases that too great a reliance on foreign supply is dangerous, and that in determining certain parts of our tariff policy domestic considerations must be borne in mind which are political as well as economic.

Among the industries to which special consideration should be given is that of the manufacture of dyestuffs and related chemicals. Our complete dependence upon German supplies before the war made the interruption of trade a cause of exceptional economic disturbance. The close relation between the manufacture of dyestuff on the one hand and of explosives and poisonous gases on the other, moreover, has given the industry an exceptional significance and value.

Although the United States will gladly and unhesitatingly join in a program of international disarmament, it will nevertheless be a policy of obvious prudence to make certain of the successful maintenance of many strong and well-equipped chemical plants. German chemical industry, with which we will be brought into competition, was and may well be again a thoroughly knit monopoly, capable of exercising a competition of a peculiarly insidious and dangerous kind.[18]

It's obvious from this quote that the danger posed by cartels and their monopoly agreements were well known at the highest levels of government. Yet the most stunning aspect of the aftermath of WWI was the speed at which IG Farben reestablished its cartel agreements. This could only have occurred with the full cooperation of Republican administrations and the leaders of corporate America.

Even during the peace conference, there were those in this country who acted fraudulently, if not treasonously. Throughout the war, lawyer John Foster Dulles sought to protect the Kaiser's assets from seizure by the Alien Property Custodian, the APC. Dulles sought to subvert the peace conference by smoothing the way for cartels. As a member of the postwar U.S. War Trade Board, Dulles had good information for sale. He was well aware that German bribes went all the way to the Harding administration's crooked Attorney General, Harry Daugherty. In a later corruption trial, Daugherty's defense counsel pointed out a bigger crook behind the bribery scandal — John Foster Dulles, "who strutted about the Peace Conference promoting himself as [Secretary of State] Lansing's nephew while carrying a 'bag looking for a bribe,' misdirecting his clients and comporting himself as a man who should be disbarred."[19]

In other words, a right-wing element at the peace conference was willing to sabotage the interests of world peace for personal and private gains. Dulles continued to work his mischief in the corrupt Harding administration, where he had access to its highest levels of power. Later, as WWII approached, he and his brother, Allen, helped hide Nazi ownership of, and involvement in, American corporations from the U.S. government.

Daugherty was not the only Harding administration member seeking to form alliances and cartel agreements with IG Farben. Before becoming Secretary of Treasury, Andrew Mellon controlled interests such as Alcoa, and formed several cartel agreements with IG Farben. Mellon also supported several pro-fascist groups in the 1930s, and was part of the fascist plot against FDR in 1934.

Mellon and Daugherty were not the only officials sympathetic toward IG Farben and Germany. There were many more, some of whom became Nazi supporters in the 1930s. Besides supporters in the government, IG Farben found a multitude of support on Wall Street. Many from Wall Street later rose to high government positions, particularly in the OSS during the war, and as economic advisers during the postwar denazification period.

The first war made it obvious how dangerous the IG Farben cartel was, and the agreements were anticompetitive, a violation of trust and monopoly laws, and of the APC. However, during the Harding administration, officials openly sympathetic to IG Farben and German interests headed the two departments charged with enforcing these laws — Daugherty at the Justice Department and Mellon at the Treasury.

Mellon was Secretary of Treasury throughout the Harding and Coolidge administrations, and most of the Hoover administration. Holding his portfolio throughout the 1920s, Mellon was able to quash almost all investigations into reforming cartels. Thus, by the end of the decade, IG Farben had regained control of all its assets seized by the APC. In fact, the Mellon-owned Alcoa Corp. signed a cartel agreement with IG Farben while Mellon was still heading the Treasury.

These actions by 1920s Republican administrations had an enormous effect on the US war effort in the 1940s. Cartel agreements signed in the 1920s caused supply shortages of many vital materials and production delays of munitions during WWII. Particularly damaging was a shortage of aluminum, the result of the cartel of IG Farben and Alcoa. Only recently has information surfaced on this damage to the second war effort, as evident from a recent Newweek.com article:

> The fresh look at wartime culpability may extend to other American icons. In 1940 one of the nation's most prestigious law firms, Sullivan & Cromwell, joined together with the Wallenberg family of Sweden — famed for producing Raoul, a Holocaust martyr who saved Jews in Budapest — to represent Nazi German interests, says Abe Weissbrodt, a former Treasury Department lawyer who prosecuted the case in 1946. The scam? Sullivan & Cromwell drafted a voting trust agreement making the Wallenbergs' Enskilda Bank a dummy owner of the U.S. subsidiary of Bosch, a German engine-parts maker, so the Nazis could retain control. The papers were drawn up by John Foster Dulles, a Germanophile who later became Secretary of State and whose name today graces Washington's international airport. (The scheme worked during the war, but in 1948 Bosch was finally auctioned to a U.S. buyer.) "The record is compelling in terms of warranting questions about Dulles' motives and his own allegiances," says historian Masurovsky. "One might say about him what Treasury said about Chase and J.P. Morgan, that they had allegiance to their own corporate interests and not to their country."[20]

Sullivan & Cromwell was established by Algernon Sullivan in New York following the economic panic of 1857 which had bankrupted his practice in Indiana. The young Sullivan had just married a George Washington descendent from Virginia. Before the Civil War broke out, Sullivan built his firm based on his wife's southern contacts. In the last two decades of the 20th century, these southern connections also played an important role in moving industry from the Rust Belt to the South. Moreover, they were key to the financial shenanigans of the Bush family.

With the advent of the Civil War, Sullivan once again saw his practice almost destroyed. In June 1861, the Confederate warship, *Savannah,* was disguised as a northern vessel to attempt to capture the *USS Perry.* However, the *Perry* captured the *Savannah* and delivered the crew to New York. Because the United States did not recognize the Confederacy as a nation, the prisoners were considered pirates who, if convicted, would have been hanged. Sullivan defended the captives, arguing that they were prisoners of war. Against all odds, Sullivan won the case.[21]

In 1870, Sullivan went back to private practice in the firm of Sullivan Kobbe and Fowler. Here, Sullivan met Cromwell, who was employed as a bookkeeper. Recognizing Cromwell's talents, Sullivan sent him to Columbia's Law School. Cromwell joined Sullivan after Kobbe and Flower left, and the firm soon flourished. When Sullivan died, Cromwell hired William Curtis as a partner and began focusing the firm on business law.

The year after Sullivan's death, Cromwell had Curtis, a New Jersey resident, work behind the scenes to change that state's laws of incorporation. Cromwell's package of changes gave much more to the corporations than to the state, and lowered incorporation fees and taxes. It further prevented shareholders from inspecting a corporation's books and interfering in corporate management. But most important, it allowed corporations to hold shares of other corporations, thus sidestepping the Sherman Antitrust Act of 1890.[22] In essence, Cromwell had designed a wholesale assault on the laws that held corporations in check. Only *Santa Clara County v. Southern Pacific Railroad Company*, the disastrous 1886 Supreme Court ruling giving corporations Fourteenth Amendment rights, was more important in creating the corporate state.

The first two companies to take advantage of the changes in New Jersey corporate law were Sullivan & Cromwell clients, the Southern Cotton Oil Co., and the North America Co. The way a firm manipulates and follows the law says a lot about its honesty and integrity. The way Sullivan & Cromwell handled the 1889 Louisiana Supreme Court decision outlawing the American Cotton Trust exposes how the firm viewed the law as a tool to be manipulated for the benefit of the wealthy. The Louisiana Court had ruled the American Cotton Trust to be an illegal association, guilty of usurping, intruding into, and unlawfully holding and exercising the franchise and privilege of a corporation without being duly incorporated.[23]

Cromwell went to Louisiana and hired the best local lawyers to argue the appeal. Then he toured the state urging members of the trusts to sell their shares to the Rhode Island Co. The Rhode Island Co., was exactly like the American Cotton Trust, but incorporated in Rhode Island, which tolerated trusts. The day the appeal was to be heard, Cromwell walked into court and announced that the company had been dissolved. Cromwell's action outraged local officials, who threatened to jail him. Cromwell wisely left town that afternoon. Cromwell then had Curtis do the same in a Texas court for the local cotton oil trust.

In 1901, J.P. Morgan used Sullivan & Cromwell to organize U.S. Steel, the first American corporation with more than $1 billion capital. Previously, Sullivan & Cromwell had organized National Tube Co. for Morgan. In 1906, Harriman sought help from Sullivan & Cromwell in gaining control over the Illinois Central Railroad. The president of Illinois Central realized the value of the north-south route of his railroad in adding to Harriman's holdings of major east-west routes. He appointed the governor of Illinois to the board and organized small shareholders against a Harriman takeover. In the mounting proxy fight, Cromwell forged alliances with two board members, coming within one vote of a majority. He then offered another board member the position of president if he would help oust the current president. In the vote of proxies, Cromwell shouted from the floor and demanded the current president cast his votes in favor of the Harriman takeover. As reported on the front page of *The New York Times,* Cromwell made a spectacle of the meeting after being attacked by the small shareholders against the takeover. Afterward, Cromwell announced there would be a board meeting in November to elect officers of the railroad. Cromwell and Harriman nursed their wounds for three weeks. The board meeting was set in New York on election day to deliberately deter the governor of Illinois from attending. The governor reluctantly attended the meeting, but to no avail; Cromwell and Harriman controlled the board. Sullivan & Cromwell worked against most of the small holders, manipulating the system to the benefit of one of the most notorious robber barons.[24]

Sullivan & Cromwell helped manipulate utility owners by placing rising profits in holding companies that, by the 1920s, had given the control of three-fourths of the nation's electric business to just 10 companies. For the firm's client, Union Electric, Sullivan & Cromwell created more than 1,000 subsidiaries. In turn, one or two individuals controlled the subsidiaries. Instead of issuing common stock, the subsidiaries issued only bonds and preferred stock that did not carry any voting rights.[25]

Sullivan & Cromwell applied the tricks developed for the utilities to the National Dairy Products Co. National Dairy had acquired a string of regional dairies across the country, and, in 1930, bought Kraft-Phoenix Cheese Co. The manipulative efforts of Sullivan & Cromwell transformed a localized industry into a multinational conglomerate known as Kraft.

By 1900, Sullivan & Cromwell emerged as the law firm of the robber barons. Cromwell was willing to use unethical means to achieve victory for any client who could afford his fees, while he worked behind the scenes to weaken corporate laws. It was at this time that Cromwell developed an interest in the Panama Canal. In 1911, Dulles' grandfather, John Watson Foster, a former Secretary of State, urged Cromwell to hire his grandson. The elder Foster had known both founding partners and had clerked for Sullivan when he was in Ohio. Cromwell complied with the request and hired John Foster Dulles.

By writing a pamphlet urging that American ships passing through the canal should have free passage, the young Dulles made a favorable impression in the firm. Sullivan & Cromwell was Panama's fiscal agent at that time.

WWI broke out during John Foster Dulles' third year at Sullivan & Cromwell. To take advantage of the war, Dulles volunteered to travel to Europe to sell risk insurance for American Cotton Oil's European shipments.

In 1915, President Wilson appointed Dulles' uncle, Robert Lansing, as Secretary of State. Lansing recruited his nephew to go to Nicaragua, Costa Rica and Panama on the pretext of company business, but in reality to sound out the Latin Americans on aiding the U.S. war effort. Federico Tinoco, a vicious dictator, led Costa Rica. Dulles advised Washington to support the dictator because he was anti-German. Dulles also encouraged Nicaraguan dictator Emianiano Camorro to issue a proclamation suspending diplomatic relations with Germany. In Panama, Dulles offered to waive the tax on Panama's annual canal fee as long as the country would declare war on Germany.

With his success in Central America, Dulles was commissioned as a captain for a position in military intelligence working for the war trade board. While on the board, Dulles recommended installing a new leader in Cuba and voiding the recent election. Dulles' concern was not for the welfare of the citizens of Cuba, but for the 13 Sullivan & Cromwell clients who held huge sugar interests there. President Wilson refused to unseat the Cuban government, but did send 1,600 marines to protect American sugar interests.

During WWI, Cromwell lived in Paris. John Foster Dulles' dealings during the peace negotiations on behalf of Germany caused him to rise in stature in Cromwell's eyes. While in Europe after the war, Dulles met with the Merton brothers in Frankfurt. The Mertons needed copper for their Metallgesellschaft business, so Dulles arranged a large loan through Goldman Sachs to allow the brothers to import American copper. It was this deal that led to charges against Attorney General Harry Daugherty. Dulles was forced to testify at the trial. He could plead innocent because Goldman Sachs backed out of the deal.

However, the real story of treason by Sullivan & Cromwell and the Dulles brothers, John Foster and Allen, begins with the end of WWI. Cromwell stayed in Paris and John Foster Dulles, while not formally in charge of the New York office, was the leading expert there. In 1926, Allen Dulles resigned from the State Department and went into private practice with his brother at Sullivan & Cromwell. In the 1920s–1930s, several Wall Street firms figured prominently in guiding investments into Germany, but almost every deal involved the services of Sullivan & Cromwell.

Coinciding with the Dawes Plan, John Foster Dulles arranged a large loan for Krupp. To obtain it, Dulles called Leland Harrison, Assistant Secretary of State, to soft-pedal the item in the news. Harrison was infuriated because the department had issued a circular asking to see foreign loans before American funds were exported. However, Dulles knew that Harrison had no authority to stop the loan. Wanting to avoid the State Department's scrutiny of German factories producing military hardware, he chose a Saturday to call Harrison. At Dulles' bidding, Sullivan & Cromwell blandly accepted Krupp's assurances that all military hardware had been destroyed.

The Krupp loan opened a new era at Sullivan & Cromwell. It was the start of a massive investment in Germany by U.S. banks, who competed with each other for the services of Sullivan & Cromwell in arranging German loans. Within a year, America had loaned Germany $150 million. Such massive lending worried both the German and U.S. governments. The State Department privately warned bankers and lawyers of the growing indebtedness of Germany. Dulles actively promoted the loans, and Sullivan & Cromwell supervised an endless stream of German bonds. Many of the prospectuses contained errors and were never proofread in the frantic pace; others were deliberately deceptive. A Bavarian bond prospectus said the country "has an excellent credit history" when, in reality, Bavaria had defaulted on its debt the year before.[26] Almost 70 percent of the money flowing into Germany during the 1930s came from U.S. investors.

Dulles gained much of his and his clients' profits from investments in Nazi Germany. In the 1930s, he created an incredible interlocking financial network between Nazi corporations, American Oil and Saudi Arabia. Here, Allen had help from his brother, Foster. Perhaps the best-known deal arranged by Dulles was between IG Farben and Standard Oil of New Jersey. What is generally not known is that IG Farben was the second largest shareholder in Standard Oil of New Jersey, second to only John D. Rockefeller.[27] Another Rockefeller-controlled corporation that Dulles worked to protect was United Fruit. Both United Fruit and Standard Oil of New Jersey continued to trade with the Nazis after the outbreak of war.

In the 1930s, Dulles arranged for the wealthy Czech family, the Petscheks, to sell their interest in Silesian Coal to George Murnane. Murnane was used merely to hide the Petscheks' interest. Dulles then sold the shares to his friend, Schacht, the Nazi economic minister. After the sale, Dulles became director of Consolidated Silesian Steel Co. Its sole asset was a one-third interest in Upper Silesian Coal and Steel Co. Friedrich Flick controlled the balance of the shares.[28] This was one of the companies seized from Prescott Bush for trading with the enemy.

Allen Dulles' role at Sullivan & Cromwell soon developed into that of a fixer. The Mellons hired him to convince the Colombian government not to confiscate their investments in the country's rich oil and mineral fields. He did so by rigging the 1932 Colombian presidential election.

By 1934, John Foster Dulles was publicly supporting Nazi philosophy. In 1935, he wrote a long article for the *Atlantic Monthly*, "The Road to Peace." He excused Germany's secret rearmament as an action to take back its freedom. Knowing what he did about Inco and Germany's munitions industry, Dulles misled his readers in asserting the wishes of Germany, Italy and Japan for peace. Later in the 1930s, Dulles helped organize the America First group, to which he gave $500 a month before Pearl Harbor. Later, he would claim no association with the organization.[29] Dulles continued his support for the Nazi line right up to the time Germany invaded Poland. Dulles' excuse for the invasion of Poland was much like blaming the victim for the crime.

After the Japanese bombed Pearl Harbor, John Foster Dulles wrote the company policy for Sullivan & Cromwell on the rehiring of those who had joined the army to fight. This policy refused to guarantee that employees could return to their former positions. Nonetheless, more than half of the firm enlisted, including four partners and 35 associates. The OSS assigned many of the enlistees to top-level positions. In an act of poetic justice, Dulles' policy to refuse to guarantee the enlistees' jobs on their return from service came back to haunt him in his 1950 race for the Senate, and figured prominently in his defeat.[30]

With the outbreak of WWII, John Foster Dulles' praise of Nazi Germany severely tarnished his image. Throughout the war, he stayed home and used sanctimonious pronouncements to rebuild his image, but he did not give up his secret Nazi ties.

The most significant action Dulles took during the war severely crippled America's war effort. The military depended on diesel motors for trucks, tanks, submarines, ships and aircraft. There was no substitute for the direct fuel injection in diesel engines. While the United States plotted to bomb Nazi diesel plants in Germany, the legal maneuvers of John Foster prevented America from manufacturing more efficient diesel engines at home.

In 1934, Dulles handled the legal end and George Murnane handled the operational end. Together they made a deal in which Bosch sold its international interests to Mendelssohn & Co., of Amsterdam, with a right to repurchase them later. In 1935, Murnane joined the board of directors of the American Bosch Co. Fritz Mannheimer, the head of Mendelssohn, was a German agent. In 1937, Murnane became chairman of the board at American Bosch. Throughout this period, American Bosch Co. tried to get the German company to reduce the 5 percent royalty it had to pay. In exchange, American Bosch volunteered information about costs, prices and other competitive data. The deal delighted the Nazi government, because it provided an outline of American war production before the U.S. entered the war.

As the war approached, the Nazis sought to further camouflage the true owner of American Bosch, and Dulles and Murnane arranged another sale. This time, the Wallenbergs of Sweden appeared to have bought American Bosch. Besides the critical fuel injectors, Bosch also produced walkie-talkies for the Third Reich. To further cloak German ownership, Dulles fabricated a maze of corporations that seemed American, without transferring control outside Germany. He had the Wallenbergs put their shares in Providentia, a Delaware corporation. Dulles was the sole voting trustee of the corporation and had full authority to dispose of the shares.

In July 1941, the Navy Department approached American Bosch on behalf of Caterpillar with the intention of manufacturing diesel equipment. American Bosch responded that it was willing to change its exclusive rights; however, the corporation's rights were indivisible and thus the company was unable to grant the request.

In May 1942, authorities confiscated American Bosch under APC. A secret government document dated Oct. 11, 1944 concluded that Dulles must have known that American Bosch was German owned.[31] Nevertheless, Dulles was successful in delaying the widespread manufacturing of diesel engines for five years during the critical period when America sought to rebuild its military might.

The Justice Department's antitrust lawyers found that other Sullivan & Cromwell clients were prominent causes of bottlenecks in war production. However, prosecution was delayed until the end of the war; otherwise, war production would have suffered adversely. In 1946, the chemical companies signed a consent decree paying a minimal fine of $5,000. A list of those who faced or signed consent decrees reads like a list of Fortune 500 corporations, including Allied Chemical, American Agricultural Chemical and Merck.

The real extent of the damage caused by John Foster Dulles, acting as an intermediary in setting up deals between the rich and the Nazis, is unknown. However, according to documents assembled from the State Department by Ronald Pruessen, Dulles acted as a fixer or intermediary in deals worth more than $1 billion. Note that the total is only for deals that Pruessen uncovered, thereby establishing a floor value. The total is most likely greater; it is unlikely the State Department would have been aware of all of Dulles' deals.[32]

To put the value of a billion dollars in 1930s context, the table below lists the gross domestic product and the gross domestic private investments throughout that decade.

Year	GDP	GDPI[33]
1929	103.8	16.7
1930	91.1	10.6
1931	76.4	5.9
1932	58.6	1.1
1933	56.2	1.7
1934	65.9	3.7
1935	73.1	6.7
1036	83.6	8.7
1937	91.8	12.2
1938	85.9	7.1
1939	91.9	9.3
1940	101.2	13.6

GDP= Gross Domestic Product, GPDI= Gross Private Domestic Investment
Numbers given in billions

In the 1930s, $1 billion ranged from 1 percent to a high of 2 percent of the GDP. Moreover, it ranges from 10 percent to 100 percent of annual domestic investments in the United States by the private sector. The money Dulles siphoned from the American economy to invest in Nazi Germany undoubtedly prolonged and deepened the Depression. To put it in another perspective, in 1940, the Nazi war machine's budget was about 5 billion marks. In effect, what Dulles alone invested was enough for almost an entire year for the Nazi war machine. (This is one way to get an airport named for you in the capital of the U.S. — as if the airport of Paris were named Adolf Hitler International instead of Charles de Gaulle.)

Likewise, Commerce Department records show that investments in Germany increased 48.5 percent from 1929–40.[34] Many U.S. companies bought direct interests in German firms, plowing profits back into the Aryanization (seizing of Jewish firms) or Nazi arms production. Among those firms: International Harvester, Ford, GM, Standard Oil of New Jersey and duPont.

In the 1944 election, Dulles advised Dewey to reject the issue of deploying U.S. troops under the command of the United Nations (note this does not refer to the present UN, but to the nations united in the war), causing a break in Allied relations. Dulles also was responsible for the extremist remark in Dewey's campaign that FDR had weakened the Democratic Party so badly that it was readily subject to capture by communist forces. Dulles also wanted to charge FDR with unpreparedness related to the Pearl Harbor bombing. However, cooler heads prevailed; George Marshall advised Dewey not to reveal the secret of the Magic Code.[35]

Besides his close ties with Dewey, John Foster Dulles wormed his way into Republican politics by befriending Arthur Vandenberg, a staunch isolationist from Michigan. Vandenberg collaborated with Dulles on the foreign policy planks of the Republican platform in 1944. At Vandenberg's insistence, Dulles accompanied him to the San Francisco organizing meeting for the United Nations. Dulles quickly leaked information to the press on the bipartisan agreement, poisoning negotiations.

In the 1950s, John Foster Dulles testified at the first Alger Hiss trial that he had asked Hiss to accept the presidency of the Carnegie Endowment for Peace. However, in the second Hiss trial, Dulles denied his previous testimony. Instead of the court charging Dulles with perjury, the inconsistency was blamed on Hiss.

At the urging of Gen. Clay, Dulles also was instrumental in getting Eisenhower to run for president on the Republican ticket. Dulles lost his earlier chance to become Secretary of State under Dewey and was eager for a second chance. Before leaving for Europe to meet with Eisenhower, Dulles studied Ike's background carefully. He learned that Eisenhower was popular with the public, but was viewed as weak on foreign policy. Dulles played on Eisenhower's aversion to American casualties during the Paris meeting by claiming that the modern strategy of preserving peace was through massive retaliation with nuclear warheads, to frighten enemies from attacking and keeping American boys from dying. Eisenhower was impressed with Dulles' views and foreign policy was never discussed.[36] The meeting cinched Dulles appointment as Secretary of State in the Eisenhower administration.

The man who arranged more deals with the Nazis than any other hand-picked the next American president and appointed himself as secretary of state.

In 1951, the Federal Trade Commission produced a 400-page secret report detailing the history of collusion in the oil market and exposing its cartel agreements around the globe. However, it wasn't until 1952 that an internal Justice Department memo noted the existence of cartel agreements that violated the U.S. antitrust laws among the seven largest oil companies. The delay was beneficial to the oil companies, since the incoming Eisenhower administration was friendlier to business than the Truman administration.

On Jan. 11, 1953, the Justice Department offered to drop criminal charges and bring a civil suit only if the oil companies would produce the documents requested for the criminal case. Arthur Dean, the attorney for the oil companies, refused the offer. Dean was another Sullivan & Cromwell lawyer.[37] It was imperative for the oil companies to avoid court hearings, where the Nazi dealings of Standard Oil of New Jersey and others during the war would be exposed. Later in the Eisenhower administration, Dean was chosen to negotiate the return of POWs in Korea.

Both Dulles brothers played a role in obstructing the Standard case before the courts. John Foster Dulles used the National Security Council to screen evidence and isolate from public disclosure evidence with "national security" implications.

The Eisenhower administration was packed with Sullivan & Cromwell employees. Another Sullivan & Cromwell lawyer, Norris Darrell, wrote the Internal Revenue Code of 1954.

As Secretary of State, Dulles used Sullivan & Cromwell to help carry on his support for former Nazi businessmen. He supported Republican Sen. Everett Dirksen's bill to return all property held by APC to its previous owners.[38] The value of the property confiscated was worth up to $200 million. The proposal horrified former Allies. Releasing the property would have returned the property to the Nazis and their collaborators.

John Foster Dulles became a director of IG Farben, while his brother served on the board of a leading German bank that became closely associated with the Nazis. Both were masters at drawing up arrangements hiding American corporations' Nazi involvement. Following WWII, as head of the CIA, Allen Dulles was in an ideal position to continue the cover-up of American corporate involvement with the Nazis, as well as helping scores of war criminals escape justice.

Following the first war, many large American investment firms and corporations invested heavily in Germany. In return for their dollars, they received bonds backed by shares in a Swiss holding company that owned shares in German banks. The banks, in turn, held shares in major German corporations that owned some of the world's most valuable patents. In effect, the German banks held a worldwide monopoly on the high technology of the time, particularly in chemicals. There was even talk of setting up a worldwide patent cartel in Germany so American investors could escape U.S. antitrust laws.

The Dulles brothers also were the masterminds behind the Dawes Plan, which had the support and backing of J.P. Morgan. Under the Dawes Plan, the United States loaned money to Germany so it could pay international reparations to England and France. In turn, England and France repaid the United States. For a while, this financial merry-go-round was successful and the Dulles brothers' clients reaped a financial windfall. From 1924–31, Germany paid the Allies about 36 billion marks in reparations, but received about 33 billion marks borrowed under the Dawes and Young Plans. This resulted in shifting the burden of German reparations to the buyers of German bonds sold by Wall Street firms at hefty commissions.

General Electric Corp. also played a tremendous role in the Dawes and the Young Plans. Owen Young was a member of GE's board and part of the brain trust behind the Dawes Plan. General Electric had large investments in Germany and benefited immensely from the Young Plan.

To fully understand its involvement in both ill-conceived German bailout plans, look at GE's management. Gerard Swope, president of General Electric, and Walter Rathenau, managing director of GE's German subsidiary, opposed free enterprise. Rathenau's views of the interwar period's new political economy are summed up in this quote:

> The new economy will, as we have seen, be no state or governmental economy but a private economy committed to a civic power of resolution which certainly will require state cooperation for organic consolidation to overcome inner friction and increase production and endurance.[39]

It is obvious that Rathenau believed corporations should hold the ultimate power and that the government's only role was to pave the way for corporate rule.

Swope held similar beliefs. He called for an antitrust law exemption for the electrical manufacturing industry. In 1931, Swope proposed forming cartel-like trade associations governed by a central quasi-governmental agency. Such laws would only serve to limit competition, as did the cartels and trade associations of Nazi Germany.

Between the cartel agreements of IG Farben and the monopolistic behavior of American robber barons, the Dulles brothers had no shortage of investors for Germany. In 1940, Professor Gaetano Salvemini of Harvard was quoted as saying that 100 percent of American big business was sympathetic to fascism. Corporate America's support for fascism was so great that U.S. Ambassador to Germany William Dodd proclaimed:

> A clique of U.S. industrialists is hell-bent to bring a fascist state to supplant our democratic government and is working closely with the fascist regime in Germany and Italy. I have had plenty of opportunity in my post in Berlin to witness how close some of our American ruling families are to the Nazi regime...
>
> Certain American industrialists had a great deal to do with bringing fascist regimes into being in both Germany and Italy. They extended aid to help Fascism occupy the seat of power, and they are helping to keep it there.
>
> Propagandists for the fascist groups try to dismiss the fascist scare. We should be aware of the symptoms. When industrialists ignore laws designed for social and economic progress they will seek recourse to a fascist state when the institutions of our government compel them to comply with the provisions.[40]

Americans have never been told the truth about the extent of corporate America's involvement with the Nazis. The media has spoon-fed Americans into believing that only a handful of companies were involved. In reality, more than 300 American corporations were illegally arming Nazi Germany during the war.

Many of these corporations took extraordinary steps to preserve communication with their German offices and to hide their Nazi involvement from the U.S. government. They could have severed all links with Nazi Germany, but instead chose to continue to support a regime at war with their own country. In doing so, these corporations became willing accomplices to the Holocaust, traitors to their country and guilty of war crimes. The traitors responsible for such actions and crimes should have received justice at the end of a hangman's noose. Sadly, not one American corporation was charged for aiding the Nazis.

The bluest of the "blue chips," IBM, actively sought business with the Nazis during the war. Dehomag, IBM's German subsidiary, supplied the Hollerith machines that played a prominent role in the Holocaust. Without Hollerith, the efficiency with which the Holocaust was carried out would have been impossible. The roundup of the Jews would have been slowed to a snail's pace by forcing the Nazis to divert more manpower to the task of locating their Jewish victims. Every concentration camp had Hollerith machines serviced by Dehomag representatives, with full approval of the New York office.

Edwin Black's *IBM and the Holocaust* details the ruthlessness of corporate America in its pursuit of profits.[41] When the Nazis came to power, IBM was under the direction of Thomas Watson, who actively sought out a contract to provide the equipment for the Nazi census.

Up until then, Watson's career had been less than ethically stellar. Watson learned his business skills from John Patterson, the ruthless founder of National Cash Register (NCR). Watson rose quickly in the ranks of NCR, learning to use trivial lawsuits against competitors. NCR placed Watson in charge of driving out of business those competitors selling used equipment. He quickly adopted the tactics of the robber barons to set up a monopoly by using predatory pricing, threats of lawsuits, bribes and even smashed storefronts. On Feb. 22, 1912, Watson was indicted for criminal conspiracy to restrain trade and found guilty.[42]

When the Nazis seized power, Watson saw an opportunity to expand in Germany for IBM. In the depths of the Depression, Watson increased IBM's investment in Germany by nearly $1 million. Even more gratifying was the secret pact Watson concluded in October 1933 that gave Dehomag commercial powers beyond the German borders. Previously, IBM confined all subsidiaries to a single country. With Dehomag now established as the de facto "IBM Europe," the Nazis were able to conduct statistical services throughout Europe. In effect, Watson had set up an IG Farben-like cartel.

In an attempt to justify the dealings with the Nazis, many suggest that Watson was not a fascist, but simply a ruthless businessman. However, evidence suggests that Watson was at least a great admirer of fascism. At a 1937 sales convention, Watson said:

> I want to pay tribute (to the) great leader, Benito Mussolini. I have followed the details of his work very carefully since he assumed leadership. Evidence of his leadership can be seen on all sides. Mussolini is a pioneer... Italy is going to benefit greatly.[43]

For years, Watson had an autographed portrait of Mussolini hanging in his living room. He was quoted as saying: "We should pay tribute to Mussolini for establishing this spirit of loyal support."

In a private letter to Reich Economic Minister Hjalmar Schacht, Watson wrote of "the necessity of extending a sympathetic understanding to the German people and their aims under the leadership of Adolf Hitler."[44]

Watson, who wrote the letter years after Hitler seized power, described Nazi aggression against neighboring countries as a dynamic policy. The letter ended with "an expression of my highest esteem for himself (Hitler), his country and his people."

Before the ink was dry on the Treaty of Versailles, American corporations were rushing to invest and support Germany. The first to support what became the Nazi line was Henry Ford. Ford began publishing an anti-Semitic newspaper in the early 1920s. He was an early financial supporter of Hitler when the Nazis were still virtually unknown.

Other early backers of Hitler and the Nazis were the duPonts. The power behind the duPont throne in the 1920s was Irénée duPont who, like Ford, was a supporter of Hitler before he was known outside Munich. Irénée duPont avidly followed Hitler's career beginning in the early 1920s. DuPont representatives traveled to Germany almost immediately after the armistice to renew their alliance with IG Farben.

In November 1919, merely months after the armistice was signed, representatives of duPont and the Badische Co., the principal corporate identity of IG Farben in Switzerland, worked out a tentative agreement for the organization of a global corporation to exploit the Haber process for ammonia and nitrate production. DuPont also sought technical help in the dyestuffs industry. Although the parties never reached a complete agreement on a grand alliance, the relationship between duPont, Vereinigte Köln-Rottweiler Pulverfabriken (VKR) and Dynamit Aktiengesellschaft (DAG) became closer. At one point, duPont had roughly $3 million invested directly in IG Farben.[45]

The most notable aspect of the November 1919 meeting and tentative agreement was the lightning speed with which the German cartels reestablished control over the all-important Haber process for ammonia and nitrate production. All parties had a stake in completing the agreement in secret, since the very nature of the agreement was in violation of the armistice. For Germany, it meant control over explosives and fertilizer production, freeing the country from dependence on Chilean nitrates. For duPont, it was a matter of profits. Before WWII, one of the most profitable periods for duPont was WWI. During that war, duPont's profits rose to $230 billion. The duPonts used the war profits to buy a controlling share of General Motors.[46]

On Jan. 1, 1926, an agreement between duPont, VCR and DAG was consummated, similar to the agreement of the same date between duPont and Imperial Chemical Industries of Britain. This agreement, debated at length in the 1934 Nye Committee hearings (see Appendix 7 for excerpts from the Nye Report), was found unsigned in duPont files. It was a gentlemen's agreement detailing exchanges of patents and technical information that could be denied if discovered. In defiance of the Treaty of Versailles banning German companies from selling military explosives, the agreement allowed duPont to sell German-produced explosives. The Nye Report provides the best summary of the agreement: "In other words, though German munitions companies cannot sell abroad, American companies can sell for them, and to our own government at that."[47]

In effect, the agreement between duPont, DAG and VCR reestablished the prewar explosives cartel between duPont, Köln-Rottweiler Pulverfabriken and the British Nobel Dynamite Trust. Under the prewar agreement, duPont agreed not to erect any explosive powder works in Europe, and the other signers agreed not to in the United States. Technical information was exchanged among the signatories, and duPont agreed to inform the others of the quantity, quality and requirements of all gunpowder sales to the U.S. government. In 1910, the Justice Department found the agreement to be a violation of antitrust laws, resulting in the breakup of the duPont explosives works and the formation of Atlas Powder and Hercules Powder. Within a few years of the 1910 ruling, duPont reorganized in Delaware, taking advantage of the state's lax regulations of corporations.

An agreement between duPont and Dynamit in 1929 controlled the production of tetrazine, a substance that greatly improved ammunition primers. When WWII began in 1939, Remington (controlled by duPont) received huge British ammunition orders. Because of a clause in the agreement with IG Farben, the British received an inferior cartridge lacking tetrazine.[48]

The Great Paper Shuffle & the Cartels

The Germans reestablished control over dyestuffs and pharmaceuticals with almost the same lightning speed with which they regained control over the Haber process. Under APC, Sterling Products bought Bayer's factories and patents. Sterling later sold the dyestuff business to Grasselli Chemical Co. This might have been a move in the right direction if not for one disturbing fact: Grasselli employed many former Bayer personnel who supported Germany during the war. Rudolph Hutz, the former manager of Bayer, became general manager at Grasselli. Hutz had been interned during the war.

In 1920, Bayer signed an agreement with Sterling covering patents and trademarks. Then, in 1923, Bayer entered an agreement to control Grasselli, even though Grasselli still held 51 percent of the stock. On March 23, 1925, Grasselli and Bayer entered an agreement with Hoechst Co., which reduced Grasselli's ownership to 35 percent. On Oct. 20, 1928, Grasselli sold its dyestuff business to IG Farben. Three days later, duPont bought out Grasselli Chemical.

The Grasselli case illustrates some of the tactics employed. IG Farben often produced an endless paper shuffle, resulting in a transfer of ownership in name only while employing the same personnel. This was common to many post-WWI deals, where the American firm would retain 51 percent ownership in order to appear that it was in control, while in reality, IG Farben held overall control of pricing, plant expansion and export policies.

In 1929, IG Farben merged most of its interests in the United States into an umbrella company, American IG. It combined Grasselli Dyestuffs, General Aniline, Agfa-Ansco, Winthrop Chemical, Magnesium Development and others. In April 1929, Wall Street offered $30 million of American IG debentures to investors; within an hour of their release, the offering was oversubscribed. The agreement between Magnesium Development and IG Farben would figure prominently at the onset of WWII in delaying aircraft production.

Sterling Drug was part of the maze of front companies that IG Farben and Bayer used to regain control over assets seized during the war. In 1918, the APC sold Bayer at a public auction. Sterling was the winning bidder at $5.31 million. Earl McClintock, an APC staff attorney, arranged the details of the sale. One of Sterling's first acts was to hire McClintock at more than triple his government salary.

Under laws governing APC sales, a buyer faced a $10,000 fine, 10 years imprisonment, or both, for acting for an undisclosed principal or reselling to or for the benefit of a noncitizen. The buyer also forfeited the property to the U.S. government.[49] The sale of Bayer to Sterling clearly fell within the scope of the law.

The original connection between Sterling and Bayer remains secret. However, it is well established that months after the purchase, Sterling president William Weiss met with Bayer executives in Baden Baden. An informal agreement of cooperation was reached and, shortly after, Sterling formed Winthrop Chemical. In 1923, Winthrop entered a cartel agreement, and was assigned all of Bayer's patents. Once again, the familiar 50-50 split was part of the agreement.

In 1925, IG Farben and Sterling-Winthrop brought Metz into the Sterling orbit. The result of all the stock transfers and paper shuffling was that IG Farben regained control of the U.S. pharmaceutical business for a mere $2 million.

APC also seized the Hoechst-Metz Co. Metz claimed that he had bought back the assets of the company, but it was commonly believed to have been a dubious stock transaction. In 1921, a court ruled in favor of Metz. In his bizarre rambling ruling, Judge Julius M. Mayer said:

> As seizure by the Alien Property Custodian is likely to carry the suggestion to those not informed in respect of the controversy, that the demandee (Metz) in some manner may have been improperly associated with the enemy, it is desirable at the outset to state that no such situation exists here. The Transactions here took place long before our entry into the war and indeed before the European war started and had no relations to either. That Metz should deliberately by his testimony falsify the true transaction is not to be thought of. Stock ownership would not affect the apportionment of profits. This testimony of Hauser can only be rejected upon the theory that both Hauser and Metz have willfully deceived the court by false testimony.[50]

Soon after the ruling, the Harding administration appointed Judge Mayer to the Federal Circuit Court. What Mayer lacked in legal shrewdness was offset by his political correctness. Mayer ordered the deportation of Emma Goldman, ruling that aliens had no rights under the Constitution. In another ruling, a pamphlet about the relationship between big business and war was written by an author named Scott Nearing and published by the American Socialist Party. Mayer found Nearing innocent and the publisher guilty of obstructing the war. This was a sleight of hand; if he had found the author guilty, it would have constituted a violation of his free speech rights, but as an organization, the American Socialist Party lacked this protection. Other victims of the good judge were IWW members, who could expect to receive the harshest sentences possible in his courtroom.

Judge Mayer's rulings were a reflection of the prevailing attitudes and beliefs of contemporary business leaders. His rulings were extremely pro-business and anti-union. He showed no tolerance for those who held different political beliefs.

George Sylvester Viereck and his Burgerbund campaigned extensively for Harding during the 1920 presidential election. After the election, Viereck demanded a political payoff, but Harding was noncommittal.[51] Viereck became the man behind the notorious Nazi publisher Flanders Hall, and was later indicted for sedition.

By 1925, IG Farben had made powerful allies inside the Republican administration. Then Secretary of Commerce Herbert Hoover appointed a nine-member Chemical Advisory Committee, including Walter Teagle of Standard Oil of New Jersey; Lammont duPont; Frank Blair, president of Sterling Drug; and Henry Howard, vice president of Grasselli. Despite the extensive ties these four had with IG Farben, they sat on a board meant to help America's chemical industry fight off the IG Farben cartel.[52]

In 1928, Sterling's Weiss brought the entire drug industry together in one giant cartel. With Louis Liggett, he put together Drug Inc., a holding company for Sterling-Winthrop. Drug's properties included United Drug, Liggett, Bristol Myers, Vick Chemical and Life Savers. The Richardson family, which owned the Vick Chemical Co., is one of the many hard-right foundations that promoted impeaching President Clinton and is closely associated with the Bush family.[53]

Liggett was the Republican National Committee member from Massachusetts who made the false claim that, under President Coolidge, the Department of Justice had approved the creation of Drug Inc. It was not until 1933, after the defeat of Hoover in the 1932 election, that Drug Inc., was dissolved.

Also tied to the illegal cartel of Drug Inc. was the notorious Dr. Edward Rumely. Rumely was imprisoned for pro-German activities during the first war. When President Coolidge released him, he went on to become director of Vehex Inc., another corporation formed by Weiss.

Throughout the maze of paper shuffling and stock transfers, the accounting firm of Price Waterhouse collected fat fees for auditing the books of two of IG Farben's American affiliates, Sterling and Standard Oil of New Jersey.[54] Audits from Price Waterhouse helped sanitize the records of Drug Inc. and other IG Farben front companies.

From 1929 until Drug Inc. was dismantled, Ted Clark, President Coolidge's private secretary, was its vice president for government relations. While on Drug Inc.'s payroll, Clark also served a short time as Hoover's secretary. In 1942, Clark's files were suddenly withdrawn from auction and donated as a sealed gift to the Library of Congress. Those who had seen the files noted correspondence with Coolidge's Assistant Attorney General Col. William Donovan, and with Charles Hilles, former Chairman of the Republican National Committee and a close associate of the Morgans.

The timing of the file withdrawal is highly suspicious. Donovan was closely involved with both Drug Inc. and IG Farben. He became director of the OSS in June 1942, about the time the files were sealed.[55] Donovan spoke patronizingly about IG Farben at Hoover's second conference on the chemical industry: "So far as it presently appears, the so-called chemical entente and Franco-German dyestuff agreement appear to involve no attempt to exploit this market. In fact, we have authentic assurances that these arrangements are not directed against the market."[56]

IG Farben had learned its lessons well during the first war. Its American interests were vulnerable to seizure in wartime. In a move that should have set off an alarm about Germany's designs on war, IG Farben made an effort to further cloak its ownership of American IG. Even with Walter Teagle, president of Standard Oil of New Jersey, and Edsel Ford on its board of directors, American IG was vulnerable to seizure if war broke out. By a conjuring trick, American IG assets were transferred to a German-controlled corporation based in Switzerland, Internationale Gesellschaft für Chemische Unternehmungen (IG Chemie). From then on, American IG loudly proclaimed it was Swiss-owned and controlled, and free from German interests, even though, until 1940, the president of IG Farben, Herman Schmitz, also was the president of IG Chemie.[57]

The ruse of masking German control through various Swiss concerns soon became a favorite tactic of IG Farben. With the storm clouds of war on the horizon by the late 1930s, it also became a favorite tactic of the Dulles brothers in helping American investors hide their dealings with the Nazis.

Another German firm seized during WWI was Rohm & Haas, which was sold to Tanner's Products. The tanning industry at that time played an important role in support of war-related chemical facilities. In 1924, the original German owners regained control. Technically, Rohm & Haas of Philadelphia was independent of Rohm & Haas of Germany; the same stockholders merely owned both. In 1927, the two firms signed an agreement about the division of territories. The agreement was typical of German cartel arrangements in that it restricted American companies from South America and Europe, granting those areas to the German corporation.

During the 1920s and 1930s, Rohm & Haas' primary business involved the production of general chemicals, particularly methyl methacrylate or Plexiglas. By 1934, Plexiglas reached commercial practicability and a new agreement was reached between IG Farben, Rohm & Haas of Philadelphia, and Rohm & Haas of Germany. The new agreement further restricted Rohm & Haas of Philadelphia's territory and banned the firm from entering six business areas: photography, dyestuffs, synthetic rubber, pharmaceuticals, abrasives and celluloid masses.

In 1939, Rohm & Haas cross-licensed to duPont its process for making cast sheets of methyl methacrylate. However, the terms of the license limited duPont's production to half of Rohm & Haas' production. By 1940, the market for methyl methacrylate had exploded with wartime applications. DuPont was receiving enormous orders for Lucite and Plexiglas that far outstripped the restricted production agreement. On Aug. 10, 1942, a grand jury indicted both Rohm & Haas and duPont for restricting war munitions production.

Besides producing methyl methacrylate for airplane canopies, Rohm & Haas also produced Tego glue film, used to produce the plywood needed for aircrafts and marine vessels, such as PT boats. Once again, Rohm & Haas had a production agreement with a German firm covering Tego.

There are literally thousands of examples of IG Farben and other German firms regaining control over vital industrial processes in the 1920s. Among the most startling were two areas in which American industry dominated: aluminum and magnesium.

In 1907, the Pittsburgh Reduction Co. reorganized as Alcoa, the Aluminum Company of America. The Mellon, Davis and Hunt families owned Alcoa through closely held shares. Alcoa held two patents for making aluminum: the Hall and Bradley patents, which expired in 1906 and 1909, respectively. Theoretically, the expiration of the patents would have allowed others to enter the aluminum business. To keep its monopoly, Alcoa took steps to ensure control of the aluminum market by buying up the raw bauxite supply. Until 1915, Alcoa was a member of every world aluminum cartel.

By 1928, Alcoa owned 32 subsidiaries, including railroads, bauxite mines, fabricators and power companies in and out of the United States, such as Duke Power of Canada. Alcoa also controlled more than 20 other companies.

Also that year, Alcoa created the Aluminum Co. Ltd. of Canada (Alted), selling its subsidiaries all of its foreign properties, except for its Dutch Guiana bauxite mines. The controlling interest of Alted remained the same, with E.K. Davis as president. Alted's creation was a ruse used by Alcoa to keep its monopoly. It also freed Alcoa to enter additional European cartel agreements through its Alted subsidiary. When the war clouds appeared and the United States began a defense build-up, the result of Alted's creation became clear. The United States was no longer the world's largest aluminum producer; Germany was now No. 1.[58]

Intertwined with German control over the aluminum industry was its control over magnesium, another industry in which America was either dominant or competitive with Germany by the end of WWI. Magnesium is used in tracer bullets, flares and incendiary bombs, and magnesium alloys are indispensable in aircraft production.

During WWI, eight American companies produced magnesium. With the end of the war and the decrease in magnesium demand, only two companies stayed in the business: Dow Chemical and American Magnesium Co. (AMC). AMC was a wholly owned subsidiary of Alcoa. In 1931, Alcoa and IG Farben penned the Alig Agreement, which became the charter of the magnesium industry. Once again, the agreement formed a joint company in which each firm held a 50 percent share. IG Farben shareholders had the right to limit the production capacity of any company in the United States, and to restrict total U.S. production to 4,000 tons a year.

In 1933, after continuous pressure, Dow affirmed AMC as its preferred customer. In 1934, IG Farben entered an agreement with Dow to buy 600 tons of magnesium the next year, with options for the same amount in 1936 and 1937. The agreement restricted Dow from selling in Europe, except for sales to IG Farben and British Maxium. Under this arrangement, Dow sold magnesium to IG Farben at 20 cents a pound — 30 percent less than it charged American companies.[59]

The above cartel agreements are only a few examples. A complete account of all cartel agreements and how they hindered the war effort would fill volumes. More than 100 American corporations had cartel agreements with IG Farben. None of the agreements were legal under U.S. trust laws, as all monopolized or restricted trade. Many were also illegal under Alien Property Custodian laws, since they transferred control to IG Farben and other German corporations seized during WWI.

Once war broke out in Europe, cartel agreements had an enormous impact on global geopolitics. Almost all cartel agreements banned American corporations from South America. Germany did not need to fight for South American markets; American businesses willingly handed them over to IG Farben when they signed the cartel agreements. It was only after war broke out that the cartel agreements allowed American corporations to expand their markets into South America, and then often only to German firms already there.[60]

It was through these South American outlets that American corporations continued to supply Nazi Germany during the war. They served as the method of choice to evade the British blockade. By using a South American firm, either under the control of IG Farben or one of its American cartel partners, shipments to Germany were first exported to a so-called neutral country, such as Spain or Switzerland, and then to Germany. It was through a South American subsidiary that Standard Oil of New Jersey continued to supply Nazi Germany with oil and munitions. The company also distributed pro-Nazi propaganda throughout South America during the war.

Corporate apologists try to dismiss these cartel agreements simply as good business practices. However, legal documents from IG Farben suggest they were an integral part of Germany's war plan. The following excerpts from its legal department leave no doubt about IG Farben's plans:

… After the first war, we came more and more to the decision to tarn (German for hood or camouflage) our foreign companies in such a way that participation of IG in these firms was not shown. In the course of time the system became more and more perfect.

… If the shares or similar interests are actually held by a neutral who resides in a neutral country, enemy economic warfare measures are ineffectual; even an option in favor of IG will remain unaffected.

… Protective measures to be taken by IG for the eventuality of war should not substantially interfere with the conduct of business in normal times. For a variety of reasons it is of the utmost importance that the officials heading the agent firms, which are particularly well qualified to serve as cloaks, should be citizens of the countries where they reside.

… In practice, a foreign patent holding company could conduct its business only by maintaining the closest possible relations with IG, with regard to applications, processing and exploitation of patents it is sufficient to refer to experience.

Adopting these measures offered protection against seizure in the event of war.

… In the case of winning this war, the mightful situation of the Reich will make it necessary to re-examine the system of Tarnung. Politically seen, it will often be wished that the German character of our foreign companies is openly shown.

After the outbreak of war, IG's legal department continued discussing *Tarnung*.

… Only about 1937 when a new conflict became apparent did we take pains to improve our camouflage in endangered countries in a way that they should, even under wartime difficulties, at least prevent immediate seizure.

… Camouflage measures taken by us have stood us in good stead, and in numerous cases have even exceeded our expectations.[61]

A Treasury report on espionage and saboteurs made in 1941–42 is equally vivid:

In the twenty year period between 1919–1939, German interests succeeded in organizing within the United States another industrial and commercial network centered in the chemical industry. It is unnecessary to point out that these business enterprises constituted a base of operations to carry out the Axis plans to control production, to hold markets in this Hemisphere, to support fifth column movements, and to mold our postwar economy according to Axis plans. This problem with which we are now faced is more difficult than, although somewhat similar to, the problem faced by us in 1917. The background is vastly different from that which existed in 1917.

Certain individuals who occupied a dominant place in business enterprises owed all of their success to their business contacts in the past with IG Farben.[62]

The Treasury report went on to discuss IG Farben's practice of sending spies and agents into the United States to become citizens. The report also discusses the need of dismissing 100 American citizens from General Aniline, including five key executives, as Nazi spies or agents.

IG Farben's employment of spies and its relationship to the Gestapo were made vividly clear to Congress months before the attack on Pearl Harbor. Richard Krebs, a former Gestapo agent, testified before the Dies Committee on Un-American Activities. Later chapters will discuss how the Dies Committee subverted the investigation of Nazis.

From his personal knowledge of German cartels, Krebs testified at length about the organization of Nazi propaganda, espionage and sabotage in the Western Hemisphere. In his testimony, Krebs stated that Hamburg-Amerika Lines and Zapp Transocean News Services were nothing more than appendages of the Gestapo. Hamburg-Amerika was one of the firms seized from Prescott Bush for trading with the enemy. Krebs detailed how businesses in the United States employed Gestapo agents who were placed in other firms that were not a part of pro-Nazi cartels.

Krebs' testimony revealed that the Gestapo's Industrial Reports Department had special schools to train Germans and Americans of German descent to work in the U.S. as mechanics, engineers, drafters, newsmen and even teachers. Krebs specifically stated that the relationship of IG Farben with the Gestapo was "to obtain information about our security program and to produce choke points, or to sabotage our war efforts. In 1934, IG Farbenundustrie was completely in the hands of the Gestapo. It went so far as to have its own Gestapo prison on the factory grounds of the large works at Leuna and, particularly after Hitler's ascent to power, began to branch out in the foreign field through subsidiary factories. It is the greatest poison gas industry in the world, concentrated under the title of IG Farbenindustrie."[63]

While there was less sabotage during WWII than in WWI, the new tactics were just as useful in delaying the production of war equipment and munitions. For example, Standard Oil of New Jersey managed to delay any increase in toluol production until 1941 out of obedience to IG Farben. Toluol is the vital starting material for producing both TNT and butadiene, the feedstock for synthetic rubber.

There is at least one report that Standard Oil of New Jersey intended to resume its cartel link with IG Farben following WWII. In May 1942, Walter Winchell stated that CBS effectively silenced a news reporter covering both the Truman and Boone Committees. This reporter had included in his script reports that Standard Oil of New Jersey intended to resume ties with IG Farben when the war ended. A CBS censor who killed the item reportedly told the reporter to "go easy on Standard, you know we carry plenty of their business."[64]

By the time Pearl Harbor was bombed, support for fascism was widespread, especially within large corporations. Some of the support was the direct result of IBM President Tom Watson's tenure as president of the International Chamber of Commerce (ICC), which enthusiastically promoted trade with Nazi Germany. In 1937, the International Chamber of Commerce held its world congress in Berlin, during which Schacht presented Watson with Hitler's medal. Watson later returned the medal, but only after it was clear that war was imminent.

Throughout the 1930s, several large newspaper chains were openly pro-Nazi, as were many members of Congress. By the end of 1942, the proclaimed list of blacklisted companies (Nazi front corporations in Europe and South America) grew to more than 5,000.[65] In the process, many American corporations were shown to be still trading with the Nazis. None of these companies would ever face charges, because by 1942, support for fascism and the corporate state was thoroughly entrenched in American corporate culture.

Support for fascism within the corporate community can be traced back to the period immediately following WWI into the 1920s. None of the cartel agreements would have been possible without the voluntary cooperation of America's corporate leaders. Many, such as duPont, actively sought out cartel agreements following WWI. Others, such as Standard Oil Of New Jersey, were willing to reach new cartel agreements with IG Farben and Germany after WWII ended. The widespread enthusiasm to enter such agreements can only be understood by exploring the attitudes of America's corporate leaders following WWI.

The Red Scare of 1919

WWI had been good for American corporations' bottom lines; many reaped fat profits. In fact, leaders of corporate America were spoiling for a fight. Prices were frozen during the war and the government seized many corporations for trading with the enemy because of their illegal, trade-restricting cartel agreements with IG Farben. Moreover, before the war, corporations had suffered under the great trustbuster Teddy Roosevelt. Businesses were eager to raise prices once the government lifted the wartime controls. The leaders of corporate America saw themselves as victims of the political atmosphere of the previous 20 years.

The muckrakers largely fueled the liberal and progressive movements that ushered in the new century. The press had exposed the robber barons and their practices for all to see. The attack on organized capital and the rich elite (such as Rockefeller, Morgan and Mellon) was fully justified. Their policies were universally detested by the public.

Naturally, corporate America resented the attacks and sought to resume its old methods. Business as usual meant recreating the huge trusts and reestablishing their monopolies. Inking new cartel agreements with IG Farben was merely reinstituting their imagined right to rule the world. The likeness of the cartel agreements to the behavior of the robber barons cannot be underestimated.

At the end of WWI, the leaders of corporate America saw two threats to their dreams of grandeur looming on the horizon: organized labor and the Bolshevik Revolution. Out of these threats, the Right Wing launched one of the most shameful periods of political repression, the infamous Red Scare of 1919. Having experienced firsthand the power of the press, corporate America employed the media in a full-scale assault to regain its stature. It used the three most successful propaganda methods ever devised: patriotism, religion and anti-communism.

To fan the Red Scare flames, every possible asset was employed to destroy the threats of unionism, communism and socialism. J.P. Morgan laid the groundwork for this assault before war's end by buying editorial control of the media. According to Rep. Oscar Callaway in the Congressional Record:

In March, 1915, the J.P. Morgan interests, the steel, shipbuilding, and powder interests, and their subsidiary organizations, got together 12 men high up in the newspaper world, and employed them to select the most influential newspapers in the United States, and the sufficient number of them to control generally the policy of the daily press of the United States. These 12 men worked the problem out by selecting 179 newspapers, and then began, by an elimination process, to retain only those necessary for the purpose of controlling the general policy of the daily press throughout the country. They found it was only necessary to purchase the control of 25 of the greatest papers. The 25 papers were agreed upon; emissaries were sent to purchase the policy, national and international, of these papers; an agreement was reached; the policy of the papers was bought, to be paid for by the month; an editor was furnished for each paper to properly supervise and edit information regarding the questions of preparedness, militarism, financial policies, and other things of national and international nature considered vital to the interests of the purchasers... This policy also included the suppression of everything in opposition to the wishes of the interests served.[66]

In 1919, the Morgan family and its allies also bankrolled the creation of the American Legion and crafted it into a union-busting organization of thugs. The first acting officers of the legion were bankers, stockbrokers and the like.

The Legion took on a fascist character almost from its inception and, in the 1930s, played a prominent role in the fascist plot against Roosevelt. In 1923, the Legion's Commander, Alvin Owsley, openly embraced Mussolini and approved fascism as a policy for the United States. In the *Journal of the National Education Association*, Owsley equated the Legion in America with the Fascisti in Italy.

... the American Legion stands ready to protect our country's institutions and ideals as the Fascisti dealt with the destructionists who menaced Italy... The American Legion is fighting every element that threatens our democratic government — soviets, anarchists, I.W.W., revolutionary socialists and every other Red... Do not forget that the Fascisti are to Italy what the American Legion is to the United States.[67]

The Legion took on a racist character through the 1920s and 1930s, and served as a recruiting base for the rebirth of the Ku Klux Klan. In the South, many Legion posts were also local Klan cells.

This should not be taken as a besmirching of those who have honorably served their country. In fact, disgruntled veterans who resented the wealthy elite for using them as cannon fodder went on to create the Veterans of Foreign Wars (VFW). It was the VFW that led the fight for early payment of veterans' bonuses after the 1929 stock market crash. The American Legion stood idly by, supporting the failed policies of Wall Street and the Hoover administration.

The importance of the Legion's anti-union activity is obvious in the events leading up to the 1919 Red Scare. By the end of 1919, the buying power of the 1913 dollar had shrunk to 45 cents. Food costs had increased by 84 percent; clothing, 114.5 percent; and furniture, 125 percent. By the end of 1919, the cost of living had risen 99 percent in the preceding five years.[68] Wages during this time rose, at most, 5 percent–10 percent for salaried employees. In fact, workers such as salaried clerks, police and others in similar positions were worse off than any time since the Civil War.

Organized labor had made large gains during the earlier, more liberal times with such bills as the Clayton Act, the Seamen's Law and the Adamson Act. Membership in the American Federation of Labor increased from about 500,000 in 1900 to more than 4 million by 1919. Unions kept an effective truce with management, but with the war's end, they went on the offense. Many employers were willing to grant moderate wage increases, but refused to negotiate or even recognize the workers' rights to join unions.

President Wilson had foreseen the upcoming struggle of unions, as shown in his remark to Secretary of the Navy Josephus Daniels in 1917, just before the United States intervention in the war in Europe: "Every reform we have won will be lost if we go into this war. We have been making a fight on special privilege. War means autocracy. The people we have unhorsed will inevitably come into control of the country for we shall be dependent upon steel, ore and financial magnates. They will ruin the nation."[69]

However, the industrialists and leaders of corporate America wanted a return to "normalcy," meaning freedom from government regulation, unions and public responsibility. Thus, the stage was set for a full-scale assault against organized labor, which, in 1919, had more than 4 million workers involved in 3,600 strikes. The strikes were only occasionally successful, with most winning no concessions.

Secondary to the plight of organized labor, but central to the 1919 Red Scare, were various espionage laws passed during the war aimed at German agents and cartels. After the war, politicians and law enforcement officials used these laws against leftists and the leaders of the labor movement.

During the war, hysteria was fanned by independent agencies, such as the National Security League, the American Defense Society and the government-sponsored American Protective League. These organizations converted otherwise sane Americans into raging superpatriots. More often than not, these superpatriots and their organizations were blights on freedom, and used by the Right Wing to gain and preserve power.

These superpatriot groups garnered strength from the Right Wing, not the public; their financial support came directly from corporations and the rich elite. The National Civic Federation received most of its support from V. Everit Macy, August Belmont and Elbert Gary. The National Protective League was supported by T. Coleman duPont, Henry Frick, J.P. Morgan and John D. Rockefeller.[70] While union leader Matthew Woll was acting president of the National Civic Federation, the group collaborated closely with Nazi agents in this country.[71] Another group from the 1920s that underwent the transformation from nativism to fascism was Harry Jung's American Vigilant Intelligence Federation.[72]

In effect, these superpatriot groups and the American Legion were bridging the chasm between the rich elite and the general population. They appealed to a large part of the population by invoking a false sense of patriotism, while the directors and managing officers remained fully under the control of the elite. They also fostered a conservative economic agenda. Except for the National Civic Federation, they were all virulently anti-union. As an umbrella group of business and union leaders with a few trade unionists on its board of directors, the NCF acted much like a company union, vigorously pursuing an aggressive, open-shop policy.

In the postwar period, the membership of these patriot groups was relatively small. However, they exerted an influence that far outstripped their numbers. Their propaganda efforts were well funded and organized. The National Security League sent pamphlets to schoolteachers, clergy, business leaders and government workers. In every major city, they formed a flying squadron of speakers to whip up public sentiment against radicalism, which included unionism.

Central to the hysteria were three federal acts. The first was the 1917 Espionage Act. This act made it illegal to convey false reports with the intent to interfere with the operation or success of U.S. military forces, to promote the success of its enemies or to attempt to cause insubordination, disloyalty and mutiny. The second was the Sedition Act of 1918, which made it illegal to utter, print, write or publish any disloyal, profane or abusive language about the U.S. government, the Constitution or the military. The third act, passed in October 1918, excluded from admission into the United States all aliens who were anarchists or who advocated assassinating public officials.

While only a handful of pro-Nazis ever faced charges under these laws during WWII, thousands of individuals were rounded up because of them in 1919. These laws, and the plight of labor, would now play a central role in the events leading up to the mass hysteria of the Red Scare of 1919, launched by the Palmer Raids.

One of the first victims of the espionage laws was Victor Berger, a founder of the Socialist Party. The socialists opposed the war, as did Berger. In 1918, officials arrested Berger under the Espionage Act for his statements, such as: "Personally, I was against the war before war was declared. But now since we are in the war, I want to win this war for democracy. Let us hope we will win the war quickly. The war of the United States against Germany cannot be justified. The blood of American boys is being coined into swollen profits for American plutocrats.[73]

Berger was arrested for his criticism of war profiteering, which threatened the leaders of corporate America. While awaiting trial, Berger ran for his old seat in the House of Representatives, winning it back on a peace platform. In January 1919, the court found Berger guilty of conspiracy to violate the Espionage Act and sentenced him to 20 years at Leavenworth. His conviction was only the beginning of the destruction of the Socialist Party. Party Secretary Charles Schenck, who had ordered leaflets that discouraged enlistment, was convicted shortly after Berger.

Many other prominent members of the Socialist Party were arrested for violations of the Espionage Act. In June 1918, Eugene Debs delivered a scathing speech denouncing the arrests of such prominent

Socialists as Charles Ruthenberg, Alfred Wagenknecht, Kate Richards O'Hare and Rose Pastor Stokes. Soon after, officials arrested Debs.

The arrests of prominent Socialists were systematic, and before the hysteria of the 1919 Red Scare was over, the party was destroyed. Sincere Socialists were punished for patriotism, while cunning capitalists reaped the rewards of trading with the enemy, of prolonging the war, of the victory, and of postwar chaos.

Closely associated with the Socialist Party in the minds of the public were members of the International Workers of the World, nicknamed the Wobblies. Founded in 1905 in protest over the conservative American Federation of Labor, the Wobblies were aggressive in both demands and actions. Like the Socialists, they were singled out during the Red Scare for annihilation.

Before the war's end, corporate America enlisted the press in its defense, using perhaps the most effective propaganda tool available — the bogey of communism. The press attacked the Bolsheviks for the Brest-Litovsk Treaty, as well as their views on capitalism. Using the wild claims of the superpatriot groups, church magazines, business and financial journals, and the general press struck out against Bolshevism. The term "Bolsheviks" soon became interchangeable with criminals, German agents, anarchists, Wobblies, Socialists and economic imbeciles. In the eyes of the press, there was no difference between a Wobbly and a Bolshevik. Both were tantamount to treason.

Claims made in the press about the Bolsheviks were ludicrous. One particular horror story made the staggering claim that in Petrograd, the Bolsheviks had an electric guillotine that could behead 500 people an hour. The press portrayed Bolsheviks as wild, bloodthirsty murderers.

Perhaps the most astounding success of the propaganda about Bolshevik bloodletting was in mustering support for a U.S. intervention in Russia. Many of the same right-wing forces in the U.S. that opposed entry into a war with Germany now supported intervention in Russia. The overwhelming majority of Americans were isolationists, yet right-wing pressure was strong enough that President Wilson sent a small contingent of forces into Russia, with the curious stipulation that they could not intervene in domestic affairs.[74] Tagging along as a missionary was William Dudley Pelly, who later founded the Silver Shirts, a pro-Nazi group.

The combination of media propaganda with the real plight of labor was a recipe for trouble. Three events — the Seattle general strike, the bombings and the Boston police strike — triggered the epidemic hysteria in late 1919.

During the war, inflation hit Pacific Northwest workers hard. Seattle had been a hub of wartime shipbuilding, which caused a dislocation of peacetime industries, housing shortages and extreme inflation. As a result, the Pacific Northwest became a hotbed of activity for the IWW. Even before shipyard workers walked off the job, area newspapers were busy asking whether strikes were for wages or Bolshevism. On Jan. 21, 1919, 35,000 shipyard workers went on strike in violation of their contract, which had two months to run. The director of the Emergency Fleet Corp., Gen. Charles Piez, refused to discuss any conditions of employment.

On Feb. 3, the Seattle Central Labor Council announced that a general strike in support of the shipyard workers was to begin in three days. Consequently, mass hysteria gripped the city. The public, fearing shortages from the strike, went on a buying frenzy. Drug, department and grocery stores were swamped with customers stockpiling goods. Hardware stores had more orders for guns than they could fill. The Labor Council quickly ran an editorial to calm the hysteria, stating the Strike Committee would run all industry necessary to the public health and welfare, and that law and order would be preserved.

Scores of articles in the local media compared the pending strike to Bolshevism, further inflaming the public. On the morning of Feb. 6, 60,000 workers went out on strike. The unions granted exemptions to garbage, milk and even laundry trucks. At no time during the strike was Seattle without food, coal, water, heat or light. Even more remarkable, no violence marred the strike.

Among the alarmists was Seattle Mayor Ole Hanson, who had run unsuccessfully for the Senate the year before. Originally a Republican, Hanson switched to the Progressive Party in 1916 and supported Wilson. He harbored an intense hatred for the IWW, believing it was at the root of all labor unrest. His fear reached a fever pitch when the general strike was called. He had no doubt that it signaled the beginning of a revolution "to take possession of our American government and try to duplicate the anarchy of Russia." Hanson also had no doubt that the man who ended this anarchy would have a promising political career.

At Hanson's request, federal troops from Fort Lewis were dispatched to Seattle on Feb. 6. Ever the ambitious politician, Hanson personally led the troops into the city with a huge American flag draped over his car. The following day, Hanson declared that unless the strike ended, he would use the troops to crush it and to run all the essential enterprises. Hanson's words framed the hysteria to come later in the year: "The time has come for the people in Seattle to show their Americanism. The anarchists in this community shall not rule its affairs."[75]

Seattle newspapers continued a barrage of condemnation against the strikers, calling for "no compromise now or ever."[76] In the face of criticism fueled by the fear of revolution, the strike ended on Feb. 11 with Hanson proclaiming: "The rebellion is quelled, the test came and was met by Seattle unflinchingly."[77]

Banner headlines and editorials across the nation labeled the strikers as Reds. The *Chicago Tribune* warned its readers, "it's only a middling step from Petrograd to Seattle."[78]

Hanson was not the only politician who saw a bright future in denouncing unionism and strikes as Bolshevism. Minnesota Sen. Knute Nelson declared that the Seattle strike posed a greater danger than strikes during the war. Utah Sen. William King said strike instigators were Bolsheviks. Washington Rep. William King said: "From Russia they came, and to Russia they should be made to go."[79]

Within a few months of the strike, Hanson resigned as mayor of Seattle and toured the country lecturing on the danger of domestic Bolshevism. The lecture circuit proved financially rewarding; in seven months, Hanson netted $38,000, more than five times his annual mayoral salary.

The Seattle general strike was a fundamental cause of Red Scare hysteria because it focused America's attention solely on what became known as radicalism. Any strike after Seattle was framed the same, each with ever- increasing hysteria. The most successful propaganda ploy of the right wing in America had been successfully launched.

Both foreign and domestic events kept the fear of Bolshevism alive. On Feb. 20, the press reported a Bolshevik agent wounded French Premier Clemenceau. Four days later, Secret Service agents arrested four Wobblies in New York City. The press immediately seized on the arrests, alleging they were part of a worldwide plot to kill American and Allied officials.

In March, the *Chicago Tribune* reported uncovering a plan for planting bombs in Chicago. On April 1st, the New York Times reported a Department of Justice agent had infiltrated a conspiracy by anarchists in Pittsburgh to seize the arsenal and use the explosives to lay the city in ruins. It wasn't until April 28 that any bomb physically emerged. On that day, Hanson's office in Seattle received a package. Hanson was in Colorado on a Victory Loan tour, and aides left the package containing a homemade bomb unopened on a table. The wrapping was torn in transit and acid leaked, damaging the table.

The following day, a maid lost both hands when she opened a similar package that exploded. She worked for a former senator from Georgia, Thomas Hardwick. An alert postal clerk who read of the bombings supposedly remembered setting aside 16 similar packages for insufficient postage just days earlier. He located the packages and told authorities. Postal officials later found 18 additional bombs in transit. The packages were addressed to, among others, Attorney General Palmer, the Secretary of Labor, Chief Justice Holmes, John D. Rockefeller, J. P. Morgan, and several senators and immigration officials.

Russian and Italian anarchists were blamed, yet none of the bomb plots were ever solved. There are many resemblances here to the 1970's "strategy of tension" in Italy. Bombings were arranged by police agents working for fascist elements within the upper echelons of government. The terrorist acts were then used to suppress unions and keep the Italian Communist Party out of the government.

The nation was now timed and primed for May Day violence. In Boston, police arrested 116 socialists when violence erupted during a May Day parade. The police arrested only socialists. In New York, riot soldiers raided the Russian People's House and the offices of *The Call*, a liberal magazine. Other cities saw similar events. Cleveland erupted in an orgy of violence, with more than 40 socialists injured and another 106 arrested.

Yet another month later came the trigger for mass hysteria, the June 2 bombing of Attorney General Palmer's home. A copy of *Plain Words,* an anarchist pamphlet, was placed near the doorstep. Palmer was an ambitious politician with an eye on the 1920 presidential nomination. While President Wilson remained healthy, Palmer was held in check, but as Wilson's health declined, Palmer began to assert more power. It was not until the President was bedridden that Palmer was able to unleash his assault on unions and socialists. Meanwhile, the press sensationalized fears of a Red Scare with each strike.

The Winnipeg general strike in June further heightened tensions. It was given the same Bolshevik label as the Seattle strike. Newspapers ran scare headlines to shock the public and harden opinion against unions. Further inflaming the public was labor's insistence on the Plumb Plan for government ownership of the railroads.

By late summer, the public was nearly hysterical with fear of Bolsheviks and unions. Each event led to greater anxiety and fear, and ratcheted up the hysteria. Then the Boston Police went on strike. Police in other cities had already unionized, but police commissioner and former mayor Edwin Curtis was virulently anti-union. He stated that a police officer could not simultaneously belong to a union and perform his sworn duties. Massachusetts Gov. Calvin Coolidge backed Curtis and took a hard line toward the striking police officers. Soldiers and volunteers took to the streets to police Boston, and the city announced that none of the strikers would be rehired. Coolidge's harsh approach to unions immediately placed him in the national spotlight.

In September, coal miners went on strike. With President Wilson's health failing at an alarming rate, Attorney General Palmer argued for invoking an injunction under the Lever Act. Organized labor had supported the Lever Act and its use of injunctions to stop strikes in the event of war. Wilson had given labor the express promise the government would never use the act in times of peace. The betrayal outraged labor leaders and workers. Without the approval of the entire cabinet, Palmer invoked the act and issued an injunction on Oct. 30, signed by federal Judge Albert Anderson.

Against this backdrop, the Massachusetts governor's race took on national significance. Coolidge's harsh stance in the Boston police strike was fresh in everyone's mind, and he became the unanimous choice of the Republican Party for reelection. The Boston police strike became the focal point of the race, with the press loudly framing the election as a battle between Bolshevism and law and order. Coolidge handily won reelection with his anti-union message; the following year, he was selected as the vice presidential candidate.

Anti-unionism reached hysterical levels in fall 1919. Newspapers proclaimed that anything other than the open shop was un-American. The anti-union campaign of big business was bearing fruit. Clergymen such as David Burrell of Marble Collegiate Church in New York City claimed the Bible not only proved the closed shop was unpatriotic, but also unchristian.[80]

Clergy and churches that supported the rights of labor soon fell victim to attacks by the superpatriot groups. The superpatriots singled out for unusually harsh treatment the National Welfare Council, the Federation for Social Service of the Methodist Church and the Commission on Church and Social Services. Many clergymen sympathetic to labor were labeled "parlor pinks." This was the beginning of the radicalization of religion to the hard right's viewpoint. Liberal and moderate church leaders were purged.

By the end of 1919, the Red Scare was reaching critical mass. Palmer, ever more confident of his future political achievements, believed the best solution was to deport radicals. Colluding with certain Labor Department and immigration officials, Palmer assured himself of greater success.

Palmer issued orders on Dec. 27 for the FBI to arrange meetings on Jan. 2, 1920 of the groups it had infiltrated. During the raids, field agents were to obtain all necessary documentation, such as charters, meeting minutes, membership lists and books. No person arrested was allowed to communicate with anyone unless Palmer, William Flynn or J. Edgar Hoover granted permission. Palmer had appointed Flynn as chief of the Bureau of Investigations, the forerunner of the FBI.

The results were spectacular. The Bureau of Investigations, with help from local police, arrested more than 4,000 suspected radicals in 33 U.S. cities. Arrests were often made without warrants. The bureau turned the arrested Americans over to state authorities for prosecution under syndicalism laws. Prisoners were denied legal counsel and held under inhuman conditions. Brutality by arresting officers and jailers was widespread.

The mass hysteria even reached into the halls of Congress where, at the urging of Palmer, 70 sedition bills were introduced. Eventually, cooler heads prevailed and none of the peacetime sedition bills passed. Nevertheless, many states passed sedition laws that made it easier to prosecute the IWW. In New York State, five Socialist Party members of the legislature were disbarred.

The full extent of the hysteria and brutality is best be illustrated by the Centralia Massacre that followed the steel and coal strikes. In 1919, there were only two IWW halls open in the state of Washington; the others had been suppressed or closed by the police or local mobs. The Centralia IWW hall had just reopened after a local mob raided it during a Red Cross parade the year before.

On Oct. 20, 1919, a group of local business leaders formed the Centralia Protective Association to safeguard the small town against undesirables. Rumors inside the IWW hall were rampant that it would be raided. On Armistice Day, the parade route led directly past the hall. The Wobblies, seeking to protect themselves from mob violence, stationed armed members inside the hall, across the street and on a hilltop overlooking the street. Parade marchers included the local post of the American Legion led by Warren Grimm of the Centralia Protective Association. At first, it appeared that violence would be averted, but some legion members moved toward the IWW hall. In self-defense, the Wobblies opened fire and wounded several legionnaires, including Grimm. Another legionnaire was shot in the head as he burst through the door.

The Wobblies responsible for the shootings were quickly rounded up and jailed, except for Wesley Everest, who escaped toward the Skookumchuck River. A posse chased Everest and overtook him as he tried to ford the river. Everest refused to surrender and soon emptied his revolver, killing another legion member. Before taking him to jail, the posse beat Everest and knocked out his teeth with a rifle butt.

That night, the lights went out in Centralia. Under the cover of darkness, a mob broke into the jail, seized Everest and took him to the Chehalis River. On the way, one of his captors castrated him. At the river, he was dragged from the car pleading for the mob to shoot him. He was hung from the bridge, but the first rope was too short. Somehow, Everest remained alive through two attempted hangings. On the third try, the mob stomping on his fingers as he desperately clung to the bridge, Everest finally succumbed.

After making sure their work was done, the mob turned their headlights on the dangling body and riddled the corpse with bullets. After several days, Everest was cut down and displayed in the jail as an example to other Wobblies. Since none of the town's undertakers would care for the body, four of Everest's fellow IWW members were forced to dig his grave in a potter's field. No inquest was ever held; the corner ruled the death a suicide. In the end, eight Wobblies were found guilty of murder and imprisoned.

The Centralia Massacre followed a long string of attacks on strikers and unions dating back to at least the post-Civil War era. By 1914, the attacks had become commonplace. On April 20, 1914, in an effort to break a strike against the Rockefeller-owned Colorado Fuel and Iron Co., more than 40 striking miners and their families were murdered in Ludlow, Colo., by the Colorado National Guard and Rockefeller-hired thugs from the Baldwin-Felts detective agency.[81] Another massacre of Wobblies occurred in Everett, Wash., on Nov. 5, 1916.[82]

Superpatriot groups sprang up like mushrooms after a rain, and would continue distributing literature throughout the 1920s. No group with liberal tendencies remained untouched. The Lusk Committee branded *The Survey*, a national liberal magazine, as approved by revolutionary groups. Other liberal magazines such as *The Nation, New Republic, Dial* and *Public* were the subjects of similar attacks. The ACLU was condemned as a Bolshevik front. Even the National League of Women Voters became labeled as a tool of radicals.

The infamous Lusk Committee followed on the heels of a report from the U.S. Senate Overman Committee. The Overman Committee began hearings on Feb. 11, the day the Seattle general strike ended. The 1,200-page report showed little evidence of communist propaganda in the United States, and even less of an influence on American labor.

The Lusk Committee sprang from a report leaked to the public by prominent New York lawyer Archibald Stevenson. Stevenson was serving in the Military Intelligence Division, and supplied a list of 62 individuals to the Overman Committee whom he had branded traitors. Stevenson's report on radicalism in New York City determined that Bolshevism was rampant among New York workers.

On March 26, the New York legislature appropriated $30,000 for the Lusk Committee and appointed Stevenson as assistant counsel. On June 12, the Justice Department raided the Russian Soviet Bureau and hauled off 2 tons of propaganda material for the Lusk Committee for review. Following the raid, New York Sen. Lusk declared there were at least 50 radical publications in the city. At the same time, New York State Attorney General Charles Newton claimed the Soviet Bureau was the clearinghouse for all radical activity in the United States.

On June 21, the Lusk Committee struck again, this time raiding the Rand School of Social Science and the local IWW office. The committee claimed that documents from the Rand School showed that radicals were in control of at least 100 trade unions. Stevenson even claimed the documents showed that the Rand School was propagandizing for blacks.

With no supporting evidence, Lusk charged the Rand School was the headquarters for Bolshevik radicals and quickly took steps to close it. The renewal of the school charter was delayed until July 30, when the Supreme Court Justice of New York threw out the case for lack of evidence.[83]

Preachers & Klansmen

In 1924, the Hearst papers, the American Legion and the Ku Klux Klan led the charge for the "Americanization" of schoolbooks, loyalty oaths for teachers and harsher immigration legislation. The three organizations became deeply tied to fascism in the following decade. Several members of the American Legion were involved in the fascist plot of 1934 against FDR. The Hearst papers became an open propaganda outlet for the Nazis and fascism. The Klan went on to form an alliance with the American Bund.

W. J. Simmons, a former Methodist circuit rider from Atlanta, established the second Klan in 1915. The original Klan had died out and disbanded. (The second Klan would be disbanded later, only to be reborn once again.) In the first four years of rebirth, the Klan was relatively small. Not until 1920 did it grow mammoth.

Two factors with roots in the late 1800s set the stage for the rebirth of the Klan. The first was massive immigration from Europe. The American Protective Association, formed in 1887, was virulently anti-alien. The group was particularly strong in the Midwest, where the Klan gained strength in the 1920s. The other reason was the populist movement of the 1890s, which sought to unite blacks and poor whites against mill owners and the conservative elite of the South.[84]

It was not until Simmons met publicists Edward Young Clarke and Elizabeth Tyler in 1920 that membership increased, peaking around 4.5 million. Simmons had a contract with the two, giving them 80 percent of all membership dues. Clarke and Tyler promoted the Klan as rabidly pro-America, antiblack, anti-Jewish, anti-union and, most importantly, anti-Catholic.

The huge increase in Klan membership was largely a product of the Red Scare. Another factor were the race riots in the summer of 1919, in Chicago; Washington, D.C.; Elaine, Ark.; Charleston; Knoxville and Nashville Tenn; Longview, Texas; and Omaha.

Through the first half of the decade, the Klan would be a serious force in both the North and South. The message from the new Klan was that it meant business. Besides blacks, Jews and immigrants, the Klan attacked bootleggers, dope dealers, nightclubs and roadhouses, violations of the Sabbath, sex and so-called scandalous behavior.

The early 1920s saw a rash of lynchings, shootings and whippings; the victims were most often black, Jewish, Catholic or immigrant. "Women of scandalous behavior," as determined by the Klan, were subject to abuse. In Alabama, a divorcee was flogged for remarrying. In Georgia, the Klan, led by a minister, administered 60 lashes to a woman for the vague charge of immorality and failure to go to church. In Oklahoma, Klansmen whipped girls found riding in automobiles with young men. In the San Joaquin Valley of California, the Klan flogged and tortured women for morality charges.[85] In Chicago, Mildred Erick was beaten nearly unconscious and had crosses carved on her arms, legs and back by Klansmen. The attack was provoked by her conversion to Catholicism.[86]

In November 1921, a case in Asheville, N.C. became the focus of the national media. Rev. Abernathy of the First Christian Church sent a letter to city officials calling for a purity campaign and the arrest of two women, Etyln Maurice and Helen Garlington, and two black men, Louis Sisney and Maurice Garlington. The women were charged with prostitution, fornication and adultery. Both women received a sentence of one year in the county jail. The campaign was similar to an earlier one in Athens, Ga., launched by the Rev. M.B. Miller of the First Christian Church. Miller headed the Klan in Athens.

Scores of women received much harsher treatment. Asheville got national attention because it was the home of William Dudley Pelly and the Silver Shirts. Many regions where the Klan was strong in the 1920s later became centers of pro-fascist groups in the 1930s. Pelly moved his Silver Shirt organization to Indiana, an area that had a strong Klan in the 1920s.

With its antiblack, anti-union, anti-communist, anti-socialist, anti-Jew and extreme nationalist agenda, the Klan's platform was remarkably similar to that of the Nazis. By the 1930s, the Klan served as a bridge between nativist groups and fascists. On Aug. 18, 1940, the Klan formalized an alliance with the American Bund at the Nazi encampment of Nordland in Andover, N. J. Before this, a Nazi agent offered former Grand Wizard Hiram Evans $75,000 to control the Klan's voice. When James Colescott succeeded Evans, the Klan began its collaboration with the American Bund.

After forming the alliance, the Klan embarked on a plan to infiltrate unions in an effort to Americanize them. After Pearl Harbor, the Klan intensified these efforts, particularly in the Detroit area. Once inside the unions, Klansmen spread pro-fascist literature and succeeded in provoking wildcat strikes to hinder the war effort. Their efforts went so far as organizing opposition to buying war bonds.

Probably the Klan's most successful effort to disrupt the war effort was the Detroit riot, an attempt to prevent blacks from occupying their new homes in the Sojourner Truth Settlement housing project. The riot left several dead, interrupted war production and was propaganda for America's enemies. Germany and Japan seized on the riot, airing lurid broadcasts of it to demoralize American troops.[87]

Today, one cannot understand the Detroit area without looking at the influence of fascism there. The Klan provoked the riot and was closely associated with the Bund at that time. However, many other fascist organizations were active in Detroit, including the Black Legion, the Wolverine Republican League, and Father Coughlin and several other fundamentalist ministers of hate. Michigan was one of the hot spots for fascism, electing several of the strongest supporters of fascism in the halls of Congress.

Detroit was not the only riot inspired by the Klan that was designed to stop war production. Another race riot occurred on June 15, 1943 in Beaumont, Texas. A mob of more than 4,000 attacked the black section of the city, looting stores and burning buildings. The riot killed 21 people and war production in the area was slowed for months.

Today's modern Klan formed an alliance with neo-Nazis domestically and in England, Sweden, Canada and Australia. An American sergeant stationed in Bitburg served as the Klan's recruiting officer in Germany. Currently, much of the hate and pro-Nazi literature in Germany (where it is illegal) comes from the United States.[88]

In the 1920s, Klan-inspired lynchings and riots were common. More than 450 people were lynched; almost all were black.[89] Lynchings became so frequent that Rep. L.C. Dyer of Missouri introduced a bill in 1921 to make them a federal crime. The bill passed the House, but was killed in the Senate by a southern filibuster. On Dec. 9, 1922, a mob in Perry, Fla. burned a black man at the stake after accusing him of murder.[90]

The most noted act of Klan-inspired violence was in Rosewood, Fla., which was chronicled in a recent movie. In January 1923, the tiny town of Rosewood came under attack by a mob incited by a report of a black man assaulting a white woman in the nearby town of Summer. The riot resulted in several murders of Rosewood residents; the black portion of town was burned to the ground. Fearing for their lives, black residents fled into the nearby swamps. No charges were ever filed against the mob, which was reported to have included several Klansmen from outside the area.

Although Rosewood is the most widely known race riot of the 1920s, it was not the bloodiest. The Tulsa, Okla. riot of 1920 was far more horrific. A mob of more than 10,000, some wielding machine guns, attacked the black section of the city, destroying 35 square blocks and leaving more than 300 dead. The mob used at least eight airplanes to spy on the blacks and possibly to bomb some areas.[91]

Listing all the race riots and lynchings of the 1920s would fill several volumes. Many, such as Rosewood, were reported nationally. *The Nation* reported "the state of Florida was unconcerned about the fate of Negroes." A few northern newspapers condemned the massacre, but most adopted a more apologetic view of the Klan and its violence. *The Tampa Times* justified it by proclaiming that blacks "are anything but a Christian and civilized people." *The Gainesville Sun* went even further, stating that lynchings would prevail as long as criminal assaults on innocent women continued, and equating the massacre with the death of a dog.

Today, most peoples' image of the Klan is one of a violent gang of racists dressed in bed sheets, a pariah of some sort. Even with the rise in membership since 1980, the Klan is still a shadow of its former self. However, its real legacy is not the symbols of hooded nightriders or cross burnings, but in developing what is now the Religious Right.

It was commonplace in the 1920s for ministers to lead the local Kaverns. The same holds true today. One such example is the Rev. J.M. Drummond, who was the keynote speaker at a Klan rally near Estill Springs, Tenn., on July 7, 1979.[92] Drummond is an Identity minister, as is Pete Peters, another minister closely associated with the Klan.

The Identity religion teaches that Aryans are the true Jews of the Bible, and that Jews, blacks and other minorities are children of Satan. Two of the more influential developers of the Identity religion began their ministries in the 1920s.

The Red Scare of 1919 resulted in purging anyone holding even the mildest of liberal views, clergy included. With few liberal clerics remaining, the result was a chasm into which the Klan and the radical right moved, shifting the spectrum to the far right. The result is visible today in the link between racism and religion.

The evolution of the present Religious Right from the 1920s Klan can best be shown by the careers of Gerald Winrod and Gerald Smith. Winrod established the Defenders of the Christian Faith in Salina, Kan. in Nov. 1925, an extremely conservative sect. In April 1926, he began publishing a monthly magazine, *The Defender*. Winrod supported prohibition and rabidly opposed the theory of evolution.

The Scopes "monkey trial" would become a watershed event in shaping later movements. The issue of teaching evolution defined the evolution of the Religious Right itself. Although there were fundamentalists before the 1920s, the Scopes trial revitalized and redefined the fundamentalist religious movement. In fact, the term "fundamentalist" was coined in the 1920s. Many early fundamentalists, such as John Franklyn Norris, were openly sympathetic to the Klan. Norris was a Baptist preacher from Texas with a parish in Detroit. He also ran a seminary with a notable graduate, John Birch. Birch's death at the hands of Chinese communist forces in the late 1940s spawned the formation of the John Birch Society in the 1950s.

In 1926, Winrod led a campaign to ban teaching evolution locally, as well as in California and Minnesota. He appointed a committee to examine textbooks, and in Minnesota, he helped William Bell Riley draft the bill introduced in the Minnesota legislature. Riley was a force in the conservative wing of the Baptist Church during the 1920s.

Like Winrod, Riley rabidly opposed teaching evolution, and was also extremely anti-Semitic. In 1934, he published the *Protocols of the Elders of Zion*, and an article on communism, attempting to show they were part of a conspiracy at work in Roosevelt's New Deal. Riley preached: "Today in our land many of the biggest trusts, banks and manufacturing interests are controlled by Jews. Most of our department stores they own. The motion pictures, the most vicious of all immoral, educational and communistic influences, are their creation."[93]

This quote from one of Riley's sermons is indistinguishable from Hitler's propaganda. It is a clue that if Riley was not outright pro-Nazi, he certainly harbored sympathy for fascism.

Riley was not the first cleric to tout the Protocols. On Feb. 12, 1919, the Rev. George Simons testified in front of the Senate's Overman Committee, shocking listeners with the tale of a secret, worldwide Jewish conspiracy. Simons cited the Protocols as evidence. It is generally assumed that Simons got his copy of the Protocols from Dr. Harris Houghton of military intelligence. Houghton got his copy from the Czarist immigrant Boris Brasol.[94]

With his congregation of 3,500, Riley exerted tremendous influence in the upper Midwest. Jewish leaders regarded his church as the center of anti-Semitism in the area, but Riley's influence extended far beyond. In 1902, Riley founded Northwestern Bible Training School, which in 1935 became the Northwestern Theological Seminary. He also assisted in preparing *The Fundamentals*, a statement of fundamentalist belief. Just before his death, Riley placed the leadership of Northwestern under Billy Graham's direction.

On March 2, 2002, the ghost came home to roost on the head of Riley's chosen successor. On that day, an additional 500 hours of Nixon tapes were released. In a 1972 conversation between Nixon and Graham, the preacher expressed his contempt for, as he saw it, Jewish domination of the media. Graham is heard on tape referring to a Jewish newspaper owner: "His stranglehold has got to be broken or this country is going down the drain."

Later in the conversation, Graham says of Jews: "They swarm around me and are friendly to me. Because they know I am friendly to Israel and so forth. But they don't know how I really feel about what they are doing to this country, and I have no power and no way to control them."[95]

In response to the new revelations, Graham apologized profusely, claiming no memory of the incident. Yet this example of Billy Graham's anti-Semitism should come as no surprise to those who have followed his career.

Graham had earlier been embroiled in a similar scandal. His portrait graced the cover of the January 1957 issue of *The American Mercury*. The magazine was owned by his friend Russell Maguire, who had acquired a huge fortune from oil and munitions. The owner of the Thompson submachine gun company bought the *Mercury* in 1952.

In 1951, Maguire gave $75,000 to Billy Graham to produce a film praising the virtues of free enterprise development of God-given natural resources: *Oiltown, USA*. Graham continued his friendship with Maguire after producing *Oiltown* and wrote several articles for the *American Mercury*. By the time Graham's portrait appeared on the cover, the magazine had earned a reputation as overtly anti-Semitic and hard right. Maguire and the *Mercury* were ardently anti-communist, calling for abolishing the income tax, the UN, NATO, the ACLU and Zionism. Throughout the 1950s, the *Mercury* under Maguire's guidance supported Sen. Joseph McCarthy.

Other writers for the *Mercury* included J. Edgar Hoover, Ralph de Toledano and George Lincoln Rockwell, founder of the American Nazi Party. De Toledano resigned from the OSS after refusing to work with liberals. Maguire was an open backer of fascism and fascist organizations, and an early supporter of Rockwell. Rockwell often complained about Maguire's miserly donations.

By January 1957, the *Mercury* was at loggerheads with the Anti-Defamation League over charges of anti-Semitism. Despite their public apologies, the Religious Right and Billy Graham cannot rid themselves of their past support of fascism and anti-Semitism any more than a leopard can change its spots.

Conservative theological circles today still regard William Bell Riley highly, carefully sweeping under the rug his collaboration with the Jayhawk Nazi Winrod. Anti-Semitism is still present in the Baptist Church, but like many right-wing groups, today the Baptist Church cloaks its anti-Semitism behind a thin veil. It comes bubbling to the surface in the position the church has adopted in recent years of reaching out to Jews so they may be converted to Christianity. Jewish leaders describe this program as condescending. Paradoxically, it is also manifested in their strong support for Israel, which is based on the misguided beliefs of many fundamentalists. The reconstructionists are a sub-branch of the Religious Right who believe the end of the millennium marks the end of time and the approaching battle of Armageddon, with the conversion of Jews to Christianity.

Winrod's lingering influence and anti-Semitism also were readily apparent in the 1980s in Kansas. At that time, Kansas became a hotbed of support for the Posse Comitatus, a far right-wing, extremely anti-Semitic group. A former Silver Shirt leader founded the Posse Comitatus, which subscribes to the Identity faith.

This was not the end of Winrod's influence. In the 1960s, his son, Gordon, began buying land in Ozark County, Mo., and eventually opened a church he called Our Savior, in which he preached his hate for the Jews. Winrod's congregation consisted mostly of his adult children and a few followers. Two or three times a year, despite many complaints, he would mail every resident of the county his Winrod Letter. During his trial, he repeatedly referred to the proceeding as a "Jewdiciary."[96]

The Posse's rise to popularity in the Midwest and in Kansas, in particular, provides another example of how old prejudices, hate and fascist leanings linger for generations. Indeed, racism in Kansas can be traced back before the Civil War. Winrod's lingering influence is seen in the 1999 attempt by the Kansas Board of Education to ban the teaching of evolution.

Although Winrod claimed he was not a member of the Klan, he did nothing to oppose the group.[97] During the 1920s, an estimated 100,000 Kansans were Klansmen. In the 1924 race for governor, both Democratic and Republican candidates sought the Klan's support. There was a solid base of support in Kansas at that time for candidates who attacked Catholics and Jews. Winrod would depend on that base in his later run for the Senate.

It was not until the 1930s that Winrod adopted full-blown fascism. After 1934, Winrod accepted the Nazis' justification for their anti-Semitic policies. His view was the Nazis were only acting to save Germany from Jewish radicalism, economic exploitation and racial lust. In 1935, he called Hitler a devout Catholic. Eventually, in the 1940s, Winrod was indicted for sedition.

An even more direct link between the 1920s and today's far right groups can be established by tracing the origin of the Identity religion. It is based on racial hatred, and has been adopted by many current far right groups, including the Aryan Nations, the Posse Comitatus, various Klan klaverns and militias.

Reuben Sawyer, pastor of East Side Christian Church in Portland, Ore., was the first to combine the Klan with Identity religion. He was instrumental in the British Israel Federation, and during the 1920s, was a popular speaker in the Pacific Northwest. It was out of the British Israel Federation that the Identity religion emerged. Sawyer was a leader of the Klan in Oregon and the founder of its women's auxiliary. He also was the first to combine anti-Semitism with anti-communism, as in the following quote:

Jews are either Bolshevists, undermining our government, or are shylocks in finance or commerce who gain control and command of Christians as borrowers or employers. It is repugnant to a true American to be bossed by a sheenie. And in some parts of America the Kikes are so thick that a white man can hardly find room to walk on the sidewalk. And where they are so thick, it is Bolshevism they are talking. Bolshevism, and revolution.[98]

From such views the Identity religion developed. Among those credited with its founding was a young minister, Gerald Smith. Smith began his ministries in Soldier's Grove, Wis., by revitalizing a Disciples of Christ congregation. In 1923, He accepted a pulpit at a church in Indianapolis, and soon built the congregation to more than 1,000. At that time, the *Christian Evangelist* noted that Smith was a prominent figure among the Hoosier Disciples. Throughout the 1920s, he moved to other pulpits in the Indianapolis area and, in 1929, left Indiana for the Kings Road Christian Church in Shreveport, La.

While at the Kings Road church, he worked with the Klan, not against it. Smith's self-promotion and social activism soon alienated many of his wealthy backers. It wasn't long before Smith aligned himself with one of the populist Huey Long. In 1934, he resigned his pulpit at Kings Road to work with Long's Share the Wealth organization. In 1936, Smith endorsed for reelection Eugene Talmadge, the racist governor of Georgia, and aligned himself with another well-known fascist, Francis Townsend.

In 1939, Smith met Merwin Hart, head of Utica Mutual Life, and soon received support from the New York Economic Council. No doubt, Smith's campaign against the CIO union figured prominently in the decision to support him. Living in Michigan at that time, Smith began broadcasting on WJR, a station owned by a Roosevelt enemy. There he received further support from leading industrialists, such as the Dodge and Olds brothers. In 1938, he supported the campaign of Arthur Vandenberg, a senator with fascist leanings. Smith also cultivated a friendship with Henry Ford.

In 1942, the FBI received a tip that Winrod helped Smith start *The Cross and Flag*, a notorious fascist publication that continued well into the 1960s. Following WWII, Smith moved to California and founded what has become the Identity religion. In the 1960s, he moved to Arkansas, and started several grandiose projects, one of which, the *Christ of the Ozarks*, was completed in 1966. It was soon followed by a Bible museum. His legacy is the Identity religion, which has become almost universal among far right groups today. It acts as the glue holding various factions of the far right together and justifying their hate.

American Eugenics

A more sinister aspect rose alongside racism in the early part of the 20th century — eugenics. Eugenics as applied in the 1920s can be defined as the creation of the prefect Aryan race and the elimination of all inferior individuals and races. It is so intertwined with racism in America that it is impossible to separate them. IQ tests were developed as an offshoot of the eugenics movement, as was Planned Parenthood. Moreover, eugenic laws passed in the United States served as the model for the Nazi Nuremberg Laws.

Most Americans have little understanding of the eugenics movement. Surviving groups have sought to outwardly distance themselves from a movement associated with the Nazis. It is commonly assumed the movement died beside the Third Reich, but this is not only wrong, it also is dangerous, because the eugenics movement is still alive and well today.

Author Edwin Black has traced the origins of eugenics back to biblical times and the Judeo-Christian concept of charity. After the Roman Empire adopted Christianity, the Canones Arabicia Nicaeni mandated the expansion of hospitals and other institutions for the needy in 325 A.D. Such institutions were also needed in England, and the church supplied them. Starting in the early 1500s, English agriculture underwent a change from small to large estate farming, idling thousands of farmers and contributing their numbers to the masses of needy. In 1530, King Henry VIII seized church property because the church refused to allow his marriage to Catherine of Aragon. Charity had now become a state responsibility. Although tending to the needs of the poor was expensive, the alternative of riots and revolutions was less appealing to the nobility.

By the end of the century, a distinct pauper class had emerged in England. Compulsory poor law taxes were assessed to each community to pay for housing the poor. The pauper class was viewed largely as arrogant and ripe for riots or revolution. The advancing Industrial Revolution only compounded the problems, as the poor were concentrated in urban slums, where sweatshops sprang up to exploit cheap labor. For 300 years after Henry VIII, many reforms were made in the poor laws, and the ruling class became ever more resentful of the poor tax. By the 1800s, they looked down on the poor as subhuman.

In 1798, English economist Thomas Malthus published a watershed theory on the nature of poverty and the social economic system. Malthus believed the population was growing at a geometric rate, while the food supply was only increasing linearly. The solution he called for was population control. He also maintained that charity promoted generation-to-generation poverty. Many of his supporters ignored his criticisms of an unjust social and economic system, and instead merely rejected the value of helping the poor.

Since the 1980s, the same attitude has been a mainstay of the Republican Party. Yet even in the Great Depression of the 1930s, there was no shortage of food, coal or any of the needs for a normal living standard for every American. There wasn't even a money shortage. The Depression was the result of an inequitable distribution of wealth, with no means of delivering food to the hungry other than through private charity soup kitchens.

In 1851, Herbert Spencer, an editor on the free-trade journal The Economist, published his *Social Statics*. Spencer argued that man and society followed the laws of science, not of a caring God. He popularized the familiar term: "survival of the fittest." He argued that the fittest would continue to prosper while the poor would become more impoverished until they died out naturally. Spencer denounced charity and aid to the poor. In 1859, Charles Darwin published his famous theory of evolution in *Origin of Species.* Spencer then published *Principles of Biology* in 1863, arguing that heredity is under the control of physiological units. In 1886, the Moravian monk Gregor Mendel published his classic experiments with peas from which he modeled a predictable heredity system.

Heredity provided a false basis for eugenics. In 1869, Francis Galton, the father of eugenics, published *Hereditary Genius*. Galton had never finished his medical studies at London's King College, but instead had studied mathematics at Cambridge, where he became a devotee of the emerging field of statistics. Galton distinguished himself by recognizing patterns. In his book, Galton studied the genealogies of eminent scholars, artists and military men. He found that many of them were descendents of the same family and decided the frequency was too impressive to ignore. Galton then assumed that not only physical characteristics, but also mental, emotional and creative qualities were hereditary. Further, Galton reasoned that talent and quality could be sharpened by judicious marriages in a few generations into a race of highly gifted individuals. Galton suggested that by selective breeding of the very best, the human race could evolve into a prime species. Galton hoped to develop a regulated marriage process in which members of the finest families only married carefully chosen spouses.

Galton developed a protoscience in search of justifying data. His ideas of marriage became known as positive eugenics. However, with the 20th century arrived, a new form of eugenics developed: negative eugenics, calling for sterilization of the unfit. The spotlight of eugenics soon shifted from England to the United States, where it immediately took on a racist characteristic.

Breeding humans had been part of America from pre-colonial slave trade days. Only the strongest could survive the journey from Africa. On their arrival, the slaves were paraded about on the auction block for examination. Following the Civil War, America was primed for eugenics. In 1865 in upstate New York, the utopian Oneida Community declared in a headline that human breeding should be the foremost question of the age. As news of Galton's work reached American shores a few years later, the Oneida community began its first human breeding experiment with 53 female and 38 male volunteers.

As the new century approached and the number of emigrants from eastern and southern Europe increased, eugenics became more popular as a means to purify American society. However, one would be amiss to blame the rise of eugenics in America solely on the massive immigration during the last half of the 19th century. Contributing to its rise was a good deal of racism and group hatred. American Indians were isolated on reservations. The isolation of groups judged as unfit became a cornerstone of negative eugenics. In the Southwest, much of the race hatred stemmed from the Mexican-American War, and absorbing thousands of Mexicans in the territory taken by the United States. On the West Coast, the race hatred took the form of the Chinese Exclusion Act barring immigration from China and blocking naturalization of those already here. In the South, race hatred reached a feverish peak, and a network of Jim Crow laws were passed to keep society pure.

In 1891, Victoria Woodhull, a leading feminist of the day, published a pamphlet with the unapologetic title *The Rapid Multiplication of the Unfit*. It called for both positive and negative eugenics. In 1896, former census director Francis Walker published "Restriction of Immigration" in *Atlantic Monthly,* evoking the specter of racial suicide beneath a rising tide of non-Anglo-Saxon immigration. Roughly 18 million immigrants arrived between 1890–1920.

By the turn of the 20th century, women were still barred from voting, and racial hatred was the norm. Reservations isolated Native Americans. White society considered blacks and Asians as second-class citizens and undesirables. Vigilantes often dispensed what passed for justice at the end of a hangman's rope: from 1889–1918, mobs lynched 3,224 people. More often than not, the victims were black; 702 were white. Moreover, trivial reasons such as staring at a white woman, offensive language or other such minor infractions often sufficed as provocation for hanging a nonwhite person.[99]

Eugenics was touted as a cure-all for society's problems. Criminal analysis would move racial hatred and criminal behavior into the realm of heredity and eugenic cleansing. Eugenics considered disease and physical afflictions, such as tuberculosis and epilepsy, as hereditary disorders.

One of the first benefactors of eugenics in the United States was the Carnegie Institute. Following an infusion of bonds and other assets totaling $14 million from the founder in 1901, a special act of Congress in 1904 rechartered the institute. The new charter established the institute as one of the premier scientific organizations of the world. Twenty-four eminent individuals from science, government and finance were selected as trustees, including Elihu Root, Cleveland Dodge and John Billings. John Merriam was appointed president. The Carnegie Institute soon added a new science to its principal areas of investigations — negative eugenics.

Charles Davenport emerged as the driving force behind the American eugenics movement. Davenport, a sad character with a Harvard degree in zoology, came from a long line of Congregational ministers. His father was a real estate man who had founded two churches. He raised his family harshly, forcing members into long hours of Bible study.

Davenport approached the Carnegie Institute in 1902 to fund a study of evolution at the biological experiment station at Cold Spring Harbor where he worked. In 1903, the American Breeders Association (ABA), a group created by the Association of Agricultural Colleges and Experimental Stations, elected Davenport to its five-person permanent oversight committee. Davenport also was successful in pushing the ABA to adopt the views of negative eugenics. In 1904, the Carnegie Institute formally inaugurated the evolution center at Cold Spring Harbor, with Davenport as director.

Davenport's work impressed the wealthy elite of New England and attracted more funding from the Carnegie Institute and Mary Harriman, the widowed heir to the railroad fortune of E.H. Harriman. Others who jumped aboard the movement were Henry Ford, John Kellogg, Clarence Gamble, J.P. Morgan and E.B. Scripps.

Davenport soon enlisted the help of Harry Laughlin, a Missouri schoolteacher and minister's son. Davenport structured the Eugenics Records Office to further Laughlin's career. At Cold Spring Harbor, Laughlin set out to identify the most defective and undesirable Americans, which he estimated at about 10 percent of the population. He toured Sing Sing and got the records of the inmates to prove for all time that criminal behavior was hereditary. He also toured New York's State Asylum and the Connecticut school for the feebleminded. He then started training field workers to produce more eugenics records. Laughlin also targeted epileptics.

In early May 1911, the ABA created a special committee to study the best practical means of cutting off the defective germ-plasma of the American population. The stage was now set for removing undesirables. The ABA appointed Laughlin secretary of the committee. The advisory panel included Dr. Alexis Carrel of the Rockefeller Institute for Medical Research, Chief of the Bureau of Statistics O. P. Austin, and immigration expert Robert DeCouncy Ward, among other prominent advisers.

In mid-July 1911, the special committee met in Manhattan and systematically plotted a campaign to purge the blood of American people of the declining influence of these undesirable antisocial classes. The committee identified 10 classes of the socially unfit: feebleminded; pauper; alcoholics; criminals, including petty criminals; epileptics; the insane; the constitutionally weak; those predisposed to certain diseases; the deformed; and the blind and deaf. Not only did the ABA target the individuals afflicted, but also their extended families. The group agreed that sterilization of the extended families was desirable.

The eugenic committee supported an ambitious plan with priority on sterilizing those receiving custodial care, including those in poorhouses, insane asylums, prisons and other state agencies. This group comprised roughly 1 million people. The plan called further for sterilization of borderline cases of 7 million people judged by the ABA to be unfit to become useful parents or citizens. The estimated 11 million people targeted for the first wave was over 10 percent of the population. After completing the first wave, the plan called for sterilizing the extended families of those judged unfit.

The committee sought to bypass the courts in ordering the sterilization. It tried to define sterilization as a police function. In its view, once a eugenic board ordered sterilization of an individual, police would simply enforce the decision. Laughlin and his committee also suggested polygamy and systematic mating to increase the bloodline of the desirables, and harsh laws to prevent births to any judged unfit. They called for restrictive marriage laws, forced segregation of undesirables and compulsory birth control in a global movement.

It was only a short step from theory to carrying out the plan. The first sterilizations occurred outside the law in parallel with the development of eugenics. In Kansas in the 1890's, F. Hoyt Pitcher surgically asexualized 58 children confined in the Kansas Home for the Feebleminded. The citizenry denounced the doctor, and the board of trustees, which staunchly defended Pitcher and his work, reluctantly removed him. The doctor did not face charges.

About the same time, Dr. Harry Clay Sharp was castrating inmates at the Indiana Reformatory to cure convicts of masturbation. Again, the procedure was conducted outside the law. In 1899, Sharp read an article in the *Journal of the American Medical Association* (JAMA) written by Dr. Albert Ochsner, who recommended vasectomies for all convicts. After reading the article, Sharp performed the procedure on scores of inmates without anesthetics.[100]

By 1906, Sharp claimed to have performed 206 vasectomies, even though the procedure was not legal. While Sharp was influential in the passage of Indiana's sterilization law, he was by no means alone.

Rev. Oscar McCulloch of the Plymouth Congregational Church in Indianapolis was a leading reformer and promoter of public charity, while harboring a deep hate for the poor. Indiana law specified compulsory servitude for its paupers. They could be farmed out to the highest bidder.

McCulloch performed his own genealogical survey of Indiana's wandering paupers called the Tribe of Ishmael, which quickly became a centerpiece of eugenics studies. McCulloch preached to his congregation that paupers were parasites, preordained to be nothing more.

While there were many evangelical ministers who served as officers in the eugenics movement and more were members, the connection to religion seems informal, depending solely on the individual minister involved. Yet few ministers spoke out against eugenics, and those who did so waited until the 1930s, after it was discredited and associated with the Nazis. The connection between eugenics, the Klan and religion is an area open to further research.

David Jordan, president of the University of Indiana, also lectured his students that paupers were parasites. In 1902 in his book *Blood of a Nation,* he first proposed the concept of blood as the immutable basis for race. Jordan left Indiana to accept a position as the first president of Stanford University.[101]

Besides Jordan and McCulloch, Dr. J. N. Hurty, a staunch believer in eugenics, headed the Indiana State Board of Health. Hurty would later rise to become head of the American Public Health Association. In 1907, at the repeated urging of Sharp and Hurty, Indiana became the first state to pass eugenic laws calling for sterilizing undesirables. In 1905, legislators in Michigan first proposed sterilization laws; the next year in Pennsylvania a similar bill was introduced. Both measures failed, but the Pennsylvania bill was used as a model in Indiana. It passed with little debate in the Indiana House, 59–22 votes; in the Senate, 28–16.

In 1909, Oregon Gov. George Chamberlain vetoed a sterilization bill, noting that it did not require enough safeguards. That year, eugenic sterilization laws failed in several other states, including another attempt in Michigan and a first try in Wisconsin. But that year, sterilization laws did pass in three more states.

Washington State mandated sterilization of habitual criminals and rapists. Connecticut passed a law allowing medical staff to examine patients of two asylums for the feebleminded and their family trees to decide whether to sterilize. California passed a bill to allow castration or sterilization of convicts and residents of the state home for the feebleminded.

In the next two years, more states passed eugenic sterilization laws, including Nevada, New Jersey and New York. Iowa passed perhaps the most inclusive regulations, allowing the sterilization of criminals, idiots, feebleminded, imbeciles, drunkards, drug fiends, epileptics, and moral or sexual perverts.

Nonetheless, the American Breeders Association and the Eugenic Record Office remained frustrated with the progress of removing undesirables from the gene pool. Although several states had laws allowing forced sterilization, they were scarcely applied. Only in California, where more than 200 were sterilized, had the law been applied to more than a couple individuals. Moreover, public support for sterilization laws was lacking across the nation.

Following the death of Galton in 1911, the First Eugenic Conference was organized in London. Winston Churchill was scheduled to introduce the king at the conference and reportedly was concerned about the rising number of people judged to be mental defects. The organizers wanted Secretary of State P. C. Knox to send an official delegation. The State Department could not comply because the conference was a nongovernmental meeting, but Knox sent invitations to prominent American leaders on official letterhead. Knox, a former lawyer for Carnegie Steel, effectively used the State Department as the eugenics post office. American race theories dominated the conference held at the University of London.

The next big stride forward for the American eugenics movement came with the U.S. entry into WWI. Officials struggled with the task of classifying the 3 million draftees. Robert Yerkes, president of the American Psychological Association, and other eugenic activists pleaded for intelligence testing of the new draftees. They developed two tests for the army — the beta test for those who could read and write English, and a pictorial alpha test for those who could not read. The questions centered largely on popular culture.

Urbanites could pass the exam easily, while draftees from rural, isolated areas failed miserably. Even the questions in the pictorial tests were drawn from the latest pop culture. In the pictorial test, the subject was to draw in what was missing. Predictably, the results were dismal: 47 percent of all whites 89 percent of all blacks failed. Nonetheless, Yerkes claimed that feeblemindedness was the lowest in the following Anglo groups: 0.1 percent in the Dutch, 0.2 percent in Germans and less than 0.05 percent in Swedes.[102]

During the war, eugenic groups multiplied in America. In 1914 the Race Betterment Foundation was founded by Dr. John Kellogg, a member of the corn flakes family and the Michigan state board of health. The group attracted some of the most radical elements in the eugenics movement.

The next big advance for eugenics came on May 2, 1927, in a Supreme Court ruling of Buck vs. Bell. The case revolved around Carrie Buck and the sterilization law of Virginia.

Shortly after WWI, Virginia confined Carrie's mother, Emma, to a home for the feeble–minded. Virginia had a well-established program of sweeping social outcasts into such homes. Carrie's mother was a destitute widow convicted of prostitution, making her an ideal candidate for the home for the feebleminded, where she remained for the rest of her life.

Carrie, an only child, was placed with the Dobbs family. Although she was a good student, she was taken out of school when she reached sixth grade. In 1923, Carrie became pregnant after she was raped – by a relative of the foster parents. The Dobbses filed commitment papers, declaring Carrie feebleminded and promiscuous.

In 1924, Virginia passed a sterilization law for the feebleminded. The case attracted the attention of Laughlin and other prominent individuals from the eugenics movement. To further their efforts and strengthen their court case, they had Carrie's daughter declared feebleminded at age 3 – although she did well in school. Eventually, the case reached the Supreme Court. Chief Justice was William Howard Taft. Only Justice Pierce Butler ruled against sterilizing Carrie. The opinion written by Justice Oliver Wendell Holmes Jr. closed with words that still echo throughout time: "Three generations of imbeciles are enough."[103] Yet in 2000, the Court elected George W. Bush, a fifth-generation racketeer, to be president.

Until the Buck ruling, many states with sterilization laws avoided using them. Of the 23 states with such laws, Maine, Minnesota, Nevada, New Jersey, South Dakota and Utah recorded no sterilizations. Idaho and Washington State recorded one each; Delaware recorded five cases. Kansas had recorded 335; Nebraska, 262; Oregon, 313; and Wisconsin 144. California recorded 4,636 cases.

From 1927–40, the totals increased at a horrific rate. North Carolina recorded 1,017 cases of forced sterilization; Michigan, 2,145; Virginia, 3,924; and California, 14,568. In total, no less than 35,878 people were sterilized. [104] Following Laughlin, the Nazis adopted a law in 1933 that opened the way to sterilizing more than 350,000 people. "Laughlin proudly published a translation of the German Law for the Prevention of Defective Progeny in The Eugenical News. In 1936, Laughlin was awarded an honorary degree from the University of Heidelberg as a tribute for his work in 'the science of racial cleansing.'"[105]

Throughout the 1920s, the eugenics movement attracted people from diverse causes. The leading proponent of birth control, Margaret Sanger, was committed to Social Darwinism and eugenics. Through her radical oratory and her publication, *Birth Control Review,* she helped to legitimize the appeal of eugenics.

The eugenics movement attracted another leading figure of the time, Lucien Howe, a pioneering ophthalmologist. As a leading expert, Howe was well aware that hereditary blindness is rare. Yet Howe supported sterilizing the blind, banning marriage of anyone blind, and even led the charge to extend sterilizations to relatives of the blind.

With the gathering strength of the eugenics movement, Harry Laughlin sought to integrate the movement inside various government agencies. One long-standing target for Laughlin was the Census Bureau. The bureau ignored Laughlin's suggestion that each person be classified by race, such as German Jew or Dutch Jew. It did allow Laughlin to conduct a survey of those in state custodial and charitable facilities, as well as jails.

Unable to gain further inroads into the Census Bureau, Laughlin turned to other government agencies. He found ready acceptance in Virginia, largely due to Walter Plecker, the registrar of vital statistics. Plecker, an extreme racist, soon used his hatred of race mixing, or "mongrelization of the white race by lesser races," to shape one of the nation's most restrictive marriage laws. With the help of Anglo-Saxon clubs, the 1924 Virginia legislator passed the Racial Integrity Act, labeling anyone with more than one-sixteenth nonwhite blood as a nonwhite. Originally, the act called for one sixty-fourth, but the legislature amended it because too many of the leading families of Virginia boasted of their Indian ancestry. The penalty for falsely registering one's race was a year in jail.

The dilution of the bill incensed Plecker. His fury was further inflamed when Congress granted citizenship to all Indians not already naturalized, less than two weeks after the passage of Virginia's Racial Integrity Act. Plecker's problem was with Indians mixing with both whites and blacks, so under the act, they could claim exemption from being classed as non-white. Most of Virginia's Indian population were poor and lived in rural areas, making them an easy target for reclassification as Negroid, despite vigorous protest. In one case, Plecker ruled that if a comb could pass through the hair of an individual, he or she would be classified as Indian; if not, as Negroid. The comb test was perhaps as good as any other method Plecker used in reclassifying Virginia's Native Americans. He used his racist tactics to expunge the Indian as a racial classification in Virginia.

The eugenics movement was largely unable to penetrate the federal government and affect policy decision, with one notable exception, the immigration law. After 1890, the American eugenicists considered the immigrants arriving from Europe to be genetically inferior. The massive number of people fleeing Europe heightened their fears. More than 8 million immigrants arrived between 1900–09. The newly arrived came mostly from southern and eastern Europe. Many of them were Catholic or Jewish. The influx of immigrants contributed to the urbanizing of the country. The 1920 census revealed for the first time that more people lived in urban rather than rural areas. The resulting reapportionment was hard-fought. The House increased the number of representatives to 415 to preserve as much as possible the old districts and power structure. The Red Scare and the rise of the Klan added further fuel to the fury.

A key figure in the success of eugenicists on immigration policy was Albert Johnson, a fanatic racist and eugenicist. He was raised at the edge of the Mason-Dixon Line in Illinois during the turbulent post-Civil War reconstruction period. He later became a big city newspaperman before moving to the small town of Hoquiam, Wash. In 1912, Johnson ran for Congress and won a seat in the House. In 1919, he began a 12-year tenure as chairperson of the Immigration and Naturalization Subcommittee in the House.

While there had been immigration restrictions before Johnson's chairmanship, these were reactionary in nature and not eugenically motivated. Johnson took a dim view of all immigration, and tried to restrict it on eugenics grounds. One of his first actions was to appoint Laughlin as his eugenics expert. Laughlin and other eugenicists had long urged the classification of immigrants along strict biological and racial lines, with intelligence testing before they left Europe. The goal was to restrict immigration using quotas before the mass arrivals started in 1890.

Laughlin's inflammatory rhetoric, supported by funding from the Carnegie Institute, began producing results in Congress. Due to the political explosiveness of the issue, Congress wavered. In 1923, Labor Secretary James Davis signaled a willingness to cooperate in setting up an overseas eugenics network. Laughlin then toured Europe as a special immigration agent.

In 1924, President Calvin Coolidge signed an immigration act that called for vast changes. For instance, the Italian quota was cut from 42,000 a year to just 4,000. The act limited immigration to just 2 percent of the reported national origin of the 1890s census. However, the act produced a firestorm in Congress, with many arguing the validity of the data used to set the quotas.

The act required the Census Bureau report its methods in fixing base figures to a quota board, made up of Secretary of Commerce Herbert Hoover, Secretary of State Frank Kellogg and Secretary of Labor James Davis. In 1927, the quota board sent a letter to Coolidge, cautioning that the figures were not satisfactory.

Laughlin was only partially successful in setting up his European testing centers. The system was installed in Belgium, England, Ireland, Holland, Poland, Italy, Czechoslovakia, Denmark, Germany and Sweden. On average, roughly 80 percent of would-be immigrants from those countries were eugenically inspected; about 88 applicants out of every 1,000 were rejected as mentally or physically defective. However, Laughlin's inspections were short lived due to a shortage of funding and government objections from Europe.

Nevertheless, Laughlin's major achievement in establishing eugenics as part of immigration was the passage of the 1924 Immigration Act and the setting of quotas. Both stood as national policy until 1952.

The American Breeders and the Eugenic Society were not content with sterilization and segregation methods as a gradual means to eliminate the defective. By 1910, they also were proposing euthanasia using a lethal chamber. The forerunner of the modern gas chamber was thought to be humane.

Euthanasia was listed as the eighth of nine methods of eliminating defectives from society. Many prominent professional people in both medicine and psychology came to support euthanasia, including Margaret Sanger and others within her birth control movement.

On Nov. 12, 1915, euthanasia and eugenics became front-page news across the country. One Dr. Harry Haiselden refused to provide treatment for a newborn suffering from extreme intestinal and rectal abnormalities. There was a question if the baby could be saved; yet the doctor withheld treatment. Emboldened by some favorable press coverage, the doctor admitted to euthanizing others. Haiselden later brought to light the case of the Illinois Institution for the Feebleminded in Lincoln. The institute fed patients with milk from its cows, knowing the herd was infected with tuberculosis. Eugenicists believed death from tuberculosis was the result of defective genes.

However, the real story behind the gates of this home for the feebleminded was euthanasia by neglect. Between 1904–09, 12 percent of Lincoln residents died. As many as 30 percent of the epileptic children died within 18 months of admission, and many residents died before age 10. In 1930, the life expectancy of those judged feebleminded was just 18.5 years; today, the rate for those classed as mentally retarded is 66.2 years.[106]

Euthanasia through neglect was all too common in America in the 1920s and 1930s. In fact, it is still commonplace in America today where adequate health care has now become a luxury only affordable by the wealthy. An excellent example is the case of Legionnaires disease. The discovery of the disease occurred in 1976, with an outbreak among attendees of an American Legion celebration of the bicentennial. It took researchers more than six months to discover the bacteria responsible for the outbreak that caused numerous deaths and a near panic. Yet further investigation of blood samples from other deaths showed that a previous outbreak of the disease had occurred in 1965 at St Elizabeth's Psychiatric Hospital in Washington, when 14 patients died.

The legionnaires were upright citizens and voters, while the residents of St Elizabeth's were weak and expendable. No uproar ensued on their deaths, which were checked off as routine.[107]

Neglect of the poor and weak characterizes the right wing in America. It serves the same purpose as eugenic euthanasia of bygone days. Further, it provides society with a guiltless solution and the excuse of being unaware, like the good German citizens living next to a concentration camp.

As mentioned earlier, the American eugenics movement began to attract global attention at the First Eugenic Conference in London, where American views dominated. Plans for further conferences were made. The second was held in Paris, but World War I forced postponement of the next one.

Following the war, Germany would not cooperate with the International Federation of Eugenic Organizations because of bitter animosity remaining between Germany and England, France and Belgium. However, German eugenicists' bonds with Davenport remained firm, due largely to generous funding of German eugenic research by the Rockefeller Foundation and the Carnegie Institute. American laws soon became an inspiration for the German racists, including Adolf Hitler. While in prison for the Beer Hall Putsch, Hitler studied textbooks that quoted Davenport and other American eugenicists. The president of the American Eugenic Society received a letter from Hitler praising *The Passing of the Great Race* by Madison Grant, which Hitler described as his bible. It called for eliminating the unfit. [108]

It would be unwise to attribute Hitler's extreme racist views to the American eugenics movement. Nonetheless, by cloaking his racism in science, Hitler was able to attract additional followers who would have otherwise remained neutral. The intellectual view of eugenics that Hitler adopted was strictly from the American eugenics movement. One of the books that Hitler studied was *Foundation of Human Heredity and Race Hygiene,* written by three American eugenicists. In Germany, Julius Lehmann published the book. Lehmann was at Hitler's side during the Beer Hall Putsch. It also was Lehmann's villa where Bavarian officials were held hostage in the immediate aftermath of the failed coup.

The influence of the American eugenics movement on Hitler can be seen in several quotes from *Mein Kampf*.

The demand that defective people be prevented from propagating equally defective offspring is a demand of the clearest reason and if systematically executed, represents the most humane act of mankind.
It must see to it that only the healthy beget children ....
The prevention of procreative faculty in sufferers from syphilis, tuberculosis, hereditary diseases, cripples, and cretins is no crime... A prevention of the faculty and opportunity to procreate on the part of the physically degenerate and mentally sick, over a period of only six hundred years, would not only free humanity from an immeasurable misfortune, but would lead to a recovery which today seems scarcely conceivable ....
... The result will be a race which at least will have eliminated the germs of our present physical and hence spiritual decay.
Speaking English, wearing good clothes and going to school and to church do not transform a Negro into a white man. Nor was a Syrian or Egyptian freedman transformed into a Roman by wearing a toga and applauding his favorite gladiator in the amphitheater.
... since it restores that free play of forces which must lead to a continuous mutual higher breeding until at last the best of humanity, having achieved possession of this earth, will have a free path for activity in domains which lie partly above it and partly outside of it.
... that the state represents no end, but a means. It is, to be sure, the premise for the formation of a higher human culture, but not its cause, which lies exclusively in the existence of a race capable of culture.
Every racial crossing leads inevitably sooner or later to the decline of the hybrid product as long as the higher element of this crossing is still existent in any kind of racial unity.[109]

The first quote from *Mein Kampf* above is an eerie echo of the Justice Holmes majority opinion in the Buck case:

It is better for all the world if instead of waiting to execute degenerate offspring for crime, or to let them starve for their imbecility, society can prevent those who are manifestly unfit from continuing their kind. The principle that sustains compulsory vaccination is broad enough to cover cutting Fallopian tubes. Three generations of imbeciles are enough.[110]

Hitler was acutely aware of the progress of eugenics in the United States, as evident in *Mein Kampf* in which he notes the passage of quotas for immigration. Hitler attributed the superior culture of the United States compared to South America to a large Germanic population that did not interbreed with the lesser, native population like the Spanish. Throughout the pages of *Mein Kampf,* one can note the similarity of Hitler's rantings to the policies of the American eugenicists. Perhaps the best summarization of Hitler's views comes from *Mein Kampf*: "The Germanic inhabitant of the American continent, who has remained racially pure and unmixed, rose to be master of the continent; he will remain the master as long as he does not fall victim to defilement of the blood."[111]

During the first two decades of the 20th century, American eugenicists led the way. With the rise of Hitler in Europe, Germans became copartners in eugenic research, but it was American money that kept German eugenic research and science alive during the hyperinflation of the early 1920s. One noted beneficiary of Rockefeller Foundation money was the Kaiser Wilhelm Institute for eugenic research, with its own institutes for psychiatry, anthropology and brain research.

Throughout the 1920s, German eugenicists continued to gain stature in the global movement. On Jan. 30, 1933, Germany assumed the leading role in the eugenics movement with Hitler's rise to power. It did not take Hitler long to impose his eugenic views. On July 14, 1933, Hitler issued the Reich Statute Part 1 No. 86, the Law for the Prevention of Defective Progeny, calling for compulsory sterilization of defectives. The nine categories listed were feebleminded, schizophrenia, manic-depressive, Huntington's cholera, epilepsy, hereditary body deformities, deafness and hereditary blindness. Alcoholism, the last category on the list, was optional to avoid confusion with ordinary drunkenness.

The Nazis announced that 400,000 Germans would be subjected to the law immediately. The program began on Jan. 1, 1934. The Nazis created a massive sterilization infrastructure with more than 205 local eugenic courts and 26 special eugenic appellate courts. The law required doctors to report suspected patients and to provide their confidential records.[112]

The law was essentially the same one that Davenport and Laughlin proposed for the United States and passed in a majority of states. While most of the world reacted in shock and horror to the inhumane regime of the Nazis, American eugenicists covered developments in Germany with fascination and joy. The *Journal of the American Medical Association* reported on the Nazi law as if it were a routine health measure, like vaccines. The Rockefeller Foundation continued to fund additional Nazi eugenics studies until the outbreak of war in Europe.

In 1933, after an aggressive campaign to secure a contract with Germany, IBM designed the first Nazi census. It was IBM technology that aided the Nazis in carrying out the Holocaust. It would have taken an army of workers years to manually sort through all the records, but with the IBM's Hollerith machines, the same task could be completed in hours.

It was not until 1936 that the eugenics movement experienced a decline due to the Nazi threat in Europe. By then, Germany was considered a threat to the peace in Europe, and refugees were flooding the world.

Central to eugenics studies was research on twins. Several small studies on twins were conducted in England and the United States. However, with the rise of Nazism, the lead in twin research would pass to Germany, now in the forefront of eugenics research. Still, the seed money came from the Rockefeller Foundation, as the following telegram of May 13, 1932, from the foundation's headquarters to its Paris office reveals:

JUNE MEETING EXECUTIVE COMMITTEE. NINE THOUSAND DOLLARS OVER THREE YEAR PERIOD TO KWG INSTITUTE ANTHROPOLOGY FOR RESEARCH ON TWINS AND EFFECTS ON LATER GENERATIONS OF SUBSTANCES TOXIC FOR GERM PLASMA. NATURE OF STUDIES REQUIRES ASSURANCE OF AT [Rockefeller's director of science in Europe — Augustus Trowbridge][113]

The chief beneficiary of the Rockefeller seed money was Dr. Otmar Freiherr (Baron) von Verschuer. Von Verschuer was a violent anti-Semitic and German nationalist who had taken part in the Kapp Putsch in 1920. In 1922, he outlined his nationalistic eugenic position in a student article, "Genetics and Race Science as the Basis for National (Völkische) Politics." By the time of the Beer Hall Putsch, von Verschuer was lecturing that fighting the Jews was integral to Germany's eugenics battle. In 1935, he left the Institute of Anthropology to establish Frankfurt University's new Institute for Hereditary Biology and Racial Hygiene. By 1937, von Verschuer gained the trust of the Nazis and, within two years, was describing his role as pivotal to Nazi supremacy.

After the Nazis seized power, the American eugenicists and medical media still praised von Verschuer's work. Such prestigious American medical journals as the *Journal of the American Medical Association* cited his research. Rockefeller money continued to flow to him. It was not until 1936, after Raymond Fosdick became president of the Rockefeller Foundation, that funding for German eugenics research slowed. However, funds were readily available if the research omitted the word eugenics and was repackaged as research in genetics, the brain, serology, etc.

In June 1939, the Rockefeller Foundation tried to deny that it was funding Nazi science. This was a lie, because the Rockefeller trust was sending money through the Emergency Fund for German Science. The sleight of hand provided the foundation with a window of deniability. Funds to von Verschuer continued through the war years, supporting several concentration camp experiments. In 1943, he received funding from the German Research Society for experiments packaged under the label of serology. The experiments required large volumes of blood from twins at Auschwitz.[114]

Most readers have probably never heard of von Verschuer, yet everyone is aware of the horrendous and hideous experiments carried out on Auschwitz prisoners at his beckoning by a former Ph.D. candidate of his, who remained his collaborator throughout the war. This former student who provided the blood samples for the study was Dr. Joseph Mengele, the notorious "Angel of Death." Hence the trail of Rockefeller money leads directly to the gates of Auschwitz and some of the most gruesome experiments ever carried out on humans.[115]

While Mengele escaped to South America to avoid war crimes charges and a sure date with the hangman, the Allies never charged von Verschuer with war crimes or crimes against humanity. In 1946, the *Die Neue Zeitung,* an organ of the U.S. occupying power, published an article listing all the doctors who fled Germany. On May 3, it followed with accusations against von Verschuer by Robert Havemann, a communist and chemist who had resisted the Nazis. He openly accused von Verschuer of using Mengele to get eyeballs and blood from those murdered at Auschwitz. Von Verschuer dictated a sworn statement to the occupation-appointed administrator of the Kaiser Wilhelm Institute that he had always opposed racial ideas. He further swore that Mengele himself was transferred to Auschwitz against his will. In fact Mengele could not wait to get involved in the war, and enlisted.

Havemann organized a committee of scientists at Kaiser Wilhelm Institute to examine the evidence against von Verschuer. The committee concluded that he had engaged in despicable acts in concert with Mengele. The report was sealed for the next 15 years. Then a second board found von Verschuer innocent of committing any crimes or transgressions against inmates of Auschwitz. Von Verschuer's record was expunged of any transgressions, and he soon became a respectable scientist in Germany and the United States.

In 1949, Verschuer became a member of the American Society of Human Genetics, newly created by eugenicists. The first president of the society was Hermann Muller of Texas, a former Rockefeller fellow who had worked at the Kaiser Wilhelm Institute in 1932. In 1960, under international pressure to continue the hunt for Nazis, an investigation opened to examine the connection between von Verschuer and Mengele. It concluded there was none. Von Verschuer's record, like those of so many other Nazis, had been completely whitewashed. In 1969, he was killed in a car accident; he never faced justice for his crimes.[116]

It was not until 1940 that the Carnegie Institute stopped funding Laughlin and the Cold Spring Harbor Center. In 1947, a Carnegie administrator overseeing the dismantling of Cold Spring contacted the Dight Institute, an independent eugenics research organization at the University of Minnesota. In 1948, the Dight Institute agreed to take the records about individual traits and family documents if Carnegie defrayed the shipping cost. Six months later, the Minnesota Historical Society agreed to take a half-ton of books and family genealogical books. The New York Public Library took an additional 1,000 volumes of family genealogical books.

In December 1946, the United Nations passed Resolution 96 (I), which embedded genocide into international law. It reads as follows:

"Genocide is a denial of the right of existence of entire human groups, as homicide is the denial of the right to live of individual human beings; such denial of the right of existence shocks the conscience of mankind, results in great losses to humanity in the form of cultural and other contributions represented by these human groups and is contrary to moral law and the spirit and aims of the United Nations."

Shortly after the passage of Resolution 96, the UN ratified the Treaty Against Genocide. The treaty listed five categories of genocide:

Killing members of the group.

Causing serious bodily harm or mental harm to members of the group.

Deliberately inflicting on the group conditions of life calculated to bring about its physical destruction in whole or in part.

Imposing measures intended to prevent births within the group.
Forcibly transferring children of the group to another group.[117]

Under the categories listed above, aspects of past and present policies of the United States and Canada, including ghetto-like reservations, are considered genocidal under the international treaty. Also, the policies of many international companies, especially those engaged in oil exploration and mining, are equally guilty of genocide in the remote areas of South America, Asia and Africa. However, the UN has failed to pursue a single case of genocide against any corporation.

Eugenics, like fascism, did not die with the end of WWII. Rather, during the war, it began to morph into more socially acceptable forms. In fact, one of the largest sterilization campaigns in the United States took place in 1946–47, in the North Carolina's Winston-Salem school district.

In 1941, the American Eugenic Society helped set up a Department of Medical Genetics at Wake Forest Medical School with money from the Carnegie Institute. Eugenics Research Association Vice President William Allan chaired the new department. Following Allan's death in 1943, Dr. C. Nash Herndon took over. Herndon was an advocate of forced sterilization. By 1943, he claimed to have sterilized about 30 individuals, mostly blacks.

In 1946, the Bowman Gray (Memorial) Medical School in Winston-Salem was founded by Gordon Gray, a close friend and frequent golfing partner of Prescott Bush. The school kept extensive eugenic records of children with diseases believed to be inherited, which included low IQ children.

Herndon and Gray, with the help of Dr. Clarence Gamble, heir to the Procter and Gamble soap fortune, began a program to administer an IQ test to all Winston-Salem schoolchildren. Below some arbitrary cut-off point in the test scores, children were selected for sterilization. The program extended to nearby Orange County with money from James Gordon Hanes, a trustee of Bowman Gray Medical School and underwear mogul. Hundreds of children in North Carolina were sterilized in the program. Wake Forest is still uncovering its past association with the eugenics movement.

The Bush Family & Eugenics

In 1950–1951, John Foster Dulles, chairman of the Rockefeller Foundation, led John D. Rockefeller III on a world tour, focusing on the need to stop the expansion of the nonwhite populations. In the fall of 1952, Rockefeller and Dulles established the Population Council with money from the Rockefeller fortune. The American Eugenics Society soon moved its Yale University headquarters into the offices of the Population Council, and the two groups merged. In 1953, Dr. Herndon became president of the American Eugenic Society, and its work continued to expand with money from the Rockefellers.

In the early 1950s, Gordon Gray was appointed as the first director of the Psychological Strategy Board under Truman. Later in 1958, Gray became National Security Adviser to Eisenhower. Gray's son, C. Bowden, served as legal counsel to George H. W. Bush (Prescott's son) throughout the evolving Iran-Contra scandal.

In 1958, Prescott Bush and Gordon Gray, who were President Eisenhower's frequent golfing partners, helped secure an appointment for William Draper to chair a committee advising Eisenhower on the use of military aid to other countries. He was a relative of Wickliffe Draper. Dillon and Read employed him the 1930s. He helped Prescott Bush float the largest bond issue for Nazi Germany, and later served in postwar Germany as head of the economic unit in charge of dismantling the cartel system.

Draper was a racist and major funding source for the eugenics movement. He used his position as committee head to direct its focus away from military aid to the danger of overpopulation in third world countries. The Eisenhower administration dismissed his racist views. Draper went on to fund the Population Crisis Committee with money from the Rockefellers and duPonts. In the 1960s, he served as an adviser to LBJ. He was instrumental in getting the Johnson administration to use the overseas aid program to fund birth control in nonwhite countries.

The Bush-Rockefeller connection goes back before WWI to Samuel Bush, president of Buckeye Casting. Samuel Bush also was director of several Ohio and Pennsylvania railroads that worked closely with the Ohio-bred Standard Oil. Standard held a minority interest in Buckeye Castings, and Rockefeller required railroads transporting Rockefeller oil to buy all their couplings and related railroad equipment from Buckeye.

George H. W. Bush, Prescott's son, was a vocal supporter of Draper's policies. In 1964, he campaigned in Texas against the Civil Rights Act. In 1969, as a member of Congress, Bush arranged hearings on the dangers posed by the birth of too many black babies.

In 1972, as ambassador to the United Nations, George H. W. Bush arranged the first official contract between the American government and the Sterilization League of America. By then, the league had changed its name, yet again, to the Association for Voluntary Surgical Contraception. This contract burdens the United States taxpayer with the cost of sterilization programs in the nonwhite third world. Dr. Clarence Gamble later set up the Pathfinder Fund, whose primary objective is to break down the resistance to sterilization in third world countries.

In the 1980s, as vice president, George H. W. Bush urged Reagan to appoint William Draper's son Bill as administrator of the United Nations Development Program, an organization connected with the World Bank and charged with supervising population control. Bush also was in on the appointment of Bill Draper to the Export-Import Bank. During the 1980s, the Export-Import Bank, at the urging of the Reagan administration, served as a funnel to provide Saddam Hussein with funds and credits during the Iran-Iraq war.

The Bush and Draper families shared close friendships going back to the 1920s. Bill Draper was co-chairman for finance and head of fund raising for the 1980 George H. W. Bush for President campaign. The Pioneer Fund was established by Wickliffe Draper. Charles Murray, the Pioneer Fund's best-known expert, has served as adviser to many of George W's top consultants, and is often quoted by them. He directly influenced the repressive welfare programs of Tommy Thompson and NYC Mayor Giuliani, and was a consultant to Thompson on changes in the Wisconsin welfare system. Murray's books, *The Bell Curve* and *Losing Ground,* both about the inferiority of blacks, serve as bibles for the school privatization and anti-welfare movements in the United States. Thus the racist policies of the Bush family extend into George W. Bush's administration.

It will be noted from the foregoing what a tight, small group the postwar eugenics movement is. American fascism is not broadly based; it is concentrated in a few key wealthy families, with links by marriage to a larger circle. Many of these people also had key posts in the Eisenhower administration. Ike was certainly no supporter of fascism; he expressed hatred for the Nazis, and Germans in general, countless times in letters to his wife. Yet his administration was littered with Nazi supporters. In essence, he was duped. However, the old general was not a complete fool. In his farewell address, he forewarned about the military-industrial complex, a polite description for postwar fascism.

It is undeniable that the tentacles of eugenics extend into such causes as birth control, population control and Planned Parenthood. When such organizations and policies are under democratic control, they can do much to alleviate poverty, human misery and famine.

However, the Cold Spring Harbor Laboratory is still operating. Currently, it is a leader in the human genome project. While the genome project will undoubtedly provide many future medical benefits, it could equally provide weapons of mass destruction, such as bioweapons or even more evil genome-specific bioweapons. The *Project for the New American Century* (PNAC) describes genome-specific weapons as politically useful tools. PNAC serves as the blueprint for the George W. Bush administration, with many members closely associated with PNAC.

With the Bush administration's disregard for human rights and the ban on nuclear testing, it is cause for alarm to find Cold Spring Harbor firmly controlled by the same families involved in the American eugenics movement. Current directors William Gerry and Allen Dulles Jebsen are the grandsons of Averell Harriman and Allen Dulles, respectively. When such policies and organizations slip under the control of families like the Bushes and Rockefellers they can be used as modern-day weapons of genocide.

The legacy of the 1920s is not one of flappers and speakeasies. Its true legacy is one of brutal repression. The leaders of corporate America were successful in purging socialists and union organizers through a network of hard-right "patriotic" groups. The seeds of fascism were successfully sown in the 1920s, and grew into full-blown fascist groups during the economic turmoil of the 1930s.

In 1929, the economy sank into a deep depression, a fitting tribute to the failed laissez-faire economic policies of the decade's three Republican administrations. In May 1932, WWI veterans came to Washington D.C., demanding payment of their deferred bonuses to help them survive the Depression. On May 24, Gen. Alfred Smith, Chief of G2 (Army intelligence), and Gen. Douglas MacArthur met to consider carrying out Emergency Plan White, designed to suppress domestic unrest. Charged with preparation was Gen. George Van Horn Moseley, who held extreme views on eugenics and immigration; following his retirement, he became a pro-Nazi figure.[118] He and MacArthur were convinced the Bonus Marchers had fallen under communist control. Moseley was insistent on removing the marchers by force.

In one of the most hateful acts of all time, President Hoover ordered the army to expel the Bonus Marchers from Washington, D.C. Late in July, the army attacked the marchers using tear gas, cavalry, sabers and bayonets. Two officers involved in the attacks were George Patton and Dwight Eisenhower.

Summing up, the Nazis' plan for world domination involved several facets, like a many-headed hydra. The cartel agreements went far beyond establishing monopolies and, in fact, were a major part of the Nazi war plan readily entered into by the leaders of corporate America. With fascism's support for big business came extreme anti-unionism.

Cartel agreements had two effects on WWII. First, they hindered production of munitions. Second, they shifted the geopolitical balance in South America to the Nazis. Most of the cartel agreements excluded American companies from expanding into South America, while German firms were free to do so. Once the war started, these German firms in South America were used to evade the British blockade, prolonging the war.

Nazi influence in South America continued after the war. Once safely in South America, Nazi war criminals became military advisers and trained their host country's security forces. The result has been a series of coups overthrowing reformist governments, followed by brutal dictatorships with their accompanying death squads. The Nazi influence in Argentina was apparent as recently as the Falkland Islands War, in which the Argentine air force achieved some success. The Argentine aircraft industry is the direct product of ex-Nazi engineers.

Chapter 4, The 1930s:
Nazis Parading on Main Street

The Plot to Remove Roosevelt

For many readers, the 1930s evoke images of the Great Depression and the Dust Bowl. However, this decade of wrenching world economic turmoil involved far more serious events. Events conspired to unleash the horrors of World War II and the unfathomable inhumanity of the Holocaust. WWII shaped the geopolitical scene for the rest of the century. Claims arising from the Holocaust would still be front-page headlines as the world entered the 21st century.

The 1930s was a decade in which Nazis openly paraded, unopposed, in the streets of America, supported by many. Many details about fascism in the 1930s are still shrouded in secrecy. It has been over a half-century since the end of the war, yet news is still surfacing concerning corporate America's dealings with the Nazis. No one has yet comprehensively exposed the connections between the fascists of the 1930s and today's American right wing. Many of the events of the decade have been quietly swept under the rug, such as the plot against Roosevelt. The press downplayed the assassination attempt at that time and today, most people have never heard of it.

Just as economic hardships in Germany helped the rise of Hitler, many Americans hit by the Depression joined the fascist ranks. Similarly, the long and deep recession of the 1980s led to a reemergence of fascism, in the United States and worldwide, with the transition from the industrial age to the information age.

In the 1930s, membership in fascist groups expanded, with some claiming more than a million members. This influence extended to the end of the 20th century. Many of today's far right extremist groups were founded by the pro-Nazis of the 1930s, like the Posse Comitatus established by former Silver Shirt leader Henry Lamont Beach. Others like the World Anti-Communist League, are havens for former pro-Nazis and even Nazi war criminals. The ethnic heritage groups set up by the Republican Party under Nixon are also such havens. The American Security Council, founded in the 1950s by elements from three pro-Nazi groups of the '30s, exerted a serious influence on the Reagan administration.

The wild-eyed claim current in militia groups about Russian or UN troops massing on the Canadian border is nothing but recycled rhetoric from past generations of fascists. The 1960s right-wing group, the Minutemen, made a similar claim. Its version had the Red Chinese massing along the Mexican border for an invasion. This, too, can be traced back to the '30s, when fascists claimed Jews were on the Mexican border.

Except for Russia, Hitler never invaded a country without first unleashing his agents to foment domestic unrest. The United States was targeted too; the Nazi web of intrigue extended far beyond the use of spies and noisy street agitators, such as the Silver Shirts. The Nazis found willing accompanists in the media, the halls of Congress and corporate boardrooms.

Fortunately, the fringe right has always been badly fragmented; indeed, it would be a cause for great concern to see a consolidation today among the various groups. The fragmentation of the 1930s was even greater than it is today.[1] More than 700 different fascist groups existed during the decade. The American National Socialist Party, German-American Bund, Christian Front, the Silver Shirts, America First Committee, the Christian Mobilizer, National Worker's League and the Committee of One Million were some of the more prominent fascist groups at that time. Many factions of the Mother's Movement were also openly fascist.

There are many similarities between the fascist groups of the 1930s and today's far right groups: the intense hatred of minorities and unions, isolationism, and the use of destructive division, nationalism and religion. The Identity religion common to so many of today's far right groups evolved directly from fascist groups of the '30s. These parallels are as striking as they are disturbing, and should stand as a warning of the hidden agenda of the right wing in this country. However, the real story of fascism from the '30s and '40s is one of traitors and seditionists escaping justice after the war's end, as seen in the following quote from *Facts and Fascism* by George Seldes:

> Only the little seditionist and traitors have been rounded up by the FBI. The real Nazi Fifth Column in America remains immune. And yet there is evidence that those in both countries who place profits above patriotism — and fascism is based entirely on profits although all of its propaganda speaks of patriotism — have conspired to make America part of the Nazi Big Business system. Thurman Arnold, assistant district attorney of the United States, his assistant, Norman Littell, and several congressional investigations, have produced incontrovertible evidence that some of our biggest monopolies entered into secret agreements with the Nazi cartels and divided the world among them. Most notorious of all was Alcoa, the Mellon-Davis-Duke monopoly which is largely responsible for America not having sufficient aluminum with which to build airplanes before and after Pearl Harbor, while Germany had an unlimited supply. Of the Aluminum Corporation sabotage, and that of other leading companies, the press said very little, but several books have now been written out of the official record.[2]

It is this unbridled corporatism that is the heart of fascism. Notice how the words of George Seldes written in 1943 still hold true today about those who place profits above patriotism. The stated objective of the first Bush administration was to discover which corporations were responsible for supplying Iraq with the equipment to produce chemical and biological weapons, and to bring them to justice. Ten years after the Gulf War, not a single corporation has been charged, and the media has quietly swept that pledge under the rug. As Seldes stated, they are immune.

More odious is Dick Cheney, Secretary of Defense in the first Bush administration and the current Vice President, who sold Iraq dual-use equipment during his tenure as CEO of Halliburton. As Secretary of Defense, Cheney awarded several contracts to Halliburton's subsidiary, Brown and Root Services, for reports about how private companies could provide logistical support to troops in potential war zones. From 1992–99, with Cheney at Halliburton's helm, Brown and Root was awarded $1.2 billion in defense contracts. Here again is a revolving door between corporate America and government, a door leading to heady profits from corruption for the few and disenfranchisement for the masses. Not a single mention of these deals was made in the press during the 2000 election campaign.

Here we have the heart of the problem of the 21st century: corporate power. Corporations have become so powerful, they openly flaunt our labor and environmental laws. This has reached the point where society now serves the corporations rather than corporations serving society.

In short, as we progress into the new century, the right-wing issues at the forefront of today's political scene are merely recycled pro-fascist issues of the '30s. It is an agenda of corporate rule. The GATS treaty currently being negotiated and the now-dead Multilateral Investment Agreement are attempts to go global with fascist corporatism.

Due to the depth of the Depression, the early 1930s were rife with grandiose plots. During the fall of 1933, Americans learned of a sensational plot by Gen. Art Smith and his Khaki Shirts. Smith, a soldier of fortune and raging Judeophobe, had formed a tight-knit band of 30–100 followers. As his reputation grew, so did his ambitions. Smith, whose idol was Mussolini, boasted that a million men would follow him and kill every Jew in the United States. He announced he would march on Washington and seize the government, much as Mussolini had done in Italy. Fortunately, Smith was arrested on a tip to police about an arms cache.[3]

A good place to begin studying the fascism of the 1930s is with the one common factor at the heart of all the fascist groups — the visceral hatred of Roosevelt and liberalism. This was echoed in the 1990s with the Republican attack on President Clinton, which again showed how far right-wing extremists will go to gain power and subvert democracy.

The attempted coup d'état against Roosevelt was financed by Irénée duPont, J.P. Morgan and a few other wealthy industrialists of the time: Robert Clark, heir to the Singer sewing machine corporation; Grayson Murphy, director of Goodyear; and the Pew family of Sun Oil. During WWII, all three of these corporations aided the Nazi empire. Singer's plant, located on the east bank side of the Elbe, made machine guns for the Nazis.

Central to the plot against Roosevelt were two groups: the American Legion and the Liberty League. The American Legion was formed and financed by Morgan and Murphy in 1919 primarily to break strikes. Two former state commanders of the American Legion were involved in the plot: William Doyle, and Gerald MacGuire.

Irénée, the power behind the duPont throne at that time, held a controlling interest in General Motors. He was an avid fascist and supporter of Hitler, closely tracking his career since the 1920s. On Sept. 7, 1926, duPont gave a speech before the American Chemical Society in which he proposed creating a race of supermen by injecting special drugs into them during childhood. Not every child would receive them; duPont insisted that only those of pure blood would get the injections.[4]

Throughout the 1930s, the duPonts invested heavily in Hitler's Germany. General Motors, controlled by the duPont family, invested $30 million into IG Farben alone. Wendell Swint, duPont's foreign relations director, knew that IG Farben and Krupp arranged to contribute half a percent of their payroll to the Nazi Party. Swint testified before the 1934 Munitions Hearings that duPont was fully aware that it was financing the Nazis through the Opel division of General Motors. Even more telling is the financial backing the duPonts provided pro-Hitler groups in the United States. Starting in 1933, duPont financed the American Liberty Lobby, Clark's Crusaders (which claimed 1.2 million members) and the Liberty League.[5]

In 1934, Irénée duPont and William Knudsen, president of General Motors, with friends of the Morgan Bank and others, set in motion a plot to overthrow FDR. They provided $3 million in funding for an army of terrorists, modeled after the French fascist group, Croix de Feu.[6] The objective of the plot was to either force Roosevelt to take orders from this group of industrialists as part of a fascist-style government or to execute him if he chose not to cooperate.

The plotters selected Gen. Smedley Butler, a WWI hero, to head the plot, although Butler overtly opposed fascism and, in 1931, denounced Mussolini as a murderer and thug. The Italian government demanded an apology and President Hoover complied, placing Butler under arrest for court martial proceedings. Roosevelt, then governor of New York, spoke out against the charges against Butler. Roosevelt had been responsible for awarding Butler's Second Medal of Honor for his service in Haiti. Hoover then backed down and Butler received a mild reprimand for refusing to retract his statement.

The plotters selected Butler because of his great popularity among veterans. Butler had spoken words of encouragement to the Bonus Marchers and was relentless in his pursuit for better treatment of American veterans. Gerald MacGuire and Bill Doyle, both wounded WWI veterans, first approached Butler at his home. The pair played on Butler's sympathy for veterans. However, Butler was not an easy man to fool. After they exchanged pleasantries and discussed each other's service in WWI, MacGuire worked up the nerve to present his plan to Butler.

According to MacGuire, they wanted Butler to attend an American Legion convention and give a speech in favor of the gold standard. Butler immediately asked about the bonus for the veterans. The best answer MacGuire could produce was that they wanted the veterans to be paid in gold and not "rubber" money. Butler was suspicious; both MacGuire and Doyle were dressed in fancy tailored suits and they arrived in a chauffeured limousine. With his suspicions aroused, Butler refused to give them an affirmative reply, but he left the door open to learn more.

The plotters failed to realize that Butler was a man of honor who believed in the constitution and democracy. He had a reputation of absolute honesty and was careful how his name was used. Stringing

MacGuire along, Butler attended several more meetings with him before he left for Europe. MacGuire was a bond salesman for Clark, who sent him to Europe to study how fascists in Europe used veterans.

On his return, MacGuire once again sought out Butler. More meetings followed, including one in which MacGuire laid out 18, $1,000 bills to prove that he had enough funding and to ease any of Butler's concerns. At the same meeting, MacGuire wanted Butler to come with 200 friends to an American Legion convention and give a speech in favor of the gold standard. This aroused Butler's suspicions of ulterior motives, and he refused. Butler also refused MacGuire's offer of an extra $750 per speech if he would refer favorably to the gold standard on his tour of 20 speeches to the VFW around the country; instead Butler lambasted the American Legion leaders.

In one meeting, MacGuire implied that they had men inside the Roosevelt administration who kept them fully informed. Butler noted that MacGuire had correctly predicted the dismissal of administration officials, the American Legion endorsement of the gold standard, and other events.

In another meeting, MacGuire threatened that if Butler did not accept leadership of the plot, Gen. Douglas MacArthur would take his place. MacGuire claimed the Morgans favored MacArthur, but that he had held out for Butler. Another name mentioned, in case Butler refused to head the plot, was former American Legion head Hanford MacNider of Iowa. MacArthur was extremely unpopular among the veterans for leading the charge against the bonus marchers. MacNider also was unpopular for opposing early payment of the bonus. MacGuire noted this and told Butler that MacNider would soon switch his view on the bonus. Within a week, MacNider did switch.

There were other meetings with Butler, who eventually demanded to meet with the leaders of the plot. Clark then met with Butler and offered him a bribe to read a speech to the American Legion. The speech, again favoring the gold standard, was written by John W. Davis, a former Democratic presidential candidate, and chief counsel to J. P. Morgan. Butler bristled at being offered a bribe. Clark backed off and announced that he was withdrawing his own support from the effort. In response, the plotters brought in Frank N. Belgrano Jr. to head the American Legion. Belgrano was a senior vice president of Giannini's Bank of Italy that handled Mussolini's business accounts. Giannini also founded the Bank of America. Belgrano remained an official of Bank of America until after the death of the founder, then went on to found Transamerica.

Eventually, MacGuire had to confess to Butler the plot involved replacing Roosevelt. MacGuire suggested that Roosevelt was tired and needed an assistant to run the country while he attended to ceremonial activities much like the King of Italy, who had relinquished power to Mussolini. Again, Butler bristled at the idea.

In July, the Morgan Mellon-controlled press, including Henry Luce's *Fortune* magazine, unleashed a propaganda blitz praising the virtues of fascism. In August, the American Liberty League appeared. As part of the plot, Butler had been informed earlier of this group.

Morgan and duPont cronies, including John J. Raskob, funded the Liberty league. On its advisory council were Dr. Samuel Hardin Church, who ran the Carnegie Institute in Pittsburgh; W.R. Perkins of National City Bank; Alfred Sloan, CEO of GM; Joseph M. Proskauer, former New York Supreme Court Justice and the general counsel to Consolidated Gas Co.; J. Howard Pew of Sun Oil and financier of the openly fascist Sentinels of the Republic; and David Reed, the Republican senator from Pennsylvania who remarked on the floor of the Senate in May 1932: "I do not often envy other countries and their governments, but I say that if this country ever needed a Mussolini, it needs one now."

Fearing the plot was about to climax with the appearance of the Liberty League, Butler wanted to go public with what he knew. However, he knew he would be ridiculed without someone to corroborate his story. Butler had a newspaper reporter he trusted, Paul French, interview MacGuire. In the interview, the talkative MacGuire confirmed what he had told Butler, as well as his ebullience for fascism: "We need a fascist government in this country… to save the nation from the communists who want to tear it down and wreck all that we have built in America. The only men who have the patriotism to do it are the soldiers, and Smedley Butler is the ideal leader. He could organize a million men overnight."[7]

Once French confirmed the plot, Butler informed the Roosevelt administration. Roosevelt realized that with the backing of such a plot from powerful business leaders, he could not dismiss it as a crackpot scheme. Yet, Roosevelt also was well aware that arresting the leaders of such industrial powerhouses of the day could create a national crisis that could abort the fledgling economic recovery and perhaps trigger another Wall Street crash.

To foil the plot, FDR had news of it leaked to the press, and formed a special House committee to investigate the matter. The McCormick-Dickstein Committee agreed to hear Butler's story in a secret session that met in New York City on Nov. 20, 1934. In four days, the committee heard Butler and French present the details of the plot and the testimony of MacGuire.

Both McCormick and Dickstein described MacGuire's testimony as eminently self-incriminating. The committee, which caught MacGuire lying several times, determined that he did have in his possession the thousand-dollar bills and was in the locations cited. George Seldes noted that all the principals in the case were American Legion officials and conservative financial backers. Other administration officials urged the committee to get to the bottom of the case. McCormick indicated that Butler's evidence was not the first of the plot; in fact, the committee had been in possession of other evidence for five weeks.

With many of the country's leading papers openly pro-fascist, any coverage of the plot was buried or dismissed as the ravings of a madman. On Nov. 22, the Associated Press struck a low blow at Butler in the headline "'Cocktail Putsch' Mayor says."[8] Mayor LaGuardia had come out against Butler.

However, Butler received fresh support from VFW head James Van Zandt, who told the press that the plotters also approached him. Van Zandt claimed that MacArthur, Theodore Roosevelt Jr., and MacNider had all been sounded out. After announcing that Clark would be subpoenaed to appear before the committee as soon as he returned from Europe, the committee quickly adjourned without calling more witnesses. Not a single name mentioned in all the testimony ever appeared before the committee. Writer John Spivak learned that Frank Belgrano had been called to testify, but never did.

The committee formally dissolved on Jan. 3. No other witnesses ever appeared before the committee. Apparently when one is rich enough, one is immune from the laws of the country, regardless of damning evidence. On Feb. 15, the committee released its preliminary findings.

In the last few weeks of the committee's official life it received evidence showing that certain people had made an attempt to establish a fascist organization in this country. No evidence was presented and this committee had none to show a connection between this effort and any fascist activity of any European country. There is no question that these attempts were discussed, were planned, and might have been placed in execution when and if the financial backers deemed it expedient. This committee received evidence from Maj. Gen Smedley D. Butler (retired), twice decorated by the Congress of the United States. He testified before the committee as to conversations with one Gerald C. MacGuire in which the latter is alleged to have suggested the formation of a fascist army under the leadership of General Butler. MacGuire denied these allegations under oath, but your committee was able to verify all the pertinent statements made by General Butler, with the exception of the direct statement suggesting the creation of the organization.

This, however, was corroborated in the correspondence of MacGuire with his principal, Robert Sterling Clark, of New York City, while MacGuire was abroad studying the various forms of veterans' organizations of Fascist character. This committee asserts that any efforts based on lines as suggested in the foregoing and leading off to the extreme right, are just as bad as efforts which would lead to the extreme Left. Armed forces for the purpose of establishing a dictatorship by means of Fascism or a dictatorship through the instrumentality of the proletariat, or a dictatorship predicated on racial and religious hatreds, have no place in this country.[9]

The press muffled Butler's vindication. *The New York Times* failed to report the committee's findings. Instead, it chose to report on the committee's recommendation of registering all foreign propagandists. Buried deep in the pages of the *Times* was a brief acknowledgment that Butler's story had been proven true. It was much the same in the rest of the nation's newspapers. The press simply did not report it. John Spivak, a veteran Washington correspondent, was told that a Cabinet member decided to censor the report. The implication was that the release of certain names would embarrass the Democratic Party. At least two prominent Democrats who had been presidential candidates had been involved: John Davis, a lawyer for the Morgans, and Al Smith, a crony of the duPonts. About a week after receiving the tip, Spivak accidentally stumbled across the uncensored report. Spivak copied the uncensored version and then compared it with the official version. The censored portions of the testimony by Butler and French are in *The Plot to Seize the White House.*[10]

Even more curious is the fact that no one ever faced charges. Spivak went to the Justice Department and was told it had no plans to prosecute. The American Civil Liberties Union issued an angry statement on the lack of justice stemming from the committee's findings.

The congressional committee investigating unAmerican activities has just reported of a Fascist plot to seize the government ... was proved; yet not a single participant will be prosecuted under the perfectly plain language of the federal conspiracy act making this a high crime. Imagine the action if such a plot were discovered among Communists! Which is, of course, only to emphasize the nature of our government as representative of the interests of the controllers of property. Violence, even to the seizure of government, is excusable on the part of those whose lofty motive is to preserve the profit system... [11]

Obviously, powerful forces were brought to bear on the committee — forces more powerful than the government, forces immune from the country's laws.

Spivak offered an interesting explanation of why the plot failed:

The takeover plot failed because though those involved had astonishing talents for making breathtaking millions of dollars, they lacked an elementary understanding of people and the moral forces that activate them. In a money-standard civilization such as ours, the universal regard for anyone who is rich tends to persuade some millionaires that they are knowledgeable in fields other than the making of money. The conspirators went about the plot as if they were hiring an office manager; all they needed was to send a messenger to the man they had selected.[12]

Four years after it was formed, the congressional committee released a white paper concluding that certain persons tried to establish a fascist government. Further investigations disclosed that more than a million people had contracted to join the putschist army and that Remington, a duPont subsidiary, would have supplied the arms and munitions.[13]

As the duPonts saw their plot crashing in around them, they chose to work within the system to gain power, just as Hitler did after the failed Beer Hall Putsch. In the 1936 presidential race, the duPonts and the American Liberty League backed Alf Landon.

The fascist groups initially agreed to back Father Coughlin's third-party candidate, William Lemke. Fritz Kuhn, the leader of the American Bund, then visited Germany before the election and conferred with the leaders of the Nazi Party. At the urging of Hitler's henchmen, he returned to back Landon, and urged other fascists to do the same.

Republicans, Nazis & Elections

With its pro-business agenda and views of the leaders of corporate America, the Republican Party was soon laden with fascists.

Even before the Nazis seized power in Germany, they were already actively involved in American politics and elections. The shocking twist is that they did not have to infiltrate the Republican Party. Many of them were already employed at high levels in the national or state party organizations.

Nazis were seen working for the Republican Party almost from the start. The earliest known instance came in the 1920 election. George Sylvester Viereck and his Burgerbund campaigned extensively for Harding. Following the election, Viereck demanded a political payoff, but Harding was noncommittal. Viereck would become the man behind the notorious Nazi publisher, Flanders Hall, and later, during the 1940s, was charged with sedition.

In October 1928, Edmond Furholzer, a pro-Nazi publisher from Germantown, N.Y., offered to deliver the German vote to Hoover for $20,000. With his chances looking good late in the campaign, Hoover turned down Furholzer's offer.

Furholzer was hardly an obscure Nazi. He was a leading figure in the hard right of Yorkville, a predominantly German neighborhood of Manhattan. In 1928, the Republican State Committee adopted many of Furholzer's proposals. Four years later, when Hoover's chances were dismal, the campaign gladly accepted Furholzer's help. In fact, during the 1932 campaign, Furholzer worked endlessly for the Republican National Committee, campaigning tirelessly for Hoover in New York State. He smeared Roosevelt as the new Wilson, the man who destroyed Germany.[14] In 1933, Furholzer returned to Germany.

By 1934, the Nazis had only been in power for less than a year, but already were active in placing their agents or pro-Nazis in positions of power. On Feb. 22, 1934, Sen. Daniel Hastings of Delaware and Rep. Chester Bolton announced the Republican Party had merged their Senatorial and Congressional Campaign Committees into a single organization, independent of the Republican National Committee. Just before the merger, the two campaign committees hired Sidney Brooks, longtime head of research at International Telephone and Telegraph (ITT). ITT was one of many American corporations that went to extraordinary means to continue trading with the Nazis after war broke out.

Brooks soon made a frantic visit to New York. On March 4, 1934, he went to Room 830 of the Hotel Edison, rented to Mr. William Goodales of Los Angeles, who was actually William Dudley Pelly. The meeting ended with an agreement to merge Brooks' Order of 76 with the Silver Shirts. Then Brooks stopped at 17 Battery Place, the address of the German Consulate General.

The Order of 76 was a pro-fascist group. Its application form required the fingerprints and certain biographical details of applicants. Brooks' application revealed that he was the son of Nazi agent Col. Edwin Emerson, and that he chose to use his mother's maiden name to hide his father's identity.[15] Emerson was a major financial backer of Furholzer and his paper. The Republican Party was employing Nazi collaborators and pro-fascist groups at a high level.

On Oct. 22, 1936, the *New York Post* broke the following story:

Nazi Publicist on G.O.P. Payroll

To win votes for Landon and Bleakley, the Republican State Committee is employing on its payroll a staff of propagandists identified with local Nazi organizations, the Post learned today.[16]

On October 30, 1936, *New York World-Telegram* revealed more details.

U.S. Nazi Attack on Jews Is Laid to Republicans

Anti-Semitic Radio Speeches by Griebl, Others Sponsored by G.O.P.

Fritz Kuhn Among Speakers in Regular Broadcasts Over WWRL

The Republican Party had been sponsoring radio broadcasts by American Nazis to win German votes, it was disclosed today. One of the recent speakers was Dr. Ignatz T. Griebl, a national Nazi leader and pronounced anti-Semitic ...[17]

The second quote shows that the Republican Party leadership was willing to promote Nazi racism. In fact, an integral part of the Nazi battle plan was promoting racial riots or division within the United States to weaken or prevent the nation from entering the war. Such collaboration with the Nazis was tantamount to treason. Hitler and his agents in the U.S. must have been very pleased that leaders of the Republican Party were willing to promote and incite civil unrest by spreading anti-Jewish propaganda.

This example of vicious anti-Jewish campaigns by Republican leaders was not an isolated incident. In fact, it was commonplace. In the 1938 Minnesota governor's race, leading officials of the Republican Party conducted another vicious anti-Jewish campaign to defeat Gov. Elmer Benson of the Farmer-Labor Party.

Benson's inaugural address on Jan. 5, 1937 had placed him on the left of the New Deal spectrum. FDR endorsed Benson in 1936, and the Republican Party considered this a declaration of war. Among the measures Benson supported were:

- A two-year extension on the mortgage moratorium for farmers
- A technical assistance program to assist and promote cooperatives
- Union wages for state employees
- Creation of a state commission on youth
- Free transportation for rural high school students
- Repeal of the criminal syndicalism laws (Remember the Wobblies?)
- Creation of a state housing agency
- Development of a state-owned cement plant
- Increased benefits for the disabled, people on relief and the aged
- A constitutional amendment enabling the state to produce and sell electrical power to municipalities
- A state liquor dispensary
- New provisions in the state's unemployment benefits, including striking workers[18]

Few of Benson's proposals became law, as the state senate effectively blocked his program. Central to Benson's programs was a restructuring of the tax code, which passed the state House of Representatives intact. Some of the provisions were:

- Complete removal of the state tax levy on homes and homesteads up to the value of $4,000.
- Taxing the net income of individuals and corporations on a graduated basis so state income tax revenues would replace a large share of local school taxes.
- Increased taxes on accumulated wealth, including mining companies, to balance the state budget; increased taxes on chain stores.[19]

Conservatives in the Senate ignored the House tax bill until a few days before the legislative session closed, resulting in a special session. The Twin City press ran article after article denouncing the Farmer-Labor Party, while citing such business leaders as Charles Fowler of Northern States Power, Mr. Montague representing the Steel Trust, Aleck Janes of Great Northern Railroad, and Aaron Youngquist of Minnesota Power and Light. The press acted as a puppet of the business leaders, who were claiming the Farmer-Labor Party was driving business out of the state. Because of the bad press over the Farmer-Labor Party, Benson's tax proposals failed to pass the Senate, setting the stage for a bitter election campaign the following year.

In 1938, the Republican Party, with Harold Stassen heading the state ticket, ran two campaigns: a high-road campaign by Stassen, and a dirty campaign headed by the old guard in the Republican Party. Led by Ray P. Chase, this second campaign set new lows. Chase's vehicle for running it was the Ray P. Chase Research Bureau. Financing his efforts were some of Minnesota's business elite: George Gillette, president of Minneapolis Moline; J. C. Hormel, the meat packer; James Ford Bell, Northwestern Bank; Col. Robert McCormick, owner of the *Chicago Tribune*; and George Belden of the Citizens Alliance.

To achieve his goal, Chase used both legal and illegal methods. Files were stolen from the State Relief Department and Farmer-Labor members were scanned for communist activity. Dean Edward Nicholson supplied data about left-wing student organizations on the University of Minnesota campus. One of the students labeled as a dangerous radical was Eric Sevareid. Chase produced and distributed the Red-baiting pamphlet, *Are They Communists or Catspaws*. In it, Chase launched into a vicious anti-Jewish attack about an alleged conspiracy, equating Judaism with communism and Gov. Benson's role in it.

Chase's attack went beyond Minnesota. Using the services of Cyrus McCormick, Chase managed to get U.S. Rep. Martin Dies to hold hearings in late October on communist influence in the Farmer-Labor Party.

To understand how the Republican Party could run election campaigns based on intense and vicious racist platforms, one needs to understand the attitude in the country toward Jews at that time. A few days after Kristallnacht, Roosevelt expressed his anger and horror publicly. A Gallup poll that month revealed that 94 percent of the people disapproved of the Nazi treatment of Jews, but 97 percent of the people also disapproved of the way Nazis treated Catholics. A Roper poll that same month revealed the depth of anti-Semitic views in America. The poll found that only 39 percent of the people believed that Jews should be treated as everyone else; 53 percent believed that Jews were different and should be restricted; and 10 percent believed Jews should be deported. In the winter of 1938-39, many had denounced aid for "refu-Jews." Polls revealed 71 percent-85 percent opposed an increase in immigration quotas; 67 percent opposed admitting any refugees, and 67 percent opposed a one-time admission of 10,000 refugee children.

Turning away the refugees aboard the *St. Louis* was a low point in the Roosevelt administration and arguably indefensible because of the Holocaust, but Roosevelt hardly acted in a vacuum. Public opinion was decisively against admitting Jews. One can only guess how much of the anti-Semitism prevalent at that time was the direct result of the various campaigns conducted by the Republican Party, which often equated Judaism with communism, as in the example of the 1938 Minnesota election.

The pattern of collaboration between the Republican Party and the Nazis extends further. On Nov. 23, 1937, executives of General Motors and other corporate and political leaders met with Baron Manfred von Killinger and agreed on a total commitment to the Nazi cause. The secret agreement also called for replacing Roosevelt, preferably with Burton Wheeler of Montana. It was leaked to George Seldes who published it in his newsletter *In Fact*. The entire text of the agreement can be found in *Facts and Fascism*. Here is an excerpt:[20]

> The substance of the German suggestion amounts to changing the spirit of our nation as expressed by recent elections. That is possible but by no means easy. The people must become aware of the disastrous economic effects of the policies of the present administration first. In the wake of reorientation of the public opinion a vigorous drive must start in the press and radio. Technically it remains a question as to whether this drive may center on the Republican National Committee.

> Farsighted businessmen will welcome conferences of this kind. A tremendous inspiration might come out of them. There is no reason why we should not learn of emergencies similar to those prevailing in our own country and the methods by which farsighted governments were trying to overcome them. It is also clear that manufacturers, who usually contributed to the campaigns of all candidates, must realize that their support must be reserved to one, in whose selection they must take an active hand.

Each section of the document was written by one of the participants. A member of the U.S. Senate wrote the first paragraph of the quote above; a representative of General Motors wrote the second. Once again, it is clear from the first paragraph that leaders of the Republican Party were collaborating with the Nazis. It further establishes the pattern of collaboration between the Nazis and Republicans over several years. Nor would this be the last involvement of Nazis in the Republican Party. In 1940, a group of Republican congressmen accepted money from Hitler for their election campaigns.

The second paragraph above is of paramount importance. The leaders of corporate America did follow the prescription above for subverting democracy.

After the failure of Landon in the presidential race, and in defiance of Roosevelt's desire to improve working conditions for the average person, Knudsen and duPont launched a speed-up system at General Motors. The system forced men to work at a horrifying pace, and many line workers died of the heat and pressure.

Irénée duPont personally paid almost $1 million to hire armed storm troopers modeled after the Gestapo and equipped with gas to sweep through his plants and beat any rebellious workers. He also hired Pinkerton to look through his industrial empire to spy on left wingers, "malcontents" or labor leaders. Concurrently, he started to finance the notorious Black Legion in the Detroit area. He encouraged foremen at General Motors to join this group of terrorists.

The prime purpose of the Black Legion was to firebomb union meetings, murder union leaders and terrorize all workers to prevent unionization. The Black Legion was linked to the Klan and to the even more terrifying Wolverine Republican League. Members of this later group included several big business leaders. The Black Legion murdered at least 50 people, many of them black.[21]

The backers of fascism in the United States were rich industrialists, as were Hitler's backers in Germany. Corporate America willingly entered cartel agreements, which, in effect, granted them a monopoly. Big business was also attracted to fascism's extreme anti-unionism. Professor Gaetano Salvemini of Harvard was quoted in the undergraduate daily that a new fascism threatened America — the fascism of corporate business enterprise in this country. He also believed that 100 percent of American big business was in sympathy with fascism.[22] Support for fascism was widespread among industrialists in the U.S., as shown by the remarks of the Ambassador to Germany in the *New York Times*, cited on p. 86. [23]

Collaboration between the Republican Party and the Nazis was a continuing effort throughout the 1930s. However, it would not reach epidemic proportions until the 1940 election. With the European continent already embroiled in war, and President Roosevelt espousing pro-British views, the Nazis were desperate to keep the United States out of the war. In a bizarre plot full of intrigue involving Texas oilman William Rhodes Davis, labor leader John L. Lewis, and Mexico, Nazis provided extensive funding to the Republican Party for the 1940 election.

W.R. Davis of Texas Oil had been supplying the German navy with oil since 1936. He was the owner of Eurotanker, a huge German refinery. For the complete story of Davis, the reader should see Dale Harrington's *Mystery Man*.[24] Davis had arranged a deal to supply the Nazis with oil from Mexico. Mexico had nationalized its oil fields, including some owned by Davis. Led by Standard Oil of New Jersey, big oil boycotted the Mexican oil market. Therefore, the German deal was vital for the Mexican economy.

The outbreak of war in Europe jeopardized Davis' road to riches. He used his friendship with John L. Lewis to arrange a meeting with Roosevelt early in 1940, in which he proposed a far-out peace plan. Roosevelt was cool to the proposal and told Davis that any peace plan would have to come through official channels. Davis then traveled to Germany to meet with Goering. Central to his plan was the removal of Hitler; the Nazis would remain in power under Goering. On Davis' return, Roosevelt refused to meet with him.

Besides the peace plan, the talks between Goering and Davis centered on the upcoming presidential election. The Nazis were desperately seeking the defeat of Roosevelt, although they were less than enthusiastic about the Republican candidates. They agreed the best chance of defeating Roosevelt was to back the Republicans rather than run a third party. Davis knew that Lewis opposed another war and told the Nazis that Lewis had control over the election with his large block of union voters. Lewis was not pro-fascist. Instead, he feared that a new war would lead to a dictatorship and placing the CIO under emergency laws. Because of the Red Scare of 1919, one can hardly blame Lewis for his fears.[25] Talks soon settled on how much money was needed to defeat Roosevelt; the final sum settled on was $5 million.

Joachim Herslet of the Reich Foreign Economic Ministry carried the plan to the United States. To obtain dollars, Goering persuaded the Italians to release money used to finance fascist propaganda and espionage. An Italian courier, Luigi Podesta, delivered the money to the German consulate in New York. Herslet told the charge d'affaires of the German Embassy in Washington of his mission, and that he had $5 million at his disposal. With some of the money from Herslet, Davis opened accounts in the Bank of Boston, Irving Trust, Bank of America, and the Bank of Germany in Mexico City.

On the eve of the Republican National Convention, money from this Nazi slush fund was used in a propaganda blitz for the isolationists. One Republican member of Congress received $3,000 for heading a contingent of 50 isolationists. The Nazi money was well spent, because the convention closed with a party platform plank firmly opposing U.S. involvement in the war. The Nazis were especially pleased to note the platform plank was taken almost verbatim from the full-page German propaganda ads placed in the *New York Times* on June 25.[26] The Nazis paid Stephen Day thousands of dollars to form the committee publishing the ad. Maloney named Day, a Republican representative from Illinois, as a fascist collaborator. Reps. Samuel Pettingill, Harold Knudsen, John O'Conner and Hamilton Fish, and Sens. Edwin Johnson Bennett Clark, David Walsh, Burton Wheeler and Rush Holt signed the ad.[27] Both Lewis and Democratic Sen. Burton Wheeler, a leading isolationist, spoke before the convention.

With this success behind them, the Nazis then decided to spring a similar effort on the Democratic convention. Davis distributed $100,000 to buy 40 delegates from Pennsylvania to vote against Roosevelt. The Nazi press agent, Kurt Sell, arranged for several other Democratic congressmen to attend the convention on German Embassy funds. Sell also funded several anti-war ads in the *Chicago Tribune* on July 15.

Although the Nazis were not enthused over Willkie's nomination, they thought any president would be better than Roosevelt. With their slush fund of $5 million, the Nazis surreptitiously helped Willkie through secret donations to various pro-Willkie clubs. Thomsen, the charge d'affairs of the German embassy, destroyed all receipts, so it may never be known how much money the Nazis funneled into the Republican Party, or to whom. It is not clear if it all was spent. Supposedly, $3 million was found in the embassy when the FBI seized it in December 1941. Nevertheless, the embassy had other sources of funding than Herslet's funds. In fact, Thomsen did not cooperate with Herslet and ran his own campaign.

Perhaps the best summary of this plot is a quote from a report to the German Foreign Ministry by German Ambassador Thomsen:

> Roosevelt's prospects of being elected a third time have declined... At this juncture John L. Lewis [chief of the CIO] enters the arena with approximately 8 to 10 million votes controlled by him. He is determined to make ruthless use of his influence, and will do so in favor of strict isolationism. Lewis is pursuing that policy not indeed because of any pro-German sentiments, but because he fears that America's involvement in a war would mean the establishment of an American dictatorship and the placing of his organization under emergency laws. He is negotiating with Republicans at present and will support them in the campaign if Willkie publicly declares himself for keeping America out of all European conflicts. Lewis can throw his strength at will to Republicans or the Democrats, but this much is certain that he surely will not use it for Roosevelt. He may even, as he has already threatened to do, organize a third party of disgruntled Democrats, the Peace party, and in the person of closely allied Senator Wheeler put up a suitable candidate.[28]

While $5 million seems a trivial amount today in a presidential campaign, in 1940, it was significant; the total expenditures by the Republican Party were slightly less than $15 million.

The amount of Nazi funds spent on the Republican 1940 campaign may never be known. From the funds recovered in the embassy raid, it is clear that at least $2 million was spent from the slush fund alone. A major proportion of the Republican 1940 campaign funds came directly from the Nazis. Since the major industrialists were active supporters of the Nazis and also large donors to the Republican Party, more than half of the 1940 Republican campaign funding came either directly from Nazis in Berlin or their sympathizers in the United States.

Davis donated at least $48,000 to Willkie, bypassing the $5,000 federal limit by donating to individual state parties. He also bankrolled the radio address of Lewis on Oct. 21, in which he announced his support for Willkie. In late October, Davis forwarded copies of his documents about his proposed peace plan to leaders of the Republican Party, including Willkie, former President Hoover, Sam Pryor and Verne Marshall. Willkie decided not to use the material, fearing it might backfire. In the end, labor chose to remain loyal to FDR and Roosevelt won the election with 27 million votes to Willkie's 22 million votes.[29]

Top Republican leaders, including former President Hoover, closely collaborated with high-level Nazi officials in Berlin to bring about Roosevelt's defeat. Postwar interviews of Goering and Ribbentrop confirm Hoover connived with the Nazis in the 1940 election. Hoover was also a secret member of the fascist America First group, dedicated to Roosevelt's defeat.

Captured Nazi documents confirm the close association of the Republican Party with the Nazis. In one captured document written in anticipation of defeat, the Nazis expressed hope for a Republican victory so they might achieve an "easy peace." A short excerpt from the document in Appendix 10 follows:

> Right now, the chances for a separate peace with the West are a little better, especially if we succeed, through our propaganda campaign and our confidential channels, to convince the enemy that Roosevelt's policy of unconditional surrender drives the German people towards Communism.

> There is great fear in the U.S.A. of Bolshevism. The opposition against Roosevelt's alliance with Stalin grows constantly. Our chances for success are good, if we succeed to stir up influential circles against Roosevelt's policy. This can be done through clever pieces of information, or by references to unsuspicious neutral ecclesiastical contact men.

> We have at our command in the United States efficient contacts which have been carefully kept up even during the war. The campaign of hatred stirred up by Roosevelt and the Jews against everything German has temporarily silenced the pro-German bloc in the U.S.A. However, there is every hope that this situation will be completely changed within a few months. If the Republicans succeed in defeating Roosevelt in the coming presidential election, it would greatly influence the American conduct of war towards us.

With the Battle of the Bulge raging in Europe, the Republican candidate, Dewey, lashed out against Roosevelt, saying that his call for unconditional surrender was prolonging the war and costing American lives.

The Nazi involvement in the 1940 election was extensive, including congressional races. Evidence gathered by British intelligence on Americans at Roosevelt's request also netted information about FDR's political enemies, confirming that seven U.S. senators and 13 representatives received campaign contributions from the Nazis. Berlin directly financed much of the isolationist wing of Congress.[30]

From at least 1932, the Nazis were deeply involved in the U.S. political process, although the extent of that involvement is still shrouded. Somewhere in the vaults of the United States and England lie incriminating files that will expose the collaboration of many more individuals and corporations with the Nazis.

Fascism and Unions

Wall Street and corporate America built Hitler's war machine. Once war was threatened and the Roosevelt administration started to build up American defenses, corporate America went on strike. Many of the deals between corporate America and the Nazis border on treason. Most of these were cartel agreements, similar to the establishment of monopolies.

Before U.S. entry into the war, the biggest scandal was in aviation. The government awarded contracts for 4,000 planes in 1940, but by Aug. 9, corporate America had only built 33 planes. General Motors, controlled by the duPonts, dominated the aviation industry. The press suppressed the real story of a "sit-down strike" by big business and distracted the public's attention by blaming labor. In fact, it was a capitalist's strike, and until big business got special tax breaks, it refused to produce planes.[31] For six months, from May to October 1940, corporate America produced no airplanes at all. It was using the aviation industry as a front to thwart President Roosevelt's plan.

Throughout this strike, the press failed to mention the refusal of General Motors to accept contracts already awarded for planes. The strike by corporate America had the support of the newspaper chains, as well as the War and Navy departments.

During WWI, the automobile industry came close to committing treason. Throughout 1917, the auto companies refused to cut production by 25 percent in the second half of the year, thereby denying the defense industry production space and a substantial amount of iron and coal that was needed for defense production. In 1941, General Motors announced it would produce no new models until 1943. General Motors quickly broke that pledge in 1942.

On March 26, 1942, Sen. Truman accused Standard Oil of treason for delivering the new tetraethyl lead gas additive to both Germany and Japan. Standard was the major supplier of oil to both the Nazis and Japanese. In his appearance before the Senate committee, Farish, the president of Standard, was asked if his company delivered the oil to Japan that made the attack on Pearl Harbor possible. He answered that Standard Oil was an international company. Standard buffed its image with an advertising campaign that promoted the virtues of its products, helped along by the major papers.[32]

Like oil, steel is a highly strategic material, and the one most needed in arms productions. The record of big steel was one of sabotage, as shown in some of the following quotes pulled from *Labor,* a union magazine published by Seldes:[33]

"Sabotage of war program charged to Steel magnates," *Labor,* July 7, 1942. Subtitle: "More interested in keeping monopoly than with beating Axis, declares Senator O' Mahoney."

"Truman Accuses Steel Companies of Sabotage," PM Magazine, June 6, 1942. Subtitle: "Senator Black charges that big corporations hamstring production."

Labor, April 28, 1942: "It has become clear as the noonday sun that the vicious attack which has been made on the nation's workers in recent weeks was actually a red herring designed to divert attention from the treasonable sabotage of the nation's war program by Big Business, which is being exposed by congressional committees and defense agencies. Proof of that statement may reasonably be drawn from the sensational and unbelievably shocking disclosures of a cold-blooded betrayal of national welfare by men whose only flag is the dollar sign."

"One of the most shameful chapters in our history."

The Carnegie-Illinois Steel Corp., a subsidiary of U.S. Steel, and the Jones and Laughlin Steel Co. were charged by the War Production Board with having refused to fill government armament orders while diverting iron and steel to favorite civilian customers for nonessential purposes. The result is that shipbuilding and other war construction have been held up.

The President directed the Navy to take over three plants of the Brewster Aero Co., accused of sabotaging the aviation program.

The United States faces a shortage of critical war materials because the outstanding industrial concerns have contracts with German monopolists restricting production here.

One of the necessary war materials hamstrung by these cartel agreements was carboloy or cemented tungsten carbide. Carboloy's abrasive properties were vital in the machining of hardened steel products. Without it, parts for tanks and other instruments of war were next to impossible to machine. General Electric held the patent, with a cartel agreement with Krupp that limited the production and restricted sales.

As soon as General Electric cemented its deal with Krupp, the price of tungsten carbide jumped from $48 a pound to $453 a pound. With the cartel agreement in place, General Electric used its position to buy out or cripple domestic competition in the abrasive market. General Electric paid royalties to Krupp on every pound of carboloy produced. Not only did this arrangement tell the Nazis how much carboloy America was using in its build-up for war, but the royalties, in effect, ended up in Hitler's war chest.

In September 1940, following a complaint by the Firth-Sterling Steel Co., the agreement was broken up when the court issued two federal antitrust indictments against General Electric and Krupp. Firth-Sterling had run afoul of General Electric's price levels as it sought to sell shell-turning blanks to the U.S. Army. The cartel's hindrance of war production outraged the Senate Committee on Military Affairs.

On Jan. 26, 1947, the trial of General Electric resumed in New York City. Under indict–ment were GE Vice President Zay Jeffries; President W.G. Robbins of the Carboloy Co.; Walter M. Stearns, former GE trade manager; and Gustav Krupp. Krupp was not present; he was under arrest in Germany for war crimes. Ironically, during the trial, Jeffries accused union leaders of having "un-American objectives" and denounced high wages.

Throughout the trial, General Electric's lawyers fought bitterly against the introduction of captured Nazi documents. In one such document, Walter Stearns was quoted as telling the Germans that while GE intended to fix prices, "this must never be expressed in the contract itself or in any correspondence which might come into the files of GE." Other documents quoted Jeffries threatening the president of a competitor: "We'll either buy you out or break you."

The jury found General Electric, its subsidiaries and company officials guilty on five counts of criminal conspiracy. Ironically, no further charges, such as sedition or hindering the war effort, were leveled. Despite pleas from the Department of Justice for heavy sentences, Judge John C. Knox handed down only minor fines. The court fined Stearns and Jefferies $2,500 each; Robbins, $1,000. Judge Knox fined GE and Carboloy $20,000 each; Inter–national General Electric, only $10,000. Once again, the rich and powerful escaped justice with a mere slap on the wrist.

The fine for General Electric was particularly lax, considering the firm had made millions on carboloy. In 1935 and 1936 alone, General Electric's subsidiary that made and sold carboloy realized a $694,000 profit. Newspapers failed to cover the trial and the convictions, but found plenty of space on their front pages for General Electric's charges that members of the Union of Electricians working at atomic energy plants were potential security risks. The union's *UE News* was the only paper to report on the trial and convictions.

Aluminum Corp. had an agreement with IG Farben that restricted production of aluminum and magnesium, which hindered building fighters and bombers. The record from that era makes it clear that corporate America was doing its damnedest to sabotage the war effort. Newsweek has reported that at least 300 corporations were doing business with the Nazis during the war.[34]

A career spokesman for native fascist sentiment was Merwin Hart, a Harvard classmate of FDR. His National Economic Council opposed the New Deal. Hart admired Franco, and many big businessmen supported his American Union for Nationalistic Spain, one of many pro-fascist groups he formed. It garnered the support of reactionaries like James Rand of Remington-Rand; Lammont duPont; A.W. Erickson, chairman of a New York advertising agency; Alfred Sloan, president of General Motors; and J.H. Alstyne, president of Otis Elevators.

Hart wholeheartedly followed the fascist line. He opposed the 44-hour week, fought against the unemployment and the child labor acts and, even more odiously, demanded that only those people not on relief be allowed to vote. According to Hart: "Democracy is the rallying cry under which the American system of government is being prepared for despotism. If you find any organization containing the word 'democracy' it is probably directly or indirectly affiliated with the Communist Party."[35]

Next to the duPonts and their friends, Henry Ford was the most notorious pro-Hitler backer. In 1919, he first announced, "International financiers are behind all wars. They are what is called the International Jew: German-Jews, French Jews, English-Jews, American-Jews. ... the Jew is the threat."[36]

Again, the same rhetoric is familiar today with many right-wing groups, particularly the Posse Comitatus. The quote above is almost unchanged from the Posse's rhetoric in the 1980s. They uses code words, such as international bankers to mean Jews. Similarly, they and others still promote *The Protocols of the Elders of Zion*, a malicious anti-Jewish pamphlet based on a known forgery, first published in this country by Ford in his *Dearborn Independent*.

Ford's involvement went much further than publishing anti-Jewish propaganda. He was an early financier of Hitler. Getting hard evidence of funding for Hitler is a rarity, but with Ford, it is irrefutable. The most credible evidence comes from Hitler's treason trial after the failed Beer Hall Putsch, from the testimony of Herr Auer, vice president of the Bavarian Diet (Parliament) on Feb. 7, 1923.[37][38]

The Bavarian Diet has long had information that the Hitler movement was partly financed by an American anti-Semitic chief, who is Henry Ford. Mr. Ford's interest in the Bavarian anti-Semitic movement began a year ago when one of Mr. Ford's agents, seeking to sell tractors, came in contact with Diedrich Eichart the notorious Pan-German. Shortly after, Herr Eichart asked Mr. Ford's agent for financial aid. The agent returned to America and immediately Mr. Ford's money began coming to Munich.

Herr Hitler openly boasts of Mr. Ford's support and praises Mr. Ford as a great individualist and a great anti-Semite. A photograph of Mr. Ford hangs in Herr Hitler's quarters, which is the center of the monarchist movement.[39]

Like Hart, Ford supported the Nazi agenda, harboring a rabid hatred of Jews and unions. One of the myths that Ford successfully created was that he paid his workers more than other firms. In fact, he paid less; the United Autoworkers printed tables showing that wages for every category of worker were lower than those paid by Chrysler and Briggs (General Motors). The maximum wage paid by Ford was below the minimum wage of the union.[40]

Ford was not known to be generous or supportive of charities, either; he never contributed any large sum to anyone, with one exception: the Moral Re-Armament Movement led by Dr. Frank Buchman, a notorious fascist and a Lutheran minister.[41]

Buchman preached a philosophy of pacification of labor through the use of force. Followers of Buchman read like a who's who in the anti-union movement, such as Harry Chandler, the reactionary publisher of the *Los Angeles Times,* and Louis B. Mayer. With his program for pacifying labor, Buchman rabidly opposed communism and praised Hitler: "I thank heaven for a man like Adolf Hitler, who built a front line of defense against the anti-Christ of Communism."[42]

While many of his apologists claim Hitler deceived him, Buchman never renounced fascism or changed his fascist views of labor. The main reason the Moral Re-Armament group has persisted to the present, despite its controversial views, are the pro-business and anti-labor stance, and the support it received from such leaders as Ford. Buchman also was the founder of Alcoholics Anonymous.

To deal with labor, Ford employed Harry Bennett, who had one of the largest spy and thug services in America, which battered, killed and otherwise intimidated workers. Wherever Ford located a plant, there was a long record of murders and beatings of workers at the hands of Bennett's thugs. Ford even went so far as to fire workers who took part in the 1932 hunger march. Bennett employed Father Coughlin, the rabid fascist radio priest, to undermine the efforts to unionize Ford. Coughlin bribed United Auto Workers leader Homer Martin to betray the workers by pushing for a company union rather than join the AFL or CIO.[43]

The plight of the American worker during the '30s is hardly imaginable today. Working conditions were so intolerable that numerous congressional committees held hearings on the issue. Employers routinely used spies, and hired stool pigeons, thugs, gangsters and murderers. They were well equipped with arms, including Thompson machine guns and "poisonous gas," the term at that time for tear gas. The visceral hatred of labor and unions by employers is documented in the many volumes of the La Follette reports on corporate America. George Seldes lists the following seven facts from the reports:

1. American business employs a vast espionage system whose purpose is to fight labor.

2. 200 agencies employ 40,000–50,000 spies in industry.

3. $80 million a year is spent by big corporations in fighting labor, employing spies, buying gas and guns, hiring gangs.

4. Almost all the great corporations are in the spy racket, including Ford, General Motors, U.S. Steel, Bethlehem Steel, Consolidated Edison, Weir, Frick, Coke, etc.

5. 2,500 companies comprising what Sen. La Follette called the "Blue Book of American Industry" are part of the American Gestapo.

6. The National Association of Manufacturers, U.S. Chamber of Commerce, Merchants and Manufacturers Association, National Metal Trades Association are the chief organizations engaged in native fascism.

7. The American press still gives its front pages and its approving editorials to smears, exaggerations and falsehoods of the Dies Committee. And similar committees that employ reporters to attack labor, especially those labor unions which are progressive and militant and put up a strong fight for the rights of labor, suppressed almost all the hearings and findings of the La Follette Committee, which constituted an exposure of fascism in American industry.[44]

Here is the heart of fascist ideology of the 1930s and of the far-right, corporate rule today. It is the basis for the visceral level of hate for unions, fueled by the corporate elite and their propaganda organizations. There is no better example to show the power of the pro-fascists in the United States than to compare the plight of the American worker with his counterpart in the rest of the industrial nations. In every category, the American worker comes up short. For example, the American worker earns 44 percent less than his German counterpart and 15 percent (1994 figures) less than his Japanese counterpart.[45] While the average American worker is lucky to receive a two-week vacation, his European counterpart typically enjoys five weeks vacation and a list of benefits the U.S. worker can only dream about. An exception is the UAW, one of the most successful unions in gaining workers' benefits; nonunion workers and members of other unions in America earn far less.

Nor has the plight of the worker seeking to unionize changed much from the 1930s–1940s. Today, corporate America outsources security to private, non-union companies, which can be used as hired thugs and union busters. Although muggings and factory death squads are not as great a threat today, corporate America still has no qualms about murdering union organizers in other countries. A recent report revealed that Coca-Cola hired right-wing death squads to murder union organizers in Columbia.[46] The United Steel workers union filed suit in Miami alleging that Coca-Cola and Panamerican Beverages, its principal bottler in Latin America, waged what union leaders describe as a campaign of terror, using paramilitaries to kill, torture and kidnap union leaders in Columbia.

The intensity of workplace spying is greater today than in the 1930s and 1940s. Workers and job applicants are routinely forced to take drug tests. Their financial and medical records are open books to employers. In a recent case, Burlington Northern Santa Fe Railway was found to have ordered genetic testing of an employee as a follow up to his surgery for carpal tunnel syndrome. There is no gene for carpal tunnel syndrome. The employee was not informed of the testing and did not give permission for it. Such information could be used to deny promotions, or to trigger firing the employee because he had a predisposition to cancer or other inheritable disease.[47]

Even more onerous are the private blacklists. The American Security Council[48] was formed in the late 1950s to provide member companies with background checks on employees or applicants, particularly those believed to foster anti-free enterprise views. It is directly linked with the pro-fascists of the 1930s, and had a great influence on the Reagan administration. Another such group, the Church League, was founded in the 1930s. Indeed, almost every right-wing group keeps some sort of blacklist to deny employment to anyone holding unacceptable views on such topics as union activism or leftist politics.

The standard tactic of fascists like the duPonts was to finance a legitimate group that would be widely accepted, like the American Security Council, then use it to further their aims by focusing media attention on it. Another good example was the American Legion in the previous chapter.

In some regards, labor has advanced. But overall, labor has lost the high ground of the 1950s that coincided with a peak in union membership. Today, it is commonplace to hear of raids on sweatshops, where workers are held virtually at gunpoint. Child labor is now a bigger problem than it was in 1900. The nation's largest retailer, Wal-Mart, is notorious for demanding employees work off the clock. Wal-Mart has also been found guilty of keeping evening employees locked in at the end of their shift when no supervisor is around to unlock the front door.

The wide differences in pay and benefits between U.S. workers and their European counterparts reflect not only greater unionization abroad, but also political systems that are friendlier to unions and workers. Many anti-union laws were passed since WWII through the efforts of fascist groups. The wide disparity in wealth in the United States is one result. No other highly developed nation has such a wide gap between rich and poor.

In the secret 1937 agreement between U.S. corporations and Baron Manfred von Killinger calling for a total commitment toward the Nazi cause, the section written by a General Motors executive declared:

> We must just as well recognize that business leaders of this country must get together in the present emergency. By now they must have realized that they cannot expect much from Washington. We will have to resort to concrete planning. We can agree that it is desirable to convince our business leaders that it is a good investment to embark on subsidizing our patriotic citizens' organization and secure their fusion for the common purpose. Unified leadership with one conspicuous leader will be a sound policy. We will be grateful for any service our German friends may give us in this respect.[49]

This agreement is essentially a call to subvert and destroy democracy in favor of a total commitment to the Nazis. Note the "patriotic organizations" referred to, groups like the Silver Shirts and Black Legion. As already noted, many of the pro-fascist groups received financial support from the backers of the plot against FDR. By 1942, the plan of corporate America was in full force.

The Press Sells Out to the Nazis

Besides funding pro-fascists groups like the Silver Shirts, corporate America sponsored several other groups that preserved a semblance of respectability. One such organization that figured prominently in spreading the propaganda was the National Association of Manufacturers (NAM). Its first president was Samuel Bush, father of Prescott and grandfather of George H.W. Bush. Organizations like NAM served as bridge groups between the rich corporate owners and the public.

NAM and the National Industrial Information Committee picked up the banner of duPont's free enterprise dogma. It was Fulton Lewis Jr. who became the mouthpiece for NAM, his former employer. Using his radio program on the Mutual Network, Lewis spread NAM propaganda to 3 million people daily. Lewis denied the truth put forth by the La Follette and Truman committees, and instead aired NAM's propaganda under the guise of "Your Defense Reporter."[50] At its 1942 convention, NAM went on record in support of duPont's Free Enterprise. The convention adopted a plank of full support for free enterprise, even if it hindered the war effort. In contrast, the 1942 CIO convention went on the record for winning the war first, ahead of any union issues.[51] In other words, labor was willing to make the sacrifices needed to win the war, while big business put profits first.

The Chamber of Commerce and the American Legion served to bridge the gap between workers and the American elite during the 1920s. NAM served a similar role from the 1930s into the 1950s. The top officials of the John Birch Society in the 1950s were all former NAM officials. The Birch Society also acted as a bridge group.

The media were overtly pro-fascist during the 1930s, especially the major newspaper chains. Hearst admired Mussolini and even paid him to write articles for his upstart United Press wire services. Mussolini received $1,750 for each article, an amount equivalent to about $17,000 today. The articles were poorly written by Margherita Sarfatti, Mussolini's mistress.

Hearst attempted to hire Hitler to write for him, too. According to U.S. ambassador to Germany Dodd, Hearst met with Hanfstangel and Rosenberg, two of Hitler's most trusted propagandists, in September 1934 at Baden Baden. After leaving Baden Baden, Hearst traveled to Berlin, where he met personally with Hitler. A deal was sealed between Hearst and Goebbels worth $400,000. After receiving the money, Hearst quickly ordered all of his writers for his International News Service to present all events in Germany in a friendly manner. Following the agreement, Hearst papers printed uncensored propaganda from the Nazis throughout the 1930s.[52] The Hearst press consisted of 25 daily newspapers, 24 weekly newspapers, 12 radio stations, and two world news services. The other major newspaper chains owned by McCormick and Scripps-Howard also presented pro-fascist views.

Many members of the National Publishers Association were also members of NAM. William Warner, publisher of *McCall's* and *Redbook,* was the head of NAM. P.S. Collins represented the Curtis Publishing Co., publisher of the *Saturday Evening Post* and the *Ladies Home Journal*. Collins also was a spokesman for W.D. Fuller, a NAM president. The Luce family publications of *Time, Life* and *Fortune* were closely associated with NAM.

Most people can reach informed and just decisions if provided with a balanced view. However, Seldes pointed out that during the 1930s, with only three or four exceptions, all the large newspaper columnists and radio commentators were right-wing reactionaries.[53]

In their effort to propagandize the American people, omissions were more important than the pro-fascist views the media expressed. For example, the press failed to mention the Senate report investigating airpower. The report concluded: "It is apparent that American aviation companies did their part to assist Germany's air armament. It seems apparent also that there was not an adequate check on the foreign shipments … ."[54]

Part of the evidence included a letter from the president of Curtiss-Wright to his sales agents:

We have been nosing around in the bureau in Washington and find that they hold as most strictly confidential their dive-bombing tactics and procedure, and they frown upon our even mentioning dive-bombing in connection with the Hawks, or any other airplanes to foreign powers.

It is also unwise and unethical at this time, and probably for some time to come, for us to indicate that we know anything about the technique and tactics of dive-bombing.

It may be alright … to put on a dive-bombing show to show the strength of the airplanes — but to refer in contracts to dive-bombing or endeavor to teach dive-bombing is what I am cautioning against doing...[55]

Curtiss-Wright demonstrated its dive-bombing planes in air shows in Europe, helping the Nazis to develop the Stuka. In the first six months of 1933, Pratt & Whitney's sales jumped to almost $1.5 million, as the Nye report exposed the company as one of the largest smugglers of planes to Hitler. Other suppliers of aircraft parts to Hitler in the early years included Curtiss-Wright and Douglas.

Another scandal left unreported was the sale of defective wire by Anaconda. One notable newscaster of the time who failed to report the story was Lowell Thomas. Pew, owner of Sun Oil, sponsored Thomas' broadcasts. Thomas had also worked for NAM.

The *St. Louis Star-Times* accused U.S. Cartridge Co. of producing defective cartridges and had submitted its findings to the Office of Censorship. The AP wire failed to pick up the story and, thus, it went unreported outside the St. Louis area.

The capitalists' strike to delay and reduce war munitions production was blamed on labor. The press made no mention of the Tolan Committee. Testifying before the committee, the United Autoworkers president stated that of 1,577 machine tools, 337 were not in use, and he urged coordination. The autoworkers secretary reported 64 percent machine tool idleness, labeling it a crime against civilization and democracy. These idled tools could have been turning out war material. Any shortage of war material was not the result of a shortage in labor or equipment, but the result of corporate fraud.

The press certainly did not report on the profiteering by corporate America. James Hayes, general counsel for the *ILWU Dispatcher*, testified before the Congressional Merchant Marine subcommittee, giving proof of the obscene profiteering in shipping. Due to the sit-down strike by corporate America, the government was forced to lease private ships. The American Foreign Steamship Corp. made a profit of $895,974 on two voyages. The American Export Line made a profit of $1,572,144 on ships worth only $232,350. The American President Line made a profit of $814,242 on ships worth $307,828 in three trips.

The situation remains unchanged in the 21st century. Columnists and radio mouthpieces are almost all hard right in their views. The news fails to report on the health risks and costs of on-the-job injuries and disease. Whenever new laws are proposed, media coverage comes from the Chamber of Commerce or another pro-business organization. The costs discussed are those to the corporation; no mention is ever made of the costs to the worker.

Today, the media is even more consolidated than in the 1940s; six corporations control more than 80 percent of the airwaves and press. Republicans have repeated the lie that the media are biased to the left so often that many people buy into the mantra, even though the reverse is true. In fact, corporations censor the media. Two-thirds of editors questioned reported that their advertisers threatened to withdraw because of the content of news stories. In a 1992 survey, 75 percent report that large advertisers have tried to influence the content of news stories.

In 1965, a Procter & Gamble executive testified to the Federal Communications Commission that his company would only sponsor programs meeting strict standards: "There will be no material in any of our programs which could in any way further the concept of business as cold, ruthless and lacking all sentiment or spiritual motivation."[56]
At $7.6 billion, P&G's yearly advertising budget is the world's largest.

The anti-union coverage of some of the major strikes in the late 1990s should come as no surprise. Coverage of the UPS strike focused only on how the strike was hurting various businesses. The press made no comments on the cause of the strike, the use of excess part-time workers and the attempted money grab of the union's pension fund, nor on the way corporations have raided pension funds and left retired workers holding an empty bag.

During the GM strike, coverage focused on how the strike was hurting car sales. The press didn't mention how GM violated the terms of the union contract by sneaking the stamping dies out of the plant in the middle of the night over the Memorial Day holiday.

It was thanks to the pro-fascist press and trade organizations that duPont succeeded in creating an illusion of free enterprise as a freedom to be upheld. Bennet and others in the Ford empire openly boasted to Rimar, a former member of the Ford Gestapo, that no newspaper would print his version of the truth during his trial. Indeed, none did and no publisher would take his book *Heil Henry!—The Confession of a Ford Spy*, which contained these statements.

For years I have been one of the key men in the Ford Gestapo. Within the Ford's domain I soon found there was no liberty, no free speech, no human dignity … the vast power of Ford extended into the courts, schools, prisons, clubs, banks, even into the national capital, enveloping us all in a black cloud of suppression and fear.

Our Gestapo covered Dearborn with a thick web of corruption, intimidation and intrigue. The spy net was all embracing. My own agents reported back to me conversations in grocery stores, meat markets and restaurants, gambling joints, beer gardens, social groups, boys' clubs, and even churches.[57]

The quote points out the extent of Ford's anti-union activities and the willingness of corporations to use any means available to spy on and intimidate their workers.

Corporations are now able to access more information than ever about their employees. In this country, corporations are allowed to read the private e-mail and search lockers of employees. Some corporations even maintain the right to search employees' cars parked in a company lot. In effect, American workers must give up all their constitutional rights, including the right to privacy, free speech, and the right to assemble, the minute they walk through the corporate door seeking a job.

Media that are subservient to their advertisers and media divisions owned by defense contractors have helped promote public anti-union sentiment. When OSHA sought to set new workplace standards to prevent repetitive stress injuries, the media aired the views of the Chamber of Commerce, but no information from doctors. No union data was presented to reveal the extent of the problem, the debilitating effects of this menace to employees forced to work at ungodly speed.

In the 60 years following WWII, the Republican Party and far right-wing extremists have adopted the philosophy at the heart of fascism — corporate rule. It is the basis for the intense hatred of unions and working people. In the entire eight years of the Reagan administration, the minimum wage was not raised once, although inflation raged through the early '80s. When he fired the striking PATCO workers, Reagan sent a signal to corporate America that he would not seek prosecution of union busters. The situation improved slightly under President Clinton. However, under George W. Bush, the plight of workers has become acute. He threatened injunctions against unions planning to strike.

An insight into the plight of labor in the '30s comes from the Robert La Follette committee:

The committee found that purchasing and storing arsenals of firearms and tear and sickening gas weapons is a common practice of large employers of labor who refuse to bargain collectively with legitimate labor unions, and that there exists a large business of supplying gas weapons to industry... During the years 1933 through June 1937, $1,255,392.55 worth of tear and sickening gas was purchased by employers and law enforcement agencies, chiefly during or in anticipation of strikes ... all of the largest individual purchasers are corporations and their totals far surpass those of large law-enforcement purchases. In fact the largest purchaser of gas equipment in the country, the Republic Steel Corp., bought four times as much as the largest law-enforcement purchaser.[58]

This was during the Depression, when a new car sold for less than $1,000.

Failing physically to beat labor into submission, the fascists turned to legal tactics, such as the anti-union right-to-work law. Those laws are still highly regarded in right-wing circles today, but few know that the fascist group, Christian America, first sponsored it in the early 1940s.[59] The forces behind the Christian American group were wealthy Texans tied to the Kirby family. Vance Muse formed Christian America after Kirby's death. Both Kirby and Muse had a long history of opposing the New Deal and supporting racism. Muse was an associate of Gerald Smith.

Another member of the Christian America was Lewis Ulrey, who took over the distribution of Gerald Winrod's propaganda, in which he openly advocated a 12-hour workday. Ulrey penned the following for Gerald Winrod's *Defender*:

Into this bedlam and chaos in Germany Adolf Hitler injected himself as a new ... messiah to lead ORDERLY GERMANS from political confusion to SYSTEMATIC UNITY.
Hitler put it up to the Germans to decide between the Jewish ownership and domination of the country or DOMINATION AND OWNERSHIP BY THE NINETY NINE PERCENT OF THE GERMAN POPULATION.
HUMAN NATURE BEING WHAT IT IS, IT IS NOT STRANGE THAT THE GERMANS DECIDED AGAINST THE JEWS AND IN FAVOR OF HITLER.
OUR PRESIDENT HAS SENT TWO INSULTING MESSAGES TO HITLER AND A NUMBER OF HIS PINK CABINETEERS HAVE MOST BLATANTLY AND VIOLENTLY BROADCAST SILLY INSULTS TO THE GERMAN GOVERNMENT.[60]

The Christian America group was the leading lobbyist for right-to-work laws throughout the South and Midwest in the early 1940s. It was well funded and prone to use heavy-handed lobbying tactics on state legislatures. Perhaps the best summary of their tactics comes from a remark by Arkansas Rep. Chambers from Columbia, Ark. On the day of voting for the right-to-work law in that state, he pointed to Val Sherman, the associate director of Christian America, and said, "I'm not branding Mr. Sherman as a disciple of Hitler, but he's a graduate of his school. Hitler would be glad to charter a submarine to Texas and solicit his services."[61]

Others associated with Christian America were Alfred Sloan, CEO of GM; the duPonts; bankers George and Joseph Widener; and Wall Street lawyer Odgen Mills.

It is a common misconception that after the bombing of Pearl Harbor, the pro-fascists folded their tent and went home quietly. Instead, they went underground. In fact, Archibald MacLeish, Librarian of Congress, accused the pro-fascist press, represented mainly by Hearst, Scripts-Howard, McCormick and Patterson, of treason in a speech before the American Society of Newspapers. Even though the speech was broadcast, newspapers failed to cover it, or when they did, they censored it heavily. Although MacLeish did not name anyone, he mentioned treason twice. The follow-up in *The New York Times* deleted those two paragraphs. In many other reports, the mention of treason was deleted and the articles were buried in the back pages.[62]

The 1942 American Newspaper Publishers Association convention voted for a "second front now" and went on to denounce the fascist appeasement forces in America, naming the McCormick-Patterson chain, *The Chicago Tribune, The New York Daily News, The Washington Times-Herald* and the Hearst chain. It accused the American press of anti-unionism, suppressing and slanting the news to fit the publisher's views. William Green, president of the AFL, confirmed the depth of this support for fascism:

Recently a bitter campaign of malicious propaganda to poison the public's mind against organized labor has been carried on by the subsidized press which is composed of reactionary daily newspapers controlled, through ownership and advertising, by exploiting profiteers and union haters. Together with the bourbon politicians, idle rich and anti-labor columnists, they are the real parasites of our country... By peddling falsehoods about labor, the subsidized press is creating factionalism, disunity and class hatred. If Hitler were not so busy running away from a victorious Russian army he would take time to pin medals on the editors and columnist who are misleading the public. The reactionary editors of the newspapers are doing just what Hitler predicted he could accomplish here through his agents.[63]

Congressman Elmer Holland of Pennsylvania characterized Joseph Patterson, owner of the *New York Daily News,* and Eleanor Patterson, owner of the *Washington Times-Herald,* as America's No. 1 and No. 2 exponents of the Nazi propaganda line.[65]

In 1942, *The Chicago Tribune* and part of the McCormick chain were on trial for betraying secrets to the Japanese by publishing the names and locations of the ships in the Battle of Midway, a clear case of treason. The *Tribune* got the information through one of its war correspondents, Stanley Johnson, who was sailing aboard the *New Orleans* en route to Hawaii and had seen a decrypt of JN25 (a Japanese naval code) on the captain's desk. It revealed what the U.S. Navy knew of the Japanese fleet deployment and strategy. The headline in the *Chicago Tribune* published three days after the battle read *"Navy Had Word of Jap Plan to Strike at Sea."* The *Tribune* avoided conviction by claiming that part of the article was false and much of it had been faked. Roosevelt and the Justice Department were hamstrung and could not prosecute the case fully. In a rigorous trial, the government would have had to reveal that it had indeed broken the Japanese naval code. Protecting that secret and the lives of American GIs was worth far more than bringing the traitors to justice.[64]

Tribune owner McCormick was a leading isolationist and vicious Roosevelt hater. He had published the Rainbow 5 top secret battle plans just before Pearl Harbor, in an effort to embarrass Roosevelt and paint him as a war monger.

Congressmen & Seditionists

A common misunderstanding about Roosevelt and the 1930s is lack of awareness of the opposition Roosevelt faced. While he enjoyed tremendous popularity among the electorate, he had many powerful and influential enemies, both in and out of the government.

When it comes to enemies, the Roosevelt and Clinton administrations have several similarities. Clinton was plagued by the vicious smears inspired by Richard Mellon Scaife, while it was Irénée duPont hatching the plots against FDR. Both leaders faced a hostile press and bitter opposition from Republicans. Neither enjoyed much bipartisan support.

The Republicans, many of them openly pro-fascist, opposed Roosevelt's efforts to prepare for the coming war. Roosevelt had many bitter enemies in Congress. Throughout the 1930s, the German Nazis sought a cause that would ignite the native fascists in America and keep the United States out of the war. They mistakenly believed all Americans of German ancestry would rally behind the American Bund and the fascist cause.

The American Bund's connection with the Third Reich was complex. Hitler's top priority was to keep the United States neutral and to preserve at least amicable diplomatic relations. High officials in Berlin were embarrassed by the Bund's rallies, with their bellicose speeches and storm troopers attacking anyone challenging the organization. Most Americans regarded the Bund as financed by and controlled by Berlin.

Hitler banned the Bund from receiving aid from Germany. Nevertheless, funding continued because the Bundesleiter, Fritz Kuhn, proved adept at pitting one Nazi organization against another. Hans Dieckhoff, the German ambassador to the United States and brother-in-law of von Ribbentrop, was one of the Nazis who viewed the Bund as a hindrance to German-American relations. Acting on instructions from Berlin, Dieckhoff ordered all German citizens to withdraw from the Bund in an effort to improve diplomatic relations. He was infuriated to learn that Kuhn got funds from SS Lt. Gen. Werner Lorenz's organization, Volksdeutsche Mittelstelle. At its peak, the Bund probably consisted of no more than 6,500 activists and another 20,000 sympathizers. About 1.5 million Americans were German-born. While the Bund remained a force, it was largely ineffectual as a rallying point for German-Americans, who chose to be loyal to their adopted country.

The Nazis were also unable to exploit the great racial and ethnic differences in America enough to keep the U.S. out of the war, in spite of some successes in provoking Judeophobia and even race riots after the Bund and Klan united. The one cause the German Nazis did find to unify the opposition behind was "Get Roosevelt."[66]

Many but not all of Roosevelt's opponents in Congress were pro-fascist. However, some members of Congress left little doubt of their support for fascism by their actions.

Two of Roosevelt's greatest enemies in Congress were Republican Sen. Gerald Nye from North Dakota and Democratic Rep. Martin Dies from Texas. Both headed congressional committees vital to war preparation. Burton Wheeler of Montana was a close third. All abused their franking privileges, mailing propaganda against the war or even from pro-fascist groups to thousands of constituents.

Nye opposed all major defense measures in the Senate. He led the fight against Lend-Lease, and openly collaborated with many groups seeking appeasement, regardless of their political leanings. On the floor of the Senate, he charged that British — not German — submarines had sunken the *Robin Moor;* only later did he withdraw the baseless charge. He started a probe of Hollywood, but the investigation failed after he admitted that he had not seen the movies that he labeled "war propaganda." He arranged for a Bund member to air his defeatist views before the Senate and later used his congressional frank to mail copies of the speech to thousands. He was one of the biggest boosters of the America First Committee, and praised the virulent Judeophobe Gerald Smith for publishing *The Cross and the Flag.*[67]

Dies, the first chairman of the Committee on Un-American Activities, immediately set out to sabotage the investigations of subversion by pro-fascist groups. His first chief investigator, Edward Sullivan, was exchanging confidential messages with the German High Command in 1938, the year of his appointment. Sullivan was high in the ranks of the Ukrainian-American fascist groups. He greeted members of the Bund with a "Heil Hitler," and denounced FDR's administration as a Jewish Communist plot. He was a former labor spy for the Railroad Audit and Inspection Co. J.B. Sullivan was replaced by Matthews, another right-wing extremist, and on leaving the Dies committee, he immediately rejoined a fascist Ukrainian group.

Instead of examining pro-Nazis, the committee investigated and compiled an extensive blacklist of liberals and antifascists. Throughout the war, the committee carried on a vicious attack on the Roosevelt administration, charging that Reds packed various agencies, and denouncing America's fighting allies.

An example of the opposition Roosevelt faced can be found in the fight over the draft. Nye led the battle and succeeded in greatly reducing what FDR had envisioned. Originally, Roosevelt had planned on two years of universal service for all Americas, in the armed forces or in government agencies. To be fair, support for the draft was bipartisan, as was opposition, which came mainly from the Midwest and northern plains. The bill, passed on Sept. 16, 1940, approved the draft for one year only. The following year, the bill to extend the draft passed the House by a one-vote margin, with 182 Democrats and 21 Republicans voting for, 65 Democrats and 133 Republicans voting against the draft.

One fascistic Congressman was Republican Rep. John Schafer from Wisconsin. His congressional record was one of complete opposition to any defense measure. In an interview with Carlson, an investigative reporter posing as a pro-fascist, Schafer spoke of a revolution against democracy: "The bloody kind. There will be purges and Roosevelt will be cleaned right off the earth along with the Jews. We'll have a military dictatorship to save the country."[68] He belonged to the Steuben Society, a German-American ethnic association.

Republican Rufus Holman from Oregon openly praised Hitler on the floor of the Senate.

I doubt if the right is all on one side among the present belligerents. At least Hitler has broken the control of the international bankers and traders over the rewards for the labor of the common people of Germany.

In my opinion it would be advantageous if the control of the international bankers and traders over the wages and savings and the manner of living of the people of England could be broken by the English people, and if the control of the international bankers and traders over the wages and savings and the manner of living of the people of the United States could be broken by the people of the United States.[70]

Holman also inserted several pro-Nazi propaganda pieces into the Congressional Record. As Oregon's state treasurer, his praise for Hitler's sterilization program resulted in amending the state's sodomy law in 1935 to include all moral degenerates and sexual perverts, whether they committed a crime or not. Oregon at that time used castration rather than vasectomy.[71]

Republican Sen. Thomas Schall from Minnesota entered material in the Congressional Record from James True, a notorious Jew baiter and inventor of the infamous Kike Killer, a nightstick.

Republican Rep. Louis McFadden of Pennsylvania also supported True. McFadden believed in the international Jewish conspiracy, and that Jews were not being persecuted in Germany under Hitler. He was virulent in his opposition to Roosevelt's plan to allow 200,000 Jews to immigrate to the United States. He believed the plan's supporters, like Secretary of Labor Frances Perkins, were part of the conspiracy by the "Jewish-controlled administration." McFadden believed Perkins' real name was that of a Russian Jewess, Matilda Wutski.[72]

Another pro-fascist was Sen. Robert Reynolds, a Democrat from North Carolina, who also openly praised Hitler on the floor of the Senate. Reynolds was a resident of Asheville, the home of Pelly's Silver Shirts. Reynolds spoke glowingly about fascism:

The dictators are doing what is best for their people. I say it is high time we found out how they are doing it, and why they are progressing so rapidly. Hitler has solved the unemployment problem. There is no unemployment in Italy. Hitler and Mussolini have a date with destiny. It is foolish to oppose them so why not play ball with them.[73]

Reynolds was friends with Gerald Winrod and the American Nazi George Deatherage. Backed by Burton Wheeler, he rose to become chairman of the Senate Committee of Military Affairs. In April 1940, Reynolds provided Nazi agent Simon Koedel with detailed confidential information about French ports,[74] an act of treason.

Reynolds believed that aliens were at the heart of all of America's problems, and he organized a posse of youths aged 10–18 called the Border Patrol, to catch alien crooks. He kept his position in the Senate until 1944. By then, the Democratic Party had enough of the fascist infiltrator and chose another figure popular in North Carolina to run for his seat. Rather than face certain defeat, Reynolds retired.

Another fascist supporter in Congress was Democrat Sen. Rush Holt from West Virginia. Holt was the youngest person ever elected to the Senate. He won election in 1934 as a backer of the common man and the New Deal, but soon thereafter, he began criticizing the New Deal, and eventually became one of the harshest critics of FDR. By the end of his term, he was a supporter of fascism. In the 1940 primary, Holt faced two other challengers for his seat after losing support from the Democratic National Committee, and finished third.[75]

The examples of Holt and Reynolds provide a stark contrast between the Democratic and Republican parties. The Democratic Party tried to purge fascists from its ranks in the primary, unlike the Republican Party, which made no such attempts, and even encouraged the Nazis with anti-Semitic campaigns.

Contrary to popular belief, the Japanese attack on Pearl Harbor did not fully unite the country. On Jan. 27, 1942, with the memory of Pearl fresh in everyone's mind, Rep. Clare Hoffman, Republican from Michigan, delivered a vicious attack on Roosevelt. His address to the House was titled "Don't Haul Down the Stars and Stripes," better known as "Roosevelt is Judas." Hoffman, long an outspoken critic of Roosevelt and a member of the Impeach Roosevelt Committee, ordered 145,000 copies of his speech, and used his congressional frank to mail 105,000 copies.[76]

The best evidence showing that several members of Congress had ties to the Nazis came from a Department of Justice investigation that led to the bungled sedition trial of 1944. There is a fine line between free speech and sedition. Simple opposition to war is not sedition, but accepting funds from the enemy to conduct espionage or to spread propaganda clearly steps over the line of free speech.

Grand jury investigations conducted in 1940 produced abundant evidence that several members of Congress received funds from Nazi sources. The sedition trial stemmed from three separate grand jury investigations. The special assistant to the Attorney General William Maloney convened the first on which finished on July 21, 1942, indicting 28 individuals and listing 30 publications and 26 organizations.

Because of intense pressure from several sides, including from Sen. Burton Wheeler, the Justice Department removed Maloney from the investigation. Wheeler used his position as chairman of the Senate Judiciary Committee to exert extreme pressures on Attorney General Biddle for Maloney's removal.

Maloney called several of the pro-Nazi members of Congress to testify before the grand jury. One of the suspected representatives was Ernest Lundeen, the populist senator from Minnesota. Hoover had an FBI agent tailing Lundeen. On Aug. 31, 1940, Lundeen and the FBI agent died in a plane crash. Lundeen's secretary, Harriet Johnson, reported later that on the day of his death, the congressman had arrived unusually early and was clearly distraught. Lundeen told her that he had gone too far and there was no turning back. She sensed he was referring to his Nazi connections. He also told her that, despite a storm, he had to fly back to Minneapolis at once to see his wife.

Johnson then drove Lundeen to the airport, and reported that several times he cried. FBI agent J.J. Pasci followed the pair to the airport and boarded the same plane. Johnson said that after Lundeen boarded, she saw several passengers in a struggle with him. Shortly after takeoff, the pilot lost control of the plane in the storm and crashed just 36 miles west of the capital.

The day after his death, Johnson opened the representative's locked files and discovered many documents that revealed that Lundeen was in the direct pay of the Nazis. The next day, Lundeen's widow arrived and asked by name for the Viereck files. Harriet Johnson then reported it to the FBI, which forwarded it to Maloney.

Maloney only had a partial view of the Nazi connections. He determined that seven senators and 13 representatives had been bribed, or acted in collusion with Nazi Germany, aiding and encouraging them, and that four more members of Congress were guilty of collaboration. These congressmen had used their franking privileges to distribute isolationist speeches, many written or edited by Viereck.[77] Those whom Maloney listed as collaborators with Viereck were Stephen Day (Republican, Illinois), Hamilton Fish (Republican, New York), Rush Holt (Democrat, West Virginia) and Ernest Lundeen (Farmer-Labor, Minnesota).

The remaining 20 were: John Alexander, R-Minnesota; Philip Bennett, R-Missouri; Usher Burdick, R-North Dakota; Worth Clark, D-Idaho ; Cliff Clevenger, R-Ohio; Henry Dworshak, R-Idaho; Clare Hoffman, R-Michigan; Edwin Johnson, D-Colorado ; Bartell Jonlman, R-Michigan; Harold Knutson, R-Minnesota; Robert La Follette, R-Wisconsin; Gerald Nye, R-North Dakota ; Robert Reynolds, D-North Carolina; Paul Shafer, R-Michigan ; Henrik Shipstead, R-Minnesota; William Stratton, R-Illinois; Martin Sweeney, D-Ohio; Jacob Thorkelson, R-Montana; George Tinkham, R-Massachusetts; and Burton Wheeler, D-Montana [78]

The congressmen Maloney listed as dupes of the Nazis have several interesting characteristics. First, members of the Republican Party dominate the list. This should not be surprising because the Republican Party employed known Nazis in election campaigns. Two of the Democrats on the list, Holt and Reynolds, were removed by party leadership.

Most of these members of Congress came from the upper Midwest, especially Minnesota and Michigan where there were strong anti-union movements, and several ministries that preached the Nazi line of hatred of Jews. The Teutonia Association, founded in Detroit on Oct. 12, 1924, was something of a forerunner of the American Bund.

Viereck was the highest-ranking Nazi agent arrested during the two world wars. He was a V-agent or "Vertrauensleute" (confidant) for the Abwehr. Following the war, another exposed V-agent was William Rhodes Davis, the Texas oilman.[79] Very little is known about Viereck and the network of V-agents because the Nazis destroyed most of their files. Documents on most known V-agents suggest they were employed to spread propaganda.

What is certain is that Viereck received more than $500,000 from the charge d'affairs of the German embassy, Thomsen, to bribe, corrupt and undermine members of Congress, and spread propaganda.[80] Viereck also received funds from Hansen Sturm, chairman of the Romanoff Caviar Co., and from General Aniline and Film. Thomsen had valuable friends in high places, including Assistant Secretary of State Breckingridge Long and Ambassador to France William Bullitt. Long had publicly approved Mussolini's invasion of Ethiopia.

Lundeen was secretly pro-Nazi, and received money directly from Viereck, the German Board of Trade and the Steuben Society. Maloney determined that other members of Congress had accepted Nazi money in deals to publish books through the notorious Flanders Hall, a fascist publisher closely associated with Viereck: Burton Wheeler of Montana, Gerald Nye of North Dakota, Jennings Randolph and Rush Holt of West Virginia, and William Stratton of Illinois.

On June 13, 1940, Thomsen reported to Germany that it was necessary to take literary countermeasures against Roosevelt. In this plan, Thomsen contacted New York literary agent William Lengel and proposed a series of five books. One by Theodore Dreiser was to warn of the dangers of intervention, another by Sylvia Porter was to provide a woman's perspective about what the war would mean. The other three were to be written by journalist George Creel, novelist Kathleen Norris and publicist Burton Rascoe. Pearl Harbor preempted the deal before any were written.

In September 1941, Maloney convened a grand jury to investigate the Congressional Nazi connections. The results of the grand jury were classified for years. Viereck was indicted, as was George Hill, a mailroom aide to Hamilton Fish. Maloney was deeply annoyed that he could not get indictments against any congressmen. Once again, the little, expendable people were prosecuted, while the powerful were protected.[81] Many of the congressmen Maloney subpoenaed managed to avoid testifying until after Pearl Harbor. After the attack, public interest was directed to the war effort, and prosecution of the pro-fascists was neglected.

Maloney successfully prosecuted George Hill and was getting ready for Viereck's trial when Judge Allen Goldsborough suddenly told Maloney he only had two weeks to prepare. Goldsborough was associated with the extreme elements of the right wing. Maloney was successful in having Goldsborough replaced after swearing out an affidavit giving details of their meeting and the demand by Viereck's attorney, Daniel Colahan, that Goldsborough handle the case. He also successfully prosecuted Viereck, who received a prison term of two to six years. On March 20, presiding Judge Letts reduced Hill's sentence. One year later, the Supreme Court reversed Viereck's conviction, and both he and Hill were set free.

Although no charges were brought against the pro-Nazi members of Congress, their plot was exposed. Nonetheless, they continued to use their franking privileges to spread pro-Nazi propaganda. After Pearl Harbor it was not possible for them to do so directly, and they used organizations like the Republican Nationalist Revival Committee, the National Economic Council, or *Western Voice,* edited by fundamentalist minister Harvey Springer from Engle–wood, Colo. Springer, "the cowboy preacher," praised fascist Gerald Smith as a real man of Christ and denounced the Federal Council of Churches as dominated by communists. He was also a vicious Judeophobe, but is still highly regarded as a theologian in Baptist circles.

One of the more striking aspects of the history of fascism in the United States was the removal of people like Maloney from office. Maloney was relentless in his pursuit of native fascists. After getting indictments on July 21, 1942 against 28 suspects, he was depicted as a stooge of the International Jewish bankers by Joe Kamp, a pro-Nazi propagandist. Sen. Burton Wheeler demanded that Attorney General Biddle remove Maloney. When Biddle objected to such pressure, Wheeler announced he would blow the whistle on the Department of Justice. It is unknown what leverage Wheeler had on the Department of Justice, but Biddle immediately dismissed Maloney and made it clear that he could not act even as a consultant to his successor.[82] His successor, John Rogge, was a capable and able prosecutor who handled the sedition trial in 1944. He also was abruptly removed.

Without exception, those who sought to expose the fascists and bring them to trial were forced from office or otherwise discredited. Gen. Butler, who exposed the fascist plot against Roosevelt, was mocked in the press in a successful effort to discredit him. Meanwhile openly pro-fascist operators continued to rise in power.

Of the three separate grand jury indictments, the third listed the most organizations and publications for sedition, but certain organizations were dropped from the third list:

The America First Committee

National Committee to Keep America Out of Foreign Wars (a group associated with Fish)

Citizens Committee to Keep America Out of War

Make Europe Pay War Debts (a Viereck committee)

War Debts Defense Committee (a Viereck committee)

Coalition of Patriotic Societies

Crusading Mothers of America

Citizens No Foreign War Coalition

Constitutional Education League
We, the Mothers United
We, the Mothers, Mobilize for America [83]

Those names of those indicted by the three different grand juries also differed.

Indictments returned on July 21,1942	Indictments returned on Jan. 4, 1943	Indictments returned on Jan. 3, 1944[84]
Court Asher	Court Asher	***
David J. Baxter	David J. Baxter	David J. Baxter
Otto Brennermann	Otto Brennermann	***
H.V. Broenstrupp	H.V. Broenstrupp	H.V. Broenstrupp
Oscar Brumback	Oscar Brumback	***
Prescott F. Dennett	Prescott F. Dennett	Prescott F. Dennett
C. Leon De Aryan	C. Leon De Aryan	***
Hudson de Priest	Hudson de Priest	***
Hans Diehel	Hans Diehel	Hans Diehel
Elizabeth Dilling	Elizabeth Dilling	Elizabeth Dilling
Robert E. Edmondson	Robert E. Edmondson	Robert E. Edmondson
Elmer J. Garner	Elmer J. Garner	Elmer J. Garner
James F. Garner	James F. Garner	***
William Griffin	William Griffin	***
Charles R. Hudson	Charles R. Hudson	Charles R. Hudson
Ellis O. Jones	Ellis O. Jones	Ellis O. Jones
William Kullgren	William Kullgren	***
Wm. R. Lyman Jr.	Wm. R. Lyman Jr	Wm. R. Lyman Jr.
Donald McDaniel	Donald McDaniel	***
Robert Noble	Robert Noble	Robert Noble
William D. Pelly	William D. Pelly	William D. Pelly
Eugene Sanctuary	Eugene Sanctuary	Eugene Sanctuary
Herman M. Schwinn	Herman M. Schwinn	Herman M. Schwinn
Edward J. Smythe	Edward J. Smythe	Edward J. Smythe
Ralph Townsend	Ralph Townsend	***
James C. True	James C. True	James C. True
George S. Viereck	George S. Viereck	George S. Viereck
Gerald B. Winrod	Gerald B. Winrod	Gerald B. Winrod
***	Frank W. Clark	Frank W. Clark
***	G.E. Deatherage	G.E. Deatherage
***	Frank K. Fernenx	Frank K. Fernenx
***	New York Enquirer	***
***	P. de Shishmareff	***
***	Lois de Lafayette Washborn	Lois de Lafayette Washborn
***	***	Garland Alderman
***	***	Lawrence Dennis
***	***	Ernest F. Elmhurst
***	***	August Klapprott
***	***	Joe E. McWilliams
***	***	E.J. Parker Sage

The common thread among the organizations dropped from the list was association with certain members of Congress. Several of the members listed above, including Fish and Wheeler, and many prominent business leaders were closely associated with the America First Committee. The National Committee to Keep America Out of Foreign Wars was also close to Fish. The two groups associated with Viereck could have opened charges against many of the congressmen above. Wheeler as chairman on the Senate Judiciary Committee brought strong pressure on Attorney General Biddle. A trial would have exposed all those connected to additional charges of sedition. The big fascists had to be protected.

The end to the prosecution of seditionists and Nazi collaborators came with the death of Judge Eicher on Nov. 30, 1944 in the midst of the trial. The next morning, the new judge declared a mistrial. The trial had been delayed and disrupted by the defendants since its start in February.

Rogge, like Maloney, was relentless in his pursuit of Nazi supporters. In spring 1946, he received news from U.S. Army Capt. Sam Harris, a member of the prosecuting team at Nuremberg, of indisputable evidence linking the former Nazi government with leading citizens of the United States. On April 4, Attorney General Tom Clark allowed Rogge and four aides to fly to Germany. Over the course of 11 weeks, Rogge and his team questioned 66 people, including Goering and Ribbentrop, and dozens of other top Nazi officials, including friends of William Davis. Rogge's findings were decisive and explosive:

> Our investigation showed us that we had completely underestimated the scope and scale of Nazi activities in the United States. When I went to Germany I felt that the biggest threat to American democracy emanated from the machinations of persons like the defendants in the sedition trial (i.e. the little fascist crackpots). I found that a far more dangerous threat lay in the inner-connection between German and American industrialists, and that some of the best known names in America were involved in Nazi intrigue.[85]

On returning to the United States, Rogge started preparing a comprehensive report for Attorney General Clark. In July, Rogge submitted the first draft. Clark was clearly distraught over the references linking business and political leaders with the defeated Nazi government. Clark specifically mentioned the links to Sen. Burton Wheeler, a close friend. A Clark aide then asked that he omit all names of American politicians and business leaders. Rogge refused, already realizing the report would never be published.

On Sept. 17, 1946, Rogge submitted the final draft with the explosive recommendation that the Department of Justice open an investigation of collaboration between American and Nazi industrialists before the war. Not surprisingly, Clark refused to publish it. However, to Rogge's surprise, within days Drew Pearson's column published portions of his report.

Shortly after, Rogge was granted a two-week leave of absence to make a lecture tour on the fascist menace. Clark was adamant that Rogge not mention his report. Speaking before an audience at Swarthmore College, Rogge revealed some of his discoveries. He stated that Goering and Rubbentrop told him that John L. Lewis, William Rhodes Davis, Sen. Burton Wheeler, former Vice President James Garner, former Postmaster General James Farley, and former President Herbert Hoover had all conspired with the Nazis to defeat Roosevelt in the 1940 election and to keep the United States out of the war.

On Oct. 25, Rogge left from New York on a flight bound for Seattle. Due to bad weather, the flight made an unscheduled stop in Spokane. There, an FBI agent named Mr. Savage handed Rogge a terse dismissal letter from Tom Clark. The day before, Sen. Wheeler had met with President Truman and demanded Rogge be fired. Wheeler was concerned Rogge's charges would derail his hopes for an appointment to the federal bench.[86] Wheeler never did get the appointment.

Maloney and Rogge suffered the identical fate because of their staunch opposition to fascism. The fascists in the government were too strong to allow an investigation into their treasonous acts. Only a few cries of protest were ever voiced in the press about Rogge's dismissal. To further discredit the relentless Nazi hunter, the fascists besmirched his brilliant and honorable career by labeling him a communist. FBI

Director J. Edgar Hoover himself was giving speeches around the country denouncing various Americans as communists, with little or no evidence to back the charges.

There was little attempt to prosecute traitors or Nazi war criminals after the war. A brazen example was that of Martin Monti, one of Father Coughlin's followers. Monti was drafted and sent to Italy. On Oct. 13, 1944, he stole a P38 aircraft and flew it across German lines, landing in Milan. He surrendered to the Germans and offered to help them. They transferred him to Berlin, where he broadcast pro-Nazi propaganda, often quoting Father Coughlin. After the war, he was court-martialed for desertion and theft of the plane. The normal sentence in such cases was death, but Monti received a 15-year suspended sentence. He reenlisted as a private and by 1946, had risen to the rank of sergeant.[87]

The Allied armies won the war in Europe against fascism, but the United States was losing it at home. In their rabid hatred of communism, the native fascists now plotted the Cold War. Everyone was needed to fight the new menace, and justice for old scores could be sacrificed.

The Pro-Nazis of the 1930s

After the fall of France, a speech by Lindbergh aroused the fiery Secretary of Interior Harold Ickles to form his own investigation committee exposing Nazi propaganda. T.H. Tetens headed this group. The three-member task force soon presented Ickles with shocking evidence that Nazis in Germany were financing far-right groups in the U.S., including the Christian Mobilizers, Silver Shirts, Father Coughlin and others. Ickles presented the evidence to the attorney general and in the next year, these groups found themselves under investigation. FDR knew of Ickles' plan and encouraged selective leaks to the media and to the FBI.[88]

A good example is George Eggleston. In 1941, he began publishing *Scribner's Commentator,* a mass-circulated magazine secretly subsidized by the German embassy. Eggleston had access to laundered funds from the estate of Charles Payson, a millionaire admirer of Lindbergh. He located his publishing headquarters at Lake Geneva, N.Y. There, he received instructions from Germany via short-wave radio for a second publication he undertook, *The Herald.* It was even more pro-Nazi and smacked of Goebbelsian propaganda. It impressed Thomsen, charge d'affaires of the German Embassy, who wanted to get it into the hands of American soldiers.

Following Pearl Harbor, the America First Committee officially disbanded. However, at a Dec. 17, 1941 meeting in the home of Sibley Webster, a wealthy Wall Street broker, a few key America First members, including Charles Lindbergh, reformed under a new name, Americans for Peace. The following quote from that meeting is from Horace Haase.

> It is obviously necessary for the leaders of the America First like Wood and Webster to keep quiet. But the organization should not be destroyed. I have never been in the limelight and have nothing to lose. I can remain active in a quiet way. I should like to offer to keep the files. We must get ready for the next attack which must be made upon this communistic administration.[89]

Four days after the Japanese attack on Pearl Harbor, the National Copperheads, a West Coast group closely associated with the America First Committee, met in Los Angeles. Appearing before the meeting, Ellis Jones stated that "the Japanese have a right to Hawaii. I would rather be in this war on the side of Germany than on the side of the British."[90]

Thus began the battle for the minds of the people. Similar calls, combined with cries to impeach Roosevelt, were repeated across America. Many followers, sensibilities firmly offended, deserted the pro-fascist groups in droves. However, the hard-core fascists and their leaders resorted to a whispering campaign to destroy the morale of the soldiers and the public. Among the often-heard comments: Our armed forces are weak. The war will bankrupt the nation. The Chinese and British will make a separate peace with Japan and Germany. Stalin is getting too strong, and Bolshevism will sweep over Europe.

Pro-fascist newspaper chains went into overdrive after the Pearl Harbor attack: "This great war seems to be in the hands of inexperienced civilians who have proven uniformly unsuccessful in managing the country's affairs in time of peace, and are now displaying a more dangerous incompetence in time of war... Of course Russia is not a full partner of the United Nations. She is a semi-partner of the Axis." (Hearst's *New York Journal-American*, March 17, 1942)[91]

But starting in February 1942, the pro-Nazis had their hopes dashed. There was no panic in America, just anger directed at the Axis nations and their conspirators, and fifth column agents inside the country. Beginning that month, the FBI arrested and sent to prison several unregistered agents for Germany, the most notable being Laura Ingalls. By April, the postal service banned Father Coughlin's *Social Justice* and William Pelly's *The Galilean* newsletters because of seditious content. Special grand juries met across America to investigate propaganda and seditious acts.

The opposition to the war climaxed on July 23, 1942 when the Department of Justice indicted 27 men and one woman for sedition, although the legal process was sabotaged at the highest levels. Some were found guilty and sentenced to jail terms, including Pelly (in another trial). Dilling and others were found innocent. A review of the list reveals that none of the real leaders or financial backers was brought to justice. Those indicted were low-level leaders, or mere noisy gadflies. The only trial that ever charged any of the real leaders was the one previously mentioned against the *Chicago Tribune*. After 60 years, only a few of the names of those indicted warrant more than a footnote in history.

One of those indicted, William Dudley Pelly and his group, the Silver Shirts, warrant a closer look. Pelly founded the Silver Shirts on Jan. 31, 1933 in Asheville, N.C., the day Hitler took power in Germany. He described it as a Christian militia. Throughout the '30s and until Pelly's indictment for sedition, the Silver Shirts were one of the largest and most violent pro-Nazi groups. Pelly was the son of a Methodist minister who believed that Jews were the children of Satan.[92] He acquired his intense hate for Jews from White Russians during his missionary work with the American Expeditionary Force in Russia at the end of WWI. This hatred was later reinforced when Pelly was fired as a Hollywood screenwriter.

Due to their extreme racism and Judeophobia, the Silver Shirts became popular in areas of the country where the Klan was strong during the 1920s, especially in the Pacific Northwest, where they filled the void left after the Klan split apart in Oregon and Washington. The Silver Shirts were openly pro-Hitler, and formed alliances with the American Bund and the Klan.

If not for their lingering influence on fascist groups in America, they would be as forgettable as any of the more than 700 fascist groups from the 1930s. However, many of today's far-right groups can trace their ancestry to the Silver Shirts. Posse Comitatus founder Henry Lamont Beach was a leader of the Silver Shirts in Oregon. Richard Butler, founder of the Aryan Nations in Hayden Lake, Idaho, was a Silver Shirter and Klansman.[93] Butler still used the Nazi salute at Hayden Lake years after the end of the war.[94]

Gerald L. K. Smith, one of the founders of today's Christian Identity, was perhaps the most influential former Silver Shirt. Identity religion, the belief that the Aryans are the real descendants of the Hebrew tribes, is a common bond among many right-wing extremist groups today,[95] such as the Posse, the Aryan Nations, and many militias and Klan groups.

Religious fundamentalism, intolerance and blinding hatred of minorities link today's right-wing extremists to the fascists groups of the 1930s. Much of the hate today goes back to those ministries of hate . Today's televangelists hark back to the 1930s. The medium may have changed from radio to television, but the style is the same Father Coughlin used. The number of listeners to his radio broadcasts and followers in his organizations reached into the millions. His sermons were filled with virulent hatred of Jews, communism and Roosevelt. Pat Robertson, Jerry Falwell or any of the other televangelists follow the same format today. Only today, they carefully disguise their hatred for Jews and substitute hate for gays, welfare, abortion, unions or any other liberal program designed to help the poor or workingman. And, of course, Clinton and other liberals have replaced Roosevelt as objects of their scorn.

Coughlin was the most influential of all the preachers during the '30s. He commanded the largest following, and was something of a central figure or uniter of the various groups. One such group of followers was the Christian Crusade, whose goal was to establish a so-called Christian government, modeled on the corporate-clerical state of Franco.[96] Other groups associated with him were the Christian Front, many of the various mothers' groups, and the America First Committee. Politically, Coughlin opposed aid to Britain, the draft and any bill that would be a deterrent to Germany and Hitler. His opposition often bordered on sedition, although he was never charged. His ministry of hate ended with the attack on Pearl Harbor.

Three other ministers of hate from this period deserve special mention — Gerald Smith, Gerald Winrod and Wesley Swift. Swift, who had direct connections to the Nazis, is credited with leading the Identity movement. He also was a member of the Klan. Billy Hargis, who later gained fame in the 1950s and early '60s, was a Winrod associate.

Both Winrod and Smith were Coughlin disciples. Winrod came close to winning election as a senator from Kansas and, at that time, was often called the Jayhawk Nazi. Smith closely associated with Huey Long and, after his death, tried to take over the governor's political machine. Smith also was a member of Pelly's Silver Shirts.

Although Coughlin was the most widely recognized religious figure from the Nazi movement during the '30s, Gerald K. Smith may have been the most influential in the long term. Smith was well known in the 1930s, and though he did not have as large a following as Coughlin, his influence is seen in many right-wing groups today.

Smith was an assistant in Coughlin's Christian Front and an associate of Henry Ford. He was an ordained minister in the Disciples of Christ Church and a virulent Judeophobe who gained notoriety by staging a Passion Play in Louisiana. While Coughlin disappeared from the national scene by the end of the war, Smith went on to found the Christian Defense League (CDF), a survivalist offshoot of the Klan. The CDF pamphlet, *The Cross and the Flag,* was among the first to present the Identity religion.

One of Smith's assistants in his Christian Anti-Communist Crusade was Wesley Swift, widely regarded as an icon of the Identity religion today. Swift was one of the first to assert a need for paramilitary groups, and he formed the racist California Rangers, a core group of the Minutemen. He also founded the Church of Jesus Christ-Christian in 1946. Later, after a disagreement with Butler, he moved his hate ministry to Hayden Lake, Idaho, where it formed the basis of varied racist groups, such as the Aryan Nations and the former order.

Swift associate Col. William Gale ran for governor of California in 1958 on a pro-segregation ticket, and was a former aide to Douglas MacArthur. He also founded a church based on the Identity religion, the Ministry of Christ. Gale was a founder of the Posse Comitatus. Both Swift and Gale recruited Richard Butler, the head of the Aryan Nations.[97]

This clear line of succession from Smith to the present sets up an irrefutable link between the pro-Nazis of the 1930s and the far-right groups of today.

The association between fascism and religion extended beyond the fringe religious hacks of the 1940s and included mainstream religion. For example, the Southern Baptist leader and minister M. E. Dodd of Louisiana made headlines for attending the 1934 Baptist World Convention in Berlin. Dodd was an extreme racist who praised the Nazis. Dodd justified Hitler's Gestapo tactics by linking Jews with communism.[98] He considered the Jews in Germany to be outside agitators similar to racial agitators in the South. To be fair, some Baptists did denounce the Nazis, but the Alabama Baptists followed Dodd's views.

Dodd also was the first Baptist minister to preach a sermon over the airwaves on Jan. 5, 1941.[99] With people like Dodd holding leading positions of authority in the South, it should not be surprising that until the 1960s, the churches were a bulwark of segregation. Dodd's views on Jews may linger on with

Southern Baptists, who attended the 1997 Fourth Annual Super Conference of Christian Israel Churches in 1997. Pastor Everett Ramsey of the Faith Baptist Church of Houston, Mo. hosted this conference promoting the Identity religion.[100] This close association with the Identity religion led to the recent announcement by the Baptists to try to convert Jews to Christianity.[101] Jewish leaders have described the proscribed guidelines of this Southern Baptist conversion as insulting and condescending.

Many of the far-right groups today are trying to distance themselves from their racist roots or at least cloak them to attract followers, yet the the common bond of the Aryan Identity religion remains.

There are other sources for today's racism, including the alliance between the Klan and the American Bund in the 1930s. Some have credited this alliance with the increase in violence in the Identity movement. Nevertheless, the Klan is a mere shadow of its former self. One should not dismiss the threat posed by Klansmen, but from a political point of view, they are marginal now. A Gallup Poll released on July 27, 1970 showed that only 3 percent of the public viewed the Klan favorably, while 75 percent regarded the Klan in an unfavorable light.[102] In the 1980s, that favorable number probably rose slightly with the increase in right-wing extremist groups, but for most Americans, the Klan is still a pariah.

A greater source of concern is the Pioneer Fund, a group that had direct links to Hitler and the Nazis. In 1937, Wickliffe Draper, heir to the giant textile machinery manufacturer, Draper Corp., established the Fund. Draper was an extreme racist and a staunch anti-unionist as early as the days of the Sacco and Vanzetti trial of the 1920's. Other objects of his hatred were the United Nations, John Kennedy, the Nye Committee and liberals. His hatred for the members of the Nye Committee for trying to charge the duPonts with war profiteering led to his deliberate persecution of Alger Hiss between 1948–51.

Draper and associate Harry Laughlin created The Model Eugenics Laws in America, which Hitler used to write the Nuremberg Laws. In 1936, Laughlin received an honorary degree from the University of Heidelburg. Both Draper and Laughlin advocated the involuntary sterilization of institutionalized Americans. Twenty-four states adopted such laws that led directly to sterilizing more than 75,000 Americans.[103]

However, the real danger of the Pioneer Fund is in the political clout and financial backing it has to spread racism. Among the original directors of the Pioneer Fund who supported the policies of eugenics was John Marshall Harlan II. Eisenhower appointed Harlan to the Supreme Court in 1957.[104]

On Sept. 12, 1963, the Mississippi State Sovereignty Commission received notice from Morgan Guaranty Trust Co. that it received an anonymous gift of $100,000 to fight against civil rights. Additional money was forthcoming from the Pioneer Fund and used in a broadside attack on civil rights. The Pioneer Fund also was a source of funding for anti-bussing programs.[105] It is also the source of much of the funding for book titles like *The Bell Curve*, a piece of racist drivel disguised as science. *The Bell Curve* is inherently false and used much of the work provided by the Pioneer Fund. One of the chief beneficiaries of the Pioneer Fund has been Roger Pearson, who is closely linked to the Liberty Lobby. In addition, the Pioneer Fund was one of the driving forces behind Proposition 187, the anti-alien measure on the 1994 California ballot. Presently, two noteworthy Republican politicians are linked with the Pioneer Fund: Jesse Helms [106] and Steve Forbes.[107]

After 30 years, it is difficult to find direct links in any political group. People die and ideology evolves, and, at best, one can only show an evolving linkage. Yet in this case, the linkage is direct, with Draper still expounding his racist Nazi views.

The Pioneer Fund was established on racial hate and remains an institution based on hate. An example from the 1930s comes from a member of the Mother's Movement, Lucinda Benge. Benge charged that white sailors were given blood transfusions from blacks and "Orientals," making them ill and likely to father black or yellow children.[108]

One of the most influential right-wing political groups today was formed from the remnants of three fascist groups of the 1930s. The American Security Council (ACS) was constituted in 1955 by members of the pro-fascist America First Committee, the American Vigilante Intelligence Federation, and the American Coalition of Patriotic Societies.[109] The American Vigilante organization was the product of the notorious pro-fascist Harry Jung, while the Coalition of Patriotic Societies was closely associated with eugenics and the Pioneer Fund. The American Vigilant Intelligence Foundation, founded in 1927, collected large sums of money from such corporate donors as Sears, A.B. Dick, International Harvester and First National Bank.[110] The person most responsible for establishing the America First Committee and ACS was the reactionary head of Sears Roebuck, retired Gen. Robert Wood.

The America First Committee was the brainchild of a young Yale College student, Douglas Stuart Jr., the son of the first vice president of Quaker Oats. The nut never drops far from the tree, as Quaker Oats was a later member of ACS. One of the founding members of the Church League was a vice president of Quaker Oats. Stuart attended the 1940 Republican Party convention and consorted with the isolationists.

Charles Lindbergh had already shown interest in Stuart's idea of uniting all opposition to the forthcoming war under one umbrella group. With Lindbergh's advice, the young Stuart sought aid from Gen. Wood, a strong isolationist and apologist for Hitler. Soon after, the America First Committee incorporated, with Wood at the helm. William H. Regnery was one of the signers of the incorporation.[111]

Big business leaders underwrote the America First group and John Foster Dulles wrote the charter. Eight business leaders supplied more than $100,000 each, including H. Smith Richardson and William H. Regnery. Both Regnery Publishing Co. and the Smith Richardson Foundation played prominent roles in the effort to derail the Clinton administration.

William R. Castle, a former under secretary of state under Hoover, also was instrumental in launching the America First Committee. Castle was a scion of a wealthy family from Hawaii. He believed that only the wealthy should serve in the diplomatic corps. Castle opposed sending any aid to China, despite Japanese aggression there. Former President Hoover remained a secret member of the committee.

The America First Committee was not founded to help the Nazis, but under Gen. Wood's direction, the group soon let pro-Nazis join, including Dudley's Silver Shirts and Klan members, and it became the mouthpiece of their propaganda. Even Laura Ingalls, the Nazi agent, was a member. Ralph Townsend, who held a leadership role in San Francisco, also was a paid agent of the Japanese government. Garland Alderman was in a leadership role in Michigan, and was a member of the Nazi-inspired National Workers League. He was later indicted on sedition charges. Dellmore Lessard was the Oregon chairman of the America First Committee, but was forced to resign after it was disclosed he had accepted funds from the Nazi-controlled Kyffhaeuserbund.[112] The America First Committee was successful in bringing many of the pro-fascist groups under one umbrella group.[113]

America First grew quickly, reaching a membership of around 800,000, thanks in part to wealthy founders and slick promotion. It benefited from the publicity operations of Quaker Oats, Sears and Hormel. Thanks to the ties with Hormel, the large advertising firm of Batton, Barton, Durstine and Osborn also contributed to the group's promotion.

FDR had his own sources of intelligence about America First. One was Walter Winchell, who told Roosevelt learned that Thomas Dewey was negotiating to take over the group. Dewey's presidential ambitions forced him to back off and distance himself somewhat.[114]

Such background on the America First Committee makes it difficult to defend as a patriotic organization. However, in a venom-laced diatribe in response to former mayor of New York Ed Koch, perennial presidential candidate Pat Buchanan did just that. Buchanan himself has other embarrassing ties to fascism. In his response, Buchanan named four people who signed a recruiting poster for the America First Committee at Yale Law School: Bob Stuart, Eugene Loche, Potter Stewart and Gerald Ford. He also listed three other members: Sen. Peter Dominick, Sargent Shriver and Kingman Brewster.[115]

Brewster later became president of Yale, a university that has employed former Nazi war criminals. At Yale, Brewster appointed Tracy Barnes as a special assistant for community relations. Barnes, an OSS operations officer during the war, resigned from a high-level CIA position to accept the offer. At the CIA, Barnes organized the overthrow of the Arbenz government of Guatemala and selected E. Howard Hunt as his political officer for the team.[116]

William Regnery also was one of the founders of the American Security Council; his son, Henry, later replaced him. The American Security Council had a great influence on the Reagan administration, and on many of the more hotly debated issues of the 1950s–1980s. Regnery and two other isolationists began broadcasting "Human Events" and, in 1947, started Regnery Publishing. Interestingly enough, the first two titles published by Regnery were critical of the Nuremberg Trials. The third was another pro-Nazi book attacking the Allied air campaign. In 1954, Regnery published two books for the John Birch Society. He also was the publisher of William F. Buckley Jr.'s *God and Man at Yale*. According to Howard Hunt, the CIA subsidized Regnery Publishing because of its pro-Nazi stance.

Henry Regnery and Bunker Hunt funded Western Goals, an organization that is now dead. Western Goals reportedly compiled lists of people judged subversive. In 1986, Reagan appointed Alfred Regnery to help dismantle the Justice Department's Office of Juvenile Justice.[117] In the 1990s, the Regnery publishing house released many venomous smears attacking President Clinton.

Few Americans know about the concerted efforts of the Nazis to create domestic turmoil in the United States. Fewer still know about the fascist plot to overthrow Roosevelt, or understand how the indigenous fascist groups of the 1930s still exert influence on our daily lives and the political climate.

Hitler's dream of uniting all German-Americans under the fascist American Bund was a resounding failure because most chose to remain loyal to their adopted country. Hitler's grandiose plan of creating widespread racial strife met with only limited success. The Detroit, Michigan and Beaumont, Texas race riots were both inflamed by the Nazi-affiliated Klan and other fascist groups. Hitler must have been overjoyed to see Republicans conduct vicious anti-Jewish campaigns in several states.

In this brief look at the fascists in the 1930s, fewer than 20 of the more than 700 fascist groups operating in the '30s have been covered in any depth. Many of these groups received money directly from Nazi Germany and from the same wealthy industrialists who were knowingly building the Third Reich's war machine.

The fascist influence extends to this day in the form of anti-labor legislation, such as the right-to-work laws and the Taft-Hartley Act. Both have direct connections with fascism. Right-to-work laws were passed largely due to lobbying efforts of the fascist group Christian America. Republican House member Fred Hartley was an open advocate of Japan and Germany in the halls of Congress right up to the moment Pearl Harbor was bombed. Today, the United States is the only major Western government that outlaws a general strike, and is in violation of UN policy on unions and labor. General strikes are commonplace in France and the rest of Europe. This extreme anti-labor agenda is still readily obvious today in the Republican Party.

Hitler's greatest success in creating domestic unrest came in the halls of Congress. Under the banner of isolationism or pacifism, many conservatives in both parties were openly pro-fascist, and were influential in delaying war production and aid to the Allies. Several pro-Nazi members of Congress received funds directly from Nazi Germany, others indirectly through Viereck and Flanders Hall in the form of royalties for books.

Clear evidence has been established of collusion between the high-ranking officials of the Republican Party and known Nazi agitators in every election year throughout the 1930s.

As John Rogge learned in Europe, the Nazi infiltration was much more extensive than he had believed as prosecuting attorney for the sedition trial. He learned that ex-President Herbert Hoover, a former vice-president of FDR, a United States senator and other high-ranking officials conspired with the Nazis to prevent Roosevelt's election in 1940.

Earlier, Gen. Smedley Butler suffered the same fate after revealing the fascist plot against Roosevelt. The press labeled him a crackpot for saving the country from fascism. This pattern of dismissal of those who strongly opposed fascism was repeated time and again. By 1943, with the Nazis clearly defeated on the battlefields of Europe, it reached epidemic proportions. Meanwhile, the careers of those who aided the Nazis steadily advanced.

An exhaustive review of all the fascist groups of the 1930s is beyond the scope of any single book. Further review of these groups would only confirm the findings so far and expose more. In this brief chapter, the roots of today's far right-wing groups have been traced back to the fascist groups of the 1930s. Most notably, the American Security Council that exerted a large influence on the Reagan administration was formed from remnants of three pro-Nazi groups. Other groups, such as the Aryan Nations and the Posse Comitatus, have their roots in the fascism of the 1930s.

Some of the connections made in this chapter may be more embarrassing than ideological, particularly the link between Gerald Ford and America First. Other figures like Regnery consistently confirmed their fascist ideology. The mention of a group does not imply that all its members are fascist ideologues, but that a significant element of the organization is either fascist or predisposed to fascist ideology.

One of the greatest deterrents to exposing further connections is that so much evidence is classified as secret in government vaults. The efforts of Congresswoman Elizabeth Holtzman to have all documents from that era open to public scrutiny should be applauded.

After passage of the 1998 Nazi War Crimes Disclosure Act, three million pages of previously classified documents have been released. Those released in April 2001 included documents on Emil Augsburg, a member of the Wannsee Institute, the Nazi think tank that plotted the massacre of Jews. Augsburg became part of the Gehlen network of ex-Nazis employed by the CIA after the war, when he should have been tried as a war criminal. With each release of additional files, a clearer picture will emerge of the relationship between the CIA and the Nazis, of how vast the fascist network was, and how justice was subverted.[118]

What these documents may reveal is best summed up by the Nazi War Criminals Interagency Working Group, a site maintained by the U.S. government:

> Clearly the information contained in these still classified files will prove to be embarrassing to our government. In the name of containing Soviet aggression, many hard-core, high-ranking Nazis were welcomed into the camp of the Western Allies. Men like *General Adolf Heusinger,* who served as Deputy Chief of Operations and Planning for the entire German armed forces. A man so close to Hitler that he was literally standing next to him on July 20, 1944 when the room they were in blew up in what ultimately proved to be a failed assassination attempt. * Nevertheless, Heusinger was welcomed by the Western Allies after the surrender and rose to new heights in the postwar period when, on April 1, 1961, his appointment as Chairman of the Permanent Military Committee of "NATO" with an office in the Pentagon was announced by none other than President John F. Kennedy.[119]

The second deterrent comes from the media itself, both the popular broadcasting networks and the publishers, and their lack of enthusiasm, respectively outright sabotaging of efforts to expose the connections. The Internet has put a dent in the propaganda monopoly of the corporate-owned popular media and press. This is a two-edged sword, with far-right groups quick to adapt to new technologies. Nevertheless, even now there are those who advocate censorship of the Net. We must help fight to keep the Internet free of both government and private censorship.

Hitler did not rise to power in a revolution. As Huey Long once remarked, "Of course we will have fascism in America, but we will call it democracy!"

Chapter 5,
The War Years

Magic and Pearl Harbor

Sept. 1, 1939, the day Hitler unleashed his Panzer tanks against Poland, marked the formal beginning of World War II. For another six years, a brutally savage war lashed the European continent, in a conflict so horrific that millions perished; reportedly six million Jews died in the Holocaust alone. With the aid of new technology, an entire civilian population was targeted for destruction. War spread into North Africa and China, and engulfed the South Pacific.

No single event of the 20th century brought forth more geopolitical changes than WWII. Almost every European country saw a change in government during or after the war. New governments and nations were born worldwide as the British Empire dissolved. The United States was propelled from a second-tier nation to a superpower and world leader.

War brought forth a sea of changes within the United States, too. As the only Allied country to escape large-scale damage, the United States catapulted into the role of an economic powerhouse. Moreover, with the fears of the Red menace reignited, the U.S. bid farewell to an isolationist policy, choosing an interventionism verging on imperialism. For the first time, the United States kept a large standing army.

For Americans, the war did not begin until Dec. 7, 1941, the "day of infamy." It was a two-front war, perhaps best symbolized by the Marines raising the flag on Mount Suribachi and GIs wading ashore at Normandy. The war meant ration cards, collection drives for scrap metal and other materials in short supply, and images of Rosie the Riveter. It is this home front of the war that is grossly misunderstood by Americans today. Most Americans mistakenly believe the country was totally united in its war efforts, yet nothing could be further from the truth, as we saw in Chapter 4.

To understand the many events of WWII, both on the battlefield and on the home front, a brief look at the Allies' deadliest weapon is needed, too. The marks of this weapon were behind every headline throughout the war, and traces of it were even found in domestic events. This remarkable weapon fired no bullets and dropped no bombs; it simply was the Allied ability to break the Japanese and German code. Nevertheless, wrapped behind a shroud of secrecy, Magic and Ultra decrypts were undoubtedly the Allies' ultimate weapon. They provided the edge in the great sea battles in the South Pacific and on the battlefields of Europe. Without codebreaking, the war would have undoubtedly lasted much longer at a terrible cost of human lives.

Although every student of WWII knows the importance of codebreaking, few know of the bizarre and childish way the military branches handled the information it yielded. Frank Rowlett of the Signal Intelligence Service broke the Japanese code Purple on Sept. 20, 1940. The rivalry between the Army and Navy led to a bizarre routine by which Roosevelt received the messages. The traffic over Magic was too great for Army cryptanalysts to handle alone. As a result, naval code breakers shared the task of decrypting the messages. Each service had an officer who decided which messages to pass on to the administration. This task fell to Army Col. Rufus Bratton and Alwin Kramer of the Navy. The military limited distribution to the President, Secretaries of State, War and Navy, Army Chief of Staff, Directors of Military and Naval Intelligence, and Chiefs of Naval Operations and War Plans.

The bizarre way in which the military delivered the decrypts to FDR arose from the intense rivalry between the Navy and Army. After a prolonged dogfight, the two branches reached a solution of sorts. On odd-numbered months, an Army courier delivered the decoded messages to the President; on even-numbered months, a naval courier delivered them.

The level of absurdity increased in summer 1941. In June, Col. Bratton noticed a Magic decrypt of the Japanese diplomatic code Purple in the wastebasket of Pa Watson, FDR's military aide who was in charge of appointments. He alone determined who would see the President. Watson had, indeed, been careless with the decoded message and was not on the list of those approved to see Magic decrypts. The overzealous colonel reported Watson's carelessness to his superior, Gen. Sherman Miles. The general then decided not to trust the White House any longer with decrypts. For the balance of June, FDR received the decrypts from the naval courier. However, starting in July, the Army refused to deliver any of the decoded messages to the White House. By August, the Navy managed to work out a new agreement with the Army. The naval courier would read the messages to the President, then summarize them; however, he was prohibited from showing the decrypt to the President.

A more serious leak arose in the State Department. According to the Magic distribution scheme, only Secretary of State Cordell Hull was to receive the intercepts. However, Hull gave copies to six of his top aides, one of whom shared the decrypts with four more members in the Far Eastern Division. Joseph Dugan, who was in charge of the mimeograph room, was a strict isolationist opposed to FDR. Dugan discussed and even showed the decoded messages to a friend of his inside the State Department. However, Dugan's friend was in the pay of Hans Thomsen, the German chargé d'affaires in Washington who conspired to fix the election in 1940. Thomsen reported to Berlin that the Americans had broken the Japanese code.

Remarkably, on May 6, Magic code breakers decrypted a message from the Japanese ambassador Baron Hiroshi Oshima in Berlin, relaying Thomsen's report of the broken code to Tokyo. Even more remarkable, after a nonchalant investigation, the Japanese determined their code to be unbreakable and continued to use it. By November, Roosevelt had tired of the psychotic manner in which he received the Magic decrypts. He demanded to see the full text of the messages and ordered that only naval couriers deliver them.[1]

Breaking the Magic and Ultra codes led directly to one of the most controversial questions of WWII: Was Roosevelt forewarned of the attack on Pearl Harbor? The controversy has raged for more than 60 years. The first to level such a charge was the *Chicago Tribune*. This was the same anti-Roosevelt paper that published the secret Rainbow 5 war plans. The same paper was charged with treason in revealing the location and names of the ships involved in the battle at Midway. This paper also scuttled the plans for making the OSS a permanent agency at the end of the war. The best evidence so far suggests there was no such warning. Right up to the hour Pearl Harbor was bombed, the White House and the military planners expected the attack elsewhere in the Pacific, such as the Philippines.

Writers after the war concocted a similar story on the other side of the Atlantic. According to British writers, the Allies were willing to go to extremes to protect the secrets of Magic and Ultra. British critics claimed Churchill had foreknowledge of the attack on Coventry. According to the overactive imagination of these writers, Churchill was willing to allow the city to be destroyed rather than tip off the Germans that their code had been broken. Ultra did yield that the Japanese planned a massive attack, but the intercept was not translated until three days later; and even then, the location was not mentioned. The final message of the Japanese also failed to name the location of the attack.

While there is more than enough blame to go around, Gen. Shorts and Adm. Kimmel must share most of it. It was their command and they failed to take proper actions following the war-warning message in late November. Such a message should have alerted both officers of the need to take full defensive measures, like manning antiaircraft guns, having scout planes in the air at all times, and rotating and separating the fleet. Washington shares some of the blame in failing to follow up to ensure that the commanders had taken suitable actions. Much of the blame can be placed on the insane rivalry between the Army and Navy in the way they handled Magic. Dec. 6 was an Army day to decode the messages, and the Navy wasted time by sending the intercept to the Army. Since the Army decoders had already left for the weekend, further delay occurred when the intercept was returned to the Navy for decoding.

Finally, much of the blame was simply old-fashioned American arrogance. No one from the President on down believed Japan could attack American soil. No one believed that torpedo bombs could be used at Pearl Harbor. Naval experts simply dismissed the idea because they believed the harbor was too shallow. Before the bombing, the Navy never used any torpedo nets inside Pearl Harbor. Yet, of all the bombs dropped there, the torpedoes probably were responsible for more damage than the conventional bombs.

The Internment

In November 1941, in an attempt to strengthen security, Roosevelt sent his own man, news reporter John Carter, to the West Coast to assess the loyalty of the Japanese residents there. Roosevelt employed him essentially as a spy, and set up a small special intelligence unit under him. Carter picked Curtis Munson, a Chicago businessman, for this assignment. Munson reported that up to 98 percent of the Japanese were loyal. However, his report alerted FDR to the dangers of dams, bridges, power stations and other such unguarded targets. Roosevelt spent considerable time worrying about espionage, similar to what had occurred during the first war. He could not shake the image of an act of sabotage like the explosion of the Black Tom munitions depot during WWI.

In the period immediately following the Pearl Harbor bombing, OSS director William Donovan contributed to Roosevelt's fears of a fifth column. He reported to the President that German saboteurs were about to descend on American shores, supported and aided by U.S. bands of storm troopers. Donovan also forwarded a report to FDR claiming Japanese soldiers disguised as civilians were mobilizing to attack San Diego, and that Los Angeles was in danger of an imminent Japanese air strike. Perhaps the most damning statement came from Naval Secretary Frank Knox. On Dec. 15, Knox stated: "I think the most effective fifth column work of the entire war was done in Hawaii."[2]

Immediately after the Pearl Harbor bombing, panic gripped the West Coast. Local civilians formed coast watcher groups from San Diego to Seattle. The Army also put in place armed coast watchers. Both sets of coast watchers were prone to shoot first. The worsening news contributed to the near-hysteric conditions along the coast. On Dec. 23, just six miles offshore, a Japanese submarine sank an oil tanker leaving the port of San Luis, California. The Philippines had fallen and the Japanese were now in firm control of the South Pacific. More Japanese submarines were sighted, particularly off the Oregon coast. On Feb. 23, 1942, a Japanese submarine surfaced a mile offshore and shelled the Richfield Oil Co. The next night, the skies of Los Angeles resembled a Fourth of July celebration lit by search–lights, tracer bullets and antiaircraft fire. An uncontrolled fear gripped the city with people thinking it was under attack. But there was no attack.

In Washington State, a power line from one of the dams suddenly went dead. The gun shops and hardware stores in the towns affected by the power outage had a bonanza selling ammunition. The streets were soon empty of adult males because everyone was in the backwoods hunting Japs. With power soon restored, these patriotic Jap hunters came straggling home. Miraculously, none of them suffered any injuries greater than severely bruised egos. The power company located the problem and repaired the damage caused by cows in a nearby pasture.

As tension and fear continued to mount on the West Coast, Roosevelt was soon under intense pressure to do something about the Japanese living there. Gen. DeWitt, the West Coast Army Chief, California Gov. Culbert Olson and Earl Warren, California's Attorney General, led the call for internment. The governors of Washington and Oregon were squarely behind internment, too. Both states were Klan hotbeds in the 1920s. Only a single state west of the Mississippi, Colorado, would accepted the relocation of the Japanese without confinement. With political pressure reaching a feverish pitch, Roosevelt signed executive order 9066 on Feb. 19, 1942, launching one of America's more grievous sagas, the internment of Japanese citizens.

The political pressures on Roosevelt were immense, and the roots lie deep in American racism. Prejudice against the Japanese was seen in a 1924 report prepared by the Labor Department during the Coolidge administration. Because the Oriental Exclusion Act was pending in Congress, the report was suppressed. Tennessee Democratic Sen. Thomas Stewart, the prosecutor in the Scopes trial, released the report, which was a study conducted on the strike against the sugar planters in Hawaii. The report noted the Japanese in Hawaii were settling near strategic military areas and otherwise imperiling national defense. Sens. Stewart Maybank of South Carolina and Rufus Holman of Oregon said the report should have been publicized at that time and the nation put on guard about the compromised defenses of Hawaii.

Anti-Asian legislation goes back further to 1882, when President Chester Arthur signed the Chinese Exclusion Act, barring Chinese immigration for 10 years. In 1892, Congress extended the law for another decade and, in 1902, made the ban permanent. In 1907, the Unites States struck a deal with Japan to limit immigration and prevent Japanese immigrants from ever gaining citizenship. Without citizenship, the immigrants could not legally own land. The WWII internees were despoiled of their property.

While ultimately the burden for issuing the executive order rests squarely on Roosevelt's shoulders, it was rooted in America's sordid racist past. While the internment of the Japanese is shameful and indefensible, they might have suffered attacks from the civilian coast defense groups, who tended to be overzealous patriots dispatching vigilante justice. Prejudices against Asians were well engrained on the West Coast, and civilian coast watchers could assume a Japanese fisherman to be a spy and shoot him on the spot. Any disruptions such as a power outage would have been blamed on the local Japanese, resulting in vigilante attacks.

Native Fascists

The war years saw the beginning of the transformation and polarization of both major parties. Before the war, each party had a conservative and liberal wing. By the end of the 1960s, they were fully polarized, with the Republicans as the party of conservatives and the Democrats the party of liberals.

The war forced the native fascists to adapt to preserve their ideology too. The first change came with the Pearl Harbor bombing. The second change began around mid-1943, when everyone realized Nazi Germany was defeated and it would be only a matter of time before surrender.

Pearl Harbor forced them to abruptly change their tactics. America was fighting back; it was not giving up. Open pro-fascist rallies and parades were now out of the question. Membership quickly dwindled, leaving only the hard core, who went underground to wage an all-out propaganda war. The fascist agenda was now cloaked under a false banner of patriotism with its new goddess of "free enterprise" for America to worship.

In November 1940, FDR set aside a week as National Bible Week. The National Bible Association organized the observances. It had an elitist agenda, with roots in the National Committee for Religious Recovery, founded in 1940 by New York business interests. *Newsweek* described the National Committee as a group of "a few Wall Streeters." In 1941, the National Committee changed its name to The Laymen's National Committee. Its first chairman was Lambert Fairchild. He described the agenda: "For God and Country, you're going to see religion and business formed into a solid phalanx. Let no rabble-rousing communist tell you anything else, you security-holders who want security for your holdings."[3]

Fairchild was trying to fuse business with religion interests, a common theme in the conversion of nativists to groups that adopted fascism as part of their ideology. Although there is a parallel to the role of religious groups in the Red Scare of 1919, the new development was much deeper, with direct links to corporate funding, which was largely lacking during the Red Scare.

Fairchild had close ties with several fascist organizations, including the American Bund, the Christian Mobilizers and the Christian Front. After *Newsweek* exposed his pro-Nazi associations, he was replaced by Howard Kiroack, who also had ties to several pro-fascist groups. The full extent of both individuals' involvement can be found in Carlson's book, *The Plotters*.[4] In 1945, the National Committee for Religious Recovery presented an Annual Award of Merit to the pro-fascist newspaperman William Randolph Hearst.

The National Bible Association has preserved close ties with the elitists, as shown in its list of chairmen over the years. Past chairmen have included William Grede (CEO of Grede Foundries, anti-unionist, and founding member of the John Birch Society), Charles Hook (Armco Steel), Edward Werle (New York Stock Exchange), J. Peter Grace (W.R. Grace & Co), C. Fred Fetterolf (Alcoa) and Richard DeVos (Amway). In other words, most of the past directors were CEOs of large corporations, rather than prominent religious leaders.

No organization or institution was free from fascist infiltration. In the capitalist environment, fascism is insidious; its tentacles reach out and infect all organizations and groups. After the Klan formed an alliance with the American Bund, members were urged to join unions and incite strikes that would stop war production. The press and even Congress had their share of native fascists.

As the real power of the fascist movement in the United States lay with the leaders of corporate America and their Wall Street cronies, the evolution of fascism took two predictable forms. One form became virulently anti-union; the other became fanatically anti-communist. This transformation came about largely through various groups financed by the leaders of corporate America. They provided financial support to the gamut of fascist groups, from the extremely violent Black Legion to the more subdued America First group.

Most of the fascist groups remained active during the war and continued to receive corporate funding. In their struggle to further the fascist cause, they found many allies in the press, in Congress and in various government agencies, including Hoover's FBI.

After WWI, fear of Bolshevism added to the existing nativism and fear of immigration, leading to uniquely American, strident forms of anti-communism and anti-unionism. Donner describes this transformation of the anti-union movement:

> The root of the anti-subversive impulse was fed by the menace. Its power strengthened with the passage of time, by the late twenties its influence had become pervasive and folkish. Bolshevism came to be identified over wide areas of the country by God-fearing Americans as the Antichrist come to do eschatological battle with the children of light. A slightly secularized version, widely shared in rural and small-town America, postulated a doomsday conflict between decent upright folk and radicalism – alien, satanic, immorally incarnate. The enemy was perceived with the kind of retching horror evoked by the biblical cry "Unclean."[5]

Unionism was regarded as an alien idea imported by lazy and unclean foreigners. The trial of Sacco and Vanzetti came in 1920. Despite strong alibis from witnesses placing Vanzetti at a location other than the scene of the robbery, the jury found both men guilty and sentenced them to death. The jury was unable to overlook Vanzetti's political views.[6]

The roots of anti-unionism extend back to the Civil War and the Pinkerton Agency. After the war, employers used the agency as a weapon against the labor unions.[7] Pinkerton had the most success in the 1870s when it smashed the Molly Maguires for the Reading Railroad. It was a short step from labor intervention to espionage. Agencies like Pinkerton transformed into institutional tools for class warfare. Since unionism involved political events of the time, surveillance of union activity invariably embraced political targets. It became fashionable and politically expedient for pro-business politicians to associate labor with violence, conspiracy and the communist revolution.

Much of the violence was caused by employers, who stockpiled tear gas and Thompson submachine guns, urged a local sheriff to murder IWW members in Everett, Wash., and provoked violence in Lawrence, Mass.

In the 1930s, religious fundamentalist and anti-communist groups began to take on a fascist flavor. The transformation was often subtle. Anti-union groups went from mere opposition to unions to promoting and protecting corporations, monopolies and cartels. An increase in anti-Semitic views marked the fundamentalist religious groups. Almost all the nativist groups shifted from isolationism to global interventionism.

Powerful forces protected the fascists behind the scenes. As in Germany, where the leaders of the large corporations put Hitler in the chancellor's office in a backroom deal, and the leaders of corporate America wielded such unbridled power that they could attempt a plot against FDR to install a fascist government. Although the participants were exposed and the evidence was damning, Roosevelt was powerless to bring them to justice, and the plotters were never arrested.

Roosevelt's Secret Plan

The U.S. government was ill-prepared to deal with fascism and the threat it posed. Congress made a feeble attempt by setting up a committee to look into American fascism. Rep. Martin Dies quickly seized the committee and converted it to a Red-baiting squad. Any efforts at examining fascism were quickly sabotaged.

The only other government agency with a role in domestic investigations was the FBI, led by the patron saint of the right wing, J. Edgar Hoover. While Hoover's racist and anti-Jewish views are known, much mystery still surrounds his role in fascism during the war years. Hoover was always a politically ambitious seeker of seeking power and control. His first important experience came in 1919 with the forerunner of the FBI, in the repressive Palmer Raids. Hoover was an overly enthusiastic participant, sensing that anti-communism and anti-unionism were means to further his career and increase his power. Donner summed up Hoover's true legacy: "Out of nativism, anti-communism, super-patriotism, religion and political conservatism, he forged an ideology of capitalism in the American grain, a blueprint for American fascism."[8]

Evidence of Hoover's sympathy for fascism is plentiful. His most open political ties were with "respectable" super-patriotic conservative groups, including various veteran organizations, the Daughters of the American Revolution, the American Security Council (formed in the mid-1950s from members of three pro-Nazi groups of the 1930s), and the Freedom Foundation. Hoover also kept links with various right-wing or conservative churches.[9]

Until the 1940 election, Hoover spent more time spying on British agents and communists than on Nazi operatives. As early as 1939, Roosevelt allowed British agents to wiretap Americans believed to be aiding the Nazi cause. Master spy Sir William Stephenson, better known as Intrepid, headed the British operation. By the time the United States entered the war, Stephenson had uncovered a web of Nazi-American financial ties.

The wiretaps were illegal, of course, and evidence gathered from them was not admissible in court, but they provided the British with the means to stop the flow of American support to Hitler. Usually, this meant intercepting shipments of war materials to Germany. However, there also is evidence that Intrepid also murdered some fascist agents in the United States. British agents may have poisoned William Rhodes Davis, the Texas oilman and Nazi supporter.

Roosevelt planned to leak the information gathered by the British operation to the media after the war to create a public uproar about treason, and then launch a full investigation without harming the war effort. As part of this secret scheme between Roosevelt and British intelligence, he deliberately placed suspected individuals in positions in which they could easily be monitored. It was no accident that after his appointment to the OSS, Allen Dulles' office in New York was one floor below the British wiretapping office.

Dulles' appointment was a deliberate setup. It placed him in a position in which he would be tempted the most to continue aiding the Nazis. After the war, Roosevelt meant to use this information to help prosecute Dulles, but two unforeseen events scuttled his plan. First, someone tipped Dulles off. The leak is commonly attributed to Vice President Henry Wallace, and it was the motivation for dumping him from the ticket in 1944. Second, the death of Roosevelt killed the plan, because FDR never told Truman about it.

Dulles was not Roosevelt's only target; the many other wealthy Wall Street investors included Joseph Kennedy. Before his death, former Supreme Court Justice Arthur Goldberg confirmed that Roosevelt set up Dulles.[10]

During the war, Goldberg served in the labor division of the OSS. His knowledge of the set-up suggests that the OSS, or at least one of its branches, was likely involved with Roosevelt's secret plan of placing people suspected of aiding the Nazi cause under surveillance. OSS involvement would have been illegal since its charter banned spying in the United States. The evidence would have been inadmissible in court, but was in keeping with Roosevelt's plan to leak the information to the press. The OSS involvement suggests the plan was far-reaching and that many more Nazi sympathizers were being watched.

While Roosevelt's relationship with J. Edgar Hoover was reportedly harmonious, the operation was kept secret from and the FBI, a hint that he did not trust Hoover fully, and may have even suspected his loyalties.

In addition to the British import-export office, 30 Rockefeller Plaza housed the offices of Western Continents Corp., founded on Aug. 14, 1941 as a "research and analyzation work and export and import" business by George Muhle. A Dun and Bradstreet report carried a brief outline of Muhle's life. It also listed Council of Foreign Relations member William Diebold Jr., as treasurer.

What the Dun and Bradstreet report failed to note was that George Muhle's real name was George Muhle Mertens. The outline of the Dun and Bradstreet report omitted a significant part of Mertens' life in the otherwise correct summary. From 1926 to 1927, Mertens had been the head of Germany's Bureau of Investigations for Anti-Democratic Activities. The bureau was a government intelligence organization formed to counter leftist and rightist organizations in Germany. Goering dismissed Mertens from all his posts in the Nazi government and charged him with high treason.

For a while in 1936, Mertens worked for the Commerz Bank in Berlin. The counselor of the American Embassy in Berlin, Prentiss Gilbert, aided Mertens' entry into the United States. Gilbert had joined the Schering Corp., believing the Nazis had sold it to legitimate owners, only to find that it was merely a front for continued Nazi activity.

Mertens contacted the Roosevelt administration through Adolf Berle, who passed him along to Francis McNamara of the Alien Property Division of the Department of Justice. McNamara, feeling legally bound, finally put Mertens in contact with Donovan and William Stephenson. It was Stephenson's Intrepid organization that put up the front money to form Western Continents.

In 1942, control of Western Continents passed from Stephenson to Donovan. By that time, Mertens had mapped out the Nazi commercial structure in the United States and its relationship with the Sicherheitsdienst (SD). Mertens also exposed Nazi front companies in South America and how they interacted with their North American counterparts. He presented a detailed exposure of the SD and the personal financial arrangements of the fascist French prime minister Pierre Laval and his associates, including the Bank of Worms.[11] The information gained from Mertens proved that the Intrepid operation was not only successful, but also far reaching, including the top levels of foreign governments friendly with the Nazis.

The scheme with the British was only one of many of Roosevelt's intelligence channels. He often asked his friends to take on special missions for him, many of which ended in failure, such as Vincent Astor's voyage in the South Pacific. Another recruit into FDR's private spy network was John Carter, a writer for the fledging *Time* magazine.

Joseph Kennedy, like Dulles, was placed in a position where he could be watched carefully. Roosevelt had sent the Irishman to England as an ambassador. Churchill's son Randolph confirmed that Kennedy was under electronic surveillance. It revealed that a lowly code clerk named Tyler Kent had passed secret documents to one Anna Wolkoff. She passed the information on to the Italian foreign minister, who forwarded it to the Nazi foreign office. After an argument during a weekend meeting at Hyde Park, Roosevelt abruptly terminated Kennedy's ambassadorship. Britain tried Kent, an American citizen, in secret proceedings in the Old Bailey on Oct. 23, 1940. The court sentenced him to seven years.[12]

The FBI and Hoover

Hoover's spying on the British was a fence-sitting maneuver on his part, due to his great ambitions. It was a position that left him largely neutral, or leaning to the Nazis. Loftus claims the fascist forces in the Republican Party offered Hoover an appointment as Attorney General, a position he coveted, if Roosevelt lost the 1940 election.[13]

With Roosevelt's reelection, Hoover had to hurry to mend fences with the White House by offering files on Nazi sympathizers. However, Hoover had spent so much time spying on the British and chasing suspected communists that he had no central index of suspected pro-Nazis. Hoover then went begging to the Anti-Defamation League for its records. The British, of course, had better files, but refused to share them with Hoover and the FBI, fearing the right-wing faction in the bureau would leak word of the wiretap operation. Hence, it is clear that MI6, the top intelligence service of the world at the time, believed the FBI was infested with Nazis and Nazi sympathizers.

Many believe Hoover's opposition and refusal to cooperate with the OSS was due to of his ambitious aims for the FBI. In reality, it was Hoover's thin skin and his tendency to hold grudges. His opposition to the OSS goes back to the 1920s, when Coolidge appointed William Donovan as an Assistant Attorney General. During his tenure in the Department of Justice, Donovan became aware of Hoover's wiretapping of politicians' telephones for his private files for blackmail purposes. Attorney General Stone nearly fired Hoover over the incident, and Hoover never forgot who embarrassed him.[14]

Even more damaging was Hoover's sabotage and obstruction of the fledging intelligence network before and during the war, which was corroborated by Dusko Popov, a British master spy who had earned the confidence of the Nazis as a double agent. In 1941, the Germans sent him to the United States to reorganize and run their spy network. For a double agent, it was the chance of a lifetime to deceive the Nazis on a grand scale. However, Hoover disapproved of Popov's playboy lifestyle, and refused to help preserve his cover.

Popov brought with him important intelligence from Germany that included the Japanese interest in the defenses and fortifications of Pearl Harbor. This information was received just four months before the attack. Hoover was neither equipped to understand the value of the information nor could he find a publicity use for it. He quickly buried the report without sending it to the War Department or the White House.[15]

Included in Popov's documents was information about the German microdot, or encryption via microphotography, which Hoover did find useful. In April 1946, he published an article in the *Reader's Digest* claiming credit for capturing the secret of the microdot from an enemy spy. This was a lie; a British agent gave it to him. But even more damning, the article contained a diagram exposing Popov's source, a Brazilian diplomat. In 1946, South America was the destination of many of the Nazi war criminals. In his effort to seek the spotlight, Hoover exposed a useful source who could have provided information on war criminals in South America. *Reader's Digest* has always held an extreme right-wing bias, so much so that George Seldes in *Facts and Fascism* devoted an entire chapter to it. Seldes charged that Dewitt Wallace, the owner of the *Reader's Digest,* told his staff that he did not want Hitler defeated. Edited by a pro-Hitlerite from the Hearst papers, *Reader's Digest* consistently published anti-union and fascist propaganda. The following quote from *Facts and Fascism* sums up Seldes' opinion of the *Reader's Digest* and its owner:

> It pretends to be an impartial reprint magazine, selecting the best items from all others, but it is in fact a skillfully manipulated publication spreading the reactionary views of a powerful nobody named DeWitt Wallace... DeWitt Wallace is either a knave or a fool. Either he is so stupid that he doesn't know that he is spreading fascism, or he is a Machiavellian knave who has devised a wonderful and sinister method, far superior to any known to Herr Goebbels.[16]

Hoover apparently saw nothing politically or morally wrong with the Nazis. Only three days before the Pearl Harbor bombing, on Dec. 4, 1940, Hoover finally broke relations with Interpol, an agency controlled by the Nazis, and then only after other top FBI executives urged him to do so.

In short, the top echelon of the FBI saw no danger from fascism, but upheld a visceral hatred for communism and Russia, as well as for FDR, the New Deal and liberalism. The FBI's top intelligence officer during the war and until 1954 was D. Milton Ladd, who claimed FDR was a Comintern agent.[17]

The FBI's policy under Hoover during the war years was openly antagonistic to our Russian ally, and to liberalism in general, including the New Deal. No one from the Department of Justice, including the Attorney General, tried to muzzle Hoover. Everyone knew of Hoover's inclination for keeping files on his enemies in Congress and throughout the federal bureaucracy. It seems certain that Hoover was taping his known and potential enemies to a far greater extent than previously thought. For example, Hoover kept a file on Frank Murphy over a 10-year period that contained derogatory information from his private life, even after Roosevelt appointed Murphy as Attorney General in 1938.

Hoover was solely responsible for transforming the crime-fighting agency into a domestic intelligence agency with a gut-level hate of the Left. From 1940 to 1945, Hoover gave more than 50 speeches on the dangers of communism, many of them openly critical of his superiors and their values. In effect, he was able to transform the FBI into a vast propaganda agency.[18]

Throughout his lifetime, Hoover's favorite whipping boys were communists. He supported Joe McCarthy's witch hunts of the early 1950s. Likewise, Hoover desperately tried to associate the civil rights leaders of the 1960s and the Vietnam War protesters with communism. The FBI's persecution of the Left in the '60s through its COINTELPRO operation was a grave injustice. Like the Palmer Raids, these operations depleted the Left of leadership and created a vacuum of moderating forces, allowing fascism to rise up in the 1930s and again in the 1980s. In any other country, the Palmer Raids, the McCarthy witch hunts and COINTELPRO would be condemned as purges. McCarthy is a hero to the right-wing media, and the mainstream media kill the COINTELPRO story by not reporting it.

Given the antagonistic views of the director and the top echelon of the FBI, the pursuit of fascists and seditionists was paralyzed. With the Department of Justice handicapped by the FBI's lack of interest, most of those indicted for sedition went free. In any case, the defendants were only minor scapegoats; neither the power and money behind them was exposed, nor did the FBI have any interest in looking into the leaders and money used to support the fascist groups. There was no mass arrest of fascists during the war, unlike the mass arrests of the Palmer Raids following WWI or in the following McCarthyism era.

Hoover's efforts to spread propaganda extended beyond the FBI. In the 1940s, he fed information to Father John F. Cronin. During the 1940s, Cronin was the assistant director of the Social Action Department of the National Catholic Welfare Conference. With Hoover's aid, Cronin became an expert on communism, and later a close associate of Richard Nixon. The Chamber of Commerce secretly retained Cronin to write and distribute pamphlets critical of unions, communism and liberalism. The 1947 pamphlet, *Communism Within the Labor Movement,* led to the drive to require union leaders to sign a noncommunist affidavit.[19] No one should harbor the misconception that the FBI is a crime-fighting agency. It has always been America's Gestapo with a mission to destroy the Left. That record extends from the Palmer Raids and COINTELPRO to the present day.

A Fascist in Congress

Another individual aiding the fascists was H. Ralph Burton, Chief Counsel to the House's Military Affairs Committee. Burton was a racist and an anti-Semite with a long history of associations with fascists. At one point, he was the lawyer for William Ludecke, who bragged he was Hitler's No. 2 Nazi in the United States. Burton also was a special counsel to the DAR during their flagrant Red-baiting days, and a close associate of Walter Steele, editor of the fascist *National Republic.*

In the mid-1930s, Burton was general counsel for Father Coughlin's National Union of Social Justice in Maryland. Burton's son, Robert, also had close associations with fascists. His son was a frequent guest at the Japanese Embassy and was often observed in the company of other Nazis under surveillance. In 1939, Burton was an investigator for the WPA subcommittee, and was determined to show Jews controlled and ran the WPA for the benefit of fellow Jews.

How a man such as Burton with known Nazi sympathies was able to keep a sensitive position when the country was at war with Germany is a mystery, and there were hundreds more like him. Yet anyone with the slightest tinge of socialism or communism was rapidly removed from any position within the government.

While Burton served in the Military Affairs Committee, he continued to make himself a thorn in the side of Army officials. He would scan lists of draft deferments, skipping over ethnic surnames looking for Jewish ones. Burton would then call the local draft board demanding they be drafted.

Burton's most damaging role was in wrecking the Army's Orientation Course after the issue of Program 64. The Orientation Course was set up to teach recruits what they were fighting for and to offset the fascist propaganda circulating at the time. At first, the Orientation Course was general in nature, but as more and more recruits demanded more definitive information, it became specialized. Program 64 contained the following definition of fascism:

If we don't understand fascism and recognize it when we see it, it might crop up again — under another label — and cause another war.

Fascism is a way to run a country — it's the way Italy was run, and the way Germany and Japan are run. Fascism is the precise opposite of democracy. The people run democratic governments, but fascist governments run the people.

Fascism is government by the few and for the few. The objective is seizure and control of the economic, political, social, and cultural life of the state. Why? The democratic way of life interferes with their methods and desires for: 1. Conducting business; 2. Living with their fellow men; 3 having the final say in matters concerning others as well as themselves.

The basic principles of democracy stand in the way of their desires; hence — democracy must go! Anyone who is not a member of their inner gang has to do what he's told. They permit no civil liberties, no equality before the law. They make their own rules and change them when they choose. If you don't like it, it's T.S.

They maintain themselves in power by use of force combined with propaganda based on primitive ideas of blood and race, by skillful manipulation of fear and hate, and by false promises of security. The propaganda glorifies war and insists it is smart and realistic to be pitiless and violent.[20]

It is hard to imagine that such a statement caused an outburst of protest on Capitol Hill, yet it touched a nerve. Several representatives made indignant speeches on the floor of the House. Clare Hoffman of Michigan and John Rankin of Mississippi were outraged over Program 64, as were other pro-fascist members. Their indignation soon led to the discontinuance of the top-rated Orientation Courses. The pro-fascists in Congress did not want the GIs to know what they were supposedly fighting against.

Another factor was the average GI's general lack of education, which created the need for programs such as the Army's Orientation Courses. In 1947, the average education for all U.S. adults was only 8.6 years; 75 percent did not complete high school. In 1947, only 19 percent of the voters had a generally correct view of the Wagner Act, according to a Gallup poll. 69 percent simply had no idea; the rest gave wrong answers.

In 1951, only 8 percent of adults could properly define monopoly, antitrust suit, the Sherman Act and interlocking directorates.[21] This low level of education left 80 percent susceptible to anyone's propaganda. In short, most of the voters were dupes for whoever could shout the loudest. The pro-fascist bloc in Congress soon replaced the Orientation Course with an anti-communism program.

Rainbow 5 and the Great Sit-Down Strike

As the support for fascism crystallized among the nativist groups during the war years, so did the support for fascism among the isolationist members of Congress. In the previous chapter, the removal of Maloney as prosecutor of the seditionists by Sen. Wheeler and the pro-fascist members of Congress contributed to the failure of the trials of even the minor fascists. Father Coughlin was not even indicted. However, it was on the eve of the war with Germany that Wheeler overtly revealed himself as a traitor and a fascist. On Dec. 4, 1941, the pro-fascist *Chicago Tribune* and its sister publication, the *Washington Times Herald,* printed the plans for the top secret Rainbow 5 Plan.

Rainbow 5 was the battle plan developed by the military in case war broke out. Publishing the plan or leaking information about it would be the equivalent of publishing or leaking the battle order of the Pentagon during the Cold War – unquestionably, an act of treason. In Hitler's speech declaring war against the United States on Dec. 11, 1941, he cited the final straw: "With no attempt at an official denial there has now been revealed in America, President Roosevelt's plan by which, at the latest in 1943, Germany and Italy are to be attacked in Europe by military means."[22]

The government failed to charge anyone with treason or sedition: neither the *Chicago Tribune*, nor Wheeler nor the Army officer who delivered the papers to him, despite an FBI investigation. Fewer than a dozen copies of the top secret contingency plan existed.

The author of the report on Rainbow 5 was Col. Albert Wedemeyer, who had been educated at the German War College. While in Berlin, he rented an apartment with a member of the Nazi Party. Wedemeyer became a close friend to Gen. Ludwig Beck, Chief of the German General Staff. He was friendly with Lindbergh and acted as his interpreter when the aviator toured Germany. He also was close to Gen. Robert Woods, president of America First.[23] Wedemeyer attended several America First meetings.

Hoover strongly believed that Wedemeyer leaked the plans to Wheeler. Of special note, Reagan resurrected Wedemeyer's career as a special military adviser in the 1980s, yet another of the many seemingly innocent connections between Reagan and the Nazis.[24]

One clue appears in the book *A Man Called Intrepid*, where Sir William implies that he was authorized to leak the Rainbow 5 plans.[25] As already mentioned, FDR allowed the British to keep watch on certain individuals known to be friendly with the Nazis, particularly those associated with Wall Street. Two that Roosevelt appointed so they could be monitored were Allen Dulles and Nelson Rockefeller. FDR's plan was to charge them with treason and sedition following the war. Wheeler may very well have been another of those being watched. Wheeler was connected to the Rockefellers through Anaconda, which delivered substandard copper wire to our Allies and our own military.

By leaking the files to the *Chicago Tribune*, Wheeler ensured that they would be published. The *Tribune* was openly pro-fascist before the attack on Pearl Harbor and rabidly opposed to Roosevelt. It later faced charges of treason for publishing the names of the ships involved in the battle of Midway.

Wedemeyer's career deserves scrutiny. He was part of a military circle that was anti-Jewish. A few years after the war, Wedemeyer wrote in a letter to his close friend, retired Col. Truman Smith, that Zionists, the British and communists made America's entry into the war certain. Later, Wedemeyer stated that "most of the people associated with communism in the early days were Jews."

He further claimed that Roosevelt's Jewish advisers did everything possible to spread venom and hatred against the Nazis. He stated that during his attendance at the German War College in 1936, his eyes were opened to the number of Jews in the American government by reading the *Die Frankfurter Zietung* and *Die Berliner*. The Nazis controlled both papers.[26]

In 1937, Wedemeyer linked the shortage of food in Germany to the Jewish question. Using the embassy's attaché stationery, Wedemeyer wrote to friends dismissing the food shortage as caused by poor weather and crop failures. He claimed that Jews in other countries had bought up the enormous quantities of foodstuffs and intentionally diverted the shipments from Germany.

As late as 1958, Wedemeyer was still voicing pro-Nazi opinions. He ignored the Nazis' racial ideology, describing *Lebensraum* as merely a national movement to win living space. Wedemeyer used the same historical analogies as the Nazi propagandists, comparing the German invasions and expansions eastward with the American expansion westward.

The two people with the greatest influence on Wedemeyer's career were Truman Smith and Wedemeyer's father-in-law, Deputy Chief of Staff Stanley Embrick. Embrick was the most outspoken isolationist general in 1939. Many of the officers in Wedemeyer's circle harbored pro-fascist leanings and an extreme hatred of Jews. Such views had been ingrained into the officers since the 1920s and would affect how the war was conducted, as well as the postwar period.

In 1939, Truman Smith was the military attaché in Berlin and warned against allowing the Jewish question to interfere with German-American relations. After returning to Washington that year, Smith became Gen. George C. Marshall's German specialist. Smith conferred extensively with Lindbergh, as did Col. Hamilton, the head of the German section of G2, or Army intelligence. Lindbergh's isolationist views were well known through his radio broadcasts. Two weeks after the German invasion of Poland, Smith delivered a confidential message from Roosevelt offering Lindbergh a cabinet position in aviation if he would halt his radio broadcasts. Both Smith and Lindbergh scoffed at Roosevelt's offer.

In November 1939, Smith's assistant attaché in Berlin, Maj. Percy Black, also returned to Washington. Black had accompanied the German army into Poland a short time before. Like Smith, Black talked glowingly of the prospect for a negotiated settlement. Even more disturbing was his discounting of Nazi brutality. In May 1940, the Nazi invasion of France proved him wrong.

Wedemeyer opposed creating the State of Israel, as did Black and other members of his circle of friends. After retiring, Wedemeyer became a writer for the John Birch Society and a member of the American Security Council.

The most astonishing aspect of the publication of the Rainbow Plans was that charges of treason were never brought, even after the war. Few Americans even know this page of history. It is another example of how high-level fascists in the United States were immune from prosecution.

The strongest support for fascism and opposition to the war came from the leaders of corporate America. They were behind the plot to seize the White House and install a fascist government. They built the Third Reich's war machine, as noted by U.S. Ambassador to Germany William Dodd. And it would be the leaders of corporate America who went on a sit-down strike to prevent the production of war munitions, first for the Lend-Lease program, and then for our own troops once war was declared.

Between 1940 and 1945, there was a dramatic evolution in the tactics employed by the native fascists in America. Corporate America opposed Lend-Lease and the entry of the United States into the European war, and rejected several contracts to supply Britain with war munitions. One example: Ford Motor Company's rejection of a contract to build Rolls Royce engines for the RAF. Other corporations hid behind the terms of the cartel agreements with IG Farben and other German corporations, as with duPont supplying the British with inferior cartridges lacking tetrazine. Most damaging aspect was the sit-down strike of 1940 .

As clouds of war gathered on the horizon, the need for aircraft was one of the most pressing. Aircraft production requires massive amounts of aluminum, and the Aluminum Company of America (Alcoa) owned by Andrew Mellon held a virtual monopoly in the United States. Alcoa signed a cartel agreement with German interests in the late 1920s. Seldes recorded the following about Alcoa:

> "If America loses the war it can thank the Aluminum Corporation of America" – Secretary of Interior Harold Ickles, June 26, 1941.

> By its cartel agreement with IG Farben controlled by Hitler, Alcoa sabotaged the aluminum program of the U.S. Air Force. The Truman Committee heard testimony that Alcoa's representative, A.H. Bunker, a dollar-a-year head of the aluminum section of the OPM [Office of Production and Management] prevented work on our $600,000,000 aluminum expansion program.

> Congressman Pierce of Oregon said in May 1941: "To date 137 days or 37.5 percent of a year's production has been wasted in the effort to protect Alcoa's monopolistic position. This delay translated into planes means 10,000 fighters or 1,665 bombers."

> This of course is the answer to the boys on Guadalcanal and in Tunisia and not absenteeism, the 48-hour week or wage increases to meet the cost of living.[27]

Not only did Alcoa own almost all the plants that produced aluminum, but it also controlled most of the high-grade bauxite ore. Aluminum production requires massive amounts of electric power, and Alcoa controlled much of the hydropower, too. In a radio broadcast on March 22, 1941, Assistant Secretary of State Adolf Berle declared:

> The Lord Almighty so built the continent of North America that most of the water in the northeast quarter of the continent forms streams and rivers which flow into that huge collection of reservoirs we call the Great Lakes. This is an enormous amount of water. All of it funnels out to the sea through a single great millrace, which is the St. Lawrence River. If that water is ever harnessed, it will make the largest and cheapest supply of electricity available anywhere in the world.[28]

However, the St. Lawrence was unharnessed and would remain so. Andrew Mellon owned all the land on the American side and much of the land on the Canadian side of the International Rapids stretch. Along this 49 miles, the river falls 92 feet and could be used to generate electricity at a cost of one-tenth of a cent a kilowatt-hour. Only last-minute fights by New York governors, Charles Hughes in 1907 and Alfred Smith in 1926, prevented Alcoa from exercising absolute control over it. By 1940, Roosevelt failed to gain passage in Congress of a treaty negotiated by Herbert Hoover for the joint development of the St. Lawrence. The Alcoa lobby was too strong to break. Both Ontario and New York drew electrical power from Niagara. The Canadian power was generated by a public-owned system and charged $0.85 a kilowatt-hour. On the New York side, the power was produced by the private Niagara Hudson at a cost of $1.59 for a kilowatt-hour.[29]

This example of the conglomerate gouging New Yorkers at almost twice the rate of cost of the Canadian public utility should serve to remind us that some services and materials are too valuable to ever be entrusted to private hands. And even this price gouging was miniscule compared to the energy shortage contrived by Enron in California during the winter of 2001, or to the profits that Alcoa generated during the war. In a long antitrust suit in 1940, a government brief stated that Alcoa's highest profits came from producing sheets of 24S and XA 24S alloys, both of which were used extensively in aircraft. According to the Justice Department, as the sole supplier of these alloys, Alcoa was realizing a profit of

181 percent.[30] Alcoa's cartel agreement with a German corporation in the 1920s allowed Germany to produce 165,600 tons of aluminum in 1938; total U.S. production was only 103,129 tons. Alcoa had also invested heavily in plants in Italy, Spain, Hungary, and Norway, countries with their own fascist regimes, or that had fallen under the boot of the Third Reich. No investigation of Alcoa's dealings with the Nazis was ever made.

Mellon not only controlled aluminum production through Alcoa, but he also sought to prevent competition through his cronies in the Office of Production and Management (OPM). E.R. Stettinius, head of the board of U.S. Steel and the OPM, was in charge of the Industrial Materials Section. Stettinius issued glowing reports assuring that a satisfactory supply of raw materials was available. Many of the materials, such as antimony, manganese, mercury, tungsten, nickel, chromium and tin, came from the South Pacific Islands and Malaya, and would be vulnerable to a supply cutoff. Nor were stocks on hand adequate for a two-year supply because buying did not begin until 1940.

In May of 1941, the truth of the shortages was exposed in a report from the Metals Reserve Corp. The report detailed the amount bought, in transit and delivered. With zinc, a vital material in producing the brass cartridges, the report was dismal. Only 50,000 tons were ordered from Newfoundland (less than a month's supply). Because of the war production, zinc consumption rose to 70,000 tons a month (7,000 tons more than domestic production). One thousand rounds of 30-caliber shells consumed 16 pounds of zinc; 1,000 rounds of 75-mm shells, 3,800 pounds of zinc. During the war, production of small arms ammunition reached 4 billion rounds a month.[31]

Aluminum production is the best example of how the dollar-a-year men like Stettinius hindered the war effort. At the onset of the war, there was only one aluminum refiner in the U.S., Alcoa. In 1941, Alcoa could produce a maximum of 642 million pounds of aluminum in a year. Roosevelt's plan to produce bombers alone required 1.6 billion pounds a year.

At that time, Reynolds Aluminum was a small upstart, merely a fabricator of aluminum products which had never produced a single ingot of virgin aluminum. Foreseeing the shortage in aluminum and unable to get a full supply of aluminum from Alcoa, Reynolds agreed to mortgage all of his property to start refining in his own plants if the government would lend him the money. The Reconstruction Finance Corp. (RFC) approved his loan within 30 days for $15 million, and later increased it to $20 million.[32]

Reynolds soon had a plant in Lister, Ala., that produced 40 million pounds, and another plant in Longview, Wash., that produced 60 million pounds, but considerable pressure was brought against Reynold's loan application. W. Averill Harriman and a delegation of War Department officials pressured Secretary Ickles to deny Reynolds a share of electrical power from Bonneville. Behind the scenes, Stettinius and his consultant, Grenville Holden, vigorously opposed Reynold's entry into aluminum refining.[33]

With the Ickles' help, Reynolds persevered despite the objections and backroom intrigues of Stettinius and Holden. To protect Alcoa, they blocked other new entrants from producing aluminum and from using new methods. In March 1941, the Bohn Aluminum Co., sought a loan to produce aluminum, which Holden denied. Although OPM had been ladling out millions of dollars to help businesses expand for the war effort, Holden told Bohn: "The Army is not disposed to finance expansion of industrial capacity with government funds as long as any company is prepared to expand with private funds." Holden was likewise uninterested in expanding aluminum production even when a private company from Switzerland sought to enter the market.[34] He opposed the use of low-grade ore in an effort to protect Alcoa, which controlled all the high-grade ore. With the increased demand for aluminum for bombers, the only North American high-grade ore deposit was exhausted in two years.

From May to October 1940, corporate America engaged in a sit-down strike. Led by the aviation industry, defense contracts were left unsigned until the corporations received special tax privileges. Unlike labor strikes, the sit-down strikes of corporate America had the support of the news media, the

War and Navy Departments, and the new Defense Commission. The media labeled any strikes by labor as treason. No labor strikes were launched against any aviation corporation, yet hardly any planes were produced.

A look at the ships in service on Jan. 31, 1941 only confirms the serious lack of Navy war vessels. In three of the five categories listed, the total tonnage falls short of what Congress authorized in 1934.

	Authorized 1934	In Service 1941[35]
Battleships	525,000 tons	464,300
Aircraft Carriers	135,000 tons	134,800
Cruisers	343,770 tons	328,973
Destroyers	190,000 tons	217,390
Submarines	68,298 tons	107,960

The inadequacy of the Navy's procurement of warships is glaring in comparison to fleets of the Axis powers.[36]

	Jan. 1, 1941		Jan. 1, 1943	
Ships	U.S.	Axis	U.S.	Axis
Battleships	15	20	18	28
Aircraft Carriers	6	8	7	8
Cruisers	37	75	45	101
Destroyers	159	271	219	325
Submarines	105	284	133	500

Except for destroyers in 1941–43, the U.S. shipbuilding industry barely outpaced the losses suffered in the first year of the war. Fortunately, England's Royal Navy was up to the task of ruling the seas.

In May 1940, the financial editor of the *New York Sun* was astonished by the British 100-percent excess-profits tax. Corporate America, which built Hitler's war machine in violation of the Treaty of Versailles, was in no hurry to arm the United States or its Allies. The July 29, 1940 issue of *Barron's Financial Weekly* reported: "The attitude of some defense industries that they must be assured of a profit is souring many Washington dispositions, even in the pro-business War and Navy Departments." Unlike GIs who were drafted and defended their country for the paltry sum of $21 a month, the aviation industry reaped millions.

In June 1940, Congress changed the Vinson-Trammell Act of 1934 to limit profits on competitively bid contracts to 8 percent; 7 percent on other contracts. Roosevelt signed the bill on June 28, 1940, but by July 10, he had to surrender to corporate America and its sit-down strike.

Besides dropping the limits on profits, corporate America demanded and received legislation that enabled companies building new plants or equipment to amortize the investment in five years. Assistant Secretary of War Louis Johnson sent out a letter to all plane manufacturers asking for work to begin immediately, even though it took 60 days for the new bill to pass through Congress. The plane manufacturers waited.

Even with the special tax breaks, corporate America chose to invest little of its own money in new plants and equipment, choosing instead to let the government directly finance the expansion. By April 13, 1941, the proportion of private funds invested in expanding various defense industries was minuscule, as shown in the table below.

Tanks and Vehicles	24%
Aircraft	16%
Guns and Parts	12%
Ammunition	6%
Ship Construction	3%

Of the $2.8 billion in planned expansion of defense factories, private capital only accounted for $773 million. The average government spending for plant expansion was $6 million, while the average spending of private capital under the five-year amortization was $60,000. Corporate America was holding the free world hostage. The figures in the table above are enough of a testament to bury the myth that private enterprise built America and created a "Fortress of Democracy." In fact, it was all done with taxpayers' money.

Industry after industry, the story was much the same as it was for aluminum. In the critical machine tool industry, corporate America continued to drag its feet and delayed war production. General Motors could have made available about 15 million man-hours of machine tooling if it had foregone a model change. If the entire auto industry had foregone model changes in 1942, more than 30 million man-hours of machine tooling could have been freed up for the war effort. General Motors promised to give up a model change and then quickly went ahead with it anyway.

Against Roosevelt's call for full production, survey after survey found machine tools sitting idle. According to the March issue of *Monthly Labor Review*, a publication of the Department of Labor, weekend shutdowns were common. A survey of 45 machine tool plants found only 14 running three shift. Another 19 ran two shifts, but the number of workers on the second shift was less than 20 percent of the day shift. In plants with three shifts, only 25 percent of workers were on the second and third shifts.

The AFL Machinist's Union charged that the major obstacle was the strong anti-unionism of the Metal Trade Association and its fear of hiring new, pro-union workers. In May 1941, a Bureau of Labor Statistics study revealed a high ratio of workers had quit the machine tool industry because of the repressive working conditions. There was no labor shortage. In 11 categories of skilled machinists, there were only prospective shortages of labor in four.

Further complicating the shortage in machine tools was the industry's widespread reluctance to subcontract work to small shops. In this they were protected by the dollar-a-year men. In one case, community and labor leaders in Beaver County, Pa. were concerned with the war effort, and prepared a 60-page booklet listing the production plants and labor supply available. The booklet was delivered to Sidney Hillman's division of the Defense Commission in charge of labor, the only division actively interested in farming out defense contracts to small firms.

The Defense Commission ignored the Beaver County booklet. The factories of Beaver County's small businesses went unused. The idle factories in Beaver County included five modern machine shops that, together, could handle large contracts, and seven extra plants with partially available production for alloy iron, steel, brass and aluminum castings. Also available: seven pipe and tube mills; two plants producing machine tools parts; two plants for metal stampings; four plants for light steel fabrication; two producing rivets, bolts and nuts; five plants for all kinds of wood packaging crates. It was not until May 1941 that Beaver County received its first subcontract, a mere $1,500 for nuts and bolts, despite pleas from Roosevelt to use all available production plants.

The dollar-a-year-men staffing the Defense Commission and OPM were not interested in small firms. Instead, they sought to protect their former corporations, many of which held cartel agreements with IG Farben. With a stranglehold on wartime production, large corporations held the nation hostage. By the end of the war, only 31 corporations ran 50 percent of the government-built plants. The 100 largest ran 75 percent of them.[37]

Labor statistics confirm how the largest corporations used the war to the disadvantage of smaller firms. In 1939, firms with fewer than 500 employees employed 52 percent of all manufacturing workers. Five years later, these firms employed only 38 percent. Corporations employing more than 10,000 employees accounted for less than 13 percent of all workers in 1939, but by 1944, they accounted for 31 percent of the workforce. The war against fascism became a war for corporatism.

Only in aluminum did the RFC finance a competitor to break a production monopoly, and then only at the beginning of the transformation to a war economy. By 1940, with war raging in Europe, the large corporations were in the catbird seat. Roosevelt was powerless to assert control over war production, as the repeal of the changed Vinson-Trammell Act attests. Men could be drafted to serve their country, but capital was exempt. Any attempt to draft capital would have been met with immediate cries of communism from the right-wing and pro-Nazi groups. The nation's security was held hostage by the same corporations that built Hitler's war machine, and whose senior management and owners supported many of the pro-fascist groups.

The Battle for the Home Front

By mid-1942, the war news was gloomy. Rommel's Panzers raced across North Africa and were within 60 miles of the Nile. On the Eastern Front, Hitler's forces were at the gates of Stalingrad. The Luftwaffe was pounding London into rubble. Ships from the United States bound for England were disappearing under the waves of the Atlantic at an alarming rate, victims of Hitler's wolf packs. The Philippines had fallen to the Japanese.

It was during this time, our darkest moment of the war, that the most devastating blow was struck. No ships were sunk, no planes lost and no soldiers killed. This was a different assault, a battle for the minds of Americans. It would open the third front of the war on the home shores. It would be a battle that free people could hardly afford to lose.

Wrapped up in an electioneering jingle and cloaked behind a false flag of patriotism, Lammont duPont hid the very heart of fascism. Behind a thin veil of false patriotism and free enterprise lurked the root of fascism — corporate rule. Thus began the most blatant fraud ever perpetrated against the American people. In effect, duPont dressed up fascism with a smiley face to mollify the American people. To accomplish this horrific swindle of freedom and liberty, all resources were deployed. It became a full-scale assault on the rights of the American people that continues to this day. Under the banner of this feckless new goddess of free enterprise, the fascists in the United States launched a multipronged attack against our freedoms. One prong questioned the patriotism of anyone not subscribing to unbridled corporations; another prong attacked unionism; and the third attacked socialism and communism.

This forgotten campaign launch by one of the most notorious fascists of his time is imperative to understanding fascism in America following the war. It clearly marks the beginning of the right wing's adoption of the fascist ideology. Before Eisenhower's troops ever started marching across North Africa and before the Marines ever started island-hopping one bloody atoll after another toward the Japanese homeland, a third front of the war was raging in the American homeland for the control of the people. Tragically, the heroic efforts of the war against fascism were lost as quickly as the Third Reich crumbled into ashes. While our armies were victorious on the battlefields of Europe and the South Pacific, the battle for the homeland was lost. The new goddess of free enterprise replaced democracy in America. Instead of corporations serving the general interest of society, society was now forced to serve the interest of corporations.

DuPont's political slogan of "free enterprise" had been invented by the National Manufacturers Association (NAM) during the 1930's, in an attempt to avoid the negative connotations of the word "capitalism," such as the blame for the Depression. There is no such right listed in the constitution nor does the constitution grant any rights to corporations. While the founders believed in an economy based on property rights, they were hardly foolish enough to allow trade to go on unregulated. A third of the populace during the revolution had been indentured servants to British corporations, and the states regulated corporations closely. However, unregulated corporationism was precisely what duPont meant by free enterprise.

The agenda of "free enterprise," as envisioned by Lammont duPont, can be seen from his speech before a secretive meeting of the resolution committee for the National Manufacturers Association (NAM) on Sept. 17, 1942.

The way to view the issue is this: Are there common denominators for winning the war and the peace? If there are, then, we should deal with both in 1943. What are they? We will win the war by reducing taxes on corporations, high-income brackets, and increasing taxes on lower incomes, by removing unions from any power to tell industry how to produce, how to deal with their employees or anything else, by destroying any and all government agencies that stand in the way of free enterprise.[38]

DuPont's calls to overthrow any government agency that hindered him were subversive and treasonous. It is the same agenda followed by Hitler on taking power. As we enter the 21st century, it is the same agenda put forward by the Republicans and the right-wingers.

The media immediately began praising the virtues of free enterprise, while ignoring duPont's funding of the pro-Nazi Liberty League and Black Legion and involvement in the fascist plot against the White House a decade before. This was a full-scale assault against the New Deal and responsible government. The timing of this campaign for free enterprise coincided with the 1942 election that reduced the Democrats' majority in Congress. In effect, it left Congress under the control of the Republicans and conservative "Dixiecrats."

Throughout the 1920s and into the 1930s, the duPonts and other munitions makers were embroiled in congressional investigations into war profiteering. As the battle for Midway raged, the duPonts were already covering up their crimes of war profiteering and their dealings with the Nazis, with the help of the media.

The major newspaper chains and media outlets were openly pro-fascist. The Hearst papers published the most notorious Nazi propaganda unedited. The Chamber of Commerce, the American Legion and the National Association of Manufacturers (NAM) quickly adopted the false goddess of free enterprise, especially NAM with its mouthpiece Fulton Lewis broadcasting over the airwaves. Lewis was one of Hoover's media allies who often received leaked information from the FBI. This became a standard form of attack by Hoover and the FBI against a group or an individual. Lacking information to convict, Hoover would seek to destroy his targets by leaking rumors to his press allies.[39] Nixon and Joe McCarthy later adopted the tactic.

NAM performed a central propaganda role. Seldes, arguably the best investigative reporter of the 20th century, devotes two chapters in *Facts and Fascism* to exposing NAM and Fulton Lewis.[40] Frederick C. Crawford headed NAM. During the 1930s, Crawford was a director of Associated Industries, a strikebreaking agency. Three congressional committees investigated NAM. The Garrett Committee exposed its lobby as secretive and reprehensible. The lobby functioned to defeat members of Congress who opposed its policies of illegal strikebreaking and other actions. The O'Mahoney Investigation showed that 200 industrial firms and 50 financial families owned, controlled and ruled the United States. Of these families, 13 were the most powerful.

In congressional hearings on March 2, 1938, evidence showed 207 firms controlled and financed NAM. Leading the list of firms were General Motors, duPont, Chrysler, National Steel and Pennsylvania Railroad. The leading contributors to NAM also were the leading contributors to many pro-Nazi groups, such as the American Liberty League, the Crusaders, Sentinels of the Republic, and the National Economy League. In the Senate report produced by Sen. Black, *Special Committee to Investigate*

Lobbying Activities, letters from members of the Sentinels stated: "the old line Americans of $1,200 a year want a Hitler," "the New Deal is communist" and "the Jewish threat is a real one."[41]

At the same secret meeting of the resolution committee in which duPont was quoted above, NAM hammered out its agenda for the future. The platform included a fight against any management-labor committees. These committees were a prominent part of wartime contracts. They were indispensable in overcoming obstacles and bottlenecks in production. Freeing Wall Street from all controls and driving women out of industry after the war figured prominently in the NAM platform.

More disturbing was the call to launch a propaganda campaign in high schools and colleges, and to abolish the social programs of the New Deal. Even more ominous was a threat to sabotage war production and to undermine Roosevelt's prestige unless NAM's demands to make the poor pay for the war were met.

A quick look at the officers of the National Industrial Information Committee, the propaganda arm of NAM, reads like a Who's Who of fascists. J.H. Rand, president of Remington Rand, used newspapers to propagate lies about big labor during strikes. Walter D. Fuller, president of Curtis Publishing, was the man responsible for the pro-fascist attitude of the *Saturday Evening Post.* The pro-Franco and pro-fascist H.W. Pretis, president of Armstrong Cork, was listed by Attorney General Jackson as un-American. Sen. Gillette exposed Howard Pew of Sun Oil as the main subsidizer of the Republican Party in Pennsylvania. Pew also was a large financial contributor to the Sentinels, Crusaders and other pro-fascist groups. With his threat to pull a big ad contract, Pew was responsible for the *New York Times* going Republican in 1940. Colby Chester and William Warner, CEOs of General Foods and McCall Corp. respectively, headed NAM when the La Follette investigation found the association guilty of employing spies.

The power behind NAM was the Special Conference Committee, comprised of 12 corporations: ATT, Bethlehem Steel, E.I. Du Pont de Nemours, General Electric, General Motors, Goodyear Tire, International Harvester, Irving Trust, Standard Oil of N.J., U.S. Rubber, United Steel and Westinghouse.[42] The secretive business organization was dedicated to destroying unions and promoting the NAM agenda. With one possible exception, all the corporations supplied the Nazis with arms.

In 1943, Colombian University professor Robert Brady described the Special Conference Committee:

The most important line of policies within NAM, in short, seems to be traceable directly or indirectly to this inside clique within the inner councils of the organization ... Nowhere else is shown so clearly the dominating positions in the NAM of ... members of the Special Conference Committee. Public relations techniques were born, nurtured and brought to flower within these ranks." They met in the offices of Standard Oil, 30 Rockefeller Plaza.[43]

The Civil Liberties report produced by a Senate committee led by La Follette and Thomas described the Special Conference Committee as a secret coalition in direct furtherance of the specific forms of company unions used by the Rockefeller-owned Colorado Fuel and Iron, which resulted in the Ludlow massacre.

According to Seldes, the 13 most powerful families in the United States and members of NAM are: Ford, duPont, Rockefeller, Mellon, McCormick, Hartford, Harkness, Duke, Pew, Pitcairn, Clark, Reynolds and Kress. Of these, five were involved in the plot of against Roosevelt: duPont, Mellon, Pew, Pitcairn and Clark. With the possible exception of three, all of these families had close connections with fascism and arming Hitler.

NAM was more than just a mouthpiece for the fascist elite. It also was a bridge group between classes, as in Germany, where rich financial backers held the real power behind the Nazi movement. The legions of Brown Shirts making up most of the Nazi membership came from the lower classes, while the upper classes maintained control and directed the party's policies. In the United States, NAM bridged the class gap with the Black Legion and, even more importantly, by linking the nativist groups with fascism.

Members of the Black Legion in Michigan's Oakland County were mostly unskilled and semi-skilled workers who had migrated to the Detroit area from the hill country of the South. They were unused to an urban environment. The insecurity and monotony of factory work made them eager to join an organization that promised power and adventure. The following quote characterizes the average Black Legion member.

He came from a small farm in the South. He had gone through grammar school, though he had not received a high school diploma. Married, the father of two children, working on construction or as unskilled labor in a steel plant or auto assembly line, he never came to reconcile himself to city life or industrial work. His greatest concern was obtaining and holding a job for his family's sake. To the general insecurity of the times was added the fear that alien labor might displace him. Detroit had a large immigrant labor population and this offered further justification for the traditional nativist dislike of alien groups.[44]

The upper levels of NAM made public references to the alien nature of unions, calling them un-American and anti-American, playing on the fears foremost in the mind of the average Black Legion member. Many of the top John Birch officials, including Robert Welch himself, were also NAM officers. The John Birch Society was a group of far right-wing extremists created by NAM and controlled by former NAM officials to appeal to the poor and middle class. The JBS chain of bookstores in the late 1950s and early 1960s were directed specifically at the lower middle classes and served as propaganda centers for the hard right. The Black Legion did not have the same type of direct link to NAM, but was directed and controlled by the automakers in the Detroit area.

With almost unlimited power, corporations were able to create and fund many fronts to hide their support for fascism. Often these fronts would have a claim to respectability. While NAM was at the forefront of propagandizing the new goddess of free enterprise, other groups figured prominently as well, especially the Chamber of Commerce. During the 1920s and 1930s, the Chamber of Commerce took on a fascist character and was sympathetic to both Hitler and Mussolini.

The Chamber of Commerce wrote the 1934 report, *Combating Subversion Activities in the United States,* which became a blueprint for repressing the Left in the 1950s and the McCarthy Era.[45] The report demanded the passage of anti-subversive legislation, including a sedition law, and urged that a special agency in the Justice Department be created to investigate subversive activities, with special attention to communists.

In 1948, the Chamber of Commerce published a pamphlet, *Program for Community Anti-Communist Action,* that contained detailed instructions for developing and keeping a system of files which was nothing more than a blacklist.[46] These lists have their roots in nativism and serve as an ideological resource for the promoters of corporate America. They are common among the various groups that have comprised the far right since the end of the war. The Church League and the American Security Council were two of the largest compilers of such blacklists.

By most measures, duPont's campaign for free enterprise was an overall success. Even more remarkable is the relatively short time in which it was accomplished. The press suppressed all efforts to oppose this fascist campaign, including Roosevelt's State of the Union Address on Jan. 11, 1944, in which he proposed an economic bill of rights:

The right of a useful and remunerative job in the industries, or shops or farms or mines of the nation.

The right to earn enough to provide adequate food and clothing and recreation.

The right of every farmer to raise and sell his products at a return which will give him and his family a decent living.

The right of every businessman, large and small, to trade in an atmosphere of freedom from unfair competition and domination by monopolies at home or abroad.

The right of every family to a decent home.

The right to adequate medical care and the opportunity to achieve and enjoy good health.

The right to adequate protection from the economic fears of old age, sickness, accident and unemployment.

The right to a good education.[47]

The media also suppressed the "Century of the Common Man Speech" by Roosevelt's Vice President, Wallace. Note the sweeping success of the Republicans and hard right in denying these basic rights to the American people: more than sixty years later, Americans still have not gained a single one. The right wing actively opposes increases in the minimum wage law; agrobusiness corporations are replacing the remaining family farmers, and social welfare has been reduced to inadequate levels. We still have no national healthcare plan that ensures everyone's basic right to satisfactory medical treatment. Former Mayor of New York City Rudy Giuliani even adopted a program in which the homeless who refused work were denied shelter and their children were made wards of the fascist state. Big corporations dominate the economy . Republicans and right-wingers are feverishly trying to destroy one of the most successful programs created under FDR — Social Security. George W. Bush has eliminated overtime pay for many workers. This is the sad state of America today. Republicans grant billions in corporate welfare to corporations, but grudge to spare a red cent for a poor man. They are condemning millions to a life of poverty with no hope of ever bettering themselves.

In the 1946 election, Republicans gained a majority in both the Senate and the House, and immediately set out to attack labor and unions on all fronts. At one time, there were no fewer than 200 anti-union bills in the House. The Taft-Hartley Act emerged out of the fray, over President Truman's veto. Republican Fred Hartley from New Jersey proposed the bill in the House. Hartley had been more than friendly with the Hitler regime and Japan, if not an outright fascist right up to the day the Japanese bombed Pearl Harbor.[48] The act severely restricted the activities of unions, and gave corporations the right to interfere with union organizing and to propagandize their employees. Writing the bill were lobbyists for large corporations, such as General Electric, Allis-Chalmers, Inland Steel, J.I. Case and other large industrials. Congress added several amendments favoring small businesses to ensure passage over Truman's veto. It soon became known as the Slave Labor Act. Thus, in four short years, the fascist agenda of the duPonts was marching swiftly forward, destroying the rights of labor and setting a course for corporate rule.

The passage of the Taft-Hartley Act was closely associated with the Allis-Chalmers strike of 1946–47. Local CIO 248 succeeded in uniting its workers through tough times and solidified the support of labor. Members of the local looked forward to increasing wages and better working conditions. Allis-Chalmers had anticipated the end of the war and was spoiling for a confrontation, to break unionism in Wisconsin.

Much as the media played a major role in union busting during the Red Scare of 1919, they now fanned the flames of a new Red Scare. On Sept. 23, 1946, the *Milwaukee Sentinel* launched an expose, "Communists in Local 248." An Allis-Chalmers' speechwriter secretly wrote the article. Company management soon got another boost from Charles Wilson, head of General Electric and former Vice Chairman of the War Production Board, who stated: "The problem of the United States can be captiously summed up in two words: Russia abroad and Labor at home."

Allis-Chalmers conflated elements of communism and labor to break one of the nation's most important postwar strikes. Right-wing extremists controlled the company. Maz Babb and Walter Geist headed the management; successive presidents of the corporation were leaders of the pro-Nazi America First group. Harold Story headed labor relations at Allis-Chalmers and was instrumental in writing several of the provisions of the Taft-Hartley Act. After leaving the company, Story was elected to the Milwaukee School Board and led the anti-integration forces.

Several states passed right-to-work laws after intense lobbying pressure from the fascist group, Christian America, linked to the Kirby family of Texas. By 1950, labor had clearly lost; it would be another eight years before union membership peaked.

When the Freedom Train began to roll across America in 1947, it touted the right to free enterprise. Two freedoms that FDR held dear, freedom of speech and freedom from fear, were replaced with this nonexistent freedom. Before the Freedom Train completed its journey across country, displaying the Constitution, Declaration of Independence and Bill of Rights on stops in all 48 states, the right of unions to assemble was severely curtailed with the passage of the Taft-Hartley Act. No mention was made of FDR's Economic Bill of Rights. Ironically, one of the other freedoms — free speech — was trampled the most in the following years by Joe McCarthy. Freedom of religion was employed in the war on the home front for free enterprise and fascism. Including this display in the Freedom Train served only to spread the propaganda for the false god of free enterprise.

The second-prong attack on communism was even more successful. The adoption of fascism's basic tenets by the Right Wing in America in 1942 eventually led the world to the brink of a nuclear holocaust during the Cold War. It also led to one of the most repressive decades in the history of the country, the 1950s and the McCarthy Era. Rich industrialists and the CIA with its reliance on Nazi war criminals led the right-wing embrace of fascism in the postwar era.

The DuPont plot against freedom by duPont would not have succeeded without the aid of the pro-Nazi members of Congress like Fred Hartley.

The Nazis Run for Cover

Perhaps the most influential pro-fascist member of Congress who aided the duPonts' "free enterprise" was Martin Dies. Dies set about sabotaging the search for fascists by the House committee and, instead, started a witch hunt for Reds, including any ideology to the left of fascism, just as in the Great Red Scare of 1919. Previously, a Republican committee from Minnesota, led by some of the leading industrialists of that state, asked Dies to explore the communist influence in the Farmer-Labor Party. Both the FBI and the Dies committee were guilty of chasing Reds over fascists. Although both investigated a few fascists, the emphasis was on communists.

Ironically, the communists posed only a minor threat compared to the fascists, as the results from the 1936 election readily testify. In 1936, the pro-fascist candidate, Lemke, polled 882,479 votes, 11 times the vote total of the communist candidate.[49] In fact, the Communist Party vote in 1936 declined 20 percent from the 1934 election. Other polls from the era confirm the threat was from the Right and fascism, not communism or the Left. Polls of college professors of that time reveal a deep intolerance. One poll showed that 35 percent of professors omitted facts from textbooks that might lead to criticism of the social order. Another poll found that 48 percent of the professors favored deportation of aliens who criticized the constitution.[50]

Hoover was estranged from Dies after the congressman leveled charges that the FBI bungled the mass arrest of Spanish Civil War veterans that resulted in dismissed indictments. The arrest of these veterans who volunteered to fight fascism while the Right Wing was still apologetic to Hitler's cause stands as one of the great injustices of the 20th century. Their arrests were based solely on their political views, since most members of the Abraham Lincoln Brigade were either socialists or communists.[51] Their only crimes were their political views. Veterans of the Brigade suffered throughout their lives at the hands of Hoover and the FBI. As late as the 1990s, the FBI was still keeping them under surveillance. Dies even went so far as to Red-bait Attorney General Jackson, citing his support for such groups as the American League for Peace and Democracy, and the League of American Writers.

To further the duPonts' free-enterprise enterprise, the same whipping boy — menacing hordes of godless Reds — was recycled from WWI to protect the interests of the rich elite, which magnified and encouraged the fascist groups. Just as after WWI, labor unions were among the first groups charged with communist infiltration. One of Dies' first and primary targets was the longshoremen's leader Harry Bridges. He was finally deported in 1945 after 10 years of harassment by the Dies Committee and the FBI. Dies extended his attack on Bridges to a sweeping attack against Labor Secretary Frances Perkins.[52]

Dies and his committee also attacked the New Deal, extending their attack on communism to include liberal elements. One target was Eleanor Roosevelt. The FBI covertly leaked derogatory information about her to right-wing publicists.[53]

Other targets of Dies were California Democratic nominee for governor Culbert Olson, and Sen. Sheridan Downey. Charges were brought before the committee from the private sector, by Harper Knowles. He claimed to be a representative of the Radical Research Division of the American Legion; in reality, he represented a fascist-connected organization, Associated Farmers Inc. The Radical Research Division was created in the 1920s during the Red Scare to target union organizers and any group from the Left seen as a threat to business. Most of these radical research groups in the Legion formed after WWI and were partially responsible for fanning the flames of the Great Red Scare of 1919.

Downey's Republican opponent in the election was a millionaire landowner and member of the Associated Farmers, which worked to ban John Steinbeck's *Grapes of Wrath* from California public libraries. Knowles went on to found the Western Research Foundation, a blacklist operation that figured prominently in the 1970s and 1980s.[54]

A final example will prove just how psychopathic Dies was, as well as the extent of his Red hysteria. The case centered on J.B. Mathews' charges of communist influence in the consumer movement. Mathews and Fred Schlink were consumer advocates until Schlink's employees unionized and formed a rival Consumer Union. Mathews timed his release to coincide with a 1939 Federal Trade Commission (FTC) decision to cite Hearst's *Good Housekeeping* for fraudulent advertising. At least one manufacturer claimed the seal could be obtained simply by placing ads in the magazine. Other manufacturers claimed *Good Housekeeping* would withdraw its seal if the manufacturer discontinued their ads. The FTC decided to act after complaints from retailers and manufacturers. Hearst launched a massive anti-communist advertising blitz, and Dies threatened to open an investigation into the consumer groups.[55] Since these housewives and other manufacturers were threatening corporate America, they were branded as communist and discredited. It simply never occurred to Dies that housewives could have legitimate complaints about a product. They had to be godless Reds and their movement silenced.

In 1944, Dies chose not to seek reelection. However, this was not the end of his radical right-wing activities. During the late 1950s and early 1960s, he was a contributing editor of *American Opinion*, the tabloid published by the John Birch Society. Another contributing editor was Hans Sennholz, a former Luftwaffe pilot who taught economics at Grove City College. J. Howard Pew, owner of Sun Oil, heavily subsidized this institution. Pew was a huge benefactor of far right groups throughout the '40s and until his death.[56]

On convening the new Congress on Jan. 3, 1945, racist Mississippian John Rankin offered an amendment to make the Dies Committee a standing committee, and to increase its membership to nine. Thus was born the most notorious congressional committee of all time. The House Committee on Un-American Activities spanned another 30 years before finally being dismantled in the mid-1970s after the Watergate and COINTELPRO scandals. Unlike the Dies Committee, Hoover and his FBI cooperated fully with the new committee, using it to launder information from illegal wiretaps, black ops, and other dubious and unconstitutional methods. Like the Dies Committee, HUAC was only interested in destroying the Left Wing; corporate America protected right-wing extremists and fascists.

Although the duPonts' fascist campaign for free enterprise was an overall success in wrestling control of Congress from the liberals in the 1942 election, the new year brought a change in the fortunes of war. The Russian ally trapped Hitler's troops at Stalingrad. Montgomery's troops defeated Rommel at El Alamein. In the South Pacific, the U.S. Navy defeated the Japanese fleet at Midway and in the Coral Sea. The Axis was clearly defeated; it was only a matter of time before they would be forced to surrender.

With the imminent defeat of Nazi Germany pending in 1943, corporate America had to cover its tracks. The same corporations that were guilty of delaying war production in the sit-down strike and sponsoring pro-fascist groups at home also were guilty of knowingly trading with the Nazis during the war. A massive change in tactics was required to protect them from sedition or treason charges after war's end.

The change in tactics is clearly marked by three notable aspects. First, it marked the beginning of targeting those in the government who fully opposed fascism. Many of those in the Roosevelt administration or in the halls of Congress who called for the complete destruction of fascism were discredited, forced to resign or targeted for defeat in elections by corporate America. Several dedicated public servants who fought passionately against fascism were dismissed or otherwise discredited at the hands of the native fascists.

Below is a sampling of these individuals and the dates of their dismissals. The list is by no means complete; hundreds of others suffered the same fate.

Individual	Year Removed
William Maloney	1942
John Rogge	1946
Summer Wells	1943
Jerry Voorhis	1946
Norman Littell	1944
Harry Dexter White	1948

Second, it marked a distinct change in an openly aggressive, antagonistic attitude toward our Russian ally by the Right Wing in America. From 1941 to 1945, J. Edgar Hoover crisscrossed the country delivering speeches on the evils of communism. Each speech was more inflammatory and the threat more urgent than the one before. The House's Un-American Activities Committee stepped up its attacks on communists, leading to the McCarthy Era. Finally, many Nazis recruited by the CIA intensified the fear.

Finally, the change in tactics signaled a frantic effort for a negotiated peace. While there had been previous efforts for a negotiated peace, most notably by Texas oilman William Rhodes Davis in 1940, the new attempts clearly marked the beginning of the cover-up of corporate America's treasonous behavior. Allen Dulles and Prince Hohenlohe began the most significant peace plan during this time. In 1943, Dulles began meeting with Prince Hohenlohe, a Nazi. Dulles falsely claimed to speak for Roosevelt and agreed with Hohenlohe that postwar Germany should be the leader of industrial production in Europe to preserve a bulwark against Russia. Dulles was lying because Roosevelt was leaning toward the Morgenthau Plan calling for complete dismantling of German industry.

Dulles agreed with the prince that it would be unbearable for any European to think that Jews might return to positions of power. Dulles also said that Americans were only continuing the war to get rid of the Jews and that there were people in America who were intent on sending the Jews to Africa.

During his talks with Hohenlohe, Dulles gave away the entire battle plan for Europe. He told the Nazi prince that the Allies would not land in Spain, but instead, after conquering Tunisia, would advance toward Ploesti to cut off the German oil supply. This information was extremely useful to the Nazis. Besides freeing any troops needed to guard the Spanish frontier, it meant the Nazis' supply of tungsten from the Iberian Peninsula was safe. Dulles told Hohenlohe the Allies would invade Sicily to cut Rommel off.[57]

In other meetings, Dulles spoke of Papal action in negotiations. The Vatican played a significant role in the surrender of Wolff and in helping Nazi war criminals escape from Europe — and justice. In rebuilding Germany, Dulles spoke of preferring Bavaria and described a speech by Goebbels as a work of genius.

Noting that he was speaking for himself and other right-wing groups in America, Dulles disparaged Churchill and the British in their talks with the Russians over the Balkans. Finally, he requested that the American Embassy in Madrid aid Hohenlohe at any time.

Dulles spent more time giving away the Allies' battle plan than in discussing the proposed German peace treaty. He may have been stalling for time, hoping to delay the end of the war. He was well aware of the many American corporations doing a profitable business with the Nazis. He may also have hoped for a negotiated peace, or at least enough time to ferry the Nazis' ill-gotten assets out of Germany.

Dulles had several Americans in Switzerland who were willing collaborators with the Nazis. Alexander Kreuter was the American Nazi collaborator who aryanized the French Worms bank when the Nazis marched into Paris. Kreuter also had connections with Dillon and Read, the Wall Street firm that helped finance Hitler until 1934.

Another Dulles accomplice was Gerhardt Westrick, who had been a high-level German spy in Washington during WWI. He was a partner in the law firm of Westrick & Albert, which handled the German end of the lucrative reparations loan business with Sullivan & Cromwell. Westrick secured the assets of many American corporations throughout the war. His partner Heinrich Albert was head of the Ford operation in Germany. Albert received orders directly from Edsel Ford in Dearborn, Mich., to build trucks for the German army after the attack on Pearl Harbor.[58] Also included in the list of Dulles collaborators was the American Minister Plenipotentiary in Berne, Leland Harrison, who approved shipments of enemy oil through Switzerland, as well as American oil to fuel the German army.

The talks between Allen Dulles and the Nazi prince as the Third Reich collapsed were remarkably similar to the earlier peace plan by Davis in 1940. The major difference was that Himmler instead of Goering was to replace Hitler. In both cases, the Nazis remained in power and received U.S. aid to preserve a bulwark against Russia. It is not clear whether Dulles ever presented his peace plan to the White House. However, any such plans received a cold shoulder from the White House, because Roosevelt insisted on removing the Nazis from any position of power in Germany.

This was not the only peace effort advanced in 1943 by those claiming to represent Roosevelt. The head of the OSS, Bill Donovan, advanced another effort called the M Project. In July, Donovan ordered Theodore Morde, a former journalist for *Reader's Digest,* to meet the local OSS chief in Cairo. From there, Morde traveled to Turkey to meet with another OSS agent and to contact von Papen. The only condition for peace in Morde's plan was the arrest of Hitler. The plan was the same as what Dulles advanced earlier. It ended all lend-lease aid to the Soviet Union, and set up Germany as the dominating military and industrial force.

Returning to Washington, Morde wrangled a meeting with Roosevelt's speechwriter by claiming that Gen. Hurley sanctioned him to advance the proposed peace plan. The general immediately denounced Morde's initiative, calling it a thinly disguised attempt to promote *Reader's Digest*. In a memo dated Oct. 29, 1943, Donovan urged FDR to give Morde's plan serious consideration. Roosevelt quickly dismissed it.[59]

Wealthy anti-communist George Earle in Spain advanced a similar plan during the summer. After the Morde plan collapsed, Baron Kurt von Lersner proposed a new plan to Earle. Von Lersner claimed it was approved by a group of German officers, including the officer in charge of Hitler's cavalry division in East Prussia who would kidnap Hitler and make a peace proposal with only a single condition — the Soviet Union be precluded from invading Germany. Roosevelt again turned down the proposal.

In 1943, New York attorney Abram Stevens Hewitt advanced another peace plan. Like Morde and Earle, Hewitt falsely claimed to be a Roosevelt representative. The plan was once again similar to those advanced by Dulles and Morde. Early in 1944, Gabrielle Chanel, the perfume magnate, proposed yet another peace plan. Chanel tried to use her friend Lombardi's connections with the British royal family to advance it.

These secret and unauthorized negotiations reveal the extent that Dulles and others would go to sabotage the war effort. One item was common to all of these negotiations: The Nazis remained in power in Germany. By 1943, the Allies had clearly defeated Nazi Germany on the battlefield. The battles for Stalingrad and El Alamein were the turning points. Yet there was no talk of free elections in Germany. All plans centered on a more palatable replacement for Hitler, and a government friendly to corporate American collaborators.

Even more odious, these talks mark the beginning of the Cold War. Not only did these peace plans leave the Nazis in power, but they called for a rearming of Germany as a bulwark against Russia. Corporate America and the rich industrialists had to be protected at all costs against their enemies, real and imagined. The war had been profitable for them and a new war against the Soviets would be too. The benefits and profits of fair trade with Russia would be small in comparison. Corporate America was willing to risk another major war that neither the American nor the Russian people wanted, even if it meant pushing the world to the brink of a nuclear holocaust to inflate the bottom line.

Both Donovan and Allen Dulles came from Wall Street. Donovan was a prominent Wall Street lawyer involved with the Drug Inc., cartel. Dulles worked extensively for the American cartel partners of IG Farben to conceal their Nazi ownership from the U.S. government. While stationed in Switerzland he smuggled of his corporate clients' profits out of Germany to safe havens. Both Donovan and Dulles had intimate knowledge of the extensive involvement of U.S. corporations with the Nazis, and both were in ideal positions to cover up the crimes of corporate America.

In 1943, war production peaked. Thereafter, with a decline in military orders a new problem emerged — reconversion to a consumer economy. Once the military canceled its contracts, small firms wanted to go back to producing goods for the consumer. This set off a firestorm of protest among the dollar-a- year men with the War Production Board (WPG). They argued that allowing the small firms to immediately reenter the consumer market was unfair and would take business away from the larger firms that were fulfilling military contracts. In effect, big business demanded the same percent share of the market during reconversion that it had before the war. The same firms engaged in the sit-down strike were now demanding that no reconversion take place until after the war was over.

In early 1943, the War Department attempted to have WPG Chairman Donald Nelson fired. Secretaries of War and Navy, Stimson and Knox, respectively, and their under–secretaries, Patterson and Forrestal, scheduled a meeting with Roosevelt to demand that Nelson be replaced by Bernard Baruch, the choice of big business. His wartime plan rested on the assumption that industry should have the right to decide and manage the controls needed. The end of such folly was that big business would gain full control of the economy. The Baruch plan included special legislation to prevent the use of antitrust laws to penalize an overly enthusiastic exercise of that power. In effect, it would grant big businesses powers over the economy that exceeded the government's power to regulate commerce.[60] Nelson avoided being dismissed. He later brought in GE President Charles Wilson as WPG co-chairman. In the fall of 1943, Wilson made a speech warning against fascist thinking among the higher ranks of big business.[61]

On July 7, 1973, Nelson received a letter from Adm. William Leahy:

> We are disturbed over the existing lag in war production which, if it continues, may necessitate revision in strategic plans which could prolong the war.
>
> In view of the major offensive operations under way on every front, it is essential at this time that there be no relaxation in war production and that deficits in deliveries be made up at the earliest possible date.
>
> The issuance of orders at this time which will affect our ability to produce war materials is not consistent with the all-out prosecution of the war.[62]

In an unusual move, the letter was published on July 9. Of course, the letter was an appeal to the public and not to Nelson, as contracts were already being canceled or not renewed by the War Department. Leahy was hoping to panic the public into opposing the WPG's policies on reconversion.

By 1944, those supporting the fascist line of corporate rule clearly gained the upper hand. In January 1944, Charles Wilson proposed the wedding of the military to corporate America. Wilson suggested that every large corporation appoint a liaison with the armed forces with a commission of colonel or above in the reserve. The liaison would coordinate industrial production to meet the military's need. Excerpts from his proposal follow:

> First of all such a [preparedness] program must be the responsibility of the federal government. It must be initiated and administrated by the executive branch — by the President as Commander in Chief and by the War and Navy Departments. Of equal importance is the fact that this must be, once and for all, a continuing program and not the creature of an emergency. In fact one of its objects will be to eliminate emergencies so far as possible. The role of Congress is limited to voting the needed funds...
>
> Industry's role in this program is to respond and cooperate ... in the execution of the part allotted to it; industry must not be hampered by political witch hunts, or thrown to the fanatical isolationist fringe tagged with a merchants of death label.[63]

Wilson's proposal reduced the role of Congress to merely providing funds. Under such a system, no congressional investigations were possible. It removed the checks and balances provided in the constitution. Fraud would become widespread under such a system because there would be no congressional investigations into $800 toilet seats or other dubious items.

Wilson's words embraced the very heart of fascism and the power that ruled Germany the military-industrial Nazi alliance. In essence, Wilson's proposal was identical to Germany's Economic High Command that allowed the Nazis to wage total war.

Wilson's proposal formed the basis of what so alarmed Eisenhower a decade later, the military-industrial complex. It became the nerve center from which the Cold War was waged. Congress would be removed from the approval of new weapons systems, and investigating misappropriation of funds and profit mongering.

As 1944 proceeded, it became clearer that the Axis powers were defeated and orders for war munitions continued to decrease. After the war, there would be an enormous supply of government-built factories up for grabs. The same large corporations that engaged in the sit-down strike and froze smaller firms out of defense production wanted to obtain ownership of these factories. However, they had been built solely with government funds, because the large corporations refused to invest in expanding their own factories for the war effort. By the end of the war, the federal government owned 10 percent of industrial capacity. An estimated $60 billion in war surplus was up for grabs.

Large corporations had to force the government to give up control of these plants or face a formidable new competitor. The corporations did not want these plants to fall into the hands of smaller firms, either. A fire sale for large corporations was arranged, which successfully rigged the bidding process to exclude smaller firms. Competitive bids from firms other than those that had run the plants during the war were only rarely allowed. With competion successfully removed from the bidding, the low-ball bids of the large corporations were accepted. The government received only pennies on the dollar. U.S. Steel got 71 percent of the government-built integrated steel plants. Just four corporations received the synthetic rubber and polymer plants. Eventually, two-thirds of all the government-built plants went to just 87 large corporations.[64]

Corporate Traitors

The large corporations faced other problems with the war's end. Many of these corporations grew large thanks to cartel agreements with German firms that gave them exclusive production rights in the United States, while the German firms held the patents. Central to Truman's plan to preclude Germany's ability to wage war and to break up IG Farben was the removal of patents from German hands. An unnamed executive of U.S. Steel Corp. with extensive ties to Schmitz and the Krupp firm attempted to reverse Truman's policy. This executive called for immediate re-opening of the German Patent Office and a prohibition on inspections. Opening the patent office, with a ban on searches, would have been disastrous for decartelization and de-Nazification programs.[65]

War's end also could have revealed the many crimes of a corporate America willingly supplying the Nazis with munitions. Dealings with the Nazis during the war occurred with the direct knowledge of the American corporate headquarters and often at the direction from the head office. Forget the alibi that Nazis forced these poor corporations to aid them. Generally, nothing could be further from the truth. Many of these corporations went to extraordinary measures to remain in control of their assets in Germany, fully cooperating with the Nazis in violation of the law and all moral principles.

During the Allis-Chalmers strike, Charles Wilson spoke of only two problems — unions and communism. The media focused on these two issues into the next decade. Union members, government employees and teachers were forced to sign loyalty oaths. Russia was a new menace. There were no reports in the media of Ford building trucks for the Nazis, or of any other American corporation aiding Germany.

Until recently, the media has led the American people to believe that only a handful of American corporations ever invested in Germany or dealt directly with the Nazis. But a recent Newsweek article puts the number of American corporations involved in supplying the Nazis at more than 300.[66] However, even this article is shamefully apologetic to corporate America and plainly inaccurate on other accounts. It shamefully tries to exonerate some of the most notorious fascists in America during the war, the duPonts, by suggesting they did not invest in Nazi Germany after the 1930s. The reality is that the duPonts had several cartel agreements with the Nazis and were openly pro-fascist supporters in this country. The duPonts also controlled General Motors, whose Opel division in Germany built a large portion of the vehicles for the Third Reich.

According to Reuters, another article from German investigators found that 26 of the top 100 firms in the United States were guilty of serious war crimes. One report is particularly damaging to Ford and General Motors. It indicates that U.S. lawyers have direct evidence that the companies knowingly used slave labor and closely collaborated with the Nazis; evidence which gave rise to a class action suit; it was dismissed on a sovereignty pretext, and Ford settled out of court for $5 billion.[67] The report substantiates that many of the links between corporate America and the Nazis began in the 1920s.

The Newsweek article details the actions of John Foster Dulles and Sullivan & Cromwell that helped cloak Nazi ownership of the U.S. subsidiary of Bosch. They hid the real ownership by drafting a voting trust agreement, making the Wallenbergs' Enskilda Bank a dummy owner. The fraud worked throughout the war, until Bosch's American subsidiary was forced on the auction block in 1948. This is but one of many such frauds involving the actions of Sullivan & Cromwell, as well as both of the Dulles brothers.

These articles provide good examples of unlawful conduct of American corporations. The use of slave labor by Ford and General Motors, and the seizure of Jewish accounts by the Paris branch of Chase Bank are typical of the crimes corporate America committed during the war. To understand fully how such crimes against humanity have gone unpunished for half a century, one needs to follow the money trail, beginning with the Bank for International Settlements (BIS). A look at international financial intrigue paints a vivid picture of the dangers of the World Trade Organization and how it currently imperils freedom globally.

The world's central banks, including the Federal Reserve, created BIS in 1930. BIS was inspired by Hjalmar Horace Greeley Schacht, who later became the Nazi Minister of Economics and president of the Reichsbank. Schacht was raised in Brooklyn and had powerful Wall Street connections. He foresaw the rise of Hitler and the outbreak of WWII. Even before Hitler rose to power, Schacht pushed for an institution that would retain communication and collusion with the world's financial leaders in the event of war. Thus, it was written into its charter that BIS would be immune from seizure, even if its owners were at war.

One of the owners of BIS was the Morgan-affiliated First National Bank of New York. The Morgans had extensive connections with BIS, which was founded to provide the Allies with reparations from WWI as part of the Young Plan. GE board member Owen Young was a Morgan banker. One of the BIS directors was Wendell Willkie, the candidate of choice among the native fascist group to unseat Roosevelt.

Here is the crux of the power. Immune from seizure, the bank was free to act as it wished under whoever retained control. Citizens of other countries and, indeed, even governments, were powerless to oppose the bank or its actions. Instead, the bank was free to hold the world at the mercy of its knighted financial autocrats.

Granting such powers to any institution is foolhardy at best and a mistake that should never be repeated. However, after more than 50 years, the world has yet to catch on. Currently the world's financial knights are reengineering BIS in the form of the Multilateral Agreement on Investment (MAI), GATS and other free trade agreements. In effect, all of these so-called free trade agreements would override the Bill of Rights and hold a country responsible for any losses a corporation incurred from any legal action caused by the country or its citizens. Further, these trade agreements prevent a country from withdrawing by assessing penalties for lost income for up to 20 years after withdrawal. Again, the media is playing the role of an obedient lapdog for its corporate masters. The media have done such a good job in killing the story on MAI and its ramifications that most Americans have never heard of it.[68]

By the outbreak of war, BIS was under Hitler's control. BIS directors included Thomas McKittrick, an associate of the Morgans; Herman Schmitz, head of IG Farben; Kurt von Schroeder, head of the J.H. Stein Bank of Cologne and leading financier of the Gestapo; Walter Funk, president of the Reichsbank; and Emil Puhl, vice president of the Reichsbank. In May 1946 at the Nuremberg Trials, Walter Funk testified that shortly before Pearl Harbor, Chase Bank offered Puhl a major post in New York. Such an offer by Chase to a leading Nazi banker reveals the callous disregard of any moral principles. Surely at such a late date, with Europe already embroiled in war, Chase could not have been oblivious to Nazi atrocities and aggression.

The first BIS president was Gates McGarrah, formerly of Chase National Bank. During the first two years Hitler was in power, McGarrah was instrumental in financing the Nazis through BIS. In 1940, McKittrick met at the Reichsbank with Kurt von Schroeder and the Gestapo to discuss how to continue doing business if war broke out. On Feb. 5, 1942, two months after the bombing of Pearl Harbor, the Reichsbank and the German and Italian governments approved orders that allowed McKittrick to remain in charge of BIS. One of the documents of authorization simply stated, "McKittrick's opinions are safely known by us."[57] In response, McKittrick gratefully arranged a loan of several million Swiss francs to the Nazi puppet governments of Poland and Hungary.

On Sept. 7, 1942, McKittrick issued the first annual report after Pearl Harbor by reading it to an empty room. He could thereby report to Washington that no Nazi directors were present. The report itself was sheer Nazi propaganda, assuming an immediate peace in favor of Germany with a sizable distribution of American gold to stabilize the German mark. In the spring of 1943, McKittrick traveled to Berlin in violation of U.S. law, after meeting with Leon Fraser of the First National Bank of New York and the heads of the Federal Reserve. His mission was to provide Emil Puhl with secret intelligence on financial problems and high-level attitudes in the United States.[69]

On March 26, 1943, liberal California Congressman Jerry Voorhis entered a resolution in the House of Representatives calling for an investigation of BIS. Congress failed to consider the matter. Voorhis was a liberal Californian representative, a supporter of the New Deal and a relentless opponent of fascism. In 1945, Voorhis attacked the policy of placing former officers of American companies tied to IG Farben in the Office of Military Government (OMG), which was tasked with destroying IG Farben. One such person assigned to OMG was Col. Frederick Pope. Before the war, Pope had been a director or top official of more than one of IG Farben's American affiliates.[70]

Obviously, if Congress investigated either BIS or IG Farben, the risk was that many American corporations that continued trading with the Nazis would be exposed. Those Nazi sympathizers had but one choice: Voorhis had to be eliminated. The cabal of Nazi supporters selected Richard Nixon to run against Voorhis in the 1946 election.

At that time, Nixon was an unknown outside California and only a bit player in the state, yet he Nixon received financial support from the Wall Street firm Sullivan & Cromwell. With a big campaign wad, Nixon easily defeated Voorhis by branding him a communist. Nixon later offered the following "Of course I knew Jerry Voorhis wasn't a communist, but I had to win. That's the thing you don't understand. The important thing is to win."[71]

In January of 1947, Washington Congressman John Coffee introduced a similar resolution, yet BIS survived the continued protests calling for its dissolution. McKittrick was amply rewarded for his treasonous behavior with an appointment as vice president of Chase National Bank after the war.

Two of the largest U.S. banks had extensive dealings with Nazi Germany, the Rockefeller-owned Chase Bank and the Morgan-controlled National City Bank of New York. Both banks handled accounts for many of the American corporations that traded with Nazi Germany during the war, such as Standard Oil, Sterling Products, General Aniline & Film, and ITT.

In charge of European affairs for Chase was Joseph Larkin, a member of the Knights of Malta and a fascist sympathizer. (An abnormal number of Nazis and their supporters were members of the Knights of Malta.) Like McKittrick, Larkin had a long history of aiding the Nazis. Perhaps the first time was in 1936, when he refused a $4 million account for the Loyalists of Spain. When a similar account was opened in the Paris branch, he had the deposit withdrawn. Larkin gladly accepted accounts by Franco and the Reichsbank.

With the approach of war, the ties between the Rockefellers and the Nazi government solidified. In 1936, the Schroeder Bank of New York entered a partnership with the Rockefellers forming the Schroeder, Rockefeller and Company Investment Bank. *Time* magazine described the partnership as the economic booster of the Rome-Berlin Axis. Both Allen and John Foster Dulles were lawyers for the firm. Allen Dulles also was on the board of the Schroeder Bank. Six months after the start of the war in Europe, Larkin secured $25 million for the Nazi government. Accompanying the money was a detailed account of the assets and backgrounds of 10,000 Nazi sympathizers in the United States. In essence, the Nazi government was offering the sympathizers a chance to buy marks with dollars at a discounted rate through Chase Bank. This scheme was only open to those willing to return to Germany; a rush on the German mark resulted.

Chase's support of the Nazis was in outright defiance of the U.S. government and treason to the fullest extent. In May 1940, after Roosevelt froze all financial transfers to Europe, New York diamond merchant Leonard Smit began smuggling industrial-grade diamonds to Nazi Germany through Panama. A few days later, at Smit's request, Chase unblocked his account and allowed the funds to flow to Panama, then on to Nazi Germany.

In another instance, on June 17, 1940, as France was collapsing, the head of the Treasury Department, Henry Morgenthau, issued an order with FDR's approval to block French accounts in the U.S. to prevent the Nazis from looting them. Within hours, Chase officials unblocked the accounts and the funds went to Nazi Germany via South America.

On June 23, 1941, the FBI reported to Morgenthau that its monitoring of funds through Chase banks showed several payments from the Nazis to American oil companies, especially Standard Oil. The pro-Nazi publications from The German-American Commerce Association disclosed connections between Chase Bank, Emil Puhl and the Reichsbank through 1940, and the Reichsbank had accounts at both Chase and National City banks.

Larkin made great efforts to ensure the Paris branch stayed open even after Pearl Harbor. Throughout the war, Larkin allowed known Nazi collaborator Carlos Niedermann to manage the Paris branch. By May 1942, Harry Dexter White uncovered evidence that Niedermann was enforcing Nazi restrictions on the withdrawal of Jewish funds.

White, architect of the International Monetary Fund (IMF), was arguably one of the government's most important postwar economists. However, due to his liberal economic policies, as well as his relentless pursuit of the financial dealings of large corporations with the Nazis, he had to be removed. By 1948, the pro-fascists in the United States unjustly branded White as an agent of the Soviet Union. One of his chief accusers was Whittaker Chambers, who may have been a Nazi agent. Even with the recently released Venona tapes, no conclusive evidence exists that White was a Soviet agent, as claimed in several books. White died of a heart attack – three days after testifying before the HUAC committee.[72]

Additional evidence shows that Larkin was directing the actions of the Paris branch at least six months after Pearl Harbor. In fact, the Paris branch blocked American accounts while keeping Nazi accounts active. A Treasury report dated Dec. 20, 1944 revealed that Niedermann was a Nazi collaborator with Larkin's knowledge. The report further revealed that Larkin was aware of the Nazis' plan to use these accounts after the war as an instrument of German policy in the United States.

With Larkin's full knowledge, the Paris branch of Chase handled the account of Otto Abetz, the Nazi ambassador to Paris. Abetz's account was used to funnel vast amounts of money into several French companies that were collaborating with the Nazis. The money occasionally was used to support the torture of French victims. The New York office maintained constant communications with the Paris branch. The following quote from a letter from Albert Bertrand of the Chase Vichy branch to Larkin in 1942 attests to the communication and shameless collaboration between Chase and the Nazis.[73]

> The present basis of our relationship with the authorities in Germany is as satisfactory as the modus vivendi worked out with the German authorities by the Morgans. We anxiously sought and actually obtained substantial deposits of German funds ... which funds were invested by Chase in French treasury banks to produce additional income.[74]

After the war, Morgenthau's investigators in Paris found further shocking evidence of Chase's collaborations with the Nazis. They found that as Paris fell to the Nazis in June 1940, S.P. Bailey, a U.S. citizen and manager of the Paris office, offered to Larkin to immediately liquidate the branch in a patriotic gesture. Larkin quickly fired Mr. Bailey and appointed a known Nazi collaborator. In 1946, Larkin appointed the collaborationist Albert Bertrand to the board of Chase in Paris.

By 1941, it was well known that Standard Oil was supplying the Nazis with vital fuel. Maj. Charles Burrows of Military Intelligence reported to the War Department on July 15, 1941 that Standard Oil was shipping oil from Aruba in the Dutch West Indies to the Canary Islands:

> Standard ... is diverting about 20 percent of the fuel oil to the present German Government. About six

ships operating on this route are reputed to be manned mainly by Nazi officers. Seamen have reported to the informant that they have seen submarines in the immediate vicinity of the Canary Islands and have learned that the submarines are refueling there. The Informant also stated that Standard Oil Company has not lost any ships to date by torpedoing as have other American companies whose ships operate to other ports.[75]

The British blockade ran the entire length of North and South America, stopping ships bound for Germany wherever possible. To elude the British blockade, Farish sent the fuel to Russia and then transported it across Asia via the Trans-Siberian Railroad to Hitler's waiting Panzers. Once Hitler invaded Russia, Farish again eluded the blockade by shipping the oil to Vichy through North Africa.

William La Varne, a dedicated employee of the Department of Commerce, uncovered the details of Standard Oil's dealings with LATI, the Nazi airline. Not subject to boarding searches by the British blockade, LATI ferried spies into the Americas, and transported large quantities of propaganda and drugs into Latin America, all addressed to Sterling Products. Only Standard Oil could make these flights possible, because the trip from Europe to South America required refueling or high-octane fuel that it controlled. To supply LATI, Farish changed the registration of many of his ships from German to Panamanian. James Forrestal, Undersecretary of the Navy and Vice President of General Aniline & Film (another company with extensive dealing with the Nazis) quickly granted immunity.

On March 31, 1941, Sumner Welles, a State Department employee, presented a detailed report of refueling stations for Nazi vessels in South and Central America. Chief among the suppliers was Standard Oil of New Jersey and California. On May 5, 1941, the U.S. Legation in Managua, Nicaragua, reported Standard Oil subsidiaries were distributing Nazi propaganda. Further investigations by John Muccio of the U.S. Consulate revealed that Standard Oil distributed Nazi propaganda around the world.[76] Such were the dealings of Standard Oil when Nelson Rockefeller was at his post of Coordinator of Inter-American Affairs, an intelligence agency with the mission to stop Nazi influence in South America.

By 1944, America was seriously short of oil. The upcoming D-Day invasion required an even greater amount and a stable supply. Lack of oil would cancel the planned invasion or imperil the troops ashore. At that time, it cost 10 cents a barrel to bring the oil up; another 15 cents in royalties to the Sheikh of Bahrain or 20 cents for drilling in Arabia; another 21 cents in royalties to Ibn Saud. However, before the invasion, W.S.S. Rodgers of Texas Co., and Henry Collier of Standard Oil of California told Ickles the price for the government would be $1.05 a barrel, almost double the current price. The offer was take it or leave it, and Ickles was forced to accept.[77] The threat of an interruption in supply if the U.S. government intervened was explicit. Even more grievous was that Rodgers and Collier paid no income tax on their ill-gotten profits because they registered their company in the Bahamas. Their profit of $120 million was made on a $1 million investment.

Such behavior is not only criminal, but also treasonous. Standard put its own self-interest ahead of all else, putting the lives of GIs in danger and risking defeat in Europe. In effect, Standard Oil blackmailed FDR's administration for private gains. No charges of war profiteering were ever filed. As Seldes said, the big boys are immune from prosecution.

The large faction of anti-Jewish Nazi sympathizers in the State Department made such deals possible. One Nazi sympathizers with a great influence in the State Department was William Bullitt, who conducted a personal vendetta against Sumner Welles. Welles was the most powerful force in the department against fascism and was unrelenting in his pursuit of Nazis. However, Welles had a weakness that Bullitt exploited — bisexuality. Bullitt conspired with Hoover in 1940 to investigate Welles. In September, Hoover hired two Pullman porters to flirt with Welles once he was drunk aboard a train back to Washington, after attending the funeral of William Bankhead. Hoover's agents then noted his drunken conversations and sexual acts. It would take until 1943 before FDR would call for his resignation, under pressure from Bullitt. Welles' dismissal allowed the Nazi sympathizers full reign in the State Department.

Once again, a staunch opponent of fascism was removed from power. But FDR was so outraged at Bullitt that his influence was rendered impotent.

Early in 1942, the Standard Oil representative in Berlin, Karl Lindermann, held a series of urgent meetings with the two directors of American ITT in Germany, Walter Schellenberg and Baron Kurt von Schroeder. Schellenberg also headed the Gestapo's counterintelligence, and von Schroeder was a BIS director. Because of these meetings, Gerhardt Westrick, the CEO of ITT in Nazi Germany, flew to Madrid to meet with ITT founder Sosthenes Behn. The meeting centered on how links with the Gestapo and ITT could be improved, and how ITT could improve the entire German telephone system as well as a host of war munitions. Westrick, a Dulles associate, not only represented ITT, but also served as an agent for Ford, GM, Standard Oil, the Texas Oil Company, Sterling Products, Eastman Kodak, International Milk, Texaco, and the Davis Oil Co., all guilty of trading with the Nazis. The fascist government aided Behn because of his system of assuring politicians "promising plums" on his boards of directors. An example was his Spanish chairman, the Duke of Alba and a major supporter of Franco and Hitler. Behn was closely connected with the Circle of Friends of the Gestapo through Henry Mann of the National City Bank. Behn increased his donations to the Circle of Friends after Pearl Harbor. Besides owning ITT, Behn picked up a 28 percent share of Focke-Wulf Co. With the aid of ITT, Focke-Wulf was able to improve the accuracy of the German bomber squadrons, and later had a hand in the V2s that menaced England.

After Pearl Harbor, Behn entered an agreement with the German government that banned the Nazis from buying shares of ITT, but made them administrators of those shares. Behn and his directors made repeated requests for licenses to allow his companies in neutral countries to trade with the Nazis. Morgenthau refused all attempts, but Behn continued in open defiance of the U.S. government.

Besides providing as many as 50,000 fuses a month for artillery shells and bombs for Germany, Behn operated a worldwide communications network that served as a conduit for Nazi propaganda throughout the war. Nazis infested ITT's operations in South America and often were in charge of them. However, perhaps the most grievous act of ITT during the war was in providing the Nazis with sophisticated communications equipment that allowed them to break the U.S. diplomatic code.

In 1945, a special Senate committee on international communications was set up with Burton Wheeler as chairman. In the Appendix to the report, an extensive dossier revealed the co-ownership of RCA and ITT with Germany and Japan. No one noted the significance of the report. As always, the big boys supporting Nazis were immune from prosecution. In fact, shortly after the war, Behn received millions in payment for his war-damaged plants in Nazi Germany, the very same plants that made artillery shells that rained down on the GIs at Normandy and throughout the war.[78]

We have been introduced to IG Farben, the giant chemical cartel that played such a role in WWI and the rise of Nazism, and manufacturer of Zyklon gas used in the concentration camps. In 1929, Hermann Schmitz, joint chairman of IG Farben, with Max Ilgner, Walter Teagle, Edsel Ford and Charles Mitchell of National City Bank, set up the American Farben organization. In 1931, Herbert Hoover hosted Schmitz in the White House, sharing his view that Russia must be crushed. Hoover had lost his extensive oil holdings in the Russian revolution. Schmitz was able to sell $13 million of debentures through National City Bank in one morning, a considerable feat in the middle of the Depression.

In 1932, Schmitz joined forces with Kurt von Schroeder, a fanatical Nazi and director of BIS and the private bank J.H. Stein. Schroeder was an SS man linked closely with Winthrop Aldrich of Chase Bank, Walter Teagle of Standard Oil, and Behn of ITT. He set up the meeting between Hitler and von Papen that led to Hitler's appointment as chancellor, and was instrumental in setting up the Circle of Friends of the Economy, a fund for the Gestapo under Himmler's control. Representatives of ITT and Standard Oil also joined the Circle.

American IG, the American arm of IG Farben, owned General Aniline & Film (or GAF), and Ozalid, a blueprint firm. GAF supplied the Army and Navy with khaki and blue dye, respectively. This gave Schmitz's sales agents the perfect cover for spying on U.S. military bases. Also connected through General Aniline was Agfa Ansco, a huge film corporation that provided the Army and Navy with private training films and photographs of secret installations. Every blueprint from Ozalid was sent to Berlin.

In 1939, with war raging in Europe, all references to IG Farben were dropped and the company transformed into IG Chemie, a Swiss corporation controlled by Schmitz's brother-in-law with the aid of the National City Bank of New York and Chase Bank. The board of the new corporation still included William Weiss of Sterling Products, Edsel Ford and, in the place of Teagle, James Forrestal, soon to become Navy undersecretary. Another board member was former Attorney General Homer Cummings, a leading defense lawyer for the newly transformed corporation. Cummings supplied Thomsen, the Nazi government's chargé d'affaires in Washington, with Roosevelt's plans for Germany. Thomsen passed on this information in a Top Secret telegram to Germany. Eventually, General Aniline was placed under the directorship of Leo Crowley, a friend of big business and big money.

Norman Littell, an antitrust lawyer in the Attorney General's office, hounded Sterling Products relentlessly. It galled him that Sterling withheld the Bayer patent for atabrine, a quinine substitute, resulting in thousands of GIs dying needlessly from malaria. Quinine became especially scarce after the Japanese seizure of the Dutch East Indies. Atabrine was freely available to those on the list of Proclaimed Customers in South America, but Crowley refused to release it for use by American soldiers.

Like many strident anti-Nazis, Littell's enemies eventually forced FDR to dismiss him. However, just before Roosevelt's death, he asked to meet with Littell in the Oval Office. FDR told Littell that he would like to see Attorney General Biddle impeached for treason, but in his present weakened physical condition, the task would be too difficult. In 1945, Littell found support in Congress for an investigation of Sterling Drug. Al Smith of Wisconsin and Jerry Voorhis of California entered Littell's charges into the Congressional Record and demanded a full-scale investigation. The investigation never took place. Within a few days of the resolution, Biddle quietly resigned and ironically took the post of prosecutor at Nuremberg.[79] Littell faced the same fate as many other anti-Nazis in the Roosevelt administration who were forced to resign, their careers ending in shipwreck due to pressure from unseen forces.

The purge of stringent antifascists from government continued into the 1950s, climaxing with the trial of Alger Hiss. Meanwhile most of the pro-Nazis successfully managed to rehabilitate themselves, thanks to the same unseen forces more powerful than the president. Many pro-Nazi bankers received choice promotions, and pro-Nazi Congressmen remained in office for years after the war. Pro-Nazi publisher Dewitt Wallace was rewarded with an overnight stay in the Lincoln Bedroom for his pro-Nixon slant in *Reader's Digest* and his large campaign donations. Wallace personally gave Nixon more than $100,000, and contributed even more to the Nixon campaign by smuggling money through the Bahamas.[80]

Nativist Adopts Fascism

Besides a well-funded propaganda campaign by pro-fascist forces in the United States and the decidedly pro-Nazi slant of many of the nation's leading newspaper chains, the lack of education was a contributing reason for the rise of fascist groups in America. During the 1930s, most Americans lacked a high school education. Even the typical GI had only an eighth-grade education, creating the need for the Army Orientation Program. The tables below from a 1964 study relate racism with education, income and religion.[81]

Education	Percentage Prejudiced	Income	Percentage Prejudiced
8th Grade	60	Under $ 5,000	53
High School	50	$5,000-9,999	44
Some College	32	$10,000-14,999	44
College Graduate	27	$15,000 and over	40

Religion	Percentage Prejudiced	Religious Commitment	Percentage Prejudiced	Age	Percentage Prejudiced
Catholic	39	Low	38	Under 35	44
Liberal Protestant	46	Moderate	38	35-54	45
Fundamentalist	53	High	62	54 and over	55

Other polls have mirrored similar results for Judeophobia and intolerance, in spite of the Civil Rights Movement. As seen earlier, Black Legion members often were poorly educated and came from the hill country of the South. Most members held strong religious beliefs and belonged to fundamentalist churches.

The religious affiliation and the degree of commitment (or narrowness of perspective?) affect the degree of prejudice. Considering the close relations between the Klan and religion, this is not surprising. Fundamentalists show (or admit to) the highest degree of racial prejudice, in line with the heavy concentration of this tendency in the South. Churches acted as agents of segregation in the South, and the Identity religion advanced with the help of pro-Nazi preachers like Gerald Smith

Racism increased again in the 1980s after the rise of fundamentalism in the 1970s. An example was the ban on interracial dating at Bob Jones University, an issue that arose in the 2000 primary election. The right wing engaged in frantic efforts to do away with Affirmative Action and to pass hate crime legislation. Even in the 21st century, evidence still abounds of racism in religion, in the ministries of hate of people like Pat Robertson or Jerry Falwell. This does not imply that the majority of churchgoers are bigots, but rather the bigotry exists in the leaders and fanatical followers of what has become known as the Religious Right.

Some fundamentalists have carried out a 20-year campaign of terror against abortion clinics in a low-intensity urban warfare, bombing clinics and murdering staff members. If this campaign were compressed into one night, it would be no different from the Kristallnacht terrorization of the Jews at the hands of the Nazis, and voters would demand justice. The use of low-intensity tactics over years has lulled Americans into a false sense of security in the face of the inherent danger posed by these groups.

This acceptance of violence against abortion clinics was readily obvious after the terrorist attack on the World Trade Center on Sept. 11, 2001. In the aftermath, letters containing anthrax spores were delivered to several media sources and liberal members of Congress. However, abortion clinics and Planned Parenthood centers received a deluge of such threatening letters. Although none proved to contain anthrax spores, the FBI showed little interest in searching for the perpetrators. In fact, abortion centers have been receiving such threats through the mail for several years with no response from the FBI.

By contrast, one action by the Earth Liberation Front (ELF) will unleash volumes of ink in the press. The media even express outrage over peaceful protests by environmentalists. They are guilty of throwing flames at leftists while overlooking more appalling actions by rightists. Yet Oklahoma City stands as a testament that the real threat is from the right.

As a group, fundamentalists display all the major traits of fascism, anti-liberalism, anti-socialism, anti-communism, anti-labor, nationalism, and authoritarianism. Although nativist and American religious groups have always been nationalistic, until the 1930s they were isolationists. The transformation from a nativist to fascist philosophy is nearly always marked by the change from an isolationist view to a confrontational approach to communism, and more lately Arabs, Muslims and Mexicans.

To ease any further doubts of the fascistoid nature of certain fundamental religious groups, the following quote comes from a fundamentalist minister visiting the White House after returning from Guatemala in the 1980s:

The Army doesn't massacre the Indians. It massacres demons, and the Indians are demon possessed; they are communist. We hold Brother Efrain Rios Mott like the King of David of the Old Testament. He is the king of the New Testament.[82]

This is a mirror of the Nazis' war on the Jews. The first step in the Nazis' final solution was to demonize the Jews, then attack their businesses, homes and synagogues. The Nazis then seized their property, and then, finally, set up the concentration camps. It is precisely this process that makes such mad statements so dangerous. Racism is a learned trait; its early steps serve to desensitize society to cruelty. Then, left unchecked, open attacks on minority groups continue, followed by genocide. If there are any doubts of what would happen if the Religious Right ever came to power in this country, reread the quote above.

The association of various nativist religious groups with the right wing of American politics goes back to colonial times. Liberalism has always been associated with progress–iveness and change; conservatism with maintaining the status quo. No one resists change more than the various fundamental religious groups. At the first sign of change, they invoke a bloody crusade against what they sense to be an onslaught of godless behavior and the work of the devil.

Perhaps the best historical example of right-wing nativism is the anti-Catholic movement, starting about 1820 and extending through the 1850s with the Know-Nothings. The various factions of this anti-Catholic movement aligned themselves with conservative Whigs before eventually forming their own party. In essence, it was a union of convenience between the conservative elite and the bigoted, as well as a fear of Catholic immigrants who aligned themselves with liberal Democrats of that time. Nor was the anti-Catholic movement simply a battle at the ballot box. At various times, violence broke out, such as the riot in 1844 in Philadelphia in which a mob torched a Catholic Church. Again, the members of the anti-Catholic movement during this time came from the lower classes.[83]

As testimony to the zeal of religious bigotry in the United States, the Know-Nothings were the largest third party ever assembled. They succeeded in electing several congressmen to Washington and to various statehouses. Their demise only came about through their success, as the Republican Party absorbed them. The anti-Catholic movement continued after their disbandment, continuing into the 20th century and the 1960 election. Many Republicans and far right groups into the 1880s blamed the Civil War on the Catholics. Some even believed Lincoln's assassination was a Catholic plot.

The present-day infiltration of the Republican Party by the Religious Right is a dangerous repeat performance. The history of the United States is full of examples of religious bigotry used as an agent of repression. With the Republicans focused on destroying the social welfare safety net, as well as allowing churches to dispense federal aid, the future looks bleak if the country ever enters another extended economic downturn. George W. Bush has allowed Texas to support faith-based treatment centers for drug addiction, childcare and welfare services, in spite of the Constitutional separation of church and state. In his efforts to pander to the Religious Right, Bush has taken it a step further; he has exempted faith-based services from all laws. They are free to operate any way they choose[84] – to operate in unsafe buildings, hire unqualified staff and abuse the rights of those whom they pretend to help.

Even more ominous was the secret deal between the Salvation Army and the George W. Bush administration in 2001. The Salvation Army agreed to provide up to $110,000 a month to lobby for Bush's faith-based initiative. In exchange, the Bush administration exempted the Salvation Army from all federal and state anti-discrimination laws on hiring gays.[85] Such secret negotiations are shameful enough. However, the Salvation Army is a member of a larger group of fundamentalists seeking to undermine gay rights. The Christian Web portal Christianity.com hosts the Salvation Army's Web site. This portal also hosts other anti-gay sites, such as Exodus International and Pat Robertson's Christian Broadcast Network.[86] Although the media did report the secret negotiations, they quickly dropped the story or relegated it to the back pages. No mention was made in the news of the Salvation Army alliance with the anti-gay Christianity.com.

For his faith-based initiative, Bush chose two advisors connected with the CIA-connected Manhattan Institute, John J. DiIulio Jr., and Stephen Goldsmith, thus solidifying the bond between fundamentalists, hard-right ministries and the CIA. The two are also linked to Charles Murray, author of the racist *The Bell Curve*, who was also a consultant on Tommy Thompson's Wisconsin Welfare Reform Program.[87]

Mixing religion with government as Bush proposes can lead to catastrophic results, as the following quotes remind us:

Thus inwardly armed with confidence in God and the unshakable stupidity of the voting citizenry, the politicians can begin the fight for the "remaking" of the Reich as they call it.

– Adolf Hitler, *Mein Kampf*, Vol. 2 Chapter 1

Secular schools can never be tolerated because such schools have no religious instruction, and a general moral instruction without a religious foundation is built on air; consequently, all character training and religion must be derived from faith ... we need believing people.

– Adolf Hitler, April 26, 1933, from a speech made during negotiations leading to the Nazi-Vatican Concordat of 1933.

Anti-Jewish bigotry in the U.S. only began in earnest in the latter part of the 1800s, as more and more Jewish immigrants from Eastern Europe entered the country. This roughly coincides with the beginnings of the Identity religion in the United States, a religion based on racism that emerged in the 1930s from the hate ministries of Gerald Smith and Wesley Smith. With Father Coughlin, they preached about the dangers of "International Bankers," a code word for Jews. Smith and Swift were instrumental in developing the Identity religion.

More mainstream elements of the Religious Right became indoctrinated with the fascist agenda and adopted a wildly pro-business anti-union view. Fundamentalists have at times aligned themselves with and at other times against big business. As groups, fundamentalists and businesses are authoritarian by nature; thus it is only natural for the two to align more often than to oppose one another.

Other writers cite two motives for this close association: rabid fear of the Red atheist, and large financial donations. Unions were portrayed as collectivist, socialist and communist. Demagogues labeled unions as foreign and un-American. During the 1920s, the IWW became more associated with socialism and communism than with union activities. Each discovery of Reds in the early labor movement following WWI only fanned the flames. More than 6,000 people were arrested in the Palmer Raids, but in the end fewer than 600 were deported, due to lack of evidence.

Before adopting fascism in the 1930s, the ideology of the nativist groups centered on bigotry and isolationism. Between the wars, the two largest nativist groups were the Klan and the prohibitionists, with a subtle element of anti-Catholic bigotry in the prohibition movement.

After the war, the nativist fundamentalist groups all abandoned isolationism and took on a global view, with many openly calling for a new war with the USSR, while becoming fanatically anti-union, pro-corporation and anti-liberal. Most writers subscribe this conversion to large financial donations from corporations and a rabid fear of atheistic communism, but several other factors were equally important.

The abandonment of isolationism in favor of direct confrontation of communism serves as sort of a guidepost marking the division between a traditionally fundamentalist group and one that exposes the fascist ideology. Even during the Red Scare of 1919, the fundamentalist groups (although rabidly opposed to communism) did not call for direct confrontation. Instead, they believed in fortress America as a bulwark against the atheistic Red horde.

In studying this transformation, the importance of the ministers of hate during the 1930s cannot be underestimated. The influence of Gerald Winrod and Gerald Smith is still clear in the Religious Right. Many credit the present fundamentalist movement to the work of Billy Hargis, whose Christian Crusade of the 1950s and early 1960s had an enormous effect on shaping the fundamentalist or Religious Right movement. Hargis' career in many ways served as a bridge between fascism and today's fundamentalist groups. Moreover, a quick look at Hargis' career clearly verifies a link to fascism.

Politically, Hargis is best known for his rabid anti-communist views. However, his career is punctuated with links to fascist groups from the 1930s and 1940s. In 1956, Hargis distributed two pamphlets, *Our 1956 Political Crisis* and *Stevenson and Kefauver*. Both were politically motivated and timed to the election; the latter tried to label Stevenson and Kefauver as communists.

In the October 1959 *Christian Crusade Editon,* Hargis states unequivocally that he called on Winrod for help in starting his radio program. In the December 1956 issue of *Christian Crusade,* he tells of a meeting he had with the publisher of the notoriously fascist *American Mercury*. Wickliffe Draper, the founder of the Pioneer Fund, largely financed the *Mercury*. Draper was an extreme racist. In 1967, the Draper family became the largest shareholder in Rockwell International, a prime defense contractor. Like Draper, Hargis was a racist, although he loudly denounced as liars those who labeled him as such.

However, Hargis' racist views were readily obvious at his 1962 Anti-communist Leadership School. One of the invited speakers, R. Carter Pittman, said that the chief difference between blacks in American and in the Congo was that "in the Congo they eat more white people."[88]

Moreover, Hargis said in the early Civil Rights Movement of the 1950s that "segregation and racism is an artificial [issue] instigated by the Communists." Hargis used his Christian Crusade to make up a packet of information on the Civil Rights Act of 1964 that contained the following articles:

1. The cruel and naked facts concerning this proposal.
2. The similarity of the Bill to the Communist Party Platform of 1928.
3. How the Bill fulfills many of the demands of Karl Marx's Communist Manifesto.
4. The pro-communist records of the authors and supporters of this Bill.[89]

During the Little Rock school desegregation, Hargis distributed a pamphlet written by fascist Joe Kamp. Hargis also was a member of the racist Liberty Lobby and several other right-wing extremist groups. In 1961, Hargis bought the files of Allen Zoll. Zoll, an associate of Gerald Smith, founded American Patriots Inc., a fascist group that was on the Attorney General's watch list.[90]

The lingering influences of Winrod and Smith are readily clear in Hargis' career. Both Winrod and Smith cast a long shadow of influence over the fundamentalist movement. Both were close associates of Harvey Springer of Englewood, Colo. Springer was far from being just a poor country preacher; he was one of the more influential voices in the fundamentalist movement. He was a founding member of the International Council of Christian Churches (ICCC), serving on its executive committee until his death.

The ICCC opposed the liberal World Council of Churches, deriding it as communist-infiltrated. Another Smith and Winrod associate was Kenneth Goff, head of the National Organization of Christian

Youth. Winrod was connected to several other fundamentalists who were openly fascist, such as William Bell Riley, the founder of Northwestern. Winrod also was closely associated with Harry Hodge, a leading member of the fascist Christian American Association. Hodge used his friendship with Martin Dies to intercede to prevent the Dies Committee from investigating Winrod.[91]

There were many other fundamentalist ministers putting forth the Nazi line throughout the 1940s. For example, William D. Herrstrom of Minneapolis, publisher of *Bible News Flashes,* was anti-Jewish, anti-British and pro-fascist. Following the war, Herrstrom became one of the first Holocaust deniers. Other fundamentalists preaching the Nazi ideology in the 1930s and 1940s included Harry Grube of Mobile, Ala.; R.M. Parr of Detroit, Mich.; Glen Smith of Palmer Lake, Colo.; S.J. Grear of Denver, Colo.; C.K. Peterson of Phoenix, Ariz.; and W.C. Love of Hazel Park, Mich. While several of the leading theologians of the fundamentalist movement in the 1930s and 1940s were true fascists, many others were only embedded with the seed of fascism, anti-Semitism or Judeophobia.

There are other reasons for fundamentalist groups to adopt fascism. For instance, the American Bible Association was founded by fascists. In other cases, business leaders themselves started fascist-oriented fundamentalist groups. Finally, politicians or secret police would use a religious group to carry out repression, or to divide the electorate, as seen during the Red Scare and in Germany, where Hitler used religion to hold power. The purge of liberal and leftist leaders in the 1920s dissolved any liberal influence that may have been present, leaving fundamentalist groups in the hands of hard right-wing extremists. Exhausted of moderating forces, they became susceptible to fascist ideology.

The past is littered with examples of business leaders making large financial donations to church groups. Perhaps one of the largest contemporary donors to right-wing religious groups is Bunker Hunt. The Coors family also figures prominently.

In 1950, Sun Oil executive Howard Pew made a $50,000 grant to Howard Kershner's Christian Freedom Foundation. The CFF's consulting economist was none other than Percy Greaves, a researcher for New Jersey Rep. Fred Hartley of Taft-Hartley fame and board member of the Liberty Lobby. The foundation's primary aim was to indoctrinate clergy with anti-communist and libertarian viewpoints.[92] Radical libertarian views are essentially nothing more than social Darwinism, the philosophy to which Hitler subscribed.

Another case is Harding College in Searcy, Ark. One of the school's first graduates, George S. Benson, returned from a mission to to assume the presidency of Harding, which is operated by the Church of Christ and opposes most modern doctrine, including the theory of evolution. Benson began writing and speaking about fundamentalism, attracting an ever-wider audience. After the war he began promoting the free enterprise agenda of the duPonts. His main theme was that the free enterprise system would be lost unless corporate America succeeded in propagandizing citizens on the fundamentals of our way of life. Benson hit pay dirt the day Alfred Sloan, president of General Motors, heard one of his fundamentalist anti-labor diatribes. Sloan decided to bankroll Benson that very day. In 1949, Sloan bequeathed a gift of $300,000 to Harding. Other industrialists soon followed suit, including Charles Hook, chairman of Acme Steel and the Falk Foundation. By 1961, Harding's endowment fund totaled $6 million, almost all from corporate donors.

Benson opposed all welfare legislation, was virulently anti-union and attacked anything he thought smelled of socialism or liberalism. With the Sloan grant, Benson established the propaganda affiliate of Harding known as the National Education Program.[93] Its sole purpose was to produce propaganda films supporting his fascist views. The largest consumers of these films came from industrial giants such as GE, U.S. Steel, Olin Mathieson Chemical Co., and Lone Star Cement.[94] GE has made extensive use of these films, showing them to employees and promoting them throughout corporate America.

Business leaders founded other religious groups, such as the Church League in 1937. Its founders were G.W. Robnett, an ultrarightist; F.L. Loesch, chairman of the Chicago Crime Commission; and

Henry P. Crowell, chairman of Quaker Oats. The Church League was based in Wheaton, Ill. For two decades, the operating director was G.W. Robnett, an advertising man whose Institute for Special Research compiled files on suspected communists and sympathizers. The other two founders feared Roosevelt's court packing and anything else related to the New Deal.[95] The League's financial supporters included the Hearst and Coors Foundations, Howard Phillips and Gen. Robert Woods.

Religion in this country has always been a big business in itself. The extent of the wealth of churches or religion has been a tidy little secret of which few people are aware. Churches are the largest landowners after the government in this country. The extent of their wealth is mind-boggling. In 1928, the contributions to just 25 denominations exceeded $400 million. Besides this income, churches drew an added $132 million from permanent funds and legacies. The table below reveals a portion of that wealth and the power that goes with it.[96]

Denomination	Valuation in 1926
Baptist	$469,835,000
Congregational	$164,212,000
Methodist	$654,736,000
Presbyterian	$443,572,000
Episcopal	$314,596,000

A quick look at the table puts the total value of those denominations at roughly $2 billion. To put the figures in perspective, the 1926 federal budget was only $2.9 billion.

With great wealth comes power and a drive for more power. Since the rebirth of fundamentalism in the 1980s, examples of religious groups seeking to gain power abound. Almost all seek to establish a theocracy based on their beliefs. They have used the abortion and school prayer issues to ferment public strife, divide the electorate and keep alive their drive to establish a theocracy. Of all forms of governments, only a theocracy is more repressive than fascism. While not normally viewed as a religious group, the Council for National Policy (CNP) has led the drive toward theocracy. This group contains a multitude of leaders from the fundamentalists.

Another good example would be that of Pat Robertson, who is intimately tied to the CNP. Robertson sold part of his broadcasting empire, The Family Channel, to Rupert Murdoch for $1.9 billion. In his quest for power, Robertson ran for president in the Republican primaries of 1988, and vowed to control the Republican presidential nominee in 2000. He has used his ministry of hate and his broadcasting empire to advance his views and those of the Council for National Policy.

Carl McIntire best typified Robertson's counterpart from the 1940s. McIntire was expelled from the Presbyterian Church for his opposition to any liberalization in religion and politics. His views were essentially those expressed today by the Religious Right, anti-communist, anti-socialist, anti-liberal, anti-Catholic, anti-union, Judeophobic, racist and pro-business. By the mid-1960s, other leaders supplanted McIntire in the Religious Right, but during the 1940s and 1950s, he helped shape and mold it into the form it has now.

McIntire began petitioning the Federal Communications Commission in 1941 to divide the radio airtime allotted for Protestants between the fundamentalists and the mainline Federal Council of Churches.[97] Although he was soon surpassed by the broader National Association of Evangelicals, McIntire played a pivotal role in obtaining and exploiting airtime. McIntire's early recognition of the power of the media is the basis for Pat Robertson's media empire and the success of other telepreachers. McIntire's *20ᵗʰ Century Reformation Hour* aired for years before being surpassed by the new fundamentalist televangelists of the '60s. Perhaps McIntire's greatest hour came in the early 1950s with his close association with McCarthy and J. Edgar Hoover, but his more lasting impact was in furthering the careers of three other fundamentalists: Billy James Hargis, Dr. Fred Schwartz and Maj. Edgar Bundy.[98]

Review

We have seen how fascist influence was pervasive in the fundamentalist religious movement, and extended into the halls of Congress and U.S. military circles, yet it was the leaders of corporate America who headed the fascist movement in the United States.

The two preceding chapters revealed that economic sabotage and creation of civil unrest were integral parts of the Nazi battle plan from the earliest days. Neither tactic could have worked without the willing participation of corporate America. Leaders of corporate America willingly entered the cartel agreements with IG Farben that hindered the early war effort, and funded many of the pro-fascist groups of the 1930s. Then after the war, both GM and Ford shamelessly demanded reparations for damages from allied bombings of their plants. In 1967, GM received $33 million for damages sustained to its Russelsheim plant.

These same American corporations built much of the Third Reich's war machine. GM and Ford built nearly 90 percent of all the 3-ton vehicles and nearly 70 percent of all medium and heavy-duty trucks for the Reich.[99] GM built thousands of bombers for the Luftwaffe. When American forces liberated the Ford plants in Cologne and Berlin, they found destitute foreign workers confined behind barbed wire. Records show that nearly half the labor force of Ford's Cologne plant was slave labor. This was not dictated by the Nazi regime: it was nearly always the companies like Ford that lobbied the government to supply slaves. Germany had no real labor shortage, and the motive was corporate greed, not need.[100]

Both Edsel Ford and Robert Sorenson, a high-ranking official at Dearborn, served as directors of Ford Works A.G. throughout the war years. After France fell to Germany, Edsel Ford sent direct orders to Ford France that the company was to build trucks for the Nazis.

Almost all other American corporations with investments in Germany also went to extraordinary lengths to retain control, often through Swiss shell corporations. They sought the help of the Dulles brothers in cloaking their treacherous dealings from the U.S. government. By remaining in control or hiding their dealings with the Nazis, they became traitors to their country, war criminals who share moral responsibility for the resulting Holocaust and the deaths of thousands of GIs.

With the clouds of war looming, corporate America sought to delay the day of reckoning by slowing war production in the great sit-down strike of 1941. Following the attack on Pearl Harbor, the native fascists did not fold their tent and go home. Corporate America still sought ways to delay production of war munitions. Large firms essentially eliminated any small or midsize firms from producing war materiel. They failed to use their production lines to full advantage, shutting down weekends and only running skeleton crews on the second and graveyard shifts. Many jobs went unfilled, not for lack of qualified workers, but due to corporate policies, such as the barring of blacks, until Roosevelt ordered firms with defense contracts to abandon this practice.

In 1942, the darkest hour of the war, native fascists unleashed a full-scale assault on the homeland. The DuPonts, one of the country's 13 controlling families and notorious Nazi sympathizers, dressed fascism up with a smiley face and labeled it with the electioneering jingle of free enterprise. By 1943, the fortunes of war had shifted; the defeat of Nazi Germany was only a matter of time. Facing exposure with Germany's defeat, corporate America and the native fascists once again switched tactics. A blizzard of peace proposals was put forth. Common to all was that the Nazis would be left in power and only Hitler would be removed. At the same time, native fascists began a campaign to purge those who firmly opposed fascism.

By 1944, the same papers that were pro-fascist before Pearl Harbor unleashed a media blitz for an early or easy peace with Germany. The papers were full of articles and editorials proposing peace terms which would leave the Nazis in control. To distract from their past support for the Nazis, native fascists increased attacks on communism. Many of those dedicated to the war against fascism were labeled communist and removed from their positions. By the end of the war, anti-communist sentiment reached feverish proportions. A good example was the defeat of Jerry Voorhis by Richard Nixon.

However, Roosevelt remained adamant. There would be no easy peace with the Nazis. The only acceptable peace was unconditional surrender. Likewise, FDR was firm in his pledge to bring all who supported the Nazi cause to justice. In this regard, Roosevelt allowed British Intelligence to secretly spy on Americans. The British could use the information to stop shipments of war materiel and money flowing to the Nazis.

In the operation headed by master British spy INTREPID, Sir William Stephenson soon quickly uncovered damning evidence of American fascists aiding the Nazi cause. British infiltrators learned that America First had received direct funding from Ulrich von Gienanth of the German Embassy and Gunther Hansen-Sturm. The latter had paid Rep. Hamilton Fish a check, of which Stephenson had managed to get a copy. At an America First rally, Stephenson arranged for a group of antifascist infiltrators to give Fish a card with the words "Der Fuehrer thanks you for your loyalty" as cameras captured the moment.[101]

British agents soon had a wealth of information on those supplying the Nazis. Besides unearthing the many tentacles of IG Farben, British agents had information implicating Chase Bank and National Bank of New York in dealing and trading with the Nazis. Stephenson had information that Kurt Heinrich Rieth was staying in New York's Waldorf Astoria Hotel to negotiate the sale of Standard Oil's Hungarian subsidy to the Nazis. Rieth's father was Standard Oil's representative in Antwerp. Stephenson leaked the information to the press, and soon Rieth was deported for falsifying his vista. Stephenson's group also linked William Rhodes Davis to supplying the Nazis with the oil, and there is speculation that British agents may have lethally poisoned Davis. The Intrepid group also murdered key Nazi supporters in the United States when the threat they posed was critical to Britain.

In 1941, Stephenson expanded his special operations section, with particular emphasis on South America. They soon uncovered a plot to establish a fascist regime in Uruguay led by Arnulf Fuhrmann. In May 1941, a similar plot in Bolivia was uncovered. Both were foiled.

In short, Stephenson's group uncovered volumes of information on those trading with the Nazis. Many prominent Americans in government and industry were implicated. None of the information gained would be admissible in court. However, Roosevelt planned to release the information after the war. The resulting outrage would then be used to pressure Congress for a full investigation.

In a cruel twist of fate, Roosevelt died a month before Nazi Germany surrendered, and his plan died with him. None of the information was ever leaked to the press. There was no public outrage; the public would remain in the dark about corporate America's treason. There would be no trials of businessmen for trading with the Nazis.

On May 8, 1945, in a bulletin broadcast to the nation, President Truman announced the unconditional surrender of Germany. People filled Times Square with news the Nazi menace had been eliminated in Europe. It would be another four months before the Pacific would be liberated. Ticker tape parades for the returning GIs would fill the streets.

Although the Allied forces were victorious on the battlefields of Europe and the South Pacific, tragically, the war against fascism was lost on the home front. In the 1946 election, the Republicans gained control of both chambers of Congress. True to their pro-big business agenda and their past support of fascists, more than 200 anti-union bills flooded Congress. The rehabilitated Fred Hartley, who had supported Japan and Germany until the moment Pearl Harbor was bombed, coauthored the anti-union

Taft-Hartley act. The fascist group Christian America successfully lobbied several southern and midwestern states to pass anti-union right-to-work laws. One could argue that such measures were not full-blown fascism, yet that is the danger of creeping fascism. The anti-union measures were the first steps on a slippery slope. Anytime the government passes a law placing the rights of corporations or the elite ahead of the people, it is an act of fascism, or a step toward it.

Fascism is an inherent problem of any economy based on capitalism. Insidiously, as corporations grow and become more powerful, more and more laws are passed favoring large corporations and the rights of the people are damned. Fascism has never appeared at once in its full-blown totalitarian state. It took Hitler six years to consolidate his power. Fascism assumes power in gradual steps, destroying our rights one at a time until suddenly it blossoms into a totalitarian society controlled by the corporate elite.

Thousands of war criminals and pro-fascists were allowed to immigrate to the United States despite Truman's ban. The CIA's reliance on Nazi war criminals, and the native fascist's hatred of communism and anything liberal, propelled the world toward the brink of nuclear holocaust. For the fascist leaders of corporate America, the resulting Cold War served to cover their past dealings with the Nazis. For the Nazi collaborators, it was much more than just a chance to save their miserable hides. If they could induce a war between the two superpowers, the U.S. and USSR, the Nazis would then have a chance to reestablish a state in Germany.

Chapter 6,
A Pledge Betrayed

What Went Wrong at Aachen

Dawn on Oct. 21, 1944 was cool and crisp as the last traces of summer gave way to autumn. The forests around Aachen, Germany were a profusion of autumn colors. At noon, Col. Gerhard Wilck surrendered what remained of the town to the American First Army. It was the first major city of Germany captured. Of its 160,000 inhabitants, only 5,000 remained. The rest were either dead or forced by the Nazis to evacuate the city.

The American forces hoped to use Aachen as a model for the 4Ds program — demilitarization, denazification, decartelization and democratization.

On Nov. 10, *Stars and Stripes* reflected the upbeat outlook of U.S. forces in an editorial:

The Americans have come to Germany not to pat child slayers on the head or to feed SS scoundrels with Spam. The Americans have come to this land of gangsters in order to bring villains to justice.

It is not only American divisions that have entered Germany. Justice has entered Germany and not a single German will venture to cry welcome. For justice carries a sword.[1]

To organize a temporary German administration, FIG2, the military government detachment, asked the advice of the local Catholic bishop, Johann van der Velte, who had remained behind. The bishop recommended a devout Catholic and upstanding citizen, Franz Oppenhoff. According to the bishop, Oppenhoff had never joined the Nazi Party. He told the military government detachment that party membership was an irrelevant burden.

The Americans found Oppenhoff to be clean, intelligent, well dressed and seemingly respectable. Oppenhoff accepted the resulting American offer to manage the city. At first, the Americans did not question Oppenhoff's authoritarian and antidemocratic views. Nor did they question that he and his fellow business owners and managers had prospered during the Nazis reign.

American forces placed Herr Aschke in charge of the local coal mines. Again, Aschke seemed competent. No American in the occupation forces bothered to question Aschke about his use of slave labor under the Nazis or asked if he himself had been a Nazi. A few eyebrows were raised when Aschke cut wages to increase production. However, winter was coming and area residents desperately needed the coal, so the American forces allowed Aschke to continue as manager. But Aschke had been a rabid Nazi.

Oppenhoff and his leading assistants had been former officials at the Veltrup Armaments Works, and were suspected of giving large sums to the Nazis. Oppenhoff now appointed 22 former Nazis to 72 essential positions in the city. The mayor assembled 750 bureaucrats to govern the city, one bureaucrat for every 15 inhabitants. The mayor's bureaucrats were exempt from the otherwise compulsory work of clearing debris and harvesting local crops.

It was a full two months after the capture of Aachen before Saul Padover, a member of the SHAEF Psychological Warfare Division, arrived in town. He heard the local trade unionists were critical of the appointments of Oppenhoff and Aschke.

He reported to SHAEF that the U.S. military government officers assigned to Aachen were politically ignorant and morally indifferent toward the Nazis. They had made a thorough political mess by the appointments of Oppenhoff and Aschke, who were as compact a clique of ultrareactionaries and fascists as could be found anywhere in Germany.[2] Padover's report caused reverberations throughout the Allied occupation forces.

What went wrong? This had been a war for justice. The criminals were to face justice at Nuremberg. What was the war of liberation for if the occupation forces placed the Nazis they vowed to eliminate right back into positions of power?

There were no easy answers. The military government had been briefed to appoint a mayor and then leave everything to the Germans. The U.S. officers relied on technical competency, respectability and the ability to speak English in choosing their appointments. They also brought their own class prejudices, which included not choosing socialists, communists, union leaders or men not well-dressed. It never occurred to the occupation forces the Nazis sent those who opposed them to the concentration camps, leaving them homeless and dressed in rags. Relying on Bishop van der Velte was another mistake repeated across Germany, because Catholic bishops and priests had supported the Nazis. General values such as respect for clergy and the overall conservative political views that American soldiers carried with them contributed to the failure of the 4Ds program. There was no shortage of personnel, but there was a failure to assign them to the 4Ds program.

These reasons are overshadowed by a much more sinister fact that even affected the conduct of the war. Many of the wealthy and powerful in America aided Hitler and produced arms for him even after Germany declared war on the U.S. These wealthy Americans had to be protected, and they had friends in high places of power to aid them and sabotage the 4Ds programs. Since every war crime trial risked the exposure of American industrialists as Nazi collaborators, they had the war crime trials cut short. Just as they had delayed war production on the home front, they used delay and neglect to hide their Nazi dealings, and sabotaged efforts to mete out justice. Many prominent Americans – including the Dulles brothers, Prescott Bush, Averell Harriman, Henry Ford, and the Rockefellers – deserved to be tried for treason and hanged at Nuremberg.

Furthermore, the Nazis had their own plan for a comeback that depended on their friends in the United States and other countries, including coordinated efforts in the U.S. and Germany to cancel the Nuremberg trials. One of the ringleaders in the U.S. was Joe McCarthy, who received funding from a known Nazi supporter. Many seemingly innocent events such as press leaks and opposition politics from 1944 to the 1960s may be manifestations of Nazi intrigue. A careful reexamination of the way war crimes and German denazification were handled begins to expose the Nazi comeback plan and their allies.

On Nov. 11, 1944 the Joint Chiefs of Staffs in Washington issued the following directive:

The entire Nazi leadership will be removed from posts of authority and no member of the German General Staff or Nazi hierarchy should occupy any important governmental or civil position. You will not appoint the employment of active Nazis or ardent sympathizers, and no exception will be made to this policy on grounds of administrative convenience or expediency. You will remove and exclude from office any persons who act, or whom you deem likely to act, contrary to Allied interests and principles.[3]

The order was followed a month later by another directive that forbade the use of dissolved Nazi organizations for relief. Later, it was expanded to include additional categories of officials who would be subject to automatic arrest. Every school, university, courthouse and newspaper was to be closed. The new American directive horrified the British.

Con O'Neill of the United Nations War Crimes Commission commented: "Is it really necessary that we seize monuments... It is a disastrous policy to lead to total chaos. It means we do what we can, but accept no responsibility for the results, it is merely a clumsy attempt to escape criticism, although we cannot escape control."[4] These sharp differences got worse. In February, the U.S. issued another directive allowing the military to retain Nazis if needed. The justification for the new directive was that the Allied army depended on civilian water and electrical supplies. Only a small sliver of Nazi Germany lay to the east of the Rhine. Col. Bernard Bernstein immediately objected, claiming that too many detachments were taking advantage of the exception clause. He blamed the British for weakening the directives.

In March, the Twelfth Army under Bernstein's influence issued its own directive, overriding the exceptions. The new directive banned employment of anyone who had profited under the Nazis. On March 23, the White House modified the Twelfth Army's directive, allowing employment of "nominal" Nazis. Once again, Bernstein blamed the British for softening the denazification program.

When the American forces handed Aachen over to the British, the chief of SHAEF's G5, Brig. Gen. Frank McSherry, suggested to the British commanding officer that he remove Ashke from managing the mines. The miners had proven Aschke to be a fanatical Nazi supporter. The British refused, believing the coal was more important. It took the British until January 1946 to remove Oppenhoff for being a member of the VDA (League of Germans in Foreign Countries). The VDA was an organization that funded fifth column groups, such as the American Bund.[5]

There were no less than four directives on employing Nazis and more than 40 subsidiary orders. The bureaucratic maze was a perfect prescription for chaos and complete failure of the denazification program.

The failure left behind in Aachen stands in stark contrast to the liberation of Nordhausen and the success of the American T Force, part of Operation Paperclip. T Force members, known by the distinctive red T on their helmets, had priority classification and the authority to commandeer any needed equipment and entire military units, if needed.

Nordhausen, a small town in the Harz Mountains, was the site of the V2 program after Peenemunde came under Allied bombing in 1943. To ensure against future bombing, the Nazis imported thousands of concentration camp inmates to dig a vast underground network of tunnels. On April 11, Patton's Third Army liberated Nordhausen. There were 23,000 survivors in the associated Dora concentration camp, and 3,000 bodies rotting and unburied. More than 30,000 had already perished of disease, brutality or starvation.

Within hours of liberation, the T Force accompanying the Third Army had commandeered the healthier inmates to clear a mile of the main tunnel damaged in recent bombings. Meanwhile, a fleet of trucks was requisitioned, some from as faraway as Cherbourg, France. A U.S. combat engineer group rapidly rebuilt a damaged bridge. Within eight days, the T Force moved 400 tons of equipment to Antwerp for shipment to New Orleans.

Sadly, there was no war crimes unit attached to the Third Army, although Patton's forces already knew that Nordhausen depended on slave labor from the nearby Dora concentration camp. No one cared about the SS guards and officers from Dora. The Americans made no effort to arrest any of them, but simply let the SS guards walk away. It was several years before the occupation forces tracked down 39 of the SS guards for trial.[6]

Nordhausen is an ideal example of the sabotage of denazification. The army's only concern was to spirit the V2s and their assembly factory away from advancing Soviet forces as quickly as possible. For this effort, no amount of men or material was spared. It is an inconceivable breach that Patton's forces didn't arrest or hold the SS guards as POWs. SS men were in the automatic arrest category once the cease-fire was signed.

The war crimes issue had been talked to death. There were blue ribbon panels appointed to investigate and decide just what war crimes were, but they were prohibited or effectively sabotaged from taking any action.

The failure to arrest the Dora SS guards did not reflect public opinion. A 1943 British poll asked: "At the end of the war what do you think should be done with the Axis leaders?"[7]

Let them go, ignore them	1
They won't be found	1
Leave them to their own peoples	1
They should be put on trial	18
Exile them, imprison them, put them in solitary confinement	11
Hand them over to the Jews, the Poles and others who have suffered	4
Shoot them	40
Nothing is horrible enough, torture them	15
Misc., no opinion	9

American opinion was much the same. At one point in the negotiations over war crimes among the Big Three, Churchill supported summary executions. Stalin objected and insisted on trials. Later, when Patton's forces freed Dachau, some of the soldiers became so outraged over what they had seen, they started to execute SS guards. The commanding officer stopped the executions, but only after several guards were killed. An investigation followed and when confronted by investigators, Patton did the right thing and stood by his men. He tore up the investigation, ending it for all time.

In the final year of the war, the United States and London put together an ultrasecret organization, TICOM, which planted the first seed of the Cold War. This organization was so secret that in 1992, the National Security Administration extended classification of all its missions and operations until 2012. Its classification is higher than the top secret bracket, so only a handful of people have access to the files. The British government is equally secretive. Col. George Bucher, director of U.S. Signal Intelligence, formed the group in the summer of 1944. TICOM (Target Intelligence Commission) was to capture all code-making and code-breaking equipment. To this end, it seems the TICOM forces did operate behind enemy lines at times, but mostly followed advancing armies like the T Force.

They were looking for the new German FISH advance cipher machines used to replace the older Enigma devices, and any Russian code-making equipment the Germans might have captured. The Germans used FISH only for the highest-level messages.

Like the T Force, TICOM quickly snatched up people, papers or equipment, and returned them to the safety of rear guard areas for shipment to the United States. From what information there is, TICOM was as successful as the T Force. It captured a FISH coding machine and a device able to decipher the highest level Russian code. The importance of cipher machines and other coding equipment in war cannot be underestimated. It was the British ability to read Enigma transmissions that forced the Nazis to withdraw their wolf packs from the North Atlantic or risk losing their entire fleet of U-boats.

Because all TICOM documents were classified, it is unknown if the Nazi code breakers received asylum in England or the United States, or if any war criminals received new identities. However, Erich Huettenhain, a Nazi code expert, was brought to the United States.

As a result, the United States was able to read the messages of the Soviet police, military, KGB and diplomats. The U.S. knew without a doubt the condition of the Soviet Union until 1948, when the Russians discovered their code was compromised.[8] Thus General's Clay's warning of an attack that could occur at anytime should have been viewed with suspicion. His letter was directly based on reports from General Gehlen, a former Nazi general. Gehlen was following the Nazi comeback plan of provoking a crisis between the U. S. and Russia.

There is also a sinister side to the story of the T Forces and TICOM. Both groups counted on capturing equipment intact. Often the American Army raced ahead to capture a site before the Russians got there. Some equipment was captured by luck as it was being moved. Other equipment was captured in place, unharmed by the bombing campaign. It leaves open the question of why these sites were not bombed. Were they deliberately spared to capture the equipment intact, even if it meant a greater loss of GIs?

The tragic mistakes at Aachen and Dora were repeated across Germany as the Allied armies advanced. Accepted history pretends the criminals faced justice at Nuremberg. Yes, a few high officials did face trial there and were hung. However, far too many criminals escaped justice, many with the help of the Vatican and US forces.

Accepted history would lead us to believe the path to Nuremberg was straightforward. Nothing could be further from the truth. Each step of the way was paved with heated political battles, diplomatic outbursts, and geopolitical cross purposes. The primary cause was sabotage from within. Germany's defeat exposed many uncomfortable facts that had to be covered up.

GIs Died as Corporate Traitors Were Protected

The world stood aghast in the spring of 1941 at the new terror and horror unleashed by the Nazis against Yugoslavia. Hitler was enraged that the Yugoslavs had overthrown his quisling government, and he issued Military Directive 25 for an immediate invasion. Nazi dive bombers reduced Belgrade to rubble, and anything left moving was subject to strafing. To no avail, the Yugoslavian government in exile immediately petitioned the United Nations War Crimes Commission to include the bombing of civilian centers as a war crime. Note that this refers to the commission established during the war of nations united against the Nazis; it does not refer to the present United Nations. The commission did not rule on the matter.

The Allies would soon use similar tactics in even more destructive raids aimed at civilian centers. Robert Lovett, Assistant Secretary of War for air during WWII, was a lifetime advocate of bombing civilian centers. This is the way the U.S. fought the war in Vietnam and the wars in Iraq. In the end the victor determines what a war crime is, humanity and morality are forced to stand aside. In a single act the Allies unleashed a wave of total destruction on Dresden. As planned, the massive bombing set off a firestorm which wiped wiped out the entire city. Estimates of civilian deaths in Dresden are generally accepted at roughly 70,000, but some estimates range as high as 500,000. Dresden had no military value, there were no military or arms producer in Dresden. It was a civilian center crowded with refugees from the advancing Red Army. The only possible target was the rail switching center, which could have easily been disabled with a few bombs.

According to the Geneva conventions, and every principle of morality, humanity and justice, any attack on a civilian center constitutes a war crime. This includes blockades whose purpose is to starve the people into submission. Strangely the U.S. has always exerted its power to limit what may be legally considered a war crime by the Hague, which has allowed the U.S. to bomb civilian centers in Vietnam and maintain a blockade for nearly a half century against Cuba.

By 1945, the war had reduced most of Europe to rubble. This wholesale destruction came not at the hands of the Nazis, but the Allied air command. The Nazi war machine was destroyed on the battlefield, but at what cost? In Germany, the Allies estimated the bombing campaign destroyed as much as 80 percent of all housing units.

However, the effect of the air campaign against industrial centers and munitions makers was different. The Nazi war machine was producing more planes, tanks, trucks and other war material at the end of the war than in 1941. The Army estimated overall production of munitions at the end of the war to be roughly 80 percent of capacity.[9] In short, the Allied bombing campaign had been a failure.

Typical of the lack of damage to American-connected factories were the Ford and IG Farben plants in Cologne. During the war, the Allies targeted Cologne in massive air raids. One attack on Cologne involved a thousand bombers. While the British Ministry of Economic Warfare labeled the plant as a Target Category 1 ("major plants in industries of major importance"), no raid targeted the plant for 18 months. On Oct. 15 and Oct. 18, 1944, the U.S. Air Force specifically targeted the Ford plant in precision daylight bombing raids, yet the facility remained untouched. Aerial reconnaissance days later verified the raids were unsuccessful, yet the USAF scheduled no further bombings of the plant. Throughout the Allied bombing campaign, the only damage at the massive Ford complex was to a barracks for slave labor, during a nighttime aerial bombing raid by the British.[10]

In March 1945, the advancing Allied forces freed Cologne and initially estimated the damage to factories at 90 percent. The American forces made a more through investigation of factories later in March. The nearly intact Ford plant stunned the American liberators. The only damage the plant received was from artillery shells during the hopeless last stand by the Nazis. The plant was not in operation. The Nazis had removed much of the equipment and shipped it across the Rhine to hidden locations as the Allies advanced on Cologne. The wartime director of Ford Works, Robert Hans Schmidt, told the Allies that he could produce 500 trucks in a short time if they allowed him access to available material. U.S. forces allowed him to resume production because trucks were badly needed in the postwar period. On May 8, 1945, the day of Germany's unconditional surrender, an American documentary team set up its cameras to record the sight of the first postwar truck coming off the Ford Werke assembly line.[11]

The investigation of Ford Werke did not begin until June, a month after Germany's surrender and just before American forces passed control of the Cologne area over to the British. Henry Schneider headed the investigation. On Sept. 5, 1945, he presented his report on Ford Werke AG to Gen. Clay. Although Schneider's team did not learn of another set of documents kept by Johannes Krohn, the Reichskommissar for the Treatment of Enemy Property, their conclusions they made proved reliable. An excerpt from the report follows:

> The Reich used German Ford and its cooperative parent in Dearborn as a direct means of stockpiling the raw materials needed for war. Even prior to the War, German Ford arranged to produce for the Reich vehicles of a strictly military nature. This was done with the knowledge and approval of Dearborn.
>
> When war came German Ford stepped into the position of a major supplier of vehicles for the Wehrmacht. In addition, as much as 7 or 8% of total output during the war years consisted of more specialized war material.
>
> As was common in other German enterprises Ford increasingly resorted to use of prisoners of war and other slave labor who had to live behind barbed wire. The foreigners employed rose to over 40% of its labor supply in 1944. The usual Nazi discriminations in wages and working conditions were practiced. [12]

Not only did Ford willingly build trucks for the Nazis, it also helped them stockpile materials for the war with the complete knowledge of its Dearborn headquarters.

Exhibit 1 of the report was a memorandum from Heinrich Albert, a Ford Werke director, second only to Schmidt, dated Nov. 25, 1941, on the question "as to whether a complete Germanization would be necessary or advisable." In the memorandum, Albert argued against those who might wish to see "enemy property" expropriated by the Nazi state. Ford Werke, he claimed, was a fully German company that also enjoyed the privileges of membership in a global corporation. The benefits to Germany were obvious in the country's current accounts, which profited by Ford Werke's exports. The memorandum was submitted to Orvis Schmidt, a Treasury director. Orvis Schmidt returned later in June 1945 to Washington to testify before the Kilgore Committee on German penetration of the industry and finance of foreign countries. Schmidt stressed the extent of investments by American firms in various types of German industries and of the types of U.S. concerns with large interests in German industry.[13]

Despite the report on Ford Werke and the Senate investigations, no charges were ever filed against Ford for trading with the enemy. Ford Werke was now rehabilitated; it was producing trucks for the revival of the German economy as a bulwark against communism. The deaths of thousands of GIs on the battlefields of Europe were in vain. Betrayed by an elite cadre of their countrymen, the war against fascism was lost. Under a cloak of free enterprise and anti-communism, American fascists were now taking control. Today there is even more evidence of Ford aiding the Nazis.

Throughout Europe, and in Germany in particular, the scene was much the same. Large industrial plants stood unscathed amid a field of rubble, especially those plants with connections to American firms, like Ford and IG Farben. In fact, the bombing campaign left the IG Farben building in Berlin untouched, and the Allies used it as a command center. It stood in stark contrast to the rest of the city, which lay in ruins. This requires a brief look at how the Allies chose bombing targets.

During WWII, there were no laser-guided bombs that could be dropped through exhaust vents. Precision bombing was still in its infancy. Indeed, the RAF abandoned any attempt at precision bombing and switched to nighttime bombing because of heavy losses suffered in the day. Weather also presented a problem.

The definition of precision bombing used by the U.S. air force during WWII reveals how crude it was then. The United States adopted a standard of 70 percent of the bombs falling within a thousand-foot circle as precision bombing. The United States was only able to achieve even this crude standard during a single week throughout the war. Often the weather or the need to fly in formation prevented the bombs from some aircraft ever reaching the intended target. WWII precision bombing and the way it was implemented in massive bombing raids is more akin to what is termed saturation or carpet-bombing today.

The U.S. Air Force was not established as a separate branch of the U.S. military command until after the war. The term is used here to describe American airpower under the Army's command. At the cabinet level, the air force was under the control of Secretary of War Stimson. This Skull and Bones member supported an "easy peace" with Germany at the end of the war. Roosevelt allowed Stimson to choose his own staff. He chose John McCloy to act as Assistant Secretary in charge of intelligence, civilian affairs and general troubleshooter. Stimson placed Bonesman Robert Lovett as Assistant Secretary of War for air. Both McCloy and Lovett had Wall Street backgrounds. McCloy was a former Wall Street lawyer; Lovett was a partner and close friend of Prescott Bush at Brown Brothers and Harriman. It was Prescott who selected Lovett for membership in the Skull and Bones. Lovett was a fervent supporter of terror bombing of population centers all of his life, including during the Vietnam War. McCloy had an essential role in selecting targets for nondestruction, which meant other targets were selected.[14]

Another individual involved in the air force command and target selection was Trubee Davison, who also had close contacts on Wall Street. Davison had been the Assistant Secretary of War for air between the wars. However, Davison's first association with the air force was during his years at Yale during WWI. Trubee formed the special Yale Unit of the Naval Reserve Flying Corps, which was closely associated with the Skull and Bones. The Yale Unit was often snidely referred to as the millionaire squadron. While training in Florida, the pilots often were taken to their planes in wheelchairs pushed by black porters. Two other members of the Yale unit were Robert Lovett and Artemus Gates.

Since the United States was not yet at war, the unit served under British command. Robert Lovett headed the Yale unit. Trubee's father, Henry Davison, a senior partner at J.P. Morgan and Co., lavishly financed the unit, which distinguished itself during WWI.

During WWII, Trubee served directly under Lovett. From June to December 1941, Trubee was deputy chief of staff in the air force combat command with the rank of colonel. From then until his discharge in 1946, Trubee was assistant chief of staff at A-1. He was discharged as a brigadier general.

Thus the Yale Unit effectively ran the air war during WWII. Robert Lovett was Assistant Secretary of War for air. Directly under him was Trubee Davison. Artemus Gates, another member of the Yale group, served as Assistant Secretary of Navy for air.

A more interesting factor of this league is their close family ties to Wall Street and the rich elite. Robert Lovett married Adele Quarterly Brown. Miss Brown was the daughter of James Brown, a partner of Brown Brothers and Harriman, and grandson of the founder. Artemus Gates married Trubee's sister.

Trubee's father was a partner with the Morgans. However, this is only a beginning of the Davison family's connections. Trubee's wife was Dorothy Peabody, the sister of Malcolm Endicott Peabody, a former Governor of Massachusetts and the grandchild of Marianne Cabot Lee. The Davison family is related to the Rockefellers as in John Davison Rockefeller.

Trubee Davison had one other connection: Benjamin Strong may have been Trubee's brother-in-law. The author has found two conflicting reports. In one instance, there was a reported marriage of Henry Davison's daughter to Strong. The other report does not emphatically suggest a marriage, but does note that after Strong's first wife died, the Davison family raised the children. Nevertheless, there was a strong bond between Henry Davison and Benjamin Strong. It was Davison who made him a secretary of Banker's Trust and brought him in as J.P. Morgan's personal auditor. However, Strong was better known as the first director of the New York Federal Reserve Bank.

James Stillman Rockefeller served with the Airborne Command and Airborne Center as assistant chief of staff. He was a Lieutenant Colonel in the General Staff Corps when discharged in 1945.

These connections extend through time. A good example of this is Prescott Bush's connection with this circle of elites. Prescott Bush as a member of the Skull and Bones stole the skull of Geronimo. In 1986, the Apaches conducted negotiations with George H. W. Bush about its return. Representing Bush was Endicott Peabody Davison, Trubee's son.

At the top were several people with detailed knowledge of American investments in Germany. In fact, Lovett was in charge of the entire air campaign, and McCloy was deeply involved in removing targets from the selection list. Both individuals were well aware of American investments in Nazi Germany and may have had family members with such investments. Under their direct command was another layer of individuals with family ties to the Wall Street firms that invested heavily in Nazi Germany.

Without more records, which are still sealed by the government, it is impossible to assess if this group of Wall Street elites steered the bombing campaign away from American-owned targets in Germany. However, it is interesting that the only massive bombing raid directed at a specific industrial target hit the Swedish-owned S&K bearing plant deep inside Germany. The raid took a heavy toll on lives and planes. Many of the bombers lost never even reached the destination; more were lost on the return flight after receiving heavy damage over the target. There were several reasons for the heavy losses. First, the S&K plant was outside the range of any Allied fighters, so the bombers had protection for only part of the trip. Second, both antiaircraft batteries and fighter squadrons protected the plant. Planes proved to be easy targets for German fighter pilots because the bombers had no fighter protection of their own on the return trip to England.

Yet choice industrial targets such as the Ruhr steel district, were present at much shorter ranges. Damage to any of the coal mines or steel plants in the district would have limited the Nazis' ability to produce tanks and other heavy armaments. The Ruhr district was close enough for the bombers to have full fighter protection. However, many of the plants and mines in the Ruhr district had connections with American investments. These links were directly between Flick, Krupp, Thyssen and Brown Brothers and Harriman. Coal mining began again almost immediately after liberation as the example of Aachen showed, and the German coal mines supplied not only Germany but much of Europe with coal for the first few years after the war. This production level would have been impossible if the mines had been significantly damaged by bombing raids.

It is true that the motive for the S&K bombing raid was that the factory was the only major producer of bearings in Nazi Germany. Bearings are essential to any boat, plane, tank or truck. The Allies hoped that by damaging the S&K plant, German production of military vehicles could be delayed. The raid only caused minor delays in production because the Nazis easily got bearings from other S&K factories in Sweden and Switzerland.

In July 1941, the Department of War developed a plan for target selection in line with the general battle plan for potential war known as Rainbow 5, and the ABC agreement with Britain, which called for a sustained air war against Germany. The plan developed was Air War Plans Division Plan 1 or simply AWPD-1. Its primary military objective was to defeat Germany by airpower alone. If the primary objective was unachievable, the plan then called for preparing the way for a European invasion. AWPD-1 identified three vital targets in the German economy: electric power, transportation and oil, with a fourth intermediate target area, the destruction of the Luftwaffe. AWPD-1 called for 154 targets to be destroyed in the first six months.[15]

AWPD-1 was never implemented. Burton Wheeler, the pro-Nazi senator, leaked it and the Rainbow 5 battle plan to the press in the fall of 1941. Both Rainbow 5 and AWPD-1 appeared in the *Chicago Tribune* and *Washington Times-Herald*. The Nazis quickly realized the importance of both documents. On Dec. 12, 1941, Hitler issued Directive 39, which called for massing air defenses around key industrial centers. Four days later, Hitler rescinded the directive.

Early in 1942, AWPD-42 replaced AWPD-1. Besides shuffling the target priorities and including round-the-clock bombing of Germany, there was little difference between the two plans. RAF would continue with nighttime area bombing; the American air forces would use "precision" daytime bombing. AWPD-42 focused on tactical targets or targets producing equipment the German military could not do without, rather than strategic targets needed to produce war munitions.

While similar to the preceding plan, AWPD-42 placed disruption of the electrical grid only 13th on the list, in line with the emphasis on tactical versus strategic targets. Wiping out the German electrical grid would have severely limited the Nazis' ability to make war munitions, so this was perhaps the largest failure of the air campaign. The analysts mistakenly assumed that the German electrical grid could reroute power rapidly from one region to another, which, in fact, wasn't possible. Any strikes against power plants supplying industrial centers would have left those manufacturing centers idle for months.

AWPD-42 was hammered out by the Committee of Operations Analysts (COA), composed of industrialists, lawyers and various economists. The presence of industrialists is noteworthy. Almost all of America's major corporations had investments in Nazi Germany. Most of these corporations went to extraordinary means to remain in contact and to continue doing business with the Nazis after war was declared.

The committee used several criteria in deciding the suitability of the target. Essentially, they looked for bottlenecks and weaknesses in the Nazi economy that could be exploited. The makeup of the COA is interesting because of the blunder of downgrading electrical targets. The German electrical industry was closely affiliated with two American firms, GE and ITT, through cartel agreements. Plants owned by General Electric through its AEG subsidiary and those owned by ITT were only hit incidentally in area raids. The electrical plants that were bombed as targets were Brown Boveri and Siemensstadt. Neither firm had connections with GE or ITT. Furthermore, plants owned by GE like the one at Koppelsdorf also made radar equipment and would have been prime targets.[16]

At the end of the war, a team known as FIAT was sent to examine the electrical industry plants to determine the extent of the bombing damage. The team consisted of Alexander Sanders of ITT, Whitworth Ferguson of Ferguson Electric and Erich Borgman of Westinghouse. While FIAT's stated objective was to survey bomb damage, the members' actions revealed that the real goal was to get German electrical equipment back into production as soon as possible.

With the change in AWPD-42, a new bombing offensive was launched in 1942. In early 1943, the Point-Blank Directive was approved, calling for round-the-clock bombing of Germany. Again, the RAF was to bomb cities at night while the USAF bombed targets during the day. Point-Blank included a permissive clause that allowed Bomber Command to continue operations aimed at civilian morale and the general dislocation of the economy.

Shortly after the implementation of AWPD-42, RAF launched 1,000 bomber attacks against Cologne. The meat grinder was now fully operational and civilian centers were reduced to rubble. The 1943 Point-Blank Directive eased the selection of civilian centers as targets. When the RAF bombed the Ford plant at Poissy in March 1942, American newspapers published photographs of the burning facility. However, the media chains owning most of the American newspapers were eager to protect one of their largest advertisers, and never mentioned that Ford owned the plant – the truth was withheld from the American public to protect a traitor. When the Vichy government paid Ford 38 million francs in compensation, once again, the newspapers were discreet and failed to report it.[17]

One member of the COA team was Guido R. Perera, a partner in the Hutchins and Wheeler law firm in Boston before the war. He also served as trustee of the Massachusetts Investors Trust. During the war, Perera first worked on the legislative and administrative reorganization of the Army Air Corps; he then served as deputy chairman of the Advisory Committee on Bombardment and as vice chairman of the Committee of Operations Analysts. In these positions, he oversaw development of plans and target systems for bombing strategic industrial targets in Germany and Japan.[18]

Perera had connections with Massachusetts Investors Trust, the first mutual fund in America, founded by Paul Mellon in the 1920s. One of the largest holdings of the trust was Boston Insurance Co. The present owners of the Bank of Boston, Fleet Financial, are desperately trying to deny any connections between Boston Insurance and the Bank of Boston as new information surfaces linking the bank and insurance company to the Nazis. It appears that Boston Insurance was created by the bank or its directors. Erwin Pallavicini served as one of the directors of Boston Insurance Co. An OSS file describes him as a U.S.-blacklisted Nazi collaborator who also served on the board of a German insurance firm in Argentina. OSS documents also list another director of Boston Insurance, Benjamin Nazar Anchorena, as a Nazi collaborator. Newly declassified files outline the complicated financial relationships that linked First National Bank of Boston interests with Hitler's financiers, including Spanish and Mexican companies in business with Germany's Munich Re. The entire network involved around 230 German firms. Even as late as 1997, the identities of the owners of Boston Insurance remain unknown.

Quoting from an OSS report compiled in 1943: "The Boston Insurance Company is still writing all kinds of insurance of blacklisted names, and they are placing this business in the London market." That meant "the Boston," as the document referred to the insurance firm, was spreading cash and information within and between both the Allies and the Axis. The document continued: "The Boston is known to have American board members and stockholders, having been formed by interests affiliated with the First National Bank of Boston."[19] Insurance companies were ideal fronts for Nazi spies. Not only would they have detailed blueprints of the factory, but also a list of the equipment. From that information, the Nazis could reliably determine what and how much a factory could produce.

The Mellon and Rockefeller families controlled the Bank of Boston. Both were deeply involved in arming and supplying Hitler. Through Alcoa, the Mellon family had concluded several cartel agreements with IG Farben. Aluminum refining requires vast amounts of electricity. Could Perera have been one of those responsible for removing the electrical companies in Germany from the bombing list? He must have been aware of the Mellon-aluminum link, and closely associated with Mellons through Massachusetts Investors Trust. Perera also had more than the usual degree of knowledge of electric companies. After returning from the war in 1947, he served as president and later chairman of Eastern

Utilities Associates. However, without the complete records of COA, no solid conclusions can be reached.

Perera is not the only one from COA with connections to the Wall Street money that built Hitler's war machine. Arthur Roseborough, a former Sullivan & Cromwell employee from the firm's Paris office, served in Air Force Intelligence in London during 1943. This unit was created specifically to evaluate bombing damage and to recommend targets.[20]

Perera and Roseborough fall into the type of people employed by COA, so we may assume they were typical of the group. Without more COA operations files, it is impossible to decide the guilt or innocence of Perera, Rosebourgh or the COA staff in protecting the investments of American industrialists and elitists. However, the undisputed fact remains that 80 percent of the homes in Germany were destroyed; only 20 percent of industrial production. In fact, much of the reduced production capacity came from the secondary effects of the bombing campaign, such as lack of gasoline and a shortage of parts from the collateral damage to the transportation system.

After the war, a survey of the bombing concluded that it was overall ineffectual in halting German munitions production.

Greater success came with bombing the Romanian oil fields. The shortage of gasoline in the Third Reich was acute and even limited the advance of the German Wehrmacht in the Battle of the Bulge. However, Germany had always suffered from a limited oil supply, the war merely restricted it further.

The survey also found that the bombing was most successful in delaying troop deployment by disabling rail centers. Although the Nazis quickly repaired the centers, the delay was enough to give Allies an edge on the battlefield.

The massive area bombings of cities, particularly the firebombing of Dresden, raises another critical point. In essence, such bombings of civilian centers were nothing less than acts of terrorism. Estimates range from 40,000 to 500,000 killed in the Dresden firestorm. When the Nazis bombed and strafed Belgrade, Yugoslavia demanded that it be included on the list of war crimes. While much of the world considers bombings of civilian centers to be war crimes, the United States still argues they are not. It should be noted that Dresden was an ancient city and contained many unique architectural wonders. However, it was in the path of the advancing Soviet army.

Sabotaging the 4Ds Program

Unfortunately, the 4Ds program of denazification, decartelization, demilitarizing and democratization was sabotaged from the beginning. This sabotage reached epidemic proportions after the Morgenthau plan was made public following the Quebec meeting between Roosevelt and Churchill. Morgenthau was one of the few in the Roosevelt administration who pushed for a "hard peace" following the war. After the Quebec meeting, Morgenthau was viewed as the most hated man in America, largely due to Nazi propaganda from the pro-Nazi leaders of American industry. Key to sabotaging the 4Ds program was the marginalization and finally the removal of Morgenthau.

Following the success of the Normandy invasion, Morgenthau had lunch with Gen. Eisenhower in Portsmouth. Morgenthau and his aides, Dexter White and Fred Smith, were eager to sound out Eisenhower's opinions on postwar Germany. Eisenhower said: "I'm not interested in the German economy and personally would not like to bolster it, if that will make it easier for the Germans." As far as he was concerned, "the German General Staff should be utterly eliminated and the Nazi ringleaders given the death penalty." Ike felt that by supporting Hitler, German people had been accomplices to everything done in their name, and must not be allowed to escape a sense of guilt of complicity in the tragedy that engulfed the world.[21]

Eisenhower realized that Morgenthau became his severest critic after he arranged a pragmatic deal with Vichy Admiral Darlan. Nevertheless, Eisenhower was truthful in expressing his views on Germany. In letters to his wife, he often wrote of how he hated Germans. As the war progressed, Ike's view of the Germans hardened, especially after the first concentration camp was liberated.

Eisenhower also expressed his opinions on the Soviets to Morgenthau. He felt that a hard peace would motivate the Soviets to redouble their efforts to help win the European war. He staunchly felt the Russians deserved the right to capture Berlin after suffering horrendous losses. Moreover, Eisenhower was optimistic about postwar relationships with the Soviet Union. He expressed to Morgenthau that Russia had problems of its own that would keep it busy long after they were dead.[22]

On Jan. 5, 1944, with the Battle of the Bulge raging, Roosevelt's policy of unconditional surrender came under brutal assault from Sen. Burton Wheeler, the pro-Nazi demagogue, who insisted that most Americans were unwilling to sanction a peace of vengeance against Germany. Nor would they accept America acting as Europe's policeman, he said. The British embassy in Washington took note, asserting Wheeler's assault made him anti-Soviet and anti-Semitic.

On March 3, 1945, Secretary of War Stimson met with FDR and reminded him that Eisenhower had agreed to serve only for a few months as military governor of Germany after the surrender. The recent firebombing of Dresden troubled Stimson. He noted in his diary that Dresden was the capital of Saxony, the least Prussianized part of Germany. Stimson opposed a hard peace with Germany and had at one time suggested his Under Secretary, Robert Patterson, as Eisenhower's replacement. Both Roosevelt and Morgenthau approved of the idea. However, in March 1945, Stimson told FDR that after the Battle of the Bulge, the Pentagon needed to revise its war production and Patterson was needed to oversee that revision. However, Stimson took the opportunity to suggest that War Mobilization Board member Gen. Lucius Clay would be the right man.

During the summer of 1944, Morgenthau heard that John McCloy was interested in the job. He indignantly asked Hopkins how McCloy could be involved when his previous clients were firms like General Electric and Westinghouse, companies with substantial investments in Germany. McCloy knew in advance that Clay was willing to make ample use of the loophole in JCS 1067 to allow commanders to circumvent the 4Ds program.[23]

On March 10, Secretary of State Stettinius was presented by his assistant James Dunn with a document, "Draft Directive of the Treatment of Germany." Dunn had assured the Secretary of State he had merely put the Yalta decisions down on paper with no changes in policy. Four days later, Stettinius presented the paper to Roosevelt falsely claiming that Stimson had approved it. FDR initialed the document on that recommendation.

Stettinius asked Roosevelt to promote Dunn in December. Roosevelt worried about Dunn's reputation for legerdemain and his conservative views, but consented to the promotion. Dunn had been a backer of Franco and wanted to use German industrialists to rehabilitate Germany. Eleanor was outraged over the promotion.

Stettinius was unaware that Dunn had played him for a fool. The document switched Allied control from a decentralized to a centralized power concentrated in the Control Council.[24] This document upset everyone, including Stimson, McCloy and Morgenthau. The following day, Stimson asked the President why he had signed such a terrible document. Roosevelt replied that he could not remember if he had signed it. At this time, Roosevelt's health was declining rapidly and the incident raised a serious question about his ability to continue to function as president. He was constantly tired and was reported to be inattentive; within a month he died.

On March 20, Morgenthau had lunch with Roosevelt and presented him with a memo opposing Dunn's draft. FDR told Morgenthau that if he and Stimson could come up with an agreement with

Stettinius, he would revoke the draft. Before leaving, the President agreed with Morgenthau that he should fire Dunn and several others in the State Department.

On March 23, Morgenthau and Grew presented FDR with a new document to replace the Draft Directive. It was written primarily by McCloy and reflected FDR's current view of changing — not destroying — German industry. McCloy's devious sabotage of the 4Ds program extended even further than helping select the military governor and writing the control document. He made sure the military would have the upper hand and that he would not be hamstrung by a Morgenthau man. Gen. Clay also was shrewdly political and asked Morgenthau for his recommendation for an economic aide. Morgenthau recommended Bernard Bernstein, but Clay disapproved. McCloy then saw to it that his brother-in-law, Lewis Douglas, received the post.

Douglas was the heir to the Phelps-Dodge copper fortune. He had served as Roosevelt's first budget director before resigning over the President's liberal policies. Privately, Douglas complained that most of the bad things imposed by the New Deal could be traced to Jewish influence. His extreme anti-Jewish views came from his family's close business association with the Dodge family, who were active in the eugenics movement. The Phelps-Dodge Corp., was extremely anti-union, as well, and had driven their miners into the desert rather than negotiate union demands. There are enough gaps in Lewis Douglas' military files to suggest he was probably a member of the OSS. Following his appointment as economic aide to Gen. Clay, he served as ambassador to England.[25] As an economic adviser, Douglas supported revitalizing German industry.

Clearly McCloy's machinations were to cripple the 4Ds program from the start. He had his hand in selecting two of the most powerful positions in postwar Germany, the military governor and his economic aide. McCloy carefully chose both knowing that they were opposed to dismantling German industry and largely opposed to the 4Ds program. Moreover, he was chiefly responsible for rewriting the directive to ensure that German industry would not be held responsible for some of the worst crimes of the Third Reich. Later, McCloy took over as the military governor and freed most of the war criminals.

Efforts to mask Nazi assets and business arrangements began in 1943 with the realization that Germany had lost the war and it was only a matter of time before the Nazis surrendered. For the Nazis, this meant they had to transfer their stolen loot out of Germany. For American corporations, the problem was more complex. While their plants were located in Germany, they had to hide behind a thin facade of subterfuge, claiming the Nazis had seized control of their plants. They had to remove dedicated New Dealers who vigorously opposed the Nazis and replace them with dollar-a-year men and Wall Street cronies who would overlook their Nazi dealings.

By 1945, many of the New Dealers had been replaced. John McCloy and Robert Lovett had deputized numerous Wall Street financial specialists to prowl through the debris of Europe. J. Henry Schroeder Bank's vice president, Lada Mocarski, was transferred from his adviser post in the War Department to Bern, in time to take over the U.S. Consulate. Allen Dulles also was director of the Schroeder Bank.[26]

John McCloy was a former Wall Street lawyer. Perhaps his most famous case was Black Tom, in which he proved German agents sabotaged a U.S. munitions factory in New Jersey in 1916. After winning the case, he served as adviser to every president from Roosevelt to Reagan. After the war, McCloy was president of the World Bank and chairman of the Chase Manhattan Bank, the Ford Foundation and the Council on Foreign Relations. He was one of the original supporters of one world government ruled by corporations.

Robert Lovett was a Brown Brothers and Harriman employee, a close friend of Prescott Bush, and a Skull and Bonesman. He would later be the prime architect of the CIA.

The J. Henry Schroeder Bank was founded by the family of Baron Kurt von Schroeder, the radical Nazi who helped Hitler to power. Von Schroeder was a partner in the J.H. Stein Bank, which also financed the Nazis. By 1938, the London branch of J. Henry Schroeder Bank was acting as the Nazi financial agent in Great Britain. In 1933, Schroeder began representing ITT interests in Nazi Germany. In 1936, J. Henry Schroeder Banking Corp., merged with the Rockefellers to form Schroeder Rockefeller and Co.[27]

In the summer of 1945, U.S. Treasury officials uncovered evidence that Gero von Gaevernitz, a close associate of Allen Dulles, was exploiting his quasi-official position with the U.S. Legation in Bern to complete some questionable deals with E.V.D. Wright.[28]

Gaevernitz's sister married Hugo Stinnes, the vigorous Hitler-supporting banker. During the 1920s, Gaevernitz traveled back and forth between the Ruhr and Wall Street arranging deals. As late as 1941, he listed himself as an agent for Schildge Rumohr Inc., a New York dummy corporation better known as Transmares. Dulles expedited the financing for Transmares through J. Henry Schroeder Bank. The Department of Justice identified Transmares as a front for circumventing the British blockade. Gaevernitz pocketed a 30,000-franc payoff for inducing North German Lloyd to allow the cross-registration of a vessel from a Finnish to Swiss flag. He laundered the money through E.V.D. Wright in Portugal and continued to oversee Stinnes holdings in Germany and Switzerland.[29]

The obvious connections between top officials in postwar Germany and their past dealings with Nazis did not pass entirely unnoticed. As previously noted, both Treasury Secretary Morgenthau and the Kilgore Committee were alarmed, as were others in Europe. In the airgram A-1052 sent on Sept. 15, 1945 from Switzerland by Leland Harrison to the Secretary of State, the London Embassy and Robert Murphy noted the connection with the Stinnes bank:

> In view of the recent reports of the arrest of Hugo Stinnes Jr. in Germany, The Department may wish to consider, with other interested agencies, the advisability of having former Stinnes associates employed by the American government agencies to advise military as to German nationals helpful in building a democratic Germany.[30]

The airgram blindsided Dulles. In a long rambling defense of Gaevernitz, he claimed such connections were necessary to gain information. However, Dulles failed to mention the connection between Gaevernitz and Transmares.

While Dulles faced serious allegations of treason immediately after the war, he had help from the highest levels of the military occupation government. William Draper, who headed the Economic Division, was emphatically against decartelization. Draper, James Forrestal and Paul Nitze had risen to the senior management level at Dillon and Read before the war.

The Economic Division also drew heavily on the assessments of Capt. Norbert Bogdan. Bogdan was on loan to the War Department from his vice presidential post at J. Henry Schroeder Bank. He landed in Algiers with Eisenhower and went to France after it was liberated; he appeared often in Bern. In Germany, Bogdan first tried to head off the Army's Financial Division from investigating J.H. Stein Bank, by dismissing it as small potatoes. He then argued for travel orders to Cologne, even before the city fell, to cover up the Schroeder Bank records.

Donovan requisitioned Richard Helms from his job in New York of plotting Nazi submarine routes to serve in Europe. While the Helms family was not rich, his grandfather served as the first president of the Bank of International Settlements.

During the autumn of 1945, Dewitt Clinton Poole was sent to Germany to interrogate important Nazis. During the war, Poole headed the Foreign Nationalities Branch of the OSS. He directed OSS efforts to recruit agents from immigrant communities and later became president of the National Committee for a Free Europe, one of the CIA's largest propaganda efforts.

On his return from Europe, Poole met with Dulles, who was already back at work on Wall Street. After two weeks, Poole sent a long, handwritten letter to Dulles. An excerpt follows:

Department specialist Charles Kindleberger is all right as far as he goes, but he doesn't appear to control the raft of young Jew boys under him. In the fulfillment of the Potsdam program they put ahead of everything the dismantling of German plants and shipment of machinery to Russia. There had been some headway with details: Of the 100,000 Nazis now arrested, 20,000 are soon to be turned loose. The British have vigorously protested the low ceiling put on German steel production.

Since the Harry White boys continue on the job at Treasury, some change must be engineered at the highest levels; the time has come to convince the President, or at least Secretary of State Jimmy Byrnes, that to continue to ruin Germany by indiscriminate de-Nazification and unrelenting deindustrialization can only confirm Europe as a liability.[31]

After warning recipients to destroy it, Dulles circulated Poole's letter to others opposed to the decartelization of Germany. One of the recipients, Laird Bell, a Chicago banker and president of the local Council on Foreign Relations, was already on a one-man crusade against decartelization. A week later, Bell told Dulles he was developing a contact with a group centered around Notre Dame University and headed by some of the Catholic hierarchy who had formed a Save Europe Now Committee.[32]

United Nations War Crimes Commission

The Allied forces on the ground were likewise hindered from completing the denazification program by their own officers. In a meeting of the Finance Division, Capt. Norbert Bogdan, a former vice president of the Schroeder Banking Corp., of New York, argued furiously against investigations of Stein Bank. Shortly after, two of Bogdan's staff applied for permission to investigate the bank. The Intelligence Division blocked that request. ITT was closely associated with Kurt von Schroeder and wanted to hide its past help of the Nazis. An investigation of the Stein Bank would expose the connection.[33]

Unfortunately, many officers were loyal to their former employer and not their country. As IBM pressed for Treasury permission to transact business with Germany and Italy, Harold Carter, an employee of the Economic Warfare Section, took notice. Carter carefully prepared his case against IBM, but was unable to convince a court to issue a subpoena. To further complicate the matter, the Nazis only leased the Dehomag machines. A quirk in the law meant they were American property and thus entitled to protection.

Further, Watson had anticipated the war and on March 31, 1941, incorporated a new subsidiary, Munitions Manufacturing Corps. IBM bought two small canning factories to house the new unit. Within 60 days of Pearl Harbor, Watson unveiled a fully equipped manufacturing factory staffed by 250 employees. Its first product was a 20-mm antiaircraft cannon. Eventually, the subsidiary grew to produce a whole range of war munitions, including 90-mm antiaircraft gun directories, M1 rifles, gasmasks, bombing sights and other items. IBM had taken up a host of research projects for the military.

IBM arrived on the beaches of Normandy shortly after the Allies established beachheads. Mobile MRUs (Machine Records Units) made up of IBM employees and others trained by IBM became indispensable on the frontline. Their loyalty laid more with IBM than with their country. Watson received hundreds of letters from IBM soldiers, many telling of capturing Dehomag machines. However, none caused more of a stir than a letter from Lt. Lawrence Flick, written on Sept. 2, 1945. Flick told of enlisting a captain from the Property Control Division to support Hermann Fellinger, a former Nazi IBM partner. Fellinger was one of those in the Dehomag revolt who tried to overthrow the iron grip of Watson on Dehomag. Watson had no intent of reempowering Fellinger.[34]

Officers who retained a greater loyalty to their company than their country plagued the Army officer's ranks. This should not detract from the thousands that served their country honorably, but many undoubtedly thought their corporate loyalty would stand them in good stead on their return home. Others owning stock in the company were simply protecting their own investments.

As early as 1942, there were clear signals of corporate America's connivance to continue doing business with the German cartels as if the war had never taken place. In a speech on June 3, 1942 before the Illinois Bar Association, Assistant Attorney General Thurman Arnold warned:

> The secret influence of the international cartel is going to be thrown in favor of peace without victory when the first opportunity arises — just as it was thrown in that direction at Munich.

> The small group of American businessmen who are parties to these international rings are not unpatriotic, but they still think of war as a temporary recess from business as usual with a strong Germany. They expect to begin the game all over again after the war.

> It is significant that all these cartel leaders still talk and think as if the war would end in a stalemate, and that therefore, they must be in a position to continue their arrangements with a strong Germany after the war. This is not shown by their speeches, but by actual documents and memoranda of business policy which we find in their files.[35]

Arnold's words confirm the findings listed in the previous chapter. As of June 1942, corporate America had not given up hope of negotiating a peace with the Nazis. Arnold effectively predicted the outbreak of the Cold War. Perhaps, the only mistake Arnold made in his speech was in saying these treasonous corporate leaders were "not unpatriotic."

Another warning came on June 4, 1943, when Homer Boone, Chairman of the Senate Patents Committee, told the Senate Military Affairs Committee:

> The Standard Oil Co., of New Jersey directors were asked by certain stockholders to cut off all relations with Farben after the war, but (they) refused. One official said such a request was an affront. There is clear indication that after this unpleasant interlude of war they will hold hands again and resume their very harmonious and beautiful arrangements with cartels.[36]

The quotes above serve as a grim reminder to the power of the Nazi elements among us, when compared to the success of the T Forces at Nordhausen.

To fully understand the sabotaging of the 4Ds program from within, a brief look at the Nuremberg Tribunal and the personnel assigned to 4-Ds is needed. Most studies only cover the Nuremberg Trials, but there were several others. The Nuremberg Trials were a culmination of a long and complicated process, steeped in geopolitics. Since the Allies failed to reach an agreement leading to the Nuremberg Trials until mid-1945, there was no official policy in handling the Nazis as Allied forces swept across Germany.

From the beginning, the debate between Washington and London on what comprised a war crime was haunted by the failure of the trials following WWI in Leipzig.

In 1940, the exiled government of Poland first raised the question of punishing war criminals in WWII, but the British Foreign Office opposed the initiative. The issue of war crimes then remained stalled until after the German invasion of Russia, characterized by a horrendous increase in Nazi brutality. Existing international law was inadequate to address the crimes committed. An agreement was needed between the three big powers to adjust the international law to address the horrors of the war.

Periodically, the British issued statements to fortify the morale of the people trapped in occupied countries. On Oct. 21, 1940, Churchill stated that all crimes of Hitler would be on him and on all who belonged to his system. In May 1941, Foreign Secretary Anthony Eden spoke of a reckoning that would be wide and fierce. On June 12, 1941, following the Nazi invasion of Russia, Churchill stated: "These quislings, like Nazi leaders, if not disposed of by their fellow countrymen — which would save trouble — will be delivered by us on the morrow of victory to the justice of Allied tribunals."[37]

Germany's invasion of Russia marked a turning point in the relations between Poland and Britain. Britain, seeking allies against Germany, was now intent on improving relations with the Soviet Union. The exiled Polish government wanted to preserve its 1939 borders, while Moscow was insistent on keeping the Polish territory ceded to Russia following the Ribbentrop-Molotov agreement. Therefore, Polish wishes rested on the greater goals of British geopolitics.

By the autumn of 1941, the Foreign Office had to contend with growing unrest in both the Cabinet and Parliament in response to reports of German atrocities. In September 1941, Hugh Dalton, Labor MP and minister of Economic Warfare, called Eden's attention to the German practice of executing hostages whenever partisan forces attacked. Dalton proposed telling the people of Europe to keep a list of names of all those involved in executing hostages, including the commanding officer. After liberation, those on the lists would be hunted down and summarily executed. The Foreign Office remained cold to Dalton's proposal and warned against a repetition of the "Hang the Kaiser" campaign after WWI.

Recognizing the growing concern over Nazi atrocities, Eden asked the War Cabinet on Oct. 1, 1941 to approve a statement similar to the Ango-Franco-Polish declaration of April 1940. The draft declaration was a vague statement unacceptable to the War Cabinet. The Foreign Office quickly revised the declaration as follows:

> We therefore publicly declare that brutalities which are being committed in occupied countries are contrary to the dictates of humanity; are a reversion to barbarism; and will meet with sure retribution. To this end, we are united in our resolve to win freedom of the oppressed peoples and to execute justice. The methods of oppression and terror used by Hitler are such that many people, including Germans and Italians, are ignorant of the full facts. When these things are known, world opinion will not allow the criminals to escape just punishment for their crimes. The facts are being put on record so that in due time the world may pronounce its judgment. With victory will come retribution.[38]

Leaders in Parliament called for a stronger declaration. The Foreign Office did not deliver the declaration to the United States and Soviet Union until Oct. 21, which signaled the low priority it gave the war crimes issue. Four days later, in an unexpected move, Roosevelt issued a statement condemning the execution of 50 hostages in Nantes in reprisal for shooting the military commander of the region. Roosevelt's statement compelled the Foreign Office to make several quick decisions. Churchill responded immediately to Roosevelt's statement, concluding: "Retribution for these crimes must henceforth take its place among the major purposes of the war."[39]

Also plaguing the establishment of a unified war crimes declaration was the tendency of both London and Washington to dismiss the Soviet reports as exaggerations or worse, imaginary. Yet, some of the most brutal war crimes, such as the Bari Yar massacre, were occurring on the Eastern Front.

Following Churchill's remarks on Oct. 25, various Allies weighed in. The Australians thought the statement to be couched in inappropriate language and should be simplified, dropping all remarks about retributions. Governments-in-exile disagreed. The Greeks accepted the British statement in principle but insisted on adding Bulgaria's name to the war crimes declaration. The Yugoslav government wanted to include all forms of atrocities, including dive bombing, burning of villages and others. It also wanted to indict Nazi Quisling governments, including the so-called Independent Croatia.

However, the War Cabinet approved the Foreign Office stance, and the statements by Roosevelt and Churchill made a joint resolution by the Allies unnecessary. Frank Roberts, the first Acting Secretary in the Central Department of the Foreign Office, argued for keeping Britain from signing a joint declaration so as not to be committed to whatever determination the Allies might reach at the war's end. Many in the Foreign Office wanted to go further and free Britain of any commitment to making a list of war criminals or engaging in any preparation of any registry of atrocities.

Britain ultimately chose not to associate itself with the proposed declaration. Further complicating matters was a dispute among the Allies about including the Soviet Union as a signer of the declaration. The Poles, Czechs and Yugoslavs sided with England in favor, but most other governments were against. The United States, not yet at war, declined to attend any joint signing of the declaration.

The meeting of the Allies took place on Jan. 13, 1942. Representatives from nine nations took part: Belgium, Czechoslovakia, Greece, Luxembourg, the Netherlands, Norway, Poland, Yugoslavia and the French National Committee. Also present, as observers, were the United States, Britain, the Soviet Union, China, the Dominions and India. Eden addressed the group with caution, concluding that the governments of occupied territories should take the initiative in declaring the principles by which they will be guided once liberated.

While the atrocities increased in Poland, the Polish government-in-exile began demanding more than just declarations. It asked the British to conduct bombing raids in central and western Germany in retaliation for 100 hostages executed by the Nazis in Warsaw. The Foreign Office refused the request. Another Polish demand called for executing five Germans after the war for each Pole, Yugoslav or Czech killed. They further demanded creating a special air force unit for the daily bombing of a German town that had no military value in reprisal for Nazi atrocities committed in Poland.

The Poles were not the only occupied nation that demanded stronger measures from Britain. After the Nazis ravaged Lidice, the Czechs demanded that RAF raze a German village. The Foreign Office turned this demand down, too. In response to British inaction, the Czechs announced that they unilaterally would judge and punish those responsible. The Czech list included Hitler and members of his government, all representatives of Germany stationed in Czechoslovakia and their subordinates, as well as any German or Czech who aided them, even indirectly.

Objecting that it was not consulted in advance, the Foreign Office condemned the Czech action as inexcusable. Britain's rejection of the demands of the Poles and Czechs was not totally without reason. So far, Britain had fared badly in the war and there was a legitimate concern about German reprisals against captured British POWs. British mistrust of claims coming from Eastern Europe contributed to the rejections. In short, this meeting accomplished nothing except to make a show of concern about war crimes.

It was not until October 1943 that the United Nations War Crimes Commission (UNWCC) was established (not to be confused with the current United Nations, as the Allies during the war referred to themselves as the United Nations). Plaguing the commission were differences between Britain and the Soviet Union about what constituted a war crime and how to conduct the war. Just as some in the British Foreign Office opposed any war crime trials, a similar faction existed in the United States State Department. The influence of these factions is reflected by the 18 months it took for UNWCC to take shape.

Two of the biggest stumbling blocks between Britain and the Soviets were the case of Rudolf Hess and the inclusion of the Dominions. The Soviets wanted immediate trials, including that of Hess; the British wanted to wait until after the war before beginning any trials. The British also wanted to include the Dominions, such as New Zealand and South Africa, on the commission. The Soviets opposed including the Dominions unless each of the Soviet states received equal status. This also was a bedrock issue for the Soviets in forming the present United Nations. By demanding the Dominions each have a separate vote, British influence was multiplied several fold; denying the Soviet demand for a vote for each of its states weakened its overall influence.

What Is a War Crime?

The British selected Sir Cecil Hurst as its UNWCC representative. Hurst was legal adviser to the Foreign Office and sat on the Permanent Court of International Justice. The British asked both Washington and Moscow to select their representatives and proposed the American representative should chair the commission.

State Department legal adviser Green Hackwood thought the candidate should not be selected based only on knowledge of criminal law, but also on understanding of geopolitics. Secretary of State Cordell Hull wanted U.S. Attorney General Francis Biddle to fill the spot, but Biddle declined. After four months of wrangling inside the State Department, Roosevelt named his friend Herbert Pell to fill the position. Pell served in the 66th Congress as a representative from New York and as America's envoy to Portugal and Hungary. Hull accepted the nomination, despite Pell's lack of legal background. Others in the State Department immediately set out to sabotage Pell and his mission.

Despite his earlier diplomatic service, Pell was unknown in England. Ham Armstrong, a State Department official, forwarded his impressions of Pell to J. Forester of the British embassy in Washington. Armstrong charged that Pell was a disappointing political appointment who would contribute little to the commission. Forester then met Pell and decided that he was intelligent, but seemed set in his ways. The British embassy official believed Pell's knowledge of war crimes was slight, although he had already expressed certain fixed views on policy. He decided that Pell believed that war criminals should be brought before an international tribunal that should not be bound by Anglo-Saxon rules of evidence. Further, Forester stated that Pell believed there should be no appeal of sentences and death sentences should be carried out immediately after the verdict.

Following his appointment, Pell's relations with the State Department grew tenser. The State Department actively sought steps to constrain whatever policies Pell wanted to take. When Pell left for London, he decided the State Department did not regard war crimes as a legitimate concern. Pell found it surprising that not a single official in the State Department was responsible for dealing with war crimes issues.

On Oct. 20, 1943, representatives from 17 nations met in London to inaugurate the UNWCC. The Soviets were absent. The Dutch representative disagreed with the British view, which limited the commission to investigating and recording evidence of war crimes. The Dutch proposed the commission be actively involved in preparing the trials. The Chinese representative raised another troublesome point for the British. They wanted to include all war crimes dating back to the Japanese invasion of Manchuria in 1931. The British feared granting this request would open the door for the Czechs to demand investigations back to the Munich agreement, in which the British role was less than exemplary. Beyond a vote to set up the commission and the headquarters' location, nothing substantial was accomplished.

The Soviets' refusal to engage in the opening meeting did not deter Stalin from joining the Allies in a joint statement condemning German atrocities. On Nov. 1, the Big Three signed the Moscow Declaration on prosecuting war criminals. The document ended with the following words:

> Let those who have hitherto not imbrued their hands with innocent blood beware lest they join the ranks of the guilty, for most assuredly the Allied Powers will pursue them to the uttermost ends of the earth and will deliver them to their accusers in order that justice may be done. The above declaration is without prejudice to the case of major criminals, whose offences have no particular geographical localization and who will be punished by the joint decision of the Governments of the Allies.[40]

This was the only substantial agreement among the Allies about punishment of war criminals. Although its principles served as a guide for the Allies, it did nothing to bridge the differences to bring the Soviets into UNWCC. The Soviets and British remained at odds over including the Dominions vs. the various Soviet Republics. There were other obstacles to Soviet participation, especially the failure of the Allies to open a second front in 1942.

In mid-July 1943, the Soviet Union put 11 of its citizens on trial for high treason for aiding the German forces around the town of Krasnodar and for their role in helping annihilate 7,000 people. Eight Soviets were sentenced to hang; the remaining defendants were deported or sentenced to 20 years of hard labor. Moscow obviously wished to prove its commitment to punishing war criminals and to a joint policy. The Soviets held many German POWs, including many believed to be guilty of war crimes.

Several weeks after the hangings, Soviet scholar Professor A. Farrin published an English version of *War and the Working Class*. This publication hinted at being the official viewpoint of the Soviet Union. The article divided war criminals into four classes. The first class included Hitler and his cabinet ministers. The second class included party leaders and the German Army Command. Financial and industrial leaders made up the third class. The fourth group was defined as those who benefited from the Nazi plundering, such as those receiving stolen goods or those who exploited slave labor.

At Teheran, Stalin tried to translate Farrin's principles into numbers. Only two weeks after the Teheran conference, the Soviets put on trial three Germans and a Russian collaborator in Kharkov. The Soviets accused the defendants of using gas vans in which the exhaust was pumped into the compartment holding prisoners, shooting POWs and executing thousands of Soviet citizens. Once again, the trial also brought charges against the heads of the Nazi government. On Dec. 19, Russia hanged the four defendants. American reporters who followed the trial were convinced of the guilt of the defendants and of the genuineness of the charges. They also thought the Soviets had been punctilious in following legal proprieties.

The Khakov trial opened an old wound between the Soviets and London. The Soviets had always been in favor of immediate trials. The desire by Britain and the U.S. to wait until the end of the war to hold trials was unjustified by fears such trials could provoke retaliations by the Nazis against British and American POWs.

Within days of the trial, the Nazis sought to drive a wedge between the Big Three by threatening to put POWs on trial for serious breaches of international law. In January 1944, information reached Washington of protests by high military officers in Germany against any trials of American or British POWs in reprisal for the Russian trials. At the end of March, Germany published a statement saying the preparations for trials of POWs for war crimes were well advanced. Britain and the United States asked the Soviets to stop holding any more trials until after the war's end. Russia complied.

Just before the Teheran Conference, Churchill proposed a radical plan of summary executions of high-ranking Nazis accused of war crimes that were not limited to a particular geographic location. Churchill's plan allowed the nearest officer of major general rank to convene a court of inquiry, not for deciding guilt, but solely to prove identity. Once identified, the officer would order his execution within six hours.

Churchill approved a shortlist of war criminals who would be subject to his proposal. The Foreign Office opposed his plan, as did the Soviets.

The Roosevelt administration was divided on the terms of postwar Germany and war crimes. Morgenthau urged a hard peace and broad war crime investigations. Secretary of War Stimson led a faction sympathetic to Germany. The military had prepared the booklet, *Handbook of Military Government*, which reflected the views of the top military officials favoring an immediate restoration of Germany. Many of the military officers thought we were fighting the wrong enemy and should be at war with the Soviets. Under pressure from Morgenthau, Roosevelt ordered Stimson to have the booklet rewritten. Roosevelt's comments follow:

> It gives me the impression that Germany is to be restored just as much as the Netherlands or Belgium and the people of Germany brought back as quickly as possible to their pre-war state. I do not want to starve them to death but as an example, if they should be fed three times a day with soup from army soup kitchens. That will keep them perfectly healthy and they will remember that experience all their lives. The fact that they are a defeated nation, collectively and individually, must be so impressed on them that they will hesitate to start a new war.[41]

Roosevelt further criticized the document during the Aug 28 cabinet meeting, in which he named Morgenthau, Hull, Stimson and Hopkins to a committee to decide the treatment of Germany after the war. Stimson harshly opposed the hard treatment Roosevelt wanted for Germany. He passed on

Roosevelt's request to rewrite the handbook to his aide, John McCloy, who, in turn, passed it on to Murray Bernays.[42] Bernays opposed any action on war crimes fearing reprisals against American POWs. Nevertheless, in November 1944, Bernays' ideas on prosecution of war criminals were presented to FDR in a memo from Secretary of War Henry Stimson and Secretary of State Cordell Hull, *The Trial and Punishment of European War Criminals.* It was Bernays' work that provided the framework and legal theory behind the Nuremberg Trials. Although Jewish, Bernays' own doubt over the reports and inability to grasp the reality of the Holocaust played a role in his views.

On Sept. 5 Morgenthau presented Roosevelt with a comprehensive memorandum, *Program to Prevent Germany from Starting a World War III.* Known as the Morgenthau Plan, it called for complete dismantling of Germany's industrial base and severe punishment for war crimes. Since the State Department already had documents pointing out the Nazis' plans to go underground and start a new war, Roosevelt had reasons to reject an easy peace with Germany.

Stimson vigorously opposed the Morgenthau Plan and soon was joined by George Marshall and Gen. Myron Cramer. When Roosevelt left for the Quebec conference, his administration had no set policy on the course of action for postwar Germany. Roosevelt left for Quebec without any senior aides. In Quebec, it soon became obvious to Roosevelt that Churchill's main focus was on postwar aid to Britain. Consequently, Roosevelt placed a call to his Treasury Secretary and Morgenthau rushed to the conference. The Quebec conference ended with agreement on the Morgenthau Plan for postwar Germany.

Before the end of September, the press leaked the contents of the Morgenthau Plan, which came under heavy fire. With only six weeks to the election, Dewey saw his chances for victory over Roosevelt improved. Dewey charged that with such a heavy-handed plan, Roosevelt was prolonging the war and America was paying for it in blood.

Roosevelt suspected people in the State Department of the leaks to the press. The timing of the leak suggests political motivation. However, Nazi documents captured after the war suggest that such leaks may have been an integral part of Germany's planning. A March 15, 1944 directive issued by the Chief of Intelligence Division of the German High Command, Adm. Canaris, casts a suspicious eye toward Nazi intrigue:

There is great fear in the USA of Bolshevism. The opposition against Roosevelt's alliance with Stalin grows constantly. Our chances for success are good if we succeed to stir up influential circles against Roosevelt's policy. This can be done through clever pieces of information, or by references to unsuspicious neutral ecclesiastical contact men.

We have at our command in the United States efficient contacts, which have been carefully kept up even during the war. The campaign of hatred stirred up by Roosevelt and the Jews against everything German has temporarily silenced the pro-German bloc in the USA. However, there is every hope that this situation will be completely changed within a few months. If the Republicans succeed in defeating Roosevelt in the coming election, it will greatly influence American conduct of the war towards us.

The KO-leaders abroad and their staffs have innumerable opportunities of constantly referring to Roosevelt's hate policy. They must use in this campaign all the existing contacts and they should try to open new channels. We must point to the danger Germany may be forced to cooperate with Russia. The greatest caution has to be observed in all talks and negotiations by those who, as "anti-Nazis" maintain contact with the enemy. When fulfilling missions, they have to comply strictly with instructions.[43]

The quote now casts all such leaks and reports in the press in the later stages of the war as Nazi intrigue or propaganda. Such leaks may have been an integral part of the Nazis' plan, as expressed in the captured document. As shown in the previous chapters, the Nazis had willing accomplices in Congress, the military, press and industry. Also noteworthy is the passage that if the Republican Party won the election, it would alter the American conduct of the war.

In the 1940 election, Herbert Hoover collaborated with top Nazis in Berlin to try to unseat FDR. Did the Republicans again collaborate with the Nazis in 1944 and offer them an easy peace for their support in the 1944 elections? The question for now must remain unanswered. In a vault, probably marked top secret, is a document that can answer the question. However, there is no question that around 1944, the media in the United States started to print many editorials and articles supporting an easy peace with Germany. Many of those, no doubt, were the result of the Nazi directive above. Thus the heated debate for an easy peace with Germany and the deliberate sabotaging of the 4Ds program must be viewed as part of the Nazi intrigue, which directly implies that those Americans involved were traitors to their country.

In mid-December 1943, Czechoslovakia proposed that UNWCC was fully competent to handle all aspects of the war crimes tribunal. Further, the Czechs believed the tribunal should not be limited to mere examination of dossiers and compilation a list of war criminals. The resolution succeeded.

Until the end of the war, there was no accepted definition of war crimes. Without it, British Treasury Solicitor Tom Barnes told Hurst that he was unable to suggest any cases of war crimes or names of war criminals. Barnes headed the British National Office for War Crimes.

By mid-May, the committee suggested four categories of war crimes: crimes committed for preparing for war; crimes committed in Allied countries against armed forces or civilians; crimes committed against persons without regard to nationality, race, religion or political beliefs; crimes perpetrated to prevent restoration of peace.

The committee failed to supply a definition of war crimes, or to draw up an exhaustive list of them. It also could not agree before the end of the war whether a war of aggression amounted to a war crime. It never voted on this question. After the London conference, June 26–Aug 8, 1945, at the insistence of the United States, UNWCC included waging an aggressive war as a war crime.

In its first five months of operation, UNWCC listed only 70 cases of war crimes. Half of these were so incomplete, the commission could not make a determination; others were trivial. Not a single case at that time was lodged against any prominent Nazi leader. The small number of cases was due to the difficulty of getting precise information from occupied territories while the POWs and labor camps remained in Nazi hands.

At the beginning of June 1944, committee chairman Hurst met unofficially with Eisenhower's staff. Subsequently, Hurst recommended establishment of a war crimes agency attached to SHAEF, the Supreme Headquarters Allied Expeditionary Force. The Foreign Office sabotaged such a proposal and SHAEF formally rejected it.

In November 1944, the Czech government decided to list Hitler as a war criminal. The British representative opposed such a listing until the German constitution could be examined. In December 1944, the commission presented a list of 712 names of German and Italian war criminals, including the names of top Nazis such as Hitler, Himmler and 17 generals. In all, 49 top Nazis were listed.

Perhaps the Jewish issue was the most contentious to come before UNWCC. In August 1942, the Foreign Office and State Department received a report from Dr. Gerhart Riegera, a representative of the World Jewish Congress in Geneva. According to Riegera, plans were under consideration in Berlin to have all Jews in Europe deported and concentrated in the East, where with one blow they would be exterminated. Both the Foreign Office and the State Department disbelieved the report and failed to pass it on. Reports of further atrocities against the Jews continued to pile up. The British Foreign Office believed the massacres of the Jews were not war crimes. The British sought to limit war crimes to those committed against the citizens of Allied nations, and then only after the date of the Polish invasion.

Almost immediately after beginning work in UNWCC, Pell raised the question of crimes perpetrated by the Nazis against citizens of the Reich. His assistant from the State Department, Laurence Preuss, opposed the proposal. Trying to undermine him, Preuss reported Pell's actions in an unofficial and confidential letter to the State Department. In fact, it was Pell's actions that served as a catalyst for the commission to include this issue. Preuss also told the Foreign Office that Pell was making dangerous mistakes. In deference to the British Foreign Office and the U.S. State Department, the commission never included crimes against citizens of Germany before 1939. The issue led shortly to Pell's removal.

Another problem that plagued the commission was the type of court to use to prosecute war criminals. Pell told the State Department that unanimous agreement had been reached on the treatment of war crimes conducted in a single country. In crimes involving more than one country, Pell proposed that international authority should handle such cases. Pell also urged FDR to set up some machinery of justice that could act firmly and quickly.

Pell's proposal and initiative irritated Hull, who believed the commission should restrict itself to collecting evidence. Roosevelt preferred a military court and conveyed that opinion to Pell. In February 1944, a subcommittee chaired by Pell began examining the question of an international court. On Sept. 22, Pell's subcommittee formally issued the final draft on the Convention for Establishment of a United Nations Joint Court. The full UNWCC approved the draft on Sept. 26, 1944.

In January 1945, Hurst submitted his resignation after a dispute with the Foreign Office. The Foreign Office was well aware of the tireless and relentless efforts of Pell to bring the Nazis to justice. They feared Pell would be elected chairman as a replacement for Hurst. The State Department also was upset with Pell's criticism of inaction.

From the beginning, Pell's appointment had been a thorn in the side of Green Hackworth, the State Department's legal adviser. In December 1944, Hackworth told Pell the departments of State, War and Navy were considering an international court. Hackworth emphatically refused Pell's request to attend meetings at which these questions were debated.

Hackworth already knew Pell would be removed because of Congress' decision to defund Pell's $30,000 budget. The State Department, now headed by Stettinius following Hull's resignation, proposed to FDR that America's seat on UNWCC be filled with an Army officer. On Jan. 9, 1945, Hackworth and Stettinius disgracefully sacked Pell. On Jan. 29, 1945, Undersecretary Joseph Grew came under attack by the press over Pell's dismissal. One reporter questioned the State Department's record in the Senate hearings on appropriations for Pell's office. The Senate's records indicated that Hackworth's assistant, Katherine Fate, appeared before the Senate committee for funding Pell's position for less than three minutes. Once again, the invisible hands of the pro-fascists in Congress and the State Department removed a dedicated anti-Nazi from office.

The removal of both Hurst and Pell in January 1945 from the UNWCC brought strong press commentary, but the committee continued operations until March 31, 1948. In four and a half years, the commission presented 80 lists containing the names of 36,529 suspected war criminals, of which 34,270 were German. UNWCC eagerness to advance preparations for dealing with war crimes was opposed vigorously by both the British Foreign Office and the U.S. State Department. Both regarded UNWCC as a political necessity to exploit in neutralizing demands for reprisal by governments in exile. While the UNWCC was created with the noblest objectives, in reality it served no real purpose other than to talk to death the crimes of the Holocaust. It faced obstructionists from both the United States and Britain.

The Corporate Roots of the OSS

In April 1945 at London's request, FDR sent an American delegation to England to work out the differences in a common war criminals policy. Judge Samuel Rosenman headed the U.S. delegation; Viscount Simon, the British side. Rosenman's proposals included crimes committed before 1939 and against Germans citizens. To please the Americans, Simon in his proposal included a reference to crimes against Jews. Sadly, no resolution was reached due to Roosevelt's death.

Shortly after, President Truman adopted the recommendations contained in the memorandum on trial and punishment of Nazi war criminals that was first presented to Roosevelt in January 1945. Truman used the San Francisco conference to discuss and promote this list with the Allies. No decisions were reached, since the Soviets and French were not authorized to negotiate the American proposal. On June 14, 1945, the British issued a royal warrant setting the stage for arrests of war criminals by British forces. This warrant was limited to crimes occurring after September 1939. It also excluded crimes against the Jews.

It was not until after intense negotiations among the Allies from June 26 to Aug. 8 that a joint accord was reached. Under Article 6, Paragraph C, the charter established crimes against humanity, which included murder, extermination, enslavement, deportation and other inhuman acts committed against any civilian population before or during the war. Before this time, the only Holocaust crimes recognized were merely violence directed at Jews.

On Dec. 20, 1945, to set up a common basis for conducting trials in the four zones, the Allied Control Council for Germany published Law No. 10, "Punishment of Persons Guilty of War Crimes, Crimes against Peace and Humanity." The law empowered the Allied commanders of the four occupied zones to conduct criminal trials of individuals on charges of war crimes, crimes against humanity or membership in an organization that planned such crimes. In case of crimes committed by Germans against Germans or stateless persons, the military commanders were authorized to allow a trial by a German court.

Between December 1946–April 1949, there were 12 trials involving 185 defendants in the American zone. These trials became known as the Subsequent Nuremberg Proceedings. In none of these trials was the mass murder of Jews considered a separate criminal offense.[44]

In the end, the Americans tried 1,857 defendants. The military courts convicted 1,416 of 1,672 tried. The court sentenced 450 to death, 219 to life in prison, and the remaining 889 to various prison terms of five years or less. The British tried 1,085, sentencing 240 to death, acquitting 348, sentencing 24 to life, the remaining 473 to prison sentences. The French tried 2,107, acquitting 404, sentencing 104 to death, 44 to life imprisonment, the remaining 1,475 to prison sentences. The Soviets charged 14,240 with crimes, sentencing 138 to death, acquitting 142 and sentencing the balance to prison.[45]

However, these statistics fail to tell the complete story. The United States commuted many of the death sentences, and many sent to prison for long terms were free by 1951. The relatively small number of arrests made by the U.S. and Britain compared to the Soviets confirms a lack of desire to chase war criminals. This is especially troublesome because many of the Nazis went to extraordinary lengths to surrender in the West rather than to the Soviets. Further, every trial increased the risk of testimony incriminating leading industrialists and politicians.

Another factor in the failure of the 4Ds program was the OSS. In 1941, Roosevelt created the Office of Coordinator of Information (COI) with Bill Donovan at the helm. COI evolved into the OSS, the forerunner of the CIA. In assembling his team, Donovan recruited many officers from Wall Street and the top echelons of major corporations. OSS officers in Spain and Switzerland came from Standard Oil.[46] Following the Allied invasion of North Africa invasion, Standard Oil was no longer able to supply Nazi Germany through that route, so they routed it through the neutral countries of Spain and Switzerland.

It was not until Jan. 28, 1944 that the British cut off oil shipments to Spain, and then they allowed them to resume on May 2, 1944 after vigorous protests by Franco.[47]

At the beginning of November 1942, Henri Henggler and David Duvoisin, the Standard Oil bosses in Berne, asked Leland Hansen and Daniel Reagan for permission to continue shipping Nazi oil from Rumania through Switzerland. Hansen and Reagan were, respectively, the minister and the commercial attaché of the United States embassy. The request was made under the guise that the oil was used to heat the Hungarian and German embassies. The American embassy depended on German coal,[48] so a refusal would have meant the U.S. embassy went unheated.

Here is the crux of the sabotage of the 4Ds program. Many personnel in the OSS and the Office of Military Government (OMG) previously were connected with corporations that traded with the Nazis or had signed cartel agreements with German companies. The problem was systemic with U.S. intelligence personnel during the war and with U.S. occupation forces in postwar Germany.

That's not to imply that all corporate and Wall Street executives in the OSS and the occupation forces were disloyal to their country and used their positions to the advantage of their corporations. Whether former Standard executives stationed in Spain and Switzerland with the OSS played any role in shipping oil to Nazi Germany is unknown and may never be known. However, often there is no doubt many put their loyalty to their firm ahead of their country. The sabotage of the 4Ds program was widespread and sometimes can be traced back to Congress, the Department of State or the top military echelon.

Bill Donovan himself, head of the OSS and former Wall Street lawyer, had ties to IG Farben. The files of Ted Clark, vice president of Drug Inc., were withdrawn from the public shortly after Donovan's appointment to head the COI. Donovan had been associated with Drug Inc., and had expressed the view that cartel agreements did not restrict the market.

A striking development was the great number of OSS agents who later rose to positions in the political system; see the list in Appendix 12. This list should not be considered complete; it was compiled from a single source.[49] However, it reveals that an extraordinary number of ex-OSS agents received ambassadorial or other appointments in the State Department. Through the 1950s and '60s, these ex-OSS agents had excessive influence on foreign policy, and contributed to the image that our embassies were merely CIA havens.

The OSS had a role in foreign policy from its earliest beginnings. Sometimes that role was thrust on OSS officers. The State Department jealously guarded its domain while abdicating responsibility. One example was in Cairo, where the U.S. ambassador to the Greek and Yugoslav in-exile governments refused to represent the U.S. view at an Anglo-American planning committee. Instead, Turner McBaine, a California attorney and OSS officer, presented it.

After the war, McBaine became a senior partner in a San Francisco law firm and counsel to Standard Oil of California. He also served on the Asia Foundation. In 1967, it was revealed that the foundation received CIA funding and acted as a front for the agency.

In a more significant matter, OSS officers wrote the foreign policy on Thailand during the war. At that time, Thailand's Minister of Defense was Pibul Songgram, an admirer of Mussolini and Hitler. Pibul soon became Premier and bought large quantities of arms from Italy and Japan. He created a political and social model based on fascism, and when the Japanese invaded Thailand, Pibul ordered the military to offer no resistance and agreed to form a military defensive agreement. The British regarded Thailand as a fascist state and were technically at war with it. The State Department remained noncommittal on Thailand, not wishing to ruffle English feathers. Pibul's main opposition in the Thai cabinet was Phanomyoung Pridi, an admirer of the New Deal. After the war, OSS backing of Pridi and his underground army led to the creation of the free and independent state of Thailand, despite British objections and desires to control their former colony.

Donovan chose his agents from both the left and the right of the political spectrum. He hired James Murphy, former IWW organizer, and members of the Lincoln Brigade who had fought in Spain, knowing they were communists. He assigned them to Italy and France where they could work effectively with Italy's communists and the large communist faction in the French resistance. The group provided some of the best intelligence in the Mediterranean Theater.

Supposedly, Donovan assigned left-wing intellectuals and corporate executives to positions in which he could make the most of their talents. However, the corporate executives held relatively safe administrative positions, compared to the behind-the-line operations of the leftist intellectuals. Their positions also provided them with a catbird's seat to keep the lid on any embarrassing links between corporate America and the Nazis.

Other OSS members refused to work with the communist faction in France or, at best, could only offer halfhearted support.[50] Donovan assigned most of the left-wing intellectuals to operational or research roles, and most of the corporate attorneys and executives to administrative roles. Nevertheless, by hiring some agents from the Left, Donovan slated the OSS for dissolution after the war. In addition, by hiring members of the Lincoln Brigade, Donovan provided fuel for the McCarthy era.

While academia and corporations provided most of the OSS recruits, America's wealthiest families provided others. Andrew Mellon's son, Paul, served as administrative officer of the Special Operations Branch in London. William Mellon, son of the president of Gulf Oil, served in the SI Branch in Madrid – again the connection of oil and Spain. Another OSS agent from the Mellon family was David Bruce, whose wife Alisa was the sister of Paul Mellon and a cousin of the wife of Allan Scaife, who also served in the OSS.

Morgan's two sons were both OSS officers stationed in London. The duPont family also had two members serving. Alfred was one of the top OSS officials in Washington at the French desk. The Rockefeller family had members serving not in the OSS, but in military intelligence. Nelson Rockefeller was in charge of intelligence for South America. The plutocratic recruits got administrative and policy jobs; Junius Morgan was OSS Treasurer. Thus some of the families most responsible for trading with the Nazis held supervisory roles in the OSS that allowed them to quash any investigation before it started.

While some scions of the richest families undoubtedly contributed to winning the war, there is no question that many upper-class recruits were responsible for sabotaging the 4-Ds program. Despite overwhelming evidence of corporate America willingly trading with the Nazis during the war, not a single charge was ever brought. Nor were any top Nazi industrialists ever convicted of war crimes at Nuremberg. OSS members recruited from Wall Street and corporate boardrooms had intimate knowledge of the cartel agreements and were in ideal positions to squash any investigations that might expose corporate America's trading with the Nazis. The elite were protected.

Donovan's nonpartisan friendship with Roosevelt protected the OSS, he chose his recruits without regard to their political views. Still, he was not adverse to party politics. He correctly foresaw that Thomas Dewey would be the Republican candidate to face Roosevelt in the 1944 election, and suddenly recruited many former Dewey assistants. Dewey was a an anti-communist conservative. In fact, Donovan recruited so many Republicans that in some circles, the OSS was snidely referred to as that Republican Club.

Several of Donovan's recruits from the hard right were unable to fit in. Hilaire du Berrier was a hard-right journalist interned by the Japanese and rescued by the OSS. Donovan recruited du Berrier as an expert on Indo-Chinese affairs. Within a few months, du Berrier left the OSS complaining the leftists had squeezed the Right Wing out of the organization. Du Berrier later became a writer for the John Birch Society.

Another hard-right recruit who dropped out of the OSS was Ralph de Tokdano. He was selected to parachute behind enemy lines in Italy. While training for the mission, he labeled his representative, Vito Marcantonio, a communist. To be fair, Marcantonio started politics as a Republican with liberal views and was elected to Congress in 1935 from East Harlem's 20th District. In 1938, he defended his seat as an American Labor Party candidate. Marcantonio viewed the Communist Party as an American party. He also was a strong supporter of civil rights and a vigorous opponent of Joseph McCarthy. In 1944, his district was gerrymandered to include Yorkville, an area south of East Harlem whose major ethic groups expressed hostility toward left politics. During the 1930s, it had been a hotbed of support for the Nazis. The Wilson-Pakula Act of 1947 prevented him from entering the major party primaries, forcing him to run on the American Labor Party ticket that was almost universally identified as communist controlled. Marcantonio was defeated in 1950, another victim of McCarthyism. Ralph de Tokdano later became a contributing editor of William F. Buckley Jr.'s *National Review*.[51]

Donovan's warriors often experienced needless delays. The State Department objected to issuing OSS officers' passports. Ruth Shipley ran the State Department's passport division and insisted on clearly identifying officers as OSS.[52] The British Psychological Assessment Board rejected a high proportion of OSS officers assigned to write anti-Nazi propaganda. Many of those rejected were well-known screenwriters and New York advertising men. The sole reason for their rejection was that they were Jews.[53]

While Donovan allowed his agents free reign to conduct their operations, the results often ended in embarrassing moments for the OSS. In one case, OSS officers in Portugal broke into the Japanese embassy and stole a copy of the enemy's codebook, unaware that a naval intelligence team had already broken the code. The Japanese quickly changed their code after discovering the book was missing, leaving Washington and the Joint Chiefs without a source of information for several months until the new code was broken. In another high-level flap, OSS officers armed Tito's guerrillas, without first getting permission from the British Theater commander. They also sent communist agents into Spain without first notifying the American embassy in Madrid. Thus, the agents were left with no contact and had to fare for themselves.[54]

After the U.S. Army established a beachhead at Salerno, south of Naples, a group of OSS officers hatched a wild plot. Headed by a young Republican, John Shaheen, they planned to reach the Italian Naval Command and convince the admirals to surrender their fleet to the Allies. Shaheen did not realize the main body of the Italian fleet had already set sail for Malta to surrender to the British. Shaheen later became president of several international oil companies and is a large donor to the Republican Party.[55] He was embroiled in the October Surprise conspiracy in which the Reagan-Bush team conspired with Iran to hold the American captives until after the election. Shaheen also was involved in the Iran-Contra conspiracy.[56] He served with Bill Casey in the OSS and they remained close associates throughout their lives. Like many other ex-OSS agents, it is probable that Shaheen never left the fold and remained an agent throughout his lifetime.

In other cases, the embarrassment was more humorous, as in the case of an elderly former executive of General Electric briefing an OSS agent on his mission. The former executive, now a colonel in the OSS, mistakenly pronounced the name of the drop zone and spent 10 minutes searching the map for the location before an aide pointed out that it was several hundred miles north. In another case, the OSS parachuted a team into Brittany, a supposed safe zone. The zone turned out to be in the center of the German Second Parachute Division and the OSS team spent a few frantic days avoiding the Germans.[57]

Often the OSS engaged in ridiculous operations. One operation involved a Hungarian astrologer the OSS sent to the United States to shake American public confidence of the invincibility of Hitler. After reading the Fuehrer's stars, the astrologer predicted immediate doom for Hitler. The astrologer's report was carried from coast to coast in the media.

Another OSS plan stands out above all others as ridiculous. A London-based OSS group decided Nazi Germany would implode if only its leader could be demoralized. After conducting a long psychological profile of Hitler, the group decided he could be unhinged by exposure to vast quantities of pornography. The OSS group then assembled the finest collection of pornography. The material was to be dropped by plane around the Fuehrer-bunker. Hitler was to step outside and pick one up and immediately be thrown into a state of madness. But the air force liaison stormed out of the first meeting with the OSS, cursing and swearing he would not risk a single life for such an insane plan.[58]

In another incident, OSS agent Jane Foster got a large supply of condoms from a doctor in Ceylon (Sri Lanka), then stuffed them with messages urging the residents of Indonesia to resist the Japanese invaders. Submarines released hundreds of these air-filled condoms containing messages off the Indonesian coast.

One of the first hints of sabotage of justice for the Nazis and their supporters came shortly after the North Africa invasion. Charles Bedeaux was a Frenchman who became a naturalized American citizen. Known as the Speed King and hostile to unions, he amassed a small fortune in America by devising an anti-union efficiency system. He returned to France before the war and cultivated close relationships between many leading Nazis. After France fell, Bedeaux became the Vichy representative of several French industrialists in their dealings with the Nazis.

As part of his collaboration with the Nazis, Bedeaux traveled to North Africa with a plan to lay a pipeline across the Sahara from West Africa to bring cheap vegetable oil from Dakar to Hitler's Europe. Unfortunately for the enterprising Bedeaux, he became trapped in North Africa following the Allied landings in Algiers. As an American citizen, he could have been arrested for treason, but Allied headquarters took no action against the Nazi collaborator. OSS officer Edmond Taylor finally had the French arrest Bedeaux. Even after his arrest, the American authorities refused to charge him with treason.

OSS agent Arthur Roseborough, a former Sullivan & Cromwell attorney working with the Gaullists, prepared a case against Bedeaux. Allied headquarters refused to act on it. The OSS then took the case to Washington. Bedeaux was finally indicted for treason, but not before an odd attempt by the FBI to destroy the evidence. He was taken into custody and put aboard a plane to the United States. In Miami, Bedeaux supposedly committed suicide by taking poison. Many OSS agents in North Africa suspected that a group of influential Americans did not want Bedeaux to stand trial.[59] How he was able to get poison after being held prisoner for months, first by the French, then by the Americans, remains a mystery.

OSS in Europe

In late 1942, Washington received an improbable offer from the Vatican. A high Papal Secretariat offered to provide firsthand information on strategic bombing targets in Japan. The roundabout transfer of documents took only days and became known as the Vessel Project, headed in Rome by Cardinal Monsignor Giovanni Battista Montini, who later became Pope Paul VI.

Earl Brennan, a State Department veteran and a Republican New Hampshire legislator, headed the project for the OSS. Brennan had befriended the leaders of the powerful Italian Masonic Order when he was assigned to the American embassy in Italy during the first year of Mussolini's rule. Brennan also befriended some of the exiled leaders of the Italian Mafia in Canada. David Bruce, the OSS chief in London and Paul Mellon's brother-in-law, thought Brennan's connections would be useful and recruited him.

Following the Torch landings in North Africa, Brennan decided to send some of his agents into Algiers to begin planning for infiltrating Italy. The State Department denied one of his agents a passport because of his past subversive activities. Brennan then checked with Martin Dies, the chair of the House Un-American Activities Committee, about why the passport was rejected. The agent was labeled as a subversive because he had provided legal counsel for a union strike that the management labeled as communist-inspired. Once Dies removed the offending remark, Brennan's agent left for North Africa in early 1943.

Following their departure for North Africa, Brennan's remaining staff became occupied with the Vessel Project. However, the Office of Naval Intelligence preempted OSS responsibilities for Italian espionage. The Navy reached a mysterious deal with the American Mafia. In return for paroling Lucky Luciano, the Mafia agreed to use its criminal syndicate in Sicily to aid the Allies. Assistant New York District Attorney Murray Gurfein arranged the deal. Gurfein would later become an OSS colonel in Europe. Maj. George White, director of counterespionage training and a veteran official of the federal Narcotics Bureau, insisted on keeping Brennan partially informed of developments.[60]

Despite much interest in the Vessel Project, the source was never checked thoroughly and proved later to be false, causing much OSS embarrassment.

On March 13, 1945, the House Military Affairs Committee announced it was examining the loyalty of 14 soldiers labeled as communists. Among them was Lt. Irving Goff, who had left-wing sympathies and was ordered to make contact with the communist cells after the fall of Naples in late 1943. The Goff mission was to set up contacts with the communist cells in northern Italy and to establish OSS safe houses. By all standards, Goff's mission was an outstanding success. But some concerns arose in 1945 in military circles that Goff's agents were using the clandestine network to pass communist propaganda, although no evidence surfaced. Charges and countercharges flew back and forth between the military and OSS. In the end, Donovan was forced to have Goff and his men sent back to the United States in June, although no evidence ever existed that they allowed communist propaganda to flow on the network they had set up.[61]

Of all the behind-the-lines missions in northern Italy, the communist cells were the most active and fierce. It was a communist cell that captured Mussolini. Networks in northern Italy aligned under other political lines were less effective and often inactive. The communist cells' participation was crucial for the success of the final offensive launched in northern Italy on April 1, 1945. This offensive first involved a massive bombardment followed by an assault by the Fifth Army. A massive uprising by partisan forces was crucial to the success of this plan.

Goff's group first contacted and armed many of those forces. Allied forces trained more than 180,000 partisans to attack the rear of the German forces once the offensive started. Its success allowed Allied forces to drive into Austria ahead of Soviet forces.

The communist witch hunt in Congress risked the success of the invasion, the lives of thousands and a prolonged war in northern Italy. Donovan did the honorable thing in the Goff affair by standing by his men and ensuring they received the metals they deserved.

In France, Gen. de Gaulle's Bureau Central de Renseignements et d'Action (BCRA) accused the OSS of scheming to weaken and divide the underground forces all for the benefit of Gen. Henri Giraud, a rival Free French leader. BCRA traced the plot to Switzerland and Allen Dulles. Early in 1943, Dulles contacted Guillain de Benouville, a conservative Catholic once active in right-wing circles. De Benouville declared himself a Gaullist; BCRA remained suspicious due to his previous membership in a Giraud organization. While there were factions in both the United States and England that preferred Giraud, de Gaulle had already emerged as the leader of the French underground.

Before launching Operation Overlord, agents had to be placed inside France. In May 1943, Churchill and Roosevelt committed to the 1944 invasion plan. However, one thorn remained in the side of the OSS; the British MI6 intelligence unit regarded the OSS as an upstart junior partner. It was not until May 29, 1943 at the urging of David Bruce and SI chief William Maddox that MI6 granted OSS an equal partnership.

In October 1944, Allied forces overtook the Jedburgh and SUSSEX groups implanted in France by the OSS and MI6. With forces stalled at the Siegfried line, Allied headquarters was demanding intelligence reports from inside Germany. Unfortunately, the OSS had only four men inside Germany during the Battle of the Bulge. OSS then had to rely on the work of Arthur Goldberg and his labor branch. As an emergency measure, OSS gave William Casey, a former Wall Street attorney, overall control of all German projects. By the spring of 1945, OSS managed to place 150 men inside Germany at such rail centers as Leipzig.[62]

While Dulles' primary mission in Berne was German espionage, he worked closely with forces in Italy. The Allied army would have been devoid of any German intelligence had it not been for the SI branch in Italy run by Alfred Ulmer, a former Florida newspaper correspondent and advertising executive. In Italy, Ulmer set up a special section to handle German-Austria intelligence.

Dulles traveled to Washington in October 1944 for a top-level conference. There, he met an attractive Swiss-born OSS analyst, Emmy Rado, the wife of a Hungarian psychiatrist. Dulles was somewhat of a lady's man who had several affairs throughout his career, and was attracted to her. Rado proposed using Catholic and Protestant churches as a base for German political reconstruction. She thought the OSS could work effectively through the World Council of Churches to aid anti-Nazi clergy. Dulles thought the idea had merit and invited Rado to join him in Berne.[63] Reliance on the German clergy shortly proved to be disastrous, as well as a major embarrassment. In postwar Germany, the clergy proved to be mostly pro-Nazi. Pastors who opposed Hitler and the Nazis had been sent to the concentration camps.

On Dulles' return to Berne, OSS disbanded Goldberg's labor unit and reassigned personnel to the SI branch. Dulles' staff was replaced during his trip to Washington. Russell D'Oench, scion of the Grace Shipping Line, was now posted in Zurich. William Mellon was transferred from Madrid to Geneva. Russian émigré Valerian Lada-Mocarski now served as liaison officer to the Italian resistance and on the board of directors of the Nazi-affiliated Schroeder Bank with Allen Dulles.[64]

On V-E Day, J. Russell Forgan, the New York financier who replaced David Bruce as OSS commander in Europe, submitted his resignation to Donovan and suggested naming Allen Dulles as his replacement. Donovan refused, declaring Dulles a poor administrator, but Forgan and others continued pressing for him. Instead, Donovan divided the OSS operations into single-country operations and appointed Dulles to head the German office.

Unlike the British, Washington failed to integrate OSS into plans for postwar Germany. Many OSS agents received appointments as high-level advisers to the military government. However, Dulles' detachment faced formidable competition; a score of American intelligence teams representing a dozen military and civilian agencies worked at cross-purposes, searching for the same strategic information. To further hinder the OSS, many agents were being siphoned off to the Pacific.

Some of the remaining personnel lacked integrity. In the fall of 1945, Army investigators exposed an incredible black market in Berlin. The investigation rivaled the M&M Enterprises of *Catch-22* fame. Everything could be found for a price: oil, fine porcelain, cigarettes, etc. This black market, run by an OSS major and captain, involved none of the operational officers, only top-level OSS administrative personnel.

In postwar Germany, OSS was burdened with the denazification program. Military government authorities wanted a list of Nazi officials to arrest or bar from office, and names of respectable Germans to employ in administrative positions during the occupation.

Heading the Counterintelligence Branch tasked with interrogating Gestapo and Abwehr officers was Andrew Berding, who later served as Assistant Secretary of State under Eisenhower. Berding was stationed in London through most of the war. More recently, his name surfaced in an article in the June 27, 2000 edition of the *Guardian,* "Britain could have saved Italian Jews," written by Julian Borer. The *Guardian* article relates that MI6 had detailed knowledge of the Holocaust because it was decoding German radio messages throughout the war. In particular, the *Guardian* looks at the case of 8,000 Jews deported from Rome to the gas chambers. On Oct. 6, MI6 intercepted a message from German headquarters in Italy to Berlin: "Orders have been received from Berlin by Obersturm–bannfuhrer

Kappler to seize and to take to northern Italy the 8,000 Jews living in Rome. They are to be liquidated."[65]

According to the article, MI6 had intercepted a German message about the deportation. Whitehall and Washington should have received it by Oct. 11. The roundup occurred on Oct. 16. The information would have to pass through Andrew Berding before reaching Washington. It is unknown when the message reached Washington or who received it. There was enough time during which the Allies could have warned the Jews in Rome of the Nazis plan. However, there were factions in both Whitehall and Washington that ignored many of the atrocities of the Holocaust, labeling them as exaggerated.

Eli Rosenbaum, Director of the U.S. Justice Department Office of Special Investigations, said that several Nazi officers, including Karl Wolff, could have been prosecuted on the strength of the intercepts alone. Dulles was instrumental in Wolff's surrender of German forces in Italy and in protecting him from prosecution as a war criminal.

A good summation of the problems facing the denazification program was by the OSS officer Sterling Hayden, who remarked that as Allied forces advanced across Germany:

> there came squirming into the light millions of anti-Nazis. It was tough, they said, waving handkerchiefs and wringing their hands with joy, to have lived under Hitler. But, only the night before they had heated water that would quickly yield this democratic douche. The real anti-Nazis were dead or in exile, or in Besden, Auschwitz, Buchenwald. Names we thought at the time that would teach us a lesson we'd never forget.[66]

Pressed with continuous demands from the military government for anti-Nazis, Dulles and Hans Gaevernitz seized the opportunity to promote the political futures of those they worked with. Gaevernitz was a Dulles collaborator in Switzerland involved with the many so-called peace offers. Dulles had only one criterion for promotion: extreme anti-communist views, which included former Nazis.

On June 6, Rado drove Wilhelm Hoegner, Dulles' handpicked anti-communist choice to head Bavaria, from Switzerland to Germany. With the support of Dulles, the military government soon installed Hoegner as Bavaria's minister-president. Hoegner soon proved to be an embarrassment to American officials.

To continue Rado's church project, Dulles granted OSS favors to Stewart Herman, a Lutheran minister of the American Church in Berlin before the war. Herman joined OSS in 1943 as an adviser on German propaganda. After V-E Day, Herman left OSS and joined the staff of World Churches in Geneva. World Churches gave him the task of rebuilding the Protestant church in Germany. Dulles believed in using the church as a bulwark against communism. Rado soon expanded her activities to include a project code-named "Crown Jewels." The Crown Jewels was designed to counter the Soviets' return of the communist Walter Ulbricht to Germany. Rado's objective was to return to Germany as quickly as possible other political leaders opposed to communism.

As Allied forces advanced beyond the hedgerows of Normandy and started racing across France toward the Rhine, Donovan began planning a postwar role for the OSS. Although the agents' first objective was spying on the Axis, he advised them to also begin spying on both Britain and the Soviets. In August 1944, Donovan began planning an operation that evolved into "Casey Jones" and the associated "Ground Hog" operations. One of the biggest problems Allied forces faced was the lack of good maps. The Casey Jones and Ground Hog projects were joint ventures with the British. The ambitious operations proposed to photomap about 2 million square miles of Eastern Europe, including Albania, Yugoslavia, Bulgaria and all of Russian-occupied Germany.

Sixteen squadrons of American and British heavy bombers were modified for the photomapping operation. The project did not get under way until the spring of 1945. While the American planes carried markings, there is evidence that many British planes did not.

Russia noticed the purpose of Casey Jones, presumably from their spies in British and American intelligence. The Russians were very sensitive about violations of their airspace. On April 2, 1945, Gen. Nathan Twining, commander general of the Mediterranean Allied Strategic Air Force, reported six engagements with Russians who allegedly attacked the modified bombers. In one encounter, the Soviets shot down a Mustang; the pilot was believed to be safe. On the same day, the Soviets grounded all Allied aircraft in Russia and refused to let any enter or land within its borders. It lifted the ban only to allow a single DC3 flight to shuttle diplomats and freight between the USAAF base in Poltava and the Ukraine and Teheran.

In all, Casey Jones succeeded in photographing all 2 million square miles of Europe and North Africa west of the line 20 degrees East, approximately the longitude of Warsaw or Budapest. Considering the size and scope of the mission, there could be little doubt the Russians knew what was afloat. The State Department also asked the Soviets for permission on three occasions to photomap Berlin, Vienna and Prague. The operation certainly increased the tensions between the East and West in the waning days of the war.[67]

Near the end of the war, when negotiations were taking place in San Francisco to establish the United Nations, Donovan ordered his agents to infiltrate the talks. Such an action was technically against the OSS charter banning operations inside the United States.

Those recruited for this job relied mainly on hosting parties after hours, judging from the liquor bills submitted by the agents. Edward Buxton, a long-time associate of Donovan's and the OSS, headed the operation. On April 26, 1945 Buxton wrote to Donovan of a frank discussion between Shepherd, Stalin and Molotov about Yugoslavia. A short passage from that letter follows:[68]

> Shepherd related to me that he told them frankly that he is having difficulties in Yugoslavia where the prevailing sentiment is that all the brains are in Moscow and all the power in the Red Army, that furthermore there is a tendency to rely on Soviet only disregarding completely America and Great Britain.

> Molotov told Shepherd that the approach is wrong and that although Russia will try to help as much as she can after the war is over, she, Russia herself will have to seek assistance from the United States to rebuild the devastated cities and ruined economy, that they themselves will seek loans up to 10 billion to assist in her postwar rehabilitation.

> Stalin told Shepherd explicitly not to try to imitate Soviet Russia. Yugoslavia is a small country in comparison to Russia and not to carry on experimentation by establishing a Soviet regime, that they will have to get along with Western democracies and to arrange a democratic regime where the representatives are not appointed but elected … .[69]

Two bits of substantial intelligence lie buried in the passage. First and most significant was Russia's devastated condition. Such an admission should have been key to postwar relations between the United States and the USSR. Unfortunately, the message fell on deaf ears. The fascist right had gained power and was aching for a new war. It should have alerted the United States that Gen. Clay's war warning message two years later was a folly. Instead, the message of Russian weakness became lost in the propaganda coming from right-wing voices. Clay's message was taken as serious threat.

Further, this was not the only source of information about the weakness of the Soviet Union. Eisenhower remarked that a war in Europe was highly unlikely because the Russians were too busy pulling up the track from the railroads to send back to the homeland. Without railroads, Russia lacked any means to move massive amounts of equipment and troops forward. Second, the United States had captured the latest Russian coding equipment and was reading all messages.

The second piece of information explains the geopolitical postwar politics in the Balkans. Yugoslavia did go communist under Tito, but always remained alienated and independent of Russia. The CIA failed to recognize the significance of the power Tito held until after his death, and the country crumbled into various warring factions that present a threat to the peace in the area today.

Donovan should not be viewed as above suspicion. When he thought the Republicans had a good chance in the election, he packed the OSS with Republican recruits. He had his own ties with Wall Street and big money. While still in Buffalo, Donovan represented J.P. Morgan, and during the Nye Senate investigations of the 1930s on war profiteering during WWI, Donovan was the attorney for the duPonts. During the war and its aftermath, Donovan could have overlooked the connections of his former clients with the Nazis, perhaps in the belief of their innocence. However, one thing that sets Donovan apart from others Wall Streeters in the OSS hierarchy like Allen Dulles is that he was not motivated by personal gain. Unlike Dulles and the rest, Donovan died with only modest means. After his estate was settled, his wife received a check for the remaining balance of $38,000.

Dulles was suspicious of the academicians within the branch of Research and Analysis. His use of those on the left had always enraged the FBI, factions in the State Department and some members of Congress. The FBI often demanded the dismissal of members of the Research and Analysis unit. As the end of the war approached, more agents with leftist views were discharged. Only weeks before the end of the war in Europe, the House Un-American Activities Committee found a red herring in Russian-born economist Paul Baran. Once the leftist had been purged from the Research and Analysis unit, the focus shifted to preparation for war crimes trials. The United States assigned Donovan as the U.S. Deputy Prosecutor in the Nuremberg Trials until he resigned in a dispute over policy with the Chief Prosecutor, former Supreme Court Justice Robert Jackson. Ralph Albrecht, a former New York international lawyer and OSS Assistant Director, also was on the prosecutor team.

Purging leftists from the OSS hindered the investigations and prosecution of Nazi war criminals. Yet the OSS was disbanded largely because of the number of leftists it employed. In 1944, Donovan submitted a memo to FDR outlining a permanent American intelligence agency. The top secret memo was leaked to a Washington reporter with the *Chicago Times,* which printed a series of articles written by Walter Trohan critical of creating a permanent intelligence agency. Trohan presented the draft proposal verbatim even though the document was classified as top secret. However, Trohan was close to J. Edgar Hoover, who provided him with Donovan's memo.

No charges or investigation followed; some fascists were too big to be prosecuted. Once again, the *Chicago Times* published top secret documents, an act of subversion. A congressional uproar followed, led by the same pro-fascist faction that sought to keep America out of the war. Roosevelt tabled the matter, only to revive it in April 1945; a week later, he died.

No other agency had so much ridicule, embarrassment and criticism heaped on it during the war than OSS. The fate of OSS was as predetermined as if it had been created under a dark star. The embarrassing incidents, the criticism and congressional investigations served as fuel for its final death. At the center of this controversy was Bill Donovan, an intensely loyal and honest man.

Facing increasing wrath from the Republican Party and an uphill election for the Democrats in 1946, Truman had little use for an agency derisively referred to as the Republican Club throughout the war. Donovan was a Republican, but he had angered conservatives and Republicans by hiring liberals, socialists and even some communists. From the day Roosevelt appointed Donovan to head OSS, he had but one job: to destroy the Axis war machine, and he hired anyone who could help him do that. Donovan did the honorable thing and stood by his men, even in the face of a congressional investigation labeling some of his agents as communist in the Goff affair. Lesser men would have stood idly by. There lies the root cause for the short-lived fate of the OSS.

Donovan came with too much political baggage. As the Assistant Attorney General in the 1920s, he almost cost J. Edgar Hoover his job. However, Hoover was not Donovan's only heavyweight enemy. During the same period, Donovan approved a case to go to trial that charged Sen. Burton Wheeler with using influence to get oil and gas leases for a friend and client. The court acquitted Wheeler of the charges, and when he returned to Washington he never stopped attacking Donovan.[70]

FDR believed Hoover had treated Donovan badly in passing him by for a cabinet position, which was one reason he selected Donovan to head the OSS. Hoover only offered Donovan the position of Governor-General of the Philippines, which was considered a stepping-stone to greater political heights. It was the same one Taft used on his way to the White House.[71] Donovan refused the position. A myriad of reasons have been given for Hoover passing Donovan over for a cabinet position, but most likely it was due to Donovan's firsthand knowledge of the Belgium Relief Fund. This fund was merely a front to supply Germany with food and prolong World War I. Donovan had been one of the investigators the United States sent to Belgium to investigate the fund.

Donovan's lack of administrative experience (he was a poor administrator who preferred being in the field) and his opposition to prohibition were advanced as reasons for being passed over. However, Donovan's record on upholding prohibition was well known from his days as city prosecutor in Buffalo. There, he raided an elite club where he was a member. City elders were less than pleased, but to Donovan, if an Irish railroad worker could be arrested for prohibition, so could the community leaders. The law was the law and to hell with the commotion; it applied equally to the rich, and Donovan was not afraid to apply it.

Hoover also wanted to isolate Donovan outside the United States in case any of Hoover's past dealings with the Belgium Relief Fund or stock swindles surfaced. Donovan would have been relentless in investigating his boss if he was appointed Attorney General.

By 1928, Donovan also incurred the wrath of William Howard Taft. The former President and then Chief Justice wrote a letter to his son that found its way to Hoover, claiming that Donovan would be an unsuitable candidate for Attorney General.[72] Besides these heavyweight enemies, Donovan also faced opposition from the State Department and military intelligence units that viewed the OSS as infringing on their territory. Facing plentiful political foes, Truman disbanded the OSS.

The final blow to Donovan's ambitions to head a peacetime intelligence service came from the pen of Drew Pearson, the well-known columnist. Attorney General Francis Biddle was engaging in a dangerous game of passing secret documents to Pearson to discredit both Donovan and OSS. On April 27, 1945, Pearson wrote:

By the thread of one man's life hung personal relationships which affected nations. Prime Ministers and potentates, once close to Franklin Roosevelt, now must learn how to get along with an unknown gentleman in the White House. Certain Army-Navy officials, who always knew how Roosevelt would react on this and that, now must do business with a man they once criticized. To illustrate how the pendulum of fate has swung, here are some of those who will miss Franklin Roosevelt most.

Gen. "Wild Bill" Donovan of the Office of Strategic Services, sometimes called the "Cloak and Dagger Club" or "Oh So Social," will miss Roosevelt terribly. Donovan ran the giant espionage outfit which tried to find out what was going on behind enemy lines, and he had accumulated the most bizarre assortment of female spies, social register bluebloods and anti-Roosevelt haters ever seen in Washington. As an old personal friend, Roosevelt gave him free reign [sic], including grandiose plans for a postwar espionage service. Truman does not like peacetime espionage and will not be so lenient.[73]

A few days later Pearson wrote:

... the Russians are probably most suspicious of the mysterious United States espionage organization called OSS. The OSS, or Office of Strategic Services, has, strangely, distributed some of the most powerful bankers' representatives in the U.S.A. at key points where they can influence United States policy in occupied Germany.

The roster of OSS men who have been or are operating in Europe reads like a blue-stocking list of the first 60 families. It includes: Paul Mellon, son of Andrew Mellon; Junius and Henry Morgan of the House of Morgan; Alfred duPont; Lester Armour of the Chicago Armours; Gordon Auchincloss; John Auchincloss; Warwick Potter; Harold Coolidge; William Van Allen of the Astor family; and Allen [sic] Dulles, attorney for various international bankers with previous connections in Germany.

Some of these may not deserve the suspicion focused upon them. But others more than make up for it. And anyone listening for more than 30 minutes to their conversation about the next war and building up Germany as a partner in that war can understand why the Russians wrongly accused us of a deal to permit the American Army to enter Berlin first.

This is the kind of underlying suspicion which must be killed immediately and permanently if the machinery of San Francisco is to bring about permanent peace. [74]

As the world diplomats were gathering in San Francisco to form the United Nations, Pearson charged Donovan with planning a war against Russia. In reality, no plans existed until a year later, in March 1946. Even then, the Pincher series was not a real war plan. The first formal plan against Russia was devised on July 29, 1947.

Pearson was not concerned with the truth of the situation. However, his broadcast confirmed the worst fears of the Soviets and only fanned their distrust of the Allies. Excerpts from the broadcast follow:

Washington: Gen. William J. Donovan, Office of Strategic Services, has just received from his overzealous aides a detailed plan for American war on Russia. I am sure that General Donovan himself and the more responsible members of his super-spy organization had nothing to do with these plans, but I suggest that stupidity like this which, if it leaks to me, will also leak to others, including the Russians, causes distrust between the Allies just as we are trying to end this war and build up a plan to end all wars.

A series of secret cables sent by General William Donovan, of the Office of Strategic Services (nicknamed "Oh-so-Secret"), to Russell Forgan, former Chicago banker, now in Paris, is intriguing other U.S. officials. Donovan wired Forgan to interrogate directors of the giant Nazi cartel IG Farben, now seized by the United States Army.

This is the company which collaborated with Standard Oil of New Jersey and the Aluminum Corporation of America to keep vitally important patents for synthetic rubber, magnesium, and high octane gasoline from the American public at a time when it was essential to use those patents for war.

One cable from Donovan to Forgan in Paris reads:

I have already asked you to send names of IG Farben now in custody. From now on these men should be kept from one another, particularly when the interrogation begins. Files of IG Farben should be seized and sent to Paris at once in our custody. This is most important. Essential that we keep control of these men.

What intrigues other U.S. officials is that Donovan's OSS is dominated by actions of the Mellons, the J.P. Morgans and big banking and industrial houses, some of them interested in German patents ... Other Government officials are also puzzled as to why the OSS, rather than the Justice Department, should pounce upon IG Farben executives. There might be quiet probing of this.

Note — Attorney General Biddle recently told senators: "Many cartel arrangements necessarily disrupted during the European phase of the war are now being resumed. Meetings have been held, plans have been held, plans have been laid [sic], and in some cases agreements already entered into. As to some of these agreements, my department will have something to say before long." Reaction of senators is that big business never learns.[75]

The telegram sent to Donovan on April 30, 1945 over the ultrasecure Telekrypton circuit was almost the exact text of a secret signal he received. Donovan once again assigned Doering to investigate the leak. All evidence pointed to Biddle, but no charges were ever filed. Note how soon after Roosevelt's death that Biddle passed this information to Pearson.

On Sept. 20, 1945, President Truman issued an executive order disbanding the OSS, and it was dispersed among other agencies. The Secret Intelligence and Special Operations branches were transferred to the War Department and placed under the command of former OSS Gen. John Magruder. This was nothing more than a caretaker body to dismember the unit. Magruder protested the wholesale dismemberment and resigned in February.

The Research and Analysis branch headed by Aldred McCormack, a New York corporation lawyer, was transferred to the State Department. Congressional critics of OSS simply decimated McCormack's budget with the help of State Department officials. The Assistant Secretary of State for Latin America, Spruille Braden, led the charge. In front of a congressional committee, Braden stated: "We resisted this invasion of all these swarms of people ... mostly collectivists and do gooders and what-nots."[76]

Later in the 1950s, Braden became a devotee of the John Birch Society.

In March 1946, while McCormack struggled for funding from Congress, the chairperson of the House Military Affairs Committee charged that a person with strong Soviet leanings had joined the State Department. McCormack demanded a retraction. Instead, Congress cut the entire appropriation for his unit. The pro-fascist faction in the State Department convinced enough influential members of Congress that ex-OSS officers were far to the left and committed to the socialization of America and the redistribution of wealth globally.

By mid-1946, Donovan's OSS was completely dismantled and the U.S. was without an intelligence service. At first, it was suggested that private enterprise could provide the government with intelligence. A former OSS deputy director proposed to IBM's Tom Watson that he form a private intelligence service. The two men raised the initial venture capital in vain because President Truman and Congress created the CIA in 1947.

In the short span of a year, the government dissolved OSS only to recreate it under a new name. This was not a case of a vacillating government. If President Truman had not signed the executive order dissolving OSS, Congress simply would have canceled any funding for it. Disbanding OSS had an express purpose. OSS leftists served as sacrificial lambs to atone duPont's new feckless goddess on the altar of free enterprise. Those who served their country gallantly during war and were dedicated to stomping out the last vestige of fascism now became victims to the fascists in the United States. American industrialists who willingly supported Hitler during the war had to be protected.

The political climate by the end of the war had undergone a tremendous shift to the right. This change was not abrupt. Each Roosevelt administration was more conservative than the preceding. In 1944, Truman replaced Wallace as Vice President. In 1946, the Republicans gained control of both chambers of Congress. The stage was now set for a wholesale purging of leftists in the government who were dedicated to wiping out fascism.

The new CIA was a mixture of old OSS agents and military officers. OSS veterans soon became dominating forces in the new agency. The CIA had two principal divisions: Office of Policy Coordination (OPC) and the Office of Special Operations. Frank Wisner (father of U.S. diplomat Frank G. Wisner II), and Allen Dulles headed OPC. James Angleton and William Harvey headed the Special Operations division. The CIA had but one agenda: anti-communism. The fourth director of the CIA appointed by Truman was Gen. Walter Bedell Smith who, in all seriousness, once warned President Eisenhower that Nelson Rockefeller was a communist.

The top leadership of the CIA had no qualms about working with Nazi war criminals. Angleton, Dulles and Wisner all worked with and helped Nazis escape from Europe. Many immigrated to the United States after having their records sanitized by Dulles and others in the intelligence community.

The CIA instead of the FBI now had exclusive responsibility for intelligence in South America. Given Hoover's propensity to protect and expand his domain, the FBI remained cool if not frigid in its dealings with the new agency. In some South American embassies, FBI agents destroyed their records rather than giving them to the CIA.

Although the CIA was created to purge all leftists from the intelligence agency, it soon felt the wrath of McCarthyism. Loyalty oaths followed. Once again after a war, America embarked on a Red scare. The resulting Cold War was a smoke screen to cover up the crimes of fascists in the United States. No American corporation faced charges of trading with the Nazis. Not a single corporation was charged with treason. Dulles was adamant on the point. He had used his post in Switzerland to protect his own dealings with the Nazis and those of his clients. He was now in a position to further protect those American corporations that willingly supported and traded with the Nazis during the war.

The Nazi Comeback Plan

With Roosevelt's death, his pledge to bring all war criminals to justice evaporated in less than a year. The first sabotage effort came almost immediately. On April 25, 1945, Drew Pearson reported in his column that an inside group of military planners had dropped Roosevelt's plan for postwar Germany in favor of a soft peace. This small circle of military planners included representatives of big business who had served in the military planning groups during the war.[77]

This group adopted former President Herbert Hoover's plan for a "cooling-off period" and a soft peace. The Hoover administration was instrumental in helping IG Farben reestablish its cartels after WWI.

On May 16, 1945, Stimson warned President Truman of the likely pestilence and famine in central Europe, which would lead to a communist uprising. Stimson hoped Truman would appoint Herbert Hoover to review the relief situation and demand revitalization of the German economy and industrial base. In his diary, Stimson deprecated FDR and Morgenthau, referring to Hoover as a master of the subject, and FDR and his administration as amateurs.[78]

Stimson's diary reveals deep opposition to Roosevelt and a hard peace for Germany. Stimson was an integral part of the Roosevelt administration's efforts to eliminate the Nazi menace, but his diary reveals that he bitterly opposed FDR's plan for postwar peace. Truman did appoint Hoover to tour Europe to seek out a solution for relief, but Hoover used the trip to enrich himself, much as he did during WWI. One may also be certain Hoover vacuumed Europe for any incriminating evidence of his involvement with the Nazis and efforts to prolong WWI.

Within a few months, this group found a political platform in the voice of a young State Department official, George Kennan. In early 1946, Kennan's memorandum on Soviet foreign policy attracted the group's attention, and he was recalled to Washington to act as the State Department's Deputy in the newly formed War College.

Kennan's formula for rebuilding Germany as a bulwark against the East soon became policy. All subsequent decisions by leaders in the Pentagon and the State Department were based on it. The last-ditch attempt to compromise between a one-sided pro-Germany policy and one more agreeable to the Soviets was made by Secretary of State Byrnes. On Oct. 3, 1946, Byrnes proposed a program of Allied control over all of Germany for 40 years.

Byrnes' plan for a peaceful relationship with the Soviets was opposed by the policy shapers in the Pentagon, as well as by a large faction in the State Department. In 1947, George Marshall replaced Byrnes. Under Marshall, the policy-shaping apparatus of the State Department was placed in the hands of Kennan.

With the top echelon in the State Department and the Pentagon now in the hands of pro-Germany adherents, the United States was poised to rush headlong into the Cold War. Our former ally against the Nazis was now our enemy. Denazification of Germany was dead; there would be no more trials of Nazi war criminals, no investigations of corporate America and its support of the Nazi regime. The native Nazis in America had won; their crimes were swept under the rug.

Kennan was a Germanophile who studied at Heidelberg and the Hochschule fuer Politik in Berlin. He was taught and believed in the teachings of the Hochschule that Germany was a bulwark against the East. Kennan did postgraduate work in four German universities: University of Heidelberg, University of Berlin, Oriental Seminary and the Hochschule fuer Politik. All of these institutions were well known for their extreme pan-German views.

Kennan was interned with other diplomats in the Grand Hotel in Bad Nauheim, Germany, when the United States entered the war. During this time, he gave lectures expounding on the thesis that Germany's defeat would end the 2,000-year history of European civilization. What kind of U.S. diplomat would deplore the defeat of the Nazis in 1942 after the ruthless attack on Pearl Harbor? While in Berlin, Kennan had to be aware of the genocide in Poland, yet he deplored the defeat of the regime that was giving new meaning to barbaric behavior. The German newsweekly, *Der Spiegel,* confirmed that Kennan lectured his fellow inmates at the Grand Hotel about the undesirability of the defeat of the Nazis in 1952.[79]

Many officials inside the State Department and high-ranking military officials shared with Kennan the geopolitical theories of Gen. Karl Haushofer. That led to Kennan becoming the leading Cold War theorist. Unfortunately, his premise was a house of cards built on lies and deceit. By 1945, the State Department had ample evidence of extensive plans by the German High Command for a continuation of political warfare against the Allies after a military defeat. It also had files on how German authorities laid the groundwork for continuing Nazi activities in foreign countries, on preserving the German cartels, and on continuing Nazi scientific research in foreign countries.

The State Department was divided between those who favored a harsh peace and the pro-fascist faction promoting an easy peace. By the end of the war, those favoring an easy peace held the upper hand because many who vigorously opposed fascism had been removed. The State Department, now in the hands of fascist sympathizers, was busting at the seams with incriminating documents on Nazi plans to continue the war once hostilities ended. Excerpts from two of the announcements by the State Department and one from a captured Nazi document confirm the State Department was well aware of the danger. The full text of these announcements and additional captured Nazi documents are in Appendix 11.

Nazi Party members, German industrialists and the German military, realizing that victory can no longer be attained, are now developing postwar commercial projects, are endeavoring to renew and cement friendships in foreign commercial circles and are planning for renewals of pre-war cartel agreements. An appeal to the courts of various countries will be made early in the postwar period through dummies for "unlawful" seizure of industrial plants and other properties taken over by Allied governments at the outbreak of war. In cases where this method fails German repurchase will be attempted through "cloaks" who meet the necessary citizenship requirements. The object in every instance will be to re-establish German control at the earliest possible date. German attempts to continue to share in the control and development of technological change in the immediate postwar period is reflected in the phenomenal increase in German patent registrations in foreign countries during the past two years. These registrations reached an all-time high in 1944. The prohibition against exporting capital from Germany was withdrawn several months ago, and a substantial outflow of capital has followed to foreign countries.

Our investigations have yielded a considerable amount of information which indicates the schemes and devices which the Germans planned to use in order to safeguard their foreign holdings and transfer additional property abroad. In many cases, they have concealed their interests in foreign properties through holding companies as cloaks. In other cases they have abandoned formal voting control but retained a firm grip on manufacturing concerns through domination of technical processes. They have transformed their holdings into bearer shares in order to take advantage of the fact that the title to such shares can be traced only with extreme difficulty. Moreover, the Germans have also taken advantage in some countries of administrative inefficiency and corruption. The extent to which this reaches can be said in every neutral country to have been the fault of private individuals alone is problematical.

On July 27, 1943, the German Foreign Office expert on the U.S.A., the geo-politician Dr. Colin Ross, suggested in a fifteen-page memorandum a Plan for an Ideological Campaign in the United States. Recognizing Germany's inability to bring the war to a victorious end, Dr. Colin Ross proposed the immediate implementation of carefully planned psychological warfare to undermine the anticipated U.S. military victory. Dr. Ross regarded American public opinion as the weakest link because the American people seemed especially susceptible to scare propaganda hinting that a defeated Germany would join the ranks of Bolshevism. The memorandum, which was addressed to the German Secretary of State in the Foreign Office von Steengracht, became the guidepost for Germany's highly successful black-mail diplomacy in post-war America.[80]

The passages referring to German corporations confirm the idea of total warfare outlined in the chapter on the 1920s, and the success and speed with which the cartels were reestablished after WWI. Moreover, as confirmed in these documents, plans were afoot to reestablish economic control once the war ended.

The date of the third excerpt above coincides with the native fascists' desperate three-prong attack in the United States. Further, the documents in Appendix 10 confirm that Nazi agents were well placed in the U.S. to influence the political doctrine and policy.

The intent of the Nazis can best be summarized by an excerpt from a 1944 French weekly, *Combat*, written by Gen. von Stuepnagel, analyzing the causes for German military setbacks in WWII:

In the next war, which should take place within 25 years, the same mistake must not be made. The principal adversary will be the United States, and the entire effort must be concentrated against this country from the beginning... Our defeat in the present war need not be considered except as an incident in the triumphal march of Germany towards the conquest of the world, and from now on we must give a defeated Germany the spirit of a future conqueror. What does a temporary defeat matter if, through the destruction of people and material wealth in enemy countries, we are able to secure a margin of economic and demographic superiority even greater than before 1939? If we can succeed in doing this, this war will have been useful, since it will enable us, within the next 25 years, to wage another war under better conditions... Our enemies will grow weary before we do. We shall have to organize a campaign of pity designed to induce them to send us needed supplies at the earliest possible moment. Above all we must hold on to the assets we have deposited in neutral countries. The present war will thus have been victorious, in spite of our temporary military defeat, because it will have been a march forward towards our supremacy. We have not to fear conditions of peace analogous to those we have imposed, because our adversaries will always be divided and disunited.[81]

There is no more dramatic evidence of the State Department's plan of a German bulwark against the Soviets and the resulting Marshall Plan, which basically followed the Nazis' plan for a comeback. It's not that Marshall or any particular individual were Nazis. However, the State Department had reams of captured German documents and was well aware of the postwar plans of the Nazi leadership to continue the war economically and psychologically, and yet, the State Department embarked on a course that could not have pleased the Nazi leadership more. The Nazi psychological warfare campaign was extraordinarily successful in playing the Americans for fools.

While the State Department was correct in opposing the Soviet Union or any other totalitarian form of government, pushing the world to the brink of a nuclear holocaust was foolhardy. Moreover, as we learned later in the 1960s and 1970s, détente and trade were more effective weapons against the Soviets. By continuing a path of belligerence rather than peaceful coexistence, the United States forced the Soviets and their eastern European satellites to arm. The Marshall Plan propelled the world toward the nuclear brink.

Evidence the Nazis were trying to split the Allies was plentiful. Captured Nazi documents reveal the German High Command channeled proof of their secret negotiations with the Americans to Stalin through agents who were in contact with von Papen. This was the source of serious strife between FDR and Stalin in the closing months of the war. The Big Three, the U.S., U.S.S.R and U.K., had agreed to hold no secret talks separately with the Nazis. Yet, Allen Dulles was holding talks with Gen. Wolff and other Nazi officials. All reports suggest the talks held by Dulles were unauthorized. While FDR had not approved the talks and was not aware of them, the Nazis told Stalin about them. At one point before this incident, the Nazis boldly proposed that the West join them in a war against communism. The Americans who engaged in these secret talks wittingly or unwittingly played their part in the Nazi ruse. They included Allen Dulles.[82]

Besides the reams of documents the State Department had acquired, the press reported further proof that the Nazis were building an underground network. On Dec. 13, 1944, the Associated Press reported that Himmler had started such plans. The article further claimed that many party members established double identities, and the aim of their propaganda was to drive a wedge between the Allies. Evidence of the Nazi underground network and escape routes emerged as early as 1943 and was extensive by late 1944.

The Nazis made good use of their occupation of France by sending carloads of files and secret formulas over the Pyrenees to neutral Spain. Burnet Hershey, the foreign correspondent of the Hearst press, first reported on the German escape route through Spain on Jan. 25, 1943:

> Every talk I had with the Germans in Lisbon made that fact clear. They may be defeated on the battlefield, as they were in 1918, but they expect to win again at the peace table as in 1919. Of course, they will sacrifice Hitler as they sacrificed the Kaiser; but the old gang — the generals, big industrialists, phony professors of mis-education about German race superiority — will try to go underground again to lay the eggs for another war of German conquest.[83]

On Jan. 17, 1944, Harold Denny of the *Times* confirmed the early report in the following dispatch from Madrid:

> Heavy new increments of German agents have been pouring into Spain in recent days in an obvious effort by Germany to save what she can of a situation that has gone badly against her.

> A thousand Gestapo agents and other German representatives have appeared in Madrid alone in the past fortnight. Significant additions to the German population have been noted in other parts of Spain.

> They are not easy to deal with, for Germany has extensive commercial interests in Spain and many of these agents are here in the plausible guise of executives, technicians and lesser employees of these interests as well as cogs in Germany's vast diplomatic, consular and propaganda machinery.[84]

On April 13, 1944, the *New York Herald Tribune* carried a report from the British Intelligence Service and the American Alien Property Custodian about huge sums placed by high Nazi officials and industrialists in neutral and American banks. On July 19, 1944, the Office of War Information reported that Swiss officials were alarmed about recent transfers by Germans to Swiss and Portuguese banks. The money would be used to finance the resurrection of the Third Reich. On Oct. 19, 1944, *Newsweek* reported that according to diplomatic sources from Buenos Aires, German technicians and military experts were believed to be reaching Argentina incognito. On Jan. 15, 1945, according to *Newsweek,*

> Many of the men Himmler sent to Spain and Argentina to carry out Nazi plans for postwar survival, carried passports under false names and later were reported dead in Germany. All have had training in Nazi political methods and experience abroad in commercial and other posts.[85]

In fact, the names of many of those executed as plotters in the failed attempt on Hitler's life were later used as false identities for escaping Nazis. A Reuters News Wire on Sept. 14, 2000 confirmed the previous quoted documents about the Nazis planning a comeback. The new document on looted money and property was released under a Freedom of Information Act request by the World Jewish Congress. The document confirms a meeting at the Maison Rouge (Red House) in Strasbourg on Aug. 10, 1944. During the meeting, an SS general and a representative of the German armaments ministry told companies such as Krupp and Roehling that they must be prepared to finance the Nazi Party after the war when it went underground. Scheid, an SS general and director of Hermsdorff & Schonburg Co., presided over the meeting. Seven German companies, including Krupp, Roehling, Messerschmidt and Volkswagenwerk, and officials of the ministries of armaments and the navy attended the meeting.

German industry was told to make contacts and alliances with foreign firms, and lay the groundwork for borrowing large sums in foreign countries. The SS general cited Krupp's sharing of patents with U.S. companies as an example of how to employ firms outside Germany for the benefit of the Nazis. The Supreme Headquarters of the Allied Expeditionary Force sent the three-page document to the U.S. Secretary of State in November 1944.[86]

It is clear the State Department had a good idea of the Nazis' intent. Even the press was full of articles reporting on Nazi escape plans. The papers that aligned themselves as pro-fascist before the war began a propaganda blitz for an easy peace with Germany. They claimed that Roosevelt's call for an unconditional surrender delayed the end of the war; it became a campaign issue in 1944. Despite this barrage of propaganda that the Nazis may have provoked, there were thousands of articles and editorials against any appeasement of Germany and the Nazis. At the peak of this sympathy campaign for an easy peace, Maj. George Fielding Eliot wrote in the *Herald Tribune* on June 27, 1945:

> Why shouldn't the German standard of living be lower than that of Germany's neighbors? Since when has it been considered an obligation of civilized society to see to it that a criminal, in the custody of the law, must enjoy every privilege, every luxury and every article of Lucullan diet which may be available to the law-abiding members of the community?[87]

When Roosevelt's Occupational Directive 1067 was published, it had the full support of the American people. The military command kept this directive secret for months because it ran counter to its program. The essential objectives of the Allies were stated as follows in Directive 1067:

> The principal allied objective is to prevent Germany from ever again becoming a threat to the peace of the world. Essential steps in the accomplishment of this objective are elimination of Nazism and militarism in all their forms, the immediate apprehension of war criminals for punishment, the industrial disarmament and demilitarization of Germany, with continuing control over Germany's capacity to make war and preparation for eventual reconstruction of German political life on a democratic basis.[88]

During the war, the Allies solemnly agreed to remove all traces of militarism and Nazism to ensure Germany would never again wage war on the world. At Potsdam, the Allies agreed to abolish all veterans' organizations and other military clubs. The failure to continue the 4Ds program and to follow the Potsdam agreement led to additional problems for the occupying forces. The ink was barely dry on the Potsdam agreement before SS and Wehrmacht officers began setting up a close-knit society under their American captors' eyes in the prison camps. The Bruderschaft (Brotherhood) organization flourished behind the prison gates and was soon planning a Nazi comeback.

During the first two years, the Bruderschaft operated in secret. The inner circle was made up of top SS officers and important officers from the General Staff. Among the leaders: Lt. Gen. Hut von Manteuffel, former commander of the Panzer Gross Deutschland Division; Alfred Franke-Grieksch, a high-ranking SS officer; and Gottried Griessmayer, former head of Hitler Youth. The organization was well financed, reaching across Germany and extending into Italy, Spain and Argentina.

The Control Council for Germany

The question of German remilitarization first arose when Chancellor Adenauer suggested a united Europe defended by an integrated European Army. In 1948, Adenauer presented a request to U.S. authorities in secret to rearm 25 divisions. On July 30, 1948, *U.S. News and World Report* exposed the request in an article.[89]

The outbreak of the Korean War in June 1950 brought a complete change. Provisions banning military groups were no longer enforced. The Control Council allowed West Germany to set up its own

General Staff, camouflaged under the name "Blank Office." Supported by Bonn and the United States, a network of ex-Nazi officers was created to reactivate Germany's military. The man behind the plan for remilitarization was Werner Naumann. With his old party connection from the Propaganda Ministry, the SS, the Wehrmacht and the Bruderschaft, Naumann emerged in a position of power. The devoted Nazi was the directing spirit behind almost every Nazi organization and publication in 1950–51.

One of the outgrowths of this rush to rearm Germany was the Bund Deutscher Jugend (Association of German Youth). Membership in the group rose to 22,000. However, behind it was a sinister secret division of trained saboteurs and assassination squads labeled the Technical Emergency Service. Several thousand Wehrmacht and SS officers staffed this guerrilla army. U.S. agencies, the Bonn government and a few German businesses trained and equipped it.

This Nazi group would have remained lost in history among the hundreds of others in postwar Germany if it had not been for President of the State of Hesse, August Zinn. In 1952, Zinn publicly charged that the group had drawn up a blacklist of prominent politicians to assassinate in an emergency. To the dismay of the U.S. High Commissioner, evidence surfaced revealing a large-scale political assassination plot hatched in the style of the Freikorps. The Oct. 10, 1952 edition of the *New York Times* carried the story. Similar plots and illegal activities were found behind other Nazi groups, such as the Freikorps Deutschland, Bewegung Reich and scores of smaller ones.[90]

In 1952, the courts sentenced five members of a secret Hitler Action group for unconstitutional activities. Schroer, the group's leader, had been a prominent officer in Hitler's Munich headquarters. Schroer had given the order: "Act inconspicuously! Infiltrate all rightist organizations and make them ready for the final assault."[91]

American Occupation officials systematically sabotaged Directive 1067. Even Eisenhower saw the systematic way in which it was being violated and issued strong warnings to officers. As recorded in the Truman Library, Gen. Lucius D. Clay, who became Military Governor of Germany, summarized the sabotage thus.

> JCS-1067 would have been extremely difficult to operate under. If you followed it literally, you couldn't have done anything to restore the German economy. If you couldn't restore the German economy, you could never hope to get paid for the food that they had to have. By virtue of these sorts of things it was modified constantly; not officially, but by allowing this deviation and that deviation, et cetera. We began to slowly wipe out JCS-1067. When we were ordered to put in a currency reform this was in direct violation of a provision of JCS-1067 that prohibited us from doing anything to improve the German economy. It was an unworkable policy and it wasn't changed just without any discussion or anything by those of us who were in Germany. It was done by gradual changes in its provision and changes of cablegrams, conferences, and so on.[92]

Gen. Clay's words are damning. They leave no doubt the general was willingly to ignore Roosevelt's directive and conveniently twist its meaning as needed. Further, his words clearly show that he knowingly chipped away at the directive until all of its provisions were voided.

In 1948, Clay commuted the life sentence of Ilse Koch to three years. Koch, the sadistic wife of a concentration camp commandant, known by inmates as the Witch of Buchenwald, had lampshades made from the skin of inmates with distinctive tattoos. Forensics proved the various items came from human skin. However, in 1976 in a videotaped interview prepared for the George C. Marshall Research Foundation in Virginia, Gen. Clay made the following comments:

> We tried Ilse Koch. ... She was sentenced to life imprisonment, and I commuted it to three years. And our press really didn't like that. She had been destroyed by the fact that an enterprising reporter who first went into her house had given her the beautiful name, the "Bitch of Buchenwald," and he had found some white lampshades in there which he wrote up as being made out of human flesh.
>
> Well, it turned out actually that it was goat flesh. But at the trial it was still human flesh. It was almost

impossible for her to have gotten a fair trial.[93]

Ilse Koch and her lawyers never challenged the fact that the lampshades and other items were made from human skin. Such irresponsible comments as the general's contributed to Holocaust denials. Further, the Koch case shows that while the general started circumventing Roosevelt's directive by chipping away at the economic provisions, he soon intensified his sympathies to pardoning Nazi war criminals. While Gen. Clay publicly stated that Koch could not get a fair trial in an American military court, a civilian German court later sentenced her to life in prison. In 1967, the Witch of Buchenwald died in prison; the official cause of death was suicide.

Once hostilities ended in Europe, Gen. Clay was appointed as Eisenhower's Deputy Military Governor in charge of the Control Council. Following Eisenhower's retirement on March 15, 1947, Clay became the Military Governor of Germany. Eisenhower was reportedly disturbed to see his orders countermanded and expressed concern at seeing Nazis set free. Eisenhower did not need to look any further than his Deputy Governor for an explanation.

Secretary of Army Kenneth Royall opposed the denazification and decartelization plans. Royall was open in his support for rebuilding a strong Germany and was a vigorous opponent of the 4Ds program. In secret testimony before the House Appropriations Committee in April 1948, he told members of Congress that he wanted to end the war crimes trials much earlier. He claimed his major obstacle was Gen. Clay. Royall was the official responsible for halting all executions of war criminals after a false story of prisoner torture emerged in the Malmedy Massacre trial. Royall also opposed integrating the military after the war.

As Deputy Governor in charge of the Control Council, Clay was free to hire and staff the council, which had three general divisions: political, finance and economic divisions. See figure.

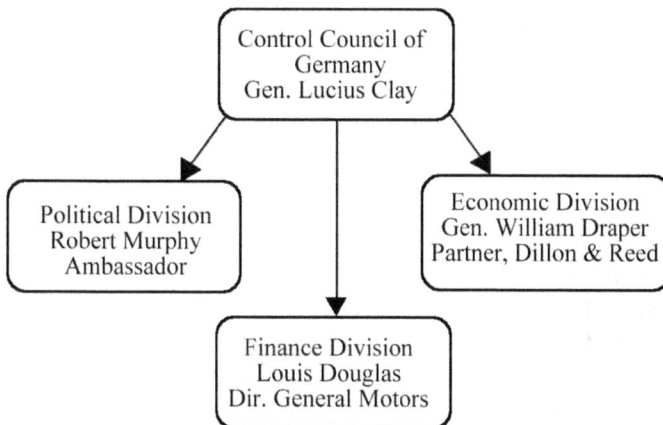

General Motors was particularly well represented on the Control Council. Besides Louis Douglas heading the Finance Division, Edward Zdunke, a prewar head of General Motors Antwerp, was appointed to supervise the Engineering Section. Col. Grame Howard, former General Motors representative in Germany and the author of a book that praised totalitarian practices and justified German aggression, was placed in charge of personnel.

The stacking of the Control Council with Wall Street and corporate executives deeply disturbed Treasury Secretary Morgenthau. Many of the firms were guilty of willingly trading with the Nazis during the war and supported pro-fascist groups at home. General Motors' Opel division was one of the largest tank manufacturers for Hitler. Dillon and Read was one of the Wall Street firms that helped finance and build the Third Reich. Morgenthau noted:

MEMORANDUM

May 29, 1945

Lt. Gen. Lucius D. Clay, as Deputy to General Eisenhower, actively runs the American element of the Control Council for Germany. Gen. Clay's three principal advisers on the Control Council staff are:

1. Ambassador Robert D. Murphy, who is in charge of the Political Division.

2. Louis Douglas, whom Gen. Clay describes as my personal adviser on economical, financial and governmental matters. Douglas resigned as Director of the Budget in 1934; and for the following eight years he attacked the government's fiscal policies. Since 1940, Douglas has been president of the Mutual Life Insurance Co., and since December 1944, he has been a director of the General Motors Corp.

3. Brig. Gen. William Draper is the director of the Economics Division of the Control Council. Gen. Draper is a partner of the banking firm of Dillon, Read and Co.

Sunday's *New York Times* contained the announcement of key personnel who have been appointed by Gen. Clay and Gen. Draper to the Economic Division of the Control Council. The appointments include the following:

1. R. J. Wysor is to be in charge of the metallurgical tatters. Wysor was president of the Republic Steel Corp., from 1937 until a recent date, and prior thereto, he was associated with the Bethlehem Steel, Jones and Laughlin Steel Corp., and the Republic Steel Corp.

2. Edward X. Zdunke is to supervise the engineering section. Prior to the war, Mr. Zdunke was head of General Motors at Antwerp.

3. Philip Gaethke is to be in charge of mining operations. Gaethke was formerly connected with Anaconda Copper and as manager of its smelters and mines in Upper Silesia before the war.

4. Philip P. Clover is to be in charge of handling oil matters. He was formerly a representative of the Socony Vacuum Oil Co., in Germany.

5. Peter Hoglund is to deal with industrial production problems. Hoglund is on leave from General Motors and is said to be an expert on German production.

6. Calvin B. Hoover is to be in charge of the Intelligence Group on the Control Council and is also to be a special adviser to Gen. Draper. In a letter to the editor in the *New York Times* on Oct. 9, 1944, Hoover wrote:

"The publication of Secretary Morgenthau's plan for dealing with Germany has disturbed me deeply ... such a Carthaginian peace would leave a legacy of hate to poison international relations for generations to come. ... the void in the economy of Europe which would exist through the destruction of all German industry is something which is difficult to contemplate."

7. Laird Bell is to be Chief Counsel of the Economic Division. He is a well-known Chicago lawyer and in May 1944, was elected president of the *Chicago Daily News* after the death of Frank Knox.

One of the men who helped Gen. Draper in the selection of personnel for the Economics Division was Col. Graeme Howard, a vice president of General Motors, who was in charge of overseas business and who was a leading representative of General Motors in Germany prior to the war. Howard is the author of a book in which he praises totalitarian practices, justifies German aggression and the Munich policy of appeasement, and blames Roosevelt for precipitating the war.[94]

Morgenthau's memorandum shows how the military systematically sabotaged the denazification program from the top down. All the firms mentioned willingly continued to trade with the Nazis during the war. Almost all took extraordinary measures to hide their Nazi trade from the United States government and to have their stateside offices remain in charge. This sabotage occurred despite clear directives from the Control Council. The relevant extracts from the Control Council follow:

You will search out, arrest and hold, pending receipt by you of further instructions as to their disposition, Adolph Hitler, his chief Nazi associates, other war criminals and all persons who have participated in planning or carrying out Nazi enterprises involving or resulting in atrocities or war crimes ...

8. Nazis and Nazi sympathizers holding important and key positions in (a) National and Gau Civic and

economic organizations; (b) corporations and other organizations in which the government has a major financial interest; (c) industry, commerce, agriculture and finance; (d) education; (e) the judiciary; and (f) the press, publishing houses and other agencies disseminating news and propaganda.[95]

The excerpt from the Control Council directive is specific. It leaves no doubt about who was to be arrested and detained. Further, the directive was explicit that there was no authority to release anyone detained until receiving further instructions from Washington. Gen. Clay's words reveal that at the very least, he was guilty of not following orders. Note the directive above included American businessmen.

While there were members like Morgenthau in the Truman administration who carried on the fight for justice, the Nazis had powerful friends in the halls of Congress to protect them. One was John Rankin. Excerpts from his speech to the House of Representatives on Nov. 27, 1947 follow:

What is taking place at Nuremberg, Germany, is a disgrace to the United States. Every other country has now washed its hands and withdrawn from this Saturalia of persecution. But a racial minority, two and half years after the war closed are in Nuremberg not only hanging German soldiers but trying German businessmen in the name of the United States.[96]

Rankin used the words racial minority to refer to Jews. He was not alone. George Dondero, R-Michigan, was mayor of Royal Oak, Mich., before his election to the House. Royal Oak was home to Father Coughlin and a hotbed for pro-Nazi groups. Dondero described the trials as a result of Jewish and communist treachery. He singled out ten lawyers from the IG Farben case, including the leading prosecutor Josiah duBois, whom he called a known left-winger from the Treasury Department, who had been a student of the Communist Party. Dondero became something of an art critic in the late 1940s and 1950s, dismissing modern art as communist inspired. He labored to censor the work of abstract artists.

Also based in Dondero's district was Dow Chemical. Dow had several cartel arrangements with IG Farben and feared the trial could lead to exposing its full collaboration with IG and the Nazis. The IG Farben trial also entangled British ICI Ltd. The British Foreign Office breathed a sigh of relief when the *Times* discreetly omitted any reference to ICI in its reporting of the IG Farben case.

The State Department largely engineered the choice of Clay and Murphy to head positions in the Control Council. Their appointments were more of a political decision, which testified to the power of the pro-fascist faction in the State Department. Clay was the only four-star general never to have conducted a combat command. While Clay served in Europe during the war, he was a rear echelon general in charge of supply.

Both Clay and Murphy were largely responsible for convincing Truman that a punitive peace was unwise, and they immediately set about sabotaging the denazification program. Once the Kennan Doctrine emerged in 1946, Clay and Murphy both embraced it. Early in 1946, Gen. Clay banned dismantling German industrial plants for reparations. Both Clay and Murphy had a great influence in escalating the emerging Cold War. In 1948, Clay issued a warning to Washington that "war may come with dramatic suddenness." His frantic message came from an exaggerated threat assessment from Gehlen, claiming the Soviets were mobilizing large numbers of troops in Eastern Europe. Gehlen was a former Nazi officer in charge of intelligence on the Eastern Front, recruited by OSS-CIA.

Hermann Abs' rehabilitation by Gen. Clay could be considered as the most damning sabotage of the denazification program. While Abs was never associated with the concentration camps or the horrors of the Holocaust, he was the one in the Nazi empire who made it all possible. Abs was the Nazi banker. Without the financial magic of Abs, the Nazis would have faced a financial crisis that would have brought down the Third Reich. Clay complained that he was never able to appoint Abs finance minister of the new German government, due to American public opinion, but he was able to appoint him to head the Reconstruction Finance Corp. (RFC). RFC was somewhat outside the realm of the government, but was the sole instrument for distributing funds for Germany from the Marshall Plan. Abs later returned to the post of Chairman of Deutsche Bank which he had held during the war, and was a key figure in the reconstruction of the German economy.

Gens. Clay and Draper

On July 30, 1947, Gen. Clay announced that extraditions from the American zone would end after Nov. 1. Three weeks earlier, the general ordered JAG to end all war crimes trials by the end of the year. At that time, there remained at least 700 murders of American airmen still uninvestigated. The reason later given for closing war crime trials was that by mid-1947, the American war crimes program was discredited, a victim of a vicious political campaign.[97] During the Battle of the Bulge, a German offensive unit was ordered to take no prisoners, and massacred 88 of the 120 American soldiers captured near the Belgian town of Malmedy. Both the *Chicago Tribune* and Sen. Joseph McCarthy engaged in the campaign to discredit the Malmedy massacre trial.

First to benefit from Clay's decision to end extradition were seven Wehrmacht and SS generals. Almost no German generals faced trial by the United States or Britain. That does not include field marshals, such as Goering. This group of German officers was wanted for destroying Warsaw in 1944 and for the murder of thousands of Poles during the German retreat. Poland requested their extradition at the beginning of 1946. Unlike in other eastern European countries, the trials in Poland had been as fair as any in the West. Western Allies extradited 1,172 men and women to Poland to stand trial. Forty-two returned after acquittal. One of the generals named in the extradition request was Gen. Heinz Reinefarth, the Butcher of Warsaw.

It is revealing to look at why some Nazi criminals were never charged with crimes, but were promoted instead to new positions of power. A typical example is the case of Theodor Ganzenmuller, who participated in the Beer Hall Putsch in 1923. As Staatssekretar in the Ministry of Transportation during the war, Ganzenmuller organized the train services for Auschwitz, Treblinka and other concentration camps. Himmler personally telephoned Ganzenmuller to work out problems in transporting the Jews.

Seeking someone to rebuild the railways in the American zone, the U.S. Transport Division shamefully proposed Ganzenmuller. Seven of the other members proposed also were in the automatic arrest category. The U.S. Transport Division withdrew Ganzenmuller's name only after the State Department wrote an urgent letter. Dorpmuller, Hitler's Minister of Transport, was appointed. Such appointments of high, former Nazis to positions of power in the postwar occupation government and the later German government were rampant. More than half of those nominated by the American Legal Division were former Nazis in the automatic arrest category.

The only American having problems finding suitable personnel to fill the new positions was Bernard Bernstein, head of the Finance Division. Gen. Bickelhaupt of the American forces appointed Hermann Geitz to head the Communications Division. Bickelhaupt was a former ATT vice president. Bickelhaupt insisted that Geitz was indispensable. Geitz had been head of the German telephone company, and before and during the war, had bought equipment from ATT. However, at the last moment, Gen. Clay stepped in and blocked Geitz's nomination.[98]

Col. Clio Straight was selected to head the prosecution of war criminals. Straight was a lawyer from Waterloo, Iowa, with no experience in criminal cases. He had been drafted and remained in charge even after career JAG officers were dispatched to Germany. Col. Claude Mickelwaite ordered Straight to wind up the trials that he presumed would last through 1948. Straight's office was handicapped by a constant demobilization effort that had reduced his staff by 50 percent. Further, Straight complained that his staff was untrained and not qualified. The constant moving of headquarters interrupted the group's work repeatedly. According to Straight, Mickelwaite saw no glory in continuing the trials, and because of their unpopularity with top Army brass, refused to ask for more personnel.

Mickelwaite faced only one obstacle in his rush to close down the trials: Damon Gunn. Gunn submitted a report to Washington on June 24, 1946 complaining that there were more than 15,000 war crimes suspects at Dachau alone, but only 63 trials had taken place involving roughly 500 of the detainees. In his report, Gunn recommended an extra 1,500 trials involving a minimum of 3,000 defendants. Gunn's recommendation was dead the day it arrived in Germany. On Mickelwaite's suggestion, Clay turned down the request.[99]

As late as 1982, Straight commented on the release of prisoners from Dachau: "I was ambivalent whether we should carry on or quit. We had established the principle and to carry on and try thousands would have been expensive. So when I got the orders, I saw the production line going. No special efforts were made. There was no method, no discussion about handing cases or bodies over to the Germans. We just plain turned them loose."[100]

Justice, it seems, died with Roosevelt. Nuremberg settled the principle of bringing war criminals to justice. However, once the Allies established that principle, they spent little effort in seeking justice for thousands of victims. American occupation forces simply turned the war criminals loose. Of course, with every new trial and every new defendant, the risk of uncovering corporate America's treason increased.

The lack of prosecution turned the American zone into a sanctuary for war criminals. Three examples will suffice. On March 23, 1948, Lt. Gen. Dratvin, Deputy Commander of the Soviet military mission, requested in writing from Maj. Gen. G.P. Hays, Clay's deputy, the extradition of 17 Russian collaborators. The Soviets charged the collaborators with shooting partisans and burning families alive in their homes. Dratvin supplied the American zone addresses of each collaborator. Hays rejected the request.

On March 31, 1948, the U.S. Legal Division approved the extradition of four German officers to Yugoslavia for a series of murders, but the Director of Intelligence canceled it on political grounds. Finally, on June 15, Army headquarters received a letter from a Lett refugee naming five former SS and SD officers living in a displaced persons camp. The reply:

> With the exception of atrocities committed in concentration camps which were located in the U.S. area of control or overrun by U.S. troops, the war crimes activities of headquarters do not entail prosecutions of criminals who committed offences against the civilian population of other countries... We thank you for bringing the matter to the attention of this headquarters.[101]

In short, no one gave a damn. Of course, Clay did not act in a vacuum in sabotaging the denazification program. The Nazis counted on support from their agents and friends, the corporations that did business with the Nazis before and during the war, and a faction in the State Department that wanted to use Germany as a bulwark against the Soviets.

This group had the means to effectively lobby and control the focus of the media. One tactic was sponsoring junkets for business leaders and politicians to Europe to study German recovery. American multinationals financed most of these trips. Draper paid close attention to these visitors and provided them with privileged information. Reports from the visits mentioned the proven impossibility of decartelization and the need to reverse the Morgenthau Plan before it was even implemented.

One of these reports that was influential in shaping policy was *A Report on Germany,* by Lewis Brown, chair of Johns-Manville Corp. The report was extremely popular, making it onto the bestseller list, and is still quoted today. Brown wrote it in 1947 after touring Germany. The experts he consulted read like a guest list for the Council on Foreign Relations: ATT's Frederick Devereux; John Foster Dulles; Herbert Hoover; Sears Roebuck President A.S. Barrowsthen, serving as U.S. Comptroller in Germany; a host of British and Swiss banking authorities; and 25 German industrialists. Brown's lists of experts omitted labor leaders, small businessmen, leaders of the resistance movement, and heads of denazification and decartelization.

In his report, Brown attacked the French and USSR punishment of Nazis as brutal and indiscriminate. He claimed the denazification program was depriving Germany of the leaders it needed to rehabilitate and rebuild. Typical delegates included the chairmen of the National Association of Manufacturers and of National City Bank, the head of the International Chamber of Commerce, and executives of Chase Bank. The one common denominator among the delegates was that all had extensive dealings with Nazi Germany, including General Electric.[102]

At that time, General Electric owned about 25 percent of AEG, Germany's own "general electric company," and had further extensive holdings in Germany. While Reed was arguing with the government against antitrust laws in Germany, GE faced 13 criminal antitrust cases in the United States.

After the war, Clay accepted a trustee position with the Alfred P. Sloan Foundation, which was connected to those who invested in Nazi Germany. The appointment immediately raises the question of a payoff for help in hiding American investments in Nazi Germany. The question, like many others raised in this chapter, cannot be answered without further documentation that may be sealed in government or corporate vaults.

While Gen. Clay's record on denazification is dismal at best, it was exemplary in comparison with Gen. Draper's. Secretary of War Stimson and Secretary of Navy Forrestal engineered Draper's appointment. Forrestal, a former president of Dillon and Read, was one of the individuals Roosevelt had under surveillance.[103] Draper was selected to head the economic division and the anticartel section. Clay often was opposed to Draper's views and actions.

Theoretically, the anti-cartel section should have had easy going in breaking up German cartels. The American JCS 1067 directive and the three-power Potsdam agreement were all adamant about destroying the concentrated German industrial strength. Unlike the debate over what constituted a war crime, there was little disagreement over the fate of cartels.

The anti-cartel section also employed Capt. Norbert Bogdan, a vice president of Schroeder Bank's New York branch. Schroeder had close ties with the Stein Bank, owned by Baron Kurt von Schroeder. Von Schroeder channeled funds to the Nazis before they seized power and was instrumental in introducing Hitler to von Papen in a meeting that opened the way for his appointment to chancellor. Allen Dulles also was a director of Schroeder's bank. Draper surrounded himself with like-minded aides. His electronic specialist was Frederick Devereux, a senior official from ATT. His steel expert was Rufus Wysor, president of Republic Steel, which had a long history of cartel agreements. Indeed, Wysor once asked a rival, "What's wrong with cartels anyhow?"

Draper was a former investment banker with Dillon and Read, which had a long history of doing business with Germany and the Nazis. While at Dillon and Read, Draper was appointed director, vice president and assistant treasurer of the German Credit and Investment Corp. (GCI). GCI served as a short-term banker for Thyssen and the German Steel Trust. Draper did not intend to ever implement Roosevelt's directive calling for dismantling German cartels and industry. In one case, Draper ordered a halt to the dismantling of an IG Farben poison gas plant.

However, in Draper's section there were three dedicated officials who worked diligently to take apart the Nazi cartels. Two of them, Russell Nixon and Bernard Bernstein, resigned by December 1945 in protest Draper's failure to carry out decartelization measures. Bernstein, who worked in the banking section, reported to Gen. Clay in September 1945 that his team had removed 9,500 employees who were proven Nazis from the banking system. However, Bernstein demanded stricter measures, including removal of U.S. officials who refused to carry out the denazification program. Bernstein claimed that too many Nazis remained in control of the banks. Clay refused to take tougher measures, and Bernstein resigned once it was clear nothing was going to be done.

James Martin chose to remain and fight for decartelization. Martin's position was undoubtedly weakened by the resignations of Nixon and Bernstein. Martin failed to take into account the strength of opposition from his own side. British and American bankers and industrialists openly worked with their Nazi partners until war broke out. Most of this continued clandestinely after the war. Investment by American corporations in Germany was staggering. In 1939, American corporations held controlling interests in German corporations worth at least $400 million.

Until mid-1946, Martin could have defeated Draper if two conditions had been satisfied. First, Martin needed information about German corporations in order to organize a breakup. Second, Americans had to control the Ruhr district in which the large steel and coal trusts were located. The Ruhr was under British control.

Draper's British counterpart was Sir Percy Mills, who arrived in Germany with no formal directive to remove Nazi businessmen. Mills was unrepentant about appointing former Nazis to control industries. He selected industrialists he had last met in 1939, who should have been under arrest, according to SHAEF.

A typical Mills appointment was Wilhelm Zangen, a Nazi Party member since 1927. Zangen employed slave labor at Mannesmann. Another appointee, Ernst Ponsgen, was selected to direct the steel industry. In 1941, Hitler awarded him with the Eagle Shield, the Nazis' highest economic award, for his "extraordinary services in arming Germany."

An estimated 100 industrialists and six major banks had controlled two-thirds of the German economy. This concentrated power made it easy for the Nazis to mobilize for war.

Martin's assessment was controversial. British and American politicians and military officials were divided about the relationship between the corporations and Nazi government.

Martin and Nixon arrived in Frankfurt at the end of April 1945. They discovered that while IG Farben's headquarters had escaped bombing, the records stored there were being dumped out of windows and burned in the courtyard. SHAEF decided to use the building as headquarters and ordered it cleared of refuse. To dismantle IG, documentary evidence was needed; those records were vital. The surviving records took two years to assemble.

The tribunal of judges on the IG Farben case in which 23 directors faced charges included Curtis Shake, Supreme Court Justice of Indiana; James Morris, Supreme Court Justice of North Dakota; and Paul Hebert, Law School Dean at Louisiana State University. From the beginning, the investigations into IG centered on two directors, Herman Schmitz and von Schnitzler. Nixon located von Schnitzler and he eventually faced trial after making several confessions and conflicting statements. Judge Curtis Shake ruled to ignore those statements in von Schnitzler's trial, claiming the accused was trying to help the Allies by telling them what he thought they wanted to hear.[104]

The decision outraged the prosecutor. The court acquitted all 23 accused of waging an aggressive war and 10 of all charges; the rest were found guilty of lesser charges. Only four were found guilty of employing slave labor. Judge Hebert wrote a dissenting opinion.

Prosecutor Josiah E. DuBois was especially irate with Judge Morris, who questioned the pace of the prosecutors' presentations and the relevancy of much of the evidence. Judge Merrell, an Indiana lawyer, was the alternate judge and agreed with Hebert. The sentences were extremely light, some being only a year and a half long. Hebert's dissenting opinion ran 114 pages. An excerpt follows:

I concur in the acquittals on charges of planning and preparation of aggressive war. I concur, though realizing that on the vast volume of credible evidence, a contrary result might as easily be reached by other triers of the facts who would be more inclined to draw the inferences usually warranted in criminal cases. The issues of fact are truly so close as to cause genuine concern whether or not justice has actually been done.

While concurring in the acquittals, I cannot agree with the factual conclusions of the Tribunal. I do not agree with the majority's conclusion that the evidence falls far short.

Utilization of [slave] labor [by Farben] was approved as a matter of corporate policy. To permit the corporate instrumentality to be used as a cloak to insulate the principal corporate officers who approved and authorized this course of action from any criminal responsibility therefore is a leniency in the application of principles of criminal responsibility which, in my opinion, is without any sound precedent under the most elementary concepts of criminal law... The evidence shows Farben's willing cooperation in the utilization of forced foreign workers, prisoners of war and concentration camp inmates as a matter of conscious corporate policy.[105]

In his criticisms of Morris, DuBois charged the judge was more preoccupied with the threat of Russian communism than in justice.

In June 1956, Draper returned to Germany from Washington with a new economic team. All were harsh critics of the punitive policies. Draper's Economic Division had not broken apart a single cartel. Among them was Lawrence Wilkinson, the new head of the industry branch. Wilkinson was sharply critical of decartelization, claiming it would hinder German economic recovery. He claimed that like denazification, it achieved nothing and only built resentment. Wilkinson aligned himself with Britain's Percy Mills. According to Martin, Wilkinson and Draper conspired with Mills to raise certain issues in the Four-Power discussions, which would give Draper a suitable pretext for seeking Washington's agreement to change American policy.[106]

In September 1946, Gen. Clay reprimanded Draper for telling visitors that denazification and decartelization were responsible for Germany's dire economic conditions. Clay's reprimand had no effect. On Nov. 13, Sir Cecil Weir cabled the American embassy in Washington that Draper assured him that it was just a matter of time before American policy fell into line with British policy. Weir soon replaced Mills. A month later, Willard Thorp, an Assistant Secretary of State, informed the British that the State Department was doing its best to keep the wild men in check. In addition, in November, the Republicans won control of both houses of Congress, tilting American policy in favor of big business and cartels. The Four-Powers law against cartels approved in January 1947 fit the lax British policy toward cartels.

Martin held off resigning until May 1947. Draper appointed Philip Hawkins, his son-in-law and a relative of the duPonts, as Martin's successor. On his return to Washington, Martin continued to fight for decartelization. He and some of the remaining members of the decartelization branch testified before the Fergusson Committee. Arrayed against him were those who produced largely false statistics to prove German industry was unused and any further breakups would force the American taxpayer to subsidize Germany. However, Fergusson's report ignored the easy choice and blamed Hawkins and Wilkinson for deliberately sabotaging the decartelization policy. The report recommended their firing.

In retaliation, Wilkinson fired Martin and one other member of the remaining decartelization team who testified against him, Alexander Sacks, who stated: "They have done whatever they could by innuendo and misstatement, to discredit a program, which they did not understand or like."[107] Wilkinson also dismissed 120 of the section's staff, leaving only 25 in Germany. Draper, promoted to Assistant Secretary of War, continued to dismantle the antitrust campaign against the Japanese multinational corporations.

While employed at Dillon and Read, Draper was in charge of the Thyssen account. He worked closely with the man in charge of this account at Brown Brothers and Harriman, Prescott Bush. (Gen. William Draper is not to be confused with Wickliffe Draper, founder of the Pioneer Fund, although they were related.) In 1932, William Draper financed the International Eugenics Congress. Doubts remain if Draper used his own money or funds from Thyssen or other corporate accounts. He helped select Ernst Ruaudin as chief of the world eugenics movement, who used his office to promote what he called Adolf Hitler's holy, national and international racial hygienic mission.

Prescott Bush shared Draper's view on eugenics. In fact, late in Prescott's first run for office in 1950, he was exposed as an activist in the old fascist eugenics movement, and Prescott lost his first bid for office as a result.

In 1958, Eisenhower appointed Draper as head of a committee to study the proper course for U.S. military aid to other countries. A year later, Draper changed the focus of the committee and recommended the U.S. government react to the threat of population explosion by planning to depopulate poorer countries. The growth of the world's nonwhite population, he proposed, should be regarded as dangerous to the national security of the United States. Eisenhower rejected the recommendation.

In the 1960s, Draper founded the Population Crisis Committee and the Draper Fund, and joined with the Rockefeller and duPont families to promote eugenics as population control. The Rockefeller family has been associated with eugenics since the turn of the century. In 1950–51, John Foster Dulles, chairperson of the Rockefeller Foundation, led John D. Rockefeller III on a series of world tours, focusing on the need to stop the expansion of the nonwhite populations. In November 1952, Dulles and Rockefeller set up the Population Council, with tens of millions of dollars from the Rockefeller family.

Gen. Draper served as George H. W. Bush's population expert. While serving in Congress, Bush chaired the Republican Task Force on Earth Resources and Population. He invited Professors William Shockley and Arthur Jensen to explain how allegedly runaway birthrates for African-Americans were down-breeding the American population. On Aug. 5, 1969, Bush summed up the testimony his black-inferiority advocates had given gave the task force. As a candidate for Congress in 1964, Bush campaigned against the passage of the Civil Rights Act.

Bush was U.S. ambassador to the United Nations in 1972, where his friends urged the U.S. Agency for International Development to make an official contract with the old Sterilization League of America. The league, which had changed its name twice, was now called the Association for Voluntary Surgical Contraception. The U.S. government began paying the old fascist group to sterilize nonwhites in foreign countries.

In Bush's 1988 campaign for president, Gen. Draper's son, William Draper III, served as co-chairman for finance. The younger Draper also was involved in United Nations depopulation efforts. Bush's Treasury Secretary was Nicholas Brady, Frederic Brandi's partner from 1954 until he replaced him in 1971. Brandi was the German who was Draper's co-director for Nazi investments and his personal contact with the Nazi German Steel Trust.

In 1958, Gen. Draper founded the first West Coast venture capital firm. His son continued in venture capital, founding additional firms in the 1960s. In 1981, Draper's son was appointed chairman of the U.S. Export-Import Bank, and four years later, was selected Administrator and CEO of the United Nations Development Program.

On July 19, 1948, Walter Lippmann summed up the sabotaging of the denazification plan:

> Though our German policy is in fact the determinant of our whole European policy, and will be decisive for peace or war, it is notorious that it has not been made by the President, or by Secretary Marshall, or by the so-called policymakers but General Clay and General Draper, and in the Pentagon ... .[108]

John McCloy

In 1949, John McCloy was appointed High Commissioner of Germany. In the 1920s, McCloy was a senior partner at Milbank and Tweed, whose most important client was Rockefeller's Chase National Bank. McCloy was not the first choice for high commissioner; it was Lewis Douglas, head of the Finance Division of the Control Council, but Douglas agreed to step aside in favor of McCloy. It appears nothing was left to chance in postwar Germany; governing was a family affair. The three most powerful men in postwar Germany: High Commissioner McCloy; Douglas, Head of the Finance Division of the Control Council; and Chancellor Konrad Adenauer were all brothers-in-law; each had married one of the daughters of the wealthy Fredrick Zinsser, a partner of JP Morgan. The Morgan empire controlled the fate of Germany.

What little justice was achieved under the Control Council and Gen. Clay was rapidly undone. Until 1940, McCloy had been a member of the law firm Cravath, de Gersdorff, Swaine, and Wood, which represented IG Farben and its affiliates. In 1940, Stimson appointed McCloy as Assistant Secretary of

War. At least three others from the same law firm turned up in the War Department. Alfred McCormick and Howard Peterson both served as Assistants to the Secretary. Richard Wilmer, commissioned as a colonel after the war started, served in a similar vein.[109] Peterson later served as the finance chairman of the Eisenhower National Committee for President, 1951–53.

McCloy was appointed by Henry Stimson, whom Roosevelt selected to head the War Department in 1940 in an attempt to make the war effort a bipartisan effort, and to blunt criticism of the coming war by the Republicans. One of Stimson's first acts on taking over the War Department was to appoint McCloy as Special Consultant to the War Department on German sabotage. Before 1940 ended, McCloy was appointed Assistant Secretary. As Secretary of State under Hoover, Stimson surely was aware of the cartels of IG Farben and how the Hoover administration aided their formation. McCloy spent most of the 1930s in Paris working on a sabotage case stemming from WWI. In 1936, he shared a box with Hitler at the Olympics.

In one of his first acts as Assistant Secretary of War, McCloy helped plan the internment of Japanese Americans. Once the war began, McCloy followed the American troops across North Africa. Such travel by an assistant cabinet secretary was highly unusual. However, McCloy's actions partly revealed his motivation. While in North Africa, McCloy helped forge an alliance with the Vichy France and Adm. Darlan.

McCloy continued to follow the advancing Allied troops across Europe and into Germany. In the closing days of the war in Europe, McCloy made one of his most noted decisions. After 16 planes bombed Rothenburg on March 31, McCloy ordered a halt to any further bombing of the city. McCloy said he wanted to preserve the medieval walled city. He also ordered Maj. Gen. Jacob L. Devers not to use artillery in taking Rothenburg. The city would have to be liberated by infantry alone, regardless of the cost in lives of GIs.

However, there are a few facts that McCloy and others have conveniently left out. For instance, just two days before the bombing, a German general with his division of troops left battered Nuremburg for Rothenburg. With the Nazi forces already stationed there, the general gave the order to defend the city to the last man. Also located in Rothenburg was Fa Mansfeld AG, a munitions maker that employed slave labor from Buchenwald.

By late 1943, the slaughter of Jews reached a feverish pace. The Allies were then in a position to bomb the concentration camps to stop the slaughter. John McCloy was almost solely responsible for blocking the bombing of the death camps. Allied planes were already bombing the industrial plants associated with Auschwitz. However, in written memos, McCloy advanced a banker's argument that the cost would be prohibitive. Such missions would risk men and planes with little damage to the Nazi war effort. McCloy even banned bombing the rail lines leading to the death camps.

In the late spring of 1944, Morgenthau was pressing the War Refuge Board to find an unused army base or some other haven to serve as a temporary home for a small group of mostly Jewish refugees from Italy. The question was put to McCloy, who responded gruffly that it was not the Army's business to take care of refugees. Outraged at McCloy's response, Morgenthau presented it at a cabinet meeting with Roosevelt. Roosevelt stated that under no circumstances should those people be turned away. Stimson dictated a memo after the cabinet meeting that someone had accused McCloy of being an oppressor of Jews. McCloy confronted Morgenthau on the charge. Morgenthau did not confess the remark directly, but happily exploited McCloy's discomfort. McCloy soon responded to Morgenthau that Fort Ontario in Oswego, N.Y., could accept 1,800 refugees.[110]

The average American at that time would probably have granted the Jews sanctuary in the United States if they had known the truth, but evidence of the Holocaust was kept from the average citizen, and even from Roosevelt. The State Department often waited for months before forwarding to Roosevelt memos with evidence of the slaughter. By the time FDR received them, it was too late to act on the intelligence. The prominent newspapers either did not print a single line about the Holocaust or, at best, relegated a few lines to the back pages. In 1943, an eyewitness described Auschwitz to Supreme Court Justice Felix Frankfurter, who was Jewish, but he refused to believe the report.

Western politicians were well aware of the massacre taking placing on the European continent. As early as 1941, military attachés were filing weekly body counts. The British were equally aware and firmly opposed to aiding the Jews. Britain's Foreign Office had a greater fear of the Nazis allowing the Jews to emigrate to the West. Undoubtedly, those fears could not be separated from British-ruled Palestine. Both Britain and the United States also were well aware of the views in the Arab world toward Jews, and the inseparable nature of a Jewish homeland and Mideast oil.

On March 23, 1943, Archbishop of Canterbury William Temple went before the House of Lords to plead for help for the Jews. In response, the British government proposed a conference with the United States on the refugee question. The British Foreign Office organized the Bermuda conference in such a way that no results were produced. The State Department refused to allow any Jewish organization to attend. Jewish leaders then sent a list of proposals.[111] Adolf Berle, Assistant Secretary of State, proposed setting up a temporary safe haven for up to 100,000 Jews in eastern Libya. The President's Advisory Committee on Political Refugees also sent a list of proposals, including using British Honduras as a sanctuary. The conference closed with no decisions reached.

Roosevelt desperately wanted to help the Jews, but was misled by his own intelligence advisers, opposed by the British and Soviets, and blackmailed by the Dulles brothers. Roosevelt was a man under secret siege, trying to avoid a rift among the Allies — a rift the Nazis would gladly exploit.

As early as 1939, the same shadow government of bigots in corporate America and their cronies in Congress led to the defeat of the Wagner-Rogers bill. Sen. Robert Wagner, a Democrat from New York, sponsored the bill. Wagner also introduced the Social Security legislation. On the House side, Edith Rogers, a Massachusetts Republican, sponsored a bill to allow 20,000 Jewish children to emigrate to the United States. In Congress, the bill was amended to require reduction of other Jewish immigration by the same amount. Out of frustration, both sponsors dropped support for the bill.

Similarly, President Truman met the same shadow government in the postwar years that blocked any attempt to allow Jewish refugees to emigrate to the United States and nearly blocked the United Nations creation of Israel. Leading the charge to block postwar Jewish emigration was none other than John McCloy.

While still in Europe as Assistant Secretary of War, McCloy helped block the executions of several Nazi war criminals. On Nov. 8, 1945, he delivered a speech before the Academy of Political Science in New York. McCloy blasted the "infamous" JCS 1067 directive and the Morgenthau Plan to prevent the decartelization of IG Farben, and decartelization in general. He belittled the operating capacity of Germany's industrial plant, although Allied bombing destroyed at most 20 percent of German industry.

Instead Congress was bombarded with a lobbying effort to go easy on Germany, and the agents of the Nazis proceeded according to the plan. Too many members of Congress were sympathetic to the Nazis. Without exception, they were all either conservative Dixiecrats or Republicans. Nebraska Sen. Kenneth Wherry, Mississippi Democrat James Eastland and Indiana Republican Homer Capehart were just some of many who stood up and denounced the decartelization of Germany. Capehart was perhaps one of the more vicious. In his speech before the Senate, he blamed Morganthau — not the Nazis — for the mass starvation of the German people. He claimed the technique of hate had earned both Morgenthau and Bernard Bernstein the title of America's Himmler.[112]

While Gen. Clay reduced the sentences of many of the war criminals, it was the High Commissioner of Germany, John McCloy, who threw open the doors of Landsberg prison. He blocked some executions of war criminals even before arriving in Germany.

Both Clay and McCloy acted with their respective advisory committees. Advising Clay was the Simpson Commission: Judge Edward Leroy van Roden of Delaware County, Pennsylvania, and Justice Gordon Simpson of the Texas Supreme Court. The committee was appointed after Lt. Col. Willis N. Everett Jr., defense counsel for the 74 defendants charged in the Malmedy massacre, petitioned the U.S. Supreme Court, claiming they had not received a fair trial. The Supreme Court ruled that it did not have jurisdiction, but Everett's petition forced Secretary of War Royall to appoint the commission. The only evidence the Simpson Commission relied on came from the defendants and German clergy who wer Nazi collaborators working to free all war criminals.

Evidence the Simpson Commission gathered regarding torture of prisoners was implausible at best. More often than not, it did not bear up to examination. In one case, the witness said he saw guards torturing another prisoner. However, the window to the torture chamber was not visible from where the prisoner said he was.

Van Roden's ludicrous claims of torture were the beginning of the revisionist movement about the Holocaust. To be fair, there were minor incidents of abuse of prisoners, but nothing to justify van Roden's bombastic claims. The Malmedy trials marked an extremely critical turning point in history. After the Malmedy trials, the factions sympathetic to the Nazis were clearly in control in both Germany and the United States. Further, efforts to disrupt the trials were coordinated in both countries.

The charges raised by the Simpson Commission were without merit. The Commission's attempt to derail justice is summed up in the words of van Roden:

> My conclusion is that the entire program of War Crimes Trials, either by International Courts, the members of which comprise those of the victorious nations, or by Military Courts of a single victor nation is basically without legal or moral authority... The fact remains that the victor nations in World War II, while still at fever heat of hatred for an enemy nation, found patriots of the enemy nation guilty for doing their patriotic duty. This is patently unlawful and immoral. One of the most shameful incidents connected with the War Crimes Trials prosecutions has to do with the investigations and the preparation of the cases for trial. The records of trials which our Commission examined disclosed that a great majority of the official investigators, employed by the United States Government to secure evidence and to locate defendants, were persons with a preconceived dislike for these enemy aliens, and their conduct was such that they resorted to a number of illegal, unfair, and cruel methods and duress to secure confessions of guilt and to secure accusations by defendants against other defendants. In fact, in the Malmedy case, the only evidence before the court, upon which the convictions and sentences were based, consisted of the statements and testimony of the defendants themselves. The testimony of one defendant against another was secured by subterfuge, false promises of immunity, and by mock trials and threats.[113]

Judge van Roden's words belie his objectivity. He disagreed fully with the premise of the war crimes trials. Also, he sought to confer on the defendants the legal rights present in civil cases. Neither Churchill nor Roosevelt intended the trials to be anything more than a military tribunal in which civilian rights need not apply fully. On returning to Texas, Simpson was offered the job of vice president and general counsel of the General American Oil Co.

An obstacle to justice at Nuremberg was the quality of the judges and their own political motives. One Nuremberg judge was Robert Maguire of Oregon. In the fall of 1949, Maguire decided to run for Oregon's Supreme Court. In November 1949, the *American Bar Association Journal* published a speech delivered by Maguire, "The Unknown Art of Making Peace: Are We Sowing the Seeds of WWIII?" In the speech, Maguire argued against further trials.[114] His speech was an effort to appease the right wing of the Republican Party in Oregon to strengthen his election chances.

McCloy was advised by the Peck Commission: David Peck, a judge in the New York Appellate Division; Fredrick Moran, chairman of the New York Board of Parole; and Brig. Gen. Conrad Snow. The Peck Commission was only authorized to reduce sentences, not to challenge the legal decision of guilt. While the Simpson Commission was limited to reviewing the trials held at Dachau, the Peck Commission was limited to the trials at Nuremberg.

It was not until after McCloy's appointment as High Commissioner that he opened the doors of Landsberg Prison. McCloy insisted until his death that releasing the war criminals was not politically motivated, but nothing could be further from the truth.

The industrialists' trial, once considered of equal importance to the main Nuremberg Trial, ended because the Soviets blockaded Berlin. Even as the convicted directors of Krupp and IG Farben were being taken to Landsberg, they knew there was little prospect of serving their sentences. Germans and the fascists in America believed that they were just the innocent victims of left-wing fanatics. The Nazis' allies in the United States were successful in smearing the trial as such. In Landsberg, the prisoners settled into a comfortable routine. Flick controlled his empire through weekly visits from his lawyers and business associates. He chose Hermann Abs as his financial adviser. Abs, already "rehabilitated" by Gen. Clay, headed the Reconstruction Loan Corp.

When McCloy arrived as High Commissioner, there already was a concerted drive to rebuild German industry as a bulwark against the Soviets. Abs informed McCloy that the key to Germany's recovery and cooperation was the release of the industrialists from Landsberg. McCloy also was told the same by Karl Blessing, a war criminal whom Allen Dulles saved. In fact, McCloy could have been told that by any German citizen.[115]

On Aug. 28, 1950, McCloy received the recommendations of the Peck Commission. The commission, appointed on March 20, 1950, was controversial from the beginning; indeed, under various state laws, it was illegal. Some of the cases the commission examined had already been reviewed three times. Under most state laws, it was illegal to appoint a second appellate court to reexamine the findings of a primary appellate court. Nor would an appellate court have the authority to pardon criminals; it would be limited to reducing the sentence or commuting death sentences to life in prison, but the Peck Commission had the power to grant pardons.

The Peck Commission reported it had examined the judgments on all the prisoners, and interviewed them and their lawyers. While that sounded reasonable enough to the inexperienced, it was not.

Even in a clemency hearing in front of a governor, the views of the district attorney and trial judge are presented. Yet, not a single prosecutor or judge from the tribunals was consulted. Nor had the Peck Commission opened a single page of the transcripts and documentary evidence. In fact, the crates of transcripts and evidence available to the commission were never opened. The only materials from the trials that were reviewed were the verdicts, which spanned 3,000 pages. Reviewing all the material from the trials was an impossible task in the time McCloy allotted the Peck Commission. Transcripts, excluding briefs and documents, spanned some 330,000 pages. At the rate of 1,200 words a minute, a speed-reader would need 17 months to get through the Nuremberg transcripts.[116]

In reality, the Peck Commission served as nothing more than a politically motivated blue-ribbon panel. McCloy used the commission's recommendations as an excuse to justify freeing war criminals.

Both the Simpson and Peck commissions were politically motivated. The Nazis were counting on their agents and sympathizers in other countries, including the United States, to do their bidding after the war. The conservative faction of Congress did not disappoint them. By the end of the 1940s, conservative Republicans succeeded in perpetrating the myth that the Nuremberg war criminals were victims of Roosevelt. By the end of the decade, many people came to accept that myth. This conservative faction was roused to action by the Malmedy Trial and the false charges made by Nazis in Germany of torture and brutality. Included in this faction were John Rankin; Harold Knutsen, the pro-fascist Minnesota congressmen; Francis Case, Republican representative from South Dakota; and John Taber, Republican representative from New York.

Freeing Krupp

Republican Sen. William "Wild Bill" Langer from North Dakota portrays the congressional politics behind the Simpson and Peck commissions. His election to the Senate in 1940 reflects the beginning of a shift to conservatism and the end of New Deal liberalism. However, Langer's seating in the Senate was not smooth.

Before running for the Senate, Langer served twice as governor for North Dakota. In his first campaign, Langer ran as the candidate for the Nonpartisan League. He had been a member of the Progressive Republicans. He made enemies within the Republican Party with Gerald Nye and William Lemke. Nonetheless, Langer received the nomination and was elected to the governor's mansion in 1932. His opponent's defense of the policies of the failed Hoover administration contributed to Langer's easy victory. Langer then cleaned out the executive departments and appointed people loyal to him.

He also openly promoted the newspaper, the *Leader.* A subscription to the *Leader* cost the subscriber 5 percent of his state pay. Langer viewed this as a legitimate way to raise campaign funds. In 1934, the court indicted Langer for soliciting and collecting money for political purposes from federal employees, and for conspiring to obstruct the orderly operation of an act of Congress. On June 17, 1934, the court found Langer guilty and sentenced him to 18 months in prison and fined him $10,000. On July 17, the North Dakota Supreme Court removed Langer from office for his felony. On May 7, 1935, the Federal Circuit Court of Appeals reversed the conviction and ordered a new trial. The first conspiracy trial resulted in a hung jury. A perjury trial in December found Langer not guilty. A second conspiracy trial, also held in December, settled the issue by finding Langer not guilty. In 1936, failing to win the Nonpartisan League endorsement, Langer ran as an independent and regained the governor's office.

More conspiracies and corruption marked Langer's second term. For example, Langer directed the State Mill and Elevator to pay 35 cents a bushel over the market price, while also appropriating nearly $6 million for general relief. Three of Langer's close friends were found buying county bonds at a discount price and selling them back to the Bank of North Dakota at full value. In 1938, the State Board of Equalization reduced the assessment on property owned by the Great Northern Railroad by $3 million. It was then revealed that an attorney for the railroad bought $25,000 of worthless stocks from Langer and never asked for their delivery. In Langer's second term, the conspiracy and corruption stories contributed to his defeat by Gerald Nye in the Republican primary.

Yet Langer was successful in his bid for the U.S. Senate in 1940. Although he had won the election, his enemies were determined not to allow him to take his seat. Langer appeared to take the oath of office on Jan. 3, 1941, but the Senate had a petition refusing to seat him. The matter was turned over to the Senate Committee on Privileges and Elections. The committee listened to much testimony, some of it damaging, about Langer's conduct. Langer was forced to admit he paid the son of the judge who presided at his second and third trials in 1935. The committee recommended 13–3 that Langer not be seated.[117]

Reflecting the shift toward conservatism, the full Senate voted to seat Langer by a vote of 52–30. He held the seat until his death in 1959. While the Democrats controlled the 77th Congress by a 66–28 margin, the vote seating Langer reflects how control of the Senate was largely in the hands of an alliance of Republicans and conservative Dixiecrats.

Embarking on his Senate career, Langer adopted a strict isolationist policy. He opposed Lend-Lease extending the draft; the NATO alliance; and formation of the United Nations. Langer did vote to declare war after Pearl Harbor.

Winston Churchill was a frequent object of Langer's scorn. In March 1949, while Churchill was touring the United States, Langer charged that Churchill had fought against the United States in the Spanish-American War. His colleagues in the Senate rebuked him when Tom Connally of Texas noted that the historical record showed Churchill was never in Cuba. In 1951, before a visit by Churchill, Langer telegraphed the pastor of Boston's Old North Church to request that two lanterns be placed in the belfry to warn Americans the British were coming.

While in the Senate, Langer served on the Judiciary Committee from 1953 to 1955, during one of America's darkest hours, at the height of McCarthyism. Langer was one of only 22 senators who voted against censoring McCarthy.

On Dec. 18, 1950, Langer blasted the Nuremberg Trials in the Senate:

These war-trials were decided on in Moscow and they are carried on under Moscow principles. These trials were essentially the same as the mass trials held in the 1930s by Stalin when Vyshinsky used treason trials to liquidate his internal enemies. At Nuremberg the Communist used war crimes trials to liquidate their external enemies. It is the Communist avowed purpose to destroy the Western World which is based on property rights.[118]

Lumping Nuremberg together with property rights was a new tack. Whether Langer was sympathetic to the Nazi movement or just a useful stooge, his actions were in line with the Nazi strategy to promote strife between the United States and the USSR.

After the war, one of the most influential Nazi agitators in the United States was Walter Becher, an anti-communist "refugee leader" from the Hitler regime. Becher joined the Nazi Party in 1931 and became an editor of *Die Zeit,* a Nazi propaganda sheet. During the war, Becher worked for Goebbels' propaganda ministry as a war correspondent.

Becher founded a pro-Nazi newspaper in Germany and sought out influence in Washington. Two of his early contacts in the Senate were McCarthy and William Jenner. Other early supporters were Francis Walter, B. Carroll Reece, Albert Bosch and Walter Judd.

His scheme was simple; as a staunch leader in the anti-communist movement in Germany, he could gain the support of leading politicians in the United States, and his prestige and stature would grow enormously at home. Among those who sent letters of support to Becher were William Langer, Prescott Bush, Strom Thurmond, Thomas Dodd, Robert Byrd, Stuart Symington, Herbert Hoover and retired U.S. Generals del Valle, Willoughby and Wedemeyer. All three generals were involved with many hard-right groups, including the lunatic fringe.

In all, Becher claimed support from more than 150 members of Congress. The list of his supporters is a virtual roster of the hard right of the 1950s. Republican Sen. William Jenner from Indiana chaired the Senate's Internal Security Committee, the counterpart to the House Un-American Activities Committee. In the 1952 presidential campaign, he led the attack on the Truman administration, charging George Marshall was soft on communism. Rep. Francis Walter, D-Pennsylvania, was a member of the House Un-American Activities. Walter accepted money from Wickliffe Draper. Republican B. Carroll Reece from Tennessee headed a committee looking into the Ford and Rockefeller foundations as agents spreading communism. Rep. Walter Judd, R-Minnesota, was a principal in the Christian Anti-Communism Crusade. Judd also was a member of the Committee for One Million and the first U.S. branch of the World Anti-Communist League, a haven for former Nazis which keeps a close relationship with Rev. Sun Myung Moon.

In 1955, Becher decided to install a permanent aide in Washington. His choice was Richard Sallet, a former Nazi diplomat who was an expert on America. Captured Nazi documents reveal his expertise. Several hundred pages testify to his success in launching an anti-Semitic campaign in the 1930s. Sallet had help from the Republican Party, which paid for broadcasts by known Nazis in New York State. Sallet also had a more limited success in undermining Americans' confidence in Roosevelt.[119]

John Grombach headed another Nazi-infested organization with close ties to this group. Grombach, a former G2 or military intelligence officer, recruited former Nazi SS officers, Hungarian Axis Quislings and Russian nationalists. His network of former Nazis produced intelligence offerings for the State

Department, the CIA and corporations. Grombach's organization originally began as a G2 operation to rival the CIA, but soon evolved beyond that. In addition to funding from the U.S. government, he received funds from Philips of the Netherlands and its American affiliate, Philips North America. One of Grombach's prized assets was Karl Wolff, a major war criminal.

Grombach had visions of grandeur with an eye on becoming Director of the CIA. High on his list of political targets were those who carried out President Truman's containment policy. Grombach viewed people such as George Kennan and Charles Bohlen as too soft on communism. He found ready allies in McCarthy and Jenner. By the 1950s, Grombach and his network of Nazis specialized in gathering dirt. He would then leak the smears to his political allies, the chief beneficiary being Joe McCarthy.

This brief look at the congressional politics of the conservatives and Republicans behind the Simpson and Peck committees leads to three significant conclusions.

First, the release of the war criminals was politically motivated by those previously sympathetic to the Nazis. Second, and more importantly, it confirms the Nazi plan to carry on the war after the hostilities ended on the battlefield. Captured documents revealed the Nazis were planning to use their sympathizers after the war to protect them and to reestablish fascism.

Finally, it proves the Cold War was largely due to Nazi intrigue. Similarly, it confirms the Nazi plans in the captured documents were well thought out, using communism as a ploy to ease peace terms and other burdens on Germany. That same faction of conservatives was the most vocal of the Nazi sympathizers and Cold War Warriors in Congress. Intertwining of the Cold War with Nazi intrigue extended well into the 1960s.

Originally, there were two trials planned for Nuremberg, both of equal importance and stature at that time. The first trial was of top Nazi officials; second was of the industrialists. The industrialists' trial at Nuremberg was canceled and held in the American zone. By the end of the first trial, chief American Prosecutor Robert Jackson succumbed to the American disease of an irrational fear of communism and spoke out against a second trial:

> A trial in which industrialists are singled out may give the impression that they are being prosecuted merely because they are industrialists. This is more likely since we would be associated in prosecuting them with the Soviet communist and the French leftists... I have some misgivings as to whether a long public attack concentrated on private industry would not tend to discourage industrial cooperation with our government in maintaining its defense in the future while not at all weakening the Soviet position, since they do not rely on private enterprise.[120]

Jackson's words were the final nail in the coffin of Roosevelt's pledge to bring the Nazis and those who aided them to justice. American corporations could now breathe easily. There would be no extended trial of Nazi industrialists to expose them.

Sen. Langer's committee forced Gen. Clay to stop the execution of all death sentences. While conservatives in the United States succeeded in swaying American opinion to view war criminals as victims of Roosevelt, it was clear by 1950 that West Germans also rejected the validity of the trials. Leading the cause of war criminals in Germany were the German Catholic and Protestant churches. Bishop Fargo Muench went so far as to call for a general amnesty.[121] Langer compared the Nuremberg Trials to the purges by Stalin.

The industrialists were among McCloy's first beneficiaries. He arrived in Germany in 1949 and, by mid-1950, the Peck Commission completed its review. On Jan. 31, 1951, *Landsberg: A Documentary Report*, with statements by McCloy and the Peck and Simpson commissions, was made public. Following the commission's recommendation, McCloy freed a third of the inmates at Landsberg. In the stroke of a pen, McCloy freed the lawyers, executives and industrialists convicted in the IG Farben, Flick and Krupp trials. Those most responsible for building the Third Reich on the backs of slave labor were now free.

McCloy was hardly in a position to grant a general amnesty after President Truman spoke in January 1951. The State Department's legal adviser, John Raymond, drafted a memo on war crimes for Truman that was a wholesale reaffirmation of the original Nuremberg and Dachau trials, and an unequivocal argument against amnesty.

The release of Krupp proved to be the most controversial. Once again, background events are important in understanding the event. The United States was already embroiled in the Korean War. A new war scare was spreading like wildfire across the American homeland. Fears of a Soviet invasion of Europe were pervasive. A debate about the vulnerability of Europe opened in Congress. Sen. Taft charged that President Truman already usurped his authority by defending Korea and had no right to increase American troop strength in Europe. Former President Herbert Hoover argued it would be pointless to try to defend Europe. News from Korea was dismal. UN forces were taking a terrible beating at the hands of the Red Chinese. MacArthur asked whether Washington considered the possibility of being driven out of Korea. The day McCloy signed the release of the industrialists, Frankfurt radio was reporting the plight of a United States-French combat regiment trapped 12 miles behind enemy lines north of Yoju.[122]

In the trial of Krupp, the prosecution decided to try Alfried and not his father, Gustav. The prosecution judged Gustav too sick to endure the rigors of a trial. After his conviction, Alfried retained the services of an American attorney, Earl Carroll. Carroll's job was to free Krupp and get his property restored. Rumors reported Carroll was to get 5 percent of everything he could recover, roughly $25 million. Some disputed that his fee was that high, but it was very handsome, so much so that once Krupp was freed, Carroll reportedly retired.

Carroll's argument for Krupp's release was based on three false assumptions. First he argued that Alfried held a junior position at the Krupp firm. Second, that under American law, assets could only be forfeited if they had been acquired illegally, which was not the case with Krupp's prewar assets. Finally, Carroll argued that Krupp was a victim of discrimination because he was the only war criminal whose assets were confiscated.

The answering brief responded to all three claims. The first claim was proven false by a 1943 interfirm circular declaring Alfried directed the entire enterprise. The second pointed out that the Nuremberg Trials acted under the law of the Four-Power coalition and not American law. The four-power agreement specified the forfeiture of assets. Finally, Krupp was not the only industrialist whose assets were confiscated. The brief noted that IG Farben was a corporation and not solely owned like the Krupp firm, and forfeiture would penalize the stockholders for the crimes of the management.[123]

Nevertheless, by freeing Krupp and returning his seized assets, McCloy justified his position by first claiming that Alfried was a playboy with no real authority in the firm. Second, McCloy portrayed Alfried's Nazi connections as indiscriminate youthful distractions. However, the record is clear that Alfried was more than a youthful playboy who hung around with a bad crowd.

Krupp was the largest employer of slave labor in Nazi Germany. By 1941, Germany faced a severe labor shortage, compounded by Hitler's dictate against employing women. Both Britain and the United States filled many jobs in their defense factories with women. American housewives turned out in droves to work in West Coast aircraft plants in response to the famed Rosie the Riveter posters. More than 3 million American women, many in their teens, worked in war-related jobs. In England, more than 2 million women worked in munitions factories. However, in Germany, fewer than 200,000 women were employed, mainly as cooks and maids. It was not until July 1944 that Hitler reversed his ban on employing women. By then, it was too late and Allied bombing disrupted the registration.

After Albert Speer turned over his labor responsibilities to Fritz Sauckel, manhunts became coordinated and routine in the occupied territories. The Nazis rounded up men and women and transported them back to the fatherland as slave laborers. Krupp was one of the most persistent customers of the new labor czar. At Nuremberg, Brig. Gen. Walter Schieber conceded that Krupp negotiated directly with the SS for concentration camp inmates.[124]

Krupp's attorneys argued Alfried had no role in enslaving foreign civilians. While in theory the roundups were official acts of the Nazi government, once concluded, industrialists were invited to take their share. Some refused, but there is no record of Krupp turning down the offer. Alfried's files were full of incriminating evidence. In the third year of the war, his files revealed the slave labor was reaching Essen two months, sometimes three months, after requisitioned. Krupp sent three executives to lodge formal protests about the dealy with the Wehrmacht, the Gestapo and the SS. Alfried appointed Heinrich Lehmann as his liaison with the German Labor Front, and as director of labor procurement and recruiting. With cooperating authorities, Lehmann drafted entire factories in France. In Holland, Lehmann drafted 30,000 ironworkers and shipwrights, many of whom were sent to Germany in chains when they showed reluctance.

Often, Alfried would complain about the quality of workers he received. In a file note from 1942 he said:

> I am under the impression that the better Russian workers are at this time being chosen for works in central and eastern Germany. We really get the rejects only. Just now 600 Russians consisting of 450 women and 150 juveniles arrived.[125]

Any complaint from Krupp drew instant attention in Berlin. On July 8, a frantic subordinate sent a report to Speer denying that Krupp was getting low-grade slaves.

> The requirements of the firm Fried Krupp A.G. for replacement for German workers drafted into the armed forces have been met currently and in time. The complaints of the Krupp firm about allegedly insufficient labor allocations are unfounded. I have once again asked Sauckel to send Krupp 3,000 to 4,000 more workers in entire convoys from the Russian civilian workers presently arriving in Service Command VI.[126]

The quotes above show that Krupp was somewhat of an antagonist, demanding more and better slaves, once again destroying the myth the Nazi Party was all-powerful. It was not the party that held the power; it was the moneyed industrialists behind the party who were all-powerful.

An excellent example was the "Jewish problem." The Nazi Party and top officials were committed to the Endlösung, the Final Solution or liquidation, and vehemently opposed enslaving the Jews. By 1942, the SS began questioning the Final Solution. It was working, but cost of ammunition was shocking and hurt the war effort. Himmler then began experimenting with gas vans. An April 25, 1942 memorandum from the Krupp headquarters noted that to produce 80 new SIGs (heavy infantry guns), expansion was needed. Alfried recommended manufacturing in the concentration camp in Sudetenland.

Four weeks later, Alfried put the question to Hitler. In his appeal to Hitler, Krupp affirmed his belief that every party member was in favor of liquidating Jews, Gypsies, anti-Nazi criminals and antisocials. However, Krupp believed they should contribute something to the fatherland before being exterminated. Properly driven, each could contribute a lifetime of work in months. Hitler hesitated, but Krupp persisted. Soon Krupp had the solution. The answer was merely economics or bribery. Krupp proposed paying the SS four marks a day for each inmate, from which seven-tenths of a mark would be deducted for food. Opposition to his new proposal vanished overnight. In September, Hitler signed the order approving the use of Jewish slave labor.

Krupp anticipated Hitler's order of Sept. 18 and teletyped a message to Sauckel's Berlin office, notifying the labor director that Krupp was ready to employ between 1,050 and 1,100 Jewish workers. In his teletype, Krupp requested workers with specific skills in metalworking. Krupp had an immediate objective: producing fuses. The Sudetenland camp was too small for mass production, so Krupp proposed to start production at Auschwitz. Assured that Auschwitz would have ample labor supplies, Krupp executives approved 2 million marks for the project.

Krupp's project was delayed largely because of the commandant's view that the work should be done by Germans. Krupp contacted Obersturmfuhrer Sommer, a junior SS officer stationed in Speer's office. Krupp requested a record of all skilled Jews, selected 500 and demanded immediate action.[127]

As the war continued and Alfried rose in power, the use of slave labor by Krupp increased. By the end of the war, Krupp employed nearly 100,000 slaves in more than 100 factories. Slaves were beaten and tortured regularly in Krupp's factories. The slightest infraction could bring on a life-threatening beating. Shelter and food for the inmates employed by Krupp was inadequate at best. Many inmates were forced to sleep on the ground, unprotected from the elements. The cruelty and barbaric treatment of the slave laborers in Krupp's camps was unsurpassed anywhere in Germany. In fact, Gen. Adolf Westhoff of the OKW, the Supreme Command of the German Armed Forces, stated that Krupp's treatment of Russian prisoners did not meet with the Wehrmacht's approval.

While there is no evidence of Krupp ordering his slaves beaten or tortured, there also is no evidence he discouraged it. There is evidence that Krupp withheld prisoners' food allotment, and proof that Alfried was aware of the beatings and torture of slaves, making him a full accomplice.

Drexel Sprecher, a prominent Washington attorney, observed the Nuremberg Trials and decided that Krupp's treatment of slave labor was far worse than any other firm, including IG Farben. Sprecher reasoned the cause lay in Krupp's one-person rule. Alfried's power was absolute.

Slavery was the most serious charge lodged against Krupp, but Krupp was equally guilty of plunder. Before the Allied invasion of North Africa, Krupp ruled a vast empire stretching from the Ukraine to the Atlantic, and from the Mediterranean to the North Sea. Most of this empire was procured from their original owners in the occupied lands. Alfried Krupp toured Europe in a Luftwaffe fighter looking for plants to add to his empire. Using subterfuge, the plants were technically purchased. The reality was the plants had been signed over to Krupp under duress and threats of death from the Nazis.

One such company was the Elmag factories in Alsace. The plants on three sites were seized and transferred to Krupp under the laws covering enemy property. What sets the Elmag factories apart from the hundreds of other looted plants were the actions taken by the workers following the Allied invasion of Normandy. Once the Allies established beachheads at Normandy, workers started to disappear into the hills at an alarming rate, to await liberation. Krupp sent roughly 60 slave laborers to build a camp for 1,250 more slaves. The workers at Elmag were so alarmed over the treatment of the slaves, they openly protested and threatened to strike. At Nuremberg, Ernst Wirtz, head of the concentration camp, was sentenced to eight years. As the Allies closed in on Alsace, Krupp removed the slave laborers and simply moved the factories to Bavaria.[128]

The actions of the workers at Elmag are noteworthy. Even under the barbaric rule of the Nazis, some men stood up and refused to be crushed by the yoke of fascist despots. Their defiance should be remembered and praised. Their actions point to the guilt of those who simply shrugged off Nazi atrocities. Cowards should have no peace.

Alfried's father, Gustav Krupp, initially opposed Hitler, but Alfried was an early supporter of Hitler and the Nazi Party. He joined the party and the SS in 1931. Throughout the 1930s, Alfried remained a loyal contributor. In the SS, he rose to the rank of colonel. McCloy's portrayal of Alfried as an indiscriminate youth was a transparent smoke screen. Born a year after Adolf Eichmann, Alfried was part of the generation that included Martin Bormann, Heinrich Himmler and Reinhard Heydrich.

Thus, it should be no surprise McCloy's pardons were met with much controversy in the United States and Great Britain. Nevertheless, this Nazi war criminal would receive an even greater reward in the span of 10 short years after walking out of Landsberg Prison. At the end of that decade, Krupp's industrial empire was the 12th largest firm in the world – and the only one of them solely owned.

"Good" Nazis like Krupp could count on being rewarded. However, the Jewish victims of Nazi war criminals could count on receiving nothing or, at best, a meager settlement for their slave labor. In 1959, under the threat of a lawsuit by an American lawyer representing Jewish survivors of the Krupp camps, Krupp announced a voluntary settlement. A fund setting aside 4 million marks would pay each survivor $750 for their ordeal. The payment was soon cut to $500 when more survivors were found than Krupp anticipated.[129] The fund ran out of money before all survivors received their meager payments.

Cover Up

Friedrich Flick was another who walked out of Landsberg Prison with Krupp. At Nuremberg, Flick was found guilty of one count of using slave labor. Generally, the judges at Nuremberg were poorly qualified and hostile to the prosecution, especially in the trials of the industrialists. Three judges ruled the director and owner of a corporation should not be held accountable for slavery and looting by his companies, unless the prosecution could prove that he personally ordered each particular crime to be carried out. This wrongful ruling allowed a defense of necessity, the corporate equivalent of acting under orders.

Amazingly, with the legal precedent set by this ruling, a 19-year-old soldier could be found guilty of war crimes for following orders, but the head of a corporation employing thousands of slaves could not.

There were other factors that contributed to such a bad decision. First, the judges brought their own prejudices to Germany. The sad state of U.S. corporate law left corporate directors and owners virtually immune from prosecution, regardless of the severity of the crime. Very few corporate executives in the United States have ever been tried for the death of an employee or consumer of the product, regardless of the severity of the crime or the complicity of the executive. The judges obviously were affected by such habits.

Second, a state of panic was already emerging over the evils of communism. The emerging fears forced the prosecution to argue the cases as crimes of individuals and not as attacks on capitalism to avoid charges of socialism and communism.

Like Krupp, Flick was a steel and coal baron who employed roughly 48,000 slave laborers from the concentration camps. An estimated 80 percent of these workers died. From 1929–32, Flick gave money to several right-wing parties, including 50,000 Reichmarks to the Nazis. He joined Himmler's Circle in 1935 and the Nazi Party in 1937. From 1936 to 1944, Flick contributed 100,000 Reichmarks annually to Himmler's Circle.

On his release, Flick immediately set about rebuilding his empire. By 1955, he owned more than 100 corporations, including a 40 percent share of Daimler-Benz AG. He was reportedly the richest man in Germany, the fifth wealthiest in the world. On his death in 1972, Flick left over $1 billion to his son. The slave laborers have yet to receive any compensation from Flick.

While rebuilding his empire, Flick cultivated and rebuilt his political connections. That influence extends to the present. In 1975, his son sold a 29 percent share in Daimler Benz, incurring a huge capital gain, taxable under German law unless the profit were reinvested before the end of 1978 in projects judged by the government to be "especially beneficial to the national economy." Although the son invested more than half the money in the United States, buying a 29 percent share in Grace Chemical, he was granted tax-exempt status.

One of the beneficiaries of Flick's empire was the Christian Democratic Party and German Chancellor Helmut Kohl. Former Nazis, including Flick, contributed handsomely to the Christian Democrats after the war. In 1972, the old leader of the Christian Democrats, Rainer Barzel, stepped down. After leaving politics, Barzel accepted a lucrative post at a Frankfurt law firm. Barzel managed to earn $700,000 in legal fees from the Flick Group for what *Der Spiegel* depicted as phantom services. Barzel's choice for a successor was none other than Helmut Kohl. Kohl admitted to accepting payments totaling $53,000 from the Flick group from 1977 to 1979. The German press reports the sums were four times larger. If the Allies had not relented in the 4Ds program, Kohl might never have come to power.

There is no question that Flick was a Nazi war criminal who exerted his influence soon after leaving prison on the policies of Germany's postwar government. There is no question of his guilt in employing slave labor, or that he refused to pay restitution to the victims of his slave labor camps. Yet within 10 years of the war's end, he was a behind-the-scenes force in German politics. One can only wonder who really won the war.

Flick's connections went far beyond the new German government, extending as far as the White House through the Bush family. On March 19, 1934 the *New York Times* reported that the Polish government was fighting American and German stockholders who controlled the Upper Silesian Coal and Steel Co., accusing the company of mismanagement, excessive borrowing, fictitious bookkeeping and gambling in securities. In December, the Polish government issued warrants for several directors accused of tax evasion. The directors accused were German, and they fled to Germany for sanctuary. They were then replaced with Polish directors. Flick retaliated by restricting credits until the new Polish directors were unable to pay the workers regularly. The *Times* noted Flick owned two-thirds of the company's stock; U.S. interests owned the other third.

The owner of the U.S. interests was none other than the Harriman Fifteen Corp. President of this American corporation was George Walker, Prescott Bush's father-in-law. The sole directors of Harriman Fifteen were Prescott Bush and Averell Harriman. Harriman also served as chairman of Consolidated Silesian Steel Corp. The holdings of Brown Brothers Harriman in Consolidated Silesian were a small part of a larger partnership between Brown Brothers Harriman and the German Steel Trust. In the 1920s, the relationship between Brown Brothers Harriman and the German Steel Trust was established through Thyssen. Flick was a major co-owner of the trust. Before 1932, the German Steel Trust also was one of the most generous donors to Hitler, the SS and SA, and it figured prominently in his appointment as chancellor. Prescott Bush and George Walker supervised the partnership between the Trust and Brown Brothers Harriman. This relationship extended to Union Bank, which made Prescott and Walker bankers for the Trust. The U.S. government seized control of Union Banking from Prescott Bush during the war.

The relationship of Brown Brothers Harriman with the German Steel Trust extended across the sea to England. Brown Brothers was an English firm that had merged with Harriman's firm after the stock market crash of 1929. In England, it continued to operate under the traditional name of Brown Shipley. The company's tradition served it well in supporting Hitler. During the Civil War, Brown Brothers were renowned for their ships running the blockade and transporting cotton from the South to England.

In 1931, the Governor of the Bank of England was Montagu Collet Norman, grandson of the boss of Brown Brothers during the Civil War. Norman was known as the most avid of Hitler's supporters within British ruling circles. When Montagu of the Bank of England visited New York, he always stayed at the home of his close friend, Prescott Bush. The Bush family dealings with the Nazis were extensive. The U.S. Property Custodian seized 23 corporations from Prescott Bush during and after the war for trading with the enemy. Much of the Bush wealth came from the Nazis.

The Allies never charged Thyssen with war crimes at Nuremberg. However, a German court later found him guilty and seized 15 percent of his empire for reparations to the slave laborers he employed during the war. By the 1970s, Thyssen had reassembled a considerable empire spanning the globe. In the United States, Thyssen Inc., was headquartered at 1114 in the W.R. Grace & Co., building.

Another holding of Thyssen's was Indian Head at 1200 Avenue of the Americas, New York City. Indian Head was a wide-ranging conglomerate with 42 plants in the United States and annual sales of $604 million. One holding of Indian Head was Peerless Pumps, bought in 1970. Another was Budd Manufacturing, purchased for $275 million in cash. By buying in cash, there were no SEC reports to file.

Indeed, neither Thyssen Inc., nor Indian Head are required to file SEC reports because they are privately held. Indian Head has since changed its name to Thyssen-Bornemiza.

Following the war, the government of Germany fervently denied the guilt of the war criminals, particularly the industrialists. The government was not alone in its denial; German business leaders were at the forefront in proclaiming German industries innocent of collaborating with the Nazis. During the Cold War, only a few pamphlets and publications condemned the Nazi industrialists. The corporations hired journalists and historians to flood the markets worldwide with material exonerating their corporations and placing full blame on the Nazi leadership. Most of the material produced was whitewash. This propaganda blitz fits the Nazis' plan.

The control former Nazi businessmen exerted over the press came almost immediately after the war. In 1949, the autobiography written by Richard Willstätter, a Jewish Nobel Prize-winning chemist, was published posthumously. Willstätter fled Nazi Germany in 1939 and wrote his autobiography in exile in Switzerland. He included a short passage critical of the anti-Semitic remarks made by Carl Duisberg, the founder of IG Farben, when Willstätter resigned from the University of Munich in 1924.

The short passage was unremarkable and would have passed through history unnoticed by all except a few scholars if executives from Bayer had not intervened. Bayer was part of IG Farben. Heinrich Hörlein, a Bayer director and retired executive, launched an all-out attack besmirching Willstätter's reputation and promoting Carl Duisberg and Bayer. Hörlein found himself in the dock at Nuremberg, but was acquitted. For a short time, an open debate persisted in Germany over the culpability of the German chemical industry and war crimes. Bayer and Hörlein soon prevailed. Under pressure, the publisher agreed to delete the short passage in all future editions and the English translation.

German corporations still protect their image in the most ruthless fashion. Twenty-three years after publishing Willstätter's autobiography, another controversy arose. In 1972, F.C. Delius, a German satirist, published a mock history of Siemens, coinciding with the company's 125th anniversary. Delius' book was not immediately recognized as a satire and, within a month, Siemens took action against the publisher. After three years of legal procedures, a provincial appeals court in Stuttgart ruled that several of the book's claims, including the Auschwitz assertion, were false, and ruled that Delius' ideas, despite being presented as satire, were damaging. In the settlement, both parties agreed to have the lines in dispute blacked out in all future editions, including the latest, published in 1995.

While some Americans may feel smug that such censorship occurred in Germany, the English translation of Willstätter's book also does not contain the passage that was offensive to Bayer. The censorship effort was global.

Perhaps the best example of historical revisionism and whitewashing comes from the United States. In several chapters, the relationship between the pro-Nazi America First group and the American Security Council is mentioned. One member of both fascist groups was the founder of Regnery Press, publisher of many of the smears made against President Clinton. The first two books published by Regnery are prime examples of pro-Nazi sympathizers whitewashing the Nazi crimes. One of the books was critical of the Allied bombing of Germany, and the other was critical of the Nuremberg Trials. Both contain many factual errors and present a revisionist view of history that in no way conforms to the truth. A review of the current officers of Regnery reveals the organization is still slanted to the hard right. Various officers are connected with fringe right-wing groups, such as the Claremont Institute and the American Enterprise Institute, as well as the Republican Party.

The censorship and whitewashing of Nazi atrocities and collusion of German business with the Nazis continue today in the Untied States. One of the largest publishers in the Untied States is the former Nazi publisher, Bertelsmann. The Bertelsmann publishing empire includes Random House, Bantam and Doubleday Dell; it is a partner with Barnes & Noble in a new Internet bookstore. Bertelsmann also holds a large share of America Online, and owns book clubs, magazines, newspapers and music labels, such as

RCA; it co-owns CLT-UFA, Europe's biggest TV and radio company. Bertelsmann owns Brown Printing Co., although that information is conspicuously missing from the Web pages of Brown Printing. Brown prints many of the popular magazines, including such titles as *Byte* and *Seventeen,* and a host of scientific journals, such as *Science* and *The New England Medical Journal.* Bertelsmann is the world's third largest media empire and the largest publisher of English-language trade books in the world.

Bertelsmann makes a concerted effort at hiding its Nazi past. In its official corporate history, Bertelsmann circulates the myth that the Nazis closed its publishing business for refusing to follow the party line. That is a lie. The Nazis did not close Bertelsmann; Bertelsmann willingly cooperated with the Nazis. When investigative reporters asked Bertelsmann to verify the claim that the Nazis closed it, the company removed all references to the era from its Web pages.

Throughout the 1930s, Bertelsmann published books favored by Goebbels. Some of the titles were *People Without Space (Volk ohne Raum)* and *Between the Vistula and the Volga.* The latter was an anti-Semitic diatribe claiming the Jews massacred Ukrainian women and children. Following the war, the Allied Control Council denied Bertelsmann's application for a publishing license. Heinrich Mohn, a founder, principal owner and chief executive, conveniently omitted his membership in SS and his support for Hitler's Youth. In 1949, Mohn stepped down as chief executive and was replaced by his son, Reinhard. Bertelsmann then reapplied for a publishing license. According to the denazification files, Reinhard served in the Luftwaffe and the elite Hermann Goering Division.[130] With the Cold War already emerging and the failure of the 4Ds program evident, the license was promptly granted.

Besides freeing the Nazi industrialists, McCloy announced a drastic reduction in the sentences of 74 of the remaining 104 cases, including commuting 10 death sentences. Even McCloy's whitewashing committee, the Peck Commission, recommended that all death sentences for members of the Einzatzgruppen were justified. Only four of the Einzatzgruppen prisoners and Oswald Pohl's death sentences were upheld.[131] The cold-blooded murderers of Malmedy would go free.

Not only did high commissioner McCloy empty Landsberg of war criminals, he also helped some of the most notorious war criminals escape justice. One benefactor of McCloy's generous protection was the Butcher of Lyon, Klaus Barbie. The French were aware that Barbie was in the American Zone and requested that the United States hand him over. McCloy's reply was brutally cold; he refused. He turned down the French "because the allegations of the citizens of Lyon can be disregarded as being hearsay only."[132] McCloy was well aware his reply was a lie, as Barbie was identified on the CROWCASS list of war criminals for immediate arrest.

Others benefiting from American protection were Eichmann and Baron Otto von Bolschwing. The latter directed the murder of Jews in Bucharest. In 1954, the CIA brought von Bolschwing to the United States. Former CIA director Richard Helms justified such action by saying: "We're not in the Boy Scouts. If we'd wanted to be in the Boy Scouts we would have joined the Boy Scouts."[133]

Throughout his reign in Germany, McCloy was bedeviled with one problem the Allied army had faced in its march across Germany: requests from priests and pastors demanding clemency for the convicted war criminals.

Cardinal Faulhaber, the head of the Catholic Church in Bavaria, was a vigorous opponent of the denazification program, and would readily offer help and protection to those whose employment was threatened by their Nazi past. The cardinal found a sympathetic ear in Col. Charles Keegan. Keegan was a soldier, but not an administrator. He welcomed any help and suggestions to organize a postwar government. Keegan had only one political adviser, and like his commander, George Patton, was indifferent to politics.

At a news conference at his headquarters in Bad Tolz, Patton made the offhand remark: "This Nazi thing is just like a Democratic and Republican election fight."[134] Patton's remark brought a stern reprimand from Eisenhower, and he was removed three days later. Nevertheless, Patton's remark characterized the common apathy of the American Army about German history and Nazi policies.

Cardinal Faulhaber was not alone in his opposition to denazification. From 1933, Catholic and Protestant churches openly supported Hitler. Despite their knowledge of Nazi crimes, they never withdrew their support. In May 1945, the German cardinals refused to accept the shared guilt of all Germans for the war and the unfolding story of the Holocaust, shamefully reaffirming the 1934 concordat. In June 1945, in the first joint pastoral message, the bishops praised the clergy for having resisted the Nazis. According to the bishops, maintaining the Catholic schools was an act of supreme resistance. The achievement was praised by Pope Pius XII. Pius XII had extensive dealings with the Nazis and, after the war, used the church as a ratline to help Nazi war criminals escape from Europe and justice.

Bishop von Galen told his flock: "If anyone says that the entire German population and each of us is implicated in the crimes committed in foreign countries, and especially in the concentration camps, that is an untrue and unjust accusation against many of us."[135] Theological support for political survival was at hand. Since the Catholic Church considers guilt is an individual matter, it denied the possibility of collective guilt.

The Protestant Church was slower to reach such a self-serving conclusion. Of all the Protestant leaders, Pastor Niemoller was the only one to accept the idea of collective guilt. Bishop Wurm did so at first, but his early acceptance of the denazification program soon turned to total opposition, largely because of Law No. 8. This law originated from Gen. Clay's anger on hearing that an Augsburg butcher, a former Nazi, still gave preferences to former party members. On Sept. 26, 1945, Clay issued Law No. 8, requiring the dismissal of any party member or sympathizer from any employment other than common labor. Ironically, the butcher was self-employed.

While Law No. 8 followed the guidelines for denazification, it was largely unenforceable. Once the law was issued, Bishop Wurm from Württemberg led the campaign against it. In the political vacuum left by Germany's defeat, the clergy held enormous power. No other body had the organization or self-confidence. As the church's opposition to the 4Ds program intensified, its influence over the people increased. Wurm's early protest against Law No. 8 was what he termed the dismissal of thousands of innocent civil servants who had been members of the Nazi Party. Wurm claimed many were politically indifferent to the Nazis and had simply joined the party to keep their job. There was some truth to this.

Nevertheless, Wurm admitted to Gen. Clay that many clergy, including himself, had joined the Nazi Party and supported Hitler, believing it might produce a religious revival. Wurm even referred to *Mein Kampf*, where Hitler had written that National Socialism and Christianity could work together. Wurm justified his beliefs by the signing of the Concordat, and the agreements between Nazi Germany and Britain before the war.

The American Religious Affairs Division listed 351 Protestant clergy as active Nazis. While the Catholic Church hid its Nazi priests in monasteries, the Protestant church refused to remove Nazis from its churches. By October 1946, only three of the 351 active Nazi clergy had been removed.[136]

Bishop Wurm also was a principal member of A Committee for Christian Aid to War Prisoners, formed illegally in 1948. A group of Nazi jurists in Munich, who served as counsel for major war criminals, formed the committee. Dr. Rudolf Aschenauer and Ernst Achenbach were two prominent leaders behind the group, whose purpose was to spread propaganda denouncing the war crime trials. The Nazis used Wurm and other leading clerics to camouflage their activities. Other prominent religious leaders in the committee were Cardinal Josef Frings, Catholic Bishop Johann Neuhaeussler and Protestant Bishop Meiser. Cardinal Frings demanded a halt in the executions.

Under the sponsorship of Frings and Wurm, the group developed a wide network to save the war criminals from the hangman. The Catholic Church and the Protestant Evangelisches Hilfswerk supported them. The latter organization provided shelter and jobs to hundreds of ex-Nazis, especially Ribbentrop's diplomats.

Frings and Wurm also headed another group, The Committee for Justice and Trade. This group consisted of ex-officers, high government officials, jurists, educators, industrialists and church leaders who raised money to aid all war criminals. The organization had a mysterious bank account (Konto Gustav) in which more than 60 industrialists regularly deposited large sums.[137]

The New German Government and Old Nazis

In January 1946, a secret report issued by the Public Safety Branch revealed the true extent of opposition that Gen. Clay and the occupying army faced. This report estimated that only one percent of the German population were committed anti-Nazis. In the same month, David Robinson, an American negotiator for Gen. Clay, reported that German political leaders admitted a free election would bring a modified Nazi government to power.

Bishop Wurm was relentless in his opposition to the 4Ds program and pushed Gen. Clay into setting up tribunals that included two German citizens to review and remove known Nazis from positions of power. Under pressure, Clay relented to the bishop's demands. The resulting tribunals made a mockery of justice.

Special Agent Charles Hick visited the villages of Marktheidenfeld and Aschaffenburg after hearing rumors the locals referred to the denazification panels as Nazi Welfare Organizations. He reported the conditions were far worse than could be imagined. The case against the Nazi wartime mayor Wilhelm Siebenlist had collapsed. Siebenlist, a long-time party member, made a fortune by exploiting his office under the Nazis. This Nazi profiteer had 14 witnesses, including 10 employees, willing to speak in his favor. There was only one witness for the prosecution, a suspected Nazi.

Hick first believed the case collapsed because of Horst Schutze, the prosecutor. Schutze had been jailed three times in three months for embezzlement. Hick also thought Heinrich Muller, the second prosecutor, might be blamed. Muller, a long-time party member, had nine charges of fraud against him. However, Julius Listmann publicly claimed credit for Siebenlist's acquittal. Listmann, the tribunal's investigator, was the proud owner of a new car from the former Nazi mayor.[138]

The Siebenlist case was not exceptional. Rather, it typified the findings of the tribunals across Germany. Much of the blame for the failure of the tribunals was due to the Catholic Church. Local priests created the impression that it was a sin to give damaging testimony. Instead, it became an honor to testify that former Nazis were good churchgoers and not Nazis. Such testimonies were known as *Fragebogen,* or questionnaires, false testimony that they had been resistance fighters. The Catholic Church even went as far as to order its members not to work in any of the tribunals.

The Catholic priest in Steinach went further, convincing a nearly illiterate panel that even the most rabid Nazis were mere followers. The panel then ranked these rabid Nazis in the "lowest threat" categories. The priest had joined the Nazis in 1925. In Uffenheim, the local priest warned his followers not to speak to the prosecutor, who was a Jew who had just returned from Auschwitz. In Unterfranken and Mittelfranken, Nazi profiteers such as Hans Glas, a former SS member, was fined only 2,000 marks. Glas had an annual income of more than 2,000 marks. Xavier Lang, another Nazi profiteer, also was fined the same paltry sum. Lang had an annual income of more than 700,000 marks.[139]

American forces failed to protect the few tribunal members and prosecutors who were anti-Nazi. Those members were subject to intimidation and assault from former Nazis. The werewolves, an underground Nazi organization that continued a guerrilla war after the surrender of Germany, murdered other tribunal members and prosecutors.

Churches seeking revitalization were very concerned about the growing menace of godless Red hordes, and former Nazis were in positions to exploit this fear. Captured documents revealed that this was precisely their plan. A quote by Bishop Wurm in the July 28, 1946 *The New York Times* provides little doubt of his fears: "Extreme left-wing elements are using denazification laws to destroy Germany's leading classes of educated men... There is something Bolshevistic about it."[140]

This was the same argument being promoted in the United States by rightists, many of whom had been Nazi supporters and sympathizers before the war. American Nazis, like their German confederates, felt the events of World War II did not lessen their right to rule.

Conditions in Germany after the failure of the 4Ds program was summed up by Strang and Steele, two British political officers who toured Germany. They reported the Nazis remained a privileged class. The failure to remove Nazi supervisors and shopkeepers left them in control of the daily lives of the German population. The anti-Nazis did not have the strength to challenge the former order. The foremost anti-Nazis had been executed by the Nazis, or perished in the concentration camps.

The views of Strang and Steele let the British lose interest in denazification further. Only American criticism prevented them from completely leaving the program.

In 1952, McCloy returned to the United States and became a consultant for the Ford Foundation, which had close ties to the CIA and the Council on Foreign Relations. In 1953, he became chairman of Chase National Bank, which soon merged into Chase Manhattan Bank. After John F. Kennedy's assassination, he served on the Warren Commission, and was involved in many dealings between the U.S. and other governments, private industry and banks.

McCloy's departure from Germany marked the beginning of a new phase of postwar Germany. Western Germany from then on was self-governed with little interference from the occupying armies. Adenauer had been elected as chancellor and his government was loudly proclaimed to be a democracy that had rid itself of the Nazi menace. This was excessively optimistic. Former Nazis filled the ranks of the Adenauer government. Adenauer himself was compromised by past associations with Nazis. He took money from Nazis that was intended to reestablish national socialists like Friedrich Flick, who gave generously to Adenauer's party.

Two of the most influential men in the chancellery were Dr. Hans Globke and Dr. Herbert Blankenhorn. Despite their loathsome records, Adenauer entrusted them men to rebuild the government. Hans Globke served the Nazis as the top official in the Office for Jewish Affairs in the Ministry of Interior. He was involved in forming the racial laws and drafting the text of Hitler's race laws. Globke also was the author of the notorious commentary that interpreted the Nuremberg laws, easing the way for the Holocaust. When the Nazis decided on mass extermination of the Jews, Globke's superior resigned as a matter of conscience. Globke filled his position. As chief legal adviser and head of Jewish Affairs, Globke was a direct participant in the Holocaust.

On Sept. 28, 1960, *Der Spiegel* reported Globke had direct dealings with Eichmann. The article quoted testimony from convicted war criminal Max Marten. In 1943, Eichmann requested to send 20,000 Jews from Macedonia to Palestine. Marten needed Globke's permission for the release, but Globke refused, insisting on a strict adherence to Hitler's order for liquidation.[141]

On Oct. 30, 1955, *Die Welt* described Globke as the second in command of the German ship of state. The paper reported that he alone had access to Adenauer at all times. Globke used his power to appoint many Nazis to important government positions. Some suggested he did more to renazify West Germany than anyone else.[142]

McCloy and the Military Occupation Government had to have known of Globke's record, because there was criticism from the start. On July 12, 1950, the legal expert of the Social Democratic Party, Adolf Arndt, spoke before the Bundestag, describing Globke's record in detail, and accusing him of committing mass murder with legal paragraphs. On Oct. 16, 1951, Dr. Gerhard Luetkens, the Social Democrat's deputy, charged Globke before the Bundestag with packing the Foreign Office with ex-Nazis.[143]

On June 11, 1958, *Deutsche Zeitung* in a full-page article explained how Globke was able to keep rigid control over every ministry. As Secretary of State, Globke opened all cabinet meetings and determined the agenda. All appointments to office had to cross Globke's desk, so he was able to install loyal friends in every ministry.[144] Globke was an old friend of Reinhard Gehlen, and provided him access to Adenauer. In 1955, when the federal Republic became a sovereign state, the Bonn government openly recognized Gehlen's network of spies, a home to ex-SS and other Nazis, as an arm of the government. The network was now effectively directly under Globke.

The Federal Press Department was also under the Globke's control. Throughout the 1950s, the department became involved in several scandals involving multimillion-dollar slush funds. Globke was charged with paying journalists 1,000 or 2,000 marks for political analyses – obvious bribes to support Globke's agenda. The Federal Press Department spent other funds on friendly publishers. More than 40 million marks in additional secret funds were earmarked for discretionary use of the chancellor and secretary of state.[145] It is obvious Globke was adhering to the Nazi comeback plan.

Blakenhorn's record is as dark as Globke's. Nevertheless, the Allied occupation allowed Adenauer to appoint Blankenhorn to rebuild the Foreign Office, where he served as chief for many years. Secretary of State Stettinius warned the occupation government about him, in a letter to Robert Murphy on April 20, 1945. An excerpt:

> While in Washington, Blankenhorn is known to have been active and aggressive as a propagandist working through mainly social contacts, for the Nazi party and Hitler. Racialism was one of his favorite subjects. While professing great sympathy for the United States, he was yet an ardent and convinced member of the Nazi Party and was also a member of the SS.[146]

Stettinius sent his warning letter after receiving an OSS report from Murphy that summed up Blankenhorn as truly, thoroughly Nazi. Three weeks after the Stettinius letter, Grew sent another warning to Murphy.

Long before the surrender of Nazi Germany in 1945, Nazi diplomats made extensive plans for a quick comeback. They organized a *Niederlage* (defeat) section tasked with working out detailed plans to overcome any surrender. Many of the Nazi diplomats disappeared into harmless and previously prepared emergency shelters, such as director positions of orphanages or employment in the Evangelical Relief Society.[147] These positions seemed harmless, but their intent was not.

Many of the Nazi diplomats were heavily implicated in war crimes. However, the Allies only investigated a few of them in the Wilhelmstrasse Trial of 1949. Around that time, the *Neue Zeitung*, the official American newspaper in Germany, warned of preparations for the Ribbentrop clique to recapture the Foreign Office. In 1950, when Adenauer asked him to set up a new Foreign Office, Blankenhorn presented the nucleus of the Ribbentrop group. Adenauer must have known that Blankenhorn was implicated in war crimes of deportation and mass murder. On April 22, 1952, the Swiss newspaper, *Die Tat,* reported that in the Rademacher trial, documents implicating Blankenhorn were never introduced as evidence, despite their presence in the prosecutor's files. The article stressed that the Bonn Foreign Office pressured the court not to introduce the incriminating evidence.[148]

The persistent attacks by a few democratic papers over reactivating to the Ribbentrop group were soon echoed by the Social Democratic opposition in the Bundestag. Two broadcasts on Bavarian Radio Network by Wilhelm von Cube, a fighting democrat, aroused public anger. Von Cube proved that 85 percent of the leading officials of the Foreign Office had been Nazi Party members serving Hitler. The Bundestag then took up the investigation of 20 officials. The Bundestag report confirmed that former Ribbentrop diplomats held domineering positions in the Foreign Office, who had done the utmost to whitewash their records by exchanging affidavits – *Persilscheine* or "soap coupons," a pledge the accused was whiter than white. The report called for the immediate ouster of Werner von Grundherr, Werner von Bargen, Kurt Heinburg and Herbert Dittmann, and recommended preventing seven other former Nazis from assuming diplomatic missions abroad.[149]

In addition, the report also proved the Foreign Office conspired to protect Franz Rademacher, who was guilty of the murder of 1,500 Jews in Belgrade. The court sentenced him to only three years and eight months in prison, while allowing him to remain free pending his appeal. Rademacher quickly escaped to Argentina where he was greeted as a hero who escaped the clutches of Jewish jackals.[150]

On Oct. 23, 1952, in a debate before the Bundestag, Adenauer admitted that two-thirds of the diplomats in higher positions were former Nazis. He lamented that he could not build a Foreign Office without their skills, and quickly ignored the Bundestag's report. After the 1953 election, Adenauer presented his second cabinet members as staunch democrats. However, the truth was this cabinet was full of Nazi Party and SS members. Few were ever removed from office.

One exception was the Minister for Expellees, Theodor Overlaender, the Reichsfuehrer of the German Alliance in the East. He packed his ministry with ex-Nazis. However, he was soon at the center of a storm when it became known that he was responsible for liquidating thousands of Jews and Polish intellectuals in July 1941. A special SS task force under his command committed the mass murder when it occupied Lvov, Poland. In 1960, Overlaender was forced to resign.[151]

In the early 1960s, more than 60 West Germany ambassadors and foreign diplomats were former Nazi Party members who worked with Rademacher in organizing the Final Solution. Hans Albers, formerly assigned to Warsaw by Ribbentrop, became ambassador to Nicaragua. George Vogel, a former SS officer, served as ambassador to Venezuela. The South American appointments are noteworthy, because that continent became a favorite destination of war criminals escaping from Europe.[152]

The Nazi penetration of the Bonn government was not confined to key federal government positions. All across Germany, city governments, schools and police departments were rife with former Nazis. Nazi penetration of the police was acute in Germany's larger states, such as North Rhine-Westphalia, Scheswig-Holstein and Bavaria. On Oct. 16, 1959, the Social Democrats exposed 20 SS officers who held top police positions in North Rhine-Westphalia. The Social Democrats specifically charged that former SS officers were chiefs of criminal divisions in cities like Cologne, Dortmund and Essen. They also charged that former Nazis dominated the whole police organization, where promotions and appointments were awarded to reliable SS men.[153]

In March 1959, the government of Baden-Württemberg reported to the Diet that 152 former Gestapo officials were employed as state police. The chief of the criminal division in Stuttgart was Dobritz, a former Gestapo officer sentenced to death by a French court in absentia for torture and manslaughter.[154]

In the late 1950s, an avalanche of reports and investigations surfaced charging current police officials with war crimes. In April 1959, the State Prosecutor launched an investigation of 23 police officers in Berlin. All were suspected of the mass murder of 97,000 Jews in Bialystok, Poland. In July of 1959, officials arrested the chief of the criminal division in the district of the Palatinate, Georg Heuser, for liquidating Jews in Minsk. Then the head of the criminal division in Saarbrücken, Klemmer was arrested in 1959. Klemmer, a former Gestapo officer, admitted to ordering mass executions in the East. In January 1960, Georg Lothar Hoffmann, chief of the criminal division in the state of Hesse, was arrested and charged with mass murder in Maidanek concentration camp.

While other agencies of state and local government were just as infested by former Nazis, the infiltration of the police was an especially serious matter. No citizen could report a war criminal without fear of reprisal, especially when the criminal divisions of the police were under the control of former Gestapo and SS officers. Citizens risked their lives and freedom if they challenged the Nazi line.

There is plentiful evidence that this infestation of the police was pre-planned. The November 1957 issue of the *Frankfurter Hefte* exposed the number of news and publishing media willing to promote the Nazi line:

> In the Federal Republic there exist today 46 political associations of this character. The Nazi-militaristic wing is served by 30 newspapers, 68 Rightist book and magazine publishers, and 120 former Nazi publicists. In addition there are approximately 50 nationalistic youth organizations."[155]

The failure to denazify Germany was largely due to a deliberate sabotaging of the 4Ds program by those seeking to protect U.S. corporations that traded with Hitler throughout the war, yet one cannot overlook the Nazis' determined plan to regain power after war's end. Gen. Otto Remer, who founded the Socialist Reichs Party, denied the Holocaust ever happened, and claimed the Allies had the ovens built after the war. In 1952, Germany outlawed the Socialist Reichs Party. Within a few months, authorities found the Nazis reorganized more than 60 *tarn* (camouflaged) groups in the state of Lower Saxony.

Roosevelt's death a month before the surrender of the Nazis also contibuted to the 4Ds program failure. The burden on Truman in his first year in office was immense. In the first month alone, he had to deal with Germany's surrender and, before the summer was out, the use of the atomic bomb and Japan's surrender. When he came into office, Truman had no idea of Roosevelt's Operation Safehaven or the details of the atomic bomb. He therefore put his trust in his advisers.

One of those advisers was independent oilman Edwin Pauley. Like Forrestal, he was a spy for Allen Dulles in the Roosevelt administration and the Democratic Party. He had been part of Roosevelt's Petroleum Administration for the War, and played a role in selecting Truman as the vice presidential candidate in the 1944 election. In gratitude, Truman appointed Pauley to be the U.S. representative in the Allied Reparations Committee, despite his obvious conflicts of interest. He was simultaneously made industrial and commercial adviser to the Potsdam Conference, and given the rank of ambassador. Using his position, Pauley was able to help the Dulles brothers shift Nazi assets out of Europe. He knew that most of the Nazi assets were located in the Western zone, but deceived the Soviets long enough for Allen Dulles to spirit much of the remaining Nazis assets out of Europe.

After losing his nomination as Naval Secretary to replace Forrestal, Pauley returned to the oil business. Pauley was soon embroiled in another controversy, this one over Mexico and oil. In short, Pauley was caught running a CIA shakedown of Mexican politicians. At one point, the CIA was using Permex as a business cover and money laundry for Pauley's political contributions. The CIA-Permex connection lasted many years. One notable employee of Permex during these years was William F. Buckley Jr. Politically, Pauley played both sides, and was a committed Nixon supporter.

George H. W. Bush set up Zapata Petroleum during this time and leased oil rigs to Pauley. Pauley was Bush's best customer. In 1959, Mexico changed its laws to mandate that Mexican nationals must own oil companies. Bush stood to lose his most lucrative account. Using a fiscal sleight of hand, Bush sold the Nola 1 rig, thus hiding an American share of 50 percent. The only losers in the deal were the shareholders of Zapata, according to *Barrons*. Unfortunately, the details of the deal can no longer be scrutinized since the SEC destroyed Zapata records for 1960–66. The destruction of the SEC records occurred shortly after George H. W. Bush was sworn in as vice president in 1981.[156]

Hundreds of other cases of Nazi war criminals in positions of power in the Adenauer government could be cited. Full disclosure of all the Nazis in the new German government would literally fill volumes. Nevertheless, it is obvious from the examples cited that the Nazis were still in positions of power in the postwar government of Germany. What had gone wrong was not a mere series of errors or mistakes. Rather, it was a well-organized and well-financed plot. The understanding of the plot is critical in recognizing the rise of fascism late in the 20th century and attempts to take corporate fascism global in the form of so-called free trade and globalization of the world's economy.

James Stewart Martin of the Department of Justice's investigation team in Europe summed it up in his book *All Honorable Men.*

We had not been stopped in Germany by German business, we had been stopped in Germany by American business. The forces that stopped us had operated from the United States, but had not operated in the open. We were not stopped by a law of Congress, by an Executive Order of the President, or even by a change of policy approved by the President. ... in short, whatever it was that had stopped us was not "the government." But it clearly had command of channels through which the government normally operates. The relative powerlessness of governments in the growing economic power is of course not new ... national governments stood on the sidelines while bigger operators arranged the world's affairs.

Roosevelt understood this plot and planned accordingly. He knew the industrialists would cover up their crimes. He placed some of the suspected American supporters of fascism in positions where they could be watched closely by the British Intelligence service. He knew that evidence gathered in this manner would be inadmissible in a court of law, yet he realized this group of industrialists wielded far more power than that conferred on the president of the United States. The only chance for success in bringing this group of traitors to justice was in exposing their crimes and arousing public opinion against them. He therefore planned to leak evidence to the press and counted on the reaction of the American people to demand full investigations. He used the same tactic to foil the coup attempt against him. Unfortunately, the evidence and the plan were buried with Roosevelt, and his pledge to bring all Nazis and their supporters to justice died with him.

Moreover, there is evidence that total destruction of Germany was never part of the plan by the hidden powers. In May 1945, only days after the surrender of Germany, a small group around William Stephenson (Intrepid) formed a new company, British American Canadian Corp. S.A., based in New York and registered in Panama. On April 2, 1947, it changed its name to World Commerce Corp. The most remarkable aspect of this corporation was that with one exception, all of its directors and almost everyone associated with it had connections with British or American intelligence.

All officers of the corporation were members of either the OSS or Intrepid's network. Included in the list of officers were Sir Charles Hambro, George Muhle Merten, David Ogilvy and John Arthur Reid Pepper. The officers selected at the formation were Pepper, president; Ogilvy and Merten, vice presidents; and Thomas William Hill, Intrepid's British Security Coordinator in New York City.

Donovan apparently was not involved with either corporation until he became a director on Oct. 23, 1947, the same time that former Secretary of State Edward Stettinius joined. Stettinius had a large financial holding in the corporation. However, Donovan's law firm acted as legal advisers from the beginning. Among the legal advisers was Otto Doering.

Soon World Commerce Corp. (WCC) attracted several other prominent intelligence operatives to join as directors, officers or stockholders. Included in this group were Russell Forgan, Lester Armour, Sydney Weinberg, W.K. Eliscu, Lt Col Rex Benson and several others connected with the Canadian intelligence service. Also included were Nelson Rockefeller, former head of the agency in charge of South America intelligence; John McCloy, former Under Secretary of War; Richard Mellon; and Sir Victor Sassoon. When Frank Ryan took over as president, Stephenson provided him with connections to a group of men prominent in government, intelligence and finance. The WCC contact in Greece was a former member of the Greek and British intelligence services. In Thailand, the WCC's contact person was a former OSS agent. In short, almost all members of the WCC and its contacts were formerly connected with the intelligence services during the war.[157] Yet, this remarkable company lasted only 15 years, even with the backing of the world's financial elite. In 1962, WCC was liquidated for tax reasons.

One of the first clues about this strange corporation of former intelligence experts emerged in a letter Donovan sent to Gen. Clay, high commissioner; Robert Murphy, political adviser to Clay; and Gen. Charles Saltzman, assistant secretary for occupied areas at the State Department in November 1947. WCC's new president, Frank Ryan, wrote the letter defining the general purpose of the corporation:

In our view the restoration of economic balance in Europe is fundamentally a problem of industrial and agriculture production. The purposes to be served by such development are the maintenance of population and the creation of internationally exchangeable values, which are essential in supporting the continuance of productive operations. The restoration of production and the continuing processes which involve the international exchange of goods are the fields of primary interests to World Commerce Corporation. In these directions we are prepared to cooperate with private industry and with official bodies.[158]

Ryan advised Clay that WCC had its head office in New York City, close connections in all other major centers in the United States and representatives in 47 other countries. Ryan's letter to Clay was more specific about Germany:

WCC is prepared to provide its full cooperation to the Joint Occupying Authority toward the restoration of production in Germany. World market and price reports, industrial investigations looking toward the development and submission of specific proposals and a general commercial information service are contemplated as proper elements of cooperative activity by WCC in Germany.

WCC will submit offerings of raw materials, supplies or equipment which are required in Germany for the purposes of production.

WCC will submit bids for products of general commercial usage, which may become available for export out of German production.

WCC will develop and submit for coordinating the purchases, production and export sales of a specific plant, of a group of plants or of an industry. These proposals will look toward a specifically integrated and self-supporting operation in which the facilities of the German producers on the one hand and the WCC on the other will be joined to accomplish the require result.[159]

Here, in a nutshell, is the reason for the existence of this strange and short-lived corporation staffed by former intelligence agents connected with the wealthiest groups of the English-speaking world. The British, Canadian and United States intelligence services were running a corporation to rebuild Germany, in direct violation of Roosevelt's orders.

This corporation, formed only days after war's end by a man at the top of the British intelligence services suggests that the British never intended to destroy Nazi Germany. Including OSS members followed naturally; the OSS recruited heavily from Wall Street and families of the American industrial elite. It also is indicative that the world's financial elite, led by the British, had a plan from the beginning not to destroy Germany and to reduce the cost of rebuilding after the war to protect German industry from bombing. It cannot be stated with any certainty if the RAF's reliance on the terror bombing of civilian centers throughout the war was part of this plan until further classified government documents are made available.

Such a plan would fit with the British policy toward Europe for the previous century. Until WWI, England was the dominant power in Europe, and the British were determined to hold onto their position. England's strategic geographical location allowed it to block the sea-lanes of any European challenger. The only serious threats to British power before WWI were France and Germany. Besides the threat of a blockade, Britain fostered wars between continental rivals, thereby weakening the dominant power on the continent. In this way, England preserved her supremacy in Europe at minimal cost. Throughout the latter half of the 1700s and the 1800s, England faced no serious threat to its position. Any potential threat was quickly dealt with.

Toward the end of WWI, a new threat arose for the British – the Bolshevik Revolution, if it spread beyond the borders of Russia. Between the wars, Britain regarded the Soviets as their prime enemy on the continent. Hitler's armies had come within sight of Moscow, but at a heavy price to both the Soviets and the Nazis. Churchill delayed any invasion of Europe as long as possible. He was following the long English tradition of allowing Britain's enemies to kill each other. Rather than a cross-channel invasion, he talked Roosevelt into an invasion of North Africa, primarily to protect the Suez Canal and British shipping lanes. He further delayed the Normandy invasion by promoting the invasion of Italy. Churchill then argued for an assault through the Balkans, thereby cutting the advancing Soviets off from central Europe.

It was only faced with Roosevelt's stern demand for a cross-channel invasion after the meeting of the Big Three that Churchill agreed. Churchill favored an easy peace with Germany and only reluctantly accepted the Morgenthau Plan at Montreal. However, by this time Britain was reduced to beggar status and was desperate to hang on to its remaining empire. It was in no position to disagree if postwar aid was at stake.

Thus, the formation of the World Commerce Corp., by one of England's top intelligence officers dovetails with the British conduct of the war. Those in the top ranks of the OSS who came from Wall Street or families of leading American industrialists did not wish to see their assets in Germany destroyed, and readily climbed aboard the WCC. The motivation no doubt included decisions of empire as well as the financial interests of particular members of the elite.

Martin Bormann carefully planned the Nazi comeback plan and had the support of Hitler. The plans relied solely on two proven methods — an unyielding loyalty to the fatherland and the Nazi Party. Bormann based his plans on the two successful methods that the Germans used in WWI: the old German concept of total warfare and Tarnung, which proved indispensable during WWI and its aftermath.

Bormann's plan relied on carefully chosen Nazi agents and sympathizers placed in foreign countries. Captured documents confirm that the sabotage of 4Ds was systematic and part of Bormann's intricate and well-planned plot for the Nazis to regain power. Further conformation comes from the attitude of top IG Farben officials during their interrogation and trial. Well aware that they would not suffer any harsh penalty, they were indignant at having to suffer through the charade of an interrogation and trials.

The captured documents also confirm the distinct trends starting around 1943: the removal of officials who steadfastly opposed fascism, the rise in anti-communism and the frantic peace efforts. These were all parts of the Nazi plot to regain power. Moreover, the captured documents note the connection between the Republican Party and the Nazis. Indeed, the 1946 election played a pivotal role in the Nazis' plan as the Republicans gained a majority in Congress. Once they held the majority in Congress and the 4Ds program was dead, there would be no decartelization or harsh peace. Businesses would be free to renew their cartel ties to IG Farben and other German corporations. Standard Oil was bold enough during the war to confirm that it intended to renew its cartel agreements once the war ended.

The disruption of the Malmedy trials in both Germany and in the United States by such figures as Joe McCarthy confirms the outline of the plot as laid out in the captured documents. It is well-documented that McCarthy received election funding from known fascists. This was only the beginning of Tail Gunner Joe's role in the Nazi comeback plot. He later played a greater part in the removal of dedicated people from government offices who staunchly opposed fascism.

This chapter has presented a wealth of evidence to show the sabotaging of the denazification program was systematic and proceeded at the highest levels of the occupation army, as well as the lower ranks. The young lieutenant who wrote Pa Watson of his efforts to place a former Dehomag official in a position of power probably thought he was doing his best for his country, while putting a feather in his hat for his return to IBM. It is unlikely that he was part of this plot. It is more likely he thought that he was aiding his country. Nevertheless, his actions and those of hundreds of other young officers protected IBM and Watson from being charged with aiding the Nazis.

The real rot and corruption came at the top ranks of the occupation army and the military government. American business leaders with ties to the Nazis filled the top echelon of the military government. The Kilgore congressional committee questioned the wisdom of appointing such business leaders to the control board. The committee's 1946 report singled out Rufus Wysor, president of

Republic Steel, and Fred Devereux, vice president of ATT. Both served as section chiefs under Gen. Draper. Wysor signed several cartel agreements with Nazi steel companies and aggressively defended cartels. Yet the committee was powerless to prevent appointments or reverse decisions, so the control board could act with impunity. Gen. Draper had nothing to fear when he ordered a halt to the dismantling of an IG Farben plant. John McCloy was able to free the war criminals on the flimsiest excuses, with nothing to fear except a little bad publicity.

The sabotage conducted at higher levels was part of a larger plot on the part of the Nazi element in the United States to protect itself. As revealed in captured documents, the sabotage by Nazis was connected with, and was an integral part of, the Nazis' plans to regain power. These documents stressed that their agents and friends in the United States would help protect them. They were not disappointed when McCloy opened the gates to Landsberg prison. Once freed, Flick continued to fund Nazis in the new political system in Germany. The result was a German government composed largely of former Nazis.

At the center of the sabotage of the denazification program in the United States were three Wall Street firms: Brown Brothers Harriman, Dillon and Read, and Sullivan & Cromwell. At the very eye of this corruption were Prescott Bush, John Foster Dulles and Allen Dulles. All were traitors to their country, and all worked feverishly to cover up their own crimes and those of others. None gave up their Nazi connections; in fact, the Bush family's continuing connection to known Nazis was a campaign issue in the 1988 election.

The second part of the Nazi comeback plot involved provoking a war between the West and East. The Nazis felt secure with their *Tarnung* and hidden looted treasure, but their quickest and easiest way back to power would be by provoking a war between the United States and Soviet Union.

The Nazis recognized Americans harbored an abhorrent phobia toward communism, and were wildly successful in exploiting it. Gen. Clay's war warning from Berlin was the product of the Gehlen organization, a group of former Nazi intelligence officers and SS recruited by the OSS-CIA. It could be regarded as the first shot of the Cold War. Clay's message and the Gehlen group will be more fully discussed in a later chapter.

The Nazis were willing to provoke a war even if it meant propelling the world to the brink of a nuclear holocaust. It was the only part of the comeback plot that relied almost entirely on Nazi sympathizers in the United States. The Nazis were not disappointed. Joe McCarthy soon brought the nation to a feverish peak of mass hysteria in Red hunting. The Dulles brothers rose to positions of power to further the hysteria. John Foster Dulles had a key role in the inciting the Korean War. Any government official dedicated to fighting fascism was removed from office, often by being branded a communist.

Throughout his administration, Truman faced a hostile Congress with a Republican majority and anti-communist hysteria reigning supreme. Old fascist supporters such as Fred Hartley, who was a staunch backer of fascism and Japan on the floor of the House, were rehabilitated. In less than 10 years of having his companies seized for trading with the enemy, Prescott Bush was elected to Congress. He never faced treason charges. Bush played a pivotal role in selecting Richard Nixon as vice presidential candidate in 1952. Nixon made his first step in politics by agreeing to hide evidence from captured Nazi documents that implicated Allen Dulles as a traitor. In return, Dulles agreed to finance Nixon's first election campaign. Much of Nixon's funding for his race for the House of Representatives was provided by the same New York banks that helped to fund the Nazis. The man Nixon replaced was dedicated to removing the last traces of fascism in Europe, and was a sharp critic of the direction the 4Ds program was taking, in going soft on the Nazis and cartels. Native fascists in the United States missed no tricks in branding Voorhis as a communist.

Indeed, every Republican president and vice president since Eisenhower, with the two possible exceptions of Agnew and Cheney, have either direct ties in aiding the Nazis and Nazi war criminals, or strong family ties directly linked to the Nazi cause.

Throughout the early years of the Cold War, every brushfire or hot spot that flared up had an element of Nazi intrigue. The Cold War dragged on four decades. It was the early 1960s when the Cold War reached its feverish peak of hysteria, as the world stood on the brink of a nuclear war during the Cuban Missile Crisis. This was a turning point in the Cold War. In spite of his advisers, President John F. Kennedy chose a path of détente with Khruschev. Of course, there was no greater threat to the Nazis' plot than peaceful negotiations between the Soviets and the United States. Once détente was established between the two superpowers, the Nazi plot to regain power was dead. Indeed, following the crisis, test ban treaties were completed and the Cold War was reduced to a series of small brushfires in the Third World, with the exception of the Vietnam War. The full extent of the Nazi role in fomenting the Cold War will never be realized until all the classified documents from World War II and the postwar period are released.

The Nazi plan for a comeback had two fatal flaws. It called for a comeback about 15 years after the end of the war. They did not realize that the Allies would divide Germany. At first, the Allies planned to reunite Germany as soon as possible, but with the rising tide of anti-communism whipped up by Nazi sympathizers in the United States, the NATO Allies decided on a permanent division of Germany. The Korean War appeared too soon for the Nazis. Germany was still divided and largely in ruins; while reconstruction had advanced at a rapid pace in Western Germany, there was still a large Allied occupying force there. German reunification would be delayed until the 1980s, after the Soviet Union imploded.

With no other superpower to hold the United States in check, fascism began a rebirth in the 1980s.

The Fourth Reich indeed rose, but not in Germany.

It rose in the United States.

Chapter 7,
Nazi Gold

The Merkers Treasure

Nazi Gold! The words crackle with an electrifying terror like a bolt of lightning slicing through the sky. No two words are more liable to trigger images of Nazi intrigue and brutality. Unfortunately, there are as many false tales of Nazi loot as there are true ones. No single aspect of WWII has caused more controversy, myths and bewilderment; more than sixty years since the end of the war, a sea of controversy remains. Equally important, but seldom mentioned, is the hoard of booty collected by the Emperor of Japan. Both hoards contained enormous quantities of gold, silver, platinum, jewels, art and other valuables looted from a third of the world.

Adding to the controversy is the extreme complexity of the subject. An all-encompassing view of Nazi gold is nearly impossible because it involves Vatican, Swiss and South American banks, the Bank of England, the Federal Reserve, and Nazi plans for a rebirth. Some top Nazi officials skimmed gold and valuables into individual hoards. The Allies never reported all the gold they recovered; what the Soviet Union recovered remained hidden behind the Iron Curtain, and is only now becoming known. How much of the treasure was recovered is largely a guessing game. Bitterly disputed estimates vary widely. The only certainty is that much remains unaccounted for. A great deal was most likely spent in rebuilding Germany after the war. The wealth robbed from the victims of the Nazis helped fund the so-called European miracle of reconstruction.

The Nazis had precise plans for a comeback, resting on their ability to hide their ill-gotten loot from the Allies, and on aid from friends in foreign countries, including the United States. Some of the hoard was hidden safely in secret Swiss bank accounts; other portions were shipped to South America (mainly to Argentina) for safekeeping. One conduit to Argentina was controlled and directed by Martin Bormann. Bormann's fate is still uncertain, and valuables he sent to Argentina in project Action Feuerland are still shrouded in a fog of mystery and intrigue.

There are several accounts — some plausible, others bordering on the preposterous — about Bormann's fate. The more common and believable account had Bormann living out his life in South America, while an equally likely account had him dying in the last days of the Third Reich while trying to escape from Berlin. In a third version started by Gen. Gehlen, Bormann escaped to the Soviet Union and lived there. Gehlen claimed to have recognized Bormann in a crowd at a soccer game as a television camera panned the spectators. Most recently, one ridiculous account named Bormann as a Soviet mole in Hitler's inner circle, while another claimed a British commando unit rescued him from Berlin and he lived out his life in the English countryside.

Obviously, it would have been useful for Bormann to be declared dead in Berlin. Nevertheless, recent DNA taken from one of the skulls found in Berlin matched closely with that of an uncle of Bormann. The skull still had glass shards between the teeth, suggesting that Bormann was unable to escape from Berlin and committed suicide.

Before the advent of DNA testing, there was much controversy over the identity of the skull. It was caked with red volcanic clay not to be found around Berlin, but closely matching the soil of Paraguay. The government turned the remains over to the family, which had them cremated and the ashes scattered at sea, hoping to settle the controversy for all time, yet it still continues. There were credible sightings of Bormann in Europe, then in South America until the 1960s. The red clay suggests that Bormann died in South America and his body was moved to Berlin.

Bormann's end is of only secondary importance; what concerns us more is the fate of the assets he spirited from Germany to Argentina. Despite some factual errors that diminish their credibility, two of the best books covering Bormann and South America are *Aftermath* by Ladislas Farago and *Martin Bormann: Nazi In Exile* by Paul Manning. Manning, a reporter during WWII who has written two books regarded as classics, admits that Allen Dulles deceived him about South America. But why?

While the Nazis had concrete plans to ship much of their gold and valuables to other countries, the United States planned to recover them. A good deal of the American effort to recover the Nazi gold fell under Operation Safehaven. However, no one realized the enormous size and complexity of the task until early April 1945. Late in the evening of March 22, 1945, units of Lt. Gen. George Patton's Third Army crossed the Rhine. What at first was a trickle of soldiers crossing the river soon turned into a raging flood of troops.

By noon on April 4, the Third Army captured the village of Merkers. During April 4–5, a CIC detachment questioned displaced persons in the vicinity. Many told the CIC of unusual activity around the Wintershal AG's Kaiseroda potassium mine at Merkers. The rumor was that the Reichsbank hid its gold reserves there. CIC passed the information up to G2, which immediately issued an order to bar civilians from the area.

The next morning, two female displaced persons approached a roadblock and were questioned by the guards. One was pregnant and on the way to Keiselbach to see a midwife. After questioning, the guards drove the two women back to Merkers. The jeep driver asked the women about the Kaiseroda mine, and was told it was where the Nazis hid their gold and other valuables.

By noon on April 6, this information reached Lt. Col. William A. Russell, who proceeded to Merkers and questioned several displaced civilians who confirmed the story. In addition, Russell learned that Paul Ortwin Rave, curator of the German State Museum in Berlin, as well as an assistant director of the National Galleries in Berlin, took care of paintings there. Russell then confronted the mine officials with the information and questioned Werner Veick, the head cashier of the Reichsbank's Foreign Notes Department, who also was at the mine. Rave admitted his role as caretaker for the paintings. Veick told Russell the Nazis hid the entire gold reserve of the Reichsbank in the mine.

Military wires blazed with requests for reinforcements to guard the mine. At first, Russell ordered the 712th Tank Battalion to advance to Merkers to guard the entrances. The Ninetieth Division Military Police provided additional forces. By evening, American troops discovered five more possible entrances to the mine, and it was obvious one tank battalion was not enough. Maj. Gen. Herbert L. Earnest then ordered the First Battalion of the 357th Infantry Regiment to go to Merkers and reinforce the 712th. Russell also told an XII corps G5 officer what was going on at the mine.

On the morning of April 7, American forces placed guards at each additional entrance. At 10 a.m., Russell and two other officers with Rave and mine officials entered the main entrance, where a shaft took them 2,200 feet below the surface. In the main tunnel, they found 550 sacks of Reichsmarks, and located the main vault behind a 3-foot thick brick wall that enclosed an area at least 100 feet wide. In the center was a heavy bank vault door.

Patton was informed that a large quantity of paper money but no gold was found. As Patton's forces continued their lightning advance into Germany, he ordered the 357th Infantry Regiment, except for the First Battalion, to move out and join the Ninetieth Infantry Division. Patton also ordered the vault door blown open.

Early on April 8, Russell, with a public affairs officer, photographers, reporters and soldiers of the 282nd Engineer Combat Battalion, reentered the mine. The vault door was easily blown open and they entered Room 8. The size of the hoard was simply stunning; stretching before them was a room about 75 feet wide and 150 feet long. The room was lighted, but not ventilated.

Before them were more than 7,000 bags stretching all the way to the back of the room. The bags were laid out in 20 neat rows about knee-high and separated by roughly 2.5 feet. Baled currency was neatly stacked along one side of the room. At the back were 18 bags and 189 suitcases, trunks and boxes; each carefully marked with the name Melmer. It was obvious that these containers belonged to the SS. It also was the first clue to the complexity and scope of the Nazi looting of Europe.

Russell and his men broke some of the seals on the bags to inventory the stash: 8,198 bars of gold bullion; 55 boxes of crated gold bullion; hundreds of bags of gold items; more than 1,300 bags of gold Reichsmarks, British gold pounds and French gold francs; 711 bags of American $20 gold pieces; hundreds of bags of gold and silver coins; hundreds of bags of foreign currency; nine bags of valuable coins; 2,380 bags and 1,300 boxes of Reichsmarks (2.76 billion Reichsmarks); 20 silver bars; 40 bags containing silver bars; 63 boxes and 55 bags of silver plate; one bag containing six platinum bars; and 110 bags of currency from various countries.[1] In other tunnels, they found a large quantity of artwork. The hoard also revealed the brutality of the Nazi regime. Included in the inventory were bags of teeth containing gold fillings extracted from concentration camp victims.

Once aware of the enormous size of the hoard, Patton considered the matter to be political and immediately requested that it be turned over to SHAEF. Eisenhower appointed Col. Bernard D. Bernstein, deputy chief, Financial Branch, G-5 Division of SHAEF. On April 15, a convoy with constant overhead fighter protection moved the treasure to the Reichsbank in Frankfurt.

By mid-August, the gold was weighed and appraised. SHAEF valued the gold at $262,213,000, the silver at $270,469. A ton of platinum and eight bags of rare coins were not appraised. Early in 1946, SHAEF turned the gold over to the Inter-Allied Reparation Agency, which eventually turned it over to the Tripartite Commission for the Restitution of Monetary Gold. The Tripartite Commission returned the gold to the central banks of the countries from which it was looted. Due to the Cold War, some of the gold was not distributed until 1996.

The manner in which the Allies divided the Merkers gold is plagued with controversy. The Allies took no account of how much was from smelting dental gold. Interestingly enough, in 1948, the army microfilmed the records of the Reichsbank's Precious Metals Department and turned them over to Albert Thoms, who was working for the successor bank. These records disappeared in Germany and were not relocated again until the 1990s.

No other cache of gold and valuables found in Europe rivaled the size of the Merkers find. In the Philippines, one of the caches of the Golden Lily, the Japanese Emperor's looted treasure, reportedly unearthed by Philippine President Ferdinand Marcos, was larger. The only other possible cache from Europe that could rival the Merkers find would be the Croatian Ustashi treasure. However, the gold and valuables looted by the Ustashis have never been located. The best evidence suggests that the Ustashis smuggled them out of Europe through the Vatican-CIA ratline. How much of the Ustashi cache made it into the Vatican vaults remains shrouded in secrecy and mystery. American forces located several other smaller caches, mostly in the alpine region on the German-Austrian border, where the Nazis tried to stage a final stand.

There is no dispute about what the Merkers treasure contained. The controversy stems from where the gold came from, how the Allies divided it, and what portion of the total Nazi hoard the Merkers treasure represented.

To reach an estimate of the extent of the Nazi looting, the gold reserves of the Nazis' trading partners can be used to set an upper bound. Only a handful of countries hiding under the umbrella of neutrality continued to trade with the Nazis during the war. The following table reflects the change in gold reserves of Nazi Germany's primary trading partners.[2] The figures are in millions of dollars.

Country	1939 reserves	1943 Reserves	Increase
Spain	42	104	62
Sweden	160	456	296
Turkey	88	221	133
Portugal	79.5	447.1 (1945)	367.6
Switzerland	503	1040	537

Obviously, not all of the increase was due to the Nazis, but the figures do set an upper limit. Further, since the only currencies not accepted globally were the German Mark, Italian Lira and Japanese Yen, neutral countries continued to accept the U.S. dollar and British pound. More evidence comes from the declared deposits of Swiss banks, which soared from Swiss Francs (CHF) 332 million in 1941 to CHF 846 million in 1945. Again, not all of the increase in deposits can be attributed to the Nazis, but it does set an upper limit of half a billion dollars. Note that the dollar figure is in 1945 dollars when gold sold for $35 an ounce; the dollar value of the gold today would be more than $5 billion.

The figures above compare favorably with the latest estimates available. The report stemming from President Clinton's initiative shows the Swiss received $440 million in gold from the Nazis, of which $316 million was looted gold.[3] The Dresdner and Deutsche banks received $1 million of gold, which they sold in Turkey for foreign currency. More than $300 million in Nazi gold reached Portugal, Sweden, Spain and Turkey.

The U.K. Foreign Office conducted a vigorous campaign, warning neutral countries against accepting gold from the Nazis. The U.S. refused to support the measure until July 1943, when the alarming increase of gold reserves of the neutral countries became obvious. Even then, State Department support was cool, at best.

The above list of countries is accidents. Without their raw materials, the Nazis could not wage war. Sweden supplied vitally needed high-grade iron ore. Turkey supplied Hitler with chromate. Portugal and Spain supplied wolframite. War munitions and heavy armor production required all three metals. Chromates are used to harden steel for armor, while wolframite or tungsten ore is used primarily for machine tools. Nazi sources for both metals were extremely limited; the war forced Germany to rely almost entirely on these countries.

Considering South America was a prime refuge for the Nazis after the war, it is instructive to look at changes in the gold reserves of South American countries, particularly Argentina. Argentina's gold reserves increased from 313.83 metric tons in 1940 to 1064 tons in 1945.[4] The increase in the gold reserves of Argentina was $635 million. To put that figure in perspective, the U.S. budget for 1940 was about $9.4 billion. Brazil also saw an increase in gold reserves from 45 metric tons in 1940 to 314 tons in 1945, or an increase of about $228 million.

The reserve figures shed some light on the destination of some of the Nazis' loot. How much of the increase in South American gold reserves came from Germany towards the end of the war to finance the Nazi comeback is unknown. However, gold was only part of the plan. Even more valuable were the bearer stocks and bonds, and the Nazi front corporations set up worldwide by Bormann. They held valuable patents, and produced a steady income stream to finance the Nazi underground.

Safehaven Operations

The Allies used various methods and programs to recover Nazi gold. Poland took the first measures against Nazi looting by moving their gold reserves to Romania before they were invaded. Unluckily, the Nazis soon overran Romania too, and seized the Polish gold.

Several other European countries made similar efforts. French officials at the National Bank shipped their treasure to the United States. At the end of 1939, Belgium entrusted the French with $223 million for safekeeping. Soon after the German invasion of the Low Countries, Belgium urged France to ship its gold to London aboard military cruisers. However, the French transferred the gold to Dakar, in its West African colony of Senegal. After the fall of France and negotiations with Vichy, the Nazis got the Belgian gold.

Within the first hour of the Nazi invasion of the Netherlands, Dutch authorities shipped their gold reserves in Amsterdam to England. A second boat carrying 11 metric tons of Dutch gold reserves stored in Rotterdam struck a mine near the coastline, and was marooned. By 1942, the Nazis recovered most of the gold aboard. Other European countries failed to take any precautions, and the Nazis seized their gold reserves as soon as they were overrun. In this way, most of the gold reserves in the central banks of Europe fell to the Nazis, except for those of France and a portion of those of the Dutch.

The first action taken by the United States was Executive Order 8389, signed by Roosevelt on April 10, 1940 freezing Norwegian and Danish assets in the United States. Eventually, the United States froze the assets of every country except England, Japan and China. Freezing assets blocked Nazi accesss to them in the United States.

In July 1942, the United States issued the blacklist of individuals and companies, the Proclaimed List of Blocked Nationals, banning trade in the Americas with any party on it. Those listed were deemed hostile to the defense of the Americas. Throughout the war, the United States added to the list until it included several thousand names.

On Jan. 5, 1943, the Inter-Allied Declaration Against Acts of Dispossession Committed in Territories Under Enemy Occupation or Control, better known as the London Declaration, was announced. The measure declared the Allies would no longer recognize the transfer of property in occupied countries, even if it appeared legal. The Allies were aware that the Nazis were forcing people in occupied countries to sell or transfer their property to them. Up to then, the Nazis had painstakingly created the illusion that such transfers were legal.

On Feb. 22, 1944, the United States announced in its Declaration on Gold Purchases that it would no longer recognize the transfer of gold loot from the Axis, nor buy gold from any country that had not broken relations with the Axis. England and the Soviet Union followed with similar declarations.

In July and August of 1944, the Bretton Woods Agreement was reached, calling on the neutral countries to prevent disposition or transfer of assets in the occupied countries. On Aug. 14, 1944, the U.S., UK, and Swiss War Trade Agreement was reached, requiring the Swiss to reduce trade with the Nazis.

On Dec. 6, 1944, Operation Safehaven was organized. Four days later, the State Department released a paper urging a soft line toward Switzerland. This was the first step in sabotaging efforts to return assets to Holocaust victims. In essence, it continued a feud between the Treasury and State departments regarding peace terms and the 4Ds program.

In February 1945, the Yalta Conference agreed that reparations would be exacted from Germany. The conference also set the groundwork for the Allied Reparations Commission.

Operation Safehaven was by far the best known and biggest action the Allies launched to recover assets looted by the Nazis. Leo T. Crowley, Director of the Foreign Economic Administration (FEA), first proposed the need for a Safehaven organization in a letter to the Secretary of Treasury on May 5, 1944. Then, in a letter to Livingston T. Merchant in the State Department ten days later, William T. Stone, Director of FEA's Special Areas Branch, called for bringing in the British, as well as various other U.S. agencies. Since it involved both the Treasury and State departments, Safehaven was plagued by their intense rivalry. Thus it suffered the same fate as the 4Ds program; it was sabotaged from within.

In May 1944, Samuel Klaus, Special Assistant to the General Counsel of the Treasury Department, proposed a plan for a fact-finding mission to neutral countries dealing with the problem of hidden Nazi assets. Early planning for the trip included Klaus and Herbert J. Cummings, a State Department official. Once the Treasury Department was aware of the trip, it sent several officials to catch up with the Klaus delegation. From August to October, Klaus visited London, Stockholm, Lisbon, Madrid, Barcelona and Bilbao to encourage neutral countries to participate in Safehaven. The mission had only slight success, and canceled plans to visit Switzerland and Portugal. In his final report, Klaus outlined his current thinking on Safehaven:

> It is only in its narrowest, and relatively less important, aspects flight of enemy capital. In its most important aspects it is the use of neutral countries as bases for maintaining the assets, skills and research necessary for the conversion of Germany to a war basis at an appropriate future date. The hiding out of stolen jewels or pictures, even if it exists, is truly important from the point of view of war crimes retribution. But the presence of IG Farben personnel in Spain, the expansion of Siemens production in Sweden, or the presence of German military technicians in Argentina are of more far-reaching significance, and constitute as well the most difficult Safehaven activities.[5]

Klaus found the conditions in Spain the most troubling. There, U.S. Ambassador Carlton Hayes was unsympathetic to Safehaven's investigations, although Spain was the country most damaging to its objectives. In fact, the OSS had to work out of Portugal due to the ambassador, who identified undercover agents to the Spanish police. Hayes insisted on censoring all incoming and outgoing OSS messages. He even blocked the broadcast of Safehaven publicity material for a time.[6] Hayes was friendly to a fault with the Franco regime; however, he is credited with keeping Spain from joining the Axis, even though such an alliance probably never was part of the Nazis' plans. Just as Hitler recognized the need for a neutral Switzerland to get foreign currency and laundered gold through, the Nazis most likely recognized the need for a neutral port on the Atlantic to receive supplies, for instance, gasoline imported through Spain after Hitler invaded the Soviet Union.

Hayes was aware of Spain's oil imports. On Feb. 26, 1943, he commented that oil products in Spain were considerably easier to get than on the East Coast of the United States. The supply of gasoline and petroleum products available equaled the full capacity of Spain's tanker fleet.[7] Standard Oil supplied the gasoline from its oil fields in South America. This presented the Roosevelt administration with a Pandora's box of dilemmas. Forcing Standard to stop the shipments could have resulted in an interruption in the U.S. oil supply. At one point during the war, Standard threatened to do just that. Second, U.S. citizens suffering from gasoline rationing cards would have rebelled on learning that an American company was supplying oil to the Nazis. A similar commotion could be expected from the troops, many of whom were draftees. So the oil shipments to Spain continued. If you are rich enough, treason is no crime.

The OSS collected and evaluated most of the data for Safehaven.[i] Within OSS, Safehaven was confined to the SI (Secret Intelligence) and X2 (counterintelligence) divisions. X2 often played the

---

[i] As originally proposed, FEA was to run Safehaven with guidance from the Treasury Department on the financial and informational side, and the State Department on policymaking. However, the intense rivalry between the departments and differences with Britain weakened FEA's role. Resolution VI of the Bretton Woods Conference gave Safehaven firm legal footing. The resolution stemmed from Polish and French proposals to block funds in neutral countries to prevent the Nazis from using looted assets. On Dec. 2, the Treasury and State departments and FEA agreed to the roles of the participating agencies. Each received some measure of individual operational freedom. All the data and intelligence was to be centralized in London.

In the fall of 1944, the long-standing debate over treatment of neutrals arose between FEA and the State Department. FEA wanted to keep controls in place, while State wanted to lift the economic blockade after hostilities ended. By this time, the State Department had the stronger voice in Safehaven's actions. In October 1944, Morgenthau, Treasury Secretary; Joseph O'Connell, General Counsel for Treasury; and Dexter White,

dominant role, especially with the more important neutrals — Switzerland, Portugal and Spain. X2 was especially involved in the German effort to transfer looted assets to foreign countries.

Cooperation between the OSS and Safehaven was informal until Nov. 30, 1944, when instructions sent to all OSS stations detailed the intelligence requirement expected by the program. Safehaven was able to use already active OSS operations, redirecting them slightly toward the collection of economic data.

This made Safehaven dependent on the personalities of the various OSS station chiefs. As mentioned, the ambassador had compromised OSS missions in Spain. In Switzerland, Allen Dulles was the station chief. Dulles had already been exposed in an earlier operation, a joint program with the British, for spying on Americans, and he was suspected of being sympathetic to the Nazi cause. Roosevelt deliberately sent Dulles to Switzerland where he would be most tempted to help his clients. When Dulles reached Berne, he was aware that he was being watched. He knew he could not use official channels to help his clients in the United States. So he used his Vatican connections to help the Nazis and couriers with diplomatic immunity. The Vatican readily agreed to help Dulles in its zeal to regain its assets in Germany and further its fanatical anti-communist philosophy.

Declassified files show that Slovenian Bishop Gregory Rozman was trying to arrange the transfer of huge quantities of Nazi-controlled gold and Western currency discreetly secreted in Swiss banks during the war. The bishop was sent to Berne with the help of Dulles' friends in the intelligence service. For a few months, the Allies were successful in preventing Rozman from getting the funds. Then, suddenly, Rozman had the money for his Nazi friends living in Argentina. Dulles had fixed it. This incident may be only the tip of the iceberg. In 1945, the U.S. Treasury Department accused Dulles of laundering funds from the Nazi Bank of Hungary to Switzerland. Similar charges were made against Dulles' agent, Hans Bernd Gisevius, who worked for the OSS while serving at the Reichsbank. The State Department quickly took over the case from the Treasury, after which the investigation was silenced and dropped.[8] Gisevius also was involved in the ratlines.

Dulles' career in Berne during WWII was marked by several money-laundering cases. After the Nazis tipped off Dulles that the Swiss codes had been broken, he shifted his laundering activities to the banks of Belgium, Luxembourg and Liechtenstein. He used a roundabout route through Japan, aided by Vatican couriers.[9] After the war, all the banks in these countries refused to allow Allied investigators to look at their books. One of Dulles' dirtiest tricks may have been an effort to buy more time to move Nazi gold through Switzerland. A former East Bloc intelligence officer confirmed that Dulles warned the Nazis that their code had been broken. Shortly afterwards, the SS told the High Command to tighten code security, stop using the radio and switch to couriers. For once, the Allies had no information on German battle plans. This most likely explains how the Germans were able to launch the Battle of the Bulge as a complete surprise.[10]

Dulles and his comrades exerted a good deal of influence to ensure that U.S. investments in Nazi Germany were not seized for reparations. In Switzerland, the SS bought a large amount of stock in American corporations and laundered money through the Chase and the Corn Exchange banks. Even more brazen was the case of the Pan Am clippers hired by the W.R. Grace Corp., to transport Nazi gems, currency, stock and bonds to South America. These operations were the product of Dulles' money laundering for the Nazis.[11] Several American officers readily admit that much of the Nazi gold was never

---

Director of Monetary Research for the Treasury Department agreed that Treasury-trained agents should be dispatched to supplement embassy staffs in neutral countries.

On Dec. 6, 1944, the State Department released its long-awaited Circular Instruction to U.S. Missions about Safehaven matters. The release of the Circular marked the beginning of the political and diplomatic phases of Safehaven under the Department of State.

turned over to them. One officer tells of being in a huge vault filled with gold, gems and currency that never appeared in any U.S. files.[12]

Dulles backed Germany for a long time, seeing it as a bulwark against the Soviets. The young Lt. William Casey was another OSS agent who shared this view. Casey served in the SI division in France and the Lowlands following liberation. In a report from Paris, Casey wrote that Safehaven was a valuable field of endeavor, especially because of the potential for leverage with German financial circles.[13] After the war, Casey worked on Wall Street before becoming Reagan's CIA Director.

In 1946, Dulles' men simply changed their OSS uniforms and became the War Department Strategic Service Unit. Sometimes they were the War Department Detachment; other times, the Document Disposal Unit. In effect, there were two factions left from the OSS — a liberal faction that took orders from the president and the other under the control of Dulles. The latter faction was hoping for a conservative victory by Dewey so it could unleash an émigré army against the Soviets. Dulles had a secret ally in Region IV around Munich, where the CIC was helping to recruit ex-Nazis.[14]

Due to Dulles' close association with German industrialists, he was unwilling to give the attention to Safehaven that Washington expected. In November 1944, with the Allies now in control of France, a land route to Switzerland was reestablished, making it possible to send an X2 agent to Berne to help run the Safehaven program there. By April 1945, X2 in Berne had unearthed a great deal of information on Nazi dealings, including:

Gold and bonds looted from Europe and received by certain Swiss banks.

Additional funds sent by the Deutsche Verkehrs-Kreditbank of Karlsruhe to Basel.

Stocks and bonds held in Zurich by private firms for the Nazi Party.

Hoards of Swiss francs credited to private accounts in various Swiss banks.

Cash and property held in Liechtenstein.

More than 2 million francs held by the Reichsbank in Switzerland.

Forty-five million Reichsmarks held in covert Swiss bank accounts.[15]

This information, gleaned in less than four months by the X2 agent, only confirms other information that surfaced over the years that Dulles was working hard for the Nazis to hide their loot. Dulles was a friend of the American director of the Bank for International Settlements and top Nazi banking officials.

After the investigation into his money laundering, Dulles resigned from the OSS and returned to New York to seek out Thomas McKittrick, the former head of the Bank of International Settlements. The Nazis had moved many of their assets from Switzerland to Argentina. Dulles soon went to work for a staggering number of Argentine clients. He and Donovan agreed that every effort should be made to sabotage Truman and the liberals. To this end, Dulles inveigled Donovan into serving on the board of the World Commerce Corp., where Dulles was the lawyer. Nazi money flowed in a circle from Germany to the Vatican, then on to Argentina and back to Germany. Argentina's economy boomed from the influx. The so-called economic miracle of the 1950s came from the same money the Nazis looted from Europe in the 1940s.[16]

From the beginning, Safehaven was an ambitious project with several goals, including immediately forcing the neutral countries to stop trading with the Nazis. The secondary goals of Safehaven follow:

To restrict German economic penetration outside the borders of the Reich.

To prevent Germany from sequestering assets in neutral countries.

To ensure that German assets would be available for postwar reparations and to rebuild Europe.

To prevent the escape of those members of the Nazi ruling elite already cited for war crimes trials.[17]

For a large and ambitious program, Safehaven was terribly understaffed. With the Nazi surrender in May 1945, SI agents assigned to Safehaven had to concentrate first on strategic information before devoting any time to Safehaven. Additional well-trained agents simply were not available. Second,

Safehaven was plagued by the long-running feud between the Treasury and State departments and, to a lesser extent, by British hesitation to employ harsh measures. Finally, success was proportional to the willingness of the neutral countries to comply with Allied demands to stop trading with the Nazis. During and especially at the end of the war, Safehaven operations were left in the hands of the CIC or the CID Criminal Investigation Division of the military. While TCOM forces were well equipped and staffed, CIC and CID were poorly equipped and undermanned, as were the gold rush teams.

Bormann's Aktion Feuerland

The British Ministry of Economic Warfare (MEW) estimated that the Merkers hoard made up only 20 percent of all the gold Germany held. In August 1945, the Bank of England estimated there would only be enough gold available for a 58 percent restitution of claims. Even this only included claims by central banks, without private claims. Where did the rest of the gold go? Although the CIA still denies that the Nazis had a plan for a comeback, captured documents show otherwise. Even members of Congress and, in particular, members of the Kilgore Committee, were aware of Nazi plans. (Translations of the Nazi comeback plans are included in Appendix 10.) To understand where the missing gold went, we need to look at the German plans for a comeback.

At the center of the plan was Martin Bormann, the Reichsleiter. Bormann rose through the ranks to Party Secretary, the No. 2 spot in the Nazi hierarchy. Hitler entrusted him with ensuring the Reich would be able to stage a comeback once hostilities ended. The "Red House" meeting was the beginning of Bormann's effort to expand his plan to include industrialists and top-ranking officers. The meeting took place on orders from Bormann, who did not attend in person.[18] The Treasury Department has a transcript of the meeting conducted by an SS agent, who told the group that all industrial materiel was to be evacuated to Germany immediately because the battle for France was lost. He also assured the gathering the Treason Against the Nation Law controlling foreign exchange had been repealed. At a smaller conference that afternoon, Bosse of the German Armaments Ministry pointed out that the Nazi government would make huge sums available to industrialists to help secure bases in foreign countries. Bosse advised the industrialists to use two main banks for the export of capital: Schweizerische Kreditanstalt of Zurich and the Basler Handelsbank. He also told the industrialists about Swiss cloaks that would buy Swiss property for a 5 percent commission. A month later, Bormann countermanded Hitler's scorched earth policy, to preserve Germany's industrial base.

Bormann knew the Nazis lost the war once the Allies landed in Normandy on D-Day. He gave himself nine months to launch his flight capital program to find a safe haven for the Nazis' liquid assets. The Alsace-Lorraine area served as a microcosm for his plans. Germans owned controlling interests in many of the French banks in the area. A German majority ownership also controlled many of the factories. Bormann relied on *Tarnung* (cloaking or camouflage, see chapter 3) to hide German corporate interests. Bormann was a close friend of Schmitz, a director of IG Farben, and he studied IG's method of *Tarnung* extensively. Bormann sorted his records and then shipped them to Argentina via Spain. Already having control of the Auslands-Organisation and IG Verbindungsmänner, he began with the capital flight. Both organizations placed spies in foreign countries disguised as technicians and directors of German corporations.

By the time the Battle of the Bulge raged, Bormann had successfully moved assets out of Germany. In 1938, the number of patent registrations to German companies was 1,618, but after the Red House meeting, it rose to 3,377. Bormann also created a two-price scheme with Germany's trading partners. The lower price was cleared or settled at the end of the banking day. The neutral importers retained the higher price on their books and the difference was collected in a German account as flight capital. Under this scheme, Bormann amassed about $18 million kroner and $12 million Turkish lira. Balance sheets showed he bought seven mines in central Sweden.[19] He also created 750 new corporations scattered across the globe, representing a wide array of economic areas — from steel and chemicals to electrical companies. The firms' locations were in: Portugal, 58; Spain, 112; Sweden, 233; Switzerland, 234; Turkey, 35; and Argentina, 98. All the corporations created by Bormann issued bearer bonds, so ownership was impossible to prove.[20]

Bormann had several means of dispersing Nazi assets. He used diplomatic pouches of Nazi Foreign Policy Minister von Ribbentrop to send gold, diamonds, stocks and bonds to Sweden twice a month. A similar pattern was used to ferry valuables to South America. Bormann also allowed other Nazis to transfer their valuables through the same channels.

In Turkey, the Nazi government allowed both the Deutsche Istanbul and the Deusche Orient banks to save all their earnings rather than send them to Berlin. The earnings were mere bookkeeping items ready for transfer anywhere in the world.

In 1941, German investment in the United States held a voting majority in 170 American corporations and minority ownership in another 108. Many of these corporations were part of the IG Farben cartel. In addition, U.S. corporations had investments in Germany totaling $420 million. With his program for flight capital well on its way, Bormann gave permission for Nazis to once again buy American stocks.

Purchase of American stocks usually was done through a neutral country, typically Switzerland or Argentina. From foreign exchange funds on deposit in Switzerland and Argentina, large demand deposits were placed in such New York banks as National City, Chase, Manufacturers Hanover, Morgan Guaranty and Irving Trust. Manning reports the Nazis bought more than $5 billion in American stocks in this way.[21] These same banks were active in supporting Germany. In addition, every major Nazi corporation transferred assets and personnel to its foreign subsidiaries.

The United States and Britain never could fully grasp the extent of Nazi flight capital. John Pehle, the original director of the Foreign Funds Control, offers an interesting view as to why the United States was unable to stop Bormann and his movement of Nazi assets to neutral countries. Pehle's reasoning:

> In 1944, emphasis in Washington shifted from overseas fiscal controls to assistance to Jewish war refugees. On presidential order I was made executive director of the War Refugee Board in January 1944. Orvis Schmidt became director of Foreign Funds Control. Some of the manpower he had was transferred, and while the Germans evidently were doing their best to avoid Allied seizure of assets, we were doing our best to extricate as many Jews as possible from Europe.[22]

Pehle's explanation seems too simple. With more personnel, more could have been accomplished, but the real problem was rot and corruption in the United States. Leaders of America's largest corporations were sympathetic to the Nazis, and almost all had invested heavily in Germany. Many in Congress also sympathized with the Nazi cause. The mood in Congress was to "get the boys home and get on with business." Schmidt's testimony on the extent of Nazi infiltration of neutral countries before the end of the war fell on deaf ears in Congress:

> The danger does not lie so much in the fact that the German industrial giants have honeycombed the neutrals, Turkey and Argentina, with branches and affiliates which know how to subvert their commercial interest to the espionage and sabotage demands of their government. It is important and dangerous however, that many of these branches, subsidiaries and affiliates in the neutrals and much of the cash, securities, patents, contracts and so forth are ostensibly owned through the medium of secret numbered accounts or rubric accounts, trusts, loans, holding companies, bearer shares and the like by dummy persons and companies claiming neutral nationality, and all of the alleged protection and privileges arising from such identities. The real problem is to break through the veil of secrecy and reach and eliminate the German ability to finance another world war. We must render useless the devices and cloaks which have been employed to hide German assets. We have found an IG Farben list of its own companies abroad and at home — a secret list hitherto unknown — which names over 700 companies in which IG Farben has an interest.[23]

The list does not include the 750 companies Bormann set up. After the war, Schmidt testified again to Congress:

They were inclined to be very indignant. Their general attitude and expectations were that the war was over and we ought now to be assisting them in helping to get IG Farben and German industry back on their feet. Some of them have outwardly said that this questioning and investigation was in their estimation, only a phenomenon of short duration, because as soon as things got a little settled they would expect their friends in the United States and England to be coming over. Their friends, so they say would put a stop to activities such as these investigations and would see that they got the treatment which they regarded as proper, and the assistance would be given to them to help reestablish their industry.[24]

Here again, we see how the 4Ds program was sabotaged. In every country liberated, there was a great reluctance to disturb the machinery of money and industry connected to Germany through cartel agreements. The German presence was reduced, but not eliminated. The cloaked ownership ensured continuity for the Nazis. Even the Grand Duchess Charlotte of Luxembourg had her own ideas. On returning from exile, the Duchess dismissed the U.S. investigative team and ordered it out of the country. On June 26, 1945, the chair of the U.S. Senate Subcommittee on Military Affairs, Elbert D. Thomas, commented on Luxembourg:

We had a mission in Luxembourg which was obtaining quite a bit of information on the steel cartel until the Grand Duchess returned. Information was then blocked off from us and the mission had to retire with what information they had already collected. There was much to learn about the way in which small states like Luxembourg had been used by the cartels. The episode suggests that some rulers, whom we have befriended, may be expected to assist the cartelists in their postwar efforts to regain dominance.[25]

What the Grand Duchess learned from her finance minister was simple: Do not tamper with the cartel. Luxembourg made a vast amount of money and there was every indication that it stood to make a great deal more. All it needed to do was readjust the stock ownership to please the Allies. Powerful friends of the Bormann organization understood what was at stake and planned accordingly. Scattered across the globe in various control points, such as Wall Street, Washington, London and Paris, were members of a group of bankers well aware of the financial benefits of cooperating with the Nazi underground.

The Nazi plans rested on American fears of communism. Free enterprise and property rights were to take center stage, while war crimes and crimes against humanity were conveniently dismissed as superficial. Such was the case in the 4–1 vote by the appeals board to free Richard Freudenberg, the largest shoemaker in Germany. Freudenberg was a regional economic adviser to Bormann and a die-hard Nazi. He was in the automatic arrest category. Ambassador Murphy expressed the argument of free enterprise in his comments in defense of Freudenberg. This is the same Murphy who was part of the control council. His comments:

What we are doing here through denazification is nothing short of a social revolution. If the Russians want to Bolshevize their side of the Elbe that is their business, but it is not in conformity with American standards to cut away the basis of private property. This man is an extremely capable industrialist, a kind of Henry Ford.[26]

In testimony given at Nuremberg, Herman Schmitz praised Bormann for the manner in which he spread German assets around the globe. Of particular interest was Schmitz's view of what was ahead for the directors of IG Farben once the war ended:

We can continue. We have an operational plan. However, I don't believe our board members will be detained long. Nor will I. But we must go through a procedure of investigation before release, so I have been told by our N.W.7 people who have excellent contacts in Washington.[27]

The phrase "who have excellent contacts in Washington" should have set off alarm bells for the U.S. prosecuting team at Nuremberg. Here is direct proof of people in power in Washington collaborating with an integral part of the Nazi war machine. The N.W.7 division of IG Farben was closely connected to the SS and Gestapo, as well as the rest of Nazi intelligence. Where was the follow-up investigation to identify those contacts? There are reasons many files from WWII have not been released. Besides exposing the industrialists and congressional members mentioned in the previous chapters as traitors, such files would uncover many career employees of the State Department and the military-intelligence community as traitors.

Like so many other promising leads, it was quietly dropped. This attitude of top IG Farben directors was typical. They knew in advance that they would suffer only minor penalties. As George Seldes reminded us, there are people too powerful or too rich to be subjected to our laws, even when it involves treason. Schmitz's information was slightly inaccurate in that twelve IG Farben executives did face trial at Nuremberg. Schmitz received a four-year sentence. However, all the sentences were later reduced to time served, and all the executives returned to their previous positions.

At this point we return to the Merkers hoard. Intelligence reports since 1940 indicated the Nazis accumulated a fortune of roughly $1 billion in 1940 dollars, or about $10 billion today. The discovery of the Merkers hoard created a complex set of problems. First, the find was only about half of the estimated Nazi treasure. While the Merker's hoard was most of the Reichsbank's holdings, there was more gold and currency left in Berlin. Second, dividing the treasure presented a myriad of problems that remain controversial today.

Also troublesome were the accounts of Melmer and Max Heiliger. Interrogation of Nazi banking officials soon revealed the nature of these accounts. Albert Thoms explained the booty seized by the Wehrmacht went straight to the Reichshauptkasse or Treasury. However, the Reichsbank exclusively handled the loot seized by the SS. The bank would credit the loot to the Melmer account, assess the value, then credit the amount to the Heiliger account. Only five people were privy to the Heiliger account: Reichsbank President Walter Funk, Reichsbank Vice President Emil Puhl, Chief Cashier Kropf, Director Fronknecht and Albert Thoms, chief of the Precious Metals Department. The SS account held the earnings skimmed from the Action Reinhardt operation that began in 1943 to strip the concentration camp inmates of all gold coins, jewelry and clothing. Puhl aided this operation. Besides his Reichsbank position, he also was a director of the International Bank for Settlements. Thus, he was in a perfect position to act as an international fence after the concentration camp gold was smelted into gold bars.[28]

The Melmer account was indicative of other private accounts. Indeed, many top-ranking Nazis, from colonel on up, gathered their own treasures. Some of these private treasures, such as Goering's, were substantial in their own right, while others were more modest. The value of these private treasure hoards is unknown, as is the fate of many of them.

Additional caches were uncovered in the Merkers area. In another mine, the Allies found 400 tons of records from the German Patent Office, enough to fill 30 railroad cars. Another discovery included more than 2 million books, the records of the German High Command and much more.

Corruption Overtakes Safehaven

With the capture of Merkers, the Allies were fast closing in on Berlin. As they advanced, the Nazis made a last desperate attempt to save the remaining Reichsbank assets by moving them to southern Germany in the alpine redoubt area. Many top Nazi officials desperate to save themselves also fled to this region with the fortunes looted from their victims.

Ernst Kaltenbrunner, chief of the Reich Security Head Office, amassed one such private fortune and transported it into the Bavarian Alps to save himself and his ill-gotten gain. Only one document survives detailing the contents:

50 cases of gold coins and gold articles (each case weighing 100 pounds)
2 million U.S. dollars

2 million Swiss francs

5 cases of diamonds and gemstones

a stamp collection worth 5 million gold marks

110 pounds of gold bars[29]

Goering also transported his private hoard to the region, including a large collection of vintage wines.

The Nazis did not ship all the Reichsbank's assets to Merkers, leaving some in Berlin to pay the troops and cover other expenses in the final days of the war. Reichsbank assets left in Berlin included a prodigious quantity of paper money, 730 gold bars and millions in gold coins. The gold bars were valued at nearly $10 million.

As the Allies continued to advance with the Russians on Berlin, the Nazis shipped most of the remaining assets of the Reichsbank to southern Germany aboard two special trains, code named Adler (meaning eagle) and Dohle (meaning jackdaw).[30] Once these trains left Berlin, $3,434,625 of gold still remained in Berlin.

Because of the rapid Allied advance and air cover, the trains were unable to travel directly to Munich, and were forced to take an alternate route through Czechoslovakia. On April 16, three days after leaving Berlin, the trains were stranded about 10 miles from Pilsen, waiting for the tracks to be cleared for a final run to Munich. While stranded, the Nazis loaded some of the treasure onto trucks for the remaining trip to Munich. On April 19, the trains were just inside the Bavarian border, and the Nazis again loaded another portion of the treasure onto trucks.

By nightfall on April 19, the train was about 50 miles south of Munich at Peissenberg, where the Nazis planned to hide the treasure in a lead mine. However, the electricity was out and the mine began to fill with water. The Nazi in charge of the treasure decided to hide it in a small town named Mittenwald. At this point, it is believed the fortune consisted:

365 bags, each containing two gold bars

9 envelopes of records

4 boxes of bullion

2 bags of gold coins

6 cases of Danish coins

94 bags of foreign exchange

34 printing plates and a supply of banknote paper[31]

Even after the two trains left Berlin, a small quantity of treasure remained in the Reichsbank. On orders from Ernst Kaltenbrunner, SS Gen. Josef Spacil, head of Office II, seized the remaining Reichsbank assets at gunpoint and transported them south. Gold and gems taken in the robbery are estimated at more than $9 million.

Spacil amassed a huge private hoard, some of which he divided among Gestapo officers in the closing days. He gave Hitler's commando Otto Skorzeny 50,000 gold francs, 10,000 Spanish crowns, US$5,000, 5,000 Swiss francs and 5 million Reich marks. Skorzeny was hiding in the Austrian Tyrol. Skorzeny surfaced in Spain, where he lived palatially and ran his part of *Die Spinne* (the spider) escape route. In addition, he became an arms dealer.[32] During the 1950s, it was clear to American intelligence that Skorzeny had ample funds at his disposal. The Allies never recovered the money; Skorzeny went to work for the CIA.

American authorities later duped Spacil into leading them to a small cache containing 19 bags of gold coins, bullion worth $11,722, and paper money consisting of $160,179 and £96,614 sterling. Many other private hoards were hidden in this area of southern Germany.

Starting on April 19, 1945, the Allied gold rush teams were in full operation, headed by Col. Bernstein, Cmdr. Joel Fisher and Lt. Herbert DuBois. Helping them were Albert Thoms, chief of the

Precious Metals Department of the Reichsbank, and Emil Puhl, vice president of the Reichsbank. Gold rush teams soon located several treasure hoards. On April 26, at the Reichsbank branch in Halle, they found 65 bags of foreign currency, which included about $1 million; at Plauen, they found 35 bags of gold coins, including 1 million Swiss francs and a quarter-million gold dollars. On April 27, they learned of 82 bars of gold bullion in Aue, which was still heavily defended. On April 28, they located more than 600 silver bars and 500 cases of silver bars, which comprised the entire silver reserves of Hungary. On April 29, they found 82 gold bars at Eschwege; the following day, they found additional gold bars hidden under a manure pile at Coburg. On May 1, they found 34 cases and two bags of non-Reich gold in Nuremberg. The gold recovery teams shipped these hoards to Frankfurt.

Both combat troops and gold teams found caches of looted treasure, including the famed gold train containing treasures from Hungary. Total estimated value of the treasure recovered from the train was $500 million, including $350 million of gold.

The gold recovered from the various Reichsbank branches totaled $3 million. However, from interrogations and captured documents, the gold rush teams knew the Reichsbank branches had more than $17 million in gold. The Russians recovered roughly $3 million in Berlin. In early May, Bernstein had to return to Washington for discussions with President Truman on the decartelization program. Lt. DuBois then took charge of the recovery efforts in southern Germany.[33]

Gold rush teams failed to recover any gold from southern Germany until June 7, when a detachment headed by Maj. William Geiler (later a New York Supreme Court justice) recovered 728 gold bars. The gold was shipped to Frankfurt and properly inventoried. This recovery is commonly confused with the gold recovered by Sgt. Singleton, who recovered a stash of gold described to be around 3 feet high and 3 feet wide. Singleton's gold reached Munich, but it never reached Frankfurt and remains unaccounted for.[34]

Robert Kempner, the chief prosecutor for the Nazi diplomats' trial, expressed in a letter to Perry Lankhuff of the political division of the military government many of the problems that plagued complete recovery of the Nazi gold. The letter appears below.

In the course of our trial against Nazi diplomats which has just been concluded, it was brought to light that the German Foreign Office had — besides other gold funds — a special Ribbentrop gold fund, in gold bullion, weighing approximately fifteen tons. Leads and newspaper accounts from various countries in the Western Hemisphere indicate that unrecovered Foreign Office gold, probably in the hands of former German Foreign Office officials, is still at work for anti-American purposes. Large numbers of former German diplomats who had to do with the Foreign Office gold are still in foreign countries, e.g., Spain, Italy, Ireland, Argentina, Sweden, and Switzerland, living well from unknown resources.

It should be noted that besides other former German diplomats, a brother-in-law of Ribbentrop is living in Switzerland, and at least two other German Foreign Office officials who dealt with German gold matters.

Out of the fifteen tons, about eleven tons of Ribbentrop's Foreign Office gold was hurriedly removed from Berlin in 1945:

1. 6.5 tons to Ribbentrop's Castle Fuschl in Austria (now American Zone of Austria). The larger part of this consignment was allegedly turned over to American troops in the neighborhood of Fuschl. However German Foreign Office officials stated here in Nürnberg the amount allegedly turned over was less than the amount, which was shipped to Fuschl.

2. 2 tons to Schleswig-Holstein in the British Zone allegedly turned over to the British.

3. 3 tons to the South of Germany on the shores of Lake Konstanze, an area then in American hands. Out of the last amount, two-thirds of a ton was taken to Berne, Switzerland, in the closing days of the war. This was done in the presence of the son of the former German Minister of Foreign Affairs, von Neurath, who according to newspaper reports, arrived a short time ago in the Argentine.

About four tons were sent between 1943 and 1945 to German embassies, notably to Madrid, Spain (one ton), to Stockholm, Sweden (one-half ton), to Berne, Switzerland (three-fourths ton), to Ankara, Turkey (about 1 ton), to Lisbon, Portugal (an unknown quantity).

Since I interviewed several hundred German diplomats, including ambassadors, ministers, and fiscal and personnel administrators, I know that the summation which I made above is highly reliable.

But so far as I know there was never any check made whether gold of this amount was ever recovered or whether the amount of Foreign Office gold turned over by German foreign service people to Allied authorities at the end of the war was identical with sums indicated by my investigation.

In the course of the trial, I have from time to time pointed out the danger and the problem of this missing gold, but nobody as yet tackled the problem, and with my heavy trial work in Nürnberg, I could not devote much time to it, since no war crime was involved. I feel very strongly that this gold project should not be neglected further in these critical times, in which a large amount of uncontrolled gold constitutes a force for evil and mischief in the hands of unscrupulous opportunists working closely together and located in many countries all over the world.[35]

The only certainty about Ribbentrop's gold is that American forces only recovered a little more than 4 tons. The 6.5 tons allegedly recovered from Ribbentrop's castle vanished because no records pertaining to it exist in the Federal Exchange Depository. According to records from the Wilhelmstrasse trial, a large part of this gold was turned over to either the Third or Seventh Army on June 15, 1945. However, the books of the Allied occupation show no trace of this gold, worth $108 million today. Kempner continued to look for the missing gold. In 1950, he lobbied Congress to investigate, but it found no new information.

The disappearance of various treasure hoards recovered in southern Germany was all too common. Capt. Fred Neumann recovered a stash of paper currency from the garden of the von Bluechers. The only document of this recovery is a poorly typed receipt that Luder and Hubert von Bluecher demanded before turning the money over to Neumann. The receipt declares the von Bluechers turned over to the U.S. Army $404,840 and £405 sterling. The Army and historians suspected both Neumann and the von Bluechers in the disappearance. However, with recently released documents from government archives, it is now obvious this was part of a much larger problem, clearing them of suspicion.[36]

The problem was aggravated by the rivalry and lack of coordination between the Army and military government agencies. CID (Criminal Investigative Division) was chiefly responsible to the Army; CIC was mostly responsible to the military government. The recovery of Nazi gold involved both groups. Further, Army and military government communication was from the top down, with the bottom levels faltering, at best. Many military government commanders considered themselves free agents and ignored directives from higher-ups. Complicating the problem was the high rotation of personnel and the limited contracts the military government could offer. The military government issued one-year contracts and restricted annual pay to $10,000.

Initially, CID bore responsibility for searching for Reichsbank treasure. However, at war's end, CID was full of men counting the days before they shipped home. Most were recruited from military police units and background checks often were lacking. Several CID replacement agents had criminal records, while others were discredited police officers, which the division weeded out as soon as they were discovered.

Ultimately, all CID units were under the Command Provost Marshal, Brig. Gen. George H. (Pappy) Weems, a West Point officer whose basic branch of service was the horse cavalry. Apparently, Weems was unable to make the switch from the cavalry to armored divisions. Before his transfer to Germany, Weems was head of the military mission to Hungary. Noticeably absent in his background was any police or investigative work. Weems walked with a cane, had poor hearing and a faulty memory, and lacked the ability to understand anything complex. The general had frequent temper tantrums and often issued outrageous orders. Weems had a strange obsession with typewriters and required any case involving a stolen or missing one to be brought to his attention. In short, Weems was senile, most likely the result of a mild stroke.[37]

It was not until September 1947 that Lt. Col. William Karp replaced Weems. Obviously, Weems' inappropriate assignment handicapped CID. How Weems came to be assigned his post is left for future researchers.

Like the 4Ds program, CID was hampered by a shortage of staff and quality training, which contributed to the corruption in the Munich area. While the first gold rush teams under Bernstein lacked staff yet did an admirable job, by June 1945, most of them were discharged and replaced with new recruits.

Internal feuding among agents plagued CIC. Many agents were German-born Jews. CIC agents divided into two groups: one considered Germany their home and worked hard to rout Nazism to return to a democratic state; the other group, mostly from Eastern Europe, considered Germany a stepping-stone on the way to Palestine. Other CIC agents were first-generation Poles and Czechs, or of other Eastern European origins, with divided loyalties and even illegal alliances reaching outside CIC. By far, the CID unit was the more professional; CID agents often described CIC as a group of thugs.

From late June 1945–47, this was the sad state of affairs hampering the Garmisch case, in which gold was recovered, then lost. CID was overly compartmentalized with no clear objectives, no direction, no coordination and, most importantly, no centralized database. In short, CID allowed various units to blunder off into the dark to follow their own individual goals. The Garmisch case was complicated since no one knew exactly how much gold and currency had disappeared. It took another year and a half before the Federal Exchange Depository discovered that its Reichsbank account was short $2 million.

The recent release of classified documents shows the recovered funds were deposited in the Land Central Bank in Munich, where the gold and currency vanished. None of the recoveries around Garmisch ever reached the Federal Exchange Depository. Various American authorities in the chain from Garmisch to Frankfurt were all familiar with the proper procedures for transferring funds, but the funds would reach Munich and then disappear. After an exhaustive search, authors Ian Sayer and Douglas Botting decided that $432,985,013 from the Reichsbank was unaccounted for. Included were diamonds, securities and currencies given to Otto Skorzeny by SS General Spacil totaling more than $9.1 million, of which the Allies only recovered $492,401. In one case, Maj. Roger Rawley recovered $8 million in paper currency and turned it over to Maj. Kenneth McIntyre. From there, the funds disappeared.[38]

After Germany's surrender, the economy decayed into a black market, with cigarettes the preferred medium of exchange. One Camel cigarette was worth more than double a day's pay for a German hired to clear rubble. At first, Gen. Clay seemed unaware of the black market, but when CID reported to him that it was a security threat, he took every step to cover it up. Americans willing to engage in the black market extended all the way to the top and included Clay's wife. U.S. Customs, Florida District, made it more difficult for Gen. Clay after it sent a complaint listing landings of his personal plane in the Miami area. In each case, the pilot bypassed Customs by reporting the landings as classified. However, in Germany, the flights were logged as training missions. Charges were filed against the pilot, but it was clear he was just taking the fall for someone else.[39]

Many Americans tried to strike it rich in the black market economy, but most failed. The lucky few came predominantly from the Office of Military Government in Bavaria. The head of the Financial Division in Munich was Col. Russell Lord and his aide, Maj. John McCarthy from Property Control. Both figure prominently in the disappearance of gold and currency once it reached Munich.[40] Once the gold from Garmisch was turned over to the proper authorities in Munich, only McCarthy and Lord had access to it. An American investigator also accused McCarthy of having a hand in the drug trade in and around Garmisch and Munich.

The extent of the military government's corruption is revealed in the following passage by Lt. Kulka, an aide to Col. Smith assigned to look into the corruption in the Garmisch and Munich areas. Kulka was sent to a civilian house converted into an American bachelor officers quarters on a report that a young officer was sharing his room with his girlfriend, a baroness, which was strictly forbidden. The hausdame mistook Kulka for a courier and gave him a briefcase.

> She looked at me and said, "Oh you must be the young man who came to pick up the briefcase with the papers for Switzerland." I said, "I guess so." She said, "Oh yes, lieutenant told me that you were coming to pick it up and that you are a young pilot." So I said, "Yes." The Dame came down and handed me a briefcase and a larger attaché case, which had been sealed with a diplomatic seal. Therefore, I took them and hastily left. I took them to my room in the house and opened the diplomatic case and to my surprise found it filled with British pounds in rather large denominations and some jewelry. The briefcase I found to be filled with about ten folders which contained very neatly written columns of names of people with dates and their rank, their location and sums of money — all the instructions and records of how the money had been transported across the border. I immediately went to Colonel Smith and he was extremely interested. We went through the paperwork and found a great number of important names, including several colonels from headquarters. The one thing they all had in common was that they all belonged to units that had one time or another controlled the border crossing to Switzerland — military police, military government agencies and CIC.[41]

By the middle of July 1947, Col. Smith completed his preliminary investigation and filed his report to Gen. Clay. The report pointed out that there was enough evidence to warrant a full-scale investigation, and Gen. Clay issued an order to that effect. Fearing for his life, Smith asked for an immediate transfer. Afterward, the military governor and post commander of Garmisch were shipped back to the States and several other officers transferred out of the area. The Inspector General Office suddenly closed the investigation. Kulka alleges the order to stop the investigation came from Clay's office. He also claims half of the U.S. command would have been in trouble if the investigation continued. Files gathered by Smith and Kulka were destroyed. Kulka was ordered to keep his mouth shut, then accused of gunrunning and of harboring an alien in his quarters, who happened to be his 87-year-old grandmother. His bride-to-be was listed as a Sudeten German expellee from Czechoslovakia, not as a Jewish DP. When Kulka told his senator of the problem, so much pressure was brought on his bride-to-be and his grandmother that he had to keep quiet. Only by accident was his future bride allowed to obtain her exit permit. Col. Smith was transferred from Berlin to Ecuador. In 1978, Kulka reported that his friends' mysterious deaths and suicides were warnings to keep his mouth shut about the Garmisch affair.[42]

The Garmisch affair did not end with Smith and Kulka. In September in Bad Tohr, Frank Gammache was charged with misappropriation of military property, and disorderly and discreditable conduct. The charges were trivial compared to the criminal activity in the area. Gammache was going to be the small fall guy. Operation Garpeck opened a further investigation. Heading the operation were Victor Peccarelli and Philip von Pfluge Benzell. The case soon reached to San Francisco, where now civilian Capt. Neumann lived. The investigation into Maj. McCarthy reopened. McCarthy's influence still lingered in Munich, as files on him disappeared before investigators got to them. Shortly after they began bugging his phone, McCarthy learned of the tap and moved.

The investigation soon crossed the path of journalist Guenter Reinhardt, who came from a German Jewish banking family. At the age of 21, he came to the United States and got his first job at a bank in New York. In 1933, he became a freelance journalist who wrote a syndicated column on foreign affairs for the McClure newspapers. Various banking and civic groups commissioned Reinhardt to conduct an investigation into Germany's likely future international relations. Reinhardt turned over to the House Committee on Immigration and Naturalization the information he uncovered about Nazi activities in the United States. This led him into activities with American Intelligence. In 1934, he acted as a liaison between the McCormick Committee and the FBI. In 1942–43, Reinhardt infiltrated communist organizations for the bureau. In 1946, he joined the CIC in Germany.

By all reports, Reinhardt was an enthusiastic and dedicated agent in Europe. However, he soon began to show signs of stress and fatigue when he realized the whole system was corrupt. By the summer of

1947, he realized that his CIC career was in jeopardy. His superiors secretly arranged to send Reinhardt home. He complained about the transfer, but there was no appeal and he was forbidden to go to the Inspector General, under threat of immediate arrest. He was further warned that if he spoke with the press or tried to get another job in Germany, he would be arrested for violating security regulations. In addition, they threatened to drag his German girlfriend through the mud.

Outraged at the actions and threats, Reinhardt dictated the first of two memos. The formal 48-page report revealed the irregularities and fake intelligence reports in the Munich region, and accused CIC of widespread corruption and incompetence. The report, written in November, caused an immediate shake-up. The operations chief for Bavaria was dismissed and the executive officer was transferred. However, there also was a cover-up of two chains, one from Garmisch to Augsburg and another from Munich to Nuremberg. After he arrived in New York in December, Reinhardt wrote his second memo, a 55-page document that was divided into nine sections. The opening section, "Loot and Smuggling Situation," described how U.S. personnel continued to smuggle valuables into the States; the higher the rank, the greater the problem. Reinhardt detailed how a general's baggage contained 166 crates laden with silverware, china and other valuables looted from castles around Hesse. After his appointment as a special consultant, Reinhardt dictated his memo to Assistant Secretary of Army Gordon Gray, who later became director of the CIA.

The heart of the memo charged that a group of Americans and Germans headed by John McCarthy were involved in widespread corruption in the Garmisch area and wielded enough power to derail any investigations. The memo was sent to Gen. Clay in Germany and caused an immediate uproar. Clay hated scandals in his command. Rather than clean up the mess, he launched another vast cover-up. Gen. Weems canceled the ongoing Operation Garpeck shortly after Reinhardt's memo arrived in Germany. The Army decided the charges were overblown.

McCarthy and his superior, Col. Lord, did not escape unscathed. While they survived charges from the Reinhardt memo, their boundless greed eventually caught up with them. The pair planned to buy various IG Farben plants through a front they set up in Liechtenstein. An investigation ordered by Gen. Clay unmasked their scheme and the Army discharged them. However, Gen. Clay made no public announcement of the illegality of the scheme or its outcome.[43] Yet while the military government in the Munich area was beset with corruption, the looting of the Nazi hoard pales in comparison to the money laundered by the neutral countries.

Operation Andrew

The plot to counterfeit British pounds figured prominently in the Nazi finance plans. Perhaps one of the most understood affairs of the war, it is often mistakenly referred to as Operation Bernhard; its true name was Operation Andrew or Andreas. No one knows for certain the extent of the action, or how many bogus notes the Nazis placed in circulation.

The Bank of London had its own reasons to keep mum about the forged bills it found in circulation as the Nazis designed Operation Andrew to bring about the downfall of the British pound. The operation was the brainchild of Alfred Nanjocks, a fanatical Nazi. Nanjocks was the officer who simulated the Polish attack on the German radio station that started the war. After occupying the Low Countries, Heydrich transferred Nanjocks to the documents division of the SD, because he had earned a reputation of being too reckless and violent for his own good. Forging passports was not to the hothead's liking. However, flooding the world in bogus currency to destabilize the English economy appealed to him. Nanjocks was imagining just that.

The British were the first to try disrupting the enemy's economy using counterfeit money.[ii] The British forged German auxiliary certificates of payment for 50 Reichspfennige and dropped them from planes all over Germany.

Immediately after, Nanjocks took the idea to Heydrich, who not only approved the scheme, but also added the forging of American dollars and sought out Hitler's approval. Hitler refused to approve the forging of dollars, because at that time Germany was not at war with the United States. Funk and other bureaucrats did not like the idea much. Funk worried that destabilizing the pound could create a creditor backlash and destabilize the Reichsmark. Funk's worries testify to the degree of collusion between the Bank of England and the Nazis.

Heydrich assigned the matter to RSHA Bureau IV, which created a new division, SHARP 4, to oversee it. In the summer of 1942, the Nazis set up the forging ring inside the Sachsenhausen concentration camp headed by SS major Fredrich Kruger. The operation was formally known as Aktion1 in Berlin. The use of inmate labor limited security problems, but the group had a tough time developing a suitable paper. Max Bober, a printer by profession, headed the team of 60 inmates. The counterfeiters were isolated from the rest of the Sachsenhausen concentration camp. The Nazis provided the inmates with everything they needed, but sabotage would have resulted in their immediate death. It was not until 1943 that a Hahnemuhl plant produced a suitable paper. The factory delivered 12,000 sheets a month to the operation. Each sheet produced eight notes. Even then, the forged notes were only mediocre at best. It was not until the Nazis located Salomon Smolianoff, an expert counterfeiter, that they could produce suitable notes.

Once Smolianoff corrected the earlier mistakes, the Nazis did 15- to 20-hour print runs. The inmates examined each note and selected only the best. These notes then underwent a procedure of aging to make them look used. The Nazis counterfeiters produced all denominations, including hundred-pound notes, but the five-pound note made up 40 percent of the print runs. By mid-1943, Kruger's team had grown to 140, and was turning out about 40,000 notes a month. Unlike the rest of the camp, Kruger's inmates received enough food and even a cigarette ration.

The counterfeiters divided the notes into four categories: perfect, near perfect, flawed and rejects. They destroyed the rejects, although initially, they planned to air drop them over England. The Nazi plot reserved the perfect notes for German spies to use in neutral countries. The near-perfect and flawed notes were bundled and provided to the SS to be used in occupied countries. As the operation continued, the quality of the notes improved to such a degree that banks throughout the world accepted them. The Bank of England only stumbled across the forged notes when a bank clerk noticed the two notes she held in her hand had the same serial number.

The operation eventually shipped the equivalent of $4.5 billion in British pounds to Berlin and then all over the world. Nazi agents used the forged notes to buy legitimate objects, which they then resold for stable world currencies. German embassies in the neutral countries received some of the notes to exchange for local currency. The first attempt to distribute the notes widely was disastrous. The German military arrested their own agents when they tried to pass the forged notes, because Action1 was top secret.[44]

At some point, the underlying mission of Action 1 changed. Himmler and Lt. Grobel, head of Bureau VI, became greedy. They imagined laundering the notes on a large scale and skimming the profits for their personal benefit. To carry out the widespread distribution, Friedrich Schwend was brought into the operation. In the 1920s, Schwend was an arms dealer. He married the niece of the Minister of Exterior Baron von Neurath. Through his wife's family connections, he received an appointment as the personal administrator of the wealthy Bunge family. This is the same Bunge family that made a small fortune by

---

[ii] It was an old ruse for the British, who used it to effect in the American War of Independence, resulting in the complete debasement of the Continental currency.

shorting the market the day John F. Kennedy was murdered. In the 1930s, Schwend was working from New York managing the investments of Bunge & Born.

The operation brought Schwend into Bureau IV as paymaster of the money-laundering scheme. Bureau IV gave him a false identity as Maj. Wendig, a legal officer of the Gestapo and a member of the tank corps. In September 1943, Schwend started setting up his network and requested Col. Josef Spacil do the operation's bookkeeping. This is the same Col. Spacil involved in funding Skorzeny. Operation Bernhard is limited to this scheme of private enrichment. Schwend was skimming a third of the fake notes for this group.

Operation Andrew continued to the end of the war. The Bank of England suffered enormous losses. Even with the Russians closing in on Sachsenhausen, the operation did not shut down. It just moved to southern Germany, near the Austrian border. There, it continued to produce fake notes until about May 3. Some of the last forged notes ended up at the bottom of Lake Topltz. The Nazis hid crates of forged notes there in a midnight rowboat operation. The boxes were recovered in 2000. The fate of the balance of the notes is unknown.[45]

Sweden's Neutrality

As much as half of the Reichsbank gold remains unaccounted for. Bormann undoubtedly transferred some of it out of Germany, and top Nazi officials and U.S. personnel looted other portions of the treasure. However, a great deal of looted gold was used by the Nazis to buy munitions and raw material from neutral countries.

It was not until its Gold Declaration of Jan. 5, 1943 that the United States began an aggressive campaign toward the neutrals and their gold dealings. Aware that Nazi Germany was disposing of looted property in neutral countries, Britain started talks with the other Allies. On Jan. 5, 1945, Britain issued the Inter-Allied Declaration against Acts of Dispossession Committed in Territories under Enemy Occupation or Control. The declaration was signed by 16 nations and England. The declaration simply stated the signatory nations reserved the right to declare invalid any transaction involving property from any of the occupied territories. The declaration was largely political. Both the Bank of England and the Treasury Department doubted that the act would achieve the desired results. There was little the Allies could do to enforce the declaration without damaging their own economic situation or souring future relations with the neutrals. Technically, the act was restricted to gold dealings only. Others wanted to broaden the scope of the act to include other valuables.

Of particular concern to the United States was Switzerland. However, it was not until the tide of the war turned clearly in the favor of the Allies that the Swiss responded. On Dec. 28, 1944, Switzerland announced it had blocked all accounts from Hungary, Slovakia and Croatia. On Feb. 7, 1945, British and American delegates met with Swiss officials in Berne to negotiate an agreement on immediate economic warfare objectives and Swiss exports to Germany. In turn, the Swiss wanted help in getting raw materials and food in the form of import quotas from the Allies, and support for transit facilities across France. On Feb. 16, Switzerland announced a block on all German assets. On March 8, the Swiss signed an agreement under which the Swiss government took measures:

To ensure the territory of the Swiss Confederation should not be used as a cache for looted assets.

To conduct a census of German assets in Switzerland.

To buy no more gold from Germany except the quantity needed for diplomatic expenses.[46]

It was not until three months before the defeat of Germany that Switzerland took any action against the Nazis. Further, it was only one month before the defeat of the Nazis when the Swiss finally banned gold trades with them. The willingness of the other neutrals to take action against the Nazis followed a similar timeline. They did nothing until it was clear the Nazis were defeated.

The declarations issued on June 5, 1945, by the Four Powers and the Report of the Potsdam Conference of Aug. 2, 1945 provided the basis for the recovery of gold and Nazi assets outside Germany. The Potsdam accord stated that the Allied Control Council would take such measures as were fitting to exercise control over German assets abroad, and would exercise the right of disposal of such assets. Both acts conferred powers on the Allies that were not easy to exercise and not well received by many of the neutral countries. Legally, the Allied position was weak.

Both Sweden and Switzerland were quick to respond that such demands conflicted both with their own legislation and with their status as neutrals. The Allies failed to agree on how to deal with the neutrals until December 1945. Even then, the agreement had weak wording and offered no guidance on how to prevail on the neutrals to return Nazi assets. The United States wanted to employ sanctions while the British rejected them as unenforceable in peacetime. Eventually, Britain agreed with the United States to open negotiations with Switzerland in Washington. As leverage over the Swiss, the United States would neither unblock Swiss accounts in the United States nor remove Swiss companies from the Allied blacklist unless an agreement was reached.[47]

A brief survey follows of the neutral nations and the problems faced in each.

During the war, Sweden was openly pro-fascist, although it was one of the more cooperative neutral countries. High-grade Swedish iron ore formed the basis of a strong and profitable connection between Sweden and the Nazis, for whom this supply of ore was so vital that they delayed invading the Low Countries, going into Denmark and Norway first to protect the shipping route for the Swedish ore.

Swedish ball-bearing producer S&K also enjoyed a profitable relationship with the Nazis. S&K presented a special problem for the United States, which was equally dependent on the company for bearings. S&K did its best to delay production of war munitions in its U.S. plants, presenting the Roosevelt administration with a dilemma. The United States could impose sanctions on S&K, Sweden or both. The sanctions would most likely result in a reprisals by S&K, further limiting U.S. production of bearings, and disrupting the building of military vehicles and ships. A second alternative for the administration was to seize the plants during the war, but that would only heighten the charges of rampant communism and socialism by FDR's critics. The course followed was to allow S&K to continue business as usual. Regardless of who won the war, S&K would win big by supplying both sides.

Many other Swedish corporations that enjoyed profitable dealings with the Nazis. The one most cherished by Germany was Enskilda Bank, owned by the Wallenbergs. The Nazis borrowed funds and laundered their stolen gold there. Safehaven documents revealed that the United States was tracking the pro-Nazi activities of the Wallenbergs for several years. In February 1945, in a letter to Secretary of State Edward Stettinius, Morgenthau charged that Enskilda was making large loans to the Nazis without collateral, and covertly investing money for German capitalists in U.S. industries, in line with the Bormann plans. He further charged the bank was repeatedly connected with large black market operations.

Morgenthau identified Jacob Wallenberg as strongly pro-Nazi and rejected the claim that Marcus Wallenberg was for the Allies. Like S&K, the Wallenbergs were playing both sides. Cousin Raul Wallenberg helped to save 20,000 Jews in Budapest. When the Soviet army recaptured Budapest, Raul was arrested as an American spy. In June 1996, *U.S. News and World Report* published a review of declassified documents indicating that Raul Wallenberg was indeed a spy for the OSS.[48]

In a Feb. 7, 1945 Treasury memo, Morgenthau detailed his concerns on the Wallenberg brothers:

Jacob Wallenberg recently indicated that he was willing to sell to the Germans a Swedish plant in Hamburg for gold provided the price was high enough for possible future complications.

The following facts should be considered in evaluating the impression held in some circles that Marcus Wallenberg is strongly pro-Allied.

A. While Marcus Wallenberg was apparently sympathetic with the Allied cause, Jacob Wallenberg, his brother and partner in the Enskilda Bank was known to be sympathetic to and working with the Germans.

B. Jacob Wallenberg was the author of the Swedish-German trading agreement.

C. Jacob Wallenberg is a member of the Permanent Joint Swedish-German Trading Commission and Marcus Wallenberg is a member of the Joint Standing Committee created by the Anglo-Swedish Trading Agreement.

D. Marcus Wallenberg came to the United States in 1940 and attempted to purchase on behalf of German interest an American held block of German securities.

E. Enskilda Bank has been repeatedly connected with large black market operations in foreign currencies, including the dollars reported to have been dumped by the Germans.[49]

Britain and the United States began to enlist Sweden in the Safehaven program in 1944. Britain was in favor of restricting the program in Sweden to gold, while the United States wanted to include other assets. The United States used trade agreements as an inducement for cooperation. The Riksdag, the Swedish Parliament, voiced its approval of Safehaven and in February 1945, Sweden began an inventory of its gold and foreign currency to see how much was linked to the Nazis. By spring, the British agreed with the Americans and drafted a proposal for Sweden, which then served as a basis for talks in Lisbon and Madrid. By summer 1945, Sweden had passed several measures to restrict the sale or dispersal of German property, and expanded the range of its census to include all types of German property. In January 1946, at the urging of the Allies, Sweden broadened the laws to include German subsidiaries. In November 1945, Sweden gave the Treasury Department a report on Swedish gold transactions. From it, the Treasury decided Sweden had received $22.7 million in looted gold from Belgium. The United States soon reduced the amount to $17 million.

On Feb. 11, 1946, the U.S. Embassy told Sweden of the details of ACC Law 5 vesting the title of German assets in other countries with the occupation authorities, and invited a Swedish delegation to Washington. Sweden expressed grave concerns over the claim, but agreed to the talks. On April 5, Sweden told the American embassy the matter would have to be put to the Riksdag, where it would probably face defeat in the Riksdag in the face of beliefs that the Allied claim was invalid in international law, and therefore a violation of private property rights. Before negotiations began, Sweden also requested release of its frozen assets in the United States, and permission to inspect Swedish property in Germany. The United States denied the request.

By the end of March, after discussions with Britain and France over German assets in Sweden, the United States believed it had an almost complete picture and began to push for formal negotiations, which began in Washington on May 29. Seymour Rubin, Deputy Director of the State Department's Office of Economic Security Policy, headed the U.S. delegation. Francis W. McCombe of the Foreign Office led the British delegation. France headed its delegation with Christian Valensi, Financial Counselor of the French Embassy in Washington. Judge Emil Sandstrom headed the delegation from Sweden. From the outset, Sweden agreed to the danger of Nazi assets being used to provide a rival, but contested the legality of the Allies' claim to the assets.

On July 18, the two sides reached an agreement. Of the estimated 378 million kroner (about $90.7 million) in German assets in Sweden, Sweden agreed to divide the assets as follows: 50 million kroner (about $12.5 million) went to the Intergovernmental Committee on Refugees (later the International Refugee Organization); 75 million kroner (about $18 million) went to the Inter-Allied Reparations Agency (IARA), excluding the amounts the United States, Britain and France received; 150 million kroner (about $36 million) went for aid in preventing disease and unrest in Germany. The last sum was used in Sweden or other countries to buy essential commodities for the German economy. Moreover, the agreement allowed for Swedish and German owners of liquidated property to be compensated in German currency. It also allowed for a mission to travel to the U.S., British and French zones of occupied Germany to inspect Swedish properties. Further it called for the release of frozen Swedish assets in the

United States (estimated at the time at $200 million); the removal of any blacklists; and permission for the Allies to hold in reserve their claims to German properties in Sweden.

In the agreement, Sweden would restitute 7,555 kilograms of fine gold (roughly $8.1 million), the same quantity stemming from the Bank of Belgium. The United States would hold Sweden harmless from any claims arising from transfers from the Swedish Riksbank to third countries. Finally, the agreement banned the Allies from claims to any gold received by Sweden from Germany and transferred to third countries before June 1, 1945 or any additional claims after July 1, 1947. In his report, Rubin noted the talks advanced smoothly and without bitterness.[50]

Sweden formally approved the agreement in November 1946. Shortly before the deadline for gold claims expired on July 1, 1947, the Allies filed a request for the return of 638 looted Dutch gold bars (worth about $10 million). Sweden challenged a portion of these claims. The Swedish challenge rested on the claim that some of this gold was acquired before the London Declaration. The Allies claimed the agreement included all the gold received. The debate over the Dutch gold continued into the 1950s. Eventually, in 1955, Sweden returned about 6 tons of gold (about $6.8 million) to the Netherlands.[51]

Other problems arose in fulfilling the agreement. Sweden did not turn over the gold specified in the July 1946 agreement by the March 1948 deadline. Although Sweden quickly fulfilled its obligation to IRO in July 1947, it was not as forthcoming with the funds for IARA. Throughout the period, Sweden argued that Law 5 was invalid.

The latest investigation conducted by a bank-appointed commission revealed Sweden accepted 59.7 metric tons of gold from the Nazis. The newly discovered gold bears the same mark as that stolen from the Netherlands. The investigation also found 6 tons of gold of undetermined origin that could have come from the victims of the concentration camps. This additional find of gold was missed by the Safehaven operation. So far, Sweden has only returned 13.2 tons to Belgium and the Netherlands. The commission turned over its findings to the Swedish government. It was unclear whether that commission would have the power to recommend returning the gold. One of the investigators says Sweden has a moral but not a legal obligation to return the gold. The report was released in 1997.[52]

Portugal, Spain and Nazi Gold

Before the outbreak of WWII, Portugal held strong and long-standing political and emotional ties to Britain, dating back to the 14th century Anglo-Portuguese Alliance against Spain. England was Portugal's largest trading partner in 1938. Portugal joined the British early in WWI and sent 50,000 troops to the frontlines.

Portugal's association with Nazi Germany emerged during the Spanish Civil War. Dictator Antonio de Oliveira Salazar sided with Franco and Hitler, helped Germany smuggle arms to Franco's forces and sent Portuguese volunteers to fight. Salazar hoped thereby to achieve his long-term goal of stabilization and development of the country's economy. By the end of 1938, Germany was Portugal's second largest trading partner. However, Salazar did protest Hitler's invasion of Catholic Poland.

Salazar's choice to remain neutral during WWII had as much basis in geography as it did in any ideology. Portugal occupied a strategic position on the map of Europe. It had many ports along its Atlantic coast that would be hard for Britain to blockade. However, Salazar's main fear was an invasion of Portugal by the Nazi war machine. After occupying France, the Wehrmacht was less than 260 miles from Portugal's border. His other fear was of Hitler and Franco forming an alliance, placing Nazi troops at Portugal's border. Dean Acheson, then Assistant Secretary of State, expressed the opinion that Salazar granted favors to Germany in the trade war after computing "the relative danger of German and Allied military pressure on him."

Salazar promised both Britain and Germany open trade for Portugal's valuable domestic and colonial resources. Neutrality benefited Portugal's economy tremendously. The balance of trade went from a $90 million shortfall in 1939 to a $68 million surplus in 1942. Assets in private banks nearly doubled in the first four years of the war, while those of the Bank of Portugal more than tripled. Both the Nazis and the Allies waged economic war through threats and profitable trade deals, but Portugal could not cut its ties with the Allies because it was dependent on the United States for petroleum, coal, ammonium sulfate and wheat. In October 1942, Britain capitalized on its long-standing relationship by inducing Portugal to accept sterling in payment for goods. Britain's gold reserves were low, and both Sweden and Switzerland were demanding payment in gold.

 Portugal's economic success hinged on its rich wolframite or tungsten ore deposits. The Nazis were dependent on Portugal and Spain for this mineral. Tungsten has various uses, including light bulb filaments, but it was of particular value in producing war munitions. Germany's machining industry used tungsten carbide almost exclusively, whereas the United States was still largely using inferior molybdenum-tipped tools, mainly because of the cartel agreement GE held with Krupp for carboloy or cemented tungsten carbide. In addition, tungsten was useful in armor-piercing munitions. The Allies were not solely dependent on Portugal or Spain and could buy wolframite from other sources, but it was their goal was to deprive Nazi Germany of as much tungsten ore as possible, so they bought as much as possible from Portugal. Competition was intense and by 1943, to Portugal's benefit, the price of the ore increased 775 percent over prewar levels. Production also soared from 2,419 metric tons in 1938 to 6,500 tons in 1942.

Germany's minimum needs for wolframite were 3,500 tons a year. Considering the quantity the Nazis needed and the extraordinary means they went to ensure supplies of the ore, the Allies correctly surmised that wolframite was a vital resource for the Nazis.

To maintain its neutrality, Portugal set up a strict export quota system in 1942. It allowed both sides to export ore from the mines they owned, and a fixed percentage from independent mines. England owned the largest mine, while Germany owned two midsize and several smaller mines. France owned Portugal's second largest mine. Legal issues tied up the French mine's output throughout 1941 due to the Nazi occupation. In January 1942, Portugal closed a secret trade pact with Germany. The pact allowed the Nazis export licenses for up to 2,800 tons of wolframite. In turn, Germany was to supply Portugal with coal, steel and fertilizer, which the Allies could not supply. In 1943, the Allies tried to negotiate a new wolframite agreement. Portugal asked for price cuts in ammonium sulfate, petroleum products and other materials from the Allies. The Allies refused, and Portugal refused to increase the Allies' wolframite export licenses. At the same time, Portugal completed a new agreement with Nazi Germany.

Parallel with the wolframite negotiations were talks to gain air bases in the Azores that could prove critical for anti-submarine warfare as the battle in the Atlantic peaked. The Allies failed to take the Azores by force, fearing Germany would invade Portugal in reprisal. Invoking the old Anglo-Portuguese Alliance, Britain concluded an agreement with Portugal on Aug. 17, 1943, to use the islands starting in October. In late 1943, Portugal extended the agreement to include the U.S. Air Force.[53]

By April 1944, the United States decided to use economic sanctions to induce Portugal to cut off the Nazis' supply of wolframite. Portugal was dependent on the United States for petroleum and other products. On June 5, 1944, the Allies pressed Portugal to end wolframite shipments to Germany. The Germans immediately began to cloak their mining interests in Portugal by selling them and buying up other businesses. By June 1946, the Allies estimated the Nazis had cloaked about $2 million in hotels, cinemas and other industries. At the same time, a German U-boat seized a Portuguese vessel, increasing anti-German sentiment. The United States also began negotiations to build an air base in the Azores. Construction was delayed until after reaching an agreement on a wide range of supplies and services. On Nov. 28, 1944, the United States and Portugal signed the agreement. The United States also agreed to Portuguese participation in the campaign to free Timor from the Japanese.

On May 14, 1945, a week after Germany's defeat, Portugal passed law 34,600 freezing all German assets in the country, creating a licensing system for unblocking these assets, providing a census of these assets, prohibiting trade of foreign currency notes and establishing a penalty regime to enforce these provisions. On May 23, Portugal extended the law to include all its colonies. Included in these assets were the German government buildings. On May 6, at the request of the Allies, Portugal had seized all German government buildings. Included in the seizure were 5,000 gold sovereigns found in the German Legation in Lisbon.

While the Portuguese law gave the appearance of cooperation, the State Department feared it contained too many loopholes. For one, the census excluded participation by the Allies. The law also allowed for the transfer of blocked assets to individuals for their subsistence, and the normal exercise of commercial and industrial activity. In a report issued on June 19, 1946, the Division of Economic Security Controls decided that German firms continued to operate without any serious handicaps and many of the Nazis' assets had dissipated. Moreover, the Portuguese census failed to uncover any holdings the Allies had not already identified.

On Sept. 3, 1946, negotiations between Portugal and the Allies began on how to assess, liquidate and distribute German assets. Seymour Rubin reported to the American Ambassador to Portugal John C. Wiley. While the talks were friendly, there were serious disagreements. The negotiations stalled on four points:

Defining what German assets would qualify for liquidation
Determining how much the Portuguese could claim against Germany for wartime losses
Deciding what role each side would play in overseeing liquidation
Deciding how much gold, if any, Portugal would have to surrender to the Allies.[54]

The Lisbon talks of 1946–47 failed to resolve any of these issues. Portugal took a firm stand in 1945 that it was not responsible for returning gold it had exchanged with Germany during the war for tangible assets. Portugal claimed it never received German gold shipments from 1938 to '45. Allied intelligence decided Portugal received $143.8 million in gold from the Swiss National Bank, about half of the increase in the country's gold reserves. Of this amount, the Allies were certain that $22.6 million was from gold looted from Belgium. During the negotiations, the Allies proposed that Portugal turn over $50.5 million. The Allies contended that this amount of gold was obtained after 1942 when it was clear to everyone the German gold reserves had expanded by the looting of Europe. Portugal claimed it was not aware of such looting. Later during the negotiations, Portugal contended that all the gold it gained had been in good faith and was not looted. Throughout the long period of negotiations stretching into the 1950s, Portugal only agreed to return $4.4 million.

Recent evidence shows that Portugal's claims were, at best, disingenuous. In a confidential report, Victor Gautier, a high-ranking Swiss National Bank official, reported in his meeting with Albino Garble Peso, secretary general of the Banco de Portugal, that Portugal would not accept gold directly from the Nazis, due to political motivations and legal risks. He further noted Portuguese objections would evaporate if the money passed via the Swiss. These statements and others in Gautier's report make it clear the Portuguese wanted the Nazi gold with a clean slate from the Swiss money launderers.[55] Initially, Portugal used the Bank of International Settlements and the Yugoslav National Bank in Basel to launder the Nazi gold.

However, starting in 1941 the Nazi invasion of Yugoslavia forced Portugal to look for other routes. Also, on Jan. 8, 1942, Montagu C. Norman, Director of the Bank of England, notified Thomas McKittrick, the American Director of the Bank of International Settlements, that it would no longer recognize shipments of gold from the International Bank to Portugal. Portugal then insisted the Reichsbank sell its gold for francs to the Swiss National Bank. The Reichsbank then deposited the francs into the Banco de Portugal account with the Swiss bank. The Banco de Portugal used these francs to buy the gold from the Swiss National Bank. In addition, the Portuguese used three accounts in the Swiss bank. Portugal used one to deposit gold transferred in payment for the purchase of escudos by SNB from the Banco de Portugal. It used the second account for gold bought from the Banco de Portugal, financed with the Swiss francs. The last account closed the circle by transferring gold on orders from Berlin to the Banco de Portugal account in Zurich.

The Banco Espirito Santo also played a significant role in buying wolframite for the Nazis. An October 1945 FEA report charged that the bank was the financial agent for Nazi purchases of wolfram or wolframite (wolfram is the word for tungsten in German and other languages). After the Allies compelled the bank to forgo its German ties, the Nazis transferred their accounts to the Banco Lisboa e Acores.

A significant amount of gold was smuggled into Portugal. The German Commercial Attaché in Madrid admitted to smuggling almost $1 million in English gold sovereigns from Berlin to the German embassy in Lisbon. The coins were sent in diplomatic pouches in 1943–44. Another report noted $360,000 in gold was flown to Portugal in June–July 1944 and deposited in the Bank of Portugal under the name of the ambassador. The bank director admitted several other dignitaries had special accounts, including the brother of Franco.

While the Portuguese reached an early agreement with the Allies on German property, the issue of gold stalled the talks. Moreover, Portugal tied the property agreement to the gold issue and refused to liquidate the property. This delaying action only served to erode the value of the Nazi property seized. Talks continued off and on, formally and informally.

Recently declassified documents show the American negotiators were aware of an OSS memo dated Feb. 7, 1946 stating that Portugal had received 124 tons of Nazi gold. Nevertheless, Allied negotiators were only seeking a return of 44 tons. The Azores complicated the negotiations from the end of the war until 1953. Portugal granted the U.S. permission to build an air base in the Azores for use during the war and for five years after. By July 1947, the State Department was urging negotiators to ease the hard-line approach and seek a compromise with Portugal on the gold issue. Foremost in the change of stance at the State Department was the Azores air base negotiation. In 1945, the Joint Chiefs designated the Azores as one of nine essential strategic bases needed to preserve the security of the United States. In 1947, the United States broke off the negotiations on gold until completion of the Azores negotiations.

In 1948, Robert Lovett wrote the Treasury Secretary that "overriding political and strategic considerations of our foreign policy make it essential that the Portugal assets in the United States be unblocked." A week later, the Treasury Department weakened the licensing procedures, effectively unblocking the assets. With that action, the United States lost all leverage over Portugal. On July 17, 1951, the State Department wired the embassy in Lisbon to settle on the Portuguese terms. The State Department based the decision on the overriding importance of politico-military objectives. Portugal had become a full member of NATO. Also at stake was a long-term lease for an air base in the Azores. Based on the priority of the Cold War objectives and after consulting British authorities, the State Department recommended settling the gold issue with Portugal for a mere $4.4 million.

The Treasury Department would only agree to the terms if it received a letter signed at the Assistant Secretary level indicating there were political considerations warranting a settlement and that any agreement would not result in claims against the United States. Acting Assistant Secretary for European Affairs James Bonbright signed the letter to the Treasury. The United States finally agreed with Portugal on June 24, 1953. However, Portugal hinged the agreement on the condition of reaching an agreement with West Germany. It took until June 1958 before Germany and Portugal concluded an agreement. The next year, Portugal returned the $4.4 million in gold.

While many of the neutrals leaned toward fascism, none were fully fascist like Franco's Spain. Both Germany and Italy provided support for Franco during the Spanish Civil War. In 1941, Franco sent 40,000 volunteers to Germany. Known as the Blue Division, they served for two years on the Russian front. Although Franco declared neutrality as soon as war broke out in Europe, Spain hovered on the brink of joining the Axis powers through 1940–41. Spanish belligerency was premised on an early German victory over Britain and Germany's agreement to allow Spain to expand territorially into French Morocco, Africa and perhaps even Europe.

The Nazis recognized the strategic location of Spain early on. As early as mid-1940, the Nazis had comprehensive plans to invade Gibraltar. The plans, code-named Operation Felix, originally called for a mid-1941 operation in which two corps would move by road across Spain, with Franco's permission. Spain's rail system was a different gauge than the rest of Europe, forcing the Nazis to rely on the roads. Once in position, Gibraltar was to be attacked from both the land and air with deadly Nazi efficiency. The plans also included two extra divisions to attack Morocco once Operation Felix succeeded.

A Nazi seizure of Gibraltar would add weeks for oil tankers to reach Britain from the Mideast and give the Nazis strategic control of the Mediterranean. Franco certainly must have been aware of Britain's precarious situation in 1940. With the empire under attack worldwide, it was hardly capable of defending itself against a follow-up attack on Morocco, the country that Franco eyed. Nevertheless, the Nazis failed to get Franco's approval. Whether this was due to the intervention of the American ambassador or poor Nazi diplomacy, it has to be one of the biggest diplomatic and strategic setbacks for the Nazis.

After 1941, there were similar plans to attack Gibraltar. However, once Hitler invaded Russia, any such plans were impractical. The Germans did not have the manpower or equipment to open a new battlefront.

One of the strongest ties between Spain and Nazi Germany was the debt incurred by Spain during the civil war. Spain owed Germany for more than $212 million for war materials and other items for Franco's forces.

Britain and the United States engaged in a continuing effort to keep Spain neutral during the early 1940s. The Allies supplied Spain with grain and gasoline. Much, if not most, of the petroleum products were sent on to the Nazis. Franco played the United States for fools. He gladly accepted the gasoline, skimmed a small portion for his needs, and shipped the rest onward. Spain's neutrality hinged on the threat of a German invasion. After 1941, Spain drifted closer to the Allies. Franco provided a haven for Jews who escaped over the Pyrenees. By 1943, both American and Spanish concern about an invasion vanished, and Spain shifted to clearer neutrality.

In July 1943, the American Ambassador met with Franco and explained that there were three major aspects of Spanish policy that needed to be revised if it was to demonstrate real neutrality. Spain had to clearly announce its neutrality. Falange-controlled organs of government had to adopt the policy of neutrality already followed by the Foreign Ministry. Finally, Spain needed to recall the Blue Division. Franco responded that he could not yet fully abandon nonbelligerency, but could begin shifting toward neutrality. A 1947 State Department memo decided that Franco acted in a most non-neutral fashion for the first four years of the war, providing Nazi Germany with significant amounts of strategic goods, as well as military and intelligence support. According to intercepted messages, key to this intelligence support were the spy networks set up in the United States and Britain, run by the Spanish embassies in Washington and London. Operation of this spy network seems to have begun in 1942; the decrypted messages were available to U.S. leaders.

Besides the debt tying them to the Nazis, Spain had considerable minerals that Germany needed. Sociedad Financiera Industrial (SOFINDUS) was formed in 1936 under the name Rowak. It was a large commercial conglomerate that acted as the centerpiece of Spanish-German trade. Through special bilateral agreements in 1937 and 1939 granting German enterprises favored economic treatment, SOFINDUS built a commercial empire by the time war broke out. In a secret protocol to a 1939 German-Spanish agreement, Spain promised to serve as a conduit of supplies from South America. In

May 1940, Spain signed a three-year agreement promising supplies to Italy. By 1942, the trade between Germany and Spain shifted from mainly foodstuffs to minerals essential for warfare. Spain had rich deposits of pyrite, a high-grade iron ore that accounted for 70 percent of the mineral trade between the two countries. The Nazis also bought zinc, lead, mercury, fluorspar, celestite, mica and amblygonite or phosphate from Spain, but wolfram was the most vital. The Nazis used Spanish-flag ships to smuggle goods from South America. The Allied blockade was effective in eliminating bulk items, but small ones, such as industrial diamonds or platinum, a catalyst in producing nitrates and sulfuric acid, made up most of the smuggling trade.

Allied trade with Spain had three main objectives. The first was to obtain needed goods not readily available elsewhere. Second, by buying materials from Spain, the Allies could deny the Nazis a source for these materials. Finally, by trading materials needed by the Spanish, the Allies sought to lessen the influence of Germany. Efforts to implement this policy began in March 1940 Britain when Britain signed a six-month agreement to provide Spain with materials, such as petroleum products and fertilizer, in return for iron ore, other minerals and citrus. Britain renewed the agreement every six months throughout the war. In May 1943, the United States started to buy up materials that were being smuggled into Spain for the Nazis from their sources in South America.

However, the real competition in trade with Spain was for tungsten ore. By 1941, Germany developed most of Spain's wolfram mines and controlled the largest producer through SOFINDUS. In 1941, the Nazis bought almost all the wolframite produced. England only managed to buy 32 tons. Unlike Portugal, which had a quota system, Spain relied on an open market for wolfram that provided an edge to the Allies with their access to hard currency. Starting early in 1942, England and the United States launched a unified program to buy up as much ore as possible, causing the mines to double production from the previous year. Output increased to 2,000 tons and the price rose from $75 a ton to $16,800. In June, Spain set a minimum price of $16,380 a ton, which included a $4,546 export tax. In an effort to better compete with the Nazis, the Allies set up their own dummy corporate front and, in 1942, bought roughly half the output.

In December 1942, under pressure from the Nazis, Spain signed a new trade agreement with Germany with more explicit quotas. The agreement soon fell apart with both sides blaming the other for the failure. In February 1943, Spain signed a secret agreement in which Germany agreed to provide Spain with armaments at cost. At first the Nazis demanded a 400 percent markup on the weapons, but being desperate for wolfram and Spanish pesetas, they had to relent to Spain's demands. After the war, the Nazi negotiator commented on how strained and difficult the talks were. In August 1942, Spain agreed to pay back its debt in four installments, which the Nazis used to buy wolfram. During 1943, Germany bought roughly 35 percent of the total wolfram mined in Spain, or four to five times the level of 1940.

In January 1944, after the British Ambassador Sir Samuel Hoare met with Franco in an unsuccessful attempt to persuade Spain to suspend wolfram sales to the Nazis, the Allies imposed an oil embargo. On May 2, Spain agreed to limit the export of wolfram to Germany to 580 tons; 300 tons had already been delivered. The agreement cut German imports to half of the previous year. However, captured documents show that Germany managed to buy a total of 865.6 tons through smuggling. Wolfram exports to Germany ended in August 1944, when Spain closed the border.[56]

Operation Safehaven in Spain began in the spring of 1944. Samuel Klaus of the FEA led the team. Klaus reported that Spain was the most discouraging and difficult of all the neutrals, and that American Ambassador Carlton Hayes was unwilling to cooperate. Klaus noted the Nazis could easily cloak their businesses in Spain thanks to corrupt officials. He also pointed out that Tangiers was being used as a conduit to move Nazi assets from Spain and Portugal to Argentina. This was part of Bormann's program of flight capital.

In the fall of 1944, the Allies made their first request for Spain to stop all gold transactions involving enemy interests. Spain failed to reply. In January 1945, the Treasury and FEA wanted to link Safehaven with upcoming talks with Spain on the expired trade agreement, noting the Allies had cut off all land routes between Spain and Germany. Britain, which was more dependent on Spanish trade, adamantly opposed such linkage. It was not until May 5, 1945 before Spain issued a decree to freeze and immobilize all assets with Axis interests. After the Nazi surrender on May 7, Spain agreed to an Anglo-American trusteeship to take control of German and quasi-official properties. Problems with the trustee agreement arose immediately. By July 1947, the trusteeship had taken control of only $25.3 million out of an estimated $95 million of German assets in Spain.

Information on Spain's gold transactions came from Allied intelligence, captured German Reichsbank records, statements by Swiss banking officials and records seized from the offices of the quasi-official corporations SOFINDUS and Transportes Marion. The best estimate was that Spain received $138.2 million in gold either directly from Germany or indirectly through Switzerland. Published figures showed that Spain's gold holdings increased from $42 million in 1941 to $110 million in 1945.

Negotiations with Spain started in November 1946 in Madrid. Seymour Rubin was once again one of the lead negotiators. The negotiations dragged, and the Allies and Spain finally reached agreement on Nazi assets and the gold issue on May 3, 1948. Spain agreed to repatriate more than $114 million in gold, much of which was believed to be from the Netherlands. However, the agreement required the Allies to issue a statement that Spain was not aware the gold was looted by the Nazis.

There were two extra causes at work here that sped the negotiations to an early agreement compared with Portugal. The State Department had its usual request for an easy settlement to ease the way for military bases in Spain. More important, Spain was regarded as a pariah following the war. The Allies agreed at Potsdam to exclude Spain from UN membership for its fascist background. In December 1945, American Ambassador Norman Armour left Madrid, and was not replaced until 1951. Other nations also withdrew their ambassadors. In May 1946, a UN subcommittee presented evidence of the Spanish regime's fascist nature, its pro-Nazi activities, postwar support and sanctuary to Nazi war criminals, and political repression of opponents. The UN denied Spain membership until 1955. Spain was isolated in an unfriendly world.

Turkey on the Tightrope

Like other neutral countries, Turkey was bound to the Nazis by trade, but that is where any similarities stop. Turkey was a remnant of descended from the Ottoman Empire and was mainly a Moslem nation. During World War I, it was aligned with Germany. The nationalistic "Young Turks" overthrew the Ottoman Sultan in 1908, and began a pogrom against the Armenian minority in 1915, a charge their successors still vigorously deny. Whether the rise of the Young Turks arose spontaneously, or were sponsored by imperialist capital as the Nazis were, is a subject for further research.

Turkey began WWII bound to Britain and France by the military alliance of October 1939. It declared neutrality in June 1940 after the fall of France, and ended the war aligned with the Allies. Much of Turkey's proclaimed neutrality resulted from fears of a Nazi invasion. In June 1941, after the fall of the Balkans to the Nazis, Turkey signed a Treaty of Friendship with Germany.

Throughout the war, Turkey walked a tightrope, balancing the needs and expectations of the Nazis against those of the Allies. While Istanbul was a center of spying and intrigue during the war, Turkey took no overt action against the Nazis and, in turn, the Nazis never violated Turkey's borders. In October 1941, Turkey signed an important trade agreement with Germany. In exchange for raw material, especially chromite ore, Germany supplied Turkey with war materials and other finished goods. At the same time, Turkey maintained friendly relations with the United States and Britain, which supplied

Turkey with modern war equipment in exchange for chromite ore. Turkey's chromite ore was critical for the Nazis. Turkey was their sole source for chrome, a vital element in steelmaking. Albert Speer stated that Turkey's chromite ore was so vital to the Nazis that war production would come to a complete stop 10 months after the supply was cut off. The ore was shipped from Turkey by rail through some of the most rugged country in the world. Toward the end of the war, the Allies targeted bridges along the main rail line to stop the chromite shipments.

In 1941, the Roosevelt administration added Turkey to the lend-lease nations available to receive equipment. In January 1943, during the Casablanca Conference, FDR considered asking Turkey to enter the war. In November 1943, all three of the big leaders — Churchill, Roosevelt and Stalin — called for Turkey's entry into the war. In February 1944, after Turkey entered the war contingent on massive military aid and a significant Allied military presence, Britain and the United States stopped their aid program. By 1943, the Allies foresaw no threat from a Nazi invasion. It was not until April 1944 that Turkey stopped chromite exports to Germany, and then only after threatens of the same economic sanctions that the other neutral countries were under. In August, Turkey suspended all diplomatic relations with Germany. In February 1945, on the eve of establishing the United Nations, Turkey declared war on Germany.

Turkey was not a major recipient of gold from the Nazis. In fact, the best estimate was in the range of $15 million, most which is believed to have been looted from Belgium. In addition, two private German banks — Deutsche and Dresdner — sold gold from the Melmer account in exchange for foreign currency.

Allied efforts to recover gold from Turkey were never pursued with any vigor. Turkey's geographical location, controlling access to the Black Sea and its border with the Soviet Union made it a cornerstone for U.S. strategic interests in the coming Cold War. In 1946, formal talks were held to consider the gold received from the Nazis, as well as German assets in Turkey. The Allies estimated that German assets totaled $51 million. In March 1947, the Truman Doctrine included Turkey with Greece. In July, the United States signed a $150 million trade agreement with Turkey that dealt a deathblow to any further negotiations on restitution.[57] Turkey never turned over any gold.

Argentina, the Nazi Eldorado

Throughout the 1930s, a succession of military dictators and fraudulently elected presidents ruled Argentina. These regimes were weaken by their internal corruption and sought to legitimize themselves by reviving an ancient Hispanic alliance, the Cross and the Sword. Ties with Franco on race, religion and language were emphasized. Some even called for undoing Argentina's war of independence from Spain and for rule by a viceroy. The military leaders and the Catholic Church, urged on by the Vatican, dreamed of creating a Hispanic Catholic nation that could counterbalance the United States in the Western Hemisphere. By the time war broke out, Argentina was divided into pro-Nazi and pro-Allied camps. However, Vatican-connected operatives supporting a triangle of peace between Argentina, Spain and the Vatican controlled Argentina's foreign policy.[58]

At the onset of the war in Europe, Argentina's weak president, Ramon Castillo, announced a policy of prudent neutrality. Despite having agreed to the Havana Conference of 1940, in which an attack on any country of the Western Hemisphere would be considered an act of aggression on all American states, Argentina adhered to its neutrality policy. Argentina claimed that any action undertaken in response to an attack was a matter for each state. Argentina remained neutral during WWI and its economy benefited handsomely as a result. There was hope again that a policy of neutrality would revive the economy from the devastating depression of the 1930s.

In January 1942, Argentina agreed to the terms of the Rio Conference, severing all commercial and financial relations with the Axis powers. In June 1942, Argentina agreed to the Final Act of the Inter-

American Conference on Economic and Financial Controls, obligating all states to end commercial intercourse with the Axis. Argentina ignored the terms and continued business with the Nazis. Moreover, during 1942, Juan Goyeneche, a confidential agent of Peron, and Adrian Escobar, Argentina's Ambassador to Spain, traveled through war-torn Europe, meeting with Nazi and Vatican officials. Goyeneche collaborated extensively with the Foreign Intelligence Branch of the SS. Escobar and his consul Aquilino Lopez were collaborating with Himmler's secret service by crossing into Vichy France and reporting details on Spanish and Allied diplomats.

After extensive meetings with Vatican Secretary of State Cardinal Luigi Magione, an agreement was reached in which, once peace was established, Argentina would generously apply its immigration laws. This seemingly innocent meeting takes on critical importance at the end of the war. It proves the Vatican was planning on helping Nazis war criminals escape from Europe as early as 1942. This meeting set up the Vatican ratlines.

On Oct. 10, the Pope received Escobar and welcomed Argentina's view that it was proper for the Vatican to engage in the peace talks. Goyeneche traveled to Germany and met with Ribbentrop seeking Nazi support for the nationalist candidate in the 1943 elections. This façade of neutrality was maintained until 1943 and the colonels' revolution that eventually brought Peron to power.

Once in power, the colonels sought arms from Germany in case war broke out between Argentina and Brazil. By September 1943, the colonels gave up the idea of smuggling arms into Argentina from Germany and, instead, sought an alliance with the Nazis. The group of colonels dispatched Osmar Hellmuth and Carlos Velez to Spain to negotiate. Unfortunately for the colonels, U.S. Magic intercepts detected the upcoming mission from transmissions between the SS agent in Argentina, a Capt. Becker, and Schellenberg in Germany, and had the British seize Hellmuth when the ship docked in Trinidad.

The seizure of Hellmuth failed to deter further plots. Peron and Becker continued to plan the overthrow of neighboring governments to set up a pro-Nazi block in South America. Peron wrote in a secret manifest of the colonels:

> Forming alliances will be the first step. We have Paraguay; we have Bolivia and Chile. With Argentina, Paraguay, Bolivia and Chile, it will be easy to pressure Uruguay. Then the five united nations will easy draw in Brazil because of its type of government and its large nucleus of Germans. With Brazil fallen, the American continent will be ours.[59]

On Dec. 20, 1943, a military coup in Uruguay planned by Peron and Becker installed Gen. Gualberto Villarrod as president. American counterintelligence was aware of it through Magic decrypts of Becker's transmissions from Argentina. However, the coup was a failure for the Nazis. Using material from the decoded Magic messages, the United States threatened Argentina. Facing the U.S. threat to release the decrypts and Hellmuth's admissions from interrogations implicating Argentina's role in the coup, Argentina broke off diplomatic relations with the Nazis in January 1944. However, Argentina upheld its neutrality and did not declare war against Germany until a month before Hitler's suicide.

During the final year of the war, Argentina was a prime destination for many of the assets that Bormann spirited out of Germany for a rebirth of the Third Reich. Following the war, Argentina also was a prime destination for Nazi war criminals. Even war criminals who escaped to other South American countries generally first entered the continent through Argentina. While other South American countries generally supported the U.S. policies during the war, there was no cooperation from Argentina. Other countries adhered to the Proclaimed List and took steps to eliminate any smuggling efforts. The Treasury Department urged harsher actions toward Argentina than the State Department was willing to impose. The State Department was hampered by a fear that a harsher policy would alienate other South American countries and by a difference of opinion with the British. During both world wars, England depended on Argentina for beef. However, as early as 1942, Argentina's neutrality policy made it a leading focus of the Treasury Department and the Board of Economic Warfare.

The Nazis allowed the large number of German companies in Argentina to turn over their profits to espionage organizations for Reichsmark credits. The Treasury Department also suspected that Argentina made substantial amounts of foreign exchange available to the Axis countries, accepted the entry of large amounts of looted currency and securities into its markets, and allowed German firms to cloak their assets. An FBI report released in June 1943 described how Buenos Aires served as the Western Hemisphere outlet for U.S. banknotes stolen in occupied Europe and entered in commercial traffic in Switzerland.[60]

Throughout the war, Argentina served as a hub for Nazi smuggling. The blockade easily stopped bulk items of trade. However, critical small items, such as industrial diamonds and platinum needed by Germany, regularly were smuggled through the blockade. Immediately after Pearl Harbor, Morgenthau wanted to freeze Argentina's assets. In May 1942, he presented evidence to President Roosevelt that many Argentine companies were cloaking German funds in the United States and that Argentina had recently sent $1 million to the United States in looted currency. However, Roosevelt continued the policy set forth by the State Department. After repeated requests from the Treasury Department, the State Department agreed to an ad hoc blocking of selected Argentine accounts in October. The United States added more than 150 individuals and firms in Argentina to the blacklist.

Safehaven negotiations with Argentina started in 1944. However, the distressed relations restrained any progress in the negotiations. In February 1944, Argentine President Ramirez delegated his powers to Gen. Edelmiro Farrell. The United States failed to recognize the Farrell government and recalled the ambassador. In August and September, the State Department announced more sanctions against Argentina due to its failure to comply with denazification. In response, Argentina withdrew from the Montevideo Committee for the political defense of the continent. The Argentine Central Bank provided little help to U.S. investigators in locating German assets. After Cordell Hull resigned as Secretary of State in November 1944, the incoming Secretary, Edward Stettinius, developed an easier policy toward Argentina. Nelson Rockefeller, the appointed wartime chief of South American intelligence, also favored easier terms with Argentina. Rockefeller-controlled banks illegally transferred funds between the U.S. and Argentina from frozen accounts.

On Feb. 7, 1945, Treasury Secretary Morgenthau suggested to Acting Secretary of State Joseph C. Grew that a special Treasury representative be sent to Argentina to uncover and control Nazi external assets. Grew rejected the suggestion, citing political considerations. In early 1945, the Inter-American Conference on War and Peace held in Mexico City passed a resolution in support of Bretton Woods Resolution VI. However, the resolution known as the Act of Chapultepec did not grant control of Nazi assets in Latin American countries to multinational governing bodies. Instead, the act recognized the right of each of the American Republics, including the United States, to German property within its respective jurisdiction. Due to its continuing pro-Nazi policy, the American states excluded Argentina from the meeting. Recognizing its increasing isolation from other nations in the Western Hemisphere, Argentina declared war against Germany in the last month of hostilities.

On Feb. 11, 1946, the State Department released the famed Blue Book on Argentina. The book confirmed that the Argentine government asserted no control over German firms, delaying the efforts to seize the Nazi assets until they were dispersed elsewhere. The book also confirmed that Nazi Germany sent large sums of money to its embassy in Argentina without any serious obstacles. Some historians credit the release of the Blue Book for Peron's election as part of an anti-American backlash. On May 22, 1946, the Safehaven team reported the total value of German assets at roughly $200 million. The assets included bank balances, real estate and merchandise. The Safehaven team found no caches of art or gems, and assumed that Argentina was not a major destination of looted treasure. The team also reported that no records revealed Argentina receiving Nazi gold.

As early as 1942, the United States knew of illegal Argentina currency dealings. In April 1942, the U.S. Consulate in Switzerland reported that an Argentine diplomat was smuggling dollars stolen by the

Nazis to his homeland for sale; the funds were then transferred to Switzerland. British cables from 1944 show Argentina conducted vigorous trade with Switzerland and often the payment was in gold. By 1945, the State and Treasury departments found decisive evidence of extensive transactions involving the transfer of Argentine pesos, Reichsmarks and Swiss francs from Argentina to Switzerland. In May 1947, Argentina proposed a transfer of $170 million to its Federal Reserve account. Concern over the source of the gold only momentarily delayed the transfer. Guyatt reports that in 1973, after returning to power, Peron sold 400 tons of gold on the black market.[61] Peron code-named the sale Bormann 1345. While the Spanish government tutored the sale, the transfer agent labeled it political. Despite the massive increase in Argentina's gold reserve and the number of Nazi war criminals who found sanctuary in Argentina, even after 50 years there is little proof of Argentina accepting gold from the Nazis.

The Cold War badly compromised Safehaven investigations in Argentina. On June 3, 1947, President Truman and Argentine Ambassador Ivanissevich issued a joint announcement that the two countries would renew consultations with other Latin American countries about creating a treaty of mutual aid. In September, Argentina joined the United States and other American Republics in agreeing to the Inter-American Treaty for Reciprocal Assistance, the Rio Pact, for mutual defense against aggression. Bormann's cloaked companies in Argentina, as well as any treasure, were safe and secure. The hemisphere had to be protected from communism.

On April 10, 1941, following the Nazi invasion of Yugoslavia, the so-called independent state of Croatia was established, headed by Ante Pavelic, a member of the fascist Croat Ustashi political movement. Mussolini declared Croatia a protectorate of Italy. Both Italy and the Nazis supported Croatia. The Ustashi also were closely aligned with the Vatican. On May 18, 1941, Acting Secretary of State Sumner Welles reaffirmed the exile government of Yugoslavia did not recognize the independent state of Croatia. Shortly after, Croatia sealed the U.S. embassy in Zagreb. Since Croatia only existed as a state during the war and the United States never recognized it, the figures presented in this section are likely to be subject to revision in the future.

Postwar reports suggest the Ustashi treasury had at its disposal more than $80 million, mostly gold coins, some stolen from their victims. On May 31, 1944, Croatia deposited $403,000 in the Swiss National Bank. On Aug. 4, 1944, Croatia deposited another $1.1 million in gold. An OSS report in July 1945 concluded that Croat-owned commercial accounts in Bern totaled more than $93,000. The Historical Section of the Task Force of the Swiss Federal Department of Foreign Affairs shows that on July 24, 1945, the Swiss National Bank returned to the National Bank of Yugoslavia all 1,338 kilograms of gold in 121 ingots in the account of the wartime Croatian regime.

While bank records of deposit are not likely to change much, the gold the Ustashi carried as they fled to Austria as the war was reaching an end is very much in doubt. Estimates placed the value of gold Ante Pavelic had when entering Austria at $5 million–$6 million. Whatever the value of the loot, it is certain that much of it was used to set up and run a ratline with the Vatican. In October 1946, U.S. intelligence reported to the Treasury Department that the Ustashi had $47 million deposited in the Vatican before transfer to Spain and then to Argentina. Due to the Cold War, the Allies expended little effort in returning the thousands of war criminals from Italy to Yugoslavia. The issue of Ustashi gold received even less attention at the war's conclusion.

Switzerland, the Hub

Of all the neutral countries, none was more at the center of doing business with the Nazis than Switzerland. Geographically, the Third Reich surrounded Switzerland once France fell. Further, the preceding look at other countries has already implicated Switzerland in a pivotal role in trading with the Nazis through Swiss banks. When referring to Switzerland, most Americans think of exquisite chocolates, fine timepieces and Heidi chasing goats across alpine meadows, but it was a much different nation during the 1940s.

The 1848 constitution established the present form of Swiss government in approving three cantons, civil liberties and the parliamentary form of democracy. The franchise did not extended to women until 1971. Switzerland was ruled for decades by a center right coalition of parties. During WWII, these parties were the Christian Conservatives, Social Democrats, Liberals, and the Farmers and Artisans Party. The same coalition rules today, although some of the party names have changed. A seven-member Federal Council, the members of which parliament selects for rotating one-year terms, rules Switzerland.

Much of Switzerland's complicity with the Nazis has only recently come to the forefront from the efforts of President Clinton's appointment of Eizenstat to lead a commission to reach a just settlement with the victims of the Holocaust. While the legend of the fierce Swiss neutrality lives on, it is more of a myth, considering Swiss policy during WWII was balanced heavily in favor of the Nazis. The threat of a Nazi invasion of Switzerland has no basis in fact. As early as the 1930s, the Nazis were busy cloaking their corporations and cartel agreements with Swiss fronts. An invasion would have compromised all the hard work spent in cloaking these corporations. As we have seen in the cases of the other neutral countries, once the Nazis invaded Russia, they simply lacked the manpower and equipment to open another front. Finally, Switzerland had no strategic geographic location, unlike Spain or Turkey. Its only strategic value to the Nazis was its international banks. The Nazis could use the international banks to get hard currency and launder looted gold.

However, Switzerland was unique in comparison with the other neutral countries because it was equally dependent on Germany for coal. Once France fell, Switzerland's only source for coal for winter heating was Germany. However, the Nazis used Swiss purchases of coal for another purpose. Goods shipped to Switzerland from Germany were underinvoiced. This left a pool of Swiss francs on deposit in Swiss banks, which the Nazis used to buy foreign currency. Nonetheless, Swiss trade with the Nazis extended beyond banking and coal. Swiss manufacturers provided the Nazis with bearings, timers and other manufactured goods used in producing war equipment.

The ruling Federal Council with extra wartime dictatorial powers was responsible for setting up the economic collaboration with the Nazis. Despite the ever-present Swiss denials, the Federal Council was responsible for the most shameful act of Swiss neutrality. In August 1938, after the Anschluss the Federal Council ordered the borders closed. Fearing a mix of refugees, including Jews, the Federal Council petitioned the Nazi government in Berlin to affix a "J" stamp on all Jewish passports. The Nazis initially were not keen on the idea because they were still using immigration as a way to free Germany of Jews. Negotiations continued throughout late summer and autumn. Eventually, the Swiss threatened to require visas for all Germans entering Switzerland. The Nazis then proposed the "J" stamp on passports as a solution. Now it was a Nazi idea in the eyes of the Federal Council.

The only reason the Swiss were so intent on such a marking on passports was to make it easier for border guards to turn away Jews. Despite the myth of Switzerland being a refuge for Jews during the war, border guards turned away more than 30,000 Jewish refugees. In August 1942, the Federal Council passed another law to seal the border to Jewish refugees, despite vigorous pleas from some church members and the press. The Swiss people were not anti-Semitic and opposed the government's policy. Other than closing the border to Jews, Switzerland passed no anti-Jewish laws. The Jewish community in Switzerland was divided, with a minority favoring demonstrations to allow more Jewish immigration and a majority favoring a policy of "don't make trouble."[62]

Even if the Jewish refugees were able to get past the border guards, Swiss officials demanded to see their passports. If the passport had the "J" stamp, the officials forced the hapless Jews back into the hands of the Nazis. Border guard Grueninger received his order in 1938 not to allow in any Jews. However, Grueninger allowed 3,600 Jews entry and helped them to alter their passports so they could remain. Alerted by the Nazis of Grueninger's acts of humanity, the Swiss suspended him in December 1938. In January 1939, the government filed charges against him for forging documents. In 1941, a court found him guilty of insubordination and took away his job, retirement and severance pay, and levied a stiff fine. Afterward, he never was able to find a suitable job and was dogged by rumors that he demanded money and sexual favors from those he helped. The former boarder guard vigorously denied the unfounded rumors.[63]

Much of Switzerland's pro-Nazi bias was because of Pilet Golaz, who after the invasion of France urged the nation to adapt to the new political realities of Europe. In other words, there was much money to be made dealing with the Nazis. Swiss policy, like that of other neutrals, depended on the fortunes of war. As the Allies began their march across Europe from the Normandy beaches, Swiss policy took a turn in their favor. Even Golaz's political fortunes suffered the same fate. He was removed from office in 1944 when the tide clearly turned.

From the beginning, Swiss government officials knew of the early methodology of the Nazi genocide. The Nazis invited Swiss army doctors to serve on the Eastern Front to treat wounded Nazi soldiers in Operation Barbarossa. At that stage, roving bands of the Einsatzgruppen carried out the killings by shooting the Jews they rounded up. While the Swiss doctors did not see the killing squads, they saw the effects and reported them to the Red Cross and government officials. A 1943 National Bank Legal report mentions the deportations and persecutions of Jews.

The only area in which the Swiss displayed anything close to true neutrality was in espionage. Swiss police left both Nazi and Allied agents free to come and go. However, once France fell, there was no overland route for the Allies to travel to and from Switzerland.

The earliest news of the Holocaust to reach the West came in a telegram on Aug. 8, 1942 from Gerhart Riegner. The informant who provided the information was a Leipzig businessman, Eduard Scholte.

Received alarming report that in Fuhrer's headquarters plan discussed and under consideration according to which all Jews in countries occupied or controlled Germany numbering three and a half to four million should after deportation and concentration in the east be exterminated at one blow to resolve once and for all the Jewish question in Europe. Action reported planned for autumn; methods under discussion including prussic acid. We transmit information with all necessary reservation as exactitude cannot be confirmed. Informant stated to have close connections with highest German authorities and his reports generally reliable.[64]

Unfortunately, this report was widely disbelieved, even by Jews. Allen Dulles labeled it hysterical Jewish propaganda. Rabbi Stephen Wise, one of the recipients of the telegram, released it to the press on Nov. 24, 1942. After that, everyone was aware of the savagery and horror occurring in the Third Reich.

An article in the June 1943 *Financial Times,* written by Paul Einzig about the Allied declaration of January 1943, sent tremors through the Swiss banking community. The article detailed how all transfers of property bought by a neutral from the Nazis would be declared invalid and restoration would be sought. The bankers' concerns were over gold transfers. In July 1943, the Switzerland National Bank Committee met to decide if it should continue to accept Nazi gold. The committee took the view that Switzerland, having a gold standard, was compelled to accept. The committee agreed to ask the Federal Council for a ruling. The council was briefed in October of the issue, including the fact that the Allies advised the National Bank that some of the gold might be looted. In November, the council ruled that it was agreeing with the bank officials, thus giving a green light to Swiss banks to accept more Nazi gold.[65]

Report No. 26904, written on Jan. 30, 1945 by the Foreign Economic Administration, connected both Credit Suisse and Union Bank in supplying the Nazis with foreign currency. Attached to the memo were 28 intercepts of Credit Suisse and Union Bank communications. Nine of the intercepts concerned the financial triangle of Germany, Switzerland and Portugal regarding gold transfers. The attached memos showed that Credit Suisse alone made available to the Nazis 500,000 escudos and 200,000 kroners.[66]

A Feb. 5, 1946 report by the economic intelligence group Allied Claims Against Swiss for Return of Looted Gold provides the best estimate of gold looted from the central banks of Europe. The report estimates the total amount of gold the Nazis accumulated at $648 million. At the outbreak of the war, the best estimate of the Nazi gold reserves was $100 million. The Nazis looted the difference of $548 million from the countries of Europe. The report estimates from bank records that the Nazis sold between $275 million and $282 million to the Swiss National Bank. In addition, the Nazis sold another $20 million to commercial Swiss banks. The report proves that much of the gold ended up in Portugal and Spain after the Swiss laundered it.

A six-page report, Safehaven No. 2969, detailed the extent of Nazi assets in Switzerland. The document was sent by Americans in Bern to the Secretary of State. The report states that the Nazis owned or controlled 358 Swiss economic enterprises. In 263 of these, Nazis capital invested totaled about $114 million. The enterprises stretched across all areas of economic activity. The report listed six in textile manufacture, six in transportation manufacturing, 15 insurance enterprises, 67 retail and wholesalers, nine banks, 15 chemical concerns, 330 holding and financial companies, 11 machinery manufacturers and seven other types with less than three each. In the report, a Swiss banker estimates the banks held $110 million in Nazi assets. The estimates of German assets in Switzerland varied widely, as the table below shows.

Source of estimate	amount[67]
Treasury Department	$500 million
State Department	$250 million–$500 million
Swiss Delegation	$250 million
Press Reports	$750 million

In addition, the Nazis had large amounts of gold, currency, gems and art stored away in safe-deposit boxes. The British estimated the value of 53 paintings at $484,000. The report determined the total value of all the looted paintings at $390 million–$545 million.[68]

Cooperation of the Swiss with Allied efforts in recovering gold and ending trade with the Nazis was nearly nonexistent. In response to the United States freezing Swiss assets to prevent use by the Nazis, the Swiss cut off the coal supply to the U.S. embassy in the winter of 1941. The German embassy still received its coal allotment. Negotiations with the Swiss were always difficult. As the war progressed, it became clear to all that the Nazis were defeated. While Switzerland supplied the Nazis with many manufactured goods that took much skill to make, such as machine tools, it supplied other items, including locomotives, and even arms and ammunition. Two key Swiss exports were electric power and aluminum.

Postwar analyses by the British show that in the early years of the war, the blockade was ineffective and at no time did the Nazis experience a shortage of raw items. It was only the massive bombing campaign and large battle losses in 1944 that finally weakened the Third Reich. On June 22, 1944, Secretary of War Stimson noted the period of gentle appeasement of neutrals had passed. Following the D-Day invasion of Normandy, Allied casualties rose dramatically. Accompanying the rise in casualties was an increase in pressure exerted by the Allies on all the neutral countries.

On July 10, 1944, Bill Donovan, head of the OSS, told Roosevelt that Switzerland had agreed to buy $7 million–$10 million in gold monthly from the Nazis. Roosevelt told Donovan to take the matter up with Secretary of State Cordell Hull, and have pressure put on the Swiss. Four days later, Hull called in Swiss Minister Charles Bruggmann and reviewed the mounting casualties and cost, with a gentle hint that the United States would view continued trade with the Nazis harshly. With the success of the Normandy invasion in August 1944, the State Department commanded its legation in Berne to begin informal talks to limit the Swiss-Nazi trade. The Swiss response in late August revealed the duplicity of the Swiss:

> It goes without saying that the war as it nears the Alps changes aspect of transit problem and has a bearing on its solution. For this reason Federal authorities keep this problem under constant and careful watch. They have thus been able to observe that traffic in both directions has in general decreased and not increased since spring. In spirit of true neutrality which guides them will see to it that it follows the trend circumstances demand.[69]

Because of the pressure coming from both the United States and England, the Swiss reduced their exports of strategic materials, such as ammunition, locomotives, machine tools and other manufactured goods. The Federal Economic Administration supported stern measures against the Swiss, including withholding of food and fodder previously promised by the Allies. The Joint Chiefs of Staff also favored withholding supplies from the Swiss, but Britain opposed such stern measures. In October 1944, Under Secretary of War Patterson noted in a memo that Swiss convoys carrying shipments of goods from Spain across France to Switzerland had resumed in late September 1944. Patterson argued that such shipments should be stopped until the Swiss agreed to end all trade with the Nazis.

On Dec. 8, 1944, the executive committee of the Economic Foreign Policy approved the Allies' economic policy toward neutral countries. The policy reflected the tough stance of FEA, calling for a continuation of trade, exchange and freezing controls into the postwar period as leverage to gain support from the neutrals in achieving Safehaven objectives. Despite the approval of President Roosevelt, various government agencies and departments continued to dispute the policy.

In February 1945, after much wrangling about imposing sterner measures against Switzerland, Lauchlin Currie, assistant to President Roosevelt, headed the American delegation to Switzerland for talks on stopping the wartime trade and to begin negotiations on gold issues. William Rappard headed the Swiss delegation, although the man pulling the strings was Walter Stucki. In March, Currie reported some success. The Swiss agreed to freeze all German assets; ban importation, exportation and dealing in all foreign currencies; and restrict Swiss purchases of gold from Germany. While the Currie mission was greeted as a success, controversy soon followed. In May 1945, the U.S. Legation in Bern reported the Swiss bought 3,000 kilograms of gold from Germany. The Currie agreement clearly excluded the buy. However, the Swiss argued the gold was not looted.

In June 1945, Harley Kilgore chaired the Senate's War Mobilization Subcommittee. In the hearings, he introduced documents uncovered by Allied investigators of correspondence between German Reichsbank Vice President Emil Puhl and the German Minister of Economic Affairs Walter Funk about German-Swiss commercial discussions conducted during the Currie Mission. The treachery of the Swiss received widespread publicity. Orvis A. Schmidt, Director of Foreign Funds Control for the Treasury Department and a member of the Currie Mission to Bern, testified before the subcommittee:

> Even at this late date, the Swiss Government is loath to take the necessary steps to force banks and other cloaking institutions to disclose the owners of assets held in or through Switzerland. This means that German assets held in or through Switzerland will not be identified. Thus, the true picture of German financial and industrial penetration throughout the world will be kept a secret. By the same token, Swiss banks will continue to profit by protecting, through their secrecy laws, German's war potential and the hidden assets of it financiers and industrialists.[70]

In September, Leland Harrison, U.S. Minister in Switzerland, told Max Petitpierre, the Swiss Minister for Foreign Affairs, of U.S. dissatisfaction with Swiss efforts to complete a census of German assets and the general noncooperation of Switzerland. The Kilgore committee's revelations raised alarms in Switzerland. Some right-wing papers went so far as to claim Switzerland could not withstand another crisis like the Kilgore Committee.

In March 1946, formal talks with Switzerland, United States, Britain and France opened in Washington. U.S. negotiators held an optimistic view that the Swiss were committed to the Currie Mission agreement. On the other hand, Switzerland viewed its actions during the war as consistent with the internationally recognized obligations and rights of a neutral power. The Swiss asserted that international law granted the Nazis' seizure of monetary gold from the occupied countries (the right of occupying powers to war booty). Thus, the receipt of the gold by Switzerland was legal. Switzerland argued the Allies' claim to Nazi assets beyond Germany's border was illegal and a violation of Swiss sovereignty. In addition, Switzerland sought the removal of all Swiss companies and individuals from the Allied blacklist.

With such opposing views, the talks were set for long and hotly contested negotiations. The dispute between the United States and British about the use of sanctions to induce compliance further complicated the Allied side of the talks. Treasury briefing material for the U.S. negotiators urged a global approach to the gold issue, rather than settling the amount of looted gold in each transaction. Also, the Treasury wanted an open-end clause in any agreement, which required Switzerland to return any looted gold found in the future. Treasury Assistant Secretary Harry Dexter White insisted that Swiss funds remain blocked in the United States until the Swiss provided ironclad guarantees that they would identify and seize all accounts under German control. White estimated total of German assets in Switzerland, excluding numbered accounts and cloaked assets, to be $500 million.

The American negotiators had the benefit of two comprehensive evaluations of German gold movements during World War II. Both reports were prepared from the records of the Reichsbank. Otto Fletcher, Special Assistant to the Division of Economic Security Controls of the State Department, estimated that at the beginning of the war, Nazi gold reserves totaled $120 million. He estimated the Nazis acquired another $661 million in monetary gold during the war, most of which was looted. Fletcher also reported that all gold sold by the Nazis after early 1943 was looted. His report showed the Nazis sold or transferred $414 million in looted gold to the Swiss National Bank. The second report, prepared by James Mann of the Treasury Department, estimated the total monetary gold looted by Germany at $579 million, out of $785 million available after June 30, 1940. Mann's report decided the Swiss took $289 million in gold from the Nazis.

The Treasury's strategy for the negotiations revolved around the neutral countries recognizing the authority of the Allied Control Council's (ACC) legal right to all external German assets under the Vesting Decree. Even before the talks began, the Treasury insisted the Swiss recognize the ACC Vesting Decree and agree to return to the Allies for reparations an estimated $378 million in looted monetary gold.

Randolph Paul, special assistant to President Truman, headed the U.S. delegation in the Allied-Swiss negotiations. Paul had an important role in urging the rescue of Jews in Europe as the extent of the Holocaust became known. Seymour Rubin, Walter Surrey and senior Department of State officials responsible for economic security programs aided Paul. Walter Stucki headed the Swiss delegation.

The opening statements of all the countries revealed the chasm separating the two sides. In an effort to remove the deadlock, the Allies gave up their claim to all German assets and offered the Swiss a 20 percent share. After returning from Berne, Stucki wrote Paul regarding the Swiss legal position. He enclosed a draft agreement that accepted a role for the Allies in liquidating German assets in Switzerland by establishing a joint commission and a plan to share the revenues in some unrevealed proportion. Two days later, the Swiss released a report, *Swiss Observations With Regard to the Gold Problem* that differed markedly from Allied calculations about German gold holdings at the beginning of the war, and questioned the credibility of information provided by former Reichsbank Vice President Emil Puhl. Puhl told Allied investigators the Swiss National Bank knew the gold was looted because he had told them.

Allied reaction to the Swiss response was negative. By then, the talks were not much more than an exchange of notes and memos. Further efforts continued and other proposals arose, but none were satisfactory to either side. Finally, on April 24, Seymour Rubin told Under Secretary Acheson and Assistant Secretary Clayton that the Swiss suspended the talks. The Allies sought the return of $130 million in gold looted from Belgium and traceable to Switzerland.

On May 2, the Swiss resumed the negotiations in a meeting arranged by the Swiss ambassador in Washington, Minister Bruggmann. Stucki made his final order on his word of honor. The proposed deal provided for a 50-50 split on the sale of German assets in Switzerland and a payment of $58.1 million to settle the gold question. Paul felt the Swiss offer was the final bid. He had the benefit of U.S. intelligence reports on the flexibility, which the Swiss government had given Stucki to base his opinion on. In short, Paul already knew how much latitude the Swiss government gave Stucki in reaching an agreement. The British and French originally proposal $88 million in gold; they agreed to a settlement of $75 million. Paul felt that a better agreement could be achieved only if economic controls against the Swiss remained in place. Paul met with Stucki before he returned to Berne and agreed to the offer if the payment was raised to $70 million. Stucki not only refused, but also suggested the Swiss would subtract a 2 percent commission as a collection fee on German assets. Paul conveyed his beliefs that the Swiss had made their final offer to Assistant Secretary of State Clayton and Treasury Secretary Vinson. He said there was significant sentiment in France, Britain and the United States for elimination of controls over commercial and financial activities.

After three weeks of meetings between the Allies, the Swiss agreement was finally accepted. The Allies signed the agreement on May 26. It consisted of an accord, an annex, a gentlemen's agreement, and an exchange of letters between the Swiss and Allied delegations. On June 3, Paul sent a summary to President Truman. The major points of the agreement follow:

The Swiss Compensation Office would liquidate German property in Switzerland.

Germans whose property was liquidated would have a right to compensation in German money.

The Swiss Compensation Office would liquidate German assets in cooperation with a Joint Commission composed of Allied representatives.

Liquidated assets would be divided on a 50-50 basis between Switzerland and the Allies.

The Swiss Government would make available to the Allied Gold Pool 250 million Swiss francs ($58.1 million) on demand in gold in New York.

The United States would unblock Swiss assets and the Allies would discontinue trade "black lists" as they applied to Switzerland.

The interpretation of the accord might be settled by arbitration.

The effective date of the accord would be the date of ratification by the Swiss Parliament.[71]

On May 24, 1946, Sen. Harley Kilgore wrote a letter to President Truman urging rejection of the agreement and reversing his earlier agreement. Rep. Joseph Clark Baldwin also urged Truman to reject the agreement, but Truman accepted it. In October 1946, the United States unblocked private Swiss assets. By the end of 1948, the United States had unblocked nearly $1.1 billion in Swiss assets in the U.S. However, the Swiss continued to drag their feet in carrying out the agreement. From July–September 1946, the Swiss argued that they could not begin liquidating German assets until the Allies fixed a "fair" rate of exchange between the Reichsmark and the Swiss franc. On July 22, 1947, the Allies sent their exchange rate proposal to the Swiss. The Swiss quickly rejected it, arguing the rate could not be fixed unilaterally by France, the United States and the United Kingdom.

This was not the only case of Swiss duplicity. During the summer of 1946, the Swiss questioned the amount of gold to be returned. On Aug. 2, 1946, in a note to the State Department from the Swiss Legation, the Swiss stated that they were prepared to turn over to the Allies 50,807 kilograms of gold in payment of its 250 million Swiss franc obligation. This amount was about 800 kilograms and nearly $1 million short of the $58 million anticipated by the Allies. The Swiss arrived at the new figure by devaluating the franc. The Swiss insisted on arbitration into 1947, only to back down.

Negotiations with Switzerland continued until 1952 before reaching a final accord. Throughout the years, Switzerland displayed a disregard and contempt for the Allies' authority. Swiss duplicity marked all the negotiations, especially in the heirless assets. With heirless assets, the Swiss banks had no problems liquidating accounts for the benefit of the bank, but refused all help to Jews seeking the accounts of loved ones lost in the Holocaust. Often the banks demanded a death certificate, knowing the Nazis never issued them for concentration camps victims. This final issue was not settled until the 1990s initiative started by President Clinton and headed by Eizenstat.

Although there were renewed talks in the 1990s, Swiss duplicity still abounds. A new scandal emerged in 1997 when former bank guard Christoph Meili came forward with evidence that Union Bank of Switzerland was shredding documents about its activities with the Nazis. Meili, a night guard at Union Bank, discovered a large quantity of documents waiting to be shredded. Among them were records of accounts from the war years. The young guard turned over two books and pages ripped from another to a Jewish organization in Switzerland. Swiss law forbids destroying documents that might relate to WWII investigations. As a reward for his efforts to uncover the truth, Union Bank fired Meili. The government also is studying whether he violated any Swiss secrecy laws. The young man was threatened with the kidnapping of his daughters and has since moved to the United States. Even in the U.S., Meili still receives death threats. President Clinton signed a bill granting the Meili family permanent resident status. Christoph Meili has the distinction of being the only Swiss citizen ever granted political asylum in the United States.[72]

The Allies used the gold recovered in Germany and that returned by the neutral countries to set up a pool controlled by the Tripartite Gold Commission (TGC), which was established on Sept. 27, 1946. The Paris agreement specified the restitution of monetary gold to each participating nation in proportion to its losses of such gold. Problems stemming from the postwar economic recovery of various nations prompted the TGC to make an early distribution of monetary gold even before assembly of the Gold Pool was completed. Ten nations filed claims with TGC: Albania, Austria, Belgium, Czechoslovakia, Greece, Italy, Luxembourg, the Netherlands, Poland and Yugoslavia. On Oct. 17, 1947, TGC announced in Brussels the preliminary distribution to Belgium, Luxembourg and the Netherlands. In November and December 1947, Italy and Austria received distributions. Czechoslovakia and Yugoslavia received partial allocations in 1948. The distribution to Albania was delayed until October 1996. Overall, $379,161,426 was distributed to the claimant nations. Since the claims far exceeded the amount of recovered gold, claimants received only about 65 percent of their recognized claims. TGC now holds control of about $70 million in gold. Of that, about $47 million is stored at the Bank of England and the balance at the New York Federal Reserve Bank. The table below lists the source of the gold in the pool.

Source	Amount	Year contributed[73]
Foreign Exchange Depository	$263,680,452	1947
Switzerland	$58 million	1947
Bank for International Settlements	$4.2 million	1948
Spain	$114,329	1948
Sweden	$8 million	1949
Sweden	$7 million	1955
Portugal	$4 million	1959
Portugal	$360,000	1999

Gold Recovered in Germany

While the neutral countries must forever shoulder the shame of aiding Nazi Germany in accepting looted gold, the Allies, and in particular the United States, must also shoulder some of the shame in the recovery of stolen assets. Except for Argentina, all the neutrals claimed a threat from a possible Nazi invasion. Often, until 1941, the threat was real. However, the threat simply did not exist after that. In fact, it can be argued unequivocally that the Nazis were unable to mount another front after the Russian invasion, code-named Operation Barbarossa, because they had to delay it until after the Balkan campaign was over to free up troops. In addition, trade with the Nazis and the degree of neutrality displayed by each of the neutral nations was dependent on the fortunes of the war. This was especially true of Switzerland, which continued trading with the Nazis until the Allies were at its western border. The result was the neutral countries were willing to accept blood money for economic advantages.

However, in negotiations over the gold issue, the Allies and the United States, in particular, were equally willing to sacrifice their morality for strategic gains in the Cold War. It is readily obvious in the disregard of the Allies and the United States in handling the nonmonetary gold and victims of the Holocaust. U.S. authorities were aware of the problem from the start with the discovery at a Merkers of the Melmer account consisting of dental gold, gold watches, wedding rings, etc. Albert Thoms, head of the Reichsbank's Precious Metals Department, identified 207 bags at Merkers belonging to the Melmer account. Gen. Frank McSherry recognized the significance of the Melmer account. McSherry suggested that "this SS property contains evidence which would be useful in prosecuting SS war criminals."

The details of the Melmer account were pieced together through examinations of the Reichsbank records and by the interrogations of Thoms, Reichsbank Vice President, Emil Puhl and SS-Hauptsturmführer (Captain) Bruno Melmer. As head of the precious metals department of the Reichsbank, Thoms was able to provide the Allies with many of the details about the SS account. Thoms told his interrogators that Frommknecht sent him to Puhl in the summer of 1942. Puhl told him that the SS was about to begin the shipments to the Reichsbank containing jewelry and other items of nonmonetary gold and silver. However, because of the secrecy needed, the Reichsbank was responsible for their disposal. Shortly after this meeting, a SS-Brigadeführer (brigadier general) told Thoms that an SS officer named Melmer would deliver the first shipment in a truck. The shipment arrived on Aug. 26, 1942. The 10th delivery, in November 1942 was the first to include dental gold.

The SS first deposited the materials in the Melmer account, where the bank sorted them. Reichsbank bought the gold and silver bars, as well as currency at full value. Small items like wedding rings were sent to the Prussian Mint for resmelting. Larger jewelry items were sent to the Municipal Pawnshop, which sold the better-valued pieces. The rest of the material was sent on to Deutsche Gold-und Silber-Scheideanstalt (Degussa) for resmelting. The Nazis allowed Degussa to keep a small portion for industrial purposes, but any gold in excess was sold to the Reichsbank and the amount credited to the Melmer account.

Degussa was a large German firm engaged in metal refining and chemical production, including Zyklon-B cyanide tablets used in the gas chambers. Degesch produced the Zyklon-B tablets. Degussa and IG Farben jointly owned Degesch. Degussa also was the firm that supplied the uranium for the Nazis' atomic bomb project. Recently, Degussa spokespeople admitted ties between Degussa and IG Farben during the war. Much of the information surfacing recently about Degussa comes from a lawsuit filed in New Jersey.[74] Degussa held an exclusive contract with the Nazis for resmelting items taken from the Jews in the concentration camps, including dental gold. The Nazis were taking so much gold from the victims at Auschwitz that Degussa built a smelter there. According to Obersturmbannfuhrer Rudoff Hoss, the commandant of Auschwitz, the daily yield of gold at the camp was 24 pounds.[75]

More recently, Degussa's role in nuclear proliferation was exposed in the film documentary *Stealing the Fire*. The filmmakers document the trial of Karl-Heinz Schaab, who was tried for treason in Munich.

Schaab is the first person convicted of atomic espionage in an open trial in the last 50 years. He sold top secret documents stolen from Germany to Saddam Hussein and traveled to Baghdad many times to help Iraq build an atomic bomb. Schaab was linked to Degussa and its subsidiary, Leybold He was fined only 100,000 deutsche marks and sentenced to five years of probation.

However, there is more than just the light sentence handed out to Schaab. After the war, Gernot Zippe, known as the father of the centrifuge and an employee of Degussa, was of great interest to the militaries of several industrialized nations. Captured by the Russians, Zippe helped them build their atomic bomb. The Russians returned him to the West in 1956. On his return, the CIA immediately snapped him up to work on U.S. centrifuge technology, which is critical in separating isotopes of uranium. Through a complicated path, UN inspectors discovered a variant of Zippe's centrifuge technology in Iraq in 1996. Due to the murky underworld of arms dealing, Degussa was spared charges of treason, largely due to its connections with American defense contractors, such as duPont. Shaab was a convenient fall guy. Iraq's Scud-b missile technology can be described as 90 percent German and its atomic technology 60 percent German.[76]

In addition in 1990, Degussa was fined $800,000 for illegally exporting nuclear weapons-related material to North Korea. The firm also was implicated in exporting poisonous gas to Libya. Degussa was a large contributor to the election campaign of George W. Bush. As early as June 1999, Degussa contributed $1,950.[77] It should be noted that Degussa is a German company contributing to an American election campaign. Today, Degussa is a worldwide conglomerate reporting sales of 11.8 billion euros. Once again, a corporation associated with the Nazis has advanced, unencumbered, since the end of the war. Degussa also represents a corporation that has been so thoroughly corrupted by its past dealings with the Nazis that it is beyond reform. It should be broken up before its dealings can provoke another war. With the rise of fascism globally, the best chance of regaining control still lies in provoking another war.

The Foreign Exchange Depository decided there were 78 deliveries to the Melmer account, of which about 43 were fully inventoried by the Reichsbank. Bernstein estimated the total value of all the Melmer deliveries to be about 36.17 million Reichsmarks, with gold and silver coin and bullion accounting for 10.67 million. The controversy stems from the inclusion of gold taken from the victims of the concentration camps. The Allies judged all gold coins and bars to be monetary. Additional amounts of victim gold, classified as monetary gold, came from the resmelting of items by Degussa and from the Reichsbank after the Jews were ordered to turn in all gold and silver in 1939. This victim gold mixed with the monetary gold and some of it was sold to the neutral countries. The controversy renewed in the 1990s has shown beyond any doubt that the Allies knew of the inclusion of victim gold in the monetary gold pot. While the Allies estimated that the amount of gold taken from the victims of the Nazis was $14.5 million, only about $3 million was ever used to help the victims.

Nazi Gold Stories from Argentina

Before proceeding with the problems of heirless assets, a brief look is needed at what could be called gold stories, legends or myths, to shed more light on missing Nazi treasures. The biggest hoard still missing is that of Bormann's Aktion Feuerland project. Undoubtedly, there are as many myths as there are facts surrounding Bormann's treasure. Some have taken on legendary proportions. Thus, the reader is forewarned that what follows about this hoard may be partially false. What is known with certainty is until June 1944, Bormann transferred his loot in trucks across France to Spain. In Spain, the treasure was transferred to U-boats for the voyage to Argentina. After D-Day with the land route closed to Spain, Bormann continued his transfer of assets to Argentina by air. Author Ladislas Farago claims the complete record of this operation is preserved in the archives of Coordination Federal in Buenos Aires, in FBI files and in the archives of the British Admiralty. The latter assumed the U-boats were on regular patrol.[78] Farago claims the shipments began in 1943 and arrived every six to eight weeks. He said the money and gold were deposited in the name of Eva Peron.

According to Farago, the Perons gained control over much of Bormann's treasure, and in Eva's Rainbow Tour of Europe, she deposited more than $800 million in numbered accounts in various Swiss banks. Farago lists the treasure:

187,692,400 gold marks
17,576,386 American dollars
4,632,500 pounds sterling
24,976,442 Swiss francs
8,370,000 Dutch florins
17,280,009 Belgian francs
54,968,000 French francs
87 kilograms platinum
2,511 kilograms of gold
4,638 carats of diamonds and other precious stones.[79]

Adam Lebor has partially verified Farago's list of Bormann's treasure, specifically citing the same quantities of gold and diamonds.[80] Although Farago started the gold deliveries before the Red House meeting, the Allies first became alarmed at the Nazi gold transfers in 1943. Allied intelligence believed that much of the first gold to arrive in Argentina financed the Nazi espionage web in South America.

One legend about Argentina and Nazi gold claims that in the closing days of the war, a fleet of Nazi U-boats containing the treasure and top officials, including Hitler, left Germany for Argentina. En route, they met an Allied naval task force and a battle resulted in the loss of several Allied ships, which the United States continues to deny. Recently, more evidence surfaced in *Pravda* shedding new light on the legend.[81] In the last days of the war, the Nazis sent U-boats to Argentina. *Pravda* claims that at least five of them reached Argentina with no less than 50 top Nazis. During the trip, the U-boats sank an American battleship and the Brazilian cruiser *Bahia,* resulting in a death toll of more than 400, including U.S. citizens.

Pravda claims the U.S. ship was the *USS Eagle 56*. However, the *USS Eagle 56* was sunk on April 23, 1945 off the Maine coast towing targets for dive-bombing practice. Only 13 of the 67 crewmembers survived. Until recently, the Navy maintained a boiler room explosion sank the ship. It has now finally admitted that U-boat U-853 sank the *USS Eagle 56.* U-853 was sunk on May 6, 1945 in the North Sea, southeast of New London.[82]

The *Bahia* was sunk by U-977, which surrendered at Mar del Plata, Argentina, on Aug. 17, 1945, and was turned over to the United States for testing. Four U.S. radio operators — William Joseph Eustace, Andrew Jackson Pendleton, Emmet Peper Salles and Frank Benjamin Sparksere — were killed. The U.S. Navy still lists the men as missing in action. Brazil attributes the *Bahia* sinking to an onboard explosion.

The article in *Pravda* is based on information from Argentine researchers Carlos De Napoli and Juan Salinas. They claim that a fleet of almost 20 U-boats sailed from the Norwegian port of Bergen from May 1st to 6th. They joined another group of U-boats coming from the U.S. coasts around Cape Verde, off the western coast of Africa. There they learned of the surrender. Some scuttled their boats, others surrendered, and still others set course for Germany. However, at least six of the U-boats continued for Argentina. Further, the article claimed Churchill ordered the Argentine navy to stop attacks on German U-boats operating close to Argentina. Farago has confirmed Peron issued such an order to the navy. However, he does not mention the order came from Britain.

The *Pravda* article contains a serious error in the name of the sunken U.S. ship. Because of the controversy surrounding the boiler explosion story, when the survivors reported seeing a U-boat with a trotting horse on a red shield on the conning tower, the sinking of the *USS Eagle 56* has been thoroughly investigated. However, the article contains much information known to be true, including the listing of two of the U-boats: U-530 and U-977. U-530 surrendered in Mar del Plata, Argentina on July 10, 1945, and was turned over to the United States for testing. Other information has been partially confirmed by other investigators. Initially, the U.S. did not believe the report of Hitler's suicide and launched a search in South America for him and other missing top Nazis. After surrendering, the commander of U-977, Heinz Schaeffer, was arrested and charged with smuggling war criminals to South America.

Interestingly, U-530 was stationed around Cape Verde in 1944. On June 23, 1944, U-530 rendezvous'd with the Japanese submarine I-52 to transfer a radar detector about 850 miles west of the islands. The Allies were aware of the transfer and planes sank the Japanese sub. The I-52 was located in 1955 and still contains 2 tons of gold.[83]

More information surfaced in 1997 in Argentina. The national newspaper, *Ambito Financiero*, was contacted by a man giving his full German name and his commander's identity number.[84] He claimed he arrived in Argentina after scuttling his U-boat. In the 1970s, a different person making the same claim contacted the same paper. This U-boat commander wrote that, on Hitler's orders, 10 submarines, each with 50 officers and crew, were to sail to Argentina to help found the Fourth Reich. Recently, more information on this fleet of U-boats came from Norway. There, a person claiming to have allegedly worked in an archive department of the Nazi navy discovered additional documents that corroborate the Argentina information. The Nazis stationed a large part of their navy in southern Norway during the war. Other researchers have long claimed two U-boats were scuttled after unloading their cargo of documents and gold in shallow water, which confirms the two contacts with the paper.

Further confirmation of the Nazis' plans came from the surrender of U-234 at Portsmouth, N.H., on May 16, 1945. U-234 departed from Norway on April 16, 1945. In the North Atlantic, U-234 learned of the surrender and the order from Doenitz to abandon operations and surrender. The list of the cargo of U-234 follows:

1 ton of diplomatic and personal mail

Technical drawings and blueprints for advanced combat weaponry

Antitank weapons

Advanced bombsights and fire control systems

Airborne radar

A Me 262 jet fighter

Extra jet engines

560 kilograms of uranium oxide[85]

 In addition, the U-234 carried the following top Nazi experts:

Luftwaffe Gen. Ulrich Kessler, on his way to become German air attaché in Tokyo.

Luftwaffe Lt. Col. Fritz von Sandrart and Lt. Erich Menzel, experts in air communications, airborne radar and AA defenses.

Four Kriegsmarine officers, including a naval aviation expert, an AA expert, a naval construction engineer and a naval judge (whose job was to stamp out the last vestiges of the Sorge spy ring).

August Brinewald and Franz Ruf, experts in the technology and construction of jet aircraft whose mission was to begin production of Me 262 jet fighters in Japan.

Heinz Schlike, a specialist in radar and infrared technologies.[86]

The U-234's destination was Japan. The uranium oxide cargo was for Japan's uranium enrichment project at Hungnam in northern Korea under Nishina's direction. The technical documents helped immensely to understand Japanese defenses. The blueprints also hastened U.S. development of advanced weaponry. While the U-234 was not part of the escape to Argentina, it lends credence to the Nazis' ability to transfer their technology abroad and gives the idea of the scope of that transfer. In fact, there was a great deal more cooperation and transfer of technology between Japan and Germany near the end of the war than previously believed.

In *Gold Warriors,* the Seagraves confirm this trade of uranium between Nazi Germany and Japan. They report that Japanese cargo submarines transported gold to the Nazi sub base at Lorient, France to pay for the uranium. German U-boats and fast-surface raiders hauled the uranium to rendezvous points in Indonesia and the Philippines. From these rendezvous sites, Japanese subs hauled the uranium to its final destinations in Japan and Korea.[87]

Contacts through the Austrian Hirtenburg munitions company link Argentina with the Nazis. Hirtenburg was linked closely with New York's J. Henry Schroeder Bank through a Swiss holding company, Herbertus AG and the Argentine SA de Finanzas. The New York J. Henry Schroeder Bank was a branch of Schroeder Rockefeller Co., Investment Bankers, whose three owners during the war were Avery Rockefeller, Bruno von Schroeder in London and Kurt von Schroeder of Cologne in Nazi Germany. Nelson Rockefeller was in charge of South American security during WWII; however, he never took any steps against this conduit between Argentina and the Nazis. Tesden Corp., connected to Goering, served as a financial link between the Bahamas and Cuba with Nazi Germany. A link with the Mexican Banco Continenta, the Stein Bank of Cologne and the Bank of the Bahamas provided offshore accounts for Gestapo agents in the United States.

This brief look at the Bormann treasure transferred to Argentina readily illustrates the difficulty of sorting fact from fiction in the tales of Nazi loot. Author Uki Goni presented proof of the difficulties faced in relying on Argentina records. He found that Argentina officials purged those records of incriminating files on at least two different occasions.[88] The full truth of the Bormann treasure may never be revealed unless the United States and England declassify all WWII documents. The *Pravda* article was obviously inflated largely by Soviet suspicions of the time. However, setting aside its faults, it sheds additional light on Bormann's operation that the United States and England would like to see buried. More searches for German U-boats along the Argentine coast are already planned. Any discoveries would only serve to confirm more of the *Pravda* article, as well as the contacts made with the Argentine paper.

The Emperor's Golden Lily

While the size of the Bormann treasure is not known with any accuracy, it undoubtedly is the largest Nazi treasure the Allies failed to recover. The only other treasure remaining from WWII that could rival it in size is the Golden Lily treasure collected for the Japanese Emperor. While the Nazi treasure has been the subject of many searches and research, the Japanese treasure has been largely unexplored. While the Nazis appointed a special unit of the SS, Devisenschutzkommando, to take charge of the looting of Europe, the Japanese also had a special unit. Further, the Nazi unit employed the French to find gold and currency on a 10 percent commission. However, individuals seeking to enrich themselves, rather than the Third Reich, plagued the unit and much of the gold was siphoned off into private treasures. Seeking to avoid a similar problem, Hirohito appointed Prince Takeda Tsuneoshi as chief financial officer of the Kwantung Army. The Golden Lily involved several princes overseeing the looting to ensure the gold went to the Emperor. After the Japanese invaded China in 1937, the Golden Lily ran a parallel operation to the military campaign. The loot was amassed and trucked to Korea for shipment to the Japanese homeland.[89]

In 1939, the Japanese invaders suffered a stinging defeat at Nomonhan after a border clash with the Soviets. It's worth noting that this was the first battle in which Japanese Unit 731 employed biological warfare using typhoid bacteria. The experiment was a failure. In 1941, Roosevelt signed a secret agreement with Britain and the Netherlands to go to their defense if Japan attacked their colonies in Southeast Asia.

In 1940, the Emperor appointed Prince Chichibu to head the Golden Lily. He and Takeda traveled throughout China and Southeast Asia overseeing the looting and shipping of treasure back to Japan aboard hospital ships. By 1943, the United States submarine blockade of the home islands became effective. This forced Prince Chichibu to move his Golden Lily headquarters from Singapore to Luzon. He spent the next two and half years inventorying and hiding the treasure in a series of vaults, tunnels and caves. Chichibu hid the treasure in 172 sites.[90] The Japanese hoped to avoid surrender by arranging a cease-fire, in which Japan was allowed to keep the Philippines as a territory. Once hostilities ended, they could recover the treasure.

Besides using the Philippines to hide the treasure in the last year of the war, Japan hid gold at sea by scuttling ships. A Japanese submarine torpedoed the cruiser, *Nachii,* in Manila Bay. The submarine then machine-gunned any survivors to ensure secrecy. The *Nachii* was loaded with gold. President Marcos recovered the gold from the *Nachii* in the 1970s. In 1997, a Japanese television crew filmed the recovery of 1,800 gold bars worth $150 million. The Igorot Hill people discovered the gold. After the death of Prince Chichibu in the 1950s, a member of the Imperial family confided that the Golden Lily amassed more than $100 billion in treasure, much of which was hidden in the Philippines.[91] He also confirmed Prince Chichibu escaped by submarine from the Philippines and MacArthur's advancing forces.

The hospital ship, *Tenno Maru,* arrived at Yoksuka Naval Base loaded with casualties from the Philippines and 2,000 metric tons of gold. Days later, it moved to Maizura Naval Base, where more treasure was loaded. The ship then sailed at night. In the night, the crew was murdered and the ship sank in the bay. In a secret operation in 1987, Japan recovered the gold. The Allies mistakenly sank another hospital ship, *Awa Maru,* off the coast of China in April 1945. Aboard the ship was 40 metric tons of gold, 12 metric tons of platinum, 150,000 carats of diamonds, a large quantity of titanium and other strategic materials. Old mines in the Japanese mountains served as repositories for portions of the Golden Lily treasure. Near the Olympic Village of Nagano, the Japanese forced Korean slave laborers to dig a tunnel complex. A 10-kilometer tunnel completed the complex, in which portions of the Golden Lily treasure were hidden.[92]

The Allies made it clear that they intended to prosecute Japanese war criminals in the same manner as Nuremberg. However, unlike Germany, the Allies only convicted a few generals and admirals. The archives in Japan had vanished. The United States took exclusive control of Japan, unlike the four zones in Germany. President Truman appointed MacArthur as the Supreme Commander. For six years after the surrender of Japan, MacArthur held almost unchallenged power. As Supreme Commander, he ignored the Far Eastern commission of 11 nations. MacArthur had the power to reform the country, but instead left it in the hands of those who had bombed Pearl Harbor. The only reform imposed was the successful land reform that went ahead before it could be blocked. Washington was at least partially responsible for the lack of reforms. The liberals in Washington wanted reform while the conservatives blocked all efforts. Conservative Democrats and the Republicans held Congress until the 1946 election when the Republicans regained a majority of seats, putting Congress solidly in the conservative camp.

There were ambitious plans for reforms, such as dissolving the zaibatsu, conglomerates and banking reforms, and a new constitution, as well as restitution payments to nations ravaged by Japan. MacArthur never tried to impose any of the plans. Instead, he killed the reform efforts and started backing away from punishment of war criminals. To protect the ruling elite, MacArthur soon banned all labor demonstrations and canceled the right of labor unions to strike.

In much the same manner as the 4Ds program in Germany was sabotaged, MacArthur and his staff sabotaged the democratization of Japan with help from former Ambassador to Japan Joseph Grew and former President Herbert Hoover. Grew was appointed ambassador by Hoover in 1932 and was acting Secretary of State in 1945. His wife was a grandniece of Commodore Perry and her mother was a Cabot. Grew was from the top society of Boston and was deaf to those beneath his social status. The Grew family had longtime ties to Asia. The Grews had been bankers who underwrote the opium clipper ships of the 1800s.

Grew started sabotaging the democratization of Japan during the war. He held private talks with Japan's ambassador to Switzerland, and promised the United States would not prosecute Hirohito and would allow him to keep his throne. Both the Roosevelt and Truman administrations adamantly opposed such a promise. Both administrations called for unconditional surrender and prosecution of war criminals.

However, Grew knew he had the backing of some of the most powerful figures in American politics and high finance. He left it up to Bonner Fellers to see to it. Fellers was a former OSS agent attached to MacArthur's command. During 1941, the OSS stationed Fellers in Cairo. While there to observe the British North Africa campaign, he broadcast reports to his superiors using the black code. The Italians had broken the black code and within minutes of Feller's transmissions, Rommel knew the positions of British forces and their battle plan. Once the Allies discovered the breach in security, the Army transferred Fellers briefly to the States before attaching him to MacArthur's command.

Grew and Hoover laid out the groundwork for sabotaging peace in Japan. Friendly with both Grew and Hoover, Fellers gained a reputation of being an expert on Japan. Stationed in the Philippines in the 1930s, he made frequent trips to Japan. Hoover used Fellers during the occupation of Japan to suggest ideas to MacArthur who, in turn, used Fellers to push his presidential ambitions to Hoover and the Republican hierarchy.

As president, Hoover showed little concern about foreign affairs. However, after his defeat and as the war clouds descended on Europe, he took an active interest. In 1938, Hoover met with Hitler. Even at this late date, Hoover still would have aligned the country with Hitler to defeat Stalin. He also was a friend of Japanese royalty from his time spent in China. Hoover wanted Japan to be a conservative Pacific outpost strongly opposed to communism. He wanted an alliance with Japan for an Asian base for the Republican Party and its Wall Street cronies. Once he cleansed the Emperor and government of any guilt over the war, Japanese factories would be humming again.

Hoover and Grew's plan to cleanse the Emperor and the Japanese government of any war crimes required complete secrecy. There were still far too many bitter war memories from Pearl Harbor, the Bataan death march and Japanese forced labor camps. As late as 1945, Congress voted to charge Hirohito with war crimes. Fellers and another Grew protégé, Max Bishop, engineered the cleansing process. First, to discover the true extent of Hirohito's guilt, they questioned Japanese officials and indicted war criminals in secret. Once Grew and Bishop assembled all the facts, they sanitized each incriminating piece of information by threatening and bribing witnesses. Before the trials could begin, several witnesses who refused to be intimidated or bribed conveniently died. U.S. intelligence forced American POWs on their way home to sign documents forbidding them to talk about the harsh treatment they received at the hands of the Japanese.

While MacArthur was quietly trying to stop the trials, he received a blunt reminder from the Joint Chiefs to get serious about bringing the Emperor to trial. Despite such orders, MacArthur refused to allow a trial of Hirohito. MacArthur even put Hirohito on the public relations circuit, showing him shaking hands and portraying him as a great pacifist. Behind the scenes, MacArthur and Fellers castigated anyone not falling in line with the opinion that the war was the fault of the military.

MacArthur's list of war criminals was remarkably short. Of 300 cases investigated, only 28 appeared before the court. The Allies executed only seven Japanese war criminals. All of those hung were Choshu, not Satsuma. This may have been a payoff to the royal court from a long-standing feud dating back to the early days of the Meiji Restoration. Even postwar maps omitted the name Choshu after renaming the prefecture Yamaguchi.

Chief prosecutor was Joseph Keenan; the 11-member panel of judges consisted of a judge from each Allied nation. The Allies arbitrarily granted pardons to some of the criminals high on the list. For instance, the British decided not to prosecute a naval officer who ordered the machine gunning of 600 British sailors trying to stay afloat after their ship sank. MacArthur ordered that no information about biological warfare and Unit 731 be admitted in the trials.[93]

While Herbert Hoover kept Fellers busy in Japan nursing MacArthur's political ambitions, he guided Grew stateside. At the end of the war, Grew was resigned from the State Department and moved to Wall Street, where he became cochair of the American Council on Japan (ACJ). ACJ was a political action committee formed by wealthy conservatives immediately after the war to lobby Washington and to fight any efforts to reform Japan. *Newsweek* backed ACJ. Averell Harriman founded *Newsweek,* in 1937. His brother was a director. *Newsweek's* pro-Japanese stance had his blessing. His role as a leading fund-raiser of Democratic causes obviously came at a cost because he was looking out for his financial interests and those of his clients. The magazine hailed the Wall Street vision for Japan. Chief organizers for AJC were Harry Kern, *Newsweek* foreign editor; Compton Pakenham, *Newsweek's* bureau chief in Tokyo; and James Kauffman, a New York lawyer who served the interest of General Electric, Standard Oil, Ford, National Cash Register, Ottis Elevator, and Dillon and Read in Japan.[94]

Grew's cochairman at ACJ was another of Hoover's agents, William Castle, a wealthy plantation owner from Hawaii and former Ambassador to Japan. Until WWII, the wealthy elite regarded ambassador positions at the State Department as their own providence. Grew's assistant at ACJ was Eugene Dooman, who was raised in Japan. They regarded their mission as stopping any excesses in reforming Japan. Right-wing business leaders were careful to denounce cartels and monopolies in principle, but fought vigorously against efforts to break up Japanese conglomerates. They looked toward restoring trade with Japan, which was Asia's only industrial base. The sooner Japan's financial elite was restored to power, the quicker business could resume.

In the summer of 1947, Kauffman visited Tokyo for Dillon Read and made a personal assessment of Truman's plan to break apart the zaibatsu. Truman's plans were classified secret. However, Undersecretary of Defense William Draper leaked the documents to *Newsweek*. Draper also played a prominent role in sabotaging the 4Ds program in postwar Germany. In December, as the nation was gearing up for the presidential election, *Newsweek* denounced the overall plan for Japan as costly.

In Congress, Republican Sen. William Knowland, a wealthy newspaper publisher from California, led the attack. Knowland claimed communists wrote the Truman policy on Japan, easing the way for Joe McCarthy. Knowland and Rep. Walter Judd, a Republican from Minnesota, led the China lobby on Capitol Hill and blamed the loss of China to communism on Truman. Meanwhile, Herbert Hoover continued to lead MacArthur on about his chances to head the Republican ticket. MacArthur was particularly sensitive to *Newsweek's* charges of communism. Those charges enraged the general and he halted all further implementation of the reform program.

The final deathblow for reform in Japan came early in 1948. In February, William Draper and Percy Johnson, a Wall Street banker, toured Japan to review the policy. Johnson was chairman of Chemical Bank, which had a longtime alliance with Mitsui Bank. The outcome was predictable. Of the original list of 325 Japanese companies to be broken apart, only 20 remained on the Draper-Johnson list. Not a single Japanese bank was restructured. The Japanese banks changed their names as a precaution and hid their past.

By 1952, when the occupation ended, all leftists had been purged and the conservatives were in control of Japan. The Emperor's fortune was still in Tokyo Bay and in other locations. The first recovery of a portion of the Golden Lily is known as the Santa Romana recov. In the Philippines in the waning days of the war, Filipino guerrillas saw the Japanese hiding heavy bronze cases in a cave. An OSS major was with the group that watched the burial. After the Japanese finished hiding the treasure, they dynamited the cave entrance. The OSS agent reopened the cave and found the cases to contain gold.

From 1945–48, the United States covertly recovered the gold. William Donovan, MacArthur, Fellers, Edward Lansdale and Hoover knew of the recovery. Later, Allen Dulles learned of the gold recovery, headed by Donovan and Lansdale. The United States made no attempt to return the gold to its rightful owners. Instead, it was deposited in 176 bank accounts in 42 different countries and became the basis of the CIA's off-the-books financing. This financing was done by issuing gold certificates to influential people and binding them to the CIA. One account in Lansdale's name in the Geneva branch of Union Banque Suisse contained 20,000 metric tons of gold. The insiders squirreled some of the bullion away for private use. Documents confirm that one of the largest accounts was in the name of MacArthur.

Other documents note that Hoover had an account containing $100 million in gold bullion. One can be certain that Hoover's deep concern over Japan was based on his ability to smell a big payoff in gold from his previous experiences in China and Australia. Hoover's holdings were confirmed after his death, when his son sought government approval to dispose of a large sum of bullion. The large accounts of MacArthur and Hoover suggest that cleansing Hirohito came at a high price to the Japanese Emperor.[95]

Edwin Pauley, a rich oilman, was sent to Japan to assess its ability to pay reparations. Pauley learned about the $2 billion in gold in Tokyo Bay shortly after his arrival. Yet, he decided Japan was in shambles and could not pay its fair share of expenses of the American occupation, let alone anyone else's rebuilding efforts. Largely due to Pauley's assessment, Japan's bill for reparations came to only $1 billion. If such a sum had been distributed equally to the next of kin of the 20 million people who died because of Japan's aggression, each would have received the paltry sum of $30. In the immediate postwar scramble for reparations, the wealthy in Japan who profited from the war and hid their profits filed their own claim for reparations, totaling $5 billion. Many of these claims were paid.

Instead of cash payment to countries, the Allies ordered Japan to provide industrial equipment. Washington suspended such token payments when American firms claimed the equipment as collateral for bonds issued before the war. Two of the largest American firms making such claims were Morgan Bank and Dillon and Read. By 1950, Japan owed Morgan Bank more than $600 million in interest, penalties and principle just for the 1924 earthquake loans. In 1951, Japan arranged for refinancing of the loans through Smith Barney and Guaranty Trust. By 1952, Japan repaid all prewar investments by American corporations and compensated them for all property damage. Also, Japan repaid all prewar bonds held by companies affiliated with ACJ, while unaffiliated companies were not so fortunate. The repayment raises the question of how a country so shattered was able to pay off such a large debt in such a short time.[96]

The issue of Japan's compensation is still an issue. In 1998, one month before Prince Akihito's visit to Britain, Congress passed the following resolution:

Whereas the government of Germany has formally apologized to the victims of the Holocaust and gone to great lengths to provide financial compensation to the victims and to provide for their needs and recovery; and Whereas by contrast the Government of Japan has refused to fully acknowledge the crimes it committed during World War II and to provide Reparations to its victims: Now, therefore, be it Resolved by the House of Representatives (the Senate concurring), That it is the sense of the Congress that the Government of Japan should:

Formally issue a clear and unambiguous apology for the atrocious war crimes committed by the Japanese military during World War II; and:

Immediately pay reparations to the victims of those crimes including United States military and civilian prisoners, people of Guam who were subjected to violence and imprisonment, survivors of the "Rape of Nanking" from December 1937 until February 1938, and the women who were forced into sexual slavery and known by the Japanese military as "comfort women."[97]

One intriguing theory that sheds more light on the fate of the Golden Lily comes from author and researcher David Guyatt.[98] Guyatt theorizes the total of mined gold is deliberately understated and the supply is much larger than the 140,000 tons reported. Right-wing fascists control this additional supply of black gold. One reported trader in this market is George W. Bush.

His theory revolves around the year 1954. In 1939, Britain shut down the London Bullion Market due to a shortage of gold. Even before the war, England's gold reserves were dangerously low. The war was another drain on those reserves, as evidenced by the destroyer trade and England's reliance on the Lend-Lease program, as well as the concession of Portugal to accept the pound in trade rather than demand gold. In short, England was walking among the financially dead at the war's end. However, in 1954, just nine short years from the end of the war, England seemingly obtained enough gold to reopen the bullion market.

The Bilderberg group, founded by Prince Bernhard of the Netherlands, held its first meeting in 1954. The prince, a former officer in the SS, had worked in IG Farben's notorious NW7 group, which served as spies for the Third Reich. Bernhard belonged to the Dutch branch of the Knights Templar. In 1954, he was appointed to govern the Dutch order. John Foster Dulles was one of the most helpful Americans in setting up the Bilderberg group. Incidentally, in 1954 Dulles testified in favor of a bill designed to return vested enemy assets, such as GAF, to their previous owners. From the beginning, the Bilderberg group had several members of the intelligence community associated with it. Sir Colin Gubbins, Britain's wartime SOE head, was a founding member. Walter Bedell Smith was a co-chair of the group in the United States.

The year 1954 was significant in several other ways. A memorandum of agreement between the CIA and the Justice Department dated Feb. 18, 1954 allowed the CIA to police itself. In effect, it allowed the CIA free rein as the Justice Department turned a blind eye to matters of national security. Another noteworthy event of 1954 was the merger of Schroeder Bank and the Wagg family to form the city-based merchant bank, J. Henry Schroder Wagg & Co. Wackenhut Corp., with deep ties to both the military and intelligence communities, started operations in 1954.

Even more significant was that 1954 was the year the U.S. forecast the Soviet Union would have thermonuclear weapons. The U.S. launched a massive military buildup, costing taxpayers billions while corporations reaped fat profits. It also was the year Gen. James Doolittle finished his study of the CIA and decided the agency was not as adept as the KGB. In addition, MK-ULTRA, the mind control program of the CIA, began that year.

Perhaps the most noteworthy of all events in 1954 was a strange audit of the gold supply in Fort Knox. Each bar totaling almost three-quarters of a million dollars was weighed. In addition, a small hole was drilled into every hundredth bar and a small sample taken for assaying. To hide the extent of the audit, different assayers were used. No reasonable explanation for such a detailed and secret audit has been uncovered.

A partial list of significant events of 1954 follows: After learning about the Japanese treasures in November 1953, President Marcos started digging for gold in the Philippines. Fred Meuser, Lockheed's European director, transferred to Geneva. The Four-Power Treaty was signed in Paris to end the occupation regime in Germany. Germany joined NATO. The Geneva Accord was reached on peace between France and Indochina. In addition, in 1954 Edward Lansdale arrived in Vietnam to take over the opium trade. The Israeli Mossad and the CIA formed an intelligence "partnership." Nazi gold was moved from Argentina to the Philippines in 1954 after the Mossad determined where it was located.

Research done by the Seagraves found 172 treasure sites of the Golden Lily in the Philippines. One audited by Japanese accountants contained a staggering 777 billion yen or the equivalent of $194 billion.[99] Estimates for all 172 sites: $100 trillion. Over the years, several right-wing groups have aided and helped the CIA by laundering plundered items from the Golden Lily.

One of the latest recoveries, which raised scandalous headlines in 1994, involved former UN Secretary Gen. Kurt Waldheim, who took part in an operation involving the CIA and former Gen. John Singlaub. The operation, dubbed Nippon Star, recovered more than 500 metric tons of gold from the Philippines. Singlaub, who was active in right-wing extremist groups and political intrigue in Central and South America, headed the team. Singlaub was part of the military intelligence complex before retiring. The team consisted of Gunther Russbacher, a CIA agent, five other Americans and a handful of Filipinos. They recovered Nazi gold and gold stolen from China by the Japanese. Kurt Waldheim served as the intermediary between the Austrian National Bank and Philippine President Ramos.

What is intriguing about this sale, besides the extraordinary size, is the Knights of Malta knew details of it. A document from the Knights of Malta, *Lansdale Project,* references 500 MT (metric tons). Moreover, it refers to a meeting of Washington people to discuss the ramifications of another Lansdale project. While several former intelligence officials and military leaders are members of the Knights of Malta, their knowledge of a secret CIA operation raises further questions. Who else was in on this operation? What were the ramifications of the second Lansdale Project? Was the Vatican part of this operation? For now, those questions and others go unanswered.

The stated reason for the transfer to Austria was to provide backing for the euro. However, the presence of Waldheim as an intermediary only raises questions of connections to Nazis and fascism. Even before Waldheim took his office in the UN, the CIA and military intelligence must have known about his background as an SS officer. It is inconceivable the United States did not know he was in an automatic arrest category after the war.

A 1956 gold certificate is one of the earliest documents testifying to Marcos recovering Golden Lily treasure. This was before Marcos became a member of the Senate. Swiss Bank Corp., (Schweizerische Bank Gesellschaft M.H.C.) issued the certificate for a deposit of 7,120 metric tons of gold. Marcos collaborated with Japanese-American investigator Minoru Fukimatsu. Together, they interviewed more than 300 witnesses and somehow accessed secret Japanese government archives to discover the locations of the treasure.

The Union Bank of Switzerland issued another gold certificate on Jan. 17, 1963 to Adnan Kasogi. Adnan Kasogi was actually Adnan Khashoggi, a Marcos crony. Khashoggi's name was misspelled, but that is often the case in these certificates. Khashoggi was a Lockheed agent and partner of Yoshio Kodama. Kodama was a Japanese rear admiral during the war and a member of the Japanese Yakuza crime clan. During the war, Kodama was in charge of shipping loot to the Philippines. This gold certificate was issued to Khasoggi just before Lockheed paid the first bribe to Prince Bernhard. The CIA used Lockheed to funnel money worldwide. Moreover, Lockheed's European Sales Director, Dutchman Fred Meuser, was a member of Prince Bernhard's wartime air force squadron. Another member of the Lockheed bribe team was CIA officer Nicholas Deak. Deak founded a money-brokering firm to funnel money to Kodama. Deak's company later merged with Lionel C. Perera, who founded the money firm of Perera Manfra & Brookes. Perera was attached to the Chief of Military Government Finance Office at the Third Army's headquarters in Germany at war's end, where he interviewed Col. Rauch. Rauch was the SS colonel responsible for hiding the Reich Bank gold reserves.

With so many figures directly involved with both the Nazi and Japanese treasures, an event such as the Lockheed bribery cannot be dismissed as mere happenstance. However, the intrigue does not stop here. Marcos, Kodama and Singlaub were all members of the World Anti-Communist League, a right-wing extremist group populated with known war criminals and fascists. The Reagan administration granted the World Anti-Communist League tax-exempt status. That raises the possibility that the CIA also used the World Anti-Communist League as a front in money laundering and the drug trade.

Guyatt goes on to claim that Henry Kissinger sent a letter dated Feb. 21, 1986 to Marcos on Trilateral notepaper. Kissinger demanded that Marcos sell "63,321 tons of gold to 2,000 U.S. and European banks controlled by the Trilateral." Marcos refused and was overthrown as a result. However, Imelda Marcos chose to sell the gold to avoid criminal charges. It was transferred aboard the *USS Eisenhower* to the United States.

More evidence of Marcos recovering the Golden Lily treasure comes from the Filipino newspaper, *The Inquirer*. In 1998, the paper published an article, "Soldiers of Fortune," that revealed that all members of the 16th Infantry Battalion signed a joint affidavit declaring that, with members of the 51st Engineering Brigade, they recovered 60,000 metric tons of gold from 30 sites between 1973–85. Both units operated in strict secrecy under Marcos lackey Fabian Ver.

Whether Guyatt's theory of a secret gold treaty signed in 1954 is correct or not, it is obvious from his findings and those of the Seagraves that considerable treasure was recovered from the Golden Lily, ending up in the hands of those involved in intelligence and right-wing causes. It is most likely that a portion was skimmed for private use, while the CIA used the balance to fund clandestine operations. It is interesting to note that those connected with the secret recoveries — Herbert Hoover, MacArthur, Allen Dulles and others — were the ones who worked hardest to derail the reform of Japan and Nazi Germany. Their sole objective was to reestablish the cartels and get on with business, to hell with war crimes. Moreover, it seems certain that a large portion of the Nazi treasure and the Golden Lily financed rebuilding Germany and Japan with the direct approval of the Right Wing in America.

While the largest portions of the Nazi hoard and the Golden Lily remain shrouded in mystery and controversy, a good deal is known about smaller caches that have been recovered. Until recently, little was known about America's acquisition of treasures from the war. Much mystery remains and undoubtedly more caches will surface with time. Although Congress passed legislation requiring the return to Germany of much of this material, most of it remains stored in the American archives and private collections. Recent court rulings have supported the legislation. Only after Clinton authorized Eizenstat to reach a settlement on unclaimed assets did the New York Federal Reserve admit to holding 2 tons of Nazi gold. There has been little effort to return the war booty.

The Black Eagle Trust

Continued research by the Seagraves has revealed the United States did recover portions of the Golden Lily and Nazi treasure, and used it to clandestinely fund various right-wing causes and covert operations.[100] This enormous secret slush fund became known informally as the Black Eagle Trust.

Until September 1945, Edward Lansdale remained an insignificant advertising copywriter who spent the war producing OSS propaganda. After the OSS disbanded, he was offered an opportunity to transfer to the U.S. Army's G2 operation in the Philippines. There, he was in charge of supervising a Filipino-American intelligence officer named Severio Garcia Diaz Sanata, better known as Santy.

Gen. Tomoyuki Yamashita, the "Tiger of Malaya" sent to take over the command in the Philippines, had surrendered. He was charged with war crimes relating to gruesome atrocities Adm. Iwabuchi Kanji's sailors committed while evacuating Manila. While Yamashita was innocent, it was essential to Lansdale and his cadre of plotters that he be hanged because of his knowledge of the Japanese treasure. There was no mention of the Golden Lily or war loot during Yamashita's trial. Because of his arrest as a war criminal, it was impossible to torture Yamashita directly because it would be exposed in the resulting trial. However, Yamashita's driver fell under special scrutiny. He had driven everywhere since Yamashita's arrival in the Philippines.

Santy proceeded to torture the driver, Maj. Kojima Kashii, to find the burial sites of the Japanese treasure. Lansdale soon joined the torture sessions as an observer and participant. In October, Kojima broke down and led Santy and Lansdale to the location of a dozen sites in the mountains north of Manila. Two of the sites were easily opened and revealed a prodigious quantity of gold, precious metals and gems.

While Santy and his teams started to open the other sites, Lansdale flew to Japan to brief MacArthur and then on to Washington to brief President Truman. After a cabinet discussion, Truman decided to continue with the recovery that would be kept a state secret.

The decision was not Truman's alone. Henry Stimson, Secretary of War, first proposed using gold recovered from the Nazis as a secret slush fund during the Roosevelt administration. The Nazis had already done the dirty work and resmelted the gold, making it hard to trace its origin. Many of the owners perished in the war and much of the prewar governments ceased to exist. With many of the eastern countries falling under the influence of the Soviet Union, returning any gold to these countries was out of the question with the Cold War Warriors.

Stimson's special assistants on this were John McCloy, Robert Lovett, Clark Clifford and Robert Anderson. Anderson was a former Texas Republican legislator. In 1953, President Eisenhower appointed Anderson Secretary of Navy, and in 1954, Secretary of Defense. Some sources say his appointment as Secretary of Navy was based solely on the need to move gold from the Philippines. In 1957, Eisenhower appointed him Secretary of Treasury. In 1987, he pleaded guilty to running an offshore bank after being caught up in the BCCI scandal, which also ensnared Clark Clifford.

The Allies first discussed the idea of the Black Eagle Trust in secret during July 1944 at Bretton Woods. CIA Deputy Director Ray Cline has confirmed the secret talks. As late as the 1990s, Cline tried to control Japanese war booty sitting in the vaults of Citibank.

After briefing Truman, Stimson, Lovett and others, Lansdale returned to Tokyo with Anderson in November. From there, MacArthur and Anderson accompanied Lansdale on a secret flight to Manila. At the sites, MacArthur and Anderson strolled down row after row of gold bullion stacked two meters high. This was only the gold that had not reached Japan because of the Allied blockade of the home islands.

Cline and others have confirmed the gold recovered by Santy and Lansdale was covertly moved by ship to 176 accounts in 42 countries. Truman was informed that if such a large quantity of gold became public knowledge, the fixed $35 an ounce price would collapse. Other documents show large deposits of gold and platinum made in various Swiss banks from 1945–47.[101]

Secrecy was vital to the success of the Black Eagle Trust. The United States declared Japan was broke from the very beginning. U.S. elite led by Herbert Hoover wanted to preserve Japan as a staunch anti-communist state in the Far East. Japanese elites were hard-core conservatives alarmed by the communist threat. The most ardent of the anti-communists were the indicted war criminals. The Allies punished only a few Japanese war criminals due in a large part to interference by MacArthur in his efforts to cleanse the Emperor of all crimes.

Such secrecy led to immediate abuses and misleading of the American and Japanese people. American occupation forces left in power those most responsible for the war. Considerations for the Black Eagle Trust skewed the 1951 peace treaty between the Allies and Japan. To shield Japan from war reparations, John Foster Dulles secretly negotiated the treaty with three Japanese officials. One of them, Miyazawa Kiichi, later became Prime Minister and served repeatedly as Minister of Finance.

Article 14 of the peace treaty states:

It is recognized that Japan should pay reparations to the Allied Powers for the damage and suffering caused by it during the war. Nevertheless it is also recognized that the resources of Japan are not presently sufficient … the Allied Powers waive all reparations claims of the Allied Powers and their nationals arising out of any actions taken by Japan.[102]

By signing the treaty, Allied countries waived all rights to any claims, including those by their citizens and soldiers forced into slave labor by Japanese warlords.

Because the Black Eagle Trust and the political actions funds it spawned remain off the books and invisible, the potential for abuse in unscrupulous hands remains high to this day. In 1960, Vice President

Nixon gave one of the largest funds, the M-Fund, to leaders of the Japanese Liberal Party in return for kickbacks to his election campaign. The fund, then valued at $35 billion and now estimated as worth more than $500 billion, has served to keep the Liberal Party in power and effectively reduce politics in Japan to a one-party dictator with a block on any reforms.[103] This is readily obvious in Japan's troubled economic state. Even after sliding into an economic abyss 15 years ago, Japan has still not addressed its economic policies in any meaningful manner. In effect, Nixon's action has left Japan with an inept, corrupt and weak regime that has not even confronted its role in starting WWII.

A 1950 report prepared by MacArthur's headquarters confirmed the vast wealth of the Japanese war loot.

> Japanese owned gold and silver ... property that was acquired by Japan under duress, wrongful acts of confiscation, dispossession or spoliation ... property found in Japan and identified as having been located in an Allied country and removed to Japan by fraud or coercion by the Japanese or their agents ... great hoards of gold, silver, precious stones, foreign postage stamps, engraving plates ... precious metals and diamonds stockpiles owned or controlled by the Japanese ... 30,000 carats of diamonds in one stash, and a single find of 52.5 pounds of hoarded platinum ... .

> One of the spectacular tasks of the occupation dealt with collecting and putting under guard the great hoards of gold, silver, precious stones, foreign postage stamps, engraving plates, and all currency not legal in Japan. Even though the bulk of this wealth was collected and placed under Untied States military custody by Japanese officials, undeclared caches of these treasures were known to exist.[104]

MacArthur's staff was well aware of the Japanese treasures, including the $2 billion of gold lying on the bottom of Tokyo Bay. Another large hoard discovered in 1946 by U.S. intelligence was the $13 billion cache of underworld godfather Kodama Yoshio. Promoted to a rear admiral during the war, Yoshio oversaw the looting of the Asian underworld. After the war, Allied forces arrested and held Kodama for war crimes. To avoid trial and imprisonment, he offered the CIA a $100 million bribe. The CIA added the bribe money to the M-Fund and freed Kodama. He later financed two political parties that eventually merged into the Liberal Party.[105]

Following the death of Santy in 1974, some of the biggest black gold accounts were placed in Lansdale's name. Curiously, Lansdale retired from the CIA before 1974.

Much of the information about the Black Eagle Trust has seeped to the surface in several lawsuits that named Citibank CEO John Reed as a participant. In another, Rogelio Roxas, a Filipino locksmith, sued President Marcos for seizing a 1 ton golden Buddha that he found. In another legal battle, former U.S. Deputy Attorney General Norbert Schlei fought for his survival after being stung by the Treasury Department for asking too many questions about Japan's secret M-Fund.

Schlei was a key lawyer during the Kennedy and Johnson administrations. He was the attorney who found legal grounds for the Cuba blockade during the missile crisis, and the principal author of the 1964 Civil Rights Act. He also was the primary author of the following landmark bills: the Economic Opportunity Act of 1964, the Voting Rights Act of 1965, and the Immigration Reform Act of 1967.

The court acquitted Schlei of eight counts, including wire and bank fraud, and money laundering, but convicted him of conspiracy and securities fraud. The charges stem from Schlei negotiating a settlement for a client based on a gold certificate backed by the M-Fund. In 1998, The 11th Circuit Court of Appeals vacated the judgment, in effect admitting that Schlei was innocent of the charges and a victim of partisan politics.

While Schlei was being indicted, prosecuted and forced into bankruptcy, former Secretary of State Alexander Haig went to Japan and negotiated a certificate based on the M-Fund. This was the same action that led to Schlei's arrest. Haig carried with him a personal letter from then President George H.W. Bush.

Haig was the ideal choice to negotiate the certificate. In 1947, he served as an aide to Gen. MacArthur and undoubtedly had firsthand knowledge of the Golden Lily and the various secret funds created from it. While in Japan, Haig married the daughter of Gen. Alonzo Fox, MacArthur's deputy chief of staff.

Many aspects of WWII remain partially shrouded in fog because of censorship and government secrecy. They include the financial treachery and extortion surrounding the Golden Lily and the financial dealings with postwar Japan that are confined to a black hole of government secrecy. Western archives and databases have been purged of records of Japan's looting and economic treachery. Such reports remain classified and hidden from the public. Moreover, the reports that do exist will not be made public for another half-century. Recent efforts by Congress to force the release of documents from WWII have met with only limited success because the CIA retains the right to filter out documents that may reveal an unsavory American collusion with Japanese warlords. However, bits and pieces of the puzzle have emerged in recent years to present a partial view.

At the time the Philippines fell to the Japanese, the Philippine National Treasure consisted of more than 51 metric tons of gold, 32 metric tons of silver bullion, 140 tons of silver coins and $27 million in U.S. Treasury notes. In December 1941, the Philippine government evacuated the treasure to Corregidor and stored it in a tunnel complex. Gen. Willoughby's wife helped inventory the gold. (Willoughby will figure prominently later.) On Feb. 3, 1942, the submarine *USS Trout* arrived at Corregidor delivering munitions, food and medical supplies. Before leaving, the skipper requested ballast. The submarine was loaded with the private gold, 16 tons of silver pesos and other paper securities, including some Treasury notes. The *USS Trout* then continued its patrol, sinking two Japanese vessels before returning to Pearl Harbor. There, the Navy turned the gold and securities over to the San Francisco Mint. It never occurred to the defenders of Corregidor to hide or cloak the remaining treasure in the tunnel complex. When the Japanese captured Corregidor, the treasure was still there.

Japan used the same tactics the Nazis did in laundering looted gold. Japan moved it through Swiss banks in Tokyo, Portuguese banks in Maco, and banks in Chile and Argentina. It moved the gold to South America in large cargo submarines. The Portuguese cleverly omitted Maco in the Bretton Woods agreement.

Journalist Paul Manning had an opportunity to see Emperor Hirohito's financial records when they were still in the custody of the occupation authorities. The records showed that advisers to the Emperor began moving his gold out of Japan in 1943, about the same time Bormann began moving Nazi loot out of Germany. Historian James Mackay concludes the Emperor's accounts included $35 million in South America banks, $20 million in Swiss accounts, and $45 million in Portuguese, Spanish and Vatican accounts.[106]

Any account of the Golden Lily and Japanese war loot is incomplete without a look at Japan's use of slave labor. Slave labor, including Allied POWs, built the various treasure sites in the Philippines. Once a site was completed and ready to be sealed, the Japanese herded the slaves into the tunnels. They then dynamited the entrance, leaving the prisoners to suffocate.

The Japanese were especially brutal with their POWs, even more than the Nazis. More than 30 percent of the Allied POWs died in captivity at the hands of their tormentors. In comparison, only 3 percent of Allied POWs died in Nazi camps. The Japanese deliberately left Allied POWs to die untreated from beriberi and other tropical diseases. In a prisoner of war camp on Hainan Island, the camp commandant, Capt. Kikuchi Ichiro, withheld vitamin B capsules to prevent beriberi and calculated the minimum amount of food to keep the POWs barely alive.

The Japanese transported thousands of POWs to Japan on Hell Ships, sealed in the cargo holds under conditions so grim that it was not uncommon for 10 percent of the prisoners to die before reaching Japan. Ships carrying POWs were supposed to be marked as such, but Japan refused. When the ships were attacked and sunk, the POWs drowned, locked in the cargo holds. The Allies mistakenly sank at least 16 Hell Ships, resulting in the loss of 17,036 Allied POWs.

By mid-1942, Japan held 140,000 Allied POWs, about a half-million Western civilians, and more than 1 million overseas Chinese. The Japanese treatment of prisoners followed racial lines. They singled out the Chinese for exceptional brutality. Prisoners were forced into slave labor for various uses, including mining gold and coal. Other prisoners worked in factories, including Mitsui, Kawasaki Heavy Industries, Mitsubishi, Nippon Steel, Showa, Denko and others. Mitsui was by far the largest employer of slave labor. Operators of the Hell Ships include the following corporations: NYK Line, KKK Line and Mitsui. These corporations have never been obligated to pay compensation to their victims. Tokyo and Washington have blocked all attempts at compensation.

Japan dragooned about 1 million Chinese and another million Koreans to work in mines. The Japanese forced Korean women and young girls into prostitution. Known as comfort girls, they were slaves to the military. After capturing the Philippines, the Japanese rounded up wealthy women and young girls and raped them as many as 50 times in a day. The rapes continued until their families came up with ransoms.

After liberation, U.S. POWs in Japan were transported to Guam where they were browbeaten until they signed papers agreeing they would tell no one of their experiences.[105] For some reason, Tokyo and Washington both wanted silence surrounding the abuse of POWs. Further documentation supporting this comes from files captured by the British Royal Marines in 1945. In the files is a revealing document written by a commander of a POW camp at Taihoku in Taiwan. He received emergency instructions from the 11th Unit of Formosa: "Whether they are destroyed individually or in groups, or however it is done, with mass bombing, poisonous smoke, drowning, decapitation or what … it is the aim not to allow the escape of a single one, to annihilate them all and not to leave any traces."[107]

Obviously, Tokyo was insistent on silencing all evidence of their abuse of POWs. However, Washington's concurrence is perplexing. The war was over and Japan had been vanquished. What cities that weren't in ruins from the massive firebombing were in ashes from two atomic bombings. The only possible motives for Washington's agreement are bribery or blackmail. Meanwhile, the leaders in Washington betrayed those American GIs who suffered in the brutal slave labor camps and left them with no means of recourse.

It is almost impossible to keep something the size of the Golden Lily secret. Periodically, reports of stolen loot have surfaced. One of the first reports concerned Dutch silver. In 1946, American sources told the Dutch military mission that 110 cases of Dutch coins were transferred from Yokosuka Bank to the Bank of Japan. In 1947, Lt. Gen. Schilling of the Dutch military mission reported to his government the recovery of 30 tons of Dutch silver from Tokyo Bay. The Japanese 16th Army on Java seized this silver and shipped it aboard fake hospital ships to the Osaka Mint. Additional Dutch ingots were recovered from Etchugina Bay.

Due to postwar detective work by the former Dutch POW, Lt. A. Looijen, Japan eventually returned 187 tons of Dutch silver to the Netherlands. Looijen traced the silver bullion from Java to the Bank of Japan. Another Dutch POW, C. Broekhuizen, who was forced into slave labor, reported that it was the Japanese government's plan to hide the gold and silver until after the war, and then to melt and recast it to launder it. Other Dutch and American POWs have testified that they saw a warehouse full of coins from the various countries of Asia and the South Pacific. Standard Oil previously owned the warehouse. Still other POWs reported seeing copper coins resmelted at a Hitachi factory.[108]

POWs also reported seeing copious amounts of diamonds and other precious gems. The finest were culled and set aside, the smallest consigned for industrial use. The remaining was stored in oil drums. The Japanese hid almost all the loot in either private vaults or tunnels and bunkers. They avoided depositing all but a little in Japanese banks because the elite were not about to share the wealth with the lower classes.

The largest tunnel complex is at Matsushiro near Nagano, the site of the 1998 Winter Olympics. The tunnel complex is 10 kilometers long with more than 60,000 cubic feet of underground space. It was originally built to house the imperial family, members of the aristocracy and all government agencies. Slave labor from Korea dug the tunnel complex. No one ever saw the slaves after the complex was completed, a frequent circumstance with the Japanese treasure sites. They were probably buried alive in a side tunnel. The complex also was used to hide treasure from the Golden Lily.

After the war, Allied investigators learned that on Aug. 2, 1945, just days before Japan's surrender, 387 Allied POWs were buried alive on the Japanese island of Sado. They had been forced to work in a gold and coal mine. Lt. Tsuda Yoshiro described the event to investigators. Mitsubishi ran the mine and had a notorious reputation for brutal treatment of slave labor. In another gold mine in Sado, also managed by Mitsubishi, 1,000 Korean slave workers were buried alive. Their fate was determined from company records released in 1991. The records covered Mitsubishi's distribution of cigarette rations to its slave labor.[109]

In 1947, Gen. MacArthur brought several gemologists to Japan, including Edward Henderson. MacArthur invited him to appraise some $50 million in gems the U.S. Army recovered. According to journalist Robert Whiting, the Bank of Japan transferred roughly 800,000 karats of diamonds to MacArthur's command. No record of these diamonds has ever been found.[110]

To better understand how such a large treasure as the Golden Lily has been suppressed and how the Black Eagle Trust came into being requires a closer look at the liberation of the Philippines. While only part of the Nazi gold was ever officially recovered and returned to its rightful owners, almost none of the Emperor's loot has been returned.

The primary difference between the Asian and European theaters during the war was the OSS. Eisenhower allowed the OSS to operate in Europe. The recovered Nazi loot was due largely to the efforts of the OSS and the gold teams in Europe. Once recruits replaced the first gold teams, gold found in Europe appears to have disappeared into a black hole. However, MacArthur would not allow any OSS agent to operate in his theater of command. Lansdale arrived after the OSS disbanded and was already officially transferred to the Army.

MacArthur's intelligence branch was under the formal command of Gen. Charles Willoughby. MacArthur referred to Willoughby as his "little fascist." Born in Germany, Willoughby was a love child of Baron T. Scheppe-Weindenbach and Emma Willoughby of Baltimore, Md. After MacArthur's promotion to the U.S. Far Eastern Command, Willoughby chose to follow his idol. The Army previously assigned both men to the Philippine command. Impressed by Willoughby's loyalty, MacArthur appointed him as his Assistant Chief of Intelligence.

After Japan attacked the Philippines, Willoughby moved to Corregidor with MacArthur, then evacuated with him to Australia. Willoughby was generally inept and not even remotely prepared for many of the assignments. However, MacArthur demanded absolute control over intelligence and special operations, and Willoughby was ready and able to deliver MacArthur total control and loyalty. Willoughby also was clever at hiding his blunders and promoting his successes. Years after the war, Willoughby became a member of just about every fringe far right-wing group that came into existence.

In Australia, Willoughby set up the Allied Intelligence Bureau to run guerrilla operations in the Philippines. He also set up the Allied Translator and Interpreter Section. However, his incompetence in guerrilla warfare was too much, even for MacArthur. MacArthur appointed his personal lawyer and crony Courtney Whitney to take over the special operations and guerrilla warfare. Whitney was a rich man and well connected in the Philippines. He proved an adept officer in managing guerrilla operations. To soothe Willoughby's hurt feelings, MacArthur promoted him to general.

Severio Garcia Diaz Sanata or "Santy" was born in Luzon and educated in California, where he married the wealthy heiress Evangeline Compton. In 1930, the couple returned to the Philippines. During this time, Santy became a fringe member of the social clique around MacArthur and Whitney. During the war, Santy became one of Whitney's most effective agents in the Philippines.

Another key figure in MacArthur's Manila circle was Joseph McKickling, a law partner of Courtney Whitney. After the Japanese invasion of the Philippines, McKickling served as an officer in G2 under the command of Willoughby. He also was evacuated with MacArthur to Australia. During the torture of Maj. Kojima, McKickling was Santy's immediate superior. About the time Santy was uncovering the treasure from the Golden Lily, McKickling became fabulously wealthy. He married the wealthy heiress Mercedes Zobel McKickling and masterminded the Zobel-Ayala acquisition of global real estate, creating one of the world's great fortunes. While the Zobel-Ayala clan was far from poor, the real money in launching their world-class fortune came from McKickling.

The first detection of the Golden Lily came from a team of guerrillas smuggled into the Philippines. Disguised as a fisherman, U.S. Navy Warrant Officer John Ballinger watched a heavily laden Japanese hospital ship heading for Subic Bay. He photographed the ship and identified it as the *Hazi Maru,* a fast liner. Guerrilla hero Capt. Medina led Ballinger's unit, which watched the crew unload heavy crates from the ship onto trucks.

Ballinger's team followed the truck convoy and watched the Japanese unload the cargo in a mountain cave. Once they finished, the Japanese blew the entrance shut. It took the guerrillas several days to reopen it and find rows of boxes filled with 75-kilo gold bars. They resealed the cave and reported their findings to MacArthur's headquarters in Australia.

After the American landing of troops on Leyte, Medina's guerrillas watched the Japanese hurriedly unloading heavy boxes into a tunnel near a hospital. Medina's guerrillas attacked the Japanese and soon routed them, blowing the tunnel shut with many of the Japanese still trapped inside. Medina sent a report of this action to MacArthur's headquarters.[111]

Thus, it seems certain that MacArthur and his command staff were well aware of the existence of the Golden Lily treasure long before the Japanese surrender. What is not known is whether MacArthur was privy to Stimpson's plan to use recovered treasure to finance a global political action fund before the surrender. The extreme secrecy shrouding the POW issue from the very beginning of the surrender suggests he was. MacArthur's knowledge of Japanese treasure surely played a part in the war crimes trial of Gen. Yamashita. Yamashita was innocent of the charges, as stated earlier. However, MacArthur and his staff were eager to see the trial advance and badgered the trial tribunal, urging it to accept hearsay evidence and hasten the proceedings. Yamashita's defense team appealed the death sentence to the Supreme Court, which failed to overturn it. Justice Murphy was one of the two dissenting:

> The Petitioner was rushed to trial under an improper charge, given insufficient time to prepare an adequate defense, and there was no serious attempt to prove that he committed a recognized violation of the laws of war. He was not charged with personally participating in the acts of atrocity or with ordering or condoning their commission. Not even knowledge of these crimes was attributed to him.[112]

Judge Rutledge, the other dissenting judge, was equally critical of the conviction. Following a failed appeal to President Truman, Yamashita was hanged. Obviously Yamashita's knowledge of the treasure provided a hidden motive for MacArthur to dispose of the wrongly charged general. Charged with war crimes, MacArthur's staff could not torture Yamashita without the treatment being exposed in his trial. However, his driver, Maj. Kojima Kashii, was brutally tortured.

It is unknown how McCloy, Anderson, Clifford and Lovett managed the Black Eagle Trust in the years following the war. From the work of the Seagraves, it seems certain that Britain's reentry into the world gold market must have been based on the trust. At the end of the war, the United States held 60 percent of the world's official gold reserves. However, the rest of the world was battered and bankrupt. Thus, Washington was able to manipulate and force other countries to follow the Washington line.

By 1960, it was clear to European central banks that they soon would be holding more dollars than the official U.S. gold reserves. Until the 1960s, the U.S. gold reserves and the secret Black Eagle Trust allowed the United States to browbeat any nation into complying with U.S. wishes and desires. By 1960, the printing of fiat money nearly equaled the U.S. gold reserves. The dwindling ratio of the U.S. gold reserves to the money supply allowed other nations to escape from under Uncle Sam's heavy hand. As a result, starting around 1960, various nations began striking out on their own, most notably France. The role of gold in the Cold War is perhaps one of the most unrecognized factors in the entire era. While the Black Eagle Trust still could fix elections globally, the United States, forced by its dwindling gold stocks, eased the heavy repression of the 1950s, both domestically and globally. The result was an almost spontaneous global protest leading to one of the most tumultuous decades of the 20th century. French demands to exchange dollars for gold led to Nixon closing the gold window.

The 1948 Italian election is the first known example of the use of the Black Eagle Trust to fix an election. CIA agent James Jesus Angleton recovered Ethiopian treasure plundered by Mussolini. Angleton did not return the treasure to impoverish Ethiopia; he seized it for the CIA. He arranged for the Vatican to provide 100 million liras to back anti-communist candidates in the election. Some of the funds likely came from the Black Eagle Trust, considering the Vatican was one of the 42 recipients of shipments of recovered gold in 1946–47.[113]

Manipulating elections and other covert operations was the black side of the Truman Doctrine. Following London's appeal to Washington that it had no money for military aid to Greece and Turkey, Truman appealed to Congress for a $400 million aid package. Secretly and simultaneously, Truman sanctioned the use of funds from the Black Eagle for covert operations to defeat the communist uprising.

Frank Wisner was the man in charge of the CIA covert operation in Europe following WWII. Wisner came up with hiring ex-Nazis to create a fifth column against the Soviet Union. By 1952, he had operations in 47 countries, an official budget of $84 million and staff of 3,000. It is unknown how much funding he may have received from the Black Eagle. Wisner was supported by powerful friends: the Dulles brothers, George Keenan, Averell Harriman, and Joe and Stewart Alsop.

Likewise in Japan in the immediate postwar period, American forces used funds recovered from the Golden Lily. Three secret funds existed during the military occupation: the M-Fund, the Yoshida Fund and the Keenan Fund. MacArthur was instrumental in setting up the M-Fund, initially believed to be as large as $2 billion. Money for it came from the sale of confiscated gold, silver, gems and other strategic materials.

The M-Fund was named after Gen. William Fredi Marquat, chief of SCAP's Economic and Scientific Section. In theory, Marquat headed the U.S. unit that was to punish Japanese corporations that made obscene profits from the war. In practice, Marquat spent considerable time and effort hiding the profits for the businesses. Marquat, like Willoughby, was grossly inept. However, he was inside MacArthur's circle, where loyalty counted more than competency.

Marquat did little in the way of shutting down the profit mongers during the war. He also was in charge of bringing the war criminals from Unit 731 to justice. Unit 731 was Japan's biological and chemical warfare division that used victims as test subjects for warfare agents. Instead of fulfilling his duties, Marquat presided over the transfer of Unit 731 to Fort Dietrich. All information on the unit was withheld from the American and Japanese public, and the War Crimes Tribunal.

MacArthur and his staff created the M-Fund to buy elections. Its first big application came in the late 1940s when the socialists won. The M-Fund immediately began dispensing great sums to discredit the socialist cabinet. Later, Washington used the fund to discredit Tokyo's move to open relations with the People's Republic of China.

MacArthur and his staff set up the Yoshida Fund with a different objective. It was used to finance the Japanese underworld for "wet work," kidnapping and murder. Gen. Willoughby controlled the Yoshida Fund, where money was used to silence union leaders and organizers. Willoughby also had the job of falsifying Japanese military history to conform to the needs of American Cold War Warriors. The U.S. government published his work, *The Japanese Monographs* and *Japanese Studies in World War Two*.

Joseph Keenan, another figure from MacArthur's inner circle, controlled the Keenan Fund. Keenan was the chief prosecutor in the Tokyo war crimes trials. The sole purpose of the Keenan Fund was to bribe witnesses at those trials. Unlike the swift trial of Yamashita in the Philippines, the Tokyo trials dragged on for three years. MacArthur's staff bribed witnesses to prevent any testimony implicating the Emperor. Witnesses who could not be bribed met with violent and sudden deaths. The fund also was used to prevent testimony of Unit 731.[114]

In 1956, the Eisenhower administration used the M-Fund again to place Kishi as head of the newly merged Liberal-Democratic Party and as Japan's new Prime Minister. Kishi, a signer of the Japanese Declaration of War against the United States, was actively involved in slave labor and part of the hard-core ruling clique in Manchuria. He was one of the most prominent war criminals arrested in postwar Japan. However, he was freed with bribe money from Kodama.

Harry Kern, Eugene Dooman, Compton Packenham and other members of Averell Harriman's group groomed Kishi for 10 years. Nevertheless, Kishi lost in the 1956 election to Ishibashi Tanzan. Washington widely regarded Tanzan as the least favorable candidate. Annoyed, Eisenhower personally ordered the CIA to destroy Tanzan. After a year of paying bribes to all the factions in the Liberal-Democrat Party, the Eisenhower administration successfully placed its man in the prime minister's chair.

During Kishi's term, 1957–60, the Liberal-Democrat Party received $10 million annually from the CIA, chiefly from the M-Fund. While Nixon was negotiating the Mutual Security Treaty, he promised Kishi that he would turn over the M-Fund to the Liberal-Democrat Party, and return Okinawa to Japan in exchange for black money help in the 1960 election. On settling the security treaty, Nixon turned over the control of the M-Fund and, in 1973 as president, he returned Okinawa to Japanese rule.

In 1972, Nixon and Kissinger arranged a deal with Premier Chou En-lai to keep China out of the conflict over Taiwan. In return for standing down, Nixon offered China a large quantity of gold provided by Marcos. At that time, China's economy was in bad shape and the country lacked foreign currency to buy any foreign goods, including grain to relieve the widespread rural famine. According to CIA and Pentagon analysts, China was about to invade Taiwan to gain badly needed assets and foreign currency. At the same time, the United States was bogged down in Vietnam and the public was demanding peace.

Although the details are sketchy and the exact amount is uncertain, Kissinger apparently offered China $68 billion in gold. Supporting evidence for the deal comes from numerous bank accounts, held by members of the Black Eagle Trust, which were moved to mainland banks inside China. These rabid anti-communists would have had no other reason to move their accounts to China at the height of the Cold War.[115]

All presidents, from Truman to George W. Bush, have used the Black Eagle Trust to fund covert operations. While these black operations are odoriferous and criminal, the real danger comes in keeping the gold out of the hands of private individuals. Yet, from the beginning, the gold was held in private accounts. When President Kennedy sacked Lansdale over his operations against Cuba, Lansdale did not give up his covert activities. He merely went private. He still had enough contacts in the military and the CIA, and accounts of gold in his name to remain a player in covert operations. In practice, this left Lansdale as a private individual with the power to overthrow foreign governments and even the ability to plunge a country accidentally or deliberately into an unwanted war.

President Reagan enhanced the capacity of private individuals or groups to wage war. Early in his first term, Reagan signed Executive Order 12333 at the urging of Bill Casey. This executive order allowed the CIA and other government agencies to contract with private military firms. Furthermore, the agency did not have to reveal the contract or arrangement.

Such contracts set a dangerous precedent that allows the president to bypass the ability of Congress to declare war. Reagan immediately used it to wage war in Nicaragua. The resulting aftermath became known as the Iran-Contra scandal.

By 1980, there were plenty of individuals like Lansdale who were terminated from government service to staff private military or intelligence firms. Starting in 1972, after John Schlesinger replaced Richard Helms as CIA Director, hundreds of agents who had been engaged in the dirty tricks clique of Helms were forcefully retired. Once the CIA's involvement in Watergate and other domestic break-ins became known, Schlesinger ordered an investigation. The report, *The Family Jewels,* led to leaks about assassination programs, death squads like Phoenix and other embarrassing operations. More than 1,000 agents were terminated because of the investigation.

Further investigations in the 1970s led to more dismissals, not only at the CIA, but also the Pentagon. The Carter administration dismissed additional CIA and military personnel. Among them were Gen. John Singlaub, Ray Cline and Gen. George Keegan. Many of these men regrouped privately in such radical, far right-wing organizations as the John Birch Society, the World Anti-Communist League and the Moonies. Singlaub became an icon among the far Right.

Casey is a good example of these ex-agents. Casey was one of the original OSS crowd. He was Singlaub's case officer during WWII; Paul Helliwell was Casey's immediate superior. In addition, Casey was friendly with the Dulles brothers and worked with Cline. He became involved with Lansdale during the torture of Maj. Kojima, making Casey one of the key players in the Black Eagle Trust.

After the war, Casey founded his own Wall Street law firm. His continued involvement with former intelligence agents allowed him to form Capitol Cities in 1954, just as the CIA was pouring millions of dollars into media companies. Casey benefited from some of that money. It is likely that Casey never left the CIA. In 1973, Nixon appointed him Chief of the Securities and Exchange Commission. While serving as the SEC chief, Casey worked closely with Stanley Sporkin, whom Casey later appointed as the CIA's general counsel in the Schlei case. In 1978, Casey founded the Manhattan Institute, a think tank that absorbed several former CIA agents. In 1980, Casey left Capitol Cities to become head of the Reagan campaign. Reagan appointed Casey as CIA Director.

By 1980, private military and intelligence firms proliferated to such an extent that they became known during the Iran-Contra scandal as "The Enterprise." Marcos had connections that extended beyond the CIA into this loosely confederated network.

In the mid-1970s, Marcos became pathologically greedy. He was already a billionaire from clandestinely recovering some of the Golden Lily's treasure. However, the only means he had of selling it was through the CIA or Japan. Both would take the odd-size ingots without the standard paper trail required in the legitimate gold market, but only at a steep discount.

To bypass the CIA and Japan to sell in the open market, Marcos had to have the gold resmelted and the fingerprint from impurities altered so the gold would appear to have a Philippine origin. By 1975, Marcos had already formed the Leber group (rebel spelled backward) to uncover the Golden Lily treasure from 34 of the known 172 sites. Due to Marcos' personal fascination for psychics, the group included Olof Jonsson, a psychic from Chicago. Marcos then contacted Robert Curtis, a mining engineer from Sparks, Nev.

Curtis developed a method to extract platinum and reclaim more gold from mining tailings in the Sierras, which made him a moderately wealthy man. He also was an expert at changing the fingerprint of gold bullion. At first, Curtis turned down Marcos' offer to resmelt the gold.

However, the amount of gold discussed in the offer amazed Curtis. It was 10 times the average gold Philippine mines had ever produced. Marcos finally revealed that the gold came from Japanese looting during WWII. The idea of recovering Japanese gold fascinated Curtis and he accepted the job, arriving in the Philippines at the end of February 1975.

On March 25, 1975, Curtis signed a contract with the Leber group to supply two smelters. Curtis needed a loan to cover the expenses of the smelters and turned to a previous contact with a member of the John Birch Society. In the 1970s, Jerry Adams, Robert Welch, Jay and Dan Agnew, and Floyd Paxton contacted Curtis. Robert Welch founded the John Birch Society, a fringe group on the far right consisting mostly of wealthy businessmen, far-right politicians, and ex-military and intelligence officers. Lansdale was a member.

Birch Society members also were gold bugs. After Nixon allowed citizens to own gold, the Birch Society developed a backdoor through Canada to buy overseas gold and smuggle it into the United States. The society then used the gold to fund its own vigilante force, similar to a private FBI. The John Birch Society has always kept some type of blacklist, which is typical of all hard-right groups. Periodically, news articles have appeared about the Birch blacklist. Generally, these right-wing blacklists receive a wink and nod from the FBI that views them as helpful. Curtis was unaware the inner circle of the Birch Society knew about the Black Eagle Trust and previous recoveries of gold. It knew because one of the founding members was Col. Laurence Bunker, who had succeeded Gen. Bonner Fellers on MacArthur's staff in Tokyo.

The Birch Society arranged financing for Curtis through Washington State Sen. Floyd Paxton and his son, who ran Kwik Lok Corp. Another participant was Jerry Adams, head of the Great American Silver Corp., a company associated with the Hunt brothers. Welch and Congressman Larry McDonald told Curtis that they cleared the loan personally. MacDonald was the head of the Anti-Communist League before he died in a plane crash. The loan was unsecured except for Curtis' promise to return 22 percent of his Leber share.

By the time Curtis opened the first treasure site, the John Birch Society placed new demands on him for additional security for the loan. Curtis offered titles to his heavy equipment in Nevada. He also was obligated to give the Birchers exclusive right to market up to $20 billion of any gold recovered. The Birchers told Curtis the gold would be sold through Commonwealth Packaging Ltd., located in the Bahamas and owned by Kwik Lok. The money would be deposited in the Nassau branch of the Royal Bank of Canada and finally transferred to a branch in Kelowna, Canada. There, a key financial expert of the Birch Society would smuggle the money into the United States.

The July 4–5, 1975 columns by Jack Anderson triggered the sudden demands of the Birch Society. Anderson reported Marcos was recovering gold with the help of several Americans. Curtis barely escaped from the Philippines with his life. Later, Curtis learned that Marcos had recovered 22,000 metric tons of gold bullion. Marcos had the treasure resealed without recovering two gold Buddhas and barrels of gemstones.

While Curtis was still in the Philippines, he learned the Gold Cartel had offered Marcos a Mafia-style deal: either kill Curtis and let the cartel handle the gold or Marcos would be in trouble. The Gold Cartel refers to the alliance of prime banks, gold companies and national treasuries, including the Federal Reserve and the Bank of England, that dominate the world gold market. In the end, Curtis was left broke. Johnson-Mathey Chemicals, part of the Gold Cartel, now owned his two Philippine smelters.

Marcos was trying to blackmail the Japanese over the Showa Trust at the Sanwa Bank. The trust came from treasures recovered from the Golden Lily. At that time, the Showa Trust was so large that it was generating $1 billion a year in interest. Exposure of the trust would be embarrassing for both Washington and Tokyo. Apparently, Marcos had some success in his blackmail, as several accounts in his name appeared in the Hong Kong branch of the Sanwa Bank shortly after his negotiating team visited Tokyo.

In his first year in office, Reagan declared that he would restore the gold standard. He had ties with the Birch Society dating back to the 1950s. The Reagans also were long-time friends with Marcos. To make his plan for a new gold standard work, Reagan needed a large stock of gold. He asked Marcos privately to lend part of his hoard for the plan, but Marcos demanded a higher commission than Reagan was willing to pay.

In blackmailing the Japanese and overplaying his hand with Reagan, Marcos sealed his fate and was quickly removed from office. Once Marcos was besieged in Manila, Sen. Paul Laxalt offered him an ultimatum: forfeit the gold in return for rescue by the United States. That evening after he accepted ultimatum, barges were towed alongside the presidential palace, loaded with gold and towed to Subic Bay. Marcos was rescued and taken to Hawaii, where authorities seized billions of dollars worth of gold certificates.

The high-flying days off Marcos playing wild and loose with black gold ended in Hawaii. However, the Reagan administration's interest in the Golden Lily treasure buried in the Philippines continued. In January 1987, Alan Foringer contacted Curtis to talk about Philippine treasure.

Foringer and his aide, John Voss, told Curtis they were with the Nippon Star. Gen. John Singlaub formed the Nippon Star to search for treasure in the Philippines. Curtis wanted no part of dealing with the CIA or any CIA-connected fronts. However, Curtis was then informed in a phone call from Gen. Schweitzer that President Reagan personally supported the Nippon Star and the Phoenix Exploration groups. Reagan could not publicly approve the explorations, but had fully briefed the U.S. Embassy in Manila, and commanders at Subic Bay Naval Base and the Clark Air Force Base. Others involved in the exploration included Col. Dick Childress, Gen. Daniel Graham, Gen. Jack Vessy and Ray Cline.

Curtis reluctantly agreed to meet them in Hong Kong. However, this time he demanded that the meeting be tape-recorded. Once again, the John Birch Society was financing the operation. Curtis also discovered that Singlaub had been duped and was using false maps. Curtis retained the maps for all the sites from his earlier trip to the Philippines. Desperate to dig himself out of a financial hole, he suggested starting at a site on Corregidor. After five days of digging, Philippine Army helicopters swooped down and demanded the treasure hunters leave at gunpoint. Curtis then returned home.

Curtis returned to the Philippines a third time as a partner with Charles McDougal, a former Green Beret. Once again, as he was about to strike gold, Curtis was forced to leave the Philippines. Later, his former partners recovered roughly $4.5 billion in gold that Curtis had located.

Further evidence of the Reagan administration's involvement in recovering Golden Lily treasure comes from a suit filed by San Francisco attorney Melvin Belli over gold deposits held by Citibank. Belli concluded that Citibank's John Reed joined with President Reagan, James Baker, Bill Casey and Prime Minister Margaret Thatcher to use Golden Lily treasure to finance covert operations by the United States and Britain, and Monsanto was also linked to IG Farben. Belli referred to the plan as "The Purple Ink Document." Unfortunately, Belli died before the case could proceed. The case was still pending as of this writing.

The danger now is the Black Eagle Trust is no longer fully in the hands of the government. Instead, several far-right groups have access to it and can use it to further their radical agenda. They know more treasure is hidden in the Philippines. Undoubtedly, some of the political shift to the right in the United States since the 1980s was funded with parts of the Black Eagle Trust.

In 2001, George W. Bush sent a Navy Seal team to the Philippines to recover a portion of the loot. The younger Bush has been a player in the black market for gold for some time. His representative to purchase the gold was William S. Farish, his nominee as Ambassador to Great Britain and manager of his blind trust. George W. Bush appointed James Foley as Ambassador to Haiti before the Bush-inspired revolt in 2004. Foley was another player in the Black Eagle Trust, which leads to the question: Did money from the Black Eagle Trust finance the arming of the Haitian rebels?

Nazi Gold & the United States

Since the fall of the Soviet Union, there have been several reports of treasures looted by the Russians. Many paintings taken from Germany are in the possession of the Hermitage Museum in St. Petersburg and the Pushkin Museum in Moscow. Next to no one knows the United States had its own program of plunder, directed by Army officer Gordon Gilkey. Gilkey must have been a busy man in postwar Germany, as proved by roughly 11,000 paintings from Germany stored in the Pentagon. The most valuable of those paintings are stored in the vault at the U.S. Center of Military History.[iii]

The list of official looters ranged from government officials to private individuals. Herbert Hoover's famed postwar global tour to relieve hunger was a cover for a private mission to loot to his content. His staff plundered thousands of items for the Hoover War Library at Stanford University. One item pillaged was Joseph Goebbels' 7,000-page typed diary. Doubleday agreed with Hoover to publish part of the diary for $400,000, which could have better served hungry children of war-torn countries. Hoover's library still has the original diary. Hoover also plundered a large collection of papers and items belonging to Heinrich Himmler and the Nazi Party.[116] No doubt, Hoover saw to the removal of any incriminating files in Germany and Japan, such as those that would have revealed his collaboration with top Nazis in the 1940 election.

While it would be reasonable to expect some looting by a few GI's in the face of such enormous temptations, the swift rotation of troops out of Germany after the war hampered control of looting. Nevertheless, it appears certain there was an organized effort to sabotage the recovery and return of treasures to their rightful owners.

The pillage was not just by enlisted men. For example, in Braunes Haus in Munich, officers were not only guilty of looting, but also aided the looting by enlisted men. Underground tunnels honeycombed the three-building complex. The 1269th Combat Engineer Battalion was assigned to the T Force and charged with guarding the complex. The tunnels were full of looted items, such as silverware, paintings, party records and other valuables. Various other units also were assigned to guard the complex. Pvts. Polski and Fraser entered the complex and discovered several enlisted men and officers pocketing silverware as souvenirs. The guards did not mind. Polski joined in picking out a set of silverware with the initials AH and a swastika. Fraser picked out an 80-piece set of silverware. The two returned to headquarters and showed the booty to their commanding officer, Capt. McKee. After carefully wrapping their booty in packages, the privates had the captain label the packages "Censored by Capt. McKee." Polski mailed his booty home to St Paul, Minn.; Fraser also mailed his loot home.[117] Such looting continued unabated until the Property Control Officer ordered the complex ringed with barbwire and guards on June 10.

The treasures of all the top Nazi officials were looted to some degree. Goering hid his vast art collection in several locations. It was simply too vast to have it all transported to a final cache. He buried some of it at Carinhall, his palatial estate and hunting lodge, when the Russian advance threatened to overrun the area. The rest was transported by train to Veldenstein, Goering's castle. As the Allies approached Veldenstein on April 7, 1945 Goering once again ordered the treasure be moved by rail to Berchtesgaden, Hitler's retreat in the Bavarian Alps and the center of the redoubt area. There, Goering was able to commandeer four trains. The ease with which Goering was able to find four trains in the final days of the war was largely due to the incredible and surreal conditions surrounding the redoubt area. During the final days of the war, 14,000 freight cars arrived, many loaded with supplies and

---

[iii] A joke my father liked to tell from the postwar front: "When they found valuables, the Germans "organized" it, the Russians "liberated" it, and the Americans "took souvenirs." – *Ed.*

equipment for the Nazis' final stand in the Alps, others simply loaded with treasures collected by top officials. Wounded soldiers lucky enough to find a horse and cart filled the roads, while others laid at the roadside, unable to find transportation to a hospital, dying an agonizing death in the mud and snow. To hide some of Goering's treasure from the Allies, five freight cars laden with treasure were sent to nearby Unterstein. The rest of the treasure was left sitting on railcars that were looted by townspeople.

The 101st Airborne Division that liberated the area was soon aware that it had stumbled across Goering's art collection. After locating a hidden side room in the underground command post, soldiers blew the entrance open to Aladdin's Cave and didn't hesitate to take part of the treasure. One soldier found Goering's guest book from Carinhall. The book contained many signatures of distinguished guests, including Herbert Hoover.[118]

Gen. Patch took one of Goering's field marshal batons, which went to the West Point Military Museum when he died. Lt. Eckberg took Goering's second baton and other items, and mailed them to his mother in Chicago. Eckberg remained in Germany. His mother sold a gold medallion to a jeweler, who then placed an ad. U.S. Customs read the ad and recovered the medallion, the baton and the other items the lieutenant had mailed home. Soldiers pillaged many other personal items, such as Goering's dagger and sword. Lt. Col. Willard White, probably the most prolific looter at Berchtesgaden, helped himself to a large collection of Hitler's silverware and crystal items, mailing them home to his wife, the sister of Ladybird Johnson.[119]

Another avid looter was Lt. Col. William Brown. Brown's unit was assigned to the city and county of Weimar, Buchenwald, and the city of Apolda. Brown's collecting soon led to his questioning on June 27, 1945. His response to the statement that all property found or confiscated in an enemy country belonged to the U.S. government follows:

> Well, I am sure that I didn't know that because the general impression at that time immediately after the combat phase was that whatever people picked up they were entitled to. You know as well as I do that there's been a good deal of that going on, and there has been a good deal of picking up stuff abandoned by all troops. Anything of that kind that I was engaged in there was done with the idea that whatever things of that sort were found where there was no claimant whatever belonged to the finder. To what extent may I ask off the record well, weren't they, if they were found without any claimant? If you find the stuff lying abandoned, doesn't that belong to you?[120]

Brown was not honest in his response. Many of the items he took from claimants, such stamps from a post office he later ordered to be closed. After returning to the United States, Brown ran for the Governor of Virginia on the Republican ticket.

The best-known case of looting by American personnel was the theft of the Hesse Crown Jewels. The primary instigators of the theft were Capt. Kathleen Nash, Maj. David Watson and Col. Jack Durant, who was Nash's lover, found a fresh patch of concrete in the cellar as they explored the castle. There they found zinc-lined boxes full of jewels. The trio removed tiaras, bracelets and other items, and sold them in Switzerland. In late 1945, the trio returned to the United States. Besides the jewels and gold, they looted silverware, books and hundreds of other items. In January 1946, a member of the Hesse family reported the jewels missing. The Army's Criminal Intelligence Division determined the extent of the theft and soon arrested the trio. Durant married Nash so she could not testify against him. The court sentenced Watson to three years in prison, but he was released after four months. His family owned a large West Coast grocery store chain that obviously had connections to people in power. The court sentenced Durant to 15 years and released him after six years. However, Nash was described as a difficult prisoner and served her entire five-year sentence. Nash mailed about half of the jewels to her sister.

Nazi gold and treasures continue to be discovered. Recently, the Roman Catholic shrine of Fatima in Portugal confirmed it held Nazi gold bars in the mid-1980s. The Nazi insignia was found on four bars after the shrine requested a Portuguese bank to melt them. The bars were sold between 1982–86 to finance construction. A 1976 bank statement shows the shrine held four Nazi gold bars totaling 50 kilos. It is unknown if the shrine held more.[121]

Another treasure surfaced in 1990. It consisted of medieval works of art, including gold and silver crucifixes; rock crystal flasks; a beautiful silver receptacle called a reliquary for keeping and displaying sacred relics, inlaid with precious stones and enamels; a liturgical ivory comb; various priceless gifts belonging to warlords who ruled the old states of Germany in the 9th and 10th centuries; and perhaps the most priceless of all, a beautifully illustrated 9th-century version of the four gospels in a gold and silver binding, encrusted with gold and jewels. The treasure was discovered at the end of the war in an unused mine tunnel at Quedlinburg, a few miles south of Magdeburg in eastern Germany. U.S. Army Lt. Joe T. Meador discovered the treasure and was assigned to guard it with three other soldiers. However, Meador had other ideas. He quietly removed the items piece by piece and mailed them home. The Army launched an inquiry, which quickly ended when the area was assigned to East Germany. After Meador died in 1980, rumors quickly spread of an impending find of a remarkable medieval artwork. In 1990, the four gospels surfaced with a 1513 manuscript valued at $500,000. Further investigation in Meador's hometown of Whitewright, Texas, turned up the rest of the loot.[122]

In 1997, a vault was opened in Sao Paulo, Brazil containing more than $4 million worth of looted property – cash, gold bars and jewelry. The vault was owned by Albert Blume, a German who came to Brazil before World War II. He allegedly acted as a banker for escaping Nazis.[123]

In 2001, U.S. Treasury Secretary Paul O'Neill handed over a dozen drawings to the president of the Bremen Museum. Customs agents seized the painting four years earlier. The drawings were among 1,500 art works the Bremen Museum moved into a castle outside Berlin in 1943 for safekeeping. They first surfaced in 1993 in Azerbaijan, a former Soviet republic, where thieves stole the drawings. Four years after the July 1993 theft, Japanese businessman Masatsugu Koga approached the German embassy in Tokyo, offering to sell eight of the Bremen drawings for $12 million. By September 1997, Koga's negotiations with the museum had moved to New York City. A customs agent working undercover joined the museum negotiator meeting with Koga. Koga was arrested, but died before he could be sentenced.[124]

It would take volumes to list all the various Nazi treasures recovered since the end of the war. Undoubtedly, more treasures will be located in the future. With the fall of the Soviet Union, more Nazi treasures will surface in Russia and the other republics of the old union.

The question of victim compensation is still hotly debated. Clinton appointee Stuart Eizenstat brought many of their lawsuits to a fruitful conclusion. However, controversy remains, as victims sneer at the pitiful settlements for their time in concentration and forced labor camps. The Eizenstat study reached five major conclusions about Nazi gold:

Much of the gold passed through Swiss banks and then into other countries. The conversion of the Nazi gold into Swiss francs was the primary means by which the Nazis bought war material from neutral countries.

Trade with the neutral countries allowed the Nazis to prolong the war.

The Reichsbank knowingly incorporated into its gold reserves looted monetary gold from the national banks of other countries. This was a primary means by which the Nazis financed their aggression.

Gold from the victims of the concentration camps was mixed with monetary gold and found its way into the neutral trading parties of the Nazis.

Complete recovery of the looted gold was hampered by the indifference among neutral nations and conflicting priorities and inaction of the Allies

One is urged not to take the Eizenstat report as the final word on Nazi gold; other studies are in progress. General Motors has commissioned one such study. However, it already has been compromised by the selection of the lead investigator, author Henry Ashby Turner. The figures presented in this chapter are subject to change as more information surfaces.

While the gold rush teams did an admirable job in locating the Nazi treasures in the first few days following the end of the war, the program soon became beleaguered with ineptness and corruption. With Nazi gold, there is no direct evidence of a systematic plan to sabotage the recovery of the Nazi treasures. However, there is strong evidence that Allen Dulles aided the Nazis in transporting and hiding their looted treasures in other countries. For the Golden Lily, there is ample evidence that recovery and return of gold looted by the Japanese was systematically sabotaged by high-level intelligence officers, Herbert Hoover and elites from Wall Street.

It is equally certain the recovery of Nazi gold from the neutral countries was compromised at almost every step by the objectives of the State Department and the military. From the latest information from Argentina, it seems certain that the Perons had an enormous sum of Nazi gold at their disposal. Powerful figures in the Republican Party and business community pushed the United States into the precise trap the Nazis planned for a comeback — a war between the U.S. and Soviet Union. The shooting had hardly stopped before the pro-fascist element in the United States that opposed the war under the banner of isolation was calling for a war against the Soviets.

Justice for the victims would be sacrificed, further recovery of the Nazi gold from the neutrals would be stopped, and all resources would be employed in fighting the Red menace to protect the same corporations that built Hitler's war machine. The Nazi treasures squirreled away in neutral countries would be used to rebuild Germany as a bulwark against the Soviets.

The one definitive fact about Nazi gold is that much remains undiscovered. Perhaps the full story may never be learned. However, without the full release of all documents from this era by the United States, Britain and all parties involved, including the Vatican, the fate of the missing Nazi gold will remain clouded in a fog of mystery and intrigue.

Chapter 8,
Ratlines, the CIA and the Nazis

Operation Northwoods

The mention of the CIA commonly brings to mind images of James Bond, spy thrillers, covert warfare and Cold War Warriors fighting the evils of communism. But more often than not, the reality of CIA plots are images of the gang that could not shoot straight. Examples abound of the absurd actions of both the CIA and its forerunner, the OSS.

During WWII, the OSS became wrongly convinced that the Japanese were deathly terrified of bats. Thus, to help the war effort, Donovan of the OSS decided to test drop bats out of aircraft over the southwestern deserts before risking planes over Japan. The only fly in this ointment was the poor little critters froze almost instantly on release in the stratosphere and shattered like fine china on hitting the ground. After killing a few million bats in the skies of the southwestern desert, the plan was dropped.[1]

Harvey's "hole in Berlin" is another example of some rather shortsighted thinking by our intelligence agencies. In 1954, under the direction of Bill Harvey, a 1,476-foot tunnel into East Berlin was dug to install a phone tap on a Russian communication center. After almost a year, the Russians discovered the tap, allegedly while repairing a cable. What was not mentioned was the American spies had become so accustomed to their comforts that they turned off the air-conditioning to the tunnel during the chilly winter season. The tunnel was marked on the surface by a telltale strip of bare ground over its entire length in an otherwise snow-covered landscape.[2]

Perhaps the most bizarre case of misguided CIA misadventures is the wired kitty. During the Cold War, the CIA decided to enlist a cat to spy on the Soviets. The plan was for the cat to sit on a window ledge or bench and record any conversation. The cat went under the surgeon's knife to insert microphones, batteries and a transmitter. Agents tested the cat extensively in the lab and found it walked off the job when it was hungry. So the cat underwent surgery again and a wire was inserted to suppress its hunger. After more lab testing, the kitty was ready for field testing. Agents took the cat to a nearby park and released it, hoping to hear various conversations. Instead, they heard a screech of brakes. The cat decided to cross the street and was run over by a taxi, leaving the agents to scrape up the body and the highly classified wiring.

On March 11, 1961, President John Kennedy held a meeting with his advisers about what became known as the Bay of Pigs fiasco. (The CIA recently admitted it was responsible for the mistakes made.)[3] The original invasion was to take place some 100 miles east of the Bay of Pigs. After Kennedy demanded a site that would be more conducive to a night landing, the CIA turned to the Bay of Pigs. The original landing site picked for what was supposed to be a secret night landing was the equivalent of downtown Los Angeles. Overflights of the new landing area revealed dark forms just under the surface in the shallows of the bay. CIA experts decided they were seaweed.[4] However, they turned out to be coral reefs that could rip the bottom out of small landing craft, or leave troops high and dry like sitting ducks for any gunners onshore.

A recent episode of CIA bungling took place in the bombing of Serbia during the Kosovo crisis. By mistake, the United States bombed the Chinese Embassy. President Clinton was quick to apologize to the Chinese, and the CIA stepped forward and admitted its error. The maps had not been updated in four years. More information surfaced later. A lower-level CIA employee had warned repeatedly of the possible misidentification of that target site, but was ignored. There may have been more to the bombing than a bad map. The London *Guardian* reported that NATO deliberately targeted the embassy because it was sending messages for the Yugoslav army.[5]

The embassy bombing points to two problems. First, the agency works in total secrecy; even its budget is classified. It may be years or even decades before the truth is finally known. Second, many questioned whether the CIA was deliberately misleading President Clinton. The agency was known to pass on less-than-credible documents to higher policy making officials. During a November 1995 Senate Select Committee, it was revealed that CIA officials passed on more than 35 reports without disclosing the information came from known Soviet double agents. Between 1986–94, the CIA passed on at least 95 reports based on information from double agents without revealing the doubtful source or accuracy.[6]

At other times, the CIA deliberately defied presidential orders. During the Kennedy administration, the agency defied orders to close a training facility for Cuban guerrillas in Louisiana. Kennedy resorted to using the FBI and other agencies to close it.

Today, the CIA is perhaps the most despised agency in the government. It has overthrown governments worldwide, including those of allies such as Canada and Australia when they turned toward liberalism. In other operations, the agency has conducted gruesome operations such as Project Phoenix in Vietnam. Far too often, elements in the agency have hatched bizarre plots to achieve an agenda. One such plot was Operation Northwoods, which evolved out of the Bay of Pigs fiasco. (See Appendix 13.) While Operation Northwoods was a military operation controlled by the Joint Chiefs of Staff, it illustrates the problem with covert operations and the broader intelligence community.

In early November 1961, Robert Kennedy held a meeting in the Cabinet Room of the White House in which he announced that all responsibility for dealing with Cuba was to be shifted from the CIA to the Pentagon. This shift reflects the continuing distrust of the CIA by the Kennedy administration. The Right Wing savagely attacked the Kennedy administration for being soft on communism after the failure of the Bay of Pigs invasion. John F. Kennedy fired Allen Dulles as CIA Director over the fiasco.

Edward Lansdale and Lyman Lemnitzer directed the new Cuba operation, code-named Mongoose. Lansdale was an OSS agent during WWII who then transferred to the Army. In 1960, he was a one-star general and the deputy director of the Pentagon's Office of Special Operations. Lemnitzer was a career military officer who served as an aide to Eisenhower during the war and was appointed Chief of Staff in 1957. He helped create the NATO stay-behind network, turning Nazi agents into spies against the USSR, and infiltrating Nazi war criminals into Latin America in the 1950s.

Lansdale and Lemnitzer quietly set about exploring the possibility of doing what they wanted to do: a full-scale invasion of Cuba. The last vestiges of McCarthyism were still strong in the ranks of the military and the Right Wing. Many ranking officers believed communist agents infested the government. The John Birch Society was at its zenith. The firing of Gen. Walker for indoctrinating his troops with Birch Society propaganda in April 1961 reenergized the Right.

Walker's discharge triggered a study by the Senate Foreign Relations Committee into the dangers of right-wing extremism in the military. Its report warned of considerable danger in the education and propaganda activities of military personnel. Among the key targets were Kennedy's domestic social policies that the Right Wing deemed communist-inspired. The report concluded with a chilling warning of a possible revolt by senior military officers, and called for examination of Lemnitzer's extreme right-wing connections. Lemnitzer became increasing paranoid after Kennedy took office; he resented the youthful president. Further, Lemnitzer did not trust civilian command, which he believed interfered with the proper role of the military.

The roots of Operation Northwoods extend back to the last days of the Eisenhower administration. The Cold War was at one of its hottest points after the Soviet Union shot down Francis Gary Powers' U2. Eisenhower wanted desperately to invade Cuba. On Jan. 5, 1961, he told Lemnitzer and other aides in the Cabinet Room he would move against Cuba before the inauguration if only the Cubans would give him a good excuse. Eisenhower then suggested that if Castro failed to provide an excuse, perhaps the United States could manufacture something that would be generally accepted. Eisenhower suggested feigning a bomb attack or an act of sabotage against the United States. It was a dangerous suggestion from a president with only a few days remaining in office.[7]

Approved and signed by all the Joint Chiefs, Operation Northwoods called for acts of terrorism to be committed on American soil. Various plans included shooting innocent people on American streets, sinking boats of Cuban refugees and a violent wave of terrorist attacks launched against Washington, D.C., Miami and other cities. Using phony evidence, innocent people would be framed and Castro would be blamed.

On Feb. 26, 1962, Robert Kennedy ordered Lansdale to stop all covert planning against Cuba and to concentrate on intelligence gathering, due to the increasingly outrageous nature of Operation Mongoose. However, Lemnitzer continued with Operation Northwoods: a raft of dirty tricks like blaming Castro if the rocket carrying John Glenn into space exploded, sabotaging ships at Guantanamo or fake attacks against the base or civilians in the U.S. There was no limit to Lemnitzer's fanatical fancy. Other schemes called for bombings, hijackings, disguising a drone as a passenger plane and blowing it up, and fake attacks against the U.S. Air Force.

On March 15, 1962, President Kennedy told Lemnitzer there was almost no possibility the United States would use military force in Cuba. However, Lemnitzer persisted in his plans against Cuba to the point of insubordination. Within months, President Kennedy denied Lemnitzer a second appointment as Joint Chief of Staff and transferred him to Germany, effectively removing him from causing any further damage and ending his career.

Years later, President Gerald Ford appointed Lemnitzer to the President's Foreign Intelligence Advisory Board. Lemnitzer's aide, Brig. Gen. Craig, who helped plan Operation Northwoods, was promoted to major general and spent three years as chief of the Army Security Agency, NSA's military arm.

The Origins of the CIA

Understanding how the CIA and the intelligence-military community evolved into a hideous monster plotting to terrorize American civilians and menace freedom worldwide requires a close look at the careers of those who shaped the agency.

On Oct. 1, 1945, President Truman ordered the OSS disbanded. Bill Donovan sealed the fate of the agency when he hired liberals and socialists to fill its ranks. By the end of the war, the OSS was split into two factions in Europe. One faction vigorously hunted Nazi criminals and worked hard to decartelize Germany, while the other, led by Allen Dulles, worked equally hard to cover up war crimes and to undo any attempts at decartelization. The hard Right and Nazi sympathizers clamored to rid the nation of a spy agency full of communists.

The pool of experienced intelligence agents was reassigned to the military and other government agencies. Some, like Allen Dulles, returned to private life. Those assigned to the State Department were soon forced to return to the private sector when Congress failed to provide any funding for their positions.

On Oct. 22, 1945, three weeks after Truman's order, Secretary of War Robert Patterson created the Lovett Committee, chaired by Skull and Bonesman Robert Lovett, to advise the government on the postwar organization of U.S. intelligence activities. The new agency, which consulted with the armed forces, was to be the sole intelligence collection agency in foreign espionage and counterespionage. It had its own secret budget. On Nov. 14, 1945, Lovett appeared before the Secretaries of State, War and Navy, and pressed for a virtual resumption of the wartime OSS.

On Jan. 22, 1946, President Truman issued an executive order setting up a National Intelligence Authority, and under it, a Central Intelligence Group, the forerunner of the Central Intelligence Agency. In 1947, Congress passed the National Security Act, which mandated a major reorganization of the U.S. government's foreign policy and military establishments. The act, which took effect on Sept. 18, 1947, combined the departments of War and Navy into the single cabinet position of the (so-called) Department of Defense, and established the National Security Council and CIA.

Since 1980, there has been a steady stream of headlines indicative of America's involvement with the Nazis. Summaries from some late 1990s headlines follow:

Billions of German Marks from German taxpayers are being paid for "victim" pensions. These pensions are paid to as many as 50,000 war criminals – on top of their regular pensions. One notable recipient was Wilhelm Mohnke, a Hitler confidant and commandant of the Führer bunker. He also had a role in executing 72 POWs during the Battle of the Bulge. Germany has only reluctantly agreed to halt such payments.[8]

The prosecution of Aleksandras Lileikis as a war criminal by the government of Lithuania.[9]

Kazys Ciurinskas, a retired Indiana contractor who served as a member of the 2nd Lithuanian Schutzmannschaft Battalion, a mobile Nazi killing unit, faces deportation for lying on his immigration papers about his involvement with the Nazis during WWII. Kazys' battalion in October 1941 murdered over 10,000 people in Byelorussia [10]

Five U.S. banks: Chase, J.P. Morgan, Guaranty Trust Co., Bank of the City of New York and American Express all turned over the accounts of Jewish customers to the Nazis during the occupation of France.[11]

In an article appearing in *Newsweek* dealing with the return of the heirless assets, the cooperation of American corporations with the Nazis is exposed. Recently declassified documents show that at least 300 American firms continued to do business with the Nazis during the war.[12]

The articles suggest a faction of Americans played a much greater role in aiding Hitler and the Nazis than commonly thought. While the widespread belief is that only a handful of American companies aided the Nazis, the *Newsweek* excerpt implicates more than 300 American corporations in wartime acts of treason.

Congress passed a bill to release all documents about war criminals. However, some agencies, such as the State Department, the Department of Defense and the CIA, are still raising objections, citing national security.[13] Full disclosure of all documents about Nazi war criminals proved too embarrassing to several American corporations, powerful elite families, politicians, government agencies and programs.

In September 2000, the CIA admitted for the first time that it employed ex-Nazis. The story was only carried on the UPI wire. In the article, the CIA admitted that it employed Gen. Gehlen and his intelligence network after WWII. The acknowledgment confirmed perhaps the most widely known secret of the CIA and passed largely unnoticed. The more interesting aspect of the CIA-Nazi connection is how these former Nazis have molded foreign and domestic policies at the highest levels of government. The agency is guilty of sanitizing the records of other war criminals so they could come to the United States, then covering up these operations from Congress, federal investigators and the American public.

ODESSA

Besides the Vatican ratline, the Nazis had their own organizations devoted to helping war criminals flee Europe. The organization of former SS members, better known as ODESSA, was one part of the Nazis' plans to escape Europe. Hollywood has embellished the fabled network, which was well organized and financed with stolen loot. While the exact origins of the network are unknown, some assign its origins to the Red House meeting in 1944. Other names for ODESSA were Die Spinne, the spider; Kamradenwerk, Comradeship; der Bruderschaft, the Brotherhood.

One person known to be associated with ODESSA was Otto Skorzeny. Skorzeny's war exploits were legendary, resulting in the Allies declaring him the most dangerous man in Europe after the end of the war. Skorzeny surrendered to American forces in May 1945 and was interned at Dachau. During the war, Skorzeny trained the Werewolves, who formed the nucleus of the postwar Nazi underground and were instrumental in establishing the ratlines out of Europe.

The Allies believed the underground Nazi Werewolves functioned as commandos, conducting sabotage raids and assassinating any German who became too friendly with the enemy. There is unmistakable evidence that the Werewolves did assassinate some Germans aiding the Allies. However, it appears their primary function was to aid Nazis escaping Europe, which places the origins of the ODESSA network before the end of the war and perhaps as part of the plans evolving from the Red House meeting in 1944.

The American Army Counter Intelligence Corps (CIC) placed moles inside the camps holding Nazi prisoners. In Operation Brandy, CIC moles determined there was a well-organized, illegal POW mail service. People living close to the internment camps were eager to help the POWs escape and find money. To gain further information about the underground Nazi ratline, a CIC mole arranged for his escape with two others from Dachau. The experience confirmed the existence of the ODESSA network and clearly identified Skorzeny as its director. Polish guards at Dachau were found to be part of the network, as were some of the drivers hired to operate army trucks between Munich and Salzburg.[14]

After reaching Salzburg, the ODESSA ratline connected with the Vatican's string of monasteries reaching to Rome. There was a second ratline, ODESSA North, stretching through Norway, Sweden and Denmark. An underground network of SS veterans and Werewolves smuggled Nazi war criminals overland to ports, where they sailed to Argentina or Spain. Argentine diplomats were instrumental in easing traffic along this route.

The wholesale emigration of Nazi war criminals out of Europe could not have taken place without the approval of U.S. officials in Germany. Skorzeny was still in U.S. custody in 1948, even after being found innocent of war crimes. An American military lawyer who liked him successfully defended him; and later bragged about tricking the court to get him acquitted. However, Skorzeny still faced other charges in Czechoslovakia. Warned by American officials that a Czech government appeal to extradite him might succeed, Skorzeny plotted his escape with the help of American officials.

After escaping from the Darmstadt internment camp, Skorzeny made his way to a farm in Bavaria rented by Countess Ilse Luthje, a niece of Hjalmar Schacht. Skorzeny later married the countess before making his way to Spain. While there, Skorzeny maintained constant contact with Gehlen. The ongoing relationship between the Gehlen organization and the CIA was emblematic of a pivotal alliance with ODESSA. Former U.S. intelligence officer William Corson describes Gehlen's organization as a well-orchestrated diversion. The primary role of Gehlen's organization was to neutralize U.S. intelligence so the Nazis could continue their quest for world fascism by using the ODESSA network.[15]

In September 1948, German police noted a Skorzeny movement had sprung up in the U.S. zone and was spreading across Germany. British intelligence concluded that Skorzeny was working for U.S. intelligence and building a sabotage network. Declassified documents indicate American intelligence officials seriously considered enlisting Skorzeny, but Maj. Sidney Barnes killed the idea. Skorzeny's notoriety would expose the United States to too much potential embrassment.[16]

Little else is known about the shadowy ODESSA network beyond Skorzeny's association with it, but it appears that Francois Genoud, a Swiss resident of Pully on Lake Lausanne, functioned as the banker. In 1934, Genoud joined the Swiss pro-Nazi National Front. Two years later, he traveled to Palestine and befriended Amin al-Husayni, the pro-Nazi religious and political leader of Palestinian Muslims, who had been appointed Grand Mufti of Jerusalem in 1921 by the Zionist High Commissioner Herbert Samuel. In 1940, Genoud set up a nightclub in Lausanne to serve as a covert operation for the *Abwehr*, the German counterintelligence service. In 1941, his Abwehr contact, Paul Dickopf, sent him to Germany, Czechoslovakia, Hungary and Belgium. As part of his Abwehr services, Genoud dealt in currency, diamonds and gold, to name a few.

In 1942, Dickopf went underground with help from Genoud. Ironically, from 1968–72, Dickopf was president of Interpol. At the end of the war, Genoud represented the Swiss Red Cross in Brussels.

Using banking contacts established while working for the Abwehr, Genoud set in motion networks that later became known as ODESSA, which functioned principally for the transfer of millions of marks from Germany into Swiss banks. By 1955, Genoud was an adviser, researcher and banker for the Arab nationalism cause. He set up AraboAfrika, an import-export company that served as a cover for disseminating anti-Israeli propaganda and the delivery of weapons to the Algerian National Liberation Front. He also made investments for Hjalmar Schacht, a key postwar intermediary between Germans and Arabs. When Algerian independence was proclaimed in 1962, Genoud became director of the Arab Peoples' Bank in Algiers.

Beginning in the 1960s, Genoud helped finance and supply weapons to numerous Arab terrorists. Genoud also was a close friend of David Irving. On May 30 1996, Genoud committed suicide by taking poison.

Some sense of the scope of the CIA's involvement with the Nazis can be gathered from the table below. It presents the number of former Nazis receiving pensions from Germany, as estimated by the Wiesenthal Center. SS pensions are typically around $560 a month, three times the reparations paid to Holocaust victims. It is significant to note that more than half of those receiving pensions live in either the United States or countries of the British Empire that were committed to bringing Nazis to justice. While not all the pensioners were war criminals, a good number of them had their records sanitized.

Country	Number of Nazi Pensioners	Country	Number of Nazi Pensioners[17]
Australia	601	Austria	1,115
Argentina	128	Belgium	324
Brazil	196	Canada	1,882
Croatia	1,010	England	459
France	810	Italy	152
Romania	1,014	Slovenia	380
South Africa	152	United States	3,370

By the end of the war, many of the New Dealers who vigorously opposed fascism were replaced with more conservative officials. Nazi sympathizers now had support in the government from the growing ranks of conservatives in the Roosevelt administration and Congress. Growing support for ex-Nazis continued through the Eisenhower administration.

The Nazis also had a comeback plan of their own. It counted on support from collaborators in foreign countries, including the United States. Evidence of the plan comes from captured documents, shown in Appendix 10. The Nazis hoped to convince Americans that Roosevelt's policy of prolonging the war would drive Germany towards communism. This would help Dewey win the election and sign a separate peace with Germany. [18]

At the end of the war there were two interconnected drives by the military and intelligence operations. The first was to acquire as much German technology as possible; the other was to heighten America's phobia about communism.

American fascism has always had its roots in Wall Street and the financial elite of America. That same cadre arranged a marriage between ex-Nazis and the CIA. Previous chapters have already examined how they were able to sabotage the 4Ds program and Safehaven. The Safehaven operation was quickly stripped from the Treasury Department and Morgenthau's influence, and turned over to the State Department. There, Dulles' friends quickly shredded the Treasury Department's list of interlocking companies and blocked further investigations.

Records show that at the end of the war, CIC had two large Civilian Internment Centers, code named Ashcan and Dustbin. Both Ashcan and Dustbin served as central internment camps for POWs and Nazi collaborators. CIC identified many American internees who had remained in Germany and aided the Nazis. Much of the overwhelming, indisputable evidence for charging them with treason came directly from captured German records. But suddenly, on orders from the Department of Justice, they were released. Those in the department who spoke out were fired. The attorney who helped bury the treason cases was later promoted.[19]

Central to the Wall Street alliance with the Nazis and the OSS-CIA was Allen Dulles. Dulles played a pivotal role in helping American investors cover up their dealings with the Nazis. His reassignment to Bern from New York was a continuation of Roosevelt's secret plot, allowing British intelligence to spy on Americans believed to be aiding the Nazis. Both postings placed Dulles in a position where he would be most tempted to aid his clients. While the evidence would be inadmissible in court, it was incriminating and caused a widespread public cry for full investigations.

However, some time after Dulles arrived in Bern, the Nazis tipped him off that he was being watched. It is commonly believed the leak occurred when Vice President Henry Wallace told his brother-in-law, the Swiss Minister in Washington, about Roosevelt's secret spying. Unfortunately, the Nazis had recruited the head of the Swiss Secret Service, and in Berlin, they were soon reading any information given to the Swiss. Wallace was one of only a few in the Roosevelt administration aware of the British spying. Many of the old spies believe Roosevelt dumped Wallace from the 1944 ticket due to the leak.

The British wiretap operation originally was conducted by a special section of Operation Safehaven. Before his death, Justice Goldberg confirmed Dulles' appointment was a setup and insisted the Dulles brothers were traitors.

The British operation was extensive and included spying on Joseph Kennedy and Nelson Rockefeller. The spying on Kennedy netted his radio operator, who was tried in secret by the British and imprisoned until the end of the war. Rockefeller's appointment to an intelligence post for South America also was part of Roosevelt's scheme. Others included James Forrestal and industrialists such as Henry Ford.

Many of Rockefeller's dealings with the Nazis were conduited through shell corporations in Latin America. The dealings were facilitated by his appointment to the post of Coordinator of Inter-American Affairs by Forrestal in 1940, at his own request. This was the position of the top spy in Latin America. Rockefeller proposed to Harry Hopkins that England and Hitler fight each other to the death so that, regardless of who won, the United States could pick up the pieces to increase corporate America's economic influence. Rockefeller was only concerned with corporate America's interests. His definition of totalitarianism was limited to the USSR.

Once Nelson Rockefeller accepted the position, he told his staff that their job was to use the war to take over Latin American markets. Rockefeller also used his position to see to it that the Nazis got anything they wanted in South America, such as refueling bases, while forcing the British to pay cash. In addition, he effectively blackmailed Britain by threatening to withhold or block raw materials and food shipments. Rockefeller's chief aim was to drive the British out of Latin America and monopolize the markets. In each country, he set up coordinating committees composed of reactionary executives from Standard Oil of New Jersey, United Fruit and General Electric.[20]

Rockefeller never bothered to help the war effort; by 1945, a third of the countries in South America had still not declared war on the Nazis. Further, a pro-Nazi bloc of countries, led by Peron of Argentina, was actively involved in helping hide escaping war criminals. Peron was a friend of none other than Allen Dulles.

Allen Dulles a Traitor

Dulles reacted quickly after the Nazis told him of the Safehaven wiretaps. In January 1944, he closed down the pipeline by telling both sides that their secret messages were being intercepted. But there is a much more sinister and serious implication of Dulles' warning to the Nazis that their codes had been broken. Before the Battle of the Bulge, the Nazis began a radio blackout and relied solely on couriers to deliver orders. As a result, allied intelligence was completely blind to the Nazi battle plan for the Battle of the Bulge. Dulles' warning was a clear act of treason.

Dulles attempted to use Gero von Gaevernitz as a secret courier, but he also was under surveillance. Both Dulles and Gaevernitz were charged with laundering the assets of the Nazi Hungarian Bank through Switzerland after the end of the war, under the guise of a series of film companies. Both men managed to avoid prosecution by angry denials and subterfuge.

With the end of the war rapidly approaching, the tip-off that the Allies were intercepting his messages presented Dulles with a special problem. He could no longer use Swiss banks to launder the assets of his American clients and Nazi conspirators which were trapped in Germany. Dulles briefly shifted his money-laundering business to the Central Bank of Belgium. A significant part of the Nazi gold stocks was routed through banks in Belgium, Luxembourg and Liechtenstein. All three countries refused the Allies' postwar demand to examine their files. The Normandy invasion soon shut down this route for Nazi flight capital, leaving most of the American investors' capital still at risk in Germany. Dulles then shifted his money laundering across Austria and into Italy, where his Vatican contacts were waiting to complete the shipping to Argentina.[21]

At the end of the war, U.S.-British Combined Chiefs of Staff investigated Dulles for dereliction of duty and refusal to follow orders. Those military records have conveniently disappeared.[22] The charges stem from Dulles brokering a deal for the surrender of Karl Wolff. Dulles was ordered to break off talks with Wolff, but continued ignoring orders, even to the point of rescuing him from Italian partisans. Wolff eventually was granted amnesty with help from Dulles, despite being the highest-ranking SS officer in Italy and a war criminal. Wolff eventually went free, even though he was Himmler's chief of staff and had arranged contracts for slave labor. In addition, Wolff was the chief Nazi sponsor behind Treblinka. According to information released in 2000 by the CIA, Wolff was deeply involved in deporting Italian Jews to Auschwitz.[23]

Allen Dulles faced other serious allegations after the war. His effectiveness as a spy located in Bern was questionable at best, as shown by the following quote from a cable from Washington to Dulles in January 1944:

> We think it is essential that you be informed at once that almost the entire material supplied disagrees with reports we have received originating with other sources, and parts of it were months old. There has been degeneration of your information which is now given a lower rating than any other source. This seems to indicate a need for using the greatest care in checking all your sources. The Bern estimate of German forces is most inaccurate and misleading. It contains grievous errors regarding locations and also includes reports of non-existent divisions. Only 30 of the divisions reported are correctly identified and the remaining divisions reported are either incorrectly located or do not exist. In more than 50 instances, the classification of divisions by type is wrong.[24]

Both John Foster and Allen Dulles benefited greatly from trade with the Nazis before war broke out. Allen was a director of Schroeder Bank and John Foster sat on the IG Farben board. There also is evidence that both of the Dulles brothers made large, indirect contributions to the Nazi Party as the price to pay for influence in the Third Reich.

When the Sullivan & Cromwell office in Berlin was shut down in 1934, the Dulles brothers merely shifted their business to front men, increasing their profits as Hitler's rearmament program advanced. The buyout of Anaconda Copper by the German Giesche conglomerate is an example of how the Dulles brothers structured deals for the benefit of their clients. Anaconda bought a large block of stock in Giesche, which was secured with Anaconda's 51 percent share of Giesche's interests in Polish Silesia. Giesche provided the Nazis with funding in the early 1930s, but after they invaded Poland, he was forced to sever the American tie or face a Nazi takeover. Allen Dulles represented Anaconda. Giesche bought back its shares from Anaconda with loans from Swiss banks represented by the Dulles brothers. The Swiss banks then held stock in the German banks that arranged the loans. The net effect was to use Swiss bank secrecy as a shield from both Hitler and the American government.[25]

The treachery of the Dulles brothers was boundless. In 1940, a three-way deal was structured with their help. Allen Dulles represented Nazi buyers like IG Farben. John Foster Dulles represented the German bankers and Spanish financiers. Jack Philby represented the Saudi sellers. To understand fully the relationships in this deal requires looking at the career of Allen Dulles after WWI. Dulles was stationed in Istanbul and ran a network there that amassed a good deal of information about the potential wealth of Arabia. Jack Philby was the British Secret Service's head of intelligence for Transjordan. During this period, Philby was, in effect, rehabilitating Dulles. During WWI, Dulles was recruited by British intelligence in Bern and fell victim to a German honey trap. In return for sexual favors, he arranged for his mistress' employment in the American Legation's secret code room. The British discovered the intelligence leak and arrested both Dulles and his mistress. Dulles denied the treason and vowed to help the British if they saved his neck.

Under Philby's tutorage, Dulles' reputation as an observer solidified and he returned to Washington in 1922 to head the Near East Division. Meanwhile, Philby helped direct anti-Jewish terror and, in 1923, created the Arab Legion. In 1924, Philby aligned behind Ibn Saud. After Saud's forces captured Mecca and Medina, Philby became an adviser to the house of Saud.[26] At the same time, Allen Dulles resigned from the State Department. He found private intelligence work to be more profitable, especially when he and his brother worked out deals with the Saudis through his friend Philby.

All three men — Dulles, Philby and Ibn Saud — were known to harbor an intense hatred of Jews. Ibn Saud was the leader of the extremist Wahhabi sect of Moslems and the Arab leader who united the Arabian Peninsula.[27]

In 1936, James Forrestal brought Socal and Texaco together with the help of Dillon and Read Vice President Paul Nitze, who drew up a plan to pool the assets of the two companies "east of the Suez." Caltex became the parent company of Arabian-American Oil Co. They also involved a common shareholder, IG Farben. The Dulles brothers' client, Hermann Schmitz, was president of American IG, which later changed its name to General Aniline and Film (GAF). Forrestal sat on the board of GAF, which owned stock in both Socal and Standard, and was effectively controlled by IG Farben.

Behind the complex web of paper in the deal, Dulles' Nazi client, IG Farben, had Forrestal on its payroll and Forrestal's client, Caltex, had Saudi oil. Philby held the deal together and the Nazis had a supply of Mideast oil. The deal worked well until the entry of the United States into the war. While Harry Truman declared the buna rubber deal between Standard and IG Farben looked like treason, Standard Oil avoided all but a minor fine. Standard's principal line of defense against the government's charges was simply blackmail. Arthur Goldberg confirmed that Dulles was behind the blackmail threat to cut off the Mideast oil supply to the United States, which was already suffering from gasoline rationing.[28]

Dulles also threatened to cut off Britain's oil supplies after the British began leaking information about IG Farben. In their threat to Britain, the Dulles brothers expressed concern that British propaganda about IG Farben might involve large American companies like Standard Oil and hinder the war effort.[29]

The blackmail by Standard Oil resulting from the Dulles-Philby connection was not the end of their treachery. Ibn Saud was pro-Nazi. To stay out of British prison as a Nazi sympathizer, Philby added another angle to the 1940 deal by keeping Saudi Arabia neutral during the war for a bribe. In effect, the Saudis were paid to not pump oil for either Britain or Germany. In June 1941, James Moffett of Caltex tried the same shakedown on Roosevelt. To guarantee Saudi Arabia's oil would not fall into Nazi hands, the American government paid more than $6 million a year to Ibn Saud. However, Roosevelt turned the matter over to the British. Soon after, all Saudi oil wells were capped with cement.

After the U.S. entry in the war, rumors continued that Caltex was shipping oil to the Nazis. The Dulles brothers used their cronies in the State Department to drag the investigation out for two years. Then Forrestal proposed to Roosevelt that Caltex's loyalty to the government could be bought. They argued the British were becoming too influential in the Mideast. Roosevelt was faced with a hopeless situation; he could never get Congress to approve a government investment in Aramco. He was forced to do the next best thing and added Saudi Arabia to the Lend-Lease program to keep Middle East oil from the Nazis.[30]

The Dulles brothers had little cause to worry about the seizure of GAF, the American subsidiary of IG Farben. They had collaborators on both sides of the case. James Forrestal was vice president of GAF. The Alien Property Custodian Leo Crowley was on the payroll of the New York branch of the Schroeder Bank. Schroeder Bank was the depository for GAF, and both Forrestal and Allen Dulles were directors. John Foster Dulles even arranged his appointment as legal counsel for the Alien Property Custodian while representing another IG Farben subsidiary against the custodian.[31]

Crowley appointed Victor Emanuel to the boards of GAF and General Dyestuffs after their seizure by the Property Custodian. Emanuel, in turn, appointed Crowley to head Standard Gas and Electric at $75,000 a year. Emanuel was a director of Schroeder Bank. After James Markham replaced Crowley as Property Custodian, Emanuel appointed Markham as a director of Standard Gas. George Edward Allen was another individual owing debts of gratitude to Emanuel for appointments to private directorships after President Truman appointed Allen head of the Reconstruction Finance Corp.

Crowley also chaired the Foreign Economic Administration and sent Col. Carl Peters to Germany as part of the 4Ds program to decartelize Germany. Peters was the former president of Synthetic Nitrogen, a director of Chemnyco and an official for Advanced Solvents, all IG Farben subsidiaries. Peters was indicted in 1939 in two synthetic nitrogen cases kept secret from the public. He was eventually removed from his post in Germany by the Army's counterintelligence unit.[32]

Moreover, the section on chemicals in Crowley's Program for German and Industrial Disarmament was written by Col. Frederick Pope, a director of American Cyanamid, which was indicted and fined for conspiring with IG Farben in 1946. [33]

The Dulles brothers had little to fear from the Department of Justice. Shortly before his death, Roosevelt told a visitor that he should have fired Attorney General Francis Biddle. In May 1945, before a public hearing conducted by Sen. O'Mahoney, Biddle and Assistant Attorney General Wendell Berge testified that executives of corporations who signed and executed illegal cartel agreements with IG Farben were innocent of any attempt to injure national security and did not present any moral problem.

Biddle resigned the day before Howard Ambruster was to testify before O'Mahoney's investigation into his tenure as attorney general. Rumors at that time stated Assistant Attorney General Norman Littell forced into the record proof of Biddle's connections to Thomas Corcoran. Corcoran previously was employed by the New York law firm of the late Joseph Cotton, President Hoover's Under Secretary of

State who approved a massive loan to Germany when the Nazis rose to power. Corcoran later became legal counsel to the Reconstruction Finance Corp.[34]

The Dulles brothers were able to engineer a massive cover-up of their Nazi dealings. Their web of intrigue extended to all corners of the government. In the 1930s, they created an incredible interlocking financial network between Nazi corporations, American Oil and Saudi Arabia. Perhaps the best-known deal arranged by them was between IG Farben and Standard Oil of New Jersey. IG Farben was the second-largest shareholder in Standard Oil of New Jersey, after John D. Rockefeller.[35]

The Navy captured Nazi documents concerning the Nazi oil cartel, Kontinentale Öl AG, headed by former Reichsbank officer Karl Blessing. Dulles personally vouched for Blessing to protect German oil interests in the Mideast. Blessing and Konti were the missing Nazi link between Ibn Saud and Armco. If Blessing had been exposed, he could have taken a lot of people down with him, and the entire deal struck between the Dulles-Philby team and the Nazis would have unraveled.

The Navy assigned the documents to a young naval officer for review. Allen Dulles contacted the officer and told him to remain quiet about what he had seen and, in turn, he would arrange financing for his first congressional campaign race. This was the beginning of Richard Nixon's political career. In 1947, Nixon privately pointed out that confidential government files showed that Alger Hiss was a communist and one of John Foster Dulles' foundation employees. After the 1948 election, Nixon became Dulles' congressional mouthpiece. When McCarthy went too far in his communist witch hunt, it was Nixon who steered CIA Director Bedell Smith away from the intelligence community.[36]

The Republicans and Nazi War Criminals

An early supporter of Nixon's political career was Prescott Bush. Prescott Bush had employed the Dulles brothers to hide Nazi ownership in numerous companies. Prescott Bush also was instrumental in selecting Nixon as the vice presidential candidate in 1952. Nixon returned the favor by helping George H. W. Bush's political career. George H. W. Bush has described Nixon as his mentor.

Concealing the Konti documents was far from the end of Nixon's aid to former Nazis. For example, Nicolae Malaxa was the supplier of arms to the Iron Guard in Romania and a business partner of Goering, who was later convicted of war crimes in that country. In 1948, he formally applied for permanent U.S. residency and faced a blizzard of legal challenges. In 1951, Nixon introduced a bill in the Senate that would have granted him resident status. It failed. Later that year, Malaxa formed a shell corporation named Western Tube in Nixon's hometown. It shared a mailing address with Nixon's former law firm. The firm applied for a certificate of necessity to get top wartime priority for its material and personnel. Nixon supported granting residency to Malaxa because he was indispensable to Western Tube. Yet Western Tube never produced a single product. Others who aided Malaxa in his legal battles include John Foster Dulles and former Undersecretary of State Adolph Berle.[37]

Nixon's fraternization with Nazis continued beyond his congressional terms and into his presidency. In fact, a lasting result of Nixon's aid to Nazis has manifested in every election since 1972, including the 2004 election. Nixon, like Allen Dulles, believed the pro-Nazi émigrés from Eastern Europe would be useful in getting out the vote. Both Dulles and Nixon believed Jews were responsible for Dewey's loss to Truman. In 1972, Nixon's State Department spokesperson confirmed to his Australian counterpart that ethnic heritage groups were useful in getting out the vote in several key states.[38]

The Republican Ethnic Heritage Groups had their roots in Eastern Europe during WWII. In each of the countries, the SS funded or set up political action groups and militias. A partial list follows:[39]

Hungary — Arrow Cross
Byelorussia — Byelorussian Brigade
Romania — Iron Guard

Bulgaria — Bulgarian Legion
Latvia — Latvian Legion
Ukraine — Ukrainian Nationalist

Often these groups were more brutal and savage than the SS. Many formed active military divisions: 14th Galician, 15th and 19th divisions of the Waffen SS. All the military units from these groups played an integral role in the genocide in Eastern Europe.

Nixon's first attempt at using ethnic groups was in 1952 when he formed an Ethnic Division in the Republican National Committee. In 1953, immigration laws changed to admit Nazis, including former SS members. Nixon oversaw the new immigration policy. In 1968, Nixon promised he would create a permanent ethnic council if he won the presidential election. Until this time, the Ethnic Division surfaced only during presidential campaigns. After winning the 1968 election and appointing George H. W. Bush as chairperson of the Republican Party, Nixon delivered on his promise to the fascists. Laszlo Pasztor organized the Republican Heritage Groups Council.

During the war, Pasztor was a leader of the Arrow Cross in Hungary. Once the Arrow Cross seized power, it conducted a terror campaign against Jews until deporting them to the concentration camps. Many members of the Arrow Cross were tried and executed for war crimes. Pasztor served as a liaison in Berlin between the Nazis and the Arrow Cross government of Hungary. He was convicted of collaborating with the Nazis and served a prison sentence. Pasztor, who arrived in the United States during the 1950s and joined the Republican Ethnic Division, was one of its leaders in the 1968 Nixon-Agnew campaign.[40]

Pasztor claims he selected others for the council with similar backgrounds. The only groups approached by Pasztor from Eastern Europe were those with ties to the Nazis. There is a high degree of correlation between CIA domestic subsidies to fascists during the 1950s and the leadership of the Republican Party's ethnic heritage groups.[41] During the 1950s, while Allen Dulles directed the CIA, many immigrants registered as Republicans, and groups like the Byelorussian Republican Committee emerged. The same fascist leadership received covert CIA subsidies to buy printing presses, and dominated many of the ethnic campaign groups. The subsidy program ended after the Church Committee investigations of the mid-1970s.

The Republican Party cannot be ignorant of the fascist background of the leaders of its Ethnic Groups because Jack Anderson did a series of reports in the 1970s exposing them. According to old spies, President Ford appointed George H. W. Bush CIA Director to fend off any further congressional investigations of Nazis in the United States.[42]

Pasztor has several connections to right-wing extremist groups, such as the Heritage Foundation, the Free Congress Foundation and the World Anti-Communist League. In 1985, he gave up his seat on the Republican Ethnic Council in favor of an American-born ethnic in order to make it easier for the Group Council, an umbrella organization of ethnic heritage groups, to oppose the Justice Department's Nazi-hunting unit. In 1988, Pasztor was forced to resign from the George H. W. Bush presidential campaign after his past Nazi connections were exposed. He was one of several former Nazis serving on the Bush campaign team. However, Pasztor remains closely connected with the Bush family, as this letter from Laura Bush reveals. Clearly, the Bush family sees nothing morally wrong in associating with known Nazi war criminals.

October 3, 2002
Mr. Laszlo Pasztor
National President Emeritus
National Federation of American Hungarians
717 Second Street NE
Washington, D.C. 20002-4307

Dear Mr. Pasztor,

My thanks to you and the National Federation of American Hungarians for Stephen Sisa's book, The Spirit of Hungary. I hope you will extend to the membership my appreciation, especially for the kind inscription.

You are kind to think of me, and I am grateful for your generosity.

With best wishes,

[SIGNATURE]

Laura Bush[43]

Pasztor is typical of the immigrants from Eastern Europe admitted under the Bloodstone project. The Nazis' pasts were either buried or forgotten, and once admitted to the United States, the CIA provided them with subsidies. During the 1950s, they were recruited politically by Nixon and gradually assumed a dominant role in the Republican Party and right-wing foundations. Pasztor's career outlines the timeline, from the 1950s to the present White House.

Most of the eastern European immigrants were not Nazis, but many admitted to the United States during the late 1940s–50s were. The continuing shift to the right in America aided Dulles' efforts to enlist Nazi immigrants. The shift was marked by the removal of those who vigorously opposed fascism.

Operation Mockingbird

In September 1951, Robert Lovett replaced George C. Marshall as Secretary of Defense. Averell Harriman was named director of the Mutual Security Agency, making him the U.S. chief of the Anglo-American military alliance. A central focus of the Harriman security regime in Washington, from 1950–53, was organizing covert operations and "psychological warfare." Harriman, with his lawyers and business partners, Allen and John Foster Dulles, wanted the government's secret service to conduct extensive propaganda campaigns and mass-psychology experiments in the United States and paramilitary campaigns abroad.

The Harriman security regime created the Psychological Strategy Board (PSB) in 1951 with Gordon Gray as director. Gordon's brother, Bowman Gray Jr., chairman of R. J. Reynolds, was a naval intelligence officer, known around Washington as the "founder of operational intelligence." Gordon Gray was a close friend and political ally of Prescott Bush, and a leader in the eugenics movement in the 1920s–30s.

Shortly before the 1952 election, while the country was firmly in the grip of McCarthyism, the CIA launched a massive multimillion-dollar media blitz. The publicity campaign was designed to legitimize the expansion of U.S. Cold War operations in Europe. In essence, it was a psychological war against the American people. The program was guided by a theory of liberationism, and a major feature was the portrayal of former Nazis as freedom fighters against the USSR. The CIA's propaganda campaign inside the United States was clearly illegal, but the agency managed to cloak its role. The forefront of this campaign was known as Crusade for Freedom, which generated massive amounts of propaganda.[44]

Several other groups functioned under the Crusade for Freedom umbrella, including the Free Europe Committee, which it funded. Gen. Lucius Clay led the fundraising campaign for the Free Europe Committee and later served as one of its first directors with Allen Dulles, C.D. Jackson and Adolf Berle.[45]

While both Nixon and Dulles believed the pro-Nazi émigré groups were useful to get out the vote, the first to use them in an election was Arthur Bliss Lane. He used the Crusade for Freedom to generate enthusiasm among the émigré groups for the Republican Party in the 1952 election. By playing on the nation's phobia of communism, Republicans campaigned on a program of liberation rather than the containment policy of Truman and the Democrats.

Republican tactics in the émigré communities were almost indistinguishable from the CIA's Crusade for Freedom. Lane's specialist in the Ukrainian community was Vladimir Petrov, a Nazi quisling city administrator of Krasnodar, during the time gas trucks were introduced and used to kill at least 7,000.[46]

There is no evidence that these émigré groups were useful in swaying election results. They do point to Republican Party's continued association with fascism. As recently as 1988, several George H. W. Bush campaign employees were forced to resign once their past Nazi connections were revealed.

Dulles was able to use this illegal covert CIA propaganda campaign, casting ex-Nazis as freedom fighters, to open U.S. immigration doors. After the 1952 election he had a willing aide in Vice President Nixon.

By using foundations such as the Ford Foundation as fronts to wage the Crusade for Freedom, CIA involvement in domestic politics went undetected in the 1950s. A 1976 congressional investigation revealed the CIA funded nearly half of the 700 grants in international activities by the principal foundations. The Ford Foundation not only acted as a front for CIA propaganda campaigns, but also served to undermine the Left.

Looking at some of the past directors of the Ford Foundation from the 1950s, the connection is obvious. Paul Hoffman, who served from 1950–52, had been an administrator of the Marshall Plan. Richard Bissell served as foundation president from 1952–54, then left to become a special assistant to Allen Dulles in January 1954. Replacing Bissell was John McCloy, former High Commissioner of Occupied Germany, who set up a three-person panel to ease the foundation's connection to the CIA.

Frank Lindsay was another CIA operative who came to work for the Ford Foundation in 1953. Lindsay was an OSS veteran. As Deputy Chief of OPC from 1949–51, he was responsible for setting up the "stay-behind" groups in Western Europe. Waldemar Nielsen joined Lindsay at the foundation, where he became a staff director. Throughout his stay at the Ford Foundation, Nielsen was a CIA agent. In his various guises, Nielsen worked closely with C.D. Jackson, associated with the Psychological Strategy Board.

The foundation gave $500,000 to Bill Casey's International Rescue Committee and large grants to another CIA front, the World Assembly of Youth. The Ford Foundation is one of the largest donors to the Council on Foreign Relations. The Institute of Contemporary Arts (ICA), founded in Washington in 1947, expanded its international program in 1958 after receiving a large grant from the Ford Foundation. On ICA's board of trustees was William Bundy, a member of the CIA's Board of National Estimates and son-in-law of former Secretary of State Dean Acheson. His brother, McGeorge Bundy, became president of the Ford Foundation in 1966, coming straight from his job as Special Assistant to the President in Charge of National Security. As special assistant, McGeorge Bundy duties included monitoring the CIA.

The Rockefeller Foundation also served the CIA. Both John Foster Dulles and later Dean Rusk were presidents of the foundation before becoming Secretaries of State. John McCloy and Robert Lovett served as Rockefeller trustees. Nelson Rockefeller's service as head of South American intelligence and his central position in the foundation cemented the close link with the CIA.

The Ford and Rockefeller foundations are not the only ones that acted as CIA conduits. Former OSS agent and future CIA Director William Casey founded the Manhattan Institute. After the war, Casey also worked for another CIA front group, the International Rescue Committee.[47]

Dulles' propaganda efforts in the 1950s were massive. Besides the Crusade for Freedom, they included Free Europe, Radio Free Europe and many other programs. One measure of the scope of Dulles' effort was the CIA's $5 million contribution to anti-communist education through the crusade. While $5 million seems trivial today, at the time it exceeded all the money spent by both sides in the

Truman vs. Dewey 1948 election.[48] In 1952, Ronald Reagan became a fundraiser for the Crusade for Freedom.[49] But Reagan was tied much more deeply to the military intelligence apparatus, as the following quote indicates:

> In 1952, at MCA, Actors' Guild president Ronald Reagan — a screen idol recruited by MOCKINGBIRD's Crusade for Freedom to raise funds for the resettlement of Nazis in the U.S., according to Loftus — signed a secret waiver of the conflict-of-interest rule with the mob-controlled studio, in effect granting it a labor monopoly on early television programming. In exchange, MCA made Reagan a part owner. Furthermore, historian C. Vann Woodward, writing in the New York Times, in 1987, reported that Reagan had fed the names of suspect people in his organization to the FBI secretly and regularly enough to be assigned an informer's code number, T-10. His FBI file indicates intense collaboration with producers to "purge" the industry of subversives.[50]

The Gehlen Network

One of the first Nazis brought to America, and perhaps the one who exerted the most influence over U.S. policy, was Gen. Reinhard Gehlen. Gehlen was the Nazis' most senior intelligence officer on the Eastern Front. He began planning his surrender to American forces as early as the summer of 1944. Like all senior Nazis seeking to surrender to the United States rather than the Soviets, he offered something of value to U.S. forces in exchange for freedom from prosecution as a war criminal. Such Nazi offers were characterized by alibis that downplayed their roles in the war and war crimes.

In early March 1945, Gehlen and a small group of his most senior officers microfilmed the vast holdings on the USSR of the *Fremde Heere Ost* (military intelligence section of the German general staff). They sealed the microfilm in watertight drums and buried them in the Austrian Alps.

On March 22, 1945, Gehlen and his top aides surrendered to CIC and were taken to Camp King near Oberursel in the American zone. Capt. John Bokor, the assigned interrogator, was reportedly anti-Nazi, but claimed a great deal of knowledge about the Soviet Union and sensed the Soviets as a threat. As the two men became friends, Gehlen gradually revealed his secret microfilms and an embryonic espionage underground inside the Soviet Union. Bokor was interested in Gehlen's information, but faced several obstacles. For one, the Yalta agreements required turning over Nazis from the Eastern Front to the Soviets in exchange for help in the return of American POWs liberated by Stalin's advancing forces.

Bokor continued on his own accord and kept Gehlen's offer secret from other CIC officers. With the help of Col. William Philip, chief of the CIC interrogation center at Camp King, Bokor arranged for seven of Gehlen's senior officers to be transferred to Camp King. There, Gehlen and his senior officers set up a "historical study group" as a cover. Gehlen's microfilms were shipped to the camp without the knowledge of the CIC's chain of command. Bokor feared that if he reported Gehlen's existence too soon, he would be exposed to hostile actions from the Pentagon and military command in Frankfurt.

By the end of the summer, Bokor won the support of Gen. Edwin Sibert and Walter Bedell Smith. Bill Donovan and Allen Dulles also were aware of Bokor and Gehlen. Dulles had been tipped off about Gehlen from one of his double agents inside the German Foreign Office. OSS was jockeying for control of Gehlen and his microfilms.

Sibert shipped Gehlen and three of his aides off to Washington in August 1945 for debriefing. By December, Sibert had authority to continue at his own risk. In other words, Sibert had permission to continue with Gehlen, but if anything went wrong, the U.S. government would deny any knowledge of the operation.

Dulles' OSS Secret Intelligence Branch had direct contact with Gehlen. Frank Wisner, a former Wall Street lawyer and OSS agent, headed the coordinating team. It is unclear how much President Truman knew about Gehlen, since those documents remain classified. However, the Soviets raised vigorous protest over Gehlen at Potsdam, so it is certain Truman was at least aware of the plans to use his intelligence.[51]

Within a year, the United States set Gehlen's organization up near Pullach in a former Waffen SS training facility. He handpicked 350 former German intelligence agents to join him; their numbers eventually grew to 4,000 undercover agents. Gehlen's organization evolved into Germany's equivalent of the CIA, the Bundesnachrichtendienst (BND).

The swift recruitment of Gehlen and his rapid rise in the Western intelligence community was largely a result of U.S. fears of the Soviet Union. Once American Nazi sympathizers realized Germany had lost the war, they began stoking fears of communism and the dangers posed by the Soviet Union. The Nazis comeback plan rested on provoking a conflict between the Soviets and the U.S. To this end, Gehlen was a loyal Nazi, as suggested in the quote below:

> Their (Gehlen's organization) object was to commit the U.S. occupier on the German side and exploit the differences between Washington and Moscow in order to save the Germans from the worst consequences of the war begun by and lost by the Hitler regime.

> As early as the beginning of 1947 Gehlen had confided to one of his staff that he was reckoning on the possibility of war between Russia and America; even should there be no armed conflict, he said Europe faced a decade of growing tension. Meanwhile he was toying with a fantastic notion — that the Russians and Americans would tear each other to pieces and so give Germany the opportunity to create a new order in Europe.[52]

The extreme fear of the Soviets at the end of the war was largely illusory and more a product of vivid imaginations rather than anything of substance. Russia suffered immensely during the war, sustaining far more casualties than any other country.

Country	Population (millions)	Killed/ Missing	Wounded	Total Military	Civilian Deaths[53]
U.S.	129	300,000	300,000	600,000	0
Britain	48	400,000	300,000	700,000	60,000
Italy	44	330,000	?	?	70,000
Holland	9	14,000	7,000	21,000	250,000
France	42	259,000	350,000	600,000	270,000
Japan	72	1.75 million	?	?	350,000
Germany	78	3.5 million	4.6 million	8.1 million	2 million
Poland	35	130,000	200,000	330,000	2.5 million
USSR	194	9 million	18 million	27 million	19 million

The Ukraine and other eastern areas of the country suffered from two scorched earth policies of the retreating forces. Eisenhower once remarked to an aide that it would take several years before the Soviets would threaten Europe because it was ripping up the railroad tracks in Germany and shipping them back to Russia. Without the railroads, there was no way for the Soviets to move a massive number of troops forward for an invasion of Europe. Moreover, there is evidence that Stalin wanted peace after the war. On his return to Washington, Roosevelt's envoy to Moscow, Donald Nelson, indicated Stalin proposed a trade plan for the postwar period. The plan was for the United States to provide Russia with finished goods, such as agricultural equipment, cars, household appliances and similar items in return for raw materials.[54]

Gehlen is perhaps the man most responsible for starting the Cold War. At first, the military was skeptical of Gehlen and his reports. However, because of the meddling of Allen Dulles and postwar rivalries between the OSS and the Pentagon's Military Intelligence Service, Gehlen soon became the leading expert on the Soviets.

In the postwar period, all branches of the military and the intelligence community suffered budget cuts. Col. John Grombach headed the Military Intelligence Service in the postwar period, and was competing for scarce funds with the OSS's Research and Analysis branch. In 1945, to eliminate the OSS branch, Grombach had his men pore over captured German files looking for evidence that the agency was soft on communism. He found some, including one middle-level employee who joined the Communist Party a decade before and failed to disclose it on his application. He also found several university professors recruited by the OSS who had ties to liberal and left-wing organizations. Moreover, the OSS downplayed negative reports about the USSR and the Katyn Forest massacre to preserve the Allied coalition.

Grombach then leaked his information inside the Pentagon and to right-wing members of Congress. As a result, Congress broke the OSS's Research and Analysis branch into 17 divisions, effectively immobilizing it. With the elimination of the research and analysis group, the hard-liners were firmly in control and Gehlen's information was readily accepted. At the time, U.S. intelligence on the USSR was essentially an empty file. Even rudimentary information on the rail or road system was lacking. Gehlen was free to fan the flames of the Cold War. It's now known that his estimates of Soviet troop strength were wildly exaggerated. Paul Nitze admitted that a full third of the Russian divisions in Europe were under strength; another third existed only on paper.[55]

A former CIA chief analyst of Soviet military capabilities, Victor Marchetti, now admits that during the 1950s, Gehlen also played a part in the missile gap crisis. It was Gehlen's reports to the CIA that first triggered the alert. Walter Dornberger, another former Nazi admitted to the United States, added more fuel to the fire by publishing speculation that the Soviets might attack from the sea using short-range missiles floated in canisters. However, U2 surveillance flights failed to detect any increase in the number of ICBMs that Gehlen claimed the Russians deployed.[56]

On July 30, 1946, Chamberlin, the Army Director of Intelligence, proposed a plan to smuggle 30 ex-Nazi experts on the USSR into the United States as part of a group of 1,000 scientists. The Army wanted to shut down Operation Paperclip because of the expense of custodial duties and surveillance over the scientists. Chamberlin wanted desperately to save the Paperclip project.[57] In response , Clay issued his famous telegram to Washington suggesting a Soviet invasion of Europe was imminent:

> For many months based on logical analysis, I have felt and held that war (with the Soviets) was unlikely for 10 years. Within the last few weeks, I have felt a subtle change in the Soviet attitude ... which now gives me a feeling that it may come with dramatic suddenness."[58]

Clay's telegram was quickly leaked to the press and whipped into a full-blown war scare.

In a series of secret conferences with Gen. Clay in late 1947, Gehlen claimed the Soviet troop strength in Eastern Europe was not less than 175 divisions. He further claimed that most were combat ready and that quiet changes in Soviet billeting suggested they were preparing for a major mobilization.

In February 1948, the coalition Czech government failed, partly due to lack of U.S. support for President Edward Benes, a social democrat, on the grounds that he was not sufficiently anti-communist. Also in February, Gen. Stephen Chamberlin visited Clay and stressed that there were major military appropriation bills before Congress and there was a need to galvanize American support for increased military spending.

Gehlen's estimate of 175 divisions was accepted without question. The same troops that the 1946 Army analysis described as tied down with immediate occupation and security requirements were now described by Gehlen as highly mobile. The Army's earlier acknowledgment of Soviet troop transport and logistic problems disappeared. On Gehlen's estimates, the Soviets were now capable of simultaneously launching large-scale offensives at Europe, the Middle East and Far East. There was no reasonable voice asking where all the required divisions or logistical support would come from. The Truman administration's response was to stop any further cuts in military programs and to speed up the atomic weapons program. Operation Paperclip continued.

Initially, Gehlen's information was derived from the Nazi torture and interrogations of prisoners. Some 4 million Soviet prisoners died of starvation. While Gehlen and his men may not have engaged in the executions, he was responsible for organizing the interrogations of the Soviet prisoners, which were actually a step toward liquidating thousands of them. Many were executed or simply left to starve to death.[59]

As Gehlen's organization grew, it began to depend on interviews with émigrés from Eastern Europe, and eventually evolved into a spy web inside the Iron Curtain. Gehlen's reassurances to the United States that he would not employ any former SS men were promptly broken. At least a half dozen of his first staff of 50 were former SS men. Included were Hans Sommer, who torched seven Paris synagogues in 1941; Willi Kirchbaum, senior Gestapo leader for southeastern Europe; and Fritz Schmidt, former Gestapo chief of Kiel.[49] The earliest SS recruits enlisted with phony papers and false names. It is reasonable to suspect that some American authorities were aware of the ruse.

Gehlen privately negotiated a position for Gustav Hilger with G2's Technical Intelligence Branch in 1946.[60] Hilger's influence on American policy rivaled Gehlen's. A German diplomat assigned to Russia before the war, he developed close friendships with Americans stationed in the Moscow embassy. During the war, Hilger was directly under von Ribbentrop and served as the chief political officer on the Eastern Front. He also was a liaison between Ribbentrop's Foreign Office and the SS.

Hilger had full knowledge of the extent of the Holocaust. In December 1943, he negotiated an agreement with Italy to round up Jews into work camps. During the spring of 1944, several trainloads of Jews from these work camps were shipped to Auschwitz.

The Nazi Foreign Office also assigned Hilger to liaison with Vlasov and, by 1944, he completely integrated himself in the command structure of Vlasov's army. At the end of the war, Hilger was officially sought as a war criminal for torture. He surrendered to U.S. forces in May 1945 and, after a brief confinement at the Mannheim POW camp, was sent to Washington for debriefing because of his expertise in Soviet affairs. Hilger was eventually given asylum in the United States under the Bloodstone project. For several years, he shuttled between Washington and West Germany, becoming an unofficial ambassador for Konrad Adenauer. Hilger was instrumental in forming the Adenauer government.[61] Initially, Washington opposed Adenauer, but Hilger's contacts in the State Department eventually swayed American officials to approve it in 1949.

By 1946, Gehlen resumed funding Vlasov's army, the underground Ukrainian army and other Nazi quislings. In 1947, SS officers Franz Six and Emil Augsburg took charge of the émigré work. Both were from the Amt VI group of the SS, the combined foreign intelligence apparatus of the Nazi equivalent to the CIA. Most of Amt VI's top officers were instrumental in the mass extermination of Jews. Augsburg escaped any prosecution. Six was a major war criminal favored by both Eichmann and Himmler. Speaking at a 1944 conference on the Jewish question, Six said: "The physical elimination of Eastern Jewry would deprive Jewry of its biological reserves. The Jewish question must be solved not only in Germany but also internationally."[62] Himmler was so pleased with Six's work that he promoted him to a newly created department of his own, Amt VII.

Six eventually was betrayed, tried for war crimes, found guilty and sentenced to 20 years in prison. He only served four before John McCloy granted him clemency. Once freed, he returned to Gehlen's organization. McCloy could hardly have been unaware of Six's background when he granted the pardon.

In 1954, Gen. Arthur Trudeau, chief of U.S. military intelligence, received a copy of a lengthy report prepared by retired Lt. Col. Hermann Baun of Gehlen's staff. Baun was a highly competent officer who took a dim view of the network and hated Gehlen for forcing him out of his postwar intelligence position with the West. Baun's report listed the backgrounds of many of Gehlen's staff members. Trudeau was so annoyed with the report he took it to Konrad Adenauer during his visit to Washington. Adenauer was deeply alarmed over the report, portions of which were leaked to the press. Through meddling by the Dulles brothers (Allen was Director of the CIA and John Foster was Secretary of State at the time), Trudeau was effectively silenced by a transfer to a remote Far East post.

Listed in Baun's report was SS-Oberführer Willi Kirchbaum. Kirchbaum was an associate of Gestapo Chief Heinrich Müller and later the Deputy Chief of the Gestapo. He was in charge of deporting Hungarian Jews in 1944. Another was SS-Standartenführer Walter Rauff. Rauff supervised construction of the vans used on the Eastern Front to gas Jews, and was involved with SS Gen. Karl Wolff's negotiations to surrender the German troops in Italy in 1945. After his exposure as part of the network, Gehlen transferred him to Chile, where he functioned as an agent.

SS-Sturmbannführer Alois Brunner was another member of Gehlen's network who was a former Gestapo official working directly under Adolf Eichmann. Brunner was sentenced to death *in absentia* by a French court for instigating the notorious *razzia* carried out in France in 1942 against the Jews of Paris. Brunner was sent to Damascus as Gehlen's resident agent and lived under various aliases. Brunner later took part in a CIA-directed program to train the security forces of Abdel Nasser. U.S. officials had to know Brunner was on the CIC's wanted list.

One of the worst members of Gehlen's organization was SS-Gruppenführer Odilo Globocnik, who ran the Lublin camps in Poland. Before working for the United States, Globocnik worked for the British. He was also stationed in Damascus. Other members of the Gehlen organization included SS-Sturmbannführer Emil Augsberg, head of Treblinka and Belzec concentration camps; SS-Sturmbannführer Ernst Bibernstein, who commanded Einsatzkommando 6 of Einsatzgruppe C; and SS-Sturmbannführer Karl Döring, a staff member of the Dachau concentration camp. Döring was later postwar West German Ambassador to the Cameroons. SS-Standartenführer Eugen Steimle, the commanding officer of Einsatzgruppen B and later C, was convicted by an Allied court and sentenced to a long term in prison; he was released in 1951. Baun's list included many other SS officers who served in concentration camps or were part of the Einsatzgruppen and guilty of war crimes. Most of them had little knowledge of the Soviet Union, and their use by the CIA is indefensible.

Vlasov's Army

Vlasov's army and émigrés from other eastern European countries were the source for Frank Wisner's covert actions behind the rapidly developing Iron Curtain. Wisner, who believed in covert actions to eliminate communism rather than the containment policy of Kennan or Truman, recruited heavily from various émigré groups. The recruits were trained and often dropped across the borders into communist territory. Usually, Wisner's agents met quick fates when apprehended. The thought of a spy or a mole in their organization never occurred to them, but Vlasov's army and the Gehlen network were both infested with Soviet moles. As a result, Wisner was responsible for killing more Nazis after than during the war!

U.S. plans for a nuclear war with the USSR included integrating Vlasov's army as part of the overall strategy. The idea of using former Nazis to conduct guerrilla warfare after dropping 60–70 atomic bombs on the USSR was first proposed in 1947 by Hoyt Vandenberg. Five wings of B29 bombers were committed to the émigré guerrilla army project.[63] The Nazis were to be dropped inside the USSR after the bombings to gain control of strategic sites, as well as control of the local populace. Toward the end of 1948, Gen. Robert McClure won the approval of the Joint Chiefs for full-scale guerrilla warfare following a nuclear attack on the USSR. Until 1956, this was the attack plan. It employed thousands of émigrés from the USSR, including Vlasov's army and Waffen SS men. Documents in the National

Archives reference a top secret State Department plan to recruit a network of Albanian anti-communists who previously were denied visas as Nazi collaborators and war criminals.[64]

The United States was able to equip Vlasov's army largely with supplies from surplus war equipment. Both the CIA and the military laid claim to authority over this guerrillas force, occasionally employing them in covert operations. Such cooperation from the émigrés was later used to sanitize their records.

To hide an army of thousands in Europe, the United States simply hid them inside another army of sorts, in full view of everyone. They were hidden in labor camps known as Labor Service companies. Roughly 40,000 displaced persons were employed in these Labor Service companies, guarding POWs, removing bombing rubble from cities, locating gravesites and similar work. Officially, former Nazis were barred from these camps. But at least as early as 1946, the Labor Services recruited them. For example, Voldemars Skaistlauks, an SS general, and his top aides were part of the Latvian labor company formed on June 27, 1946. Talivaldis Karklins was another top Nazi in Madonna concentration camp. His role in torture and murders was known at least as early as 1963. He came to the United States in 1956. Finally in 1981, the office of Special Investigations — Nazi hunters in the Justice Department — succeeded in bringing charges against Karklins, resulting in a complex legal battle. He died peacefully in 1983 in Monterey, Calif.[65]

Right-wing fears of communism backfired. The hard anti-communist faction led by Allen Dulles was the prime sponsor of the Gehlen network and Vlasov's army in the Cold War. Since both groups were infested with Soviet moles, this led to greater Soviet penetration of U.S. intelligence and military organizations.

Project Overcast and Paperclip

On Dec. 1, 1944, OSS head Bill Donovan asked President Roosevelt if Nazi recruits could be given special privileges, including entry to the United States after the war. Roosevelt's blunt reply:

> I do not believe that we should offer any guarantees of protection in post-hostilities periods to Germans who are working for your organization. I think that carrying out of any such guarantees would be difficult and probably be widely misunderstood both in this country and aboard. We may expect that the number of Germans who are anxious to save their skins and property will rapidly increase. Among them may be some who should properly be tried for war crimes or at least arrested for active participation in Nazi activities. Even with the necessary controls you mention I am not prepared to authorize the giving of guarantees.[66]

The first official program to bring Nazis to the United States was Project Overcast. The Army's TICOM forces may have preceded Overcast, but those documents remain classified. TICOM forces followed the advancing Allied troops seeking the newest German cryptographic equipment code-named Swordfish, or more simply, Fish. TICOM teams managed to secure roughly 5 tons of German Sigint documents, as well as many cryptological devices. Equally important were the secret interrogations of German code breakers at the secret location code named Dustbin. The teams also secured a secret Russian cryptograph machine that allowed the American military to read Soviet transmissions. Thus, there was no need to rely solely on Gehlen and his associates for information on the Soviets. It is known the British employed several Nazi cryptographers and that Erich Huettenhain was brought clandestinely to the United States.[67]

The birth of Project Overcast had its origins in the summer of 1945 at Hotel Wittelsacher in Bad Kissingen, where German scientists from Peenemunde were held. Col. Putt soon convinced Gen. Hugh Knerr that their technical knowledge would benefit the air corps. Knerr sought permission from Washington to bring five of these scientists to the U.S. The War Department assured Truman that accused war criminals would be kept in close confinement and stern control. The deciding factor for approval was the continuing war with Japan. With the inclusion of the following phrase, Project Overcast was launched: "If any specialists who are brought to this country are subsequently found to be listed as alleged war criminals, they should be returned to Europe for trial."[68]

This restriction was soon ignored. Project Overcast only allowed for temporary visas; after the scientists completed their assigned tasks, they were to be returned to Germany. Overcast was controlled by three military intelligence agencies, which allowed it to be cloaked from the prying eyes of the public. Those agencies were the Joint Intelligence Committee (JIC), the Joint Intelligence Objectives Agency (JIOA) and the Exploration Branch of G2.

By the spring of 1946, the name of Operation Overcast was changed to Paperclip and closely coordinated with the British programs. Britain was already exploiting several groups and in March 1946, began dumping German scientists on other Commonwealth countries, including Canada and Australia. Some of those sent to Canada later entered the United States in the 1950s under Operation Paperclip. The JIOA governing committee by this time had already embarked on its own agenda. Samuel Klaus, the State Department representative, was routinely excluded from meetings. The agenda of the military officers on the governing committee was to expand the recruitment list to include POWs, militarists, SS officers and others they considered useful. Monroe Hagood, the branch chief of G2, was instrumental in hatching a plot to smuggle SS officers into the United States under Paperclip. The idea that Paperclip only recruited scientists is myth, not fact.[69]

The final policy for expanding Paperclip was presented to Truman by acting Secretary of State Dean Acheson with recommendations by him and the military to sign it. It explicitly defined the policies and procedures to be followed, including the following clause: "No person found by the Commanding General, USFET to have been a member of the Nazi Party and more than a nominal participant in its activities, or an active supporter of Nazism or militarism shall be brought to the U.S. hereunder."[70] But President Truman's directive against using Nazi Party or SS members was promptly ignored.[71]

Many Nazis were admitted under Operation Paperclip as rocket scientists, but some, like Walter Dornberger, first had to have their records sanitized. Dornberger was a major general at Peenemunde who was sentenced to hang for war crimes. England warned the United States not to admit him because he already was conniving to start another war.[72] He later rose to Vice President of Bell Helicopters; a visible post, to be sure, but even more visible after Bell announced its V22 helicopter — a surprisingly close nomenclature for someone who had been involved in the V2 program.

While most Americans realize that Wernher von Braun and other Nazi rocket scientists were brought to the United States to develop the U.S. space program, few know the extent and scope of Operation Paperclip. The GAO still perpetuates the lie that the program ended in 1947 and brought just a handful of Nazi scientists to the United States. In fact, Paperclip did not end until 1973. Under the project, more than 1,600 Nazi scientists, specialists and their dependent families were admitted to the U.S.[73] Another common misconception of Paperclip is that the only Nazi scientists allowed entry were connected with rockets, jets and the like. The hundreds of Nazi doctors from the concentration camps are never mentioned in official reports on Paperclip. Their admission led to horrifying psychochemical experiments on American soldiers and civilians, and eventually to CIA projects in mind control involving child abuse.

It has been 60 years since the end of the war and most Americans are unaware of the number of Nazi doctors and scientists who were allowed to come to the United States. Moreover, most are content to assume that the Nazi doctors have no effect on their lives. Such wishful thinking can be deadly, as in the appearance of Lyme disease in Connecticut in the mid-1970s. Two miles offshore from Old Lyme, Conn., is Plum Island, home of Lab 257, where secret biological experiments are conducted with the most deadly strains of bacteria and viruses. After WWII, the Army turned over control of the island to the U.S. Department of Agriculture (USDA). The initial charter from Congress mandated the study of animal diseases, such as hoof and mouth disease, directed to eradicating them from the nation's livestock. In 1954, the laboratory took an aggressive turn to biowarfare, seeking ways to inflict widespread disease in Soviet herds to cause a famine. Cuba alleges that bioweapons from Plum Island were used against its agriculture in the 1960s–70s.

Plum Island appears to be the site where Nazi scientists conducted experiments with disease-infested ticks. One of them was Dr. Erich Traub who received a fellowship from the Rockefeller Institute in Princeton, N.J., before the war. Traub was involved in Nazi activities in the United States during the 1930s, and was a member of Camp Siegfried and the powerful NSKK, the Nazi Motor Corps. During the war, Traub served as lab chief at Insel Riems, a secret Nazi biological warfare facility in the Baltic Sea. He served directly under Himmler, packaging weaponized hoof-and-mouth disease virus, which was dispersed from a Luftwaffe bomber onto cattle and reindeer in Russia. At Himmler's request, Traub traveled to Turkey to find a lethal strain of rinderpest virus for use against the Allies.

In 1949, Traub and his family escaped from East Germany to West Berlin. He immediately applied to work under the Paperclip Program. Within months, Traub was invited for a talk with germ warriors from Fort Detrick, the Army's biological warfare headquarters in Frederick, Md. A former declassified summary confirms the meeting occurred, but the CIA denies the summary exists and claims that if it did, it would withhold it for reasons of national security. Almost all documents concerning Traub and the Army's biowarfare at Plum Island have been destroyed or remain deeply buried in the government's secret vaults. The few documents that remain show that Traub worked with more than 40 lethal viruses on large test animals. He was at Plum Island from 1949–53 and remained an active collaborator thereafter. Reports of a Nazi scientist releasing infected ticks come from a former employee of Plum Island. The island also may be the source of the outbreak of the West Nile virus. Both the Lyme and West Nile diseases first appeared in the general area. The George W. Bush administration transferred control of the site to the Department of Homeland Security with a mission to protect the nation from bioweapons.

Scientific American dismisses the possibility of a "Nazi scientist" link to Plum Island, but documents reveal Traub was a founding member of the biowarfare program. *Scientific American* is published by Von Holtzbrinck, a firm with firm roots in the Third Reich. Von Holtzbrinck also owns Henry Holt Publishing, St. Martin's Press, MacMillan and several other major U.S. publishers.

In the race to entice Nazi scientists to the United States and thereby deprive the Soviets of their knowledge, security and screening methods were lax. The Soviets penetrated the project from the start.[74] Donald Maclean was the first secretary of the British Embassy and a Soviet mole who helped recruit Nazi scientists. Maclean supplied a list of scientists he claimed were of no value to recruit. Among them were Otto Hahn and Carl von Weizsacker, who were as well known in scientific circles as Churchill or Roosevelt in political circles. Hahn went on to win the Nobel Prize in chemistry.[75]

One of the myths about Paperclip is that German scientists were closely watched by the military, but nothing could be further from the truth. Security was lax to say the least. Often they were permitted to travel freely. Their mail was rarely checked and their phones were not tapped or monitored. For example, in the second test firing of the GE Hermes II missile, several German scientists were positioned at a distance surrounding the site to observe and to radio the command center in case the missile veered off course. The missile did veer to the south, but the German observers allowed it to continue. It landed about three miles from the main business district of Juarez, Mexico. There was evidence of sabotage, but no attempt was made to restrict the German scientists.[76] In fact, at least three of them at White Sands were known to have illegal mail drops of money from foreign sources and coded messages from South America.

Elements of the U.S. military did not wait for Project Overcast to be approved. On May 19, 1945, just two weeks after the German surrender, a military transport with blackened windows landed in Washington. Its secret cargo was Herbert Wagner and two of his aides. Wagner was the chief missile designer for Henschel Aircraft Co., and the creator of the HS-293, the first Nazi guided missile used in combat. He was smuggled into Washington by a U.S. Navy team anxious to use his guided bombs against Japan. Wagner had been a fervent member of the SA or *Sturmabteilung* (brown-shirted storm troopers) and equally ardent member of four other Nazi organizations.

The Joint Chief of Staff announced the formal beginning of Project Overcast on July 6, 1945 to exploit "chosen rare minds." The chiefs directed that up to 350 specialists, mostly from Germany and Austria, be brought directly to the United States. JIOA selected the Nazi scientists. The list of selected recruits was submitted to the State and Justice departments for final approval before they were allowed entry.

At first, the justification given for these ex-Nazi scientists was that their expertise would be useful in the war with Japan, but within a month, Japan surrendered. As early as June 1945, some were already arguing the Nazi scientists needed to be moved to the United States to deprive the Soviets of their talents. One of these was Truman's chief science adviser, RCA chief David Sarnoff. Through its subsidiary, Transradio, and with Sarnoff's full knowledge, RCA maintained a radio link between Buenos Aires and Berlin for the Nazis.

Bosquet Wev, director of JIOA, presented the first group of scientists' dossiers to the State and Justice departments about six months after Truman approved Operation Paperclip. Included were reports by the Office of Military Government (OMGUS) and the CIC. Wev's job was to guide the dossiers past the review board, which included Samuel Klaus from the State Department. Klaus was an ardent foe of the Nazis and demanded details. OMGUS reports on Wev's first batch of recruited scientists were prepared by CIC men who fought their way across Europe and saw Nazi brutality firsthand. They knew their job and reported that the first wave of scientists had been ardent Nazis entangled in war crimes. CIC was rapidly transformed and corrupted after the end of the war with the rapid demobilization of troops and replacement of agents who fought the war with those less experienced.

Wev and Klaus soon became bitter enemies. Wev excluded Klaus from JIOA meetings, demanded he approve lists he had not seen and accused him of sabotaging the project. Wev's solution was to angrily demand that OMGUS rewrite the dossiers, deleting any negative information, but not before the situation turned into a crisis.[77] One of the dossiers Wev ordered altered concerned Heinrich Kliewe. Kliewe had been in charge of the human experimentation for Hitler's biological warfare program. Kliewe was a wanted war criminal who slipped over the border into the French sector to avoid arrest.

Hamilton Robinson, Director of the Office of Controls inside the State Department, was placed in charge of the Paperclip problem. Robertson had been a law associate when John Foster Dulles was a legal adviser for the State-War-Navy Coordinating Committee which originated Paperclip. Robinson immediately rejected five dossiers, demanding more information on the scientists' background. Samuel Cummings from the State Department added to the crisis by noting differences between Wev's dossiers and the documents held in the Berlin Document Center.

Besides falsifying the dossiers, the G2 branch of the military began a smear campaign against State Department employees who rejected Nazi scientists. Eventually, Robinson was hauled before a House subcommittee on charges he was sympathetic to communists. Republican Rep. Fred Busby from Illinois filed the charges. Although the House cleared Robinson, Busby would not relent, and carried his campaign against him and the State Department to the press. On March 27, 1948, two days after a blistering attack on him and the State Department, Robinson resigned. He was the last watchdog at the State Department. The McCarran rider, which allowed the Secretary of State to dismiss any employee judged a security risk, had already led to 11 dismissals.[78]

By the spring of 1948, the floodgates to Nazi immigration cranked open. Gen. Clay sounded his war message; Busby had successfully removed men like Klaus, Cummings and Robinson from the State Department. Many Nazi scientists were already in the United States, and Gehlen's network and Vlasov's army were both fully integrated into U.S. defense plans and intelligence. The following table lists the various programs and the year they were approved.

Program	Approved
Project Overcast	1945
Operation Paperclip	1946
Project National Interest	1947
Project Bloodstone	1948
Displaced Persons Act	1948
100 Person Act	1949
Lodge Act	1950
Project 63	1950

The eight programs were used to bring Nazis to the United States. A 1978 GAO study established the CIA had a clear working relationship with war criminals among émigré groups. In a sample of 111 war criminals, the study found 20 percent had worked as informants for intelligence and security agencies.[79] Under the Displaced Persons Act, a religious or charitable group could sponsor émigrés.[80] That's how Stanislaw Stankievich entered the United States after his file was sanitized. Stankievich was a war criminal and member of the Einsatzgruppe B who ordered the murders of more than 7,000 Jews in Borissow.[81] Once in the United States, these war criminals were then free to sponsor additional émigrés. By this method, the entire Belarus Nazi quisling government came to settle around Patterson, N.J.

Project Bloodstone began operations in 1948 under the State Department. Evasion of U.S. immigration laws barring Nazis from the United States appears to be its only reason for existence. It was the first crack in the floodgate allowing Nazis into the United States. It can also be thought of as the turning point from tactical, short term or even exploitative use of former Nazis and their quislings, to more long-term, strategic objectives. Bloodstone ended in 1950, and other programs under direct CIA control superseded it.

Bloodstone primarily recruited Nazi quislings and émigrés from Eastern Europe and the Soviet Union. Many of those admitted went on to become covert saboteurs and assassins for U.S. intelligence agencies. Bloodstone was the route into the United States not only for camp guards, but also for top echelon Nazi collaborators and leaders. Its primary sponsors were Frank Wisner and Robert Lovett. Wisner initially proposed that Bloodstone allow 250 persons into the United States, with 100 assigned to the Department of State to be engaged mostly in Voice of America, and 50 assigned to each military branch.[82]

On June 10, 1948, the State-Army-Navy-Air Force Coordinating Committee initially approved Bloodstone. A month later, the Joint Chiefs approved a second interlocking program, expanding Bloodstone to include covert warfare, sabotage and assassinations. The original plan was limited to filling intelligence gaps. In June 1948, the National Security Council delivered Truman's approval of NSC10/2, which authorized the types of clandestine operations and marked a turning point in U.S.-Soviet relations. In fact, a special subcommittee of Bloodstone was created to provide false identification, cover jobs and secret police protection to immigrants.[83]

Officials responsible for the program included: Tom Clark, Truman's Attorney General; W. Park Armstrong, Director of the State Department's Office of Intelligence and Research; and John S. Earman, the CIA observer on the Bloodstone operation. Earman in later years ended several of the CIA's clandestine operations involving mind control and drugs. More than 20 senior State Department officials concerned with the Soviet Union or Eastern Europe were on the administration team. Day-to-day management of operations fell to John P. Boyd, the No. 2 man at the INS, the Immigration and Naturalization Service. Robert C. Alexander was the second in command of the State Department's Visa Division. Evron M. Kirkpatrick, husband of Jeane Kirkpatrick, handled much of Bloodstone's crucial intelligence analysis. The Kirkpatricks are joint owners of Operations and Policy Research Inc., a firm that benefited from government contracts for studies on psychological warfare, defense policies and political behavior.

Another notable member of Bloodstone was Boris Pash. He gained fame during WWII heading up the Alsos missions capturing Nazi scientists. He later headed the CIA's PB/7 team, which was responsible for assassinations.

Bloodstone started rather humbly with a yearly limit of just 250 immigrants. But the CIA, and particularly Wisner, had much grander plans. By 1950, CIA representatives asked Congress for special approval to admit up to 15,000 more agency-sponsored refugees. Congress allowed only 500 in a three-year period. The CIA then expanded its authority under NSC 86, and NSCIDs 13 and 14 to use NSC authorization to indirectly sponsor many of the same émigrés. U.S.-based programs for refugees from various USSR provinces were eager to sponsor many of the same people Wisner wanted. A number of war criminals from Latvia, Lithuanian, Belarus and the Ukraine entered in this manner.[84] Many of the Bloodstone recruits included leaders, intelligence specialists and scholars who had put their skills to work for the Nazis.

"National Interest" began in the summer of 1947 under the control of JIOA, the Joint Intelligence Objectives Agency. It allowed anyone judged to be of national interest to immigrate, unlike Paperclip, which was restricted to German and Austrian scientists. National Interest operated on two levels, employing scientists and specialists in universities and at private companies, and it operated under a veil of secrecy. The military and CIA used it to bring intelligence sources and other assets to the United States. In 1948, these individuals were under the control of the Office of Policy Coordination, the CIA's covert dirty tricks branch.

One of the beneficiaries of National Interest was Otto Ambros, a former IG Farben director. He was convicted at Nuremberg for murder and slavery, but received an extraordinarily light sentence. As soon as John McCloy pardoned Ambros, Grace Chemicals hired him as a consultant.[85] He also worked as a U.S. military consultant conducting the same type of experiments that he carried out at IG Farben, the testing of nerve gas — this time using 7,000 American soldiers at Edgewood Arsenal as guinea pigs.[86]

The Hundred Person Act was originally passed as a means to control former war criminals. The visa was to be temporary so that, if the fascist refused to work according to the agreement, he could be deported easily. The act allowed the CIA to bring in 100 people a year. The Pentagon had a similar program. In at least one case, Wisner wanted to grant a Byelorussian Nazi permanent status under the Hundred Person Act, but his file in the National Archives had him labeled as a communist.[87] How the CIA defines "no derogatory information" is the heart of the matter. Recently, a CIA official defined it as no evidence of pro-communist activities. Nazis are regarded as anti-communist, so a Nazi background is not derogatory. The CIA and FBI also use narrow definitions of employees and agents to stymie investigators and researchers. The FBI distinguishes between informants and confidential sources, casual sources and volunteers. It refuses to even release the names of confidential sources to the Assistant Attorney General of the Criminal Bureau. Intelligence agencies also regularly change their filing systems. Once old file clerks retire, all memory of the old system is gone, and even the agency cannot find records. For instance, the CIA could not find the Gehlen collection until furnished with the cryptonym.[88]

The sole purpose of Project 63 was to deny the Soviets the use of German scientists. Immigrants under Project 63 were given $5,000 and temporary visas to enter the United States for six months to seek work while staying at the Alamac Hotel in New York City. Most found employment with universities or defense contractors. The net effect was the U.S. taxpayer paid to help former Nazis get jobs with such corporations as Lockheed and Martin Marietta, among others.[89] Surprisingly, there was little exposure of the war criminals in the late 1940s–50s. Some returning military personnel were incensed at finding war criminals working at U.S. military bases. Other groups, such as the Minnesota chapter of the American Chemical Society, were outraged that émigrés were given preference for jobs over its members.[90] The Air Force did not offer a single job to engineers laid off from North American Aviation. Instead, it sent six recruiters to Germany for 35 ex-Nazis.[91]

The German government complained that U.S. recruitment of German scientists was hurting its recovery. Project 63 found a large pool of untapped expertise in Austria, despite records as war criminals or memberships in the Communist Party. In fact, Project 63 recruiters were so unconcerned about the Nazi background of the recruits that they even tried to sign up convicted war criminals in prison. An example was the recruitment of Eduard Houdremont, who was serving time for war crimes. Houdremont was a top Krupp official convicted for slave labor, but he was on the "K" list — those with talents to be denied to the Soviets. The following quote is from a brief JIOA discussion about whether to offer Houdremont a contract:

"The point to consider is whether the newspaper publicity would be adverse if he were brought over," JIOA member Max Brokaw said.

"If the man is on the K list and he should be brought over, we should do it regardless of the publicity," replied JIOA Deputy Director James Skinner.[92]

Such was the widespread disregard for background checks. In another instance, Brokaw admitted the Austrians' backgrounds had not been checked. Included in that group of recruits was an individual being investigated by the FBI. Brokaw stated the plan was to bring them to the United States and later, if some were found inadmissible, they might have to be paid off to keep them quiet. Karl Blome was one who had to be bought off. He was a major general in the SA who engaged in medical experiments during the war.[93]

After an embarrassing incident with the assassination squads in Germany, U.S. intelligence and military leaders decided it would be best if the brightest and most promising were brought to the United States. Once admitted, they were to be incorporated into the Army and cooperate in CIA special missions.

In 1950, the Army lobbied Congress to pass the Lodge Act, which initially allowed 2,500 alien nationals living outside the U.S. to enlist in the Army with a guarantee of citizenship after five years of service. Later, Congress raised the limit to 12,500. Like all the other programs, the CIA chose to mix in Nazis, including former Gestapo agents. Ironically, Jews were mostly excluded from entering the United States in this manner. The Adjutant General Office branded them as one of the more politically unreliable groups, a reference to anyone not part of what could be considered the Right Wing. The first Lodge recruits were mostly Poles and Ukrainians who arrived in October 1951. About 25 percent of the recruits were channeled into confidential posts, such as biological, chemical or atomic warfare specialists. Others were used as translators and posted to the Defense Language School in Monterey, Calif. The remainder was sent to Fort Bragg, N.C., for special guerrilla training, becoming the nucleus of the Green Berets. This explains the Nazi-style racism prevalent among the early Green Berets. By 1952, only 211 out of 5,272 applicants passed the Army's screening tests. Special Forces recruiters then lowered the language and literacy requirements to admit more recruits.[94]

The CIA and military used the above programs as ratlines to covertly allow Nazi war criminals into the United States. Although President Truman specifically barred the entry of anyone with more than nominal connections to the Nazi Party, military and intelligence agencies promptly ignored him. In a 1985 article for the Union of Atomic Scientists, Linda Hunt found that files of more than 130 Paperclip subjects had been altered. Past Nazi connections that would have excluded them from entry into the United States were deleted.

Wernher von Braun and several other Nazi rocket scientists first entered the United States as POWs shortly after the war and before Operation Paperclip. They later were allowed to reenter the United States from Canada as Paperclip recruits to gain citizenship. The military governor in Germany considered von Braun a security threat. Security files on him show how they were altered.

In the original version from Sept. 18, 1947, Von Braun's report read, in part: "He was an SS officer but no information is available to indicate that he was an ardent Nazi. Subject is regarded as a potential security threat by the Military Governor. A complete background investigation could not be obtained because subject was evacuated from the Russian Zone of Germany."

Bosquet Wev, JIOA Director,sent a letter to the European Command director of intelligence, Dec. 4, 1947 that read as follows.
1. OMGUS security reports recently forwarded from your headquarters classify (14) specialists (including Herbert Axster and Wernher von Braun) as potential or actual threats to the security of the United States...
2...
3. There is very little possibility that the State and Justice Departments will agree to immigrate any specialist who has been classified as a potential or actual security threat to the United States. This may result in the return to Germany of specialists whose skill and knowledge should be denied other nations in the interest of national security...
4. It is requested that the cases of the specialists listed in paragraph one be reviewed and that new security reports be submitted where such action is deemed appropriate in view of the information submitted in this letter.

After recieving Wev's letter, the European Intelligence unit sanitized von Braun's record. Here is the Feb. 26, 1948 version of his report.

Further investigation of Subject is not feasible due to the fact that his former place of residence is in the Russian Zone where U.S. investigations are not possible. No derogatory information is available on the subject individual except NSDAP records, which indicate that he was a member of the Party from 1 May 1937 and was also a Major in the SS, which appears to have been an honorary commission. The extent of his Party participation cannot be determined in this Theater. Like the majority of members, he may have been a mere opportunist. Subject has been in the United States more than two years and if, within this period, his conduct has been exemplary and he has committed no acts adverse to the interests of the United States, it is the opinion of the Military Governor, OMGUS that he may not constitute a security threat.[95]

Arthur Rudolph, another of Hitler's rocket scientists, directed the Mittelwerk factory at the Dora-Nordhausen concentration camp in which more than 20,000 workers died of beatings, hangings and starvation. He was an active Nazi Party member from 1931. His military file listed him as "100 percent Nazi, dangerous type, security threat, suggest internment." Rudolph later directed development of the Saturn V rocket program. In 1984, he surrendered his U.S. citizenship after the Office of Special Investigations of the Department of Justice discovered his role in persecuting slave laborers at an underground V-2 missile factory.

More grievously, a number of Nazi doctors were admitted to the United States. Hermann Becker-Freysing, Siegfried Ruff, Konrad Schaefer and Kurt Blome were all defendants at Nuremberg. All four were charged with gruesome experiments on inmates at Dachau, Buchenwald and other concentration camps. Ruff conducted high-altitude experiments on prisoners in a low-pressure chamber in which more than 80 inmates died. Becker-Freysing and Schaefer conducted experiments on inmates in which all food and water was withheld, except for processed seawater. Becker-Freysing was found guilty and sentenced to 20 years in prison. Blome was charged with participation in euthanasia, extermination of Polish TB sufferers, biological warfare and other experiments. On Aug. 21, 1951, he signed a contract to work for the Army Chemical Corps under Project 63.

Heinrich Rupp was another Nazi allowed to immigrate to the United States under Paperclip. Rupp was convicted of bank fraud. He was an operative for the CIA and deeply involved in the Savings and Loan scandals. He also is believed to have taken part in the October Surprise, sabotaging President Carter's attempted rescue of the hostages in Iran.

However, most Nazi war criminals smuggled into the United States were not scientists. For instance, Hermine Braunsteiner Ryan immigrated to Canada in 1958, then married an American and moved to Queens, N.Y. In 1963, she became a naturalized citizen and, in 1964, was exposed as a former Nazi concentration guard. One witness at the 1974 trial described how she whipped an inmate to death at Majdanek. Ryan claimed she was a homemaker and wife of a tradesman who had a hard time making ends meet. Yet for almost a decade, she was able to afford the services of the Barry law firm, one of the most expensive and experienced, specializing in immigration. While funding sources are still unknown, other incidents of interference with the prosecution have come from the judicial system. The intelligence community appears to have been Ryan's benefactor.

The example of Ryan explains two points common to the deportation cases. The defendant received top-level help, most likely from intelligence agencies. Second, the cases invariably involved low-level officials or guards. The top echelon of the former Nazi quisling governments seemed immune from prosecution, even after being exposed.

The Vatican Ratline

The CIA and military were able to smuggle many Nazi war criminals into the U.S. under various programs, but not the most notorious. Yet the military and intelligence agencies still employed Nazis like Klaus Barbie in Europe, and aided their escape to South America through the Vatican ratline.

Evidence suggests the Vatican planned on aiding the Nazi war criminals as early as 1942. On Aug. 14, 1942, Juan Carlos Goyeneche and Adrian Escobar took a flight to Rome to meet with Pope Pius XII. Goyeneche was an envoy of Juan Peron. Escobar was Argentina's Ambassador to Spain and had collaborated extensively with the Nazis. Before the meeting with the Pope, both men traveled to France and Germany to meet with top Nazis and the French puppet state. In the long meeting with the Pope, Argentina's role as a peacemaker was discussed. Afterward, Escobar was ordered to the Vatican to reaffirm Argentina's willingness to mediate peace. The talks were extensive and included the Vatican's Secretary of State, Cardinal Luigi Maglione. They agreed that once peace was established, Argentina would apply its immigration laws generously. Both sides agreed that it was appropriate for the Vatican to take part in the search for peace.[96]

While this meeting discussed applying Argentina's immigration laws generously, there is no evidence that it included Nazis or war criminals. However, both the Vatican and Argentina were aligned favorably to the fascist cause and within three years, the Vatican operated an extensive ratline for war criminals leading directly to Argentina. In fact, the Vatican route was the only one for the Croatian Ustashi.

Dulles had contacts with the Vatican before the ratline. His first were in the surrender of Wolff, and smuggling Nazi gold out of Germany through the Vatican after the D-Day invasion. Two names figure prominently in setting up the Vatican ratlines: Bishop Hudal and James Angleton. Dulles' contacts with the Vatican were mainly through the father-son team of Hugh and James Angleton. The truth behind the CIA-Nazi connection has remained buried through the efforts of such men as Allen Dulles and George H. W. Bush. As CIA director, Bush allowed James Angleton to access his own files, which he quickly destroyed. The Dulles-Angleton cover-up masked various Western financial transactions and negotiations with the Nazis during the war and helped shift postwar U.S. policy.

Hugh Angleton was a longtime business agent for Allen Dulles. The elder Angleton lived in Italy before the war broke out. He was a powerful financial broker and the European representative of National Cash Register (NCR). A former member of Sullivan & Cromwell also sat on the NCR board. Long before the war, Hugh Angleton made all the connections with the Italian fascists and the Right Wing in the State Department. He had a far-flung espionage network in Europe, but there is no evidence that it aided the U.S. before the war, nor that he was an unofficial spy for the United States, as his son claims.[97]

Some evidence suggests that Hugh Angleton acted as courier for secret financial transactions between the Vatican and Nazi Germany. At least one ex-CIA agent claims the elder Angleton personally arranged to transport Nazi gold from Germany to Italy. The younger Angleton has successfully blocked every investigation into the Dulles-Angleton smuggling system.[98]

At the end of the war, after President Truman ordered the OSS disbanded, agents simply changed uniforms and became part of the War Department's Strategic Services Unit. The OSS always had two factions. The liberal faction consisted of dedicated men who followed orders by Roosevelt and Truman. The other faction consisted of Dulles and his followers who were waiting for Dewey to be elected. By the war's end, the split between the factions was pronounced.

It was no accident that much of the gold disappeared that was recovered in Region IV in Bavaria, the area around Munich, which became a center for drug trade and smuggling. The Army's CIC agents in that area were Dulles allies and were quietly helping him recruit ex-Nazis and hide them in the region, technically an act of mutiny. For Nazi war criminals wishing to flee Europe to avoid prosecution, it was just a short trip across Austria to Italy and the waiting Vatican ratline. Many began their flight from Europe in the Munich area.

One of the first war criminals rescued by the Vatican ratline was Walter Rauff. Pius XII was extremely concerned that Italy's major industrial region would be destroyed in the Allied offensive. The Vatican eased the way for negotiations between Dulles and Rauff. With Rauff's help, Nazi commanders began a series of secret surrender negotiations with Allen Dulles in March 1945, code-named Operation Sunrise or Operation Crossword. The German army in Italy actually surrendered on April 29, 1945. The Americans arrested Rauff and within hours, a priest arrived and arranged for him to be transferred to an army hospital. Monsignor Don Giuseppe arranged Rauff's release. The monsignor also was one of the intermediaries in the surrender of German forces.[99]

Rauff was released to S Force, an OSS unit working with the British-American Special Counter Intelligence team in Italy, headed by James Angleton. Rauff was deemed a valuable asset by this OSS team, despite the Army CIC's objections that he was an unrepentant Nazi who should be imprisoned for life, if not eliminated. After extensive debriefing, Rauff was released by the OSS unit.[100] According to the French publication *Cercle Noir*, after his release Rauff contacted Archbishop Siri of Genoa and immediately went to work establishing the Vatican ratline. Rauff's contribution to Hudal's ratline may have been more financial. Rauff became a money launderer with the help of Frederico Schwend, an SS counterfeiter. Forged notes provided seed money for the ratline.

Bishop Hudal's first contact with a senior Nazi was probably his meeting with Franz von Papen on his arrival to negotiate the 1933 Concordat between Berlin and the Vatican. In 1936, Hudal published a philosophical treatise, *Foundations of National Socialism.* His pro-Nazi views were well known by then, but they did not hinder his career in the Vatican. Hudal seems to have enjoyed a close relationship with both Pius XI and Pius XII. In 1943, Hudal met Walter Rauff. By then, Rauff was a major war criminal. He had overseen development of the mobile gas vans used on the Eastern Front to kill more than 100,000 people. Rauff and Hudal became close friends. After the Allied invasion of Sicily, Bishop Hudal changed the Greater German flag on his car to the Austrian. There is no doubt of Hudal's aid to Nazi war criminals, as an excerpt from his *Römische Tagebücher (Roman Diaries)* reveals:

The Allies' war against Germany was not a crusade but the rivalry of economic complexes for whose victory they had been fighting. This so-called business ... used catchwords like democracy, race, religious liberty and Christianity as bait for the masses. All these experiences were the reason why I felt duty bound after 1945 to devote my whole charitable work mainly to former National Socialist and Fascists, especially to the so-called war criminals.[101]

From the fragments of information now available, it appears the Vatican was much more supportive of the Nazis than previously believed. Evidence of monetary backing of Hitler before his rise to power, and the 1942 plea to the Argentina ambassador and envoy to be generous with immigration once the war was over, all suggest deep support. There is also evidence the Vatican was aiding Hudal's smuggling of Nazi war criminals. In August 1944, Vatican Secretary of State Giovanni Montini (later Pope Paul VI) took up the question of extending the Vatican's charity mission to German prisoners. For a couple weeks, Americans and the British debated the Pope's request, delivered by Montini, before granting it. Within a few days, the Vatican requested that Bishop Hudal be allowed to visit German civilian internees. Hudal's pro-Nazi views were well known to American intelligence. Although Allied headquarters previously refused some Vatican requests, it granted the necessary permits for this one. Free to travel and visit prison camps, Hudal was able to spread word of his ratline.

James Angleton ensured the close cooperation of the Vatican by endearing himself to Montini. He informed Montini that one of the Vatican code clerks had been suborned by the Soviets. Angleton followed up with many acts of kindness, cultivating a close friendship with Montini.

In 1947, the Vatican was promised continuing financial aid from America to defeat the Communist Party in the 1948 election. The U.S. provided more than $350 million in civilian and military aid. In 1947, the CIA withdrew about $10 million from recovered Nazi gold laundered through a maze of bank accounts. The funds were delivered clandestinely to the Christian Democrats, often through Vatican channels.[102] Some of this money found its way to Monsignor Bicchierai, who used it to fund an underground squad of anti-communist hoodlums. Members of the squad beat leftist candidates, broke up their political meetings and rallies, and intimidated voters leaning to the Left, while the CIA sponsored well-known Italian-Americans to broadcast propaganda warnings against the communist menace.

Continued worries about popular support for the Communist Party in Italy spurred the CIA to launch Operation Gladio in the early 1950s. The Gladio network was operated by the secret services and initially funded by the CIA, which trained 622 recruits. Eventually, the network is believed to have gained as many as 15,000 members. Closely associated with the Gladio network is the secret Masonic lodge "Propaganda Due" (P2), headed by Licio Gelli. During the war, Gelli was a member of Mussolini's notorious Black Shirts, and later acted as liaison officer to the Hermann Goering SS division. By 1974, P2 had more than 1,000 members, a "who's who" of Italian political, military and economic power.

In 1974, Prime Minister Aldo Moro met with Secretary of State Henry Kissinger. Moro wished to reach an accommodation with the Communist Party in Italy, offering its leaders cabinet rank in a new centrist ruling party. Although Kissinger warned Moro that the idea was dangerous, he continued a left-centrist policy. In 1978, Moro was kidnapped and murdered, allegedly by the Red Brigades. However, evidence now exists that Moro's murder was orchestrated by P2, and that both the Red and Black brigades were heavily penetrated and run by U.S. intelligence.

In the fall of 1947, Ferenc Vajta was arrested trying to enter the United States. Vajta was a Hungarian war criminal working with Britain, France and America after the war. Truman demanded an investigation into who was smuggling Nazis into the United States. The historical record indicates that Truman was not in the know that war criminals were being smuggled in by falsified documents.[103]

Vajta's arrest and the following investigation presented Allen Dulles with a problem. He had plenty of ex-Nazis piling up in Austria and southern Germany. The number of ex-Nazis presented a security threat, as well as a source of embarrassment. He was forced to make a deal with the Vatican to move his ex-Nazis out of the area. Proof of a deal comes from an American agent, Paul Lyon, who later wrote the history of the Italian ratline for Maj. James Milano, the American officer who coordinated the operations of the ratline. Excerpts of Lyon's account follow:

I. ORIGINS

a. During the summer of 1947 the undersigned received instructions from G2 (army intelligence), USFA ... to establish a means of disposition for visitors who had been in the custody of the 430th CIC.

b. The undersigned, therefore, proceeded to Rome where, through a mutual acquaintance, he conferred with a former Slovakian diplomat (Kirschbaum, Sidor and Durcansky were all in Rome at that time) who in turn was able to recruit the services of a Croatian Roman Catholic Priest, Father Draganovich ... (who) ... had by this time developed several clandestine evacuation channels to the various South American countries for various types of European refugees.

Draganovich is known and recorded as a Fascist, war criminal, etc. ... and his contacts with South American diplomats of a similar class are not generally approved by U.S. State Department officials, plus the fact that in the light of security, it is better that we may be able to state, if forced, that the turning over of a DP to a (National Catholic) Welfare Organization falls in line with our democratic way of thinking and that we are not engaged in illegal disposition of war criminals, defectees and the like.

Through the Vatican connections of Father Draganovic, Croat, DP Resettlement Chief of the Vatican Circle, a tentative agreement was reached to assist in this operation. The agreement consists of simply mutual assistance, i.e. these agents assist persons of interest to Father Draganovic to leave Germany and, in turn, Father Draganovic will assist these agents in obtaining the necessary visas to Argentina, South America, for persons of interest to this Command... It may be stated that some of the persons of interest to Father Draganovic may be of interest to the Denazification policy of the Allies; however, the persons assisted by Father Draganovic are also of interest to our Russian ally. Therefore this operation cannot receive any official approval and must be handled with minimum amount of delay and with a minimum amount of general knowledge.[104]

Recently, an Oct. 21, 1946 Treasury Department memo surfaced linking the Vatican directly with hiding Nazi gold. The memo quotes a reliable source in Italy confirming the Vatican was safeguarding roughly 200 million Swiss Francs for the Nazis. Presumably, this gold was from the Nazi quislings, the Ustashi.[105] This recent memo suggests the agreement between Dulles and the Vatican was more extensive than previously believed. However, James Angleton jealously guarded his contact with the Vatican, going so far as refusing to identify him. Once Dulles cemented the Vatican deal, the worst of the Nazis began moving down the line to Italy and thence to South America. More than 30,000 war criminals escaped from Europe — and justice — in this manner, including some of the most notorious war criminals, such as Barbie, Mengele, Eichmann and Bormann.

A declassified top secret memo proves CIC arranged Barbie's flight to Argentina. The memo from the 430th CIC informs the State Department of the informant's real name and "shipping name." The State Department then notified the receiving country to expect his arrival.[106] Once these war criminals were reestablished in South America, many of them offered their services as military advisers or intelligence officers to some of most repressive regimes in South America. Barbie helped Bolivian dictator Banzer hang on to power by forming a mercenary army of neofascist terrorists. A Nazi colony in Chile known as Colonia Dignidad played a pivotal role in Pinochet's coup in Chile, as well as in Operation Condor, launched by Pinochet to eliminate leftists. Many other ex-Nazis also were engaged in military, intelligence or police training, torture, and the drug trade.

While Nazi war criminals had exerted considerable influence in South America, their counterparts admitted to the United States had even more, extending far beyond the space program, to shaping U.S. foreign and domestic policies, and Allen Dulles and Richard Nixon influencing elections. The use of Nazi scientists and their research has led to many abuses in medicine.

The CIA and Propaganda Corrupting Our News Media

Many of the Nazi war criminals and collaborators recruited by Project Bloodstone were placed in Radio Free Europe and Radio Liberty. Both programs were CIA fronts for psychological warfare. The seed money for the National Committee for a Free Europe came from the same pool of recovered Nazi gold used to finance clandestine operations during the Italian elections. Frank Wisner received at least $2 million of recovered Nazi loot, which he then funneled into the accounts of the National Committee for a Free Europe. Other aid, such as printing presses, radio transmitters and equipment, came from the Italian election campaign.[107]

Allen Dulles and Wisner stacked the Committee's board of directors with prominent Americans. Some early corporate notables were Peter Grace of Grace Chemical and National City Bank; H.J. Heinz of the Mellon Bank and Heinz ketchup fame; Henry Ford II; and Texas oilman George McGhee. From the beginning, the National Committee for a Free Europe depended on the silence of the media and funding from the CIA to cloak its true mission. Early members of the National Committee for a Free Europe from the media included Sig Mickelson, the first president of CBS News; Henry Luce of *Time-Life*; DeWitt Wallace of *Reader's Digest;* and C.D. Jackson of *Fortune* magazine.[108]

The net effect of this arrangement was to create a powerful lobby inside the national media that suppressed news about the propaganda operations of the CIA. The media not only blacked out CIA propaganda activities. They falsified reporting of the CIA's role in Radio Free Europe and Radio Liberty for years, leading the public to believe these operations were financed by nickel-and-dime contributions from the public. Ronald Reagan was featured in many of the fundraising ads for these programs.

By 1953, James Burnham, a psychological warfare consultant for the CIA's Operations and Policy Coordination Office, estimated the United States was spending more than $1 billion annually on various propaganda projects. To place this figure in proper context, the average hourly wage of a factory worker in 1953 was $1.75. The gross national product in 1952 was $346.1 billion, while the federal budget was $74.6 billion.[109] As a measure of the importance attached to these clandestine CIA propaganda projects, the government was spending nearly 2 percent of its annual budget on them – or 200 times the $5 million spent in the combined Truman-Dewey presidential election campaign of 1948.

While broadcasts by Radio Free Europe and Radio Liberty often included praises of Thomas Jefferson, Abraham Lincoln and other American leaders, as well as leaders of Eastern Europe, they often contained material created by the Nazis. At other times, Radio Free Europe featured Nazi collaborators and even war criminals. One of the most successful reports ever aired by Radio Free Europe was created by the Nazi intelligence service. The report referred to the "Document on Terror." The document, which falsely claimed to be a translation of a captured Soviet directive, urged the use of terror against civilians. It included sections on general terror, such as shootings and hangings, and sections on creating the psychosis of white fear or the use of agent provocateurs and other covert operations. The "Document on Terror" soon became a staple in anti-communist propaganda, becoming a widely cited source. It was recycled numerous times in *Reader's Digest* and appeared in countless newspapers.

Paul Blackstock, a noted psychological warfare expert, traced the origin of the section on disintegrating operations to a Nazi manual used for indoctrinating eastern European collaborators and troops, including the Ukrainian Waffen SS.[110] The manual was recovered from the body of a dead Nazi.

The propaganda efforts by Project Bloodstone encroaching on the American media should have triggered alarm bells, because the CIA charter restricted it to foreign operations. But the Nazi alliance inside America, driven by Prescott Bush, Averell Harriman, John Foster and Allen Dulles, wanted the government's secret services to conduct extensive propaganda campaigns and mass psychology experiments in the United States, and paramilitary campaigns abroad.

In the late 1940s, what began as voluntary cooperation between media agents and the CIA soon grew into a new CIA project. Headed by Frank Wisner, Allen Dulles, Richard Helms and Philip Graham (publisher of the *Washington Post* and a graduate of the Army Intelligence School in Harrisburg, Pa.), Project Mockingbird began buying influence behind the scenes at major media outlets and putting reporters on the CIA payroll. The CIA soon was recruiting news organizations and journalists to become spies and disseminators of propaganda. Media assets soon included all the major news sources, such as ABC, NBC, CBS, *Time, Newsweek*, the Associated Press, United Press International, Reuters, Hearst Newspapers, Scripps-Howard and Copley News Service.

In 1953, Joseph Alsop, then one of America's leading syndicated columnists, was sent to the Philippines by the CIA. Under the cover of a reporter writing about the election, Alsop was to corrupt it and ensure the winner would be Washington's favorite. He was one of more than 400 journalists who, in the past 25 years, have secretly carried out CIA assignments. In the 1950s, the CIA even operated a formal journalist school for its agents. Once trained, they were placed in major news organizations, often with the help and knowledge of media management. These trained agents acting as journalists are not counted in the 400 journalists who have worked on behalf of the CIA.

The media is riddled with close ties to the CIA. William Paley, a wartime colonel, founded CBS. Paley hired CIA agents to work undercover at the bidding of his close friend, Allen Dulles. Sig Mickelson, the first president of CBS News, served as Paley's go-between with Dulles. Joseph Ream, a former Wall Street lawyer and former deputy director of the D/DIRNSA Office of the National Security Agency (NSA), became an executive vice president at CBS on leaving NSA.[111]

William Casey, Reagan's director of the CIA, made a fortune investing in Capitol Cities Broadcasting Corp.[112]

The propaganda associated with Bloodstone and Mockingbird often portrayed the defectors from the Baltic States and Eastern Europe as tragic freedom fighters who chose to fight communism and Stalin by joining the Nazis. To some extent this was true, but it was no excuse for committing war crimes. Often these Nazi quislings were more brutal than the SS and Gestapo. Units from the Baltic States and the Ukraine committed some of the worst atrocities and war crimes in carrying out the final solution on the Eastern Front, leaving their German advisors in disbelief over their brutality.

An excellent example of the collaboration of the press associated with Project Bloodstone and Mockingbird can be found in coverage by *Life* magazine, written by Wallace Carroll. "… the Germans had millions of eager accomplices in Russia... There was no Partisan movement in their area, no sabotage, and the peasants fulfilled the German requisitions of farm products on schedule." The Nazi collaborators from Eastern Europe were extremely brutal and are associated with many of the massacres on the Eastern front, and these facts were known for a long time to Russian experts of the State Department and to a few American officers. Carroll claimed that Soviet propagandists shrewdly attributed atrocities to Vlasov's forces, as well as the numerous pro-Nazi and anti-Semitic periodicals published during the war, which were supposedly forged by the Soviets. Carroll's conclusion was, in part, that America needed to embrace the former Nazi collaborators as a central tactic in a comprehensive strategy of political warfare against the Soviets.[113]

In addition to the massive propaganda effort, the CIA launched Operation Shamrock. As early as March 1946, Eisenhower was aware of this project, which involved cooperation by the three major cable corporations to facilitate the review of all messages into and out of the United States.[114] Eventually, Shamrock evolved into a much larger eavesdropping operation, including domestic spying on SDS and other leftist elements, as well as drug dealers. With the advent of the Internet, Shamrock evolved again into a global CIA operation called Echelon to read emails. The FBI launched a parallel operation called Carnivore.

Coinciding with Project Mockingbird propaganda was a drive to fluoridate municipal water supplies. The first proposal came in 1939 from Gerald J. Cox, an Alcoa chemist. The aluminum industry produces tons of sodium fluoride as a waste product in processing ore. In 1945, two Michigan cities were chosen to take part in a 15-year comparison study to decide whether fluoride was effective in fighting children's cavities. By 1946, six more cities were permitted to fluoridate their water, and in 1947, 87 more. The Michigan study was abandoned before it was half finished because the government cited popular demand for fluoridation. The latest tests suggest fluoridation is of little value in reducing cavities.

There is a more sinister side to fluoridation. At the end of WWII, Charles Eliot Perkins, a research worker in chemistry, was sent to Germany to take charge of the vast IG Farben chemical plants. While there, he learned about a scheme by IG Farben scientists during the war and adopted by the German general staff. Water supplies in certain areas were medicated with sodium fluoride to control the people. Repeated doses in minute amounts over time can reduce an individual's power to resist domination by slowly poisoning and narcotizing a certain area of the brain, making the person submissive and easy to control. The Nazis used fluoridation in the concentration camps.

Maj. George Racey Jordan independently confirmed Perkins' findings on fluoride in Germany. Jordan, stationed at Great Falls, Mont., was in charge of overseeing the Lend-Lease shipments of sodium fluoride to Russia. When he asked his Russian counterpart what the shipments were for, he was told bluntly that it was added to drinking water in the prisoner of war camps to take away their will to resist.

Until 1945, the U.S. Public Health Service (USPHS) resisted fluoridation. Then in 1945, Oscar Ewing took over as administrator. Ewing came from a job with a much higher salary as an attorney for Alcoa.

Was fluoridation part of the Mockingbird project to ease the acceptance of the propaganda and the repression that followed in McCarthyism? The suspicions and the evidence against flouride continue to accumulate.

The extent of CIA corruption began to surface in the aftermath of Watergate. On Dec. 22, 1974, Seymour Hersh published a front-page article in the *New York Times,* "Huge CIA Operation Reported in U.S. Against Anti-War Forces." The report shocked the Ford administration. In an attempt at damage control, President Ford appointed a blue ribbon panel known as the Rockefeller Committee that included Nelson Rockefeller, John Connor, C. Douglas Dillon, Erwin Griswold, Lane Kirkland, Lyman Lemnitzer, Ronald Reagan and Edgar Shannon.

A look at the members' backgrounds shows the investigation was intended to be a whitewash. During WWII, Nelson Rockefeller headed the intelligence unit for South America, while Rockefeller-controlled companies continued to supply the Nazis. C. Douglas Dillon arranged for one of the largest bond offerings for Nazi Germany. John Connor joined Cravath Swaine & Moore in 1914. Paul D. Cravath, one of the founders, also founded the Council on Foreign Relations. In 1924, John McCloy joined the firm. During World War II, Connor was a general counsel at the Office of Scientific Research before becoming a Marine combat intelligence officer. Later, he became a special assistant to Navy Secretary James V. Forrestal, where he assisted with legislation creating the National Security Act in 1947. Connors helped create the Defense Department and the CIA. Gen. Lemnitzer was a planner for Operation Northwoods. Reagan's behavior on the commission can be taken as a proxy for the seriousness of the general investigation. He left the first meeting early and managed to miss three of the next four. In fact, he was so busy stumping that he only visited the headquarters once in the first month.

While the Rockefeller Committee was a whitewash, Congress established the Church Committee in the Senate and the Pike Committee in the House. Both committees worked diligently to uncover CIA corruption with help from Director William Colby and to the dismay of the Ford White House. By summer, the Ford administration was already planning what became known as the Halloween Massacre. A memo from Donald Rumsfeld to Ford dated July 10, 1975 outlines the possible choices for replacing

Colby at the CIA. The choices listed came from a poll conducted by Dick Cheney. Henry Kissinger suggested C. Douglas Dillon, Howard Baker, Galvin and Robert Roosa. Cheney proposed Robert Bork, followed by George H. W. Bush and Lee Iacocca. Rumsfeld proposed Bork, Dillon, Iacocca, Stanley Resor and Walter Wriston. On Nov. 2, 1975, Ford fired Colby.

Further information about the CIA's role in Greece came with the assassination of Richard Welch, the CIA chief in Athens, on Christmas day 1975. Welch had been identified as an agent in the Greek news. The "Committee of Greeks and Greek Americans to Prevent Their Country, Their Fatherland, from Being Perverted to the Uses of the CIA" denounced the agency's role in installing the reactionary Greek government.[115]

The CIA supported the revolt of the colonels in 1967 because of their strong anti-communist stance. The resulting vicious military junta was strongly embraced and aided by the Nixon administration, with Tom Pappas acting as middleman. Pappas, whose name surfaced several times during the Watergate scandal, played a part in the original fundraising scams of the Nixon gang. The Nixon tapes show Pappas provided the crucial cash to buy the silence of E. Howard Hunt and the other break-in artists. Moreover, Pappas donated $549,000 to Nixon's 1968 presidential campaign. The money came from KYP, the Greek intelligence service, which at the time was a wholly subsidized arm of the CIA. The donations broke two U.S. laws, prohibiting use of campaign funds from foreign countries and CIA use of funds in American elections.

The Nixon tapes reveal that on March 2, Haldeman told Nixon that White House counsel John Dean and Attorney General John Mitchell were getting money for the burglars from Pappas. Pappas had the great advantage of dealing in cash and, in return, he wanted to keep U.S. Ambassador Henry Tasca in Athens.

George H. W. Bush's appointment as CIA director was greeted with much misgiving. References were made to Bush's receipt of financial largesse from Nixon's Townhouse Fund and related operations. The Townhouse Fund was another of Nixon's slush funds that gave about $100,000 to Bush's losing Senate race in 1970. Bush also was deeply entangled in the Watergate scandal. However, the network established by his father Prescott Bush prevailed in securing his nomination and confirmation as CIA Director. When Sen. Church was asked about Bush's nomination, he responded in anger: "There is no question in my mind but that concealment is the new order of the day... Hiding evil is the trademark of a totalitarian government."

One of those who helped Bush secure confirmation was none other than Leon Jaworski, the former Watergate special prosecutor. Jaworski was part of the old Brown Brothers Harriman – Skull and Bones network.

On Feb. 12, Bush claimed to have removed all full-time or part-time news correspondents accredited by any U.S. news service, newspaper, periodicals, radio or TV network or station from the CIA payroll. He also claimed that there were no clergy or missionaries on the payroll. In April, the Senate Select Committee on Intelligence Activities announced that it already caught Bush lying because at least 25 journalists and reporters were still on the payroll, and the CIA was determined to keep them there. Shortly after, President Ford announced Executive Order 11905 authorizing the CIA to conduct foreign counterintelligence activities in the United States, which opened the door to many things.

The Bush-Kissinger-Ford counteroffensive against the Congressional committees began immediately. On March 5, the CIA leaked the story that the Pike Committee had lost more than 232 secret documents, which had been turned over from files of the executive branch. Anyone opposing them or investigating CIA misdeeds was held up for ridicule and branded a traitor. The CIA's dirty secrets were safe under Bush's directorship.

While Bush maintained an amiable exterior, his vicious character soon showed through. All congressional probes into the dark secrets of the CIA had to be stopped. Using Don Gregg, the CIA station chief in Seoul, Bush leaked to the press stories of Democratic congressmen receiving payments from Korea's CIA agent, Tongsun Park. This is the same Don Gregg who later served as Bush's national security adviser during his second vice presidential term, and who managed decisive parts of the Iran-Contra operations. By hyping the reports, the scandal was soon overblown. By leaking information about Koreagate which ended the careers of several members of congress, Poppy Bush was able to terrorize Congress into halting any further investigations of the CIA.

Another aid to the CIA and the Bush family has been the Smith Richardson Foundation. The foundation provided Bush with aid for the Iran-Contra scandal and during the 1950s, took an active part in psychological warfare. In the 1950s, the Richardson Foundation helped finance experiments at Bridgewater Hospital in Massachusetts, the center of some of the most brutal MK-ULTRA tortures. The foundation was established at the urging of Prescott Bush after he received a letter from Connecticut resident H. Smith Richardson, owner of Vick Chemical Co., the maker of Lifesavers candy and Vicks cough remedy. Richardson sought out Prescott's views on the foundation, which has served as a slush fund for the Bush family since then.

The Bush family knew Richardson and his wife through their mutual friendship with Sears Roebuck Chairman Gen. Robert E. Wood, leader of the America First Committee. H. Smith Richardson contributed start-up money for America First and spoke out against the United States joining the communists by fighting Hitler. Richardson's wife was a proud relative of Nancy Langehorne from Virginia, who married Lord Astor and backed the Nazis from their Cliveden Estate. Eugene Stetson Jr., Richardson's son-in-law, organized the H. Smith Richardson Foundation. Stetson was a member of the Skull and Bones secret society at Yale and worked under Prescott Bush at Brown Brothers Harriman.[116]

Besides silencing Congress, Bush also took steps to silence former agents. As CIA Director, he set up the Publications Review Board, the first peacetime government censor. The Review Board gave the CIA the power to censor all speeches and writings of former agents, as well as approve all books by them.

In the aftermath of Watergate, Congress began a series of investigations of Nazi war criminals living in the United States. Congresswomen Elizabeth Holtzman was one of those leading the investigations. Among some of the more startling facts she uncovered was that Paperclip did not end in the late 1940s as the public was led to believe; in fact, it terminated only a year or two before the 1974 start of her investigations. She also uncovered that the Displaced Persons Act barred Nazis before 1953, but a change in the law that year allowed convicted war criminals to immigrate. Holtzman proposed an amendment to close that loophole. She also lobbied hard to establish the Office of Special Investigations, the Nazi hunters in the Justice Department,[117] which was opposed by George H. W. Bush.

It was not until 1982 that the CIA openly admitted that reporters on its payroll acted as case officers to agents in the field.

As the Bush-Harriman-Dulles-Nazi alliance gained power in the postwar period, in 1951 President Truman signed the directive creating the Psychological Strategy Board. The board was established to authorize and provide for the more effective planning, coordinating and conducting of psychological operations within the framework of approved national policies. The first director of the board was Gordon Gray, a broadcast and publication media specialist. Gray was instrumental in keeping the electorate uninformed. He previously was in charge of sterilizing children in North Carolina and was a member of the Eugenic Society. Gray was a close associate of Prescott Bush. Henry Kissinger was Gray's consultant, as well as the paid political consultant to the Rockefeller family. Eisenhower signed Presidential Executive Order 10483, replacing the Psychological Strategy Board with the Operations Coordinating Board. On Feb. 19, 1961, President John F. Kennedy issued a statement abolishing the Operations Coordinating Board.

Mind Control

The Bush-Harriman-Dulles alliance went beyond propaganda into horrifying experiments in mind control. The experiments started almost simultaneously with Mockingbird and Bloodstone.

During the war, the Allies captured documents on Nazi experiments using mescaline and other psychedelics on inmates of Dachau in the search for a truth serum. Mescaline caused some people to tell their innermost secrets, but even when combined with hypnosis, the drug never gained the Nazis' confidence as a mind control drug. At the same time, the OSS conducted research on marijuana as a truth serum. Dr. Hubertus Strughold oversaw the Dachau experiments that included barbaric high-altitude tests on inmates. Strughold was brought to the United States in Operation Paperclip and became America's father of space medicine. His use of mind-altering drugs on inmates provided the foundation for CIA research into truth serums and mind control.

The U.S. Navy began some of the first experiments on mind control in 1947. The first known participation by the CIA was in 1950 with the launch of Project Bluebird. In 1953, the CIA placed its mind control under Project MK-ULTRA, an umbrella operation involving 149 subprojects. The MK prefix refers to projects sponsored by the CIA's Technical Service Division. MK-ULTRA grew to involve 185 nongovernment researchers and assistants working for 80 institutions under the direction of Allen Dulles. These institutions included 44 colleges or universities, 15 research foundations or chemical or pharmaceutical companies, 12 hospitals or clinics, and three penal institutions.

The use of Nazi doctors in MK-ULTRA is readily evident from the high correlation between the subprojects and Nazi research from the concentration camps. Various approaches used to control human behavior under MK-ULTRA included radiation, electroshock, psychology, psychiatry, sociology, anthropology, graphology, harassment substances, paramilitary devices and drugs. Project MONARCH appears to be the most prominent and hideous subproject of MK-ULTRA. Officially, the U.S. Army started MONARCH in the early 1960s. However, the project appears to have been implemented much earlier. A brief list of some of the known mind control projects:

CHAPTER: A Navy program started in 1947 that involved drug experiments.

CHATTER: A Navy program, 1950–53, in a search for a truth serum using barbiturates, amphetamines and heroin. The Bureau of Narcotics and pharmaceutical companies supplied the drugs.

BLUEBIRD: CIA Director Roscoe Hillenkoetter approved the project in 1950. Unvouchered funds paid for its sensitive areas. This began the CIA's first structured behavioral control program.

ARTICHOKE: In 1951, Project BLUEBIRD was renamed ARTICHOKE. The CIA approved a liaison with the Army and Navy to find a truth drug. Another liaison was formed with the Air Force to study interrogation techniques. Information also was exchanged with the Canadian and British governments.

CASTIGATE: A joint project by the CIA and Navy that tested a "secret potion" of a depressant, a stimulant and the active ingredient in marijuana, THC. The tests were conducted in Germany in a three-day period.

MK-NAOMI: This project that began in the 1950s was terminated, at least with respect to biological projects, in 1969, in agreement with the Special Operations Division of the Army's biological research center at Fort Detrick, Md. SOD's job was to produce germ weapons for the CIA. Its purpose was to stockpile severely incapacitating and lethal materials, and to develop gadgetry for disseminating these materials.

MK-ULTRA: Established by the CIA in 1953 as an umbrella project for the covert use of biological and chemical weapons, MK-ULTRA focused on drugs, specifically LSD.

MK-DELTA: MK-DELTA became the operational side of MK-ULTRA. MK-DELTA and MK-NAOMI already were set up before the CIA was given official permission for MK-ULTRA.

MK-SEARCH: In 1964, MK-SEARCH became a successor for portions of MK-ULTRA. Many subprojects stayed under MK-ULTRA, while the most sensitive behavioral experiments went to MK-SEARCH. These experiments were conducted on prisoners, terminal cancer patients and people described as mental "defectives." MK-SEARCH continued into the early 1970s, with more experiments performed under the Office of Research and Development. Some of these experiments consisted of implanting electrodes into the brains of cats, dogs and reptiles, and controlling the animals remotely. The following agencies were involved in behavior modification and behavioral research projects: the Defense Department; the Department of Labor; National Science Foundation; Veterans Administration; the Department of Health, Education and Welfare; National Institute of Mental Health; the Law Enforcement Assistance Administration (under the Department of Justice). All the agencies were named in secret CIA documents as providing research "cover" for MK-ULTRA.

OFTEN/CHICKWIT: A joint project between the Army Chemical Corps and the CIA's Office of Research and Development to create new drug compounds that could be used offensively. The project started in 1967 or 1968. Hallucinogens were tested on inmates in Pennsylvania.

DERBY HAT/THIRD CHANCE: The Army Assistant Chief of Staff for Intelligence (ACSI) authorized field testing of LSD in Europe and the Far East. Testing of the European population was code named Project THIRD CHANCE; testing of the Asian population was code named Project DERBY HAT.

STARGATE: Investigated the use of ESP, paranormal, remote viewing military uses of telekinesis-type research. The start date is uncertain, but it ended in 1984

MONARCH: Under MK-ULTRA, Project Monarch used trauma-based mind control.[118]

While mind control projects began steadily after WWII, it was not until the Korean War that they advanced rapidly. The first breakthrough came on September 1950 when the *Miami News* published an article by Edward Hunter, "Brain-Washing Tactics Force Chinese into Ranks of Communist Party." Hunter, a CIA contract employee operating undercover as a journalist and, later, a prominent member of the John Birch Society, had been an OSS agent in Asia. He was the first person to use the term brainwashing in print.

The military and CIA were concerned about the large number of captured Americans who signed confessions for the North Koreans. By the end of the Korean War, 70 percent of the 7,190 U.S. prisoners held in China had either made confessions or signed petitions calling for an end to the American war in Asia. Often, they accused the United States of using germ warfare in Korea, which it now appears was true.

Hunter turned out a steady stream of articles and books on brainwashing, inciting the fears of the public. The notion of a "mind-control gap" was as much of a myth as the later bomber and missile "gaps." However, the furor over mind control took on a momentum of its own. The resulting public frenzy provided cover for the CIA mind control programs in an attempt to "catch up" with the Soviets and Chinese. Ten years after the Korean War, CIA Deputy Director Richard Helms admitted the Soviet mind control research was years behind American efforts. The brainwashing scare was a propaganda effort by the CIA so it could start its mind control research.

Almost all sources of information covering the CIA's mind control programs contain errors. This is understandable, considering many of the surviving documents remain classified. In 1973, Richard Helms and Sid Gottlieb destroyed what they thought were all the records on the CIA's mind control experiments. However, a few survived. The CIA's key instrument for sponsoring basic research in psychology, sociology and anthropology from the mid-1950s to the mid-1960s was the Society for the Investigation of Human Ecology, later called the Human Ecology Fund.

Quinuclidinyl benzilate, or BZ, is a powerful hallucinogen with effects that generally last three days to six weeks. Edgewood Arsenal conducted BZ studies from 1959–75, involving as many as 2,800 soldiers as test subjects. Many of the soldiers reported never being the same afterward.

While BZ failed the Army as a mind control drug, it did become its standard incapacitating agent. BZ weapons, such as bullets, grenades, bombs and warheads for missiles, were made for the Army. Between 1968–70, these weapons were tested five times in Vietnam. For instance, in Operation White Wing, grenades filled with BZ were dropped on 500 Viet Cong; only 100 survived. The Army stored (and mostly likely still has) 50 tons of BZ, enough to "trip out" everyone in the world. Army documents suggest there is a contingency plan to use BZ as a domestic civilian riot control method. STP, PCP and hundreds of other drugs were tested for use in mind control and as incapacitating agents.

Most research involved LSD. The Army tested LSD on approximately 1,500 military personnel in the mid-1960s. Soldiers were not the only guinea pigs used by the CIA. The list of expendables: war prisoners, prostitutes, sexual psychopaths, prison inmates, certain war objectors, mentally retarded people, the elderly, terminally ill patients, schizophrenics, drug addicts, foreigners and, of course, any other man, woman or child who fit the need.

Operation Midnight Climax was a series of CIA-run brothels in San Francisco and New York. The contract agent, George Hunter White, a narcotics officer, ran the operation. He hired drug-addicted prostitutes to lure customers to CIA-financed bordellos. The prostitutes spiked the drinks of their johns and agents observed the results from behind one-way mirrors. The prostitutes were guaranteed safety and chits to get out of jail if arrested. Besides being illegal, such testing without subjects' informed consent is a violation of the Nuremberg code, a set of ethical principles regarding experiments with human subjects and other medical research, which guided the Nuremberg tribunal .

In another operation for MK-ULTRA, Dr. Harris Isabel conducted LSD research on inmates at the Lexington federal drug hospital, a treatment facility. Asked by the CIA to discover a range of synthetic drugs, Isabel began experimenting on black inmates. Anxious to please his CIA bosses, he fed his guinea pigs large daily doses of LSD, mescaline, marijuana, scopolamine and other substances. In exchange for taking part in the experiments, the inmates received injections of high-quality morphine, sometimes getting "shot-up" several times a day, depending on their cooperation. Some inmates were kept on LSD for 77 consecutive days.

The CIA's testing of LSD was so extensive that the agency can be considered one of the creators of the drug culture of the 1960s. The first "acid heads" were agents and psychologists employed by the CIA. At large universities, the CIA advertised for paid volunteers in a drug study. Most of the time, there were enough willing volunteers — and a waiting list. Harold Abranson, a CIA contractor, spoke favorably of LSD at seminars for health professionals at universities. Many of the students and professionals then tried LSD.

Ronald Stark, a CIA agent from 1960 on, was jailed for selling marijuana, morphine and cocaine. Stark manufactured 50 million hits of LSD and sold them on the black market in the late 1960s and early 1970s. Stark was released from prison after a judge learned of his CIA background.

The CIA helped underground chemists set up acid laboratories in the San Francisco Bay Area in 1967 to "monitor" events in the Haight-Ashbury district. Dr. Louis West rented a house in the district for observation purposes. West had extensive contacts with MK-ULTRA and LSD testing. Previously, he treated Jack Ruby, who he decided was insane. Ruby died in prison of cancer a few years later. Some believe Ruby's death was part of a continuing cover up of the Kennedy assassination, because one of the goals of MK-ULTRA was to find a substance that could induce cancer, and deaths from cancer would be above question.

The CIA also contracted with Eli Lilly Co., to ensure the supply of LSD. The contract signed in 1953 under Subproject 18 of MK-ULTRA totaled $400,000. George H. W. Bush was once a member of the Eli Lilly board, and the Quayle family was a large stockholder.

Many of the acid advocates in the 1960s had connections to the CIA. Ken Kesey, author of *One Flew Over the Cuckoo's Nest* and leader of the Merry Pranksters, Beat poet Allen Ginsberg, and Robert Hunter, lyricist for the Grateful Dead, first took LSD in a CIA-connected program at Stanford University. There also are suggestions that Timothy Leary received CIA-channeled money through various government agencies.

Accidental outgrowths of MK-ULTRA and its associate subprojects were all the "crazies" roaming the country. Dr. Hackney was a psychiatrist who did BeMod experiments for the CIA from 1970–75, involving how much pain a subject could withstand. These experiments were done at the Veterans Administration Hospital in Minnesota on the homeless or those who had no family. Society already considered them crazy, so no one would listen to them if they complained about the BeMod experiments. Hackney then began to figure out that these people really were not insane. Almost all of them had flashbacks involving the military, killing or learning to kill. Hackney found the stories consistent. Studies showed that these "crazies" were very conditioned and brainwashed when they were 18–21, and it worked great. The problem arose when the victims turned about 40 and all of it began to unravel. Repressed memory syndrome was offered as the diagnosis.

Shortly after repressed memory syndrome was accepted, the False Memory Syndrome Foundation appeared. The foundation's sole aim appears to be to discredit studies and research on repressed memory syndrome. Many members of the foundation have ties with the CIA and MK-ULTRA. For instance, Martin Orne, a senior CIA-Navy researcher based at the University of Pennsylvania's Experimental Psychiatry Laboratory, is one of the founding members.

One of the crazies roaming the streets was a subject of Dr. Henry Murray of Harvard. Murray was a former OSS officer deeply involved in mind control. Between 1958–62, Theodore John Kaczynski agreed to be the subject of "a psychological experiment" conducted by Murray. Kaczynski is better known as the Unabomber.

The Symbionese Liberation Army (SLA) is another group with extensive ties to the CIA and mind control. Colston Westbrook, a veteran of the CIA's murderous PHOENIX Program in South Vietnam, trained SLA leadership. Three of Westbrook's foot soldiers, Emily and William Harris, and Angela Atwood, a former police intelligence informer, were students of the College of Foreign Affairs, a CIA cover at the University of Indiana. The OSS and CIA even adopted the SLA symbol of a seven-headed cobra to designate precepts of brainwashing.

Orne was called on to examine Patricia Hearst in preparation for trial. He believed Hearst voluntarily participated in the SLA's gun-toting crime spree. Robert Jay Lifton and Louis Jolyon West shared his opinion. Lifton cofounded of the Human Ecology Fund, a front used to channel money for the CIA to various mind control researchers. West, one of the CIA's most notorious mind control specialists, currently directs UCLA's Neuropsychiatric Institute. Orne, Lifton and West unanimously agreed that Patty Hearst had been "persuasively coerced" to join SLA. She had been put through a grueling thought reform regimen, isolated and sensory deprived, raped, humiliated, badgered and politically indoctrinated with a surreal mutation of Third World Marxism. Hearst was allowed human companionship only when she was submissive.

Some of the best evidence of the CIA's mind control experiments comes from Canada, where Dr. Ewen Cameron conducted some of the most horrific experiments funded by the CIA at the Allan Memorial Institute. Much of what is known about Cameron's research has come from lawsuits by survivors. Cameron's treatment started with "sleep therapy," in which subjects were knocked out for months, then "depatterned," which included massive electroshock and LSD dosage. Depatterning was supposed to wipe out past behavior so new patterns could be installed. Finally, the subjects underwent "psychic driving," when they were heavily drugged and confined to "sleep rooms." In the sleep rooms, speakers under their pillow played a tape-recorded message over and over, 16–24 hours a day. The treatments were a failure and only messed up the lives of the victims.

The number of deaths associated with the CIA's mind control programs remains uncertain. Lack of evidence, including the known destruction of documents about mind control, cloaks all the projects. Much of what is known has come from victim lawsuits and survivors. However, due to the tenacious efforts of Eric Olson, at least one death can be attributed to the CIA's mind control projects. Olson's father, Frank Olson, was a biochemist working at Fort Detrick in the Army's biowarfare facility from 1943 until his death in 1953. At the time of his death, Olson may have been engaged in, and would have certainly known about, the biowarfare the United States was conducting in Korea.

After the war, Frank Olson met Kurt Blome at Camp King in Germany. Blome was among the defendants in the Nuremberg War Trials who would have been convicted and hanged, but for American intervention. Olson made several visits to Camp King as part of Project ARTICHOKE. Olson was present during brutal American interrogations of Soviet prisoners and suspected double agents, some of whom died under torture. Olson was deeply disturbed by what he saw. On his return from Europe, he told a friend that he was disgusted with what the CIA was doing and was determined to leave. In November 1953, Olson attended a meeting of CIA agents at a country retreat. Considered a security risk, Olson was given a drink laced with LSD and, when under the influence, was subjected to interrogation using ARTICHOKE techniques.

The cover story that has survived for more than 20 years was that after taking LSD, Olson became depressed and a week later committed suicide by jumping through a closed window on the 13th floor of a New York hotel. However, an autopsy conducted 40 years later on the exhumed corpse revealed an injury to the skull most likely caused by a blow to the head and no evidence of any cuts on the body from broken glass. It seems that Olson, exactly as recommended in a CIA assassination manual, was struck on the head and thrown from the window. His death resurfaced in the mid-1970s in the Rockefeller Commission's investigation. President Ford apologized to the family and agreed to a settlement that restricted further civil suits. Further investigation was called for, but in a White House memo, advisers to President Ford stated that this would risk revealing state secrets. Kathryn Olmstead, a California history professor, has discovered documents at the Gerald Ford library about the cover up of Olson's death. Dick Cheney and Donald Rumsfeld signed the documents.

Project Monarch and Child Abuse

One of the most outrageous and repugnant aspects of the CIA's mind control projects involved children. At least four of the MK-ULTRA subprojects document that the CIA was using children without the informed consent of parents. The more gruesome experiments on children were conducted under Project MONARCH, which may have evolved from Project MK-SEARCH subprojects, such as operation SPELLBINDER, devoted to creating a Manchurian candidate who could later be activated with a code word. Operation OFTEN was a study that attempted to harness the power of occultic forces. It may have been one of several cover programs to hide the insidious reality of Project MONARCH.

The name derives from the butterfly. When a person is undergoing trauma, like that induced by electroshock there is a feeling of light-headedness as if one is floating or fluttering like a butterfly. It also is symbolic in the transformation or metamorphosis of this beautiful insect. Moreover, occultic symbolism may give additional insight into the true meaning. Psyche is the word for both "soul" and "butterfly," stemming from the belief that human souls become butterflies while searching for reincarnation. Project MONARCH is best described as a form of structured dissociation and occultic integration to compartmentalize the mind into multiple personalities within a systematic framework.

During this process, a satanic ritual is performed to attach a particular demon or group of demons to the corresponding alter ego. In addition, drugs, sexual abuse and physical trauma, including electroshock treatments, are used to create multiple personalities. MONARCH programming involves several stages:

Alpha: The first stage, regarded as general or regular programming. It is characterized by pronounced memory retention with substantially increased physical strength and visual acuity. Alpha programming works by deliberately subdividing the victim's personality.

Beta: Sexual programming. At this stage, all learned moral convictions are eliminated, leaving the victim devoid of inhibitions.

Delta: Killer programming developed for covert operations and elite forces. Subjects are fearless and methodical in carrying out assignments. Suicide programming is layered in.

Theta: Considered "psychic" programming. Usually reserved for bloodliners or those from families with a multigenerational satanic background.

Omega: Self-destruct programming. Also known as Code Green, it generally is activated when the victim begins therapy or interrogation and too much memory is recovered.

Gamma: Another form of system protection by "deception" programming, eliciting misinformation and misdirection.

The first stages of programming usually begin by age six. Because of the trauma induced by electroshock, sexual abuse and other methods, the victim's mind splits into alternate personalities in order to cope. Formerly referred to as Multiple Personality Disorder, it is now recognized as Dissociative Identity Disorder and is the basis for MONARCH programming. Further conditioning of the victim's mind is enhanced through hypnotism; double-bind coercion; pleasure-pain reversals; food, water, sleep and sensory deprivation; and drugs. The final stage of programming usually occurs on military bases to ensure security. Several bases are implicated with MONARCH programming. In the 1980s, Offutt and the Presidio were connected to MONARCH by incidents involving children. The Presidio case dates back as far as 1982, when a military doctor warned the Army of the danger to children in its daycare center. The Army failed to follow its own regulations in allowing children to go on field trips off base without parental consent. On Aug. 14, 1984, the FBI and officers from the Army's criminal investigation division raided the home of Lt. Col. Michael Aquino looking for evidence of child molestation.

The Presidio case attracted the attention of investigative reporter and radio talk show host Mae Bruessell. During her investigation, she received several death threats. Her daughter was killed in a car wreck that she attributed to a hit. Before ending her investigation, Bruessell was struck with a rapid onset of cancer. The CIA has developed a fast-acting cancer virus. Her death may have been induced rather than from natural causes.

Linked with both Offutt and the Presidio cases is Aquino, who founded the Temple of Set, an offshoot of Anton LaVey's Church of Satan. He was attached to the DIA's Psychological Warfare Division and holds top secret security clearance for his work in military intelligence and classified psychological warfare. Aquino is obsessed with Nazi pagan rituals. He officiated at SS black magic ceremonies held at Wewelsburg, the castle once used by SS chief Heinrich Himmler to create an order of Teutonic Knights, based on the Knights Templars. His hypnotic manipulation of people made him an ideal candidate for the position of master programmer. Aquino and others were arrested for child molesting. Evidence of their guilt was overwhelming, but all charges were dropped, to the dismay of the victims' parents. Aquino has developed training tapes on how to create a MONARCH slave. He worked as a liaison between government-military intelligence and various criminal organizations and occult groups in distributing MONARCH slaves.

On Aug. 14, 1987, San Francisco police raided Aquino's home after the brutal rape of a 4-year-old girl there. The principal suspect in the rape was a Baptist minister named Gary Hambright. Hambright was indicted on charges that he committed "lewd and lascivious acts" with six boys and four girls, ranging in age from 3–7, from September–October 1986. At the time of the alleged sex crimes, Hambright was employed at a childcare center on the U.S. Army base at Presidio. Police also claimed Hambright was involved in at least 58 separate incidents of child sexual abuse. One of the victims identified Aquino and his wife as participants in the child rape. Aquino's home also served as headquarters of the Satanic Temple of Set. During the raid, police confiscated 38 videotapes, photo negatives and other evidence that the home had been the hub of a pedophile ring.

Although the evidence was overwhelming, Aquino was never charged with child abuse. On April 19, 1988, U.S. Attorney Joseph Russoniello dropped the 10-count indictment against Hambright on the grounds that there was insufficient evidence linking him or the Aquinos to the crimes. Russoniello later was implicated in efforts to cover up the links between the Nicaraguan Contras and South American cocaine trafficking.

Almost all the evidence on child abuse comes from the victims. Several from the Franklin case were later charged with felonies for refusing to recant their testimony. One of the Franklin victims told investigators that she saw George H. W. Bush pay Larry King and then leave with a young black boy. Numerous investigators on the Franklin case met sudden violent deaths. King was sentenced to 15 years for fraud in the failure of the community credit union. Yet neither he nor anyone else has faced a single charge in the pedophile sex ring.

Pedophile sex rings are the product of the CIA's mind control project MONARCH. Evidence suggests these sex rings operated continuously since the 1950s and were used by the CIA to control politicians and members of Congress. Victims have implicated at least two ex-presidents, George H. W. Bush and Gerald Ford. Evidence suggests the CIA's pedophile sex rings extend beyond the borders of the United States and may be used to also control foreign politicians. In November 2002, a similar case of child abuse emerged in Portugal. Several government ministers and the spokesperson for the opposition Socialist Party were arrested. The abused children were residents of Portugal's largest home for trouble children, Casa Pia. The investigation sparked a public outcry after it was revealed that a former president and several government ministers, as well as police, knew of the allegations as far back as the early 1980s, but failed to act. Many of the victims were deaf mutes.[132] In the late 1990's, a scandal involving a pedophile ring in Belgium forced two ministers to resign; even the King was alleged to be implicated.

In November 2003, a pedophile sex ring involving sadomasochistic orgies with children and linked to two right-wing senators of the Independent Democratic Union Party, as well as prominent businessmen and four police officers, emerged in Chile.[133]

On Jan. 28, 2003, amid the furor of the impending war with Iraq, the British press briefly reported on Operation Ore, the most thorough and comprehensive police investigation of crimes against children, before being quashed by the Blair government. Besides entangling Rock guitarist Peter Townsend of the Who, the report claimed that senior members of Tony Blair's government were being investigated for pedophilia and "enjoyment" of child-sex pornography. With the investigation reaching to senior members of his government, Blair declared a news blackout on the story.

Most information about mind control abuse also comes from former victims, such as Candy Jones and Cathy O'Brien.[119] Other information comes from Canadian lawsuits against Dr. Cameron. What little information available under the Freedom of Information Act that survived the purging of files is heavily redacted. More recently, another victim, Paul Bonaci, who survived two decades of torture under Project MONARCH, came forward. Bonaci testified about sexually abused males who were selected from Boys Town in Nebraska and taken to nearby Offutt AFB. There they were subjected to intense MONARCH programming, directed mainly by Cmdr. Bill Plemmons and former Lt. Col. Michael Aquino. Bonaci's testimony disclosed strong corroborating evidence of wide-scale crimes and corruption from the municipal and state levels, all the way up to the White House.

John DeCamp, a former Republican state senator, documented Bonaci's story that emerged in 1985 in the Omaha area.[120] The first indication that something very sinister was afoot came on July 10, 1985 when the Washington County, Nebraska Sheriff's Department contacted a state Department of Social Services social worker handling the case of three foster children. The sheriff's department picked up the three youngsters from the home of Jarrett and Barbara Webb on a child abuse complaint.

Jarrett Webb was a board member of the Franklin Community Federal Credit Union headed by Larry King. His wife was Larry King's first cousin. The Webbs cared for as many as nine foster children at a time. Although Jarrett Webb stated in March 7, 1986 that his income was only $32,000 a year, the Webb home was lavishly furnished. His wife wore a four-carat diamond ring, a full-length fur coat and custom-made dresses.[121] After social workers removed one of the young girls from the care of the Webbs, State Patrol Investigator Jane Tooley found out from her that the abuse was physical and sexual. Further investigation revealed the Webbs forced the foster children to attend parties about once every other week at Larry King's home.

The young girl told investigators there were youths from Boys Town and usually around 30 adults with about 20 children present. If a man was interested in one of the children, he would hold up a folded $50 or $100 bill and go somewhere in the house to have sex with him or her. Sometimes the sex involved more than two people and couples of the same or opposite sex. The Webbs took the money from the foster child, supposedly to keep for her.[122]

On the surface, King appeared as a benefactor of Boys Town and an upright resident of Omaha. However, underneath the façade, King had powerful underworld connections. The foster girl taken from the Webbs told investigators that, starting when she was 15, she was taken to parties hosted by King in Washington, D.C, Chicago and New York. She missed 22 days of school while on these trips. At some of these parties, only men and young boys were present and she saw acts of sodomy. She indicated that at two of the parties, one of them all-male, she saw Vice President George H. W. Bush.[123] This was the first time Bush's name surfaced in the Franklin case, and it would not be the last.

Local investigators were soon overwhelmed. What started as a simple case of child abuse evolved into a national ring of child prostitution with sensitive political overtones reaching all the way to the White House. As other victims came forward, it became clear that King was running a child prostitution ring that involved ritual murder to control the children. Other victims said that if they failed to take part in nude photographing sessions, their families would be killed. In 1988, another 15-year-old girl came forward and told investigators that King believed in devil worship. As she grew to trust the investigators, she told them of witnessing several ritual murders of young children. The young girl indicated that King first took her to what he called power meetings when she was 10. At one such meeting, she was drugged. After about eight months attending such meetings, the girl said they put her through her first test.

During the test, they locked her in a small room with an infant. Around midnight, they returned and cut the infant's head off and stuck it on the wall. They then forced the young girl to sit in front of the severed head. Later, they returned and held her down while they cut the eyes out of the severed head and then left her locked in the room another 24 hours. At another meeting, she told investigators a small child was sacrificed, fried and eaten.

The early investigation was promptly buried and covered up by local officials, with the mayor of Omaha threatening one of the police investigators with a psychiatric examination. King was well connected locally, because both the Omaha mayor and police chief were reportedly guests at some of his parties with children present. Moreover, King was a rising star in the Republican Party. He sang the national anthem at the 1984 and 1988 Republican National Conventions, and hosted a party at the 1984 convention at the South Fork Ranch.

On Nov. 4, 1988, the FBI, IRS and National Credit Union Administration raided and shut down Franklin Credit Union. Ultimately, more than $40 million was missing from the failed credit union. The failure of the credit union opened old charges that King ran a child prostitution ring and new charges of his use of the credit union as a front for the CIA.

By late 1989, Gary Caradori, the Nebraska legislator's chief investigator for the Franklin case, found four of King's victims who were willing to talk. Caradori and his son were killed in a suspicious plane crash on July 11, 1990. At least 15 others associated with the Franklin case have died suddenly under mysterious circumstances, including violent ends.[124] Former CIA Director William Colby warned his friend John DeCamp, author of the *Franklin Cover-Up*, about threats to his safety. Colby was found dead under mysterious circumstances near his home in 1996.

 In 1989, Craig Spence was found dead of an apparent suicide. Spence was involved in another case of child prostitution that broke about the same time as the Franklin case. Spence was a Republican power broker known for his lavish parties. On June 29, 1989, the *Washington Times* broke the story about Spence in an article, "Call Boys Took Midnight Tour of White House." The story entangled several top officials in the Bush administration and GOP members of Congress. Two of the ring's callboys were allegedly KGB operatives. However, all evidence pointed to a CIA sexual blackmail operation. Spence's mansion was covered with hidden microphones, two-way mirrors and video cameras. Spence hinted at his work for the CIA on many occasions, claiming he took part in covert operations in Japan and Southeast Asia. The CIA denies any connection to Spence; however, there is no question he was blackmailing several officials in the United States and Japan.

Another associate in the CIA's male prostitution network was Ronald Rosken, former chancellor of the University of Nebraska. The university board of regents fired Roskens after it verified charges of his involvement in homosexual orgies. Larry King served as one of Roskens' closest advisers. A year after his termination from the University of Nebraska, George H. W. Bush appointed Roskens to head the Agency of International Development. The agency, commonly used as a CIA front, dispenses $7 billion in nonmilitary foreign aid, thus wielding formidable clout in the geopolitical landscape.[125]

The Bush White House remained silent as the story of the White House callboys mushroomed, refusing to answer any questions about the case. After months of silence from the White House, the case faded away. Meanwhile, half a continent away in Omaha, the Franklin case was breaking. However, it suffered from a lack of publicity because of the more sensational Spence case involving top GOP officials. Moreover, the Franklin case is directly connected with Spence. As several of King's young victims stated, they were at parties in Washington that he attended. In addition, Paul Bonacci has said that he was in one of the private tours of the White House for young prostitutes conducted by Spence.[126] Bonacci told investigators that he was flown to 200–300 parties nationwide, including two in Washington and several in California. On another trip, Bonacci told investigators of being taken to Bohemian Grove where he and two boys were forced to perform sex acts on each other. After one of the boys was murdered, they were forced to eat parts of him. A snuff pornography film was made of the events.[127] At the time, Bonacci was too young to realize he was at Bohemian Grove; however, from his description of the surroundings, the location is unmistakable.

Bonacci suffers from multiple personality disorder induced by MONARCH programming. He told investigators the ring, which plunged him into Satanism, was centered at Offutt air base. He was first abused at Offutt when he was 3 years old. He described his MONARCH programming as a series of tortures, heavy drugging and sexual abuse. He also said he was trained in military arts, including assassination. In fact, his knowledge in these realms cannot be accounted for by any other means. Bonacci and others have given evidence of the central role Lt. Col. Michael Aquino played in the programming.

Bonacci and other children reported that they often were used as mules to smuggle drugs across borders. President Reagan appointed Bush to run the National Narcotics Border Interdiction System. One of Bush's key aides was Lt. Col. Oliver North, whom several children have witnessed attending King parties. James Flanery, the first reporter to investigate the Franklin case, told associates that King was running guns and money into Nicaragua, and the CIA was heavily involved. Flanery was removed from his position and sent out of state for a year.[128] King was known to have traveled several times to Jamaica, where Oliver North and other Iran-Contra figures carried out many banking transactions. King also received many phone calls from Switzerland. Tom Harvey, Franklin's chief accountant, also made several trips to Switzerland during the time money disappeared. In 1987, King gave $25,350 to Citizens for America, which sponsored speaking tours for Oliver North and Contra leaders.

The Finders case provides another connection between the CIA and child abuse. On Feb. 7, 1987, the *Washington Post* ran an article about a case of possible kidnapping and child abuse. Tallahassee police arrested two men after observing them watching several children, ages 2–7, described as neglected, covered with insect bites and extremely dirty. The investigation led to the Finders, a cult-like commune, and to properties in Washington owned by the organization. The adult males were Michael Houlihan and Douglas Ammerman. They led authorities to an old warehouse where police found color slides, photographs and photo contact sheets. Some photos revealed children engaging in bloodletting cult rituals involving animals. Other documents described "blood rituals" and sexual orgies involving children, and an unsolved murder in which the Finders might be involved. Additional documents revealed detailed instructions for getting children for unspecified purposes. The instructions included the impregnation of female members of the community, purchasing children, trading and kidnapping.

Several telex messages also were found in the warehouse. One ordered the purchase of two children in Hong Kong to be arranged through a contact in the Chinese Embassy. There was a file called "Pentagon Break-in" and references to activities in Moscow, Hong Kong, China, Malaysia, North Vietnam, North Korea, Africa, London, Germany, "Europe" and the Bahamas. Other documents identified interests in high-tech transfers to the United Kingdom, numerous properties controlled by the Finders, and interest in terrorism, explosives and evading law enforcement. The warehouse also had a video room, apparently used for indoctrination.

U.S. Customs officials verified all findings by local police. The officials soon ordered a full investigation and obtained search warrants for various locations. The investigation brought in the FBI, as well. Nevertheless, this was as far as the investigation ever got. All law enforcement agencies involved were ordered by the Department of Justice to halt their investigations on grounds of national security. It was turned over to the CIA as an "internal security matter," since the Finders is a domestic and international covert operation of the CIA. Evidence was suppressed and the abused children returned to their handlers.

The Franklin case extends beyond child abuse, with connections that associate the CIA in a wide range of nefarious activities. Bonacci reported that another prominent Nebraska resident, Harold Andersen, abused him. Andersen, editor of the *Omaha World-Herald,* is closely connected with the upper circles of the U.S. intelligence community, and close friends with another Nebraskan, Robert Keith Gray. Gray was chairman and CEO of Hill and Knowlton during the Franklin case. Hill and Knowlton was one of the largest and most influential public relations firms in the world. Gray first went to Washington during the Eisenhower administration as Ike's appointment secretary, then was assigned as secretary of the cabinet. In 1976 and 1980, Gray played a role in Reagan's presidential campaign. After Reagan's 1980 election, Gray formed his own company. Based on the strength of his ties with the Reagan administration, within a year he had built Gray and Co., into an influential powerhouse with more than $9 billion in revenue from large corporations. In 1986, Hill and Knowlton bought out the company and Gray became chairman and CEO.[129]

As the Bush administration built a case for the first Gulf War, Hill and Knowlton was the firm hired by the Kuwait government that presented 15-year-old Nayirah as a nurse who testified before Congress and news cameras how the Iraqis threw 300 babies out of the incubators to die. The young actress was the daughter of the Kuwaiti ambassador to the U.S. and a member of the royal family. Her fabricated story was constantly repeated, and has been cited as the most effective piece of propaganda for the war. Hill and Knowlton were hired to manage coverage of many scandals, including the Bank of Credit and Commerce International (BCCI), after a grand jury indicted BCCI for conspiring with the Medellin Cartel to launder $32 million in illicit drug profits.

Hill and Knowlton have a long history of association with the CIA. Former CIA agent Robert T. Crowley, the agency's longtime liaison with corporations, admits Hill and Knowlton's overseas offices are the perfect cover for agents. Crowley said the CIA uses Hill and Knowlton to distribute press releases, bypassing the law against the agency conducting domestic operations and using the media as a front. Robert Gray and Hill and Knowlton have many connections with the national and international intelligence community. International division clients of Gray and Co., were mostly right-wing governments or businesspeople tied closely to the intelligence community. Gray's associates included Edwin Wilson, William Casey, Tongsun Park (Korean CIA), Rev. Sun Myung Moon and Oliver North. In 1965, with Gray's help, Tongsun Park formed the Georgetown Club.

Gray's own homosexual leanings first surfaced in 1982. In the Watergate era, Gray served on the board of Consultants International, founded by CIA agent Edwin Wilson. According to fugitive ex-CIA agent Frank Terpil, CIA-directed sexual blackmailing operations were at a high point during the Watergate era. Terpil's ex-CIA partner Edwin Wilson ran one such operation, based in Park's Georgetown Club. The first president of the Georgetown Club was Robert Gray. Terpil claims Wilson's assignment was to subvert members of Congress by any means necessary. Wilson's blackmailing was an extension of Roy Cohn's operation during the McCarthy era.[130]

When the Reagan administration was seeking a way to circumvent a congressional ban on arming the Contras, William Casey, Robert McFarlane and Oliver North enlisted the help of Gray and Co. Gray employee Rob Owen set up a private group to raise funds for the Contras. In February 1989, Hill and Knowlton rushed to aid the image of Covenant House. The youth director, Father Bruce Ritter, was alleged to have abused children. Lauded by the Reagan administration as a showcase for privatizing social services, Covenant House expanded into Guatemala. Intelligence sources claim the sole purpose for expanding was to procure children from South America for exploitation in a pedophile ring. A former business partner of Nicaraguan dictator Somoza, Roberto Arzu, who had ties to the CIA, launched the flagship Guatemala mission of Covenant House. A top source of funds for Covenant House was Robert Macauley, founder of Americares, an institution implicated in funneling funds to the Contras. Macauley was a longtime close friend of the Bush family. George H. W. Bush's father Prescott served on the board of Americares with Father Ritter.[131]

Operation Watchtower

Edwin Wilson's pedophile blackmailing ring was only the beginning of his wicked activities. Allegedly fired by the CIA in 1971, Wilson worked the next six years for naval intelligence. With Terpil, Wilson ran a gun smuggling operation throughout the 1970s. In December 1975, Wilson and Terpil approached Col. Edward P. Cutolo, the commanding officer of the U.S. 10th Special Forces stationed at Fort Devens, Mass. After signaling he would be interested in an assignment in Colombia, Wilson and Terpil briefed Cutolo on Operation Watchtower. Cutolo commanded the second and third Watchtower missions to set up a series of three electronic beacon towers beginning outside Bogota and running northeast to the border of Panama. With the beacons activated, aircraft could fix on their signal and fly undetected, landing at Albrook Air Station. There, Panama's Col. Manuel Noriega met the planes. This route was solely for cocaine smuggling.

In 1998, Massachusetts attorney Ray Kohlman filed a $63 million lawsuit on behalf of former Green Beret Bill Tyree (Case No. 98CV11829JLT). The suit alleges the U.S. government sanctioned drug smuggling, murder and cover-up. The suit names the CIA, former Massachusetts Gov. A. Paul Celucci, former Massachusetts Attorney General Scott Harshbarger, former CIA Director and U.S. President George H. W. Bush, and government assassin D. Gene Tatum as defendants. Tyree is currently serving a life sentence for the murder of his wife. The murder is eerily similar to that of Dr. Jeffrey McDonald, a Ft. Bragg doctor framed for the murder of his wife and children in the early 1980s. Tyree's wife had been keeping a diary of her husband's secret missions. Her diary has never been found. Tyree and other Green Berets were led into Colombia as part of Operation Watchtower. Documents filed in the suit give precise details of CIA drug operations using Special Forces personnel. It also describes how Tyree was framed for the murder of his wife, and how Special Forces personnel were used to intimidate and conduct illegal electronic and physical surveillance of anyone who might expose CIA drug dealing. The documents allege the defendants, the CIA and George H. W. Bush were negligent with regard to Operation Watchtower, monitoring post-Watchtower events and seeking illegal congressional funding for the origination of FEMA.

Col. Albert Carone was a CIA paymaster and Mafia-connected money launderer who functioned as Oliver North's bagman. Carone also was a Grand Knight of the Sovereign Military Order of Malta. Carone's daughter stated that her father told her the drugs from South America went to the Colombo, Genovese and Gambino families, and that it was a joint CIA-Mafia drug operation code-named Operation Amadeus. During World War II, Operation Amadeus operated a ratline for Nazi officers from Germany into South America. It then evolved into other operations such as Operations Sunrise and Watchtower. One participant was former Gestapo officer Klaus Barbie. Drug trafficking was the principal means of funding Amadeus. Some of the drug profits were routed into funding for FEMA.

In the lawsuit, the plaintiff alleges the defendants, the CIA and George H. W. Bush, intentionally concealed the origins of FEMA. Further, the profits from CIA drug trafficking were used in some part to fund FEMA and its infrastructure. The suit also alleges that Col. Carone told the plaintiff that Col. Ollie North worked on a plan known as FEMA that would allow the U.S. military to take control of the United States in an ill-defined national emergency.

After completing the Watchtower missions, Wilson did not approach Cutolo again until 1978. Wilson explained that Operation Watchtower could be compromised if politicians, judicial figures, police and religious entities were approached or received word that U.S. troops aided in delivering narcotics from Colombia to Panama. Cutolo formed 12 Special Action Teams whose mission was to implement Army regulation 340-18-5 (file number 503-05). Cutolo's authority for this action came directly from US Army Forces Command (FORSCOM) via Wilson.

Operation Orwell's mission was to carry out extensive surveillance of politicians, judicial figures, state law enforcement agencies and religious groups. The purpose was to provide the U.S. government and Army with advance warning of the discovery of Watchtower to enable them to prepare a defense. Cutolo revealed that he began surveillance of Ted Kennedy, John Kerry, Edward King, Michael Dukakis, Levin H. Campbell, Andrew A Caffrey, Fred Johnson, Kenneth A. Chandler and Thomas P. O'Neill. As the cover-up operation became more involved in criminality, Cutolo became uneasy, and attempted to protect himself by preparing an affidavit detailing his inside knowledge. In 1980, he was killed while on a military mission in England. Cutolo's close friends allege that his investigation into the legality of these missions cost him his life. Other senior officers investigating Cutolo's death or these operations have also died in mysterious circumstances.

Within two months of grabbing power in Chile, Pinochet directed Col. Manuel Contreras to establish the Directorate of National Intelligence (DINA) or secret police. CIA station chief Stuart Burton in

Santiago established a close liaison with DINA. On Nov. 25, 1975, Chile signed the Interamerican Reunion on Military Intelligence with five other brutal right-wing regimes supported by the United States, setting up Operation Condor. Argentina, Bolivia, Brazil, Chile, Paraguay and Uruguay signed the agreement for Operation Condor, a terrorist plot to murder political opponents around the world.

In the summer of 1976, Contreras launched an operation to assassinate exiled Chilean leader Orlando Letelier. Contreras made a secret visit to Washington, where he met with CIA officials and negotiated the purchase of illegal weapons and electronic spying equipment from a firm run by Edwin Wilson and Frank Terpil. That September, Letelier was killed by a car bomb on the streets of Washington, D.C. Documents show the CIA was aware the assassination was carried out by DINA. Moreover, the CIA was forewarned of the assassination. Nevertheless, the CIA, then directed by George H.W. Bush, leaked a false report clearing Chile and DINA of any involvement in the murder.

In 1983, a federal court in Virginia convicted Wilson of selling 20 tons of C4 explosive to Libya. His defense was that he continued freelancing for the CIA after his retirement, but a denial by a top CIA official swayed the jury. On his appeal he produced 40 documents showing he was indeed still working for the CIA, and in 2003, a federal judge overturned the 1983 conviction, calling the CIA affidavit "nothing but a lie."

In 1993, a huge cache of documents known as the archives of terror was discovered in Paraguay. The documents reveal the reign of terror during the 1970s unleashed by Paraguay's dictator, Gen. Alfredo Stroessner. Besides verifying the murders of several South American leaders, the documents reveal the presence of Nazis throughout the southern cone and the assassination of Israeli agents pursuing them. They also detailed the connection of local intelligence services with drug traffickers and the CIA.

Operation Condor was wide-ranging, with the Argentina and Chile military helping Nicaraguan dictator Anastasio Somoza hold power before his overthrow in a 1979 coup. Through Condor, Argentina also helped organize death squads in El Salvador in 1979–80.

Summary

The killers in the Nazi concentration camps were trained and organized by psychiatrists and eugenicists from the T4 bureau who were, in turn, the darlings of British and American white supremacists and American finance. Both the Rockefeller and Carnegie foundations gave generously to the German eugenic and psychiatry scientists. In fact, the Rockefeller Foundation specifically funded eugenic studies on twins. How much of Joseph Mengele's butchery in the camps was directly due to Rockefeller grants is uncertain, but at the least, it was the Rockefeller Foundation that planted the seed.

Following the war, some of these Nazi doctors were spirited out of Germany under the supervision of former Bank of England Governor Montagu Norman and the Tavistock Institute Director John Rees. Other Nazi doctors, including Mengele, escaped from Europe with the help of the U.S. military and Allen Dulles through the American-Vatican ratline to South America. Still other Nazi doctors from the camps were admitted into the United States after military and intelligence officials falsified their records. The Nazi doctors admitted to the United States and the documents from others provided the basis for the CIA's Project MONARCH.

The biggest problem in determining the extent of the CIA's mind control programs comes from the extreme secrecy and destruction of files. No information is available on any newer mind control techniques.

It is a small step from mind control of an individual to mind control of the masses. The Nazis were masters at crowd control through propaganda. Recently, several unconfirmed stories have appeared suggesting the government may be using microwaves to control the masses.

It has long been established in the scientific community that electrodes implanted in the brain can control emotions and behavior. There also is good evidence that electromagnetic radiation of the right frequency can affect mood. Reports indicate the CIA conducted a program named Pandora Project focused on the use of microwaves to control behavior in monkeys. Other reports suggest this project was successful and the TETRA system for crowd control was an end result. There are reports the British are spending 2.5 million pounds on implementing the TETRA system by installing the needed microwave towers. Dr. Ross Adey was the chief researcher of the Pandora Project. The system works by broadcasting pulsed signals at 17.6 Hz that cause zombification by massive release of calcium ions in the cerebral cortex and the nervous system. However, the activated calcium ions also cause massive hormonal disturbances, which lead to frenzied imbalances, and emotional and physical states.

While these reports may be false, it is known with certainty that the government is funding crowd control research. This research is beginning to bear fruit from recent reports of nonlethal crowd control tools, such as the report of sound generators being shipped to New York during the Republican 2004 national convention. In 2005, *New Scientist* magazine reported on a new "non-lethal crowd control weapon," a microwave beam that causes intense pain within 4 seconds.

Operation Gladio and the Stay-Behind Networks

The end of WWII brought about a pronounced shift in U.S. foreign policy. For the first time in history, the country maintained a large standing army. Although U.S. foreign policy before WWII could be described as interventionist, particularly in Central and South America whenever corporate America's interests were threatened, the country still clung to isolationism after WWI. U.S. foreign policy became more interventionist, bordering on imperialist, when the CIA covertly brought about the downfall of any government leaning to the Left, including allies.

The shift was immediate and first appeared in 1947 in Greece and Turkey with the announcement of the Truman Doctrine. It appeared again in the 1948 Italian election, which the CIA covertly influenced by disrupting campaigns of communist and socialist candidates. The basis for Truman's policy was to prevent the communists from gaining power once the British withdrew from Greece. Other actions followed in rapid succession. In 1949, the CIA trained Albanian exiles on Malta, and in Rome and Athens to overthrow President Enver Hoxha. In 1950, the CIA trained rebels in Taiwan to infiltrate China, Manchuria and Tibet. Also in 1950, the CIA helped break the power of the leftist Huks and succeeded in helping elect Magsaysay president. During WWII the Huks were U.S. allies and rescued many pilots shot down behind enemy lines.

All these actions intensified the Cold War and fit into the Nazi comeback plan of provoking a war between the two superpowers. In most European countries, the United States provided support for stay-behind networks composed largely of former Nazis, which formed an integral part of the U.S. war plans against the Soviets. The stay-behind concept may have begun in Britain. When France fell to the Nazis in 1940, the British already had a guerrilla network in place there, including numerous arms caches. After the war, the stay-behind network was employed by the U.S. Joint Chiefs of Staff, and spearheaded by Allen Dulles and the CIA. The idea was to use battle-tested Nazi soldiers to fight a guerrilla war if the Soviets overran Western Europe. Thousands of former Nazi soldiers received immunity to form the nucleus of the secret guerrilla army.

The most notorious stay-behind network was in Italy, known as Operation Gladio, after the short Roman sword. In France, the network was called "Glaive " (a kind of spear); in Austria, the network was named Schwert, or Sword; in Greece, the unit was named Operation Sheepskin; and in Turkey, Red Sheepskin. The plan was later codified under the umbrella of the Clandestine Coordinating Committee of the Supreme Headquarters Allied Powers Europe (SHAPE), the military arm of NATO.

Operation Gladio formed in 1956 amid growing concern about the increasing communist influence in Italy. Initially, 622 people were recruited and trained by U.S. and British specialists in Sardinia. Eventually, Gladio may have had as many as 15,000 members. By 1972, the threat of a Soviet invasion of Western Europe subsided, and a preemptive attack on Italian communists was launched. A wave of terror bombings swept Italy, designed to shift the electorate to the Right. The bombings were carried out by members of Operation Gladio and blamed on the Red Brigade.

While former Nazi soldiers made up the army, the secret Masonic Lodge P2 (Propaganda Due) functioned as the elitist shadow government directing operations. P2 was headed by Licio Gelli, a former member of Mussolini's Black Shirts, who acted as liaison officer to the Hermann Goering SS division. By 1974, P2 had more than 1,000 members, including four cabinet ministers, three intelligence chiefs, 160 senior military officers, 48 MPs and the Army Chief of Staff, as well as top diplomats, bankers, industrialists and media publishers.

In 1974, Gelli met secretly with President Nixon's Chief of Staff Alexander Haig. The meeting in the U.S. Embassy in Rome received Henry Kissinger's blessing and a pledge for financial support for the Gladio network and its plan for "internal subversion" of Italian political life. However, Gelli needed additional funds to support P2 and operation Gladio, so he turned to P2 member Roberto Calvi, chairman of Banco Ambrosiano. Calvi began siphoning money from his bank, using the Vatican bank, the *Istituto per le Opere di Religione* (IOR), to launder it. Calvi continued to funnel a vast amount of funds to Gelli and P2, bankrupting his bank in the process.

Within months of Moro's murder, Albino Luciani was elected Pope John Paul, and less than a month later, he also died mysteriously, to the great relief to Bishop Paul Marcinkus, the American head of the Vatican bank. Marcinkus engaged in a vast web of financial skullduggery. Besides his shenanigans with Banco Ambrosiano, IOR also was known to have Mafia figures invest some of its vast wealth.

In June 1982, Calvi was found hanging from London's Blackfriars Bridge. His death was ruled a suicide. The circumstances of his death point to a Masonic ritual slaying.

The stay-behind networks also may have brought down Harold Wilson's Labor government. Wilson's surprise resignation was a result of a dirty tricks campaign operated by British intelligence at the behest of the United States. Known as operation Clockwork Orange, Army PsyOps personnel began fabricating evidence that showed senior members of the Wilson Cabinet, including the Prime Minister, were Soviet dupes. Waiting in the wings were senior military and other right-wing figures alleged to be planning a military-style coup d'état if the Labor government won the forthcoming election.

U.S. policy shifted to covert methods rather than brute military force to overthrow governments after WWII, which had shown all-out modern warfare to be excessively destructive. The Korean War with the Chinese human wave attacks only reinforced the lesson. Throughout the 1950s and into the 1960s, former Nazis in the stay-behind networks often were used covertly by the United States to overthrow regimes.

By 1950, U.S. foreign policy shifted far to the right, largely due to Nazi influence through the Gehlen network. Official U.S. policy called for containment of communism, while others called for rolling back the Iron Curtain. While it is wise and perhaps even honorable to oppose totalitarian regimes, U.S. policy after WWII only opposed leftist governments and often installed and supported brutal right-wing regimes, such as the fascist regime of Pinochet in Chile.

Coup in Iran

The dependence on an oil economy added new urgency to containing communism in the Mideast. The long Soviet border in the Mideast and its proximity to the rich Arabian oil fields prompted the United States to overthrow several governments in the region. The first U.S. intervention in the region came in Iran in 1953, precipitated by Mossadegh's move to nationalize the oil fields. The plan to overthrow Mossadegh was a joint British-American operation called Operation Ajax. Kermit Roosevelt, grandson of Teddy Roosevelt and the CIA's Mideast agent, headed the operation.

On Aug. 18, 1953, in accordance with the plan, the Shah violated Iran's Parliamentary Monarchy Constitution by dismissing Mossadegh and his nationalist cabinet without parliament's approval, and appointing Gen. Fazlollah Zahedi as Prime Minister, who had been was imprisoned during WWII for collaborating with the Nazis. The coup d'état caused three days of riots and the Shah fled. On Aug. 19, 1953, the CIA and MI6 engineered the next phase of the coup when a group of tanks led by Zahedi moved through Tehran and surrounded Mossadegh's residence. The forces behind the coup d'état also placed a large number of bribed hooligans in the streets to rally against Mossadegh. Finally, the army and police forces let the mob reach the Prime Minister's residence. After a bloody battle, Mossadegh and his top cabinet leaders surrendered, and the Shah returned to power.

With the Shah firmly in control, Iran completed a contract with an international consortium of oil companies which included Standard Oil of New Jersey, a client of Sullivan & Cromwell. Jack Anderson reported the Rockefeller family helped arrange the coup that brought the Shah to power. Anderson listed a number of ways the Shah demonstrated his appreciation.[134] The CIA also provided training for the dreaded Savak or Iranian secret police. Unfortunately, all CIA records on the Iranian intervention have been destroyed. The only other sources are Kermit Roosevelt's book and those published by the Iranians after they seized the U.S. embassy and, with it, 30 years or so of records.

The resulting government was brutally repressive. The Shah's regime suppressed any dissent. Dissenters were arrested and tortured by Savak, which maintained its own prisons. In 1979, the Shah was overthrown in a popular uprising and the U.S. embassy seized.

With the successful removal of Mossadegh, the Iranian operation became a model for the CIA's method of overthrowing governments. The pattern is always the same. First, a legally elected government proposes reforms or begins to lean to the left, threatening the profits of corporate America. The reform-minded government is then covertly overthrown and a hard-right government bordering on fascism installed. The new regime maintains power through brutality and murder with a U.S.-trained police force. This is the model the United States has followed since WWII. Often in the 1950s, ex-Nazis were employed as agents. U.S. media should be considered co-conspirators in that they cover up the bloodshed by ignoring the killing, as in Nicaragua. It is a model that has been repeated time after time in all corners of the globe. Noam Chomsky terms the resulting state subfascist.[135]

Egypt

The CIA began meddling in Egypt's affairs in 1951. The first covert actions in Egypt were led by Kermit Roosevelt to remove the government of King Farouk. Continued CIA meddling and U.S. demands forced the Nasser government to align itself with the Soviets.

During WWII, after Rommel entered Egypt, Anwar Sadat and Gamal Nasser contacted his headquarters in Libya. Both men were agents for Hitler's intelligence chief Adm. Wilhelm Canaris and members of a secret officers' association called the Ring of Iron. The British imprisoned Sadat for three years for subversive activities. Egypt was a hotbed of intrigue following the end of WWII.

In 1946, the Grand Mufti of Jerusalem settled in a luxury villa in Alexandria, courtesy of King Farouk. The Mufti had fled Palestine before the war and lived in Germany. His arrival was the prelude to a stream of Nazi veterans and war criminals coming to hide in Cairo. One of King Farouk's advisers suggested hiring Nazi veterans to upgrade the Egyptian military. Many of the Nazis recognized the political weakness of the King and began conspiring with Gamal Nasser and his "Free Officers." A 40-man contingent of Nazis shared their skills with students in the Egyptian military academies. Nasser asked them to stay on after the 1952 revolt against Farouk. Although there is no evidence the Nazi veterans initiated the coup, the participating officers were advised by them.[136]

In 1951, Kermit Roosevelt began secret talks with Nasser that ended soon after the coup. The CIA viewed Nasser as strongly opposed to communism. One of the first measures Nasser took was to come down hard on the Egyptian Communist Party, imprisoning its leaders. Several left-wing unionists were arrested and hanged after a summary trial. The CIA gladly granted Nasser's request to rebuild Egypt's intelligence service. However, Egypt and Israel were technically at war, and absolute anonymity was required, so the CIA turned to the Gehlen organization. Gehlen, in turn, turned to a reluctant Otto Skorzeny. It took a visit from a major general in the U.S. Army, as well as a CIA pay supplement, to convince Skorzeny to rebuild Nasser's intelligence system. Skorzeny used CIA funds to recruit former Nazis such as: [137]

SS Maj. Leopold Gleim, a war criminal who was sentenced to death for atrocities committed in Poland when he was Gestapo chief.
SS Gen. Alois Moser, a war criminal involved in the extermination of Jews in the Ukraine.
SS officer Alois Brunner, a senior member in Adolph Eichmann's Jewish Department.
SA Maj. Erich Bunz, an expert in the Jewish Question.
SS Capt. Wilhelm Böckler, a war criminal who took part in the liquidation of the Warsaw Ghetto.
Joachim Däumling, former Gestapo chief in Düsseldorf.
SS Gen. Oskar Dirlewanger, chief of the infamous SS penal brigade.
SS Maj. Schmalstich, who organized the transports of Jews from Paris to Auschwitz.

Once Skorzeny was under way, the operation fell under the control and observation of the CIA station chief in Cairo, Miles Copeland.

By the mid-1950s, the Nazis in Egypt evolved beyond rebuilding Egypt's military and intelligence operations into building missiles and aircraft. Wilhelm Voss was largely responsible for creating an Egyptian munitions industry with the help of Nazi scientists. He recruited several missile experts who had developed the V2 at Peenemunde. Many of the Nazi technicians were replaced with Soviets in the late 1950s when cooperation between Egypt and the USSR was at its height.

By 1960, more than 500 Germans were working in Egypt on aircraft or missile projects. Many of them went on to aid the chemical weapons projects of Libya and Iraq. For instance, Walter Busse designed missiles and jet engines for Nasser, and later worked as an adviser for Saddam Hussein's military R&D program.[138]

Skorzeny became a major arms supplier for the Salazar regime in Portugal. He worked with several firms, including the Virginia-based Interarms Co., run by former CIA agent Sam Cummings. Skorzeny was behind the formation of Bonn-based Merex Co., which was closely linked to the BND, Germany's postwar intelligence organization. Skorzeny's partner in Merex was Gerhard Mertens, a former Wehrmacht officer and an adviser to Nasser in the 1950s. Merex was a worldwide arms dealer. His principal contact in South America was Klaus Barbie, who escaped to Bolivia aided by the Vatican ratline, where he served as a security adviser to the military regimes.[139]

Skorzeny also provided training in the use of the weapons he supplied. His Paladin group was headquartered near Alicante, Spain. Its manager was Gerhard Harmut von Schubert, a veteran of Goebbels' propaganda ministry. Schubert trained security people in Argentina and Egypt after WWII. Under his command, the Paladin group provided support to Qaddafi, South Africa and the Greek colonels.[140]

The CIA's meddling in Egypt proved a resounding failure when Nasser chose to align himself with the Soviets. Much of the blame was due to the CIA's incessant demands that Egypt ally itself with the West. Nasser was a nationalist and wanted to remain neutral in the Cold War. After Egypt accepted a large arms deal from Czechoslovakia and recognized Communist China, the United States reneged on financing the Aswan Dam. The Russians generously financed it and provided further aid. However, Egypt's swing into the Soviet orbit was not entirely due to the ineptness of the CIA's demands. The CIA seemingly never considered that former Nazis might align themselves with the Soviets. Voss, the wirepuller behind the Czech arms deal, supervised the vast Skoda Works armament firm during WWII. While in Egypt, Voss recruited three of the firm's top engineers. *Der Spiegel* reported that the three engineers were communist agents. Voss' double-dealing was noted by U.S. Ambassador to Egypt Jefferson Caffery, who believed Voss aided Gen. Otto Ernst Remer's escape to Egypt. Voss saw advantages in dealing with the Soviets, as well as the West.

Moreover, the State Department was aware of the Nazis' duplicity as early as 1953. That year, a former SS veteran identified only by his code name, Kluf, warned the American consulate in Marseilles, France, of a secret international organization of former SS officers partially funded by the Soviets. The informant identified Skorzeny as an important figure and Countess Faber-Castell of the big German pencil maker as an important backer of the organization. The countess hid General Otto Ernst Remer before he fled to Egypt. Kluf told the State Department that Remer was cooperating with the Russians.

More evidence linking Skorzeny with the Soviets surfaced after British authorities arrested seven former high-ranking Nazi officials for conspiring to overthrow the Bonn Republic in 1953. H.S. Lucht Co. provided the cover for the conspirators and employed Skorzeny. The company, deeply involved in illegal trade with the Soviet bloc, was owned by Frau Lea Lucht.[141]

The Nazis played both the Soviets and the United States for dupes in funding their activities in Egypt. The plans for all parties involved in Egypt — the CIA, the Nazis and the Soviets — began to unravel in July 1956 after Nasser nationalized the Suez Canal. Three months later, British and French warplanes bombed Egyptian military targets and Israeli forces invaded the Sinai Peninsula. Worried about further Soviet encroachment in the Middle East, the Eisenhower administration denounced the bombing and pressured Israel to withdraw. Undeterred by its own ineptness, the CIA immediately turned to covert plans to remove Nasser. However, he remained the leader of Egypt until he resigned after losing the 1967 war with Israel.

Guatemala

Also in 1953, the CIA intervened in Guatemala, and regarded the action as a success. The bloody civil war to last 36 years. The legally elected government of Jacobo Arbenz Guzmán focused on land reform. In an overwhelmingly rural nation, only 2.2 percent of the population owned 70 percent of the land. Before the 1944 revolution and ousting of the dictatorship of Jorge Ubico, the army roped laborers together for delivery to lowland farms, where they were kept as debt slaves. Under the Arbenz government, the expropriation of large uncultivated tracts of land for landless peasants, the improvement in the rights of unions and other social reforms were hurting the bottom line of United Fruit. Arbenz even built a port on the Atlantic to compete against the one controlled by United Fruit; a public hydroelectric plant was constructed for the same reasons.

United Fruit was essentially a country within a country. It owned the telephone and telegraph systems, managed the only Atlantic port, and monopolized banana exports. A subsidiary owned the rail system. In the U.S., United Fruit had close ties to the Dulles brothers, various State Department officials, congressmen and the U.S. Ambassador to the UN. Former CIA Director Walter Bedell Smith was seeking an executive position with United Fruit at the same time he planned the Guatemala coup. He was later named to United Fruit's board of directors.

The first plan to oust Arbenz came during the Truman administration after Guatemala received arms from Czechoslovakia. The plan was put into effect after Eisenhower's election. International Armaments Corp. (formerly Interarmco, now known as Interarms) supplied weapons to the CIA rebels for the 1954 coup. Englishman Sam Cummings owned Interarmco. He got his start as the world's largest private provider of arms by supplying the CIA in the 1954 coup. At one point, Interarmco had enough weapons in its warehouses to equip 40 U.S. divisions.

James Atwood, a contract agent, worked closely with Cummings at times. Atwood smuggled guns into Guatemala and Nicaragua, and drugs into the United States. He also supplied arms to the IRA, as well as weapons and explosives to the Quebec Libre movement. The CIA's head of the Canada Desk at the company actively encouraged Quebec secession. Atwood was connected with both Skorzeny and Barbie, and had several former Gestapo and SD people working for him.

Atwood was involved in supplying arms to the Cuban insurgents for the Bay of Pigs. During that time, he learned the CIA was planning to use deadly toxins against the Cuban army. However, some of the toxins were accidentally released in southern Florida. Porter Goss, a CIA agent in Florida who was involved in planning the Cuban invasion, suddenly became "very ill." George W. Bush appointed Goss as CIA Director in 2005.

The Guatemala coup is an example of how the CIA manipulates American opinion. The CIA planted articles in the foreign press, which were then picked up by the news wires and newspapers in other countries. Besides the obvious multiplier effect on the potential audience, it had the appearance of independent world opinion. It was the same tactic that Bush tried to use against Clinton in the 1992 election.

The immediate effects of the coup were draconian. Within four months, 72,000 people were labeled communist, and many were tortured and murdered. U.S. Ambassador John Peurifoy had a long list of leaders the successor government was to assassinate.[142] Agrarian reform stopped and land already expropriated was given back to United Fruit. Union leaders turned up dead. Three-quarters of the population was disenfranchised with the barring of illiterates from the polls, and all political parties, unions and peasant organizations were outlawed.

Those Americans outraged at the seizing of the American Embassy in Tehran should consider John Foster Dulles' actions. Concerned that some "communists" might escape by taking refuge in foreign embassies, Dulles insisted that Guatemala arrest the refugees and deny asylum to communists. On these points Dulles lost, perhaps because the coup plotters had also sought refuge in embassies in the past.[143]

The blood bath and carnage that followed for the next 36 years can only be described as horrific. A genocidal war was carried out against the native Indians. Murders, kidnappings and disappearances became widespread, everyday events as right-wing death squads roamed the countryside. The Guatemala Truth Commission report found the army guilty of more than 200,000 deaths and disappearances – and 93 percent of the 42,000 deaths investigated in the report. Three percent were the work of the leftist Guatemalan National Revolutionary Unit; 4 percent were unresolved. The long-delayed report found that 29,000 of the investigated deaths involved summary executions; most of the victims were civilians and Mayans. The report also noted that the U.S. government trained Guatemalan officers in counterinsurgency methods to be used against the natives.

It was "clearly genocide and a planned strategy against the civilian population," said Christian Tomuschat, a German citizen who heads the three-member commission. "Government forces ... blindly pursued the anti-communist fight, without respecting any legal principle or even the most elemental ethical or religious values." In 626 massacres, the report found that government forces "completely exterminated Mayan communities, destroyed their dwellings, livestock and crops." The guerrillas were blamed for 32 such massacres.[144]

Guatemala became the first example of the right-wing death squads that have become so much a part of South American politics. The death squads and the dictators who employ them are products of the CIA-military intelligence system of the United States. They lead directly to the School of the Americas at Fort Benning, Ga. Recently, seven training manuals were released under the Freedom of Information Act. The manuals detail the use of torture, assassination and other criminal practices.

Throughout the manuals, refugees and displaced persons are highlighted as possible subversives who should be monitored. Universities are described as breeding grounds for terrorists, and priests and nuns are identified as involved in terrorist operations. Militaries are advised to infiltrate youth and student groups, labor unions, political parties and community organizations. Even electoral activity is suspect. The insurgents "can resort to subverting the government by means of elections in which the insurgents cause the replacement of an unfriendly government official to one favorable to their cause." Insurgent activity can include funding campaigns and participating in political races as candidates.[145]

In the 1980s, another aspect of these CIA interventions emerged: the association of the CIA with right-wing death squads and army leaders involved in the drug trade. The following quote illustrates the point:

The killings peaked in the early 1980s, though massacres continued to occur. By 1990, however, the military was no longer just killing for politics. It began killing for greed too. A scramble for drug profits within the Guatemalan military was under way. Guatemala, like Mexico, with which it shares its northern border, was never a major drug transshipment route before the early 1990s, when Colombians established transit operations across the entire northern isthmus. First the Medellin and then the Cali cartel came to Guatemala "because it is near Mexico, which is an obvious entrance point to the U.S., and because the Mexicans have a long-established mafia," said one Colombian drug enforcement official. "It is also a better transit and storage country than El Salvador because it offers more stability and was easier to control."

Guatemala's stability and control were achieved through cruelty unmatched anywhere in the region. Its counter-insurgency campaign was far more severe than El Salvador's. "The idea was to make the innocent pay for the guilty," said a former Guatemalan army sergeant from Quiche. The difference was that in El Salvador, military intelligence units might target a handful of young men to ensure that they killed at least one guerrilla, while in Guatemala, military intelligence units frequently killed innocent people, including children or seniors, to punish an entire village for supporting the guerrillas.[146]

The intervention in Guatemala served as a template throughout the remaining decades of the 20th century, especially in both South and Central America. Legally elected governments leaning to the left or announcing reforms that threatened corporate America were branded as communist and soon overthrown by covert support of hard-right rebellions. Invariably, the new regime was a brutal right-wing dictatorship that murdered thousands to suppress dissent. The United States soon recognized the new regime and offered support for its military and police, all in the name of combating communism and supporting freedom.

Support for right-wing guerrillas such as the Contras in Nicaragua was always sold to the American public as a fight against communist influence. The Reagan administration went so far as to question the patriotism of anyone not supporting the Contras. However, like the Conquistadors of earlier centuries, the real reason behind overthrowing reform-minded governments was to cheaply extract the natural resources and obtain cheap labor for corporate America.

The model was repeated throughout South and Central America. By 1970, the CIA had helped overthrow governments or covertly distorted elections in almost every South American country. One of the more pivotal coups removed Salvador Allende in 1973 in Chile — a culmination of a decade of covert actions by the CIA against Allende.

Chile

The CIA began covert operations in Chile following the 1958 presidential election, in which Allende came within 3 percent of winning. The next presidential election was scheduled in 1964, and Washington was determined that an avowed socialist like Allende not win.

In 1961, the Kennedy administration set up an electoral committee composed of more than 100 top-level officials from the State Department, the CIA and White House. A parallel committee was set up in the U.S. embassy in Chile. Committee operatives laid the groundwork for the election by establishing relationships with key political figures. After channeling funds to right-wing groups, the committee decided to back a centrist, Eduardo Frei of the Christian Democratic Party. The CIA underwrote more than half of the party's expenses in the 1964 election, spending an estimated $20 million.[147] The amount is about equal to the money spent by John F. Kennedy ($9.7 million) and Richard Nixon ($10.1 million) together in the 1964 election. The CIA took the Chilean election seriously.

The CIA spent the money on a scare campaign, with images of Russian tanks and Cuban firing squads, with extra attention on women and religion because, traditionally, women in Chile are more religious. The CIA produced massive volumes of propaganda to fill the airwaves and the press. Besides buying the press piecemeal, the agency subsidized wire services, magazines and right-wing newspapers from 1953–70.

One of the assets the CIA employed in the 1964 election was Roger Vekemans, a Belgian Jesuit who founded a network of social action organizations. Vekemans admits to receiving $5 million from the CIA, as well as a like amount of aid.[148] The results of the 1964 election were gratifying for the CIA. Frei won the election with a commanding margin of victory. The continued operations of the CIA propaganda network kept Allende and the socialists at bay throughout the 1960s. However, no amount of propaganda can cover the lack of needed reforms and social progress.

By 1970, Allende's popularity was high and his chances in the upcoming presidential election were good. His rising popularity did not go unnoticed by the Nixon White House, which increased anti-Allende spending by $300,000. The CIA continued to use its networks in Chile against Allende. Despite all efforts by the CIA and the Nixon White House, Allende won the Sept. 4 election.[149]

On Oct. 24, the Chilean Congress was due to confirm the winner, assuring Allende of the presidential office. This left the Nixon White House and the CIA with seven weeks to prevent him from taking office. Nixon met with Kissinger, CIA Director Richard Helms and Attorney General John Mitchell. The Committee of 40 received authorized funds to bribe Chilean congressmen to vote against Allende, but soon abandoned the effort as unfeasible. The Nixon administration concentrated on fermenting a military coup, which would cancel the congressional vote. The White House also made it clear that an assassination was not unwelcome.

The CIA and the Nixon administration launched a new propaganda campaign to impress on the military the danger of Allende taking office. Privately, military officers were threatened with a cut in aid if Allende were seated. During this seven-week period, the CIA produced more than 700 articles, broadcasts and editorials in Europe and Latin America. Journalists in the pay of the CIA from at least 10 countries traveled to Chile for on-the-spot coverage. The propaganda came with the usual communist scare tactics — fabricated stories that Allende would nationalize everything down to the small shops. The campaign was so intense that it affected the Chilean economy negatively, inducing a financial panic. The following excerpt from a CIA cable gives some indication of the scope of the campaign:

> Sao Paulo, Tegucigalpa, Buenos Aires, Lima, Montevideo, Bogota, Mexico City report continued replay of Chile theme materials. Items also carried in New York Times and Washington Post. Propaganda activities continue to generate good coverage of Chile developments along our guidance.[150]

Meanwhile, the CIA was consulting actively with several military officers receptive to a coup. It was difficult due to apolitical attitudes and support for the constitution. The prime obstacle to a military coup was the Commander and Chief of the Chilean Army, Rene Schneider, who insisted on following the constitution. The coup attempt was a direct result of a plea for action by Donald Kendall, chairman of PepsiCo, in two phone calls to the company's former lawyer, President Richard Nixon.

With time running out before Allende was seated, the CIA distributed sterilized machine guns and ammunition to some of the conspirators on the morning of Oct. 22. That same day, Schneider was mortally wounded in an attempted kidnapping. The CIA station in Santiago cabled headquarters that Schneider had been killed with CIA weapons.[151] The assassination did not result in a coup; instead, military officers rallied around the flag and the constitution. Two days later, Allende was seated as president. The Nixon administration responded by cutting aid to Chile, including loans from Export-Import Bank and Inter-American Development Bank. The following table shows the extent of the cuts:

Fiscal Year[152]	1965	'66	'67	'68	'69	'70	'71	'72	'73	1974
Total U.S. economic aid	130	112	260	97.1	8.8	29.6	8.6	7.4	3.8	9.8
USAID	99.5	93.2	15.5	57.9	35.4	18.0	1.5	1.0	.8	5.3
U.S. Food for Peace	14.2	14.4	7.9	23.0	15.0	7.2	6.3	5.9	2.5	3.2
U.S. Export-Import Bank	8.2	0.1	235	14.2	28.7	3.3	0	1.6	3.1	98.1
Total U.S. Military aid	9.9	10.1	4.1	7.8	11.8	.8	5.7	12.3	15.0	15.9
Total U.S. economic & military aid	140	122	264	105	91.8	30.4	14.3	21.3	21.9	124
Total inter-national organizations	12.4	72.0	93.8	19.4	49.0	76.4	15.4	8.2	9.4	111
World Bank	4.4	2.7	60	0	11.6	19.3	0	0	0	13.5
Inter-American Development Bank	4.9	62.2	31.0	16.5	31.9	45.6	12.0	2.1	5.2	97.3

In addition, holding what amounted to a veto, the United States denied all loans to Chile from the World Bank during 1971–73. The following U.S. banks canceled credit to Chile: Chase Manhattan, Chemical, First National City, Manufacturers Hanover and Morgan Guaranty. The CIA provided financial support to prolong strikes, and caused panic buying to further compound shortages. The CIA and the Nixon administration were determined to bring about a complete economic collapse and widespread public unrest to defeat the Allende government and prove socialism cannot work in the Western Hemisphere. The only assistance Chile received from the United States was military aid. The CIA kept in contact with its assets inside the military, relying heavily on its network to spread unrest and propaganda. Many of Chile's professionals were graduates of the Free Labor Development in Front Royal, Va., another CIA front used to spread anti-communism propaganda.

Large U.S. corporations also helped destabilize Chile in support of a coup to remove Allende. International Telephone and Telegraph (ITT) offered $1 million to Secretary of State Henry Kissinger. Officials denied the offer was accepted. However, former U.S. Ambassador to Chile Edward Korry has stated in recent interviews the offer was made by former CIA Director John McCone. McCone was a member of ITT's board at that time. The Nixon White House was well aware that ITT was illegally channeling money to the Republican Party. Korry also stated that Anaconda Copper and other multinationals, under the aegis of David Rockefeller's Business Group for Latin America, gave $350,000 to the CIA to bribe members of Congress.

In attempting to nationalize some of ITT's vast holdings, Chile was battling a financial giant larger than itself. In 1973, ITT's revenue was $10 billion, compared to Chile's GDP of less than $8.5 billion.

On Sept. 11, 1973, Allende's administration ended in a violent coup. Allende was killed after an assault on the presidential palace, where he and a group of dedicated followers made a last stand. Within twelve hours, most of the people with Allende who had survived the military assault were executed. Although there is no evidence that Americans took part in the actual assault on the presidential palace, there is plenty that the coup had ample American support. U.S. Navy ships were stationed just off the coast of Chile. There are many reports of members of the Chilean military and coup members taking part in discussions aboard the Navy ships shortly before the coup.

The U.S. School of the Americas (SOA), then located in Panama, trained many of the coup members. Gen. Ernesto Baeza, who led the assault on the palace, was an SOA alumnus. SOA has trained more than 60,000 Latin American soldiers in counter-insurgency techniques, sniper training, commando and psychological warfare, military intelligence and interrogation tactics. SOA graduates are some of the worst human rights abusers in South America. Human rights activists have tried for decades to shut down this "Death Squad U."

The Nixon administration immediately recognized the new regime and granted it $24 million in credit for wheat previously denied the Allende government. The resulting fascist regime of Augusto Pinochet was brutally repressive. Only 19 days after the coup, a briefing paper for Kissinger showed the death toll was 1,500, including 320 summarily executed. By mid-November, U.S. intelligence estimated 13,500 people had been arrested. Others were executed, disappeared or tortured, including two Americans killed in the mass executions at the national stadium.

Two months after the September 1973 coup, Col. Manuel Contreras organized the Directorate of National Intelligence (DINA), the Chilean secret police. CIA station chief Stuart Burton established a close liaison with Contreras and DINA. John Tipton, the political officer of the U.S. Embassy in Chile who cabled protests of human rights abuses back to Washington, claims the CIA and DINA were working together.

Throughout Pinochet's reign of terror, DINA was responsible for torturing, murdering and disappearing thousands. Many of the darkest deeds conducted by DINA took place at Colonia Dignidad. It was founded in 1961 by Paul Schaefer, a fanatical Nazi émigré from a colony of German immigrants who settled in the mid-1950s in an area 220 miles south of Santiago. Schaefer was an unrepentant SS veteran and former German army medic. He fled Germany to avoid arrest on charges that he whipped and molested several children at an orphanage near Bonn. After WWII, he became a Baptist-style preacher. Enthralled by his apocalyptic sermons, a sizable contingent of true believers followed him to Chile. The colony was surrounded with barbed wire and patrolled by armed guards with dogs. Those who tried to leave the colony faced various forms of psychological and corporal punishment, including prolonged isolation in small cages, beatings and drug injections.

Besides serving as a center for torturing and murdering DINA victims, Colonia Dignidad actively helped DINA locate its victims in Europe through its fascist national and international contacts, according to a recently declassified CIA document.[153] It also functioned as a shelter for Nazi war criminals in South America. Jack Anderson gave a few details about Colonia Dignidad in an Aug. 3, 1979 column, "Operation Condor, An Unholy Alliance."

Assassination teams are centered in Chile. This international consortium is located in Colonia Dignidad, Chile. Founded by Nazis from Hitler's SS, headed by Franz Pfeiffer Richter, Adolf Hitler's 1,000-year Reich may not have perished. Children are cut up in front of their parents, suspects are asphyxiated in piles of excrement or rotated to death over barbecue pits.

When Amnesty International disclosed the connection between Colonia Dignidad and DINA, several influential West German businessmen came to Schaefer's aid. In 1978, they formed a "Circle of Friends" to counter the adverse publicity from reports of human rights violations. The leading member of this Nazi support group was Gerhard Mertens, an international arms merchant who ran the Bonn-based Merex Co., founded by Skorzeny. Mertens is a longtime paid asset of the U.S. Defense Intelligence Agency and the CIA, and a collaborator with West Germany's BND spy agency, founded by Gehlen. The tentacles of Merex extend throughout South America in a network of ex-Nazi war criminals. Merex's principal contact in South America was Klaus Barbie in Bolivia. U.S. Army Counter-Intelligence Corps recruited Barbie early in the Cold War and aided his escape to Bolivia, where he advised a succession of right-wing regimes on security, while providing the CIA with information on leftist groups.

It was Merex that delivered 3 million rounds of ammunition to the Nicaraguan Contras while a ban on U.S. military aid was in effect. Lt. Col. Oliver North arranged the deal.

SS Colonel Walter Rauff, another Nazi war criminal, served as an adviser to DINA. During WWII, Rauff ran the gas vans on the Eastern Front.

In August 1975, two years after the coup, Contreras met in Washington with CIA Deputy Director Vernon Walters. The following month, Contreras asked Pinochet for another $600,000 for neutralizing the junta's principal adversaries abroad, especially in Mexico, Argentina, Costa Rica, the U.S. and Italy. On Nov. 25, 1975, delegates from Argentina, Bolivia, Paraguay and Uruguay met in Chile and established Operation Condor by an act of the Interamerican Reunion on Military Intelligence. Operation Condor did not end with pursuing leftist terrorism; it was designed to eliminate the Left in South America. Thousands of students, clergy, nuns, teachers and union leaders were brutally tortured, murdered or disappeared. It is inconceivable that Vice President Nelson Rockefeller, Henry Kissinger and CIA Director George H. W. Bush were not aware of the operation.

The resulting death toll and carnage in South America and Central America would not have been possible without the tactical approval of the United States. As national security advisor and later as Secretary of State, Kissinger sent an unequivocal signal to the most extreme right-wing forces that democracy could be sacrificed in the cause of ideological warfare. Kissinger only met Pinochet once, but during their meeting, Kissinger reassured Pinochet that human rights abuses were not a problem with the Ford administration. Kissinger's complicity with the Pinochet regime raised the possibility of Chile and other countries seeking his extradition.

George H. W. Bush deliberately misled the FBI about the existence of Condor in clearing Chile of involvement in the murder of Orlando Letelier. Operation Condor was an intelligence-sharing operation between DINA and the CIA. The FBI even provided the Pinochet regime with information on suspected associates of Chilean leftists in the United States.

Operation Condor was not confined to South America. Several people opposed to the Pinochet regime were murdered in Europe and the United States. During the summer of 1976, the CIA received information that Uruguayan military officials in Operation Condor threatened to assassinate U.S. Congressman Edward Koch because he had sponsored legislation to cut off U.S. military aid to Uruguay on human rights grounds. It was not until October, after the Letelier assassination in Washington, D.C., that CIA Director George H. W. Bush warned Koch to be careful.

In 2001, because of a meeting with an investigative journalist, Koch sought information from the CIA about why he had not been speedily warned of the terrorist threat on his life. The CIA refused to declassify the relevant documents, but sent Koch a letter suggesting initial analysis indicated the threat was nothing more than drunken bravado. Details of the threat also were deleted from State Department documents. However, the documents show the department did take action after the fact to prevent the two officers in question from entering the United States. In late 1976, Col. Fons and Maj. Gavazzo were assigned to prominent diplomatic posts in Washington D.C., but the State Department forced the Uruguayan government to withdraw their appointments.

Data on U.S. participation in Operation Condor is fragmentary at best. While President Clinton ordered the release of the documents, many still remain classified. Much of the information about Operation Condor comes from the Chilean Truth and Reconciliation Commission and the "archives of terror" discovered in Paraguay.

The Chilean commission entangled the U.S. embassy staff in Paraguay in the arrest and resulting murder of Jorge Isaac Fuentes Alarcon. The archives revealed the Condor network murdered a former president of Brazil and two Uruguayan parliamentarians, as well as hundreds of political activists. They also document the presence of Nazis throughout the southern cone of South America, and the connection of local intelligence services with drug traffickers and the CIA.

One outgrowth of the CIA's global intervention has been its involvement in the world drug trade. Thanks to *San Jose Mercury* investigative reporter Gary Webb, this issue has been placed before the American people. Webb's article, "Dark Alliance," detailed the CIA's involvement with the drug trade in Los Angeles. CIA assets in other major papers attacked the article in an effort to discredit it and distance the agency's long-rumored drug involvement. In 2004, Webb was murdered with two headshots from his own pistol.

The CIA's media assets were able to force the *Mercury* to retract the article and fire Webb, but they could not disprove his charges. There is a great deal more evidence beyond Webb's "Dark Alliance" article detailing the connection between the CIA and drugs. The CIA would need to discredit congressional testimony as well. An inkling of the CIA drug connection came on March 18, 1982, when CIA Inspector General Fred Hitz admitted before a congressional committee that the CIA maintained relationships with companies and individuals known to be involved in the drug trade. Even more damaging, he informed the congressional committee that the CIA requested and received approval from Reagan's Justice Department not to report knowledge of drug dealing by CIA assets.[155] At least one other writer traces the CIA drug trade back to the 1940s, when Col. Paul Helliwell of the OSS brought heroin from Burma and sold it in U.S. ghettos.[154]

The entire cover-up of the Iran/Contra/Cocaine scandal finally has been fully and undeniably established by the release of Volume Two of the CIA Inspector General's Drug Report on Oct. 8, 1998. To muffle congressional and public outrage, the report was released just one hour before Congress voted to hold impeachment proceedings against President Clinton. It is essentially a confession by the CIA that it engaged in a conspiracy to protect known narcotics traffickers throughout the Contra war years. The *New York Times,* in an apparent confirmation of the "Dark Alliance" article, picked a paragraph from the report that acknowledged the Contra leaders in California specifically planned to use drug money for the Contras. The *LA Times,* one of the most vicious critics of the "Dark Alliance" story, failed to print a single line on the new volume.

The report confirms the conspiratorial negotiations between the Justice Department and the CIA by first moving agents, assets and contractors into the private sector to avoid the responsibility of reporting drug dealing to Congress or anyone else. This confirms the earlier mentioned testimony of Hitz. Another portion of the report described a memorandum written by DCI Robert Gates setting down a no-nonsense policy against dealing with drug traffickers. The problem with the memorandum was it was not distributed for 15 years.[156]

Following WWII, the CIA intervened extensively in Italian and Japanese elections – U.S. allies are not immune from CIA intervention. In 1975, the CIA covertly overthrew the Australian government of Edward Whitlam. Elected in 1972, Whitlam soon withdrew Australian troops from Vietnam and ended the Aussie draft, recognized the government of North Vietnam and condemned the Nixon government.

Whitlam was a target of James Angleton, who was concerned about security and intelligence relationships with Australia. On Nov. 11, 1975, Governor-General John Kerr dismissed Whitlam as Prime Minister and dissolved both houses of parliament at the CIA's urging. It was the first time the British crown used this maneuver by the governor-general to remove a federal prime minister. It has been used only once in the history of Australia at the state level.

Economic Warfare

The record of CIA interventions leaves a bloody trail across the globe. The pattern is always the same: a popular government is legally elected and starts reforms that threaten the interests of multinational American corporations. Economic or military inducements are tried. If they fail, then the CIA begins covert methods to oust the government. These operations ended in a bloody coup in Chile and a brutal guerrilla war in the Contra revolution in Nicaragua, only two of many tactics used after all other means fail.

John Perkins in *Confessions of an Economic Hit Man* describes how multinational American corporations and the World Bank act as extended arms of the CIA.[157] Perkins, who was employed by the American consulting firm, MAIN, lays out a model of deliberate economic sabotage of countries, conducted by the CIA, the IMF and the World Bank. The first step is to coerce a country to sign a plan for economic development, which may include construction of a dam, airport, factory or other infrastructure. The plan is deliberately oversized in such way that there is no hope the country can ever repay the loan.

The country is deliberately misled by overly optimistic forecasts of the success and need for such projects. A few corrupt local politicians and rich families receive some funds to grease the way for the project. Once the economic forecasts fall short, the country slides into default on the loan. The World Bank then forces the country to accept austerity measures, which require the government to privatize property at fire sale prices, or grant other economic concessions to American corporations.

To further the economic rape of the country, the construction of the project is contracted to American corporations like Bechtel and Halliburton. While the World Bank guarantees the loan, most of the money goes straight to American contractors. In short, it is corporate welfare at the expense of the American taxpayer. Both Bechtel and Halliburton are closely linked to the Republican Party and the Bush family. Both companies have been awarded huge contracts in Iraq by George W. Bush. The ability of the United States to issue huge loans to foreign countries, never expecting repayment, depends largely on the dollar's acceptance as the world's reserve currency.[158]

One of the major reasons George W. Bush invaded Iraq was Saddam Hussein's threat to begin pricing oil in euros, undermining the dollar's reserve status and the fees of US bankers. Such a move by a major oil producer would have been greatly inflationary and wreaked havoc on the U.S. economy. It also is a major reason for the Bush regime's support of the abortive coup to remove Hugo Chavez from Venezuela, and the current claims by Chavez that the Bush administration is trying to assassinate him. It is only when the country refuses to go along with the plans that assassination squads are sent to remove the offending politician. If that fails, guerrillas are financed to remove the government or, as a last resort, American troops go in.

Ecuador exemplifies the way American corporations and the CIA engage in empire building. In the late 1960s, serious oil exploration focused on the Ecuadorian basin. A few of the local elite who ran Ecuador saddled the country with immense debt in a buying spree backed by the promise of oil revenues. Dams, industrial parks, roads and transmission lines sprang up across the country.

However, during the 1970s, protest candidate Jaime Roldos' political fortunes rose. Roldos was a university professor who took exception to the political corruption and complicity of politicians who operated with the corporations. In 1978, Roldos campaigned for president, attracting the attention of his countrymen and every nation where foreign countries exploited oil. Roldos went beyond just attacking the oil companies to include the Summer Institute of Linguistics (SIL). SIL is an American evangelical missionary group with sinister connections to oil companies. The group entered Ecuador under the pretext of studying local indigenous languages. In the Amazon basin, whenever the oil companies found a region with high probability of oil, SIL missionaries encouraged the Huaorani people to move onto reservations, where they received food and medical care in exchange for deeding their lands to the oil companies.

The mission also used an assortment of dirty tricks to encourage tribes to abandon their ancestral homeland. Often, they donated food laced with powerful laxatives, then offered medicines to cure the diarrhea epidemic. Other methods included dropping food baskets with false bottoms containing radio transmitters. U.S. military personnel monitored the radio broadcasts and whenever a tribe member was bitten by a poisonous snake or otherwise fell ill, missionaries miraculously showed up in oil company helicopters with the proper medicine.

SIL is also known as Wycliffe Bible Translators. Founded in 1934 by William Cameron Townsend, the institute began working closely with American intelligence in Mexico during WWII. It is associated with the Rockefeller family and receives funding from Rockefeller charities. Townsend worked with U.S. and foreign governments to secure the resources and pacify indigenous people in the name of democracy, corporate profit and religion, resulting in massacre and genocide.

Roldos based his oil policy on the premise that it should bring the greatest benefit to the largest percentage of people. He was the first democratically elected president of Ecuador, following a long line of dictators. After taking office, Roldos focused on Rockefeller-owned Texaco. Roldos was relentless in his attack on the oil companies and ordered SIL out of Ecuador. In 1981, Roldos formally presented his new hydrocarbon law, which would have significantly altered the relationship between oil companies and the government. It was considered revolutionary. Predictably, the oil companies reacted with anger, and soon their lobbyists were beseeching politicians in Quito and Washington. The oil companies portrayed Roldos as another Castro. Shortly after delivering a major policy speech warning all foreign interests to implement policies to help the Ecuadorian people, or else leave the country, Roldos was killed in a helicopter crash. He had been forewarned of an assassination attempt and was using two helicopters, but at the last minute, a security officer convinced him to take the decoy. Despite worldwide reaction, news of his death passed unnoticed in the United States. Osvaldo Hurtado took over as Ecuador's president, reinstated SIL, and allowed Texaco to increase drilling.[159]

After WWII, the United States had a chance to become the global leader in human rights, freedom and justice. Roosevelt planned on bringing to justice those who perpetrated the Holocaust and other war crimes, including U.S. industrialists who aided the Nazi cause. Unfortunately, he died before the end of the war, and his plans for justice died with him. Physically weakened by prolonged illness in the last years of his life, Roosevelt was unable to prevent fascist sympathizers from steadily gaining power. By the time he died, they were in places of power where they could affect policy.

At the end of the war, the OSS was badly divided between those committed to ridding the world of fascism and those sympathetic to it. Most of the OSS leadership came from Wall Street, with connections to firms that aided in building Hitler's war machine, and were now in position to protect their clients. However, Donovan also recruited agents from the labor movement, and even known socialists and communists dedicated to removing the fascist menace. After a campaign led by the *Chicago Tribune,* the OSS was promptly disbanded. Within a year, the same corporate benefactors who aided Nazi Germany created a new intelligence agency under their own control.

The Nuremberg Trials were sharply curtailed. Every trial ran the risk of exposing corporate America's crimes in aiding the Nazis. For the most part, the trials were a travesty of justice. Only a few high-ranking Nazis and low-ranking concentration guards were ever hanged for crimes in which more than 4 million Jews perished.

With the blessing of the CIA, other high-ranking Nazis had their records sanitized and were given positions of power. Thousands of Nazi war criminals were secretly recruited to work for the new agency, or for the CIA-controlled stay-behind networks. Even the most notorious war criminals were employed covertly by the agency, which helped many, such as Mengele and Barbie, escape through the Vatican ratlines to South America. Once safely in South America, the CIA employed these war criminals to overthrow popular, reform-minded governments and replace them with brutal dictatorships beholden to corporate America's interests.

This wedding of corporate interests with the new intelligence agency did not go unnoticed. While the Eisenhower administration was full of former Wall Street executives who aided the Nazi cause, the old general was not completely fooled. He had been tricked by Nazi sympathizers and beguiled with their Wall Street supporters. However, he was determined to caution the nation about the danger it faced. Shortly before leaving office, he left a rather cryptic warning:

Our military organization today bears little relation to that known by any of my predecessors in peacetime, or indeed by the fighting men of World War II or Korea.

Until the latest of our world conflicts, the United States had no armaments industry. American makers of plowshares could, with time and as required, make swords as well. But now we can no longer risk emergency improvisation of national defense; we have been compelled to create a permanent armaments industry of vast proportions. Added to this, 3.5 million men and women are directly engaged in the defense establishment. We annually spend on military security more than the net income of all United States corporations.

This conjunction of an immense military establishment and a large arms industry is new in the American experience. The total influence — economic, political, even spiritual — is felt in every city, every State house, every office of the Federal government. We recognize the imperative need for this development. Yet we must not fail to comprehend its grave implications. Our toil, resources and livelihood are all involved; so is the very structure of our society.

In the councils of government, we must guard against the acquisition of unwarranted influence, whether sought or unsought, by the military industrial complex. The potential for the disastrous rise of misplaced power exists and will persist.[160]

Sadly, the nation paid little heed to the old general's warning. The CIA was left to run amok. The information-gathering agency Truman envisioned when creating the CIA was hijacked into an agency engaged in covert operations by Frank Wisner, Allen Dulles, James Angleton, William Colby and others. It has illegally spied on Americans and suppressed dissent. It has taken over the nation's free press and become the world's largest drug importer. Even today, its budget remains secret.

APPENDICES

Appendix 1, Ch. 1: Fascism as Defined by Mussolini and Gentile

Note: This material is on the Web (www.fordham.edu/halsall/mod/mussolini-fascism.html). The reference comes from the collection of public domain and copy-permitted texts for introductory-level classes in modern European and World history.

Fascism, the more it considers and observes the future and the development of humanity quite apart from political considerations of the moment, believes neither in the possibility nor the utility of perpetual peace. It thus repudiates the doctrine of Pacifism — born of a renunciation of the struggle and an act of cowardice in the face of sacrifice. War alone brings up to its highest tension all human energy and puts the stamp of nobility upon the peoples who have courage to meet it. All other trials are substitutes, which never really put men into the position where they have to make the great decision — the alternative of life or death … .

… The Fascist accepts life and loves it, knowing nothing of and despising suicide: he rather conceives of life as duty and struggle and conquest, but above all for others — those who are at hand and those who are far distant, contemporaries, and those who will come after...

… Fascism [is] the complete opposite of … Marxian Socialism, the materialist conception of history of human civilization [that] can be explained simply through the conflict of interests among the various social groups and by the change and development in the means and instruments of production... Fascism, now and always, believes in holiness and in heroism; that is to say, in actions influenced by no economic motive, direct or indirect. And if the economic conception of history be denied, according to which theory men are no more than puppets, carried to and fro by the waves of chance, while the real directing forces are quite out of their control, it follows that the existence of an unchangeable and unchanging class-war is also denied — the natural progeny of the economic conception of history. And above all, Fascism denies that class-war can be the preponderant force in the transformation of society...

After Socialism, Fascism combats the whole complex system of democratic ideology and repudiates it, whether in its theoretical premises or in its practical application. Fascism denies that the majority, by the simple fact that it is a majority, can direct human society; it denies that numbers alone can govern by means of a periodical consultation, and it affirms the immutable, beneficial and fruitful inequality of mankind, which can never be permanently leveled through the mere operation of a mechanical process, such as universal suffrage...

… Fascism denies, in democracy, the absur[d] conventional untruth of political equality dressed out in the garb of collective irresponsibility, and the myth of "happiness" and indefinite progress...

… given that the nineteenth century was the century of Socialism, of Liberalism and of Democracy, it does not necessarily follow that the twentieth century must also be a century of Socialism, Liberalism and Democracy: political doctrines pass, but humanity remains, and it may rather be expected that this will be a century of authority … a century of Fascism. For if the nineteenth century was a century of individualism, it may be expected that this will be the century of collectivism and hence the century of the State...

The foundation of Fascism is the conception of the State, its character, its duty and its aim. Fascism conceives of the State as an absolute, in comparison with which all individuals or groups are relative, only to be conceived of in their relation to the State. The conception of the Liberal State is not that of a directing force, guiding the play and development, both material and spiritual, of a collective body, but merely a force limited to the function of recording results: on the other hand, the Fascist State is itself conscious and has itself a will and a personality — thus it may be called the "ethic" State...

... The Fascist State organizes the nation, but leaves a sufficient margin of liberty to the individual; the latter is deprived of all useless and possibly harmful freedom, but retains what is essential; the deciding power in this question cannot be the individual, but the State alone...

... For Fascism, the growth of empire, that is to say the expansion of the nation, is an essential manifestation of vitality, and its opposite a sign of decadence. Peoples which are rising, or rising again after a period of decadence, are always imperialist; and renunciation is a sign of decay and of death. Fascism is the doctrine best adapted to represent the tendencies and the aspirations of a people, like the people of Italy, who are rising again after many centuries of abasement and foreign servitude. But empire demands discipline, the coordination of all forces and a deeply felt sense of duty and sacrifice: this fact explains many aspects of the practical working of the regime, the character of many forces in the State, and the necessarily severe measures which must be taken against those who would oppose this spontaneous and inevitable movement of Italy in the twentieth century, and would oppose it by recalling the outworn ideology of the nineteenth century — repudiated wheresoever there has been the courage to undertake great experiments of social and political transformation; for never before has the nation stood more in need of authority, of direction and order. If every age has its own characteristic doctrine, there are a thousand signs which point to Fascism as the characteristic doctrine of our time. For if a doctrine must be a living thing, this is proved by the fact that Fascism has created a living faith; and that this faith is very powerful in the minds of men is demonstrated by those who have suffered and died for it.

Appendix 2, Ch. 1: The Nazi Party 25-Point Program

The Program of the NSDAP
Edited by: Dr. Robert Ley
Published by: Central Publishing House of the N.S.D.A.P.,
Franz Eher's Successors Ltd, Munich

The program is the political foundation of the NSDAP and accordingly the primary political law of the State. It has been made brief and clear intentionally.

All legal precepts must be applied in the spirit of the party program.

Since the taking over of control, the Fuehrer has succeeded in the realization of essential portions of the Party program from the fundamentals to the detail.

The Party Program of the NSDAP was proclaimed on the 24 February 1920 by Adolf Hitler at the first large Party gathering in Munich and since that day has remained unaltered. Within the national socialist philosophy is summarized in 25 points:

1. We demand the unification of all Germans in the Greater Germany on the basis of the right of self-determination of peoples.

2. We demand equality of rights for the German people in respect to the other nations; abrogation of the peace treaties of Versailles and St. Germain.

3. We demand land and territory (colonies) for the sustenance of our people, and colonization for our surplus population.

4. Only a member of the race can be a citizen. A member of the race can only be one who is of German blood, without consideration of creed. Consequently no Jew can be a member of the race.

5. Whoever has no citizenship is to be able to live in Germany only as a guest, and must be under the authority of legislation for foreigners.

6. The right to determine matters concerning administration and law belongs only to the citizen. Therefore we demand that every public office, of any sort whatsoever, whether in the Reich, the county or municipality, be filled only by citizens. We combat the corrupting parliamentary economy, office-holding only according to party inclinations without consideration of character or abilities.

7. We demand that the state be charged first with providing the opportunity for a livelihood and way of life for the citizens. If it is impossible to sustain the total population of the State, then the members of foreign nations (non-citizens) are to be expelled from the Reich.

8. Any further immigration of non-citizens is to be prevented. We demand that all non-Germans, who have immigrated to Germany since the 2 August 1914, be forced immediately to leave the Reich.

9. All citizens must have equal rights and obligations.

10. The first obligation of every citizen must be to work both spiritually and physically. The activity of individuals is not to counteract the interests of the universality, but must have its result within the framework of the whole for the benefit of all Consequently we demand:

11. Abolition of unearned (work and labour) incomes. Breaking of rent-slavery.

12. In consideration of the monstrous sacrifice in property and blood that each war demands of the people personal enrichment through a war must be designated as a crime against the people. Therefore we demand the total confiscation of all war profits.

13. We demand the nationalization of all (previous) associated industries (trusts).

14. We demand a division of profits of all heavy industries.

15. We demand an expansion on a large scale of old age welfare.

16. We demand the creation of a healthy middle class and its conservation, immediate communalization of the great warehouses and their being leased at low cost to small firms, the utmost consideration of all small firms in contracts with the State, county or municipality.

17. We demand a land reform suitable to our needs, provision of a law for the free expropriation of land for the purposes of public utility, abolition of taxes on land and prevention of all speculation in land.

18. We demand struggle without consideration against those whose activity is injurious to the general interest. Common national criminals, usurers, Schieber and so forth are to be punished with death, without consideration of confession or race.

19. We demand substitution of a German common law in place of the Roman Law serving a materialistic world-order.

20. The state is to be responsible for a fundamental reconstruction of our whole national education program, to enable every capable and industrious German to obtain higher education and subsequently introduction into leading positions. The plans of instruction of all educational institutions are to conform with the experiences of practical life. The comprehension of the concept of the State must be striven for by the school [Staatsbuergerkunde] as early as the beginning of understanding. We demand the education at the expense of the State of outstanding intellectually gifted children of poor parents without consideration of position or profession.

21. The State is to care for the elevating national health by protecting the mother and child, by outlawing child-labor, by the encouragement of physical fitness, by means of the legal establishment of a

gymnastic and sport obligation, by the utmost support of all organizations concerned with the physical instruction of the young.

22. We demand abolition of the mercenary troops and formation of a national army.

23. We demand legal opposition to known lies and their promulgation through the press. In order to enable the provision of a German press, we demand, that: a. All writers and employees of the newspapers appearing in the German language be members of the race: b. Non-German newspapers be required to have the express permission of the State to be published. They may not be printed in the German language: c. Non-Germans are forbidden by law any financial interest in German publications, or any influence on them, and as punishment for violations the closing of such a publication as well as the immediate expulsion from the Reich of the non-German concerned. Publications which are counter to the general good are to be forbidden. We demand legal prosecution of artistic and literary forms which exert a destructive influence on our national life, and the closure of organizations opposing the above made demands.

24. We demand freedom of religion for all religious denominations within the state so long as they do not endanger its existence or oppose the moral senses of the Germanic race. The Party as such advocates the standpoint of a positive Christianity without binding itself confessionally to any one denomination. It combats the Jewish-materialistic spirit within and around us, and is convinced that a lasting recovery of our nation can only succeed from within on the framework: common utility precedes individual utility.

25. For the execution of all of this we demand the formation of a strong central power in the Reich. Unlimited authority of the central parliament over the whole Reich and its organizations in general. The forming of state and profession chambers for the execution of the laws made by the Reich within the various states of the confederation. The leaders of the Party promise, if necessary by sacrificing their own lives, to support by the execution of the points set forth above without consideration.

Adolf Hitler proclaimed the following explanation for this program on the 13 April 1928:

Explanation

Regarding the false interpretations of Point 17 of the program of the NSDAP on the part of our opponents, the following definition is necessary:

"Since the NSDAP stands on the platform of private ownership it happens that the passage" gratuitous expropriation concerns only the creation of legal opportunities to expropriate if necessary, land which has been illegally acquired or is not administered from the view-point of the national welfare. This is directed primarily against the Jewish land-speculation companies.

Source: Nazi Conspiracy and Aggression Volume IV
Office of the United States Chief Counsel for Prosecution of Axis Criminality
Washington, DC : United States Government Printing Office, 1946
© 1996-2007 The Avalon Project at Yale Law School.
Document No. 1708-PS

Appendix 3, Ch. 1: Vesting Orders against Brown Bros. Harriman

Vesting orders for assets seized from Brown Brothers Harriman according to government archives on the following Web site: (www.archives.gov/iwg/ declassified_records/rg_131_alien_property/rg_131_records_03.html).

Vesting Order 7338: Certain debts owing to Good Hope Steel & Iron Works by Brown Brothers Harriman & Co.; and all rights of the former in a sinking fund held by the latter.

Vesting Order 7874: A debt owing to IGF by the Chase National Bank of the City of New York.

Vesting Order 7876: A debt owing to City of Hanover, Germany, by Brown Brothers Harriman & Co.

Vesting Order 8494: Certain securities owned by the heirs of August Thyssen Jr.; and certain debts owing to them by the Union Banking Corp.

Vesting Order 9201: Certain bank accounts and certain securities owned by Bank voor Handel en Scheepvaart N.V.

Vesting Order 9367: A debt owing to Deutsche Bank by the Chase National Bank of the City of New York.

Vesting Order 9396: Certain securities owned by Martha Obermeyer; and a debt owing to her by Brown Brothers Harriman & Co.

Vesting Order: 10742: Certain securities owned by Genossenschaft Keramik; a debt owing to them by Guaranty Trust Co.; and a debt owing to them by Brown Bros., Harriman & Co.

Vesting Order 1130: A debt owing to Fried Krupp A. G. by the Chase National Bank of the City of New York.

Vesting Order 11778: Certain securities owned by Aramo-Stiftung; and certain debts owing to them by Brown Brothers Harriman & Co.

Vesting Order 13996 & 14178: Certain securities owned by Willy Schniewind and others; and a debt owing to them by Brown Brothers Harriman & Co.

Vesting Order 14432: Certain securities owned by Willibald Bohm; and certain debts owing to him by Brown Brothers Harriman & Co.

Vesting Order 14688: Certain securities owned by Johanna Bohnenberger-Stierlin; and a debt owing to her by Brown Brothers Harriman & Co.

Vesting Order 15071: Certain securities owned by Kati Krause; and a debt owing to her by Brown Bros., Harriman & Co.

Vesting Order 15096: Certain securities owned by Deutsche Uberseeische Bank, A.G. and others; and a debt owing to Compania Argentina de Mandatos-Sociedad Anonima by Brown Bros., Harriman & Co.

Vesting Order: 15464: Certain securities owned by Theresia M. I.B.H.S.M. von Schwarzenberg; two debts owing to her by Swiss American Corp., and a debt owing to her by Brown Bros., Harriman & Co.

Vesting Order 15723: Certain securities owned by Ida Deetjen and Ella Deetjen; a bank account owned by them; and certain debts owing to them by Credit Suisse and Brown Bros., Harriman & Co.

Vesting Order 17615: 7/10 interest in certain securities owned by Albert Tottien and others; certain debts owing to them by Credit Suisse; and a debt owing to them by Brown Bros., Harriman & Co.

Vesting Order 17641: A debt owing to Willy Arend by Brown Bros., Harriman & Co.; a debt owing to him by the Chase National Bank of the City of New York and certain securities owned by him.

Vesting Order 17734: Certain securities owned by Dr. Georg Barth and others; a debt owing to them by Brown Bros., Harriman & Co.; and a debt owing to them by the National City Bank of New York.

Vesting Order 17992: Certain securities owned by Elise Probsthain and others; and a debt owing to them by Brown Bros. Harriman & Co.

Vesting Order: 18904: Certain securities, including Hugo Stinnes 4% bonds owned by L. Wenzel and a debt owing to him by the Chase National Bank of the City of New York and Herzfeld & Stern.

Appendix 4, Ch. 1: Vesting order No. 248

FEDERAL REGISTER, *Saturday, November 7, 1942* 9097

[Vesting Order Number 248]

ALL OF THE CAPITAL STOCK OF UNION BANK-
ING CORPORATION AND CERTAIN INDEBTED-
NESS OWING BY IT

Under the authority of the Trading
with the enemy Act, as amended, and
Executive Order No. 9095, as amended,[1]
and pursuant to law, the undersigned,
after investigation, finding:

(a) That the property described as
follows:

All of the capital stock of Union Banking
Corporation, a New York corporation, New
York, New York, which is a business enterprise within the United States, consisting of
4,000 shares of $100 par value common capital
stock, the names of the registered owners
of which, and the number of shares owned
by them respectively, are as follows:

Names	Number of shares
E. Roland Harriman	3,991
Cornelius Lievense	4
Harold D. Pennington	1
Ray Morris	1
Prescott S. Bush	1
H. J. Kouwenhoven	1
Johann G. Groeninger	1
Total	4,000

[1] 7 F.R. 5205.

all of which shares are held for the benefit
of Bank voor Handel en Scheepvaart, N. V.,
Rotterdam, The Netherlands, which bank is
owned or controlled by members of the Thyssen family, nationals of Germany and/or
Hungary,

is property of nationals, and represents
ownership of said business enterprise
which is a national, of a designated enemy country or countries (Germany
and/or Hungary);

(b) That the property described as
follows:

All right, title, interest and claim of any
name or nature whatsoever of the aforesaid
Bank voor Handel en Scheepvaart, and August Thyssen-Bank, Berlin, Germany, and
each of them, in and to all indebtedness, contingent or otherwise and whether or not
matured, owing to them, or each of them, by
said Union Banking Corporation, including
but not limited to all security rights in and
to any and all collateral for any or all of
such indebtedness and the right to sue for
and collect such indebtedness.

is an interest in the aforesaid business
enterprise held by nationals of an enemy
country or countries, and also is property within the United States owned or
controlled by nationals of a designated
enemy country or countries (Germany
and/or Hungary);

and determining that to the extent that
any or all of such nationals are persons
not within a designated enemy country,
the national interest of the United States
requires that such persons be treated as
nationals of the aforesaid designated
enemy country or countries (Germany
and/or Hungary), and having made all
determinations and taken all action,
after appropriate consultation and cer-
tification, required by said executive
order or Act or otherwise, and deeming
it necessary in the national interest,
hereby vests such property in the Alien
Property Custodian, to be held, used, administered, liquidated, sold or otherwise
dealt with in the interest of and for the
benefit of the United States.

Such property and any or all of the
proceeds thereof shall be held in a special account pending further determination of the Alien Property Custodian.
This shall not be deemed to limit the
powers of the Alien Property Custodian
to return such property or the proceeds
thereof, or to indicate that compensation
will not be paid in lieu thereof, if and
when it should be determined that such
return should be made or such compensation should be paid.

Any person, except a national of a
designated enemy country, asserting any
claim arising as a result of this order
may file with the Alien Property Custodian a notice of his claim, together with
a request for a hearing thereon, on Form
APC-1, within one year from the date
hereof, or within such further time as
may be allowed by the Alien Property
Custodian. Nothing herein contained
shall be deemed to constitute an admission of the existence, validity or right
to allowance of any such claim.

The terms "national", "designated enemy country" and "business enterprise
within the United States" as used herein
shall have the meanings prescribed in
section 10 of said executive order.

Executed at Washington, D. C., on October 20, 1942.

[SEAL] LEO T. CROWLEY,
Alien Property Custodian.

F. R. Doc. 42-11568; Filed, November 6, 1942;
11:31 a. m.]

Appendix 5, Ch. 1: A Timeline of Treason

1833: The Order of Skull and Bones formed at Yale.

1860: George Warde Norman is a director of the Bank of England and head of Brown Brothers during the American Civil War, when his company handles 75% of the South's cotton exports to England.

1897: Union Pacific Railroad bankrupted.

1898: Union Pacific Railroad sold to Edward Henry Harriman and his partner, Judge Robert Scott Lovett. The deal is managed by the Kuhn Loeb brokerage, of which Felix Warburg is a partner.

1902: Paul and Felix Warburg emigrate to the United States.

1904: Alfred Ploetz founds the Archive for Racial and Social Biology, which becomes the chief journal of the German eugenics or race hygiene movement. Ernst Haeckel popularizes eugenics in Germany.

John D. Rockefeller issues "Occasional Letter No.1" detailing plans to mold the people, reduce national intelligence to the lowest common denominator, destroy parental influence, traditions and customs, and eliminate science and real learning, "in order to perfect human nature".

Eugenics laboratory established at Cold Springs Harbor on Long Island. Cold Springs Harbor is also the location of the estates of both Dulles brothers. The Cold Springs facility is funded in excess of $11 million by the Harrimans and the Rockefellers.

1907: Indiana passes the first eugenics law.

Samuel Bush elected President of Buckeye Steel Castings Co. in Columbus, Ohio. For his entire career, Samuel Bush supplies Wall Street's railroads with castings. Later Bush becomes a close advisor of President Hoover and the first president of the National Manufacturers Association. (NAM). NAM has a history of supporting fascism; in the 1950s, members of NAM led by Robert Welch form the John Birch Society.

1909: The Rockefeller Foundation is established. The Rockefellers support the eugenics movement, including the Kaiser Wilhelm Institute in Germany.

1911: John Foster Dulles joins Sullivan and Cromwell.

1913: Federal Reserve Bank created. Paul Warburg serves as a governor of the bank during WWI. At the same time, his brother Max is head of the German Secret Service.

1914: With war close at hand, Percy Rockefeller takes control of Remington Arms and appoints Samuel F. Pryor as CEO.

WWI breaks out in Europe.

Adolf Hitler serves in German military intelligence.

1915: Secretary of State Robert Lansing recruits his nephew John Foster Dulles to go to Nicaragua, Costa Rica and Panama to sound out the Latin Americans on aiding the US war effort. Costa Rica is led by the vicious dictator Federico Tinoco. Dulles advises Washington to support Tinoco, who is anti-German. Dulles encourages the Nicaraguan dictator Emiliano Chamorro to suspend diplomatic relations with Germany. Dulles offers to waive the tax on Panama's annual canal fees if it will declare war on Germany.

1917: Prescott Bush joins Skull and Bones. His son and grandson George H. W. and George W. will likewise become members. Brown Brothers & Harriman is home to an exceptional number of members during the 1930s.

USA joins the war against Germany.

1918: Robert Scott Lovett elected president of Union Pacific. Samuel Bush appointed to the US War Industries Board chaired by Bernard Baruch and his assistant, Clarence Dillon.

Germany surrenders on Nov. 11.

1919: George Herbert Walker forms W. A. Harriman & Co. He is president and CEO. Averell Harriman, son of Edward Harriman is chairman. Averell later serves as US Ambassador to the USSR, 1943-1946, and as US Secretary of Commerce 1946-1948.

The Dulles brothers are involved in the treaty negotiations after WWI.

1920: Averell Harriman and George Walker gain control of the German Hamburg-Amerika Line. The deal is arranged by the chief executive of Hamburg-Amerika, William Cuno, with Max Warburg of the line's bankers. The name is changed to American Ship & Commerce Corp. Samuel F. Pryor of Remington Arms is involved in the deal and serves on the board. Cuno later becomes a heavy contributor to the Nazi Party.

1922: Averell Harriman opens a Berlin branch of W.A. Harriman. He meets with Thyssen and they agree to set up a bank for Thyssen in New York.

The Model Eugenic Sterilization Law is published by Harry Laughlin. It leads to the sterilization of over 20,000 Americans, and to the Nazi Nuremberg laws.

1923: Fritz Thyssen begins to contribute to the Nazi party.

1924: W.A.Harriman & Co invests $400,000 to set up Union Banking Corp to partner with the Thyssen-owned Bank voor Handel en Scheepvart in Holland and to transfer funds for Thyssen's United Steel. Prescott Bush is brought in to manage Union Bank. He is son-in-law of George Walker and son of Samuel Bush.

Coinciding with the Dawes Plan (see Ch. 3), John Foster Dulles arranges a large loan for Krupp.

Ethyl Corporation formed jointly by Standard Oil and General Motors.

1925: I.G. Farben has established powerful allies inside the Republican administration. Secretary of Commerce Herbert Hoover appoints a nine-member board, the Chemical Advisory Committee, whose role is to help America's chemical industry fight off the I.G. Farben cartel. Seated on the committee are Walter Teagle (Standard Oil of New Jersey), Lammot du Pont, Frank Blair (President of Sterling) and Henry Howard (Vice-president of Grasselli). All four have extensive ties with I.G. Farben.

1926: Prescott Bush promoted to Vice-President of W. A. Harriman & Co. Clarence Dillon of Dillon Read sets up the German Steel Trust with Thyssen and his partner, Fredrick Flick. Two Dillon Read representatives are on the board of the Trust. Its CEO Albert Voegler is instrumental in bringing Hitler to power. He is a director in Thyssen's Dutch bank and the Hamburg-Amerika Line. Walker, Bush and Harriman own a third of Flick's holding company.

American I.G. founded to hold I.G. Farben assets in the United States. Edsel Ford, Rockefeller and Warburg representatives are on the board.

Allen Dulles joins Sullivan and Cromwell.

1927: John Foster Dulles is director of the GAF Company (American I.G.) until 1934.

1929: Standard Oil and I.G. Farben begin cartel negotiations

1930: Dulles arranges sale of Silesian Coal Co. to his friend Schacht, the Nazi economic minister. Dulles thus becomes director of a company holding a one-third interest in Frederick Flick's Upper Silesian Coal and Steel Company.

1931: W. A. Harriman merges with the British firm Brown Brothers. Thatcher Brown, Prescott Bush and the two Harriman brothers are the senior partners. Robert Lovett, son of Robert Scott Lovett and a close friend of Prescott Bush, becomes a partner. (He will later serve as Asst. Sec. for Air during WWII, as Under Sec. of State 1947-1949, as Deputy Sec. of Defense 1950-1951 and as Secretary of Defense 1951-1953.)

Prescott Bush runs the New York office, Thatcher Brown runs the London office. Montagu Collet Norman, much like his grandfather George Warde Norman, is governor of the Bank of England and a partner of Brown Brothers. He is a close friend of Prescott Bush and a Nazi sympathizer.

Prescott Bush and George Walker host the Third International Congress of Eugenics calling for the sterilization of fourteen million Americans.

Bank of International Settlements formed.

1933: On January 4, a group of industrialists invite Hitler to the Schroeder Bank. They fund him in turn for a pledge to break the trade unions. Present at the meeting are John Foster Dulles and Allen Dulles.

Hitler assumes power.

Prescott Bush appoints Max Warburg to be the American Ship & Commerce Line representative on the Hamburg-Amerika Line board. Warburg is a long-time advisor of Nazi Economic Minister Hjalmar Schacht, a Reichsbank executive and close friend of Montagu Collet Norman.

Schacht and John Foster Dulles agree to coordinate all trade between Germany and America, in a syndicate of 150 firms set up by the Harrimans.

John D. Rockefeller appoints William S. Farish chairman of Standard Oil. He is close friends with the chairman of I.G. Farben. Farish pays for pro-Nazi propaganda in the U.S. press, for Nazi German crews on Standard Oil tankers, and for payments to the Nazi SS into 1944, when the SS will supervise the mass murder at the Standard-I.G. Farben

Auschwitz death camp, among others.

1934: The US Senate Nye Committee hearings reveal that Samuel Pryor, chairman of Remington Arms and founding director of both the UBC and the American Ship & Commerce Corp., has joined in a cartel agreement with I.G. Farben, and that the Nazis are armed with mostly American weapons.

With Hitler in solid control of Germany, Thyssen-Flick profits soar to over a hundred million and Union Bank is overflowing with money. Prescott Bush becomes its managing director responsible for German operations.

John Foster Dulles publicly supports the Nazi philosophy and German rearmament, up until the invasion of Poland in 1939.

1935: Against Washington's wishes, Standard Oil affiliate Ethyl Corporation signs a joint agreement with Nazi Germany and fascist Italy for the production of tetraethyl lead.

Nuremberg Laws are passed in Germany, paving the way for the Holocaust.

1936: The Schroeder Bank in New York merges with the Rockefellers of Standard Oil.

1937: Dulles merges all his cloaking of Nazi assets for Standard Oil and clients like Prescott Bush into an account at Brown Brothers Harriman-Schroeder Rockefeller.

1939: Hitler invades Poland; the war starts in Europe.

Farish's daughter Martha marries Averell Harriman's nephew, Edward Harriman Gerry.

Demand for slave labor by the Consolidated Silesian Steel Corporation plant in Auschwitz, Poland leads to the founding of the notorious death camp there. Prescott Bush reportedly directs a portion of the slave labor force.

1940: Allen Dulles is on the board of the Schroeder bank, with John Foster Dulles as its legal counsel. The bank acts as a financial arm of the Nazi regime.

1941: Pearl Harbor bombed and war is declared.

1942: Under the Trading with the Enemy Act, the US Alien Property Custodian seizes the shares of the Union Banking Corp. of New York, whose shareholders include the Harrimans, Prescott S. Bush, and representatives of Nazi Germany.

William Stamps Farish pleads "no contest" to charges of criminal conspiracy with the Nazis.

Standard Oil's 94%-owned subsidiary in Germany is represented in the inner circles of Nazism, Himmler's Circle of Friends, and linked to major German banks.

1945: The Treasury Department reveals to Congress that United Steel produced the following percentages of war munitions for the Nazis: Pig iron 50.8%; Pipe and tubes 45.5%; Universal plate 41.4%; Galvanised sheet 38.5%; Heavy plate 36%; Explosives 35%. Prescott Bush, Hitler's banker, is also banker for United Steel.

Allen Dulles seeks out young Naval Officer Richard Nixon who has been put in charge of captured Nazi documents which reveal Dulles as a traitor. Dulles finances Nixon's first race for office in exchange for burying the documents.

Project Paperclip begins to import Nazis into the United States.

1946: Nixon defeats five-term Democrat Jerry Voorhis for Congress, with the help of big contributions from New York banks.

1947: Authorities discover the accounts of the Silesian American Corporation in the books of Bank voor Handel en Scheepvaart. The bank manager is shocked and travels to New York to inform Prescott Bush. Two weeks later, he suddenly dies of a heart attack.

1950: Prescott Bush defeated in his Senate race due to his background of association with the American eugenics movement.

1951: Union Bank liquidated; Bush family receives $1.5 million.

1952: Prescott Bush elected to Senate. He is instrumental in the selection of Nixon as vice presidential candidate.

1953: John Foster Dulles appointed Secretary of State, Allen Dulles Director of the CIA.

With funds from Brown Brothers and Harriman, George H. W. Bush forms Zapata Oil, a CIA front.

1954: The CIA under Allen Dulles sponsors a putsch against Jacobo Arbenz in Guatemala on behalf of United Fruit. Schroeder Bank is partners with United Fruit; Dulles is still on the Schroeder board. Both Dulles brothers have a stake in United Fruit.

1961: C. Dillon appointed Secretary of Treasury.

Invasion of Cuba turns into the Bay of Pigs fiasco. George H. W. Bush is linked to the operation. In 1981, the year before Bush's election to vice president, all SEC records of Zapata between 1960 and 1966 disappear.

President John F. Kennedy fires Allen Dulles after the Bay of Pigs.

1963: John F. Kennedy assassinated.

1964: George H. W. Bush campaigns against the Civil Rights Act in his bid for the Senate, loses.

1966: George H. W. Bush elected to Congress.

1968: Nixon elected President.

1969: Zapata buys a controlling interest in United Fruit, another company with strong CIA ties and involvement in the overthrow of reform-minded Central American governments.

1971: George H. W. Bush appointed as ambassador to the United Nations.

1972: Watergate scandal erupts during Nixon's reelection campaign. George H. W. Bush appointed chairman of the Republican Party. Bush sets up ethnic heritage groups in the party as havens for Nazi émigrés.

1975: CIA Director William Colby reveals information about CIA secret domestic operations Mockingbird and MK-Ultra. Dick Cheney seeks Colby's removal.

1976: George H. W. Bush appointed CIA director by President Gerald Ford, a former member of the pro-Nazi group, American First.

George H. W. Bush allows the execution of Chilean dissident Orlando Letelier by the fascist Pinochet regime. Bush is fully informed of the Operation Condor program to execute or assassinate dissidents in South America.

1984: Arbusto Energy Inc founded by George W Bush, is sold after proving to be a failure.

1988: Silverado Savings & Loan shut down by regulators. Neil Bush, brother of George W. Bush, is a director. The seizure and investigation are delayed until after the election.

Nazi collaborators and war criminals are on the staff of the Bush campaign. William Draper is in charge of Bush campaign funding. His grandfather founded the Pioneer Fund to promote eugenics.

1989: George H. W. Bush takes oath of office as President, places his assets in a blind trust managed by William S. Farish III, grandson of the William S. Farish who supplied gas to the concentration camps.

1990: Following the Gulf War, Bahrain awards an offshore drilling contract to Harken Oil, a firm affiliated with George W. Bush. George W. sells his stake in Harken and one week later the share price collapses.

1992: George H. W. Bush pardons all of the principal players in the Iran-Contra scandal.

1996: George H. W. Bush "the Poppy" praises Sun Myung Moon in Buenos Aires. The Moon organization is full of ex-Nazis, as is its close affiliate, the World Anti-Communist League.

2000: George W. Bush appointed President by 5-4 vote of the Supreme Court.

2001: George W. Bush plays his part in the psychological warfare operation of Sept. 11th, leading to a mandate to wage war and curtail freedom.

Patriot Act restricting constitutional freedoms is passed at the urging of George W. Bush.

Appendix 6, Ch. 2: A Proposed Amendment to End Corporate Rule

Section I

The rights given to the people as set forth by the constitution and its amendments can not be construed to apply to any corporation or business entity. All business entities are paper creations of society and as such have no rights under the constitution or its amendments, with the exception of the rights granted to them in this amendment. Business entities only retain a conditional privilege to operate; a privilege which can be revoked as set forth in this amendment. This amendment applies to all business entities regardless of country of origin.

Section II

Any business entity foreign or domestic with sales exceeding one million dollars or with sales or manufacturing facilities in two or more states will henceforth be required to obtain a federal charter of incorporation within one year of passage of this amendment, and conforming to the guidelines set forth here.

Section III

Congress is given the right to alter the terms of all general charters, however Congress cannot extend a charter beyond the limits set forth here. No charter will be granted to any business entity whose revenue exceeds one hundredth of one percent of the federal budget. Business entities exceeding that limit must be broken into two or more companies within six months. Nor will any charters be granted that does not restrict the operations to a single economic activity or business. Nor will any charter be granted that does not require a seventy-five percent majority of individual stockholders for election of officers, passage of mergers, buyouts, or a change in internal governance. In such elections, each shareholder will have one vote regardless of the number of shares they may own.

Section IV

A charter of incorporation can be revoked either by the passage of a bill in Congress and signed by the president, or by a federal court. Furthermore any facility of a business entity can be closed upon passage of an appropriate ballot measure and grievance initiated by not more than 2% of the populace in the community directly or indirectly affected by the operation of the facility. The court system may grant a temporary reprieve on passage of such a measure for two years only if the management of the business entity can show they are activity working towards a solution to the grievance. If after two reprieves the ballot measure passes for the third time, the facility will be closed.

Section V

No business entity will be granted any relief or compensation in the event environmental laws, land use laws, zoning laws, or other community protection laws prevent the full use of its property.

Section VI

Business entities are given the right to sue and the right to be sued. However, the operating officers and governing boards can and will be held responsible for any gross, continuous, or frequent violations of any laws. Gross, continuous or frequent violations shall hereby be defined as more than three violations of the same law within any two-year period. Congress shall establish prison terms of not less than five years for the operating officers and governing board of directors for violations of labor, environmental and general law. No immunity from prosecution will be extended beyond the rights of the common citizen to the operating officers and governing board of any business entity in either criminal or civil law.

Section VII

No one individual can serve on more than one board of directors. Nor can any business institution have more than one of its officers serving on a board of directors.

Section VIII

No business entity may deny or restrict the constitutional rights of its employees, nor conduct a search without a warrant or other invasions of their privacy. Further, no business entity may initiate legal proceeding against citizens or groups of citizens including labor unions opposed to the operation or expansion of that entity, unless there has been criminal activity on the part of such group.

Section IX

The rights of citizens to sue business entities cannot be limited or restricted in any manner, including the award of damages. Juries of the people will have the sole discretion in awarding the amount of damages.

Section X

All shareholders will be responsible for unpaid debts up to the limit of their investment. Operating officers and members of the governing boards can be and will be held responsible for any debt without limit.

Section XI

No business entity employing more than 50 people may ever be granted any public monies or aid not available to the common citizen of that district. The government may not extend its credit for the use of or to assume the debts of any business entity. No property may be seized under the doctrine of eminent domain for the use of any business entity.

Section XII

State and federal agencies may inspect any business entity at any time without a need for a warrant. In case of a lawsuit, no corporate document enjoys the right to privacy. Once entered into a court case the documents become a public record. Nor can the case and records be sealed by the order of the presiding judge.

Section XIII

No law passed by Congress or treaty approved by Congress can override the terms set forth in this amendment.

Section XIV

In the event of war, any business entity or a subdivision thereof providing goods or services to the enemy is guilty of sedition. The operating officers and the members of governing boards of such units upon conviction in federal court shall be sentenced to life in prison. In the event of war or other national emergencies, business entities can be put to use of the nation by the President.

Appendix 7, Ch. 3: The Nye Report

The Nye Report
U.S. Congress, Senate, 74th Congress, 2nd sess., February 24, 1936, pp. 3-13.
FINDINGS

I. NATURE OF THE MUNITIONS COMPANIES

The committee finds, under the head of "the nature of the industrial and commercial organizations engaged in the manufacture of or traffic in arms, ammunitions, or other implements of war" that almost none of the munitions companies in this country confine themselves exclusively to the manufacture of military materials. Great numbers of the largest suppliers to the Army and Navy (Westinghouse, General Electric, du Pont, General Motors, Babcock & Wilcox, etc.) are predominantly manufacturers of materials for civilian life. Others, such as the aviation companies and Colt's Patent Firearms Co., supply the greatest portion of their output to the military services. In addition to the manufacturers there are several sales companies which act as agents for various manufacturers. There are also brokers dealing largely in old and second-hand supplies. In case of war, other companies, not at present producing any munitions, would be called upon to furnish them.

The Army manufactures its own rifles, cartridges, and field artillery. The Navy manufactures most of its own propellant powder, its own guns, and half of the battleships.

II. THE SALES METHODS OF THE MUNITIONS COMPANIES

The Committee finds, under the head of sales methods of the munitions companies, that almost without exception, the American munitions companies investigated have at times resorted to such unusual approaches, questionable favors and commissions, and methods of "doing the needful" as to constitute, in effect, a form of bribery of foreign governmental officials or of their close friends in order to secure business.

The committee realizes that these were field practices by the agents of the companies, and were apparently in many cases part of a level of competition set by foreign companies, and that the heads of the American companies were, in cases, apparently unaware of their continued existence and shared the committee's distaste and disapprobation of such practices.

The committee accepts the evidence that the same practices are resorted to by European munitions companies, and that the whole process of selling arms abroad thus, in the words of a Colt agent, has "brought into play the most despicable side of human nature; lies, deceit, hypocrisy, greed, and graft occupying a most prominent part in the transactions."

The committee finds such practices on the part of any munitions Co., domestic or foreign, to be highly unethical, a discredit to American business, and an unavoidable reflection upon those American governmental agencies which have unwittingly aided in the transactions so contaminated.

The committee finds, further, that not only are such transactions highly unethical, but that they carry within themselves the seeds of disturbance to the peace and stability of those nations in which they take place. In some nations, violent changes of administration might take place immediately upon the revelation of all details of such transactions. Mr. Lammot du Pont stated that the publication of certain du Pont telegrams (not entered in the record) might cause a political repercussion in a certain South American country. At its February 1936 hearings, the committee also suppressed a number of names of agents and the country in which they were operating, in order to avoid such repercussions.

The committee finds, further, that the intense competition among European and American munitions companies with the attendant bribery of governmental officials tends to create a corrupt officialdom, and thereby weaken the remaining democracies of the world at their head.

The committee finds, further, that the constant availability of munitions companies with competitive bribes ready in outstretched hands does not create a situation where the officials involved can, in the nature of things, be as much interested in peace and measures to secure peace as they are in increased armaments.

The committee finds also that there is a very considerable threat to the peace and civic progress of other nations in the success of the munitions makers and of their agents in corrupting the officials of any one nation and thereby selling to that one nation an armament out of proportion to its previous armaments. Whether such extraordinary sales are procured through bribery or through other forms of salesmanship, the effect of such sales is to produce fear, hostility, and greater munitions orders on the p art of neighboring countries, culminating in economic strain and collapse or war.

The committee elsewhere takes note of the contempt of some of the munitions companies for those governmental departments and officials interested in securing peace, and finds here that continual or even occasional corruption of other governments naturally leads to a belief that all governments, including our own, must be controlled by economic forces entirely.

III. THEIR ACTIVITIES CONCERNING PEACE EFFORTS

The committee finds, under this head, that there is no record of any munitions Co. aiding any proposals for limitation of armaments, but that, on the contrary, there is a record of their active opposition by some to almost all such proposals, of resentment toward them, of contempt for those responsible for them, and of violation of such controls whenever established, and of rich profiting whenever such proposals failed.

Following the peaceful settlement of the Tacna-Arica dispute between Peru and Chile, L.Y. Spear, vice president of Electric Boat Co. (which supplied submarines to Peru) wrote to Commander C. W. Craven, of Vickers-Armstrong (which supplied material to Chile):

> It is too bad that the pernicious activities of our State Department have put the brake on armament orders from Peru by forcing resumption of formal diplomatic relations with Chile.

When the proposal to control the international traffic in arms was made in 1924, the Colt licensee in Belgium wrote:

It is, of course, understood that our general interest is to prevent the hatching up of a new agreement plan "under such a form" (as Sir Eric Drummond says) "that it may be accepted by the governments of all the countries who manufacture arms and munitions of war."

It then proposed methods of "lengthening the controversies" and to "wear out the bodies occupied with this question."

The first great peace effort after the war was incorporated in the Treaty of Versailles and in the treaty of peace between the United States and Germany in the form of a prohibition on the manufacture, import, and export of arms by Germany. The manufacture and export of military powder by German companies, in violation of these treaty provisions first took place in 1924 and was known to the Nobel Co. (predecessors of Imperial Chemical Industries) of England and to the du Pont Co., but was not brought to the attention of the Department of State. The du Pont officials explained that the violation was allowed because of the close commercial relations between the British and German chemical companies. Later, United Aircraft licensed a German Co. for the manufacture of its airplane engines. Sperry Gyroscope also licensed a German Co. for the manufacture of its equipment. Both the engines and the equipment were of military availability. (See part V, B, secs. II and III.)

The second peace effort was made in 1922, when the Washington Disarmament Conference took place, not long after the American shipbuilding companies had received post-war awards of destroyers at a cost of $149,000,000, and while battleships whose construction was left pending in 1917 were being completed. The naval part of that conference succeeded in stopping a naval race. There was, however, no effective action taken in regard to checking the use of poison gas, which was the other main subject for consideration. The committee's record is incomplete on the activities of the munitions companies in this connection, but does show their opposition to proposals for control of the chemical industry and their interest in the choice of chemical advisers to the American delegation. The conference had been preceded by the sale of all the German chemical patents to the American companies for a small sum, extensive propaganda and expenditures for high-tariff protection on grounds of national defense, and the instigation and writing of news stories from London and Paris designed to give the American public the impression that France and England were engaged in the construction of great poison-gas factories of their own to offset the German ones. Some of these were written by a du Pont agent under an assumed name. The Washington Conference operated in this atmosphere, and contented itself with repeating the declarations of The Hague conventions respecting the use of poisonous gases in warfare which had been violated during the war. Several delegations pointed out that this was no progress at all, but simply a reaffirmation of supposedly existing international law.

The embargo placed at the request of the Central (Nanking) Chinese Government on exports of arms to China was, according to the evidence, violated by American and European munitions companies. Shipments via Europe and Panama were frequently considered as a means of evading the embargo.

The Geneva Arms Control Conference of 1925 was watched carefully by the American and European munitions makers. They knew the American military delegates to the conference several weeks before the public was informed of their names, and one of them told the munitions makers that he believed a licensing system (the sine qua non of any control) to be undesirable. Du Pont representatives made known their objections to publicity. At a conference at the Department of Commerce (prior to the convening of the Geneva Conference) the objections of the munitions manufacturers were considered carefully and reservations to the draft convention to be discussed at Geneva were made. State Department documents not entered into the record give credit to the American delegation to the Geneva Conference for weakening the proposed draft convention in two important respects. The du Pont representatives (who attended the meeting at the Department of Commerce) later remarked of the final draft of the convention regarding the arms traffic signed at Geneva in 1925:

"There will be some few inconveniences to the manufacture of munitions in their export trade, but in the main they will not be hampered materially."

The draft convention was widely advertised as a large step forward in the direction of control of the traffic in arms. It has, in 1936, not yet been ratified by sufficient States to put it into effect.

The influence of American naval shipbuilding companies on the Geneva Disarmament Conference of 1927 has been described in the committee's report on Naval Shipbuilding (74th Cong., Rept. 944). Their agent at Geneva claimed credit for the failure of that conference, which came at a time when the Big Three shipyards had been given orders by the Navy for $53,744,000 in cruisers, which would have been cut materially in case the conference had been a success. He was paid by the shipbuilders into 1929. The Navy has not denied to the committee that this agent of the shipbuilders was in possession of confidential Navy Department documents during the time of his activity at Geneva.

Following the Geneva conference an arms embargo resolution was introduced in 1928 by the chairman of the American delegation to that conference, Representative Burton of Ohio. The munitions manufacturers, cocky with their success at Geneva, consulted with such allied interests as the Sporting Arms and Ammunition Manufacturers Institute, and found it unnecessary to appear in the front ranks of opposition to this resolution. In 1932 Representative Fish introduced a resolution for a multilateral agreement renouncing the sale and export of arms. Du Pont representatives were active in lining up War and Navy opposition to it. In 1932-33 President Hoover supported an arms embargo which drew the comment from a du Pont representative: Regarding the attempts of Mr. Hoover and the "cooky pushers" in the State Department to effect embargoes on munitions sent out of the country, I do not believe there is the least occasion for alarm at present.

The munitions people were active in opposition to the arms embargo proposal which was adopted in the Senate without opposition. Senator Bingham of Connecticut succeeded in killing the bill on reconsideration and received the thanks of the munitions people and of their organization, the Army Ordnance Association. The War Department also opposed the embargo.

In 1932, another disarmament conference was held at Geneva. By this time the failure to prevent the rearmament of Germany, described above, had resulted in great profits to the French steel industry which had received large orders for the building of the continuous line of fortifications across the north of France, to the French munitions companies, and profits were beginning to flow into the American and English pockets from German orders for aviation material. This in turn resulted in a French and English aviation race, and with Germany openly rearming the much-heralded disarmament conference which convened in 1932 has failed completely. It was pointed out by a committee member that du Pont representatives were aware that "the effect of the failure to check the [Versailles] treaty violation even goes to the extent of making a subsequent disarmament convention, if not improbable in its success, at least calculated to produce only an unworkable document."

In 1934, Congress adopted a joint resolution prohibiting, in effect, sales of munitions to Bolivia and Paraguay, then engaged in the Chaco War, for a period of almost 6 years. During these 6 years, the munitions companies had profited largely from the defeat of the Burton embargo proposal, offered in 1928.

The Chaco embargo, according to indictments issued by a Federal grand jury, was violated by the Curtiss-Wright Export Corp. and the Curtiss Aeroplane Motor Co. The lower court has held the embargo unconstitutional on the ground of delegation of power to the President.

Mayrink-Veiga, agents for many munitions companies in Brazil suggested that the embargo could be evaded by the shipment of planes to Europe first, stating that to be the Curtiss and Bellanca procedure.

In 1935, after a year of hearings by the special committee, a neutrality bill was passed including an embargo on arias, ammunition, and implements of war in the event of a state of war between two or more foreign states, and including a munitions-control board with power to issue export licenses. The

Secretary of State has announced that not all the companies supposed to register under this law have done so. In 1936 an attempt was made to amend the neutrality law by holding the exports of necessary war materials (oil, copper, steel, etc.) to belligerents to normal quotas. This was defeated. Considerable quantities of those materials were already being exported to Italy, one of the belligerents in the Italo-Ethiopian War, and some of the exporting companies had connections and investments in Italy.

IV. THE EFFECT OF ARMAMENTS ON PEACE

The committee finds, under the head of the effect of armament, on peace, that some of the munitions companies have occasionally had opportunities to intensify the fears of people for their neighbors and have used them to their own profit.

The committee finds, further, that the very quality which in civilian life tends to lead toward progressive civilization, namely the improvements of machinery, has been used by the munitions makers to scare nations into a continued frantic expenditure for the latest improvements in devices of warfare. The constant message of the traveling salesman of the munitions companies to the rest of the world has been that they now had available for sale something new, more dangerous and more deadly than ever before and that the potential enemy was or would be buying it.

While the evidence before this committee does not show that wars have been started solely because of the activities of munitions makers and their agents, it is also true that wars rarely have one single cause, and the committee finds it to be against the peace of the world for selfishly interested organizations to be left free to goad and frighten nations into military activity.

The committee finds, further, that munitions companies engaged in bribery find themselves involved in the civil and military politics of other nations, and that this is an unwarranted form of intrusion into the affairs of other nations and undesirable representation of the character and methods of the people of the United States.

The export field of our munitions companies has been South America and China, with occasional excursions into Poland, Turkey, Siam, Italy, Japan, and other nations. There was less important dynamite loose in either South America or China than in western Europe. The activities of the munitions makers in Europe were of greater importance to the peace of the western world than their activities in either South America or China. It will remain for commissions with full powers in the large European nations to report on the provocative activities of their companies, particularly to investigate the statements made in the French Chamber of Deputies, that Skoda in Czechoslovakia, a subsidiary of Schneider-Creusot, financed the Hitler movement to power, which, more than any one other event, can be credited with causing the present huge rearmament race in Europe, so profitable to the European steel, airplane, and munitions companies.

In South America there have, in the post-war years, been moments of severe tension, occasionally breaking out into war. One of these moments apparently came directly after the World War, when Chile bought from Vickers a considerable battle fleet. This caused agitation in Brazil, Argentina, and Peru, with Vickers taking the lead in Chile and Argentina, and Electric Boat Co. in Peru and Brazil. The situation was apparently so delicate that an administration countermanded an offer from the United States Navy to sell destroyers to Peru inasmuch as the sale might encourage an outbreak of war between Chile and Peru (exhibits 54, 57).

Later tension developed between Peru and Chile over the Tacna-Arica matter and Aubry, the Electric Boat Co. agent, felt that if he brought the contracts for submarines for Peru — it would be a great blunder going to Argentina, for instance, via Chile (In this business we have to be tactful and a little diplomatist) and so in regard to Brazil as well as to the Argentine now that affairs are going to take place at the same time (exhibit 69).

Mr. Carse, president of Electric Boat, recognized the danger of armament when he pointed out in regard to financing Peruvian purchases "the armament which this money could purchase would not insure victory, as the other nation has much stronger armament and would tend more to bring conflict to a point than if they did not purchase the armament" (Exhibit 61). It was sold, nevertheless.

The spreading effects of such fears were reported by Vice President Sutphen of Electric Boat: It appears that there has been quite an agitation in Bolivia, as you know, and a revolution has occurred there recently, and in the opinion of the bankers it has been instigated largely by Peru to have Bolivia join with her in opposition to Chile (ex. 60).

Chile was the country which bought the original increased armaments. It was in this connection that Spear wrote Craven of the "pernicious activities" of the United States Department of State in helping the resumption of diplomatic relations between Chile and Peru.

The naval armament had its military side. Evidence read into the record during the Colt Co. hearing in 1936 indicated an arms race with intense activity on the part of all machine-gun manufacturers. The country which was credited with starting military armament "out of all proportion with that of other countries in South America" was identified as a country whose officials were the most susceptible to bribes.

The Department of Commerce obligingly furnished Colts the information that the arms race was bringing about a cabinet crisis in one of the countries reluctant to participate in it.

The statement of a Federal Laboratories salesman that "the unsettled condition in South America has been a great thing for me" is the key, and also, "We are certainly in one hell of a business where a fellow has to wish for trouble to make a living."

Colombia and Peru, at the time of the Leticia incident, were each kept well informed by the munitions companies of the proposed purchases of the other nation. The evidence of the Colt agent in Peru was that the Vickers agent, after unloading a huge armament order on Peru, had boasted to the Peruvians that he would sell "double the amount, and more modern, to the Chilean Government." When a limited amount of materiel, such as machine guns, was available, Bolivia could be forced into ordering them on the threat that unless she acted quickly, Paraguay would get them. Killing the back-country Indians of South America with airplanes, bombs, and machine guns boiled down to an order to get busy because "these opera bouffe revolutions are usually short-lived, and we must make the most of the opportunity."

In China the munitions companies report that there was a certain amount of feeling between the Central (Nanking) Government and the Canton Government. The Boeing agent was able to sell 10 planes to the Canton Government. Referring to the Nanking (recognized) Government he wrote: Their anger at us in selling airplanes to the Cantonese is more than offset by the fact that the Cantonese have gotten ahead of them and will have better equipment than they will have. In other words, the Canton sale is quite a stimulant to the sale up here.

The Co., interested in making sales also to the recognized Nanking Government, replied: If the present deal with the Cantonese can be put through, without unreasonable demands being made upon us, it is to our advantage to successfully conclude the business if for no other reason but for the effect it would have on the Nanking Government.

All this may be little more to the munitions people than a highly profitable game of bridge with special attention on all sides to the technique of the "squeeze" play, but to a considerable part of the world's inhabitants there is still something frightful in death by machinery, and the knowledge that neighboring governments have acquired the latest and fastest engines of destruction leads to suspicion that those engines are meant to be used, and are not simply for play and show.

At the time a naval bill for $617,000,000 was before Congress, the president of the Bath Iron Works in Maine asked the publisher of a string of newspapers to reprint a Japanese war-scare story, although the Chinese source of that story had been thoroughly discredited editorially by the newspaper originally publishing it, the New York Herald Tribune. He thanked the publisher for playing up the scare story (Report on Naval Shipbuilding).

Attempts to sell munitions frequently involve bribery, which, to be effective, must go to those high in authority. This is apt to involve the companies in the politics of foreign nations. Federal Laboratories, by putting itself at the disposal of the administration of Cuba and two opposing factions, all at the same time, is a case in point. The Colt agent in Peru reported on his helping overthrow the general in charge of ordnance orders. American airplane companies reported on the political influence of French and English airplane companies, in a certain European country. Sperry Gyroscope's representative reported on Vickers' (English) political influence in Spain, as did also Electric Boat Co. officials.

The political power of the companies is best indicated, however, by a letter from Mr. John Ball, director of the Soley Armament Co Ltd., of England, in which he pointed out that "the stocks we control are of such magnitude that the sale of a big block of them could alter the political balance of power of the smaller States."

V. THEIR RELATIONS WITH THE UNITED STATES GOVERNMENT

The committee first, under this head, repeats its report on naval shipbuilding, in which "the committee finds, under the head of influence and lobbying of shipbuilders, that the Navy contractors, subcontractors, and suppliers constitute a very large and influential financial group," and "the committee finds that the matter of national defense should be above and separated from lobbying and the use of political influence by self-interested groups and that it has not been above or separated from either of them."

The committee finds, further, that the munitions companies have secured the active support of the War, Navy, Commerce, and even State Departments in their sales abroad, even when the material was to be produced in England or Italy.

The committee finds that by their aid and assistance to munitions companies the War, Navy, and Commerce Departments condone, in effect, in the eyes of those foreign officials cognizant of the details of the transactions the unethical practices of the companies which characterize their foreign sales efforts.

The committee finds that the munitions companies have constantly exerted pressure on the War Department to allow the exportation of the most recent American improvements in warfare, and have usually been successful in securing it, and have also furnished plans of important new machines of war to their foreign agents in advance of any release by the War Department.

The committee finds that the War Department encourages the sale of modern equipment abroad in order that the munitions companies may stay in business and be available in the event of another war, and that this consideration outranks the protection of secrets. (General Ruggles was quoted: "It was vastly more important to encourage the du Pont Co. to continue in the manufacture of propellants for military use, than to endeavor to protect secrets relating to the manufacture.")

The committee finds that as improvements are developed here, often with the cooperation of the military services, and these improvements presumably give the United States a military advantage, we are in the anomalous position of being forced to let the other nations have the advantages which we have obtained for ourselves, in order to keep the munitions manufacturers going, so that the United States can take advantage of the same improvements which its companies have sold abroad.

The committee finds, from official documents it has not entered into the record, that the United States naval missions to Brazil and Peru have been given considerable help to American munitions makers, and that their participation and leadership in war games directed at "a potential enemy" have not advanced the cause of peace in South America, and that their activity can be misinterpreted by neighboring countries as support of any military plans of the nations to which they are attached.

The committee finds, from official documents which it has not entered into the record, that the sales of munitions to certain South American nations in excess of their normal capacity to pay, was one of the causes for the defaults on certain South American bonds; and that the sales of the munitions was, in effect, financed by the American bond purchasers, and the loss on the bonds was borne by the same people.

The committee finds that the Army Ordnance Association, consisting of personnel from the munitions companies, constitutes a self-interested organization and has been active in War Department politics and promotions.

The committee finds that the Navy League of the United States has solicited and accepted contributions from steamship companies, the recipients of subsidy benefits, and that it has solicited contributions from companies with large foreign investments on the ground that these would profit from a large navy and that its contributors have at times been persons connected with Navy supplies. The committee also finds that the Navy League together with various Navy officials have engaged in political activity looking toward the defeat of Congressmen unfavorable to Navy League and Navy views.

The committee finds, further, that any close associations between munitions and supply companies on the one hand and the service departments on the other hand, of the kind which existed in Germany before the World War, constitutes an unhealthy alliance in that it brings into being a self-interested political power which operates in the name of patriotism and satisfies interests which are, in large part, purely selfish, and that such associations are an inevitable part of militarism, and are to be avoided in peacetime at all costs.

The committee finds, finally, that the neutrality bill of 1936, to which all its members gave their support and which provides for an embargo on the export of arms, ammunitions, and implements of war to belligerents, was a much needed forward step, and that the establishment of a Munitions Control Board, under the Department of State, should satisfactorily prevent the shipment of arms to other than recognized governments.

VI. INTERNATIONAL AGREEMENTS OF MUNITIONS COMPANIES

The committee finds, under this head, that, among the companies investigated, the following have the most extensive foreign arrangements: F. I. du Pont do Nemours Co., Colt's Patent Firearms Co., Electric Boat Co., Sperry Gyroscope Co., Pratt & Whitney Aircraft Co.

The committee finds that the usual form of arrangement is a license to a foreign ally involving rights to manufacture and sell in certain parts of the world, together with more or less definite price-fixing agreements and occasionally profit-sharing arrangements, and that in effect the world is partitioned by parties at interest.

The committee finds that the granting of licenses to manufacture and sell to nations against which there were embargoes, such as Germany, was in practice a violation of the interest of such embargoes and nullified them.

The committee finds that the international commercial interests of such large organizations as du Pont and Imperial Chemical Industries may precede in the minds of those companies the importance of national policy as described publicly by the foreign office or State Department, and that such considerations of commercial interest were apparently foremost in the rearming of Germany beginning in 1924 and in the sale of a process which could he used to manufacture cheaper munitions in Japan in 1932, shortly after Secretary of State Stimson had taken steps to express the disapproval of this Nation for Japan's military activities in Manchuokuo. Several aviation companies also licensed Japan for the use of their material in Manchuokuo at a time when the United States Government refused recognition to it. Recognition by munitions companies may be far more important than diplomatic recognition.

The committee finds that the licensing of American inventions to allied companies in foreign nations is bound to involve in some form the recurrence of experiences similar to those in the last war in which Electric Boat Co. patents were used in German submarines and aided them in the destruction of American lives, and ships, and that in peacetime the licensing involves the manufacture abroad, at lower costs, of American material.

VII. THE CHEMICAL INDUSTRY AND MUNITIONS

The committee finds a general acknowledgment of the importance of the commercial chemical industry to the manufacture of such instruments of warfare as high explosives and gasses, that most of the large industrial nations have granted their chemical companies considerable measures of protection in the interests of national defense, and that no effective control has to date been established over these large military resources.

These findings were concurred in by all members of the committee.

Appendix 8, Ch. 3: US Corporations in Cartel Agreements with IG Farben

American Companies that signed IG Farben cartel agreements

Abbott Laboratories
Acetol Products Co.
Advance Solvents & Chemical Corp.
Agfa Ansco Corp.
Agfa Photo Products Co.
Agfa Raw Film Co.
Alba Pharmaceutical Co.
Allied Chemical & Dye Corp.
Aluminum Company of America
American Active Carbon Co.
American Bemberg Corp.
American Cyanamid Co.
American Enka Corp.
American Glanstoff Corp.
American IG Chemical Corp.
American Magnesium Corp.
American Potash & Chemical Corp.
American Solvent Recovery Corp.
American Window Glass Co.
American Zirconium Co.
Anaconda Sales Co.
Anglo Chilean Nitrate Corp. (N.Y.)
Ansco Photo Products Inc.
Antidolor Co.
Atlantic Refining Co.
Ayerst, McKenna & Harrison (U.S.) Ltd.
Baker & Co.

The Barrett Co.
Barnsdall Corp.
Bayer Co., Inc.
Bayer-Semesan Co.
Bell and Howcll Co.
Bernuthe Lambecke Co.
Berst-Forster-Dixfield Co.
Board of Trade for German American Commerce Inc.
Bohn Aluminum & Brass Co.
Borden Co.
Bradley & Baker
Bristol Myers Co.
Calco Chemical Co.
California Alkali Export Association Inc.
Carbide & Carbon Chemicals Corp.
Carnation Co.
Carter Oil Co.
Casein Company of America
L.D. Caulk Co.
Central Dyestuff & Chemical Co.
Central Scientific Co.
Chemical Marketing Co.
Chemnycor Inc.
Chilean Nitrate and Iodine Sales Corp.
Chilean Nitrate Sales Corp. (N.Y.)
Chipman Chemical Engineering Co.

Church & Dwight Co., Inc.
Ciba Co., Inc.
Cincinnati Chemical Works Cities Service Co.
Climax Molybdenum Co.
Columbia Chemical Co.
Commercial Pigments Co.
Consolidated Color & Chemical Co.
Continental Oil Co.
Cook-Waite Laboratories
R.B. Davis Co.
Davis Emergency Equipment Co.
Diamond Alkali Co.
Diamond Match Co.
Dow Chemical Co.
Drug Inc.
Dry Milk Co.
DuPont Cellophane Co.
E.I. duPont de Nemours Co.
Eastman Kodak Co.
Ellis Flotation Corp.
Ellis-Foster Co.
Ethyl Gasoline Corp.
Federal Match Co.
Ferrocart Corporation of America
Fezandie & Sperrle
Firestone Rubber Co.
Fitchburg Yarn Co.
Fleischmann Co.
Ford Motor Co.
Freyn Engineering Co.
Gasoline Products Co.
Geigy Co., Inc.
General Aniline & Film Corp.
General Aniline Works Inc.
General Chemical Co.
General Drug Co.
General Dyestuff Corp.
General Electric Co.
General Mills Inc.
General Motors Corp.
General Motors Research Corp.
General Tire and Rubber Co.
Glidden Co.
Goodyear Tire and Rubber Co.
William Gordon Corp.
Grasselli Chemical Co.
Grasselli Dyestuff Corp.
Greene Cananea Copper Co.
Gulf Oil Corporation of Penn.
Gulf Refining Co.
Hercules Powder Co.

Hoffmann-LaRoche Inc.
Hooker Electrochemical Co.
Household Products Inc.
Hutz & Joslin (law firm)
Hydro Carbon Synthesis Corp.
Hydro Engineering and Chemical Co.
Hydro Patents Co.
Imperial Chemical Industries (N.Y.) Ltd.
Indiana Condensed Milk Co.
Interchemical Co.
International Catalytic Oil Processes Co.
International Hydro Patents Co.
International Match Co.
International Nickel Co.
Interstate Chemical Company of Rhode Island
Jasco Inc.
M.W. Kellogg Co.
Kennecott Sales Corp.
Kerr Dental Manufacturing Co.
Koppers Co.
Koppers Construction Co.
Krebs Pigment and Color Corp.
Kuttroff Pickhardt and Co.
Lautaro Nitrate Co., Ltd.
Lever Bros.
Life Savers Inc.
Louis K. Liggett Co.
Lion Match Co.
Loose-Wiles Biscuit Co.
Magnesium Development Corp.
Marion Co.
Mathieson Alkali Works Inc.
Mead Johnson & Co.
Wm. S. Merrell Co.
Metal & Thermit Co.
H.A. Metz Co.
Metz Laboratories
Mid Continent Petroleum Corp.
Molybdenum Corp. of America
Monsanto Chemical Co.
National Aniline & Chemical Co.
National City Co.
National Distillers Corp.
National Distillers Products Co.
National Lead Co.
Nestles Milk Products Co.
New Jersey Zinc Co.
New York Match Co., Inc.
Niagara Alkali Co.
North American Rayon Corp.
Ohio Match Co.

Okonite Co.
Oldbury Electro-Chemical Co.
Owl Drug Co.
Ozalid Corp.
Ozaphane Corp. of America
Pacific Alkali Co.
Parke Davis & Co.
Penn-Chlor Inc.
Pennsylvania Salt Manufacturing Co.
Pet Milk Co.
Phillips Petroleum Co.
Pittsburg Plate Glass Co.
Plaskon Co., Inc.
Polymerization Processes Corp.
Proctor and Gamble Co.
Pure Oil Co.
Remington Arms Co., Inc.
Richfield Oil Company of California
Rohm & Haas Co., Inc.
Sandoz Chemical Works Inc.
Selden Co.
Semet-Solvay Co.
Shawinigan Chemicals Ltd.
Shell Chemical Co.
Shell Development Corp.
Shell Union Oil Co.
Sinclair Refining Co.
Skelly Oil Co.
Socony-Vacuum Oil Co.
Solvay Process Co.
L. Sonneborn & Sons Inc.
Southern Alkali Corp.
E.R. Squibb & Sons
Standard Alcohol Co.
Standard Brands Inc.
Standard Catalytic Co.
Standard IG Co.
Standard Oil of California
Standard Oil Development Co.
Standard Oil Co. of Indiana
Standard Oil Co. of Louisiana

Standard Oil Co. (New Jersey)
Standard Oil Co. of New Jersey
Standard Oil Co. of New York
Standard Oil Co. of Ohio
Standard Oil Co. of Texas
Stauffer Chemical Co.
Sterling Products Inc. (Now Sterling Drug Inc.)
Synthetic Nitrogen Corp.
Synthetic Patents Co., Inc.
Texaco Development Corp.
Texas Co.
Three-in-One Oil Co.
Titan Co., Inc.
Titanium Pigment Co., Inc.
Transamerican Match Co.
Uniform Chemical Products Inc.
Union Oil Company of California
Union Carbide and Carbon Corp.
United Drug Co.
United States Alkali Export Association Inc.
United States & Transatlantic Service Corp.
United States Rubber Co.
Universal Match Corp.
Universal Oil Products Co.
Urbain Corp.
Vacuum Oil Co.
Vegex Inc.
Vernon-Benshoff Co.
Vernon-Morner Co.
Vick Chemical Co.
Virginia Chemical Co. jhhn
Viscose Co.
Visking Corp.
Vulcan Match Co.
West End Chemical Co.
Westvaco Chlorine Products Corp.
West Virginia Match Corp.
Winthrop Chemical Corp.
Wisconsin Alumni Research Foundation Inc.
Wyandotte Chemical Co.

Appendix 9, Ch. 4: Big Donors to the Pro-Nazi Groups

The following table has been reproduced from *1000 Americans*, by George Seldes, Boni & Gaer, 1947, pp. 292-298 (reprinting 2008 by Progressive Press).

The table was originally prepared by Senator Black and is known as the 74th Congress 2nd Session Digest of Data, Special Committee to Investigate Lobby Activities. The reader is urged to remember that this list is not complete. It only represents what was known to the Senator. This table is provided to illustrate the simple fact that it was the leaders of corporate America who sponsored the many pro-Nazi groups during the 1930s. The table is also provided in hopes of aiding future researchers into fascism within the United States. To add some perspective to the dollar amounts given below; the Republican party spent roughly $15 million dollars on the presidential election of 1940. The figures in the table below total nearly five percent of that.

Name	Positions	Pro-Nazi Group	Amount in $
Addinsell, H.M.	President, Chase Harris Forbes Corp Director, Cities Services Power & Light, Philips Petroleum, U.S Electric	Crusaders American Liberty League	100 200
Allen, E. M.	President, Mathieson Alkali Works Director, Austro-American Magnesite	Crusaders American Liberty League	100 200
Armour, Lester	***	Crusaders	2,500
Ames, Thoedore	Partner, Broody, McLellan Co.	Crusaders American Liberty League	10 120
Avery, Sewell	***	Crusaders	5,000
Baker, George D.F.	First National Bank, AT&T, U.S Steel	National Economic League	1,250
Ball, George A.	***	Crusaders	5,000
Bamberger, Clarence	***	Crusaders	125
Brown, Donaldson	VP, General Motors, Director E.I. duPont Nemours	American Liberty League Crusaders	20,000 500
Carpenter, R.R.M.	VP, E.I. duPont Nemours	American Liberty League	20,000
Carpenter, W.S. Jr.	VP, E.I. duPont Nemours	American Liberty League Economists National Committee	4,834 100
Chadbourne, T.L.	Director, Zonite	American Liberty League	6,250
Chrysler, Walter	Chrysler Co.	Crusaders	876

Clayton, W. I.	Partner, Anderson-Clayton	Southern Committee to Uphold the Constitution	100
	Chairman Export Insurance	American Liberty Lobby	7,750
Copeland, Charles C.	Secretary, E.I. duPont Nemours	American Liberty League	15,000
du Pont, A.M. L	Trustee, Wilmington Trust	American Liberty League	5,000
du Pont, Henry E.	Director, Wilmington Trust	American Liberty League	20,000
		Southern Committee to Uphold the Constitution	500
du Pont, Irénée	Vice Chairman, E.I. duPont Nemours	Crusaders	10,000
		Sentinels of the Republic	100
		American Liberty League	86,750
		Southern Committee to Uphold the Constitution	100
		Minute Men and Women of Today	1,400
du Pont, Lammont	President, E.I. duPont Nemours	Crusaders	1,000
		American Liberty League	15,000
		Economic National Committee	1,000
		Southern Committee to Uphold the Constitution	3,000
		Farmers Independence Council	5,000
du Pont, Pierre S.	VP, Wilmington Trust	Southern Committee to Uphold the Constitution	5,000
	Director, General Motors	American Liberty League	5,300
du Pont, S. Hallock	***	American Liberty League	20,000
du Pont, William Jr.	President, Delaware Trust	American Liberty League	20,000
Erickson, A.W.	Chairman, McCann-Erickson	Crusaders	100
		American Liberty League	875
Echols, A. B.	VP, E.I. duPont Nemours	Crusaders	75
	Director, Wilmington Trust Grasselli Chemical	Sentinels of the Republic	25
		American Liberty league	575
		Farmers Independence Council	110
Farish, Wm. S.	Standard Oil	Crusaders	200
Greef, Bernard	Partner, P. Greef & Co	Crusaders	5
Hawkes, A.W.	Congoleum, Senator	American Liberty League	250

Heinz, Howard	President, H. J. Heinz Co.	American Liberty League	2,500
	Director, Mellon National Bank	Crusaders	5,876
Houston, George H.	President, Baldwin Locomotive Director, Standard Steel	Crusaders American Liberty League	100 500
Hutton, Edward F.	Chairman, General Foods, Zonite Director, Manufacturers Trust Co, Chrysler	Crusaders American Liberty League	500 20,000
Kemmerer, Prof E.W.	Princeton	Southern Committee to Uphold the Constitution American Liberty League	5 5
Kent, A. Atwater	***	Sentinels of the Republic	1,000
Knudsen, William S.	General Motors	American Liberty League	10,000
Kroger, Bernard	***	Sentinels of the Republic	500
La Boyteaux, W.H	President, Johnson & Higgins. Director, Grace National Bank	Crusaders American Liberty League	100 100
Lasker, Albert	***	Crusaders	5,000
Lloyd, Horatio	Partner, Morgan	Sentinels of the Republic	1000
McCall S.T	VP, American Brake Shoe, American Manganese Steel	Crusaders American Liberty League	50 100
Mellon, Andrew	Head of Mellon interests	American Liberty League	1,000
Merrick, F.A.	President, Westinghouse	Crusaders	876
Milbanks, Jeremiah	***	Crusaders	200
Moffett, George M.	President, Corn Products	Crusaders American Liberty League	7,500 10,000
Montgomery, E.W.	Director of 2 cotton mills	Crusaders American Liberty League	50 125
Morris, E.M.	President, Associated Investment	Crusaders American Liberty League	25 50
Morris, John A.	Member, Gude, Winmill & Co.	Crusaders American Liberty League Sentinels of the Republic	75 400 10
Pepper, Geo. Wharton	ex-Senator	Sentinels of the Republic	500
Pew, J. Howard	President, Sun Oil	American Liberty	20,000

	Director, Sun Shipbuilding	League	
		Sentinels of the Republic	5,000
		Crusaders	4,000
Pitcairn, H.F	***	Sentinels of the Republic	5,000
Pitcairn, Rev Theo	***	Sentinels of the Republic	3,500
Pitcairn, Raymond		Sentinels of the Republic	91,000
Pratt, John L.	VP, General Motors	American Liberty League	20,000
Raskob, John J.	VP, E.I. duPont Nemours	American Liberty League	20,000
	Director, General Motors, Bankers Trust	Southern Committee to Uphold the Constitution	5,000
Roosevelt, Nicholas	***	Sentinels of the Republic	500
Sanis, E.C.	President, J.C. Penney	Crusaders	100
		American Liberty League	100
Sloan, Alfred P.	President, General Motors	Crusaders	10,000
		American Liberty League	20,000
	Director, E.I. duPont Nemours	Southern Committee to Uphold the Constitution	1,000
Stotesbury, E.T.	Partner, Morgan	Sentinels of the Republic	1,000
Strauss, Lionel F.	Director of 11 railroads	Crusaders	200
		Sentinels of the Republic	25
Teagle, W.C.	President, Standard Oil	Crusaders	2,000
Van Alstyne J.H	President, Oliver Elevator	Crusaders	25
		American Liberty League	100
Wier, E.T.	Chairman, National Steel, Wierton Steel, Wierton Coal	American Liberty League	20,000
		Crusaders	10,125
Widener, Joseph E.	Director, Baltimore & Ohio Railroad, Reading Co.	American Liberty League	20,000
Woodward, William	Hon. Chairman, Central Hanover Bank & Trust	American Liberty League	14,000

Appendix 10, Ch. 6: Captured Nazi Psychological Warfare Plans

Directive of the German High Command on Political Warfare in the U.S.A

The following directive was issued by the Chief of the Intelligence Division of the German High Command, Adm. Walter Wilhelm Canaris, in 1944. The document lays bare the basic German strategy of scaring the U.S. with Bolshevism, but, at the same time, recommends a long-range policy of Russo-German collaboration.

SECRET STATE MATTER
OKW-Abwehr
March 15, 1944

At a meeting of the representatives of the Foreign Office, the Security Division ("SD") and the Department of Defense ("Abwehr"), the following resolutions were adopted for unified action by all our agents in foreign countries:

1. Utilize to the fullest extent all available possibilities in neutral and enemy countries, in order to support our military efforts with political and propaganda campaigns.

2. Our goal is to crush the enemy's plan, whose object it is to destroy forever the German Reich militarily, economically and culturally.

The new regulations put into effect by the political leaders for the dissolution and disintegration of the enemy bloc should be carried out more intensely. We must do our utmost to create a state of confusion and distrust among our enemies. Such a state of disunity would enable us to sue for a quick separate peace with either side. While it is true that the efforts made in that direction have failed so far due to the implacable hate policy of Roosevelt and Churchill it does not mean that some day, under different conditions, the unnatural front of our enemies could not be broken. Roosevelt's electoral defeat this year could have immeasurable political consequences.

The political and military leaders are of the opinion that Germany cannot expect any mercy from the Soviets; on the contrary, should the war take a turn for the worse, we must assume that the Slavs will do everything in order to retaliate against the harsh treatment we have inflicted upon them. In spite of everything, no effort should be spared to stir up, through carefully directed propaganda, political animosity inside the Anglo-Saxon countries which would enrage the Soviets to such a degree that, as a consequence, they would welcome a chance to conclude a separate peace with Germany.

In the event of a negotiated peace, or should we be defeated, Germany would have everything to gain — in the long run — by joining the East.

Right now, the chances for a separate peace with the West are a little better, especially if we succeed, through our propaganda campaign and our confidential channels, to convince the enemy that Roosevelt's policy of "unconditional surrender" drives the German people towards Communism.

There is great fear in the U.S.A. of Bolshevism. The opposition against Roosevelt's alliance with Stalin grows constantly. Our chances for success are good, if we succeed to stir up influential circles against Roosevelt's policy. This can be done through clever pieces of information, or by references to unsuspicious neutral ecclesiastical contact men.

We have at our command in the United States efficient contacts which have been carefully kept up even during the war. The campaign of hatred stirred up by Roosevelt and the Jews against everything German has temporarily silenced the pro-German bloc in the U.S.A. However, there is every hope that this situation will be completely changed within a few months. If the Republicans succeed in defeating

Roosevelt in the coming presidential election, it would greatly influence the American conduct of war towards us.

The KO-leaders abroad and their staffs have innumerable opportunities of constantly referring to Roosevelt's hate policy. They must use in this campaign all the existing contacts and they should try to open up new channels. We must point to the danger that Germany may be forced to cooperate with Russia. The greatest caution has to be observed in all talks and negotiations by those who, as "anti-Nazis," maintain contact with the enemy. When fulfilling missions, they have to comply strictly with instructions.

German Plan for Psychological Warfare in the U.S.A.
(Memorandum from Dr. Colin Ross to the German Foreign Office, 1943.)

On July 27, 1943, the German Foreign Office expert on the U.S., the geopolitician Colin Ross, suggested in a 15-page memorandum a "Plan for an Ideological Campaign in the United States."

Recognizing Germany's inability to bring the war to a victorious end, Ross proposed the immediate implementation of carefully planned psychological warfare to undermine the anticipated U.S. military victory. Ross regarded American public opinion as the weakest link because the American people seemed especially susceptible to scare propaganda hinting that a defeated Germany would join the ranks of Bolshevism. The memorandum, which was addressed to the German Secretary of State in the Foreign Office, von Steengracht, became the guidepost for Germany's highly successful blackmail diplomacy in post-war America. Here follow some significant parts of the memorandum.

PLAN FOR AN IDEOLOGICAL CAMPAIGN IN THE UNITED STATES
The Prerequisites for psychological warfare

1. Analyze the spiritual temper of world public opinion.
2. Evaluate correctly the ideological weapons available.
3. Put before the eyes of the world a strategic concept which will impress not only our own people, but also the neutrals and our enemies.
4. Select the most effective tactical methods for the accomplishment of the above
5. Co-ordinate the ideological campaign in support of our military and economic warfare.

The more the prospects for outright military victory diminish, the more urgent becomes the necessity for all-out psychological warfare.

In analyzing this problem we can disregard completely the possibility of total victory through military might alone, because in such a case psychological warfare is superfluous. However, in the case of total military collapse, we must continue the struggle by means of psychological warfare until the day arrives when weapons can speak again. In my opinion it is important to point to this ultima ratio now and emphasize it more than ever before. Psychological warfare will prove especially successful in the U.S.A. where many groups (weite Kreise) are fed up with the war. ...

Under all circumstances we should prepare ourselves for the worst, not in a spirit of defeatism, but in order to cope more effectively with defeatism in the hour of collapse. It is important that we see to it that our enemies, especially the Americans, should not bask themselves in the sun of victory or that they enjoy the role of being the liberators of Europe. Therefore, it is necessary to set up a far-flung organization in every country which, under enemy occupation, must carry on the task from the underground. We must do everything possible to impress upon American public opinion that after the liberation of Europe they will become involved in an endless maze of insoluble contradictions. However great their sacrifices may be they will end up in a blind alley exactly as it happened in 1918 under Wilson's grandiose planning.

We have to use the argument that if the enemy succeeds in stamping out "Fascism" or "Nazism" there will remain only Bolshevism. Thus, a Germany threatened by the Anglo-Americans with dismemberment, will throw herself completely into the arms of the Soviets, and in that way will make Bolshevism unconquerable.

This is the time to make up the balance sheet and to start with large scale preparation in order to meet the coming invasion. Our defense must not remain limited to military measures alone but must employ every available weapon of psychological warfare. The ideological offensive is the order of the day.

Appendix 11, Ch. 6-8: American Documents on Germany's Comeback Plans

On March 30, 1945 the U.S. State Department announced that reliable information collected by Allied Governments clearly indicates that the Nazi regime in Germany has developed well-arranged post-war plans for the perpetuation of Nazi doctrines and domination. Some of these plans have already been put into operation and others are ready to be launched on a widespread scale immediately upon termination of hostilities in Europe."

From the official release, the following parts are quoted:

> Nazi Party members, German industrialists and the German military, realizing that victory can no longer be attained, are now developing post-war commercial projects, are endeavoring to renew and cement friendships in foreign commercial circles and are planning for renewals of pre-war cartel agreements. An appeal to the courts of various countries will be made early in the post-war period through dummies for "unlawful" seizure of industrial plants and other properties taken over by Allied governments at the outbreak of war. In cases where this method fails German repurchase will be attempted through "cloaks" who meet the necessary citizenship requirements. The object in every instance will be to re-establish German control at the earliest possible date. German attempts to continue to share in the control and development of technological change in the immediate post-war period is reflected in the phenomenal increase in German patent registrations in foreign countries during the past two years. These registrations reached an all-time high in 1944. The prohibition against exporting capital from Germany was withdrawn several months ago, and a substantial outflow of capital has followed to foreign countries.

> German technicians, cultural experts, and undercover agents have well-laid plans to infiltrate foreign countries with the object of developing economic, cultural and political ties. German technicians and scientific research experts will be made available at low cost to industrial firms and technical schools in foreign countries. German capital and plans for the construction of ultra-modern technical schools and research laboratories will be offered at extremely favorable terms since they will afford the Germans an excellent opportunity to design and perfect new weapons. This Government is now in possession of photostatic copies of several volumes of German plans on this subject. The German propaganda program is to be an integral part of the over-all post-war program. The immediate aim of the propaganda program will be directed at removing Allied Control measures by "softening-up" the Allies through a subtle plea for "fair treatment" of Germans and later the program will be expanded and intensified with the object of giving re-birth to all Nazi doctrines and furthering German ambitions for world domination. Unless these plans are checked they will present a constant menace to post-war peace and security.

Excerpts of statement by William L. Clayton, former Assistant Secretary of State, to the subcommittee of the Committee on Military Affairs, U.S. Senate.

> The second matter I should like to discuss relates to the current and urgent problem of frustrating German attempts to hide abroad a stake for another gamble at world domination.

The Department of State has abundant evidence that the Nazis, in anticipation of military defeat, made careful plans to carry on in Foreign countries a wide range of activities necessary to support an eventual resurgence of German power. For this purpose plans were made, and carried out in part, to transfer abroad sufficient funds and specially trained personnel to carry on pan-German activities, even while the Allied armies were in occupation of Germany.

The success of German efforts to carry on in foreign countries activities inimical to the United Nations must depend on their ability to mobilize funds to support the execution of their plans. Consequently, they have made strenuous efforts to move abroad assets of all kinds, which can be converted into funds for the financing of hostile activities.

Our safehaven program is a combined effort of the Department of State, the Treasury Department, and the Foreign Economic Administration to deny to Germany, in the interests of justice and future security, the economic power arising from (a) the organized looting (to) occupied countries, (b) the flight of German capital in anticipation of defeat, and (c) the German capital investment already located abroad when the war began.

Our investigations have yielded a considerable amount of information which indicates the schemes and devices which the Germans' planned to use in order to safeguard their foreign holdings and transfer additional property abroad. In many cases they have concealed their interests in foreign properties through holding companies as cloaks. In other cases they have abandoned formal voting control but retained a firm grip on manufacturing concerns through domination of technical processes. They have transformed their holdings into bearer shares in order to take advantage of the fact that the title to such shares can be traced only with extreme difficulty. Moreover, the Germans have also taken advantage in some countries of administrative inefficiency and corruption. The extent to which this can be said in every neutral country to have been the fault of private individuals alone is problematical.

The Germans systematically looted all manner of valuable property, not only to satisfy the esthetic sensibilities of such celebrated collectors as Goering, but to acquire wealth cheaply for concealment abroad.

Looting reached its all-time low when gold was picked from the teeth of gas chamber victims. A more subtle form of looting was outright purchase with occupation currency from fearful sellers.

On July 10, 1945, **Sen. Kilgore** of the Subcommittee on War Mobilization, submitted the following report on Germany's war potential on to the Senate Military Affairs Committee:

Mr. Chairman, we have the honor to submit to you a preliminary report on the sub-committee's studies of German resources for a third world war. In its report of November 1944 on Cartels and National Security, your subcommittee found that the Germans systematically engaged in economic warfare as a prelude to military conquest. Our investigations even at that date supported the conclusion that the German aggressors have begun to pursue a strategy which they found successful a quarter century ago; they are already deploying their economic reserves throughout the world in preparation for a third attempt at world domination. ...

Germany in defeat remains a major threat to the peace of the world. The Germans, who have twice within the century launched the most devastating wars, have already set in motion plans for a third attempt to enslave the world. No peace making can be successful which does not at the outset thwart these plans and destroy Germany's potential for war making. This is the indispensable condition to peace in Europe. Lasting world peace requires also the unconditional defeat of Japan and the smashing of her war potential. ...

Germany today is better prepared to implement her plot for world conquest than she was at the end of World War I. Her major resources include (I) the world's third strongest industrial economy; (2) tremendous industrial recuperative power; (3) a world-wide network of economic and political reserves and a system of commercial interrelationships penetrating the economies of other nations; and (4) the science of aggression perfected by her leading industrialists, militarists, and politicians to reverse the decisions of the battlefield.

Germany is an industrial giant whose economy for half a century was developed by the Junker-industrialist clique as an engine of war. ... The strength of Germany's war machine lies not only in her over-expanded metallurgical and chemical industries, but in her enormous industrial flexibility and recuperative power, displayed before and throughout the war. ... It appears that if Germany had held out 6 months longer she would have been sending more destructive V-2 bombs to smash the heart of New York. Germany's recuperative power rests on her greatly expanded machine-tool industry, her reserves of skilled scientists and technicians. Except for the United States, Germany remains the outstanding machine shop in the world. German science provided the synthetic fuels and rubber which enabled her armies to drive relentlessly over Europe. German scientists and technologists created new and diabolical weapons.

In the period between World War I and World War II, Germany created economic, political, and espionage outposts throughout the world. In the United States, Germany retrieved many of the properties which had been seized during the First World War. She penetrated so deeply into key industries of Latin-American countries that a State Department official testified before the subcommittee that liquidation of the German-controlled enterprises would have crippled the economies of a number of these countries. The Germans also made strong inroads into the economies of Spain, Sweden, Switzerland, Turkey, Portugal, Finland, Bulgaria, and Roumania

... German-owned or dominated firms not only served to procure raw materials, increase German trade, and obtain much-needed foreign exchange for Germany, but they acted as centers of espionage and as intermediaries for the financing of Nazi political activities. ...

During the war, in an endeavor to maintain intact its assets in enemy countries, it used the neutral countries as a cloak for German ownership or control. ...

Despite the strenuous efforts of the United States and the cooperation of a number of the Latin-American countries, the evidence is unmistakable that German influence is still strongly entrenched in this hemisphere, particularly in Argentina. The United States itself may be one of the most important safe havens for German assets. There is over a half-billion dollars of seized assets held in unnamed Swiss accounts, which are now blocked by the United States on reasonable suspicion that these assets may in fact be German. ...

... Leading German industrialists, militarists, and politicians have at their disposal a long and carefully developed science of aggression. This science rests on a series of major deceptions: (a) that the war of aggression is the product of a few Nazi fanatics; (b) that the German economy is a normal civilian economy and should be maintained as such; (c) that the entire network of relationships between German cartels and monopolies of other countries is essential to the conduct of international trade and industrial progress; (d) that German science and German scientists are an instrument of human progress; and (e) that the Allies have less to fear from Germany than they have to fear from one another.

The evidence shows that German industry has been dominated by a number of combines and domestic monopolies, chiefly in the basic industries, and that the leaders of these combines, together with the Junkers and Nazis, were Germany's principal war makers. Constituting a kind of economic general staff, immediately after Versailles and with the assistance of the Weimar Republic which they infiltrated, they began to consolidate their position within the country and secretly to rearm Germany. By manipulating reparations, by planned bankruptcy, by Government subsidies and tariff protection, and by masterful use of international cartel relationships they disarmed their prospective victims and with the assistance of those prospective victims, perfected their own war machine. Hitler and the Nazis were late comers in these preparations. It was the cartel and monopoly powers — the leaders of the coal, iron and steel, chemical, and armament combines — who at first secretly and then openly supported Hitler in order to accelerate their ruthless plans for world conquest. By 1931 the coal cartel, one of the most powerful industrial combines in Germany, openly placed a royalty on every ton of coal sold, whether domestically or abroad, in order to finance the Nazi Party. ...

A witness before the subcommittee, who only recently interrogated some of Germany's key industrial leaders, now jailed, pointed out that these leaders confidently expect to be rescued from their present plight by powerful British and American friends who were their former cartel affiliates. ... These industrialists remain the principal custodians of Germany's plans for future war.

... Your subcommittee finds that the German economy was developed as a war economy, and that its vast industrial potential remains largely undamaged by the war; that Germany has a world-wide network — including even the United States — of commercial relationships and economic, political, and espionage outposts which she could mobilize for another war; that the leading German industrialists are not only as responsible for war crimes as the German General Staff and the Nazi Party, but that they were among the earliest and most active supporters of the Nazis, whom they used to accelerate their plans for world conquest, and that these industrialists remain the principal custodians of Germany's plans for renewed aggression. ...

The experience of the years following World War I demonstrates conclusively that without the active understanding, support, and participation of the people as a whole, the efforts of a few commissioners and even an army corps can avail nothing against the desperate schemes of a determined and skillful group of German leaders who have thoroughly indoctrinated their own people and systematically deceived the rest of the world.

Appendix 12, Ch. 7-8: OSS Personnel After the War

Joseph Alsop, unsuccessful Republican Governor candidate in Connecticut, 1962 Republican National Committeeman

Victor Anfuso, Democratic Congressman from Brooklyn 1950–62, Justice of the New York Supreme Court

Alexander Barmine, Chief of Russian Branch of the U.S. Information Agency during Eisenhower administration.

Thomas Beale, Ambassador to Jamaica, 1965–68

Andrew Berding, personal press aide for John Foster Dulles

John Blatnik, Minnesota congressman

David Bruce, Ambassador to England, France, Germany, and representative to Paris Peace Talks

Ralph Bunche, Under Secretary-General of United Nations until 1971

Oliver Caldwell, Assistant Commissioner of the U.S. Office of Education during Kennedy Administration

John Calhoun, Deputy Attorney General during Eisenhower administration

Douglas Cater, presidential adviser

Marshall Carter, Deputy Director CIA 1962–65, Director NSA code breaking 1965–69

William Cary, Chairman U.S. Securities and Exchange during Kennedy administration

William Casey, CIA Director

Ray Cline, CIA Deputy Director 1962–69, Director of State Department Intelligence 1969

William Colby, CIA Director

Philip Combs, Assistant Secretary of State during Kennedy administration

Philip Crowe, Ambassador to Ceylon, Union of South Africa, Norway

Emillo Daddario, Democratic Congressman from Connecticut elected 1958

Douglas Dillon, Treasury Secretary

Allen Dulles, CIA Director

William Eddy, Ambassador Saudi Arabia 1944–46

Alan Evans, State Department Intelligence 1947–59

Gilmore Flues, Assistant Secretary of Treasury during Eisenhower administration

John Gardener, Secretary of Health Education and Welfare 1965–68

George Garrett, Ireland Ambassador 1947–53

Arthur Goldberg, Secretary of Labor 1961–62, Supreme Court Justice 1962–65, unsuccessful Democratic Governor candidate for New York 1970

Stanton Griffs, Ambassador to Poland, Egypt, Argentina, Spain

Murray Gurfein, federal judge who ruled on the Pentagon Papers case

John Haskell, U.S. defense adviser to NATO 1955–60

Richard Helms, CIA Director

Richard Heppner, Deputy Assistant Secretary of Defense during Eisenhower administration

Roger Hilsman, special assistant to CIA Executive Officer during the Kennedy administration

Harold Hoskins, State Department Foreign Service Institute 1955–61

Lawrence Houston, General Counsel of CIA

Fisher Howe, State Department 1948–58

John Hughes, Ambassador to NATO 1953–55, Free Europe Committee 1958

Thomas Karamessines, CIA Director for Plans 1967

Paul Kattenburg, State Department, recommended total disengagement from Vietnam

Henry Kellerman, UNESCO 1956–61

Lyman Kirkpatrick, Executive Director CIA until 1965

Carl Kaysen, presidential adviser

Ridgeway Knight, Ambassador to Syria, Belgium, Portugal
William Macomber, State Department special assistant to John Foster Dulles
William Langer, Director of CIA Board of National Estimates 1950, Presidential Intelligence Advisory Board 1961
Walter Mansfield, federal judge New York City
William Maddox, Foreign Service until retirement
Edwin Martin, Argentina ambassador 1964–68
Leonard Meeker, State Department legal adviser 1965–69, Romania ambassador 1969
Clark McGregor, Minnesota congressmen elected in 1960, assistant to Nixon for Congressional relations 1970
Francis Pickens Miller, unsuccessful Democratic for Virginia Governor 1949
Robert Murphy, Ambassador Belgium, Japan, Under Secretary of State 1959–60
Joseph Rendon, unsuccessful Republican congressional candidate from New Mexico 1954, part of Guatemala coup in 1954
Theodore Ryan, Republican Minority leader and president pro tem of Connecticut State Senate 1953–57
Walt Rostow, presidential adviser 1966–69
Sidney Rubenstein, security adviser to U.S. mission to NATO
Robert Schow, Assistant Director CIA 1949–51, chief of Army Intelligence 1956–58
Walter Bedell Smith, CIA Director 1950–53
Charles Stelle, State Department 1951–56, delegate to Nuclear Test Ban Conference
Charles Thayer, State Department, resigned 1953 after being attacked by McCarthy
Marget Tibbets, Ambassador to Norway
Paul Van der Strict, Special Assistant to CIA Director until 1971
Stuyvesant Wainwright, Republican Congressman New York 1952–60
George White, investigator for Kefauver Committee
Hubert Will, federal judge Chicago
Hugh Wilson, Director of Foreign Affairs Section of Republican National Committee
John Wiley, ambassador to Colombia, Portugal, Iran, Panama
Frank Wisner, top-level CIA agent 1948–62
J. Evelle Younger, District Attorney of Los Angles 1964–68, Attorney General State of California
John Zuckerman, Deputy Director of Bureau of International Business Operations, Department of Commerce during Kennedy administration

Appendix 13, Ch. 8: Operation Northwoods

The excerpts are taken from the original 15-page U.S. Government TOP SECRET document, "Chairman, Joint Chiefs of Staff, Justification for US Military Intervention in Cuba [including cover memoranda], March 13, 1962," available at the National Security Archive Web site (www.gwu.edu/~nsarchiv/news/20010430/doc1.pdf)

TOP SECRET SPECIAL HANDLING NOFORN

THE JOINT CHIEFS OF STAFF
WASHINGTON 25, D.C.
13 March 1962

MEMORANDUM FOR THE SECRETARY OF DEFENSE

Subject: Justification for U.S. Military Intervention in Cuba (TS)

1. The Joint Chiefs of Staff have considered the attached Memorandum for the Chief of Operations, Cuba Project, which responds to a request of that office for brief but precise description of pretexts which would provide justification for US military intervention in Cuba.

2. The Joint Chiefs of Staff recommend that the proposed memorandum be forwarded as a preliminary submission suitable for planning purposes. It is assumed that there will be similar submissions from other agencies and that these inputs will be used as a basis for developing a time-phased plan. Individual projects can then be considered on a case-by-case basis.

3. Further, it is assumed that a single agency will be given the primary responsibility for developing military and para-military aspects of the basic plan. It is recommended that this responsibility for both overt and covert military operations be assigned the Joint Chiefs of Staff.

For the Joint Chiefs of Staff:

SYSTEMATICALLY REVIEWED,
BY JCS ON 21 May 84   [signed]
CLASSIFICATION CONTINUED

L.L. Lemnitzer, Chairman
Joint Chiefs of Staff

1 Enclosure
Memo for Chief of Operations, Cuba Project

RECOMMENDATIONS

8. It is recommended that:
     a. Enclosure A together with its attachments should be forwarded to the Secretary of Defense for approval and transmittal to the Chief of Operations, Cuba Project.
     b. This paper NOT be forwarded to commanders of unified or specified commands.
     c. This paper NOT be forwarded to US officers assigned to NATO activities.
     d. This paper NOT be forwarded to the Chairman, US Delegation, United Nations Military Staff Committee.

APPENDIX TO ENCLOSURE A

DRAFT
MEMORANDUM FOR THE SECRETARY OF DEFENSE

Subject: Justification for U.S. Military Intervention in Cuba (TS)

1. Reference is made to memorandum from Chief of Operations, Cuba project, for General Craig, subject: "Operation MONGOOSE", dated 5 March 1962, which requested brief but precise description of pretexts which the Joint Chiefs of Staff consider would provide justifications for US military intervention in Cuba.

2. The projects listed in the enclosure hereto are forwarded as a preliminary submission suitable for planning purposes. It is assumed that there will be similar submissions from other agencies and that these inputs will be used as a basis for developing a time-phased plan. The individual projects can then be considered on a case-by-case basis.

3. This plan, incorporating projects selected from the attached suggestions, or from other sources, should be developed to focus all efforts on a specific ultimate objective which would provide adequate

justification for US military intervention. Such a plan would enable a logical build-up of incidents to be combined with other seemingly unrelated events to camouflage the ultimate objective and create the necessary impression of Cuban rashness and irresponsibility on a large scale, directed at other countries as well as the United States. The plan would also properly integrate and time phase the courses of action to be pursued. The desired resultant from the execution of this plan would be to place the United States in the apparent position of suffering defensible grievances from a rash and irresponsible government of Cuba and to develop an inter- national image of a Cuban threat to peace in the Western Hemisphere.

4. Time is an important factor in resolution of the Cuban problem. Therefore, the plan should be so time-phased that projects would be operable within the next few months.

5. Inasmuch as the ultimate objective is overt military intervention, it is recommended that primary responsibility for developing military and para-military aspects of the plan for both overt and covert military operations be assigned the Joint Chiefs of Staff.

ANNEX TO APPENDIX TO ENCLOSURE A

PRETEXTS TO JUSTIFY US MILITARY INTERVENTION IN CUBA

(Note: The courses of action which follow are a preliminary submission suitable only for planning purposes. They are arranged neither chronologically nor in ascending order. Together with similar inputs from other agencies, they are intended to provide a point of departure for the development of a single, integrated, time-phased plan. Such a plan would permit the evaluation of individual projects within the context of cumulative, correlated actions designed to lead inexorably to the objective of adequate justification for US military intervention in Cuba).

1. Since it would seem desirable to use legitimate provocation as the basis for US military intervention in Cuba a cover and deception plan, to include requisite preliminary actions such as has been developed in response to Task 33 c, could be executed as an initial effort to provide Cuban reactions. Harassment plus deceptive actions to convince the Cubans of imminent invasion would be emphasized. Our military posture throughout execution of the plan will allow a rapid change from exercise to intervention if Cuban responses justifies.

2. A series of well coordinated incidents will be planned to take place in and around Guantanamo to give genuine appearance of being done by hostile Cuban forces.

    a. Incidents to establish a credible attack (not in chronological order):

    (1) Start rumors (many). Use clandestine radio.

    (2) Land friendly Cubans in uniform "over-the-fence" to stage attack on the base.

    (3) Capture Cuban (friendly) saboteurs inside the base.

    (4) Start riots near the entrance to the base (friendly Cubans).

    (5) Blow up ammunition inside the base; start fires.

    (6) Burn aircraft on airbase (sabotage).

    (7) Lob mortar shells from outside of base into base. Some damage to installations.

    (8) Capture assault teams approaching from the sea of vicinity of Guantanamo City.

    (9) Capture militia group which storms the base.

    (10) Sabotage ship in harbor; large fires — naphthalene.

    (11) Sink ship near harbor entrance. Conduct funerals for mock-victims (may be in lieu of (10)).

    b. United States would respond by executing offensive operations to secure water and power supplies, destroying artillery and mortar emplacements which threaten the base.

c. Commence large scale United States military operations.

3. A "Remember the Maine" incident could be arranged in several forms:

a. We could blow up a US ship in Guantanamo Bay and blame Cuba.

b. We could blow up a drone (unmanned) vessel anywhere in the Cuban waters. We could arrange to cause such incident in the vicinity of Havana or Santiago as a spectacular result of Cuban attack from the air or sea, or both. The presence of Cuban planes or ships merely investigating the intent of the vessel could be fairly compelling evidence that the ship was taken under attack. The nearness to Havana or Santiago would add credibility especially to those people that might have heard the blast or have seen the fire. The US could follow with an air/sea rescue operation covered by US fighters to "evacuate" remaining members of the non-existent crew. Casualty lists in US newspapers would cause a helpful wave of national indignation.

4. We could develop a Communist Cuba terror campaign in the Miami area, in other Florida cities and even in Washington. The terror campaign could be pointed at Cuban refugees seeking haven in the United States. We could sink a boatload of Cubans enroute to Florida (real or simulated). We could foster attempts on lives of Cuban refugees in the United States even to the extent of wounding in instances to be widely publicized. Exploding a few plastic bombs in carefully chosen spots, the arrest of Cuban agents and the release of prepared documents substantiating Cuban involvement also would be helpful in projecting the idea of an irresponsible government.

5. A "Cuban-based, Castro-supported" filibuster could be simulated against a neighboring Caribbean nation (in the vein of the 14th of June invasion of the Dominican Republic). We know that Castro is backing subversive efforts clandestinely against Haiti, Dominican Republic, Guatemala, and Nicaragua at present and possible others. These efforts can be magnified and additional ones contrived for exposure. For example, advantage can be taken of the sensitivity of the Dominican Air Force to intrusions within their national air space. "Cuban" B-26 or C-46 type aircraft could make cane-burning raids at night. Soviet Bloc incendiaries could be found. This could be coupled with "Cuban" messages to the Communist underground in the Dominican Republic and "Cuban" shipments of arms which would be found, or intercepted, on the beach.

6. Use of MIG type aircraft by US pilots could provide additional provocation. Harassment of civil air attacks on surface shipping and destruction of US military drone aircraft by MIG type planes would be useful as complementary actions. An F-86 properly painted would convince air passengers that they saw a Cuban MIG, especially if the pilot of the transport were to announce such fact. The primary drawback to this suggestion appears to be the security risk inherent in obtaining or modifying an aircraft. However, reasonable copies of the MIG could be purchased from US resources in about three months.

7. Hijacking attempts against civil air and surface craft should appear to continue as harassing measures condoned by the government of Cuba. Concurrently, genuine defections of Cuban civil and military air and surface craft should be encouraged.

8. It is possible to create an incident which will demonstrate convincingly that a Cuban aircraft has attacked and shot down a chartered civil airliner enroute from the United States to Jamaica, Guatemala, Panama or Venezuela. The destination would be chosen only to cause the flight plan route to cross Cuba. The passengers could be a group of college students off on a holiday or any grouping of persons with a common interest to support chartering a non-scheduled flight.

a. An aircraft at Eglin AFB would be painted and numbered as an exact duplicate for a civil registered aircraft belonging to a CIA proprietary organization in the Miami area. At a designated time the duplicate would be substituted for the actual civil aircraft and would be loaded with the selected passengers, all boarded under carefully prepared aliases. The actual registered aircraft would be converted to a drone.

b. Take off times of the drone aircraft and the actual aircraft will be scheduled to allow a rendezvous south of Florida. From the rendezvous point the passenger-carrying aircraft will descend to minimum altitude and go directly into an auxiliary field at Eglin AFB where arrangements will have been made to evacuate the passengers and return the aircraft to its original status. The drone aircraft meanwhile will continue to fly the filed flight plan. When over Cuba the drone will begin transmitting on the international distress frequency a "MAY DAY" message stating he is under attack by Cuban MIG aircraft. The transmission will be interrupted by the destruction of aircraft which will be triggered by radio signal. This will allow IACO radio stations in the Western Hemisphere to tell the US what has happened to the aircraft instead of the US trying to "sell" the incident.

9. It is possible to create an incident which will make it appear that Communist Cuban MIGs have destroyed a USAF aircraft over international waters in an unprovoked attack.

a. Approximately 4 of 5 F-101 aircraft will be dispatched in trail from Homestead AFB, Florida, to the vicinity of Cuba. Their mission will be to reverse course and simulate fakir aircraft for an air defense exercise in southern Florida. These aircraft would conduct variations of these flights at frequent intervals. Crews would be briefed to remain at least 12 miles off the Cuban coast; however, they would be required to carry live ammunition in the event that hostile actions were taken by the Cuban MIGs.

b. On one such flight, a pre-briefed pilot would fly tail-end Charley at considerable interval between aircraft. While near the Cuban Island this pilot would broadcast that he had been jumped by MIGs and was going down. No other calls would be made. The pilot would then fly directly west at extremely low altitude and land at a secure base, an Eglin auxiliary. The aircraft would be met by the proper people, quickly stored and given a new tail number. The pilot who had performed the mission under an alias, would resume his proper identity and return to his normal place of business. The pilot and aircraft would then have disappeared.

c. At precisely the same time that the aircraft was presumably shot down a submarine or small surface craft would disburse F-101 parts, parachute, etc., at approximately 15 to 20 miles off the Cuban coast and depart. The pilots retuning to Homestead would have a true story as far as they knew. Search ships and aircraft could be dispatched and parts of aircraft found.

ENCLOSURE B

FACTS BEARING ON THE PROBLEM

1. The Joint Chiefs of Staff have previously stated that US unilateral military intervention in Cuba can be undertaken in the event that the Cuban regime commits hostile acts against US forces or property which would serve as an incident upon which to base overt intervention.

2. The need for positive action in the event that current covert efforts to foster an internal Cuban rebellion are unsuccessful was indicated by the Joint Chiefs of Staff on 7 March 1962, as follows:

… determination that a credible internal revolt is impossible of attainment during the next 9-10 months will require a decision by the United States to develop a Cuban "provocation" as justification for positive US military action."

3. It is understood that the Department of State also is preparing suggested courses of action to develop justification for US military intervention in Cuba.

---

* (JCS 1969/303)
** (JCS 1969/313)

Index

Bibliographical Notes

Chapter 1, What Fascism Is

[1] http://quotes.telemanage.ca/quotes.nsf/QuotesByCatPerson?ReadForm&RestrictTo Category=Benito+Mussolini

[2] http://www.brainyquote.com/quotes/quotes/u/uptonsincl101370.html

[3] http://www.brainyquote.com/quotes/authors/f/franklin_d_roosevelt.html

[4] Stetson Kennedy, *Southern Exposure* (New York, Doubleday, 1946) p 189.

[5] http://www.fordham.edu/halsall/mod/mussolini-fascism.html, Note material

[6] E.A. Pillar, *Time Bomb* (New York, Arco, 1975) p 12–15. See also Henry Hook, *It's a Secret* (New York, Pamphlet Press, 1946) p 70–73.

[7] Lawrence Brita, Spring 2003, "The 14 Characteristics of Fascism," *Free Inquiry*.

[8] Henry Ashby Turner, *Hitler's Thirty Days to Power* (New York, Addison Wesley, 1996) p 159.

[10] http://en.wikipedia.org/wiki/Fascist

[94] Major work: *The World as Will and Representation*

[95] Credited with the idea of thesis and antithesis leading to synthesis.

[96] Major work: *The Protestant Ethic and the Spirit of Capitalism*

[97] "Nietzsche- A Precursor to Hitler?" http://www.newswithviews.com/Collins/phillip2.htm

[98] Peter Padfield, *Himmler* (New York, MJF, 1990) p 260.

[99] Adolf Hitler, *Mein Kampf,* p 325.

[17] Eric Hobsbawm, *The Age of Extremes* (New York, Vintage Books, 1996) p 124–25, 175.

[18] In 1928, Epp joined the Nazi Party. Several members of the Nazi leadership were members of the Freikorps.

[19] Joseph Borkin, *Germany's Master Plan* (New York, Duell, Sloan and Pearce, 1943) p 55–56.

[20] Robert Payne, *The Life and Death of Adolf Hitler* (New York, Barnes & Noble, 1973) p 137.

[21] Adolf Hitler, *Mein Kampf,* p 218.

[22] James Pool, *Who Financed Hitler* (New York, Pocket Books, 1997) p 29.

[23] Ibid, p 31.

[24] John Toland, *Adolf Hitler* (New York, Anchor Books, 1992) p 108.

[25] James Pool, *Who Financed Hitler*, p 39.

[26] Ibid, p 39-41.

[27] Ibid, p 46-48.

[29] James Pool, *Who Financed Hitler*, p 59–60.

[28] Carroll Quigley, *Tragedy and Hope* (New York, Macmillan, 1966) p 422.

[30] Robert Payne, *The Life and Death of Adolf Hitler*, p 185.

[31] George Seldes, *Facts and Fascism* (New York, In Fact Inc., 1943) p 135–36.

[32] Ibid, p 137.

[33] Ibid, p 136–37.

[34] Anthony Sutton, *Wall Street and the Rise of Hitler* (Seal Beach, Calif., 76 Press, 1976) p 100.

[35] Ibid, p 99.

[36] William Shirer, *The Rise and Fall of the Third Reich* (New York, Fawcett Crest, 1960) p 118.

[37] Robert Payne, *The Life and Death of Adolf Hitler*, p 185.

[38] Joseph Borkin, *Germany's Master Plan,* p 56–57.

[39] Robert Payne, *The Life and Death of Adolf Hitler,* p 213.

[40] Ibid, p 213.

[41] Ibid, p 214.

[42] Henry Ashby Turner, *German Big Business and the Rise of Hitler* (Oxford Press, 1985) and James Pool, *Who Financed Hitler.*

[43] Carroll Quigley, *Tragedy and Hope* (Macmillan, 1966) p 435–36.

[44] Henry Ashby Turner, *German Big Business and the Rise of Hitler,* p 83–84.

[45] Ibid, p 87–89.

[46] Ibid, p 264.

[47] Ibid, p 90–94.

[48] Ibid, p 90–94.

[49] William Shirer, *The Rise and Fall of the Third Reich*, p 118.

[50] Idid, p 203.

[51] James Pool, *Hitler and His Secret Partners* (New York, Pocket Books, 1997) p 52–53.

[52] Charles Higham, *Trading with the Enemy* (New York, Barnes & Noble, 1983) p 131–32.

[53] Robert Payne, *The Life and Death of Adolf Hitler,* p 221.

[54] George Seldes, *Facts and Fascism,* p 123

[55] James Pool, *Who Financed Hitler,* p 230.

[56] Arthur Schweitzer, *Big Business in the Third Reich* (Bloomington, Indiana University Press, 1964) p 98–99.

[57] Ibid, p 103–04.

[58] Eustace Mullins, *The World Order* (Staunton, Va., Ezra Pound Institute, 1985) p 108.

[59] Arthur Schweitzer, *Big Business in the Third Reich,* p 65.

[60] Carroll Quigley, *Tragedy and Hope,* p 437.

[61] Ibid, p 437–38.

[62] Ibid, p 438–40.

[63] Ibid, p 444.

[64] Daniel Guerin, *Fascism and Big Business* (New York, Pathfinder, 1973) p 210–11.

[65] Ibid, p 212–13.

[66] Carroll Quigley, *Tragedy and Hope,* p 453.

[67] Ibid, p 453–54.

[68] Roger Eatwell, *Fascism* (New York, Penguin, 1996) p 156.

[69] Arthur Schweitzer, *Big Business in the Third Reich,* p 146–147.

[70] John Toland, *Adolf Hitler,* p 308.

[71] Arthur Schweitzer, *Big Business in the Third Reich,* p 391, 398.

[72] Ibid, p 288.

[73] Ibid, p 344.

[74] Ibid, p 455

[75] Ibid, p 198.

[76] http://www.cdfe.org/

[77] Joseph Borkin, *Germany's Master Plan,* p 69–71.

[78] http://www.elib.com/Steiner/RSBio.php3 See also http://www.w-eich.de/hdobant.pdf

[79] http://w3.trib.com/FACT/1st.religion.alert.html

[80] Adolf Hitler, *Mein Kampf,* p 248.

[81] http://www.isrp.org/

[82] John Loftus, Mark Aarons, *Unholy Trinity* (New York, St. Martin's, 1991) p 294–95.

[83] Maureen Harrison, Steve Gilbert, *Thomas Jefferson: In His Own Words* (New York, Barnes & Noble, 1996) p 369.

[84] Jeff Jacony, 1998, What Real Hate Speech Sounds Like, *Boston Globe*, Nov. 2.

[85] U.S. Firms' Connections to Nazis Detailed, 1999, *Boston Globe*, Jan. 14.

[86] http://www.tarpley.net/bush2.htm, "The Hitler Project", Chapter 2 of Tarpley and Chaitkins' *George Bush: The Unauthorized Biography* (EIR, 1992; Reprinted 2004 by Progressive Press), a work largely ignored in the mainstream press, perhaps due to the authors' association with Lyndon LaRouche, widely considered an eccentric. However, his organization has connections extending inside the intelligence community that cannot be ignored. Tarpley's revelations concerning Prescott Bush's dealings with the Nazis are confirmed by various government documents, including the vesting orders. The dealings between Prescott Bush and the Nazis first reported by Tarpley and Chaitkin have been confirmed and extended by John Loftus and John Buchanan. Also see John Loftus, Mark Aarons, *The Secret War Against the Jews*, p 358-360.

[87] http://www.john-loftus.com/Thyssen.asp

[88] John Loftus, Mark Aaron, *The Secret War Against the Jews* (New York, St. Martin's, 1994) p 360.

[89] http://www.john-loftus.com/bush_nazi_link.asp

[90] http://www.john-loftus.com/bush_nazi_scandal.asp

[91] http://www.john-loftus.com/bushnazi_1951.asp

[92] http://www.john-loftus.com/bush_nazi_link.asp

[93] http://www.john-loftus.com/Thyssen.asp

[94] http://www.john-loftus.com/bushnazi_1951.asp

[95] http://www.nhgazette.com/cgi-bin/NHGstore.chi?user_action=detail&catalogno=
NN_Bush_Nazi2

[96] http://www.john-loftus.com/bush_nazi_scandal.asp

[97] Charles Higham, *Trading with the Enemy,* p XVII.

Chapter 2, Corporate Law

[1] http://www.rollcall.com/

[2] George Soros, *The Crisis of Global Capitalism* (New York, Public Affairs, 1998) p 102.

[3] Ralph Nader, Mark Green, *Corporate Power In America* (New York, Grossman, 1973) p 68.

[4] Jean Edward Smith, *John Marshall* (New York, Henry Holt and Co., 1996) p 436. Text of decision at
http://www.usscplus.com/online/index.asp?case=0170518

[5] http://www.constitution.by.net/Pa/PaConst38.html

[6] http://www.legislature.state.al.us/misc/history/constitutions /1875/1875_14.html

[7] http://legisweb.state.wy.us/titles/98titles/title97.htm

[8] http://www.ratical.com/corporations/CAconstArt12.html

[9] The source for this case and all that follow is the same: http://www.endgame.org/primer-history.html

[10] http://www.courts.state.wi.us/history/famous_cases.htm

[11] http://www.kings.edu/twsawyer/frankly/SS1.html

[12] Charles Lewis, *The Buying of Congress* (New York, Avon, 1998) p 184–98.

[13] Andy Pasztor, *When the Pentagon Was for Sale* (New York, Scribner, 1995) p 41–72.

[14] http://www.tompaine.com/features/2000/05/15/

[15] http://www.wtoaction.org/greenfield2.phtml

[16] http://www.theglobeandmail.com

[17] http://www.heureka.clara.net/gaia/gats.htm

Chapter 3, The Roaring '20s and the Roots of American Fascism

[1] Joseph Borkin, *Germany's Master Plan* (New York, Duell, Sloan and Pearce, 1943) p 46.

[2] Michael Sayers, Albert Kahn, *Sabotage* (New York, Harper Brothers, 1942) p 5–6.

[3] Joseph Borkin, *Germany's Master Plan,* p 22.

[4] Joseph Borkin, *The Crime and Punishment of IG Farben* (New York, The Free Press, 1978) p 5–6. See also
The Empire of IG Farben, in Antony C. Sutton, Wall Street and the Rise of Hitler, http://reformed-
theology.org/html/books/wall_street/chapter_02.htm.

[5] Joseph Borkin, *Germany's Master Plan,* p 24–25.

[6] Ibid, p 25.

[7] Ibid, p 16.

[8] Ibid, p 37.

[9] Ibid, p 46.

[10] Ibid, p 54.

[11] Ibid, p 55.

[12] Ibid, p 56.

[13] Ibid, p 56–57.

[14] Ibid, p 58.

[15] Ibid, p 75–77.

[16] Ibid, p 67–69.

[17] Ibid, p 71–72.

[18] Joseph Bendersky, *The Jewish Threat* (New York, Basic Books, 2000) p 202–04.

[19] John Loftus, Mark Aarons *The Secret War Against the Jews* (New York, St. Martin's, 1994) p 56.

[20] Newsweek.com, Dirty Business.

[21] Nancy Lisagor, Frank Lipsius, *A Law Unto Itself* (New York, Paragon, 1989) p 18–19.

[23] Ibid, p 28.

[24] Ibid, p 35–36.

[25] Ibid, p 60.

[26] Ibid, p 90–93.

[27] John Loftus, Mark Aarons, *The Secret War Against the Jews*, p 56.

[28] Nancy Lisagor, Frank Lipsius, *A Law Unto Itself*, p 128–29.

[29] Ibid, p 137–38.

[30] Ibid, p 144–45.

[31] Ibid, p 146–51.

[32] Christopher Simpson, *The Splendid Blond Beast* (New York, Grove Press, 1993) p 46–48.

[33] http://www.bea.gov

[34] Nancy Lisagor, Frank Lipsius, *A Law Unto Itself*, p 199–200.

[35] Ibid, p 156.

[36] Ibid, p 199–200.

[37] Ibid, p 202.

[37] Ibid, p 202.

[39] Antony Sutton, *Wall Street and the Rise of Hitler* (Seal Beach, Calif., 76 Press, 1976) p 50.

[40] Charles Higham, *Trading with the Enemy* (New York, Barnes & Noble, 1983) p 167.

[41] Edwin Black, *IBM and the Holocaust* (New York, Crown, 2001).

[43] Ibid, p 70.

[44] Ibid.

[45] Joseph Borkin, *Germany's Master Plan*, p 88–89.

[46] Ibid, p 86–87.

[47] Ibid, p 90.

[48] Howard Ambruster, *Treason's Peace* (New York, Beechhurst Press, 1947) p 60–61.

[49] Ibid, p 38.

[50] Ibid, p 93.

[51] Robert Herzstein, *Roosevelt and Hitler: Prelude to War* (New York, Paragon, 1989) p 128–29.

[52] Howard Ambruster, *Treason's Peace*, p 138–39.

[53] Ibid, p 41.

[54] Ibid, p 42–43. For details on Standard Oil, its German subsidiary DAPAG and its monopoly on synthetic gasoline and synthetic rubber, see Antony C. Sutton, *Wall Street and the Rise of Hitler*, http://reformed-theology.org/html/books/wall_street/chapter_04.htm

[55] Ibid, p 132–35.

[56] Ibid, p 142.

[57] Joseph Borkin, *Germany's Master Plan*, p 113–15.

[58] Ibid, p 206–11.

[59] Ibid, p 265–67.

[60] Ibid, p 152–53.

[61] Howard Ambruster, *Treason's Peace*, p 89–91.

[62] Ibid, p 272.

[63] Ibid, p 272–73.

[64] Ibid, p 322–23.

[65] Edwin Black, *IBM and the Holocaust,* p 337–39.

[66] The Congressional Record, Feb. 9, 1917, Vol. 54, p 2947-48.

[67] http://www.redthread.f2s.com/Quotations/Author/AlvinMOwsley.html

[68] Robert Murray, *Red Scare* (New York, McGraw Hill, 1955) p 7.

[69] Ibid, p 9.

[70] Ibid, p 85.

[71] http://newdeal.feri.org/nation/na37145p166.htm

[72] *The Old Christian Right,* Leo Ribuffo (Philadelphia, Temple University Press, 1983) p 16.

[73] Robert Murray, *Red Scare,* p 22.

[74] Ibid, p 40-41.

[75] Ibid, p 85.

[76] Ibid, p 63.

[77] Ibid, p 64.

[78] Ibid, p 64

[79] Ibid, p 65.

[80] Ibid, p 165.

[81] http://www.hartford-hwp.com/archives/45b/030.html

[82] http://www.epls.org/nw/emassacre.htm

[83] Robert Murray, *Red Scare,* p 94–102.

[84] http://www.unf.edu/dept/equalop/oeop11.htm

[85] http://www.unf.edu/dept/equalop/oeop11.htm

[86] http://techno.king.net/~nrrdgrrl/klan.html

[87] Michael Sayers, Albert Kahn, *Sabotage,* p 50–51.

[88] Martin Lee, *The Beast Reawakens* (New York, Routledge, 2000) p 334–35.

[89] http://hierographicsonline.org/yourhistoryonline/TheRosewood MassacreReport-I.htm

[90] http://www.displaysforschools.com/rosewoodb.html#what

[91] http://www.ncsu.edu/park_scholarships/symposium/2000/riot.html

[92] Bill Stanton, *Klanwatch* (New York, Mentor, 1991) p 36–37.

[93] http://www.aom.org/articles/israel.htm

[94] Joseph Bendersky, *The Jewish Threat,* p 63.

[95] http://www.washingtonpost.com/wp-dyn/articles/A26576-2002Mar1.html

[96] http://www.rickross.com/groups/winrod.html

[97] *The Old Christian Right,* Leo Ribuffo, p 119.

[98] Michael Barkum, *Religion and the Racist Right* (Chapel Hill, N.C., University of North Carolina Press, 1997) p 25.

[99] Edwin Black, *War Against the Weak* (New York, Four Walls Eight Windows, 2003) p 1–23.

[100] Ibid, p 63–64.

[101] Ibid, p 65.

[102] Ibid, p 75–83.

[103] Ibid, p 108–21.

[104] Ibid, p 122–23, p. 185-206.

[105] http://www.eugenicsarchive.org/html/eugenics/essay8text.html.

[106] Edwin Black , *War Against the Weak,* p 247–57.

[107] Laurie Garrett, *The Coming Plague* (New York, Penguin, 1995) p 186.

[108] Edwin Black, *War Against the Weak,* p 247–57.

[109] Adolf Hitler, *Mein Kampf* (Boston, Houghton Mifflin, 1971).

[110] Edwin Black, *War Against the Weak,* p 121.

[111] Ibid, p 275.

[112] Ibid, p 299–300.

[113] Ibid, p 297.

[114] Ibid, p 365.

[115] Ibid, p 365–67.

[116] Ibid, p 376–80.

[117] Ibid, p 404–05.

[117] Ibid, p 404–05.

[118] Geoffrey Perret, *Old Soldiers Never* Die (New York, Random House, 1996) p 154-61.

Chapter 4, The 1930s: Nazis Parading on Main Street

[1] This writer believes that one of the reasons the far right wing has always been fractured in this country is the intense hatred and intolerant views or tunnel vision of its groups and their members. The writer also believes the greater factorization during the '30s compared to today was a product of both economic conditions and the technology of the times. The groups in the '30s had to rely on the U.S. postal system to exchange their pamphlets, unlike the groups from the 1980s that were quick to develop mailing lists, and use faxes and the Internet to exchange their pamphlets in the 1990s.

[2] George Seldes, *Facts and Fascism* (New York, In Fact Inc., 1943) p 68.

[3] Robert Herzstein, *Roosevelt and Hitler: Prelude to War* (New York, Paragon, 1989) p 153.

[4] Charles Higham, *Trading with the Enemy* (New York, Barnes & Noble, 1983) p 162–66.

[5] Ibid, p 162.

[6] Ibid, p 163.

[7] http://www.korpios.org/resurgent/Coup.htm

[8] Jules Archer, *The Plot to Seize the White House* (New York, Hawthorn, 1969) p 175.

[9] Ibid, p 193.

[10] Ibid.

[11] Ibid, p 197.

[12] Ibid, p 198.

[13] Charles Higham, *Trading with the Enemy*, p 163–65.

[14] Sander Diamond, *The Nazi Movement in the United States, 1924–1941* (Ithaca, Cornell University Press, 1974) p 89, 102.

[15] John Spivak, *Secret Armies* (New York, Modern Age Books, 1939) p 75–77.

[16] Richard Rollins, *I Find Treason* (New York, William Morrow and Co., 1941) p 80.

[17] Ibid, p 81.

[18] http://freenet.msp.mn.us/people/fholson/fla3hist.htm

[19] Ibid.

[20] George Seldes, *Facts and Fascism,* p 70–75.

[21] Charles Higham, *Trading with the Enemy*, p 165–67.

[22] George Seldes, *Facts and Fascism,* p 46.

[23] Charles Higham, *Trading with the Enemy*, p 167.

[24] Dale Harrington, *Mystery Man* (Dulles, Va., Brassey, 1999).

[25] http://newsweek.washingtonpost.com/nw-srv/issue/24_98b/printed/ int/eur/ovbz0324_2.htm

[26] http://www.mthololyoke.edu/acad/intrel/nazipol.htm

[27] Charles Higham, *American Swastika* (Garden City, N.Y., Doubleday, 1985) p 45.

[28] O. John Rogge, *The Official German Report* (New York, A.S. Burnes, 1961) p 254–55.

[29] Dale Harrington, *Mystery Man,* p 137–61.

[30] John Loftus, Mark Aarons, *The Secret War Against the Jews* (New York, St. Martin's, 1994) p 74.

[31] George Seldes, *Facts and Fascism,* p 255.

[32] Ibid, p 258–59.

[33] Ibid, p 261–62.

[34] http://newsweek.washingtonpost.com/nw-srv/issue/24_98b/printed/ int/eur/ovbz0324_2.htm

[35] John Carlson, *Undercover* (New York, E.P. Dutton, 1943) p 258.

[36] Charles Higham, *Trading with the Enemy,* p 154–55.

[37] George Seldes, *Facts and Fascism,* p 135–37.

[38] Charles Higham, *Trading with the Enemy,* p 154–56.

[39] John Carlson, *Undercover,* p 235.

[40] George Seldes, *Facts and Fascism,* p 134.

[41] Ibid, p 134.

[42] http://www.bartleby.com/66/96/8996.html

[43] George Seldes, *Facts and Fascism,* p 129–31.

[44] Ibid, p 124–25.

[45] http://uaw.org/bargaining/barginfo.htm#japan

[46] http://www.indymedia.org/front.php3?article_id=54014&group=webcast

[47] http://dailynews.yahoo.com/h/wews/20010710/lo/852857_1.html

[48] Richard Dudman, *Men of the Far Right* (New York, Pyramid, 1962) p 126–28.

[49] George Seldes, *Facts and Fascism,* p 73.

[50] Ibid, p 184–90.

[51] http://www.detnet.com/wilke/antisem.htm

[52] http://sites.netscape.net/admin55/openletter3

[53] George Seldes, *Facts and Fascism,* p 184.

[54] Ibid, p 257.

[55] Ibid, p 256.

[56] http://www.fair.org/extra/9707/ad-survey.html

[57] George Seldes, *Facts and Fascism,* p 126–27.

[58] Ibid, p 281–82.

[59] E.A. Piller, *Time Bomb,* (New York, Arco Publishing, 1945) p 43.

[60] Ibid, p 52.

[61] Ibid, p 44.

[62] George Seldes, *Facts and Fascism,* p 203–04.

[63] Ibid, p 215.

[65] George Seldes, *Facts and Fascism,* p 220.

[64] Joseph Persico, *Roosevelt's Secret War* (New York, Random House, 2001) p 189.

[66] Albert Kahn, *Sabotage* (New York, Harper and Brothers, 1942) p 140.

[67] John Carlson, *Undercover*, p 232–34.

[68] Ibid, p 235.

[70] Ibid, p 238.

[71] http://www.teleport.com/~glapn/ar04001.html

[72] Robert Herzstein, *Roosevelt and Hitler: Prelude to War,* p 173.

[73] http://www.mthololyoke.edu/acad/intrel/nazipol.htm

[74] William Breur, *Hitler's Undercover War* (New York, St. Martin's Press, 1989) p 138–39.

[75] http://www.wvculture.org/history/journal_wvh/wvh51-1.html

[76] Albert Kahn, *Sabotage,* p 247–48.

[77] Charles Higham, *American Swastika,* p 38–39.

[78] O. John Rogge, *The Official German Report,* p 170–71.

[79] Dale Harrington, *Mystery Man,* p 118.

[80] Charles Higham, *American Swastika,* p 40.

[81] Ibid, p 45–47.

[82] *Ibid,* p 57.

[83] Henry Hoke, *It's a Secret* (New York, Pamphlet Press, 1946) p 14–15.

[84] Ibid.

[85] Dale Harrington, *Mystery Man,* p 206.

[86] Ibid, p 205–08.

[87] Charles Higham, *American Swastika,* p 78.

[88] Robert Herzstein, *Roosevelt and Hitler: Prelude to War,* p 386–94.

[89] John Carlson, *Undercover*, p 241.

[90] Ibid, p 243.

[91] Albert Kahn, *Sabotage*, p 245.

[92] http://www.detnet.com/wilke/antisem.htm

[93] http://hatewatch.org/who/butler.html

[94] http://www.ferris.edu/isar/Institut/pioneer/silent.htm

[95] http://www.hearnow.org/id.htm

[96] John Carlson, *Undercover*, p 55.

[97] http://www.users.interport.net/~wovoka/aarlong.html

[98] http://www.detnet.com/wilke/antisem.htm

[99] http://www.uu.edu/unionite/winter99/chlife.htm

[100] Howard Bushart, John Craig, Myra Barnes, *Soldiers of God* (New York, Pinnacle Books, 1998) p 124–25.

[101] http://www.seattletimes.com/news/nation-world/html98/bapt_19990909.html

[102] William Turner, *Power on the Right* (Berkeley, Ramparts Press, 1971) p 15.

[103] http://www.hartford-hwp.com/archives/45/022.html

[104] http://www.ferris.edu/isar/Institut/pioneer/silent.htm

[105] http://www.ferris.edu/isar/Institut/pioneer/kaukas.htm

[106] http://www.ferris.edu/isar/Institut/pioneer/helms.htm

[107] http://www.ferris.edu/isar/Institut/pioneer/forbes.htm

[108] Glen Jeansonne, *Women of the Far Right*, (Chicago, University of Chicago Press, 1996) p 105.

[109] Russ Bellant, *Old Nazis, the New Right and the Republican Party* (Boston, South End Press, 1988) p 31.

[110] Robert Herzstein, *Roosevelt and Hitler: Prelude to War,* p 154.

[111] Albert Kahn, *Sabotage*, p 200–02.

[112] Ibid, p 215–16.

[113] The following pro-fascist groups were aligned with the America First Committee: German American Bund; Silver Shirts; Christian Front; Ku Klux Klan; American Destiny Party; American Guards; American White Guards; Blackshirts and Italian Fascist Clubs; Christian Mobilizers; Ethiopian-Pacific League; Falangists; Gray Shirts Kyffhaeuser Bund; National Copperheads; National Workers League; Patriots of the Republic; Save America First; Save Our American Clubs; Social Justice Clubs; White Russian Fascist; and many elements of the mothers movement, including Dilling, Source Sabotage, p 208.

[114] Robert Herzstein, *Roosevelt and Hitler: Prelude to War,* p 386–94.

[115] http://www.theamericancause.org/pjb-99-0108.html

[116] Sigmund Diamond, *Compromised Campus* (New York, Oxford University Press, 1992) p 335.

[117] http://www.weberman.com/monica.htm

[118] Mark Fritz, 2001, CIA Opens Its Files on Third Reich Figures, *Boston Globe*, April 27.

[119] http://www.nara.gov/iwg/papers.html

Chapter 5, The War Years

[1] Joseph Persico, *Roosevelt's Secret War* (New York, Random House, 2001) p 103–07

[2] Ibid, p 167.

[3] http://atheists.org/flashline/bibwk9.htm

[4] John Roy Carlson, *The Plotters* (New York, E.P. Dutton, 1946).

[5] Frank Donner, *The Age of Surveillance* (New York, Vintage Books, 1981) p 47–46.

[6] http://www.english.upenn.edu/~afilreis/88/sacvan.html

[7] Frank Donner, *The Age of Surveillance,* p 30.

[8] Ibid, p 125.

[9] Ibid, p 118.

[10] John Loftus, Mark Aarons, *The Secret War Against the Jews*, (New York, St. Martin's, 1994) p 73–76.

[11] Anthony Cave Brown, *The Last Hero* (New York, Vintage Books, 1982) p 207–11.

[12] Joseph Persico, *Roosevelt's Secret War,* p 27–31.

[13] John Loftus, Mark Aarons, *The Secret War Against the Jews,* p 74.

[14] Burton Hersh, *The Old Boys* (New York, Charles Scribner, 1992) p 35.

[15] Frank Donner, *The Age of Surveillance,* p 86.

[16] George Seldes, *Facts and Fascism* (New York, In Fact Inc., 1943) p 158.

[17] Frank Donner, *The Age of Surveillance,* p 86–87.

[18] Ibid, p 98–99.

[19] Ibid, p 174.

[20] Henry Hoke, *It's a Secret* (New York, Pamphlet Press, 1946) p 70–73.

[21] Kim McQuid, *Uneasy Partners: Big Business in American Politics, 1945–1990* (Baltimore, John Hopkins Press, 1994) p 36–37.

[22] Charles Higham, *American Swastika* (Garden City, N.Y., Doubleday, 1985) p 135.

[23] Ibid, p 136–38.

[24] Another seemingly innocent association between fascists and Reagan was his refusal to grant a extradition request from Jim Garrison for Edgar Eugene Bradley, a right-wing preacher from North Hollywood, Calif., and part-time assistant to Carl McIntire, the fundamentalist minister who founded the American Counsel of Christian Churches. This is the only time in the history of California that a governor refused an extradition request. In one theory of the assassination of JFK, McIntire's group played a pivotal role. What is known is Bradley identified himself as a Secret Service agent to Deputy Sheriff Roger Craig in Dallas the day of the assassination, shortly after the fatal bullets were fired. Likewise, it should be noted that Bradley filed and won a libel suit over this incident. http://www.ratical.org/ratville/JFK/WTKaP.html

[25] Charles Higham, *American Swastika,* p 147.

[26] Joseph Bendersky, *The Jewish Threat* (New York, Perseus Books, 2000) p 232, 238, 274–79.

[27] George Seldes, *Facts and Fascism* p 262.

[28] I.F. Stone, *Business As Usual* (New York, Modern Age Books, 1941) p 63.

[29] Ibid, p 64.

[30] Ibid, p 73.

[31] Ibid, p 30–34.

[32] Ibid, p 84.

[33] Ibid, p 89.

[34] Ibid, p 98–102.

[35] Ibid, p 20.

[36] Ibid, p 21.

[37] Kim McQuid, *Uneasy Partners,* p 23–24.

[38] George Seldes, *Facts and Fascism,* p 99.

[39] Kenneth O'Reilly, *Hoover and the Un-Americans* (Philadelphia, Temple University Press, 1983) p 141.

[40] George Seldes, *Facts and Fascism.*

[41] George Seldes, *One Thousand Americans* (New York, Boni and Gaer, 1947) p 252.

[42] Ibid, p 252.

[43] Ibid, p 253.

[44] Lipset and Earl Raab, *The Politics of Unreason* (New York, Seymour Harper and Row, 1970) p 158–59.

[45] Frank Donner, *The Age of Surveillance,* p 50.

[46] Ibid, p 417.

[47] http://www.ssa.gov/history/fdrstmts.html#bill of rights

[48] http://www.igc.org/lpa/lpv26/lp05.htm

[49] Richard Rollins, *I Find Treason* (New York, William Morrow, 1941) p 81.

[50] http://newdeal.feri.org/students/end.htm

[51] Kenneth O'Reilly, *Hoover and the Un-Americans,* p 70.

[52] Ibid, p 50–51.

[53] Ibid, p 52.

[54] Ibid, p 53.

[55] Ibid, p 54–55.

[56] Benjamin Epstein, Arnold Foster, *The Radical Right* (New York, Vintage, 1967) p 207–08.

[57] Charles Higham, *American Swastika*, p 191–93.

[58] Ibid.

[59] Ibid, p 194–95.

[60] Bruce Catton, *The War Lords of Washington* (New York, Harcourt, Brace and Co., 1948) p 102.

[61] Ibid, p 244.

[62] Ibid, p 264.

[63] Fred Cook, *The Warfare State* (New York, Collier, 1962) p 76–77.

[64] Kim McQuid, *Uneasy Partners,* p 23–24.

[65] Charles Higham, *Trading with the Enemy* (New York, Barnes & Noble, 1983) p 222.

[66] http://newsweek.washingtonpost.com/nw-srv/issue/24_98b/printed/int/ eur/ovbz0324_2.htm

[67] U.S. Firms' Connection to Nazis Detailed, Reuters News Service, 1999, Jan. 14; Max Wallace, *The American Axis: Henry Ford, Charles Lindbergh, and the Rise of the Third Reich*, p. 334.

[68] http://www.igc.org/solidarity/atc/90Greenfield.html

[69] Charles Higham, *Trading with the Enemy,* p 1–19.

[70] Howard Amruster, *Treason's Peace* (New York, Crossroads, 1947) p 494–95.

[71] http://www.time.com/time/magazine/archive/1994/940502/940502. cover.obituary.html

[72] Fred Cook, *The Warfare State*, p 76–77.

[73] Charles Higham, *Trading with the Enemy,* p 20–31. See also Antony C. Sutton, *Wall Street and the Rise of Hitler*, http://reformed-theology.org/html/books/wall_street/index.html

[74] Ibid, p 27.

[75] Ibid, p 40–41.

[76] Ibid, p 38–39.

[77] Ibid, p 84.

[78] Ibid, p 93–115.

[79] Ibid, p 130–53.

[80] Anthony Summers, *The Arrogance of Power* (New York, Viking, 2000) p 401.

[81] Lipset and Earl Raab, *The Politics of Unreason*, p 435.

[82] Sara Diamond, *Roads to Dominion* (New York, Guilford Press, 1995) p 238.

[83] Lipset and Earl Raab, *The Politics of Unreason*, p 47–61.

[84] http://washingtonpost.com/wp-dyn/politics/news/postseries/ texasrecord/A8505-2000May4.html

[85] http://www.au.org/press/pr71001.htm

[86] http://uspolitics.about.com/library/weekly/aa071001a.htm

[87] Frank Bruni, Laurie Goodstein, 2001, New Bush Office Seeks Closer Ties to Church Groups, *New York Times,* Jan. 29.

[88] Fred Cook, *The Warfare State,* p 76–77.

[89] Harry and Bonardo Overstreet, *The Strange Tactics of Extremism*, (New York, W.W. Norton, 1964) p 197.

[90] Ibid, p 196–201.

[91] Curt Riess, *The Nazis Go Underground* (Garden City, Doubleday, 1944) p 126–27.

[92] Sara Diamond, *Roads to Dominion*, p 98–99.

[93] Fred Cook, *The Warfare State,* p 297–98.

[94] Richard Dudman, *Men of the Far Right* (New York, Pyramid, 1962) p 132.

[95] William Turner, *Power on the Right* (Berkeley, Ramparts Press, 1971) p 134.

[96] http://www.infidels.org/library/historica...dreiser/church_and_wealth_in_america.html

[97] Sara Diamond, *Roads to Dominion*, p 95–97.

[98] Sara Diamond, *Spiritual Warfare* (Boston, South End Press, 1989) p 46–47.

[99] http://www.ranknfile-ue.org/uen_nastybiz.html

[100] Max Wallace, *The American Axis: Henry Ford, Charles Lindbergh, and the Rise of the Third Reich*, St. Martin's Press (2003), p. 336. See also http://www.religioustolerance.org/fin_nazi.htm

[101] H. Montgomery Hyde, *Room 3603* (New York, Ballantine, 1962) p 80–81.

[1] Tom Bower, *The Pledge Betrayed* (Garden City, Doubleday, 1982) p 20.

[2] Ibid, p 125–27.

[3] Ibid, p 127.

[4] Ibid, p 127–28.

[5] Arthur Kahn, *Betrayal* (Warsaw, Poland, Ksiazka-I-Wiedza, 1950) p 23.

[6] Michael Sayers, Albert Kahn, *The Plot Against the Peace* (New York, Dial Press, 1945) p 31.

[7] Christopher Simpson, *The Splendid Blond Beast* (New York, Grove Press, 1993) p 356.

[8] James Bamford, *Body of Secrets* (New York, Anchor Books, 2002) p 7–23.

[9] Arthur Kahn, *Betrayal,* p 304.

[10] Reinhold Billstein, Karola Fings, Anita Kugler, Nicholas Levis, *Working for the Enemy* (Oxford, Berghahn Books, 2000) p 99.

[11] Ibid, p 118.

[12] Ibid, p 108.

[13] Ibid, p 108–09.

[14] Craig Roberts, *Kill Zone* (Tulsa, Consolidated Press International, 1997) p 154.

[15] http://www.airpower.maxwell.af.mil/airchronicles/apj/apj89/parker.html

[16] Anthony Sutton, *Wall Street and the Rise of Hitler* (Seal Beach, Calif., 76 Press, 1976) p 62–66.

[17] Ibid, p 98.

[18] http://www.capecodonline.com/obit

[19] http://www.boston.com/globe/nation/packages/secret_history/ index7_bar1.shtml

[20] Anthony Cave Brown, *The Last Hero* (New York, Vintage Books, 1982) p 324.

[21] Michael Beschloss, *The Conquerors* (New York, Simon and Schuster, 2002) p 72.

[22] Ibid, p 73.

[23] Ibid, p 190–91.

[24] Ibid, p 192–93.

[25] Ibid, p 208.

[26] Burton Hersh, *The Old Boys* (New York, Charles Scribner and Sons, 1992) p 143.

[27] Anthony Sutton, *Wall Street and the Rise of Hitler,* p 79–81.

[28] Burton Hersh, *The Old Boys,* p 144.

[29] Ibid, p 98–99.

[30] Ibid, p 145.

[31] Ibid, p 174.

[32] Ibid, p 175.

[33] Anthony Sutton, *Wall Street and the Rise of Hitler,* p 85.

[34] Edwin Black, *IBM and the Holocaust* (New York, Crown, 2001) p 409–10.

[35] Michael Sayers, Albert Kahn, *The Plot Against the Peace,* p 31.

[36] Ibid, p 30.

[37] Arieh Kochavi, *Prelude to Nuremberg* (Chapel Hill, N.C., University of North Carolina, 1998) p 10.

[38] Ibid, p 13.

[39] Ibid, p 15.

[40] Ibid, p 57.

[41] Ibid, p 82.

[42] John Loftus, Mark Aarons, *The Secret War Against the Jews,* (New York, St. Martin's, 1994) p 178–79.

[43] T.H. Tetens, *Germany Plots with the Kremlin* (New York, Henry Schunan, 1953) p 234–35.

[44] Arieh Kochavi, *Prelude to Nuremberg* (Chapel Hill, N.C., University of North Carolina, 1998) p 169.

[45] Ibid, p 244–47.

[46] R. Harris Smith, *OSS: The Secret History* (University of California Press, 1972) p 15.

[47] Charles Higham, *Trading with the Enemy* (New York, Barnes & Noble, 1983) p 61.

[48] Ibid, p 54–56.

[49] R. Harris Smith, *OSS: The Secret History.*

[50] Ibid, p 10–13.

[51] Ibid, p 18.

[52] Ibid, p 24.

[53] Ibid, p 33.

[54] Ibid, p 6.

[55] Ibid, p 88.

[56] http://www.consortiumnews.com/archive/xfile3.html

[57] R. Harris Smith, *OSS: The Secret History*, p 186.

[58] Ibid, p 222–23.

[59] Ibid, p 72–73.

[60] Ibid, p 85–86.

[61] Anthony Cave Brown, *The Last Hero,* p 706–19.

[62] R. Harris Smith, *OSS: The Secret History*, p 224–25.

[63] Ibid, p 223.

[64] Ibid.

[65] http://www.guardian.co.uk/Print/0,3858,4034066,00.html

[66] R. Harris Smith, *OSS: The Secret History*, p 235–36.

[67] Anthony Cave Brown, *The Last Hero,* p 638–44.

[68] Ibid, p 634–39.

[69] Ibid, p 639.

[70] Ibid, p 94.

[71] Ibid, p 111–15.

[72] Ibid, p 110.

[73] Ibid, p 775–77.

[74] Ibid.

[75] Ibid.

[76] R. Harris Smith, *OSS: The Secret History*, p 364.

[77] T.H. Tetens, *Germany Plots with the Kremlin*, p 183.

[78] Michael Beschloss, *The Conquerors,* p 236–37.

[79] T.H. Tetens, *Germany Plots with the Kremlin*, p 187.

[80] Ibid, p 233–38, 259–62, 266–70.

[81] Ibid, p 39–40.

[82] Ibid, p 84.

[83] Ibid, p 69.

[84] Ibid, p 70.

[85] Ibid, p 70–71.

[86] http://www.yahoo.com/text/headlines/960510/news/stories/ Reuters Nazis Plotted Post-WWII Return, 9/14/200

[87] T.H. Tetens, *Germany Plots with the Kremlin*, p 88.

[88] Ibid.

[89] T.H. Tetens, *The New Germany and the Old Nazis* (New York, Random House, 1961) p 112.

[90] Ibid, p 76–77.

[91] Ibid, p 79.

[92] T.H. Tetens, *Germany Plots with the Kremlin*, p 88.

[93] http://www.nizkor.org/features/techniques-of-denial/clay-koch-03.html

[94] Anthony Sutton, *Wall Street and the Rise of Hitler,* p 157–158.

[95] Ibid, p 159.

[96] Tom Bower, *The Pledge Betrayed*, p 321.

[97] Arthur Kahn, *Betrayal,* p 217.

[98] Tom Bower, *The Pledge Betrayed*, p 134–35.

[99] Arthur Kahn, *Betrayal,* p 219–20.

[100] Ibid.

[101] Ibid, p 221.

[102] Christopher Simpson, *The Splendid Blond Beast*, p 263–65.

[103] John Loftus, Mark Aarons, *The Secret War Against the Jews*, p 77.

[104] Arthur Kahn, *Betrayal*, p 291.

[105] http://www.court.state.nd.us/court/history/century/II.J.htm#N_244_

[106] Arthur Kahn, *Betrayal*, p 306.

[107] Ibid, p 308.

[108] T.H. Tetens, *Germany Plots with the Kremlin*, p 107.

[109] Arthur Kahn, *Betrayal*, p 308.

[110] Michael Beschloss, *The Conquerors*, p 63.

[111] John Loftus, Mark Aarons, *The Secret War Against the Jews*, p 128–32.

[112] Howard Ambuster, *Treason's Peace* (New York, Beechhurst Press, 1947) p 388.

[113] http://www.codoh.com/trials/trirecon.html

[114] Peter Maguire, *Law and War* (New York, Columbia University Press, 2001) p 208–09.

[115] Arthur Kahn, *Betrayal*, p 340–42.

[116] William Manchester, *The Arms of Krupp* (Boston, Little Brown, 1968) p 647–48.

[117] http://www.und.edu/dept/library/Collections/Langer/og19.html

[118] Peter Maguire, *Law and War*, p 219.

[119] T.H. Tetens, *The New Germany and the Old Nazis*, p 136.

[120] Tom Bower, *The Pledge Betrayed*, p 321.

[121] Peter Maguire, *Law and War*, p 213.

[122] William Manchester, *The Arms of Krupp*, p 651.

[123] Ibid, p 650.

[124] Ibid, p 463.

[125] Ibid, p 465.

[126] Ibid.

[127] Ibid, p 466–69.

[128] Ibid, p 407–08.

[129] Ibid, p 752–56.

[130] http://past.thenation.com/issue/981228/1228fisch.htm

[131] Tom Bower, *The Pledge Betrayed*, p 321.

[132] Alexander Cockburn, Jeffery St Clair, *Whiteout* (London, Verso, 1998) p 170.

[133] Ibid, p 171.

[134] Tom Bower, *The Pledge Betrayed*, p 136.

[135] Ibid, p 137–38.

[136] Ibid, p 151.

[137] T.H. Tetens, *The New Germany and the Old Nazis*, p 201–03.

[138] Tom Bower, *The Pledge Betrayed*, p 154.

[139] Ibid, p 155.

[140] Ibid, p 162.

[141] T.H. Tetens, *The New Germany and the Old Nazis*, p 38.

[142] Ibid, p 39–40.

[143] Ibid, p 40.

[144] Ibid, p 41.

[145] Ibid, p 44.

[146] Tom Bower, *The Pledge Betrayed*, p 357.

[147] T.H. Tetens, *The New Germany and the Old Nazis*, p 45. tr

[148] Ibid, p 46.

[149] Ibid, p 47.

[150] Ibid, p 48.

[151] Ibid, p 52.

[152] Tom Bower, *The Pledge Betrayed*, p 358

[153] T.H. Tetens, *The New Germany and the Old Nazis,* p 176.

[154] Ibid, p 177.

[155] Ibid, p 76.

[156] John Loftus, Mark Aarons, *The Secret War Against the Jews*, p 356–69.

[157] Anthony Cave Brown, *The Last Hero,* p 795–97

[158] Ibid, p 798.

[159] Ibid, p 800–01.

Chapter 7, Nazi Gold

[1] http://www.archives.gov/research_room/holocaust_era_assets/
research_plunder/nazi_gold_merkers_mine_treasure.html

[2] Tom Bowers, *Nazi Gold* (New York, Harper Collins, 1997) p 56.

[3] http://www.learntoquestion.com/data/difficultneutrality.html

[4] http://www.gold.org/pub_archive/pdf/Rs23.pdf

[5] http://dns.usis-israel.org.il/publish/report/ngrpt.pdf

[6] http://www.cia.gov/csi/studies/summer00/art04.html

[7] Charles Higham, *Trading with the Enemy* (Barnes & Noble, 1983) p 59–60.

[8] Mark Aarons, John Loftus, *Unholy Trinity* (New York, St. Martin's, 1991) p 277.

[9] Mark Aarons, John Loftus, *The Secret War Against the Jews* (New York, St. Martin's, 1994) p 79.

[10] Ibid, p 139.

[11] Ibid, p 111.

[12] Ibid, p 86.

[13] http://www.cia.gov/csi/studies/summer00/art04.html

[14] Mark Aarons, John Loftus, *Unholy Trinity,* p 234.

[15] http://www.cia.gov/csi/studies/summer00/art04.html

[16] Mark Aarons, John Loftus, *The Secret War Against the Jews,* p 110.

[17] http://www.cia.gov/csi/studies/summer00/art04.html

[18] Paul Manning, *Martin Bormann: Nazi in Exile* (Secaucus, N.J, Lyle Stuart, 1981) p 136.

[19] Ibid, p 132.

[20] Ibid, p 136.

[21] Ibid, p 139.

[22] Ibid, p 151.

[23] Ibid, p 152–53.

[24] Ibid, p 154.

[25] Ibid, p 155.

[26] Ibid, p 157.

[27] Ibid, p 158.

[28] Ian Sayer, Douglas Botting, *Nazi Gold,* (New York, Congdon Weed Inc., 1984) p 10.

[29] Ibid, p 20.

[30] Ibid, p 22–23.

[31] Ibid, p 26.

[32] Ibid, p 32.

[33] Ibid, p 74.

[34] Ibid, p 118–21.

[35] Ibid, p 131–32.

[36] Ibid, p 177.

[37] Ibid, p 192.

[38] Ibid, p 215–16.

[39] Ibid, p 232–33.

[40] Ibid, p 234.

[41] Ibid, p 285.

[42] Ibid, p 287–88.

[43] Ibid, p 346–50.

[44] Kenneth Alford, Theodore Savas, *Nazi Millionaires* (Havertown, Pa., Casemate, 2002) p 69–74.

[45] Ibid, p 84–85.

[46] http://193.114.50.5/events/nazigold/ngold1.pdf

[47] Ibid.

[48] http://www.copi.com/articles/nazibank.html

[49] Adam Lebor, *Hitler's Secret Bankers* (Secaucus, N.J., Citadel, 1970) p 206–07.

[50] http://dns.usis-israel.org.il/publish/report/ngrpt.pdf

[51] Ibid.

[52] http://news.bbc.co.uk/1/hi/world/40519.stm

[53] http://www.usembassy-israel.org.il/publish/report2/rpt_9806_ng_portugal.pdf

[54] http://dns.usis-israel.org.il/publish/report/ngrpt.pdf

[55] http://www.usembassy-israel.org.il/publish/report2/rpt_9806_ng_portugal.pdf

[56] http://216.239.51.100/search?q=cache:_D-rYE94qE8J:www.yad-vashem.org.il/download/about_holocaust/studies/louca_full.pdf+portugal +nazi+gold&hl=en&ie=UTF-8

[57] http://www.us-israel.org/jsource/Holocaust/assets1.html

[58] Uki Goni, *The Real Odessa* (London, Granta Books, 2002) p 2.

[59] Ibid, p 22.

[60] http://www.usembassy-israel.org.il/publish/report2/rpt_9806_ng_ argentina.pdf

[61] Sterling and Peggy Seagrave, *The Marcos Dynasty* (New York, Macmillan, 1988) p 139.

[62] Adam Lebor, *Hitler's Secret Bankers,* p 140–45.

[63] Ibid, p 138–39.

[64] Ibid, p 29.

[65] Ibid, p 52–53.

[66] Ibid, p 63–64.

[67] http://dns.usis-israel.org.il/publish/report/ngrpt.pdf

[68] Adam Lebor, *Hitler's Secret Bankers,* p 214, 106–07.

[69] http://dns.usis-israel.org.il/publish/report/ngrpt.pdf

[70] Ibid.

[71] Ibid.

[72] http://www.1939club.com/1939%20Meili-1.htm

[73] http://dns.usis-israel.org.il/publish/report/ngrpt.pdf

[74] "Nazi camp gold dispute," *The Times*, London, 1998, Aug. 21.

[75] Ladislas Farago, *Aftermath* Martin Bormann and the Fourth Reich (New York, Simon and Schuster, 1974) p 194

[76] http://www.popmatters.com/film/reviews/s/stealing-the-fire.shtml

[77] http://www.txpeer.org/Bush/Polluters_Bet_On_Bush.html

[78] Ladislas Farago, *Aftermath Martin Bormann and the Fourth Reich*, p 203.

[79] Ibid, p 216.

[80] Adam Lebor, *Hitler's Secret Bankers,* p 214.

[81] http://english.pravda.ru/world/2003/02/27/43768.html

[82] http://uboat.net/boats/u853.htm

[83] http://uboat.net/boats/u530.htm

[84] http://www.fletel.co.uk/press.html

[85] http://stonebooks.com/archives/000618.shtml

[86] Ibid.

[87] Sterling and Peggy Seagrave, *Gold Warriors* (Lodon,Verso, 2003) p 79.

[88] Uki Goni, *The Real Odessa*, p 2.

[89] Sterling and Peggy Seagrave, *The Yamato Dynasty* (New York, Broadway Books, 1999) p 172.

[90] Ibid, p 184.

[91] Ibid, p 186–87.

[92] Ibid, p 198.

[93] Ibid, p 202–18.

[94] Ibid, p 230.

[95] Ibid, p 294–95.

[96] Ibid, p 296–97.

[97] Ibid, p 293.

[98] David Guyatt, *The Secret Gold Treaty* (Solari Inc., 2000).

[99] Sterling and Peggy Seagrave, *The Marcos Dynasty,* p 139.

[100] Sterling and Peggy Seagrave, *Gold Warriors*, p 79.

[101] Ibid, p 1–5.

[102] Ibid, p 6.

[103] Ibid.

[104] Ibid, p 63.

[105] Ibid, p 8.

[106] Ibid, p 52.

[107] Ibid, p 56–57.

[108] Ibid, p 60–61

[109] Ibid, p 62.

[110] Ibid, p 63.

[111] Ibid, p 88–95.

[112] Ibid, p 89.

[113] Ibid, p 105.

[114] Ibid, p 108–14.

[115] Ibid, p 192–93.

[116] Kenneth Alford, *Nazi Plunder* (Cambridge, Da Capo, 2000) p iv–v.

[117] Ibid, p 17–19.

[118] Ibid, p 23–60.

[119] Ibid, p 61–75.

[120] Ibid, p 91.

[121] http://www.theoutlaws.com/gold4.htm

[122] http://news.bbc.co.uk/1/hi/world/34761.stm

[123] Ibid.

[124] http://www.cnn.com/2001/US/07/19/art.return/

Chapter 8, Ratlines, the CIA and the Nazis

[1] Burton Hersh, *The Old Boys: The American Elite and the Origins of the CIA* (New York, Macmillan Publishing, 1992) p 87.

[2] Ibid, p 378–79.

[3] Washington, D.C.: A key document in the history of covert warfare, the CIA's own internal investigation into the April 1961 Bay of Pigs debacle in Cuba, was made public today. The top secret, 150-page report, officially known as "The Inspector General's Survey of the Cuban Operation," castigates the agency for misinforming Kennedy administration officials, bad planning, inadequate intelligence, treating rebel leaders as "puppets," and conducting an overt military operation beyond "Agency responsibility as well as Agency capability." This quote was taken from a Web site containing the report at http://www.seas.gwu.edu/nsarchive/news/19980222.htm

[4] John Loftus, Mark Aarons, *The Secret War Against the Jews* (New York, St. Martin's Griffin, 1994) p 221.

[5] http://www.guardian.co.uk/Kosovo/Story/0,2763,203214,00.html

[6] http://parascope.com/articles/1196/nazis.htm

[7] James Bamford, *Body of Secrets* (New York, Anchor, 2002) p 72–89.

[8] http://remember.org/ideas/pensions.html, cited in Richard Boyden,
http://richardboyden.com/CIA_and_the_Nazis.htm

[9] http://secretary.state.org/www/briefings/statements/970812a.html

[10] Michael Sniffer, U.S. Moves to Deport Indiana Man for Helping Nazis, AP wire, 1998, Oct. 29.

[11] 5 U.S. Banks are Named in Report on Nazi Looting of Assets of Jews in France, AP Wire, 1999, Feb 3.

[12] http://newsweek.washingtonpost.com/nw-srv/issue/24_98b/printed/ int/eur/ovbz0324_2.htm

[13] http://www.jewishsf.com/bk980814/usbill.htm

[14] Martin Lee, *The Beast Reawakens* (New York, Routledge, 2000) p 40–41.

[15] Ibid, p 43–44.

[16] Ibid, p 42–43.

[17] http://www.wiesenthal.com/response/outrage.html

[18] T.H. Tetens, *Germany Plots with the Kremlin* (New York, Henry Schuman, 1953) p 233–35.

[19] John Loftus, Mark Aarons, *The Secret War Against the Jews,* p 100–01.

[20] Ibid, p 165–67.

[21] Ibid, p 73–80.

[22] Christopher Simpson, *The Splendid Blond Beast* (New York, Grove Press, 1993) p 205.

[23] Michael Beschloss, *The Conquerors* (New York, Simon and Schuster, 2002) p 205

[24] Christopher Simpson, *The Splendid Blond Beast,* p 218.

[25] John Loftus, Mark Aarons, *The Secret War Against the Jews,* p 60–61.

[26] Ibid, p 38–42.

[27] Ibid, p 20–21.

[28] Ibid, p 38–42.

[29] Ibid, p 67.

[30] Ibid, p 68–71.

[31] Ibid, p 65.

[32] Antony Sutton, *Wall Street and the Rise of Hitler* (Seal Beach, Calif., 76 Press, 1976) p 154.

[33] Howard Ambruster, *Treason's Peace* (New York, Beechhurst Press, 1947) p 405.

[34] Ibid, p 166.

[35] John Loftus, Mark Aarons, *The Secret War Against the Jews,* p 56.

[36] Ibid, p 221–22.

[37] Howard Blum, *Wanted!: The Search for Nazis in America,* (New York, New York Times Book Co., 1977) p 117–21.

[38] John Loftus, Mark Aarons, *The Secret War Against the Jews,* p 369.

[39] Russ Bellant, *Old Nazis, the New Right and the Republican Party* (Boston, South End Press, 1988) p 4.

[40] Ibid, p 5.

[41] John Loftus, Mark Aarons, *The Secret War Against the Jews,* p 122.

[42] Ibid, p 123.

[43] http://www.politicalamazon.com/l-pasztor.html

[44] Christopher Simpson, *Blowback* (New York, Weidenfeld and Nicolson, 1988) p 9.

[45] G. Domhoff, *Who Rules America* (Englewood Cliffs, N.J., Prentice Hall, 1967) p 76.

[46] Christopher Simpson, *Blowback,* p 232–35.

[47] John Loftus, Mark Aarons, *Unholy Trinity* (New York, St. Martin's, 1991) p 271.

[48] Christopher Simpson, *Blowback,* p 228.

[49] John Loftus, Mark Aarons, *The Secret War Against the Jews,* p 506.

[50] http://www.jfkconnections.com/cia.htm

[51] Christopher Simpson, *Blowback,* p 40–43.

[52] Heinz Hohne, Herman Zolling, *The General Was a Spy* (Coward, McCann and Geoghegan, 1971) p 93.

[53] http://web.jjay.cuny.edu/~jobrien/reference/ob62.html

[54] Bruce Canton, *The War Lords of Washington* (New York, Harcourt Brace and Co., 1948) p 286.

[55] Christopher Simpson, *Blowback,* p 63.

[56] Ibid, p 64.

[57] Linda Hunt, *Secret Agenda* (New York, St. Martin's Press, 1991) p 38–39, 138–39.

[58] Christopher Simpson, *Blowback,* p 61.

[59] Ibid, p 45.

[60] Burton Hersh, *The Old Boys,* p 250.

[61] Ibid, p 112–15.

[62] Christopher Simpson, *Blowback,* p 47.

[63] Ibid, p 138–42.

[64] John Loftus, *The Belarus Secret* (New York, Alfred Knopf, 1982) p 71.

[65] Ibid, p 88.

[66] Linda Hunt, *Secret Agenda,* p 9–10.

[67] James Bamford, *Body of Secrets,* p 15–17

[68] Linda Hunt, *Secret Agenda,* p 25.

[69] Ibid, p 36–39.

[70] Ibid, p 36–39.

[71] John Loftus, *The Belarus Secret,* p 82.

[72] http://parascope.com/articles/1196/nazis.htm

[73] Linda Hunt, *Secret Agenda,* p 1.

[74] Ibid, p 2.

[75] Ibid, p 33.

[76] Ibid, p 41–51.

[77] Christopher Simpson, *Blowback,* p 34–37.

[78] Ibid, p 115–23.

[79] Ibid, p 210.

[80] Christopher Simpson, *The Splendid Blond Beast,* p 218.

[81] John Loftus, *The Belarus Secret,* p 88.

[82] Christopher Simpson, *Blowback,* p 96–101.

[83] Ibid, p 112–15.

[84] Ibid, p 202–03.

[85] Linda Hunt, *Secret Agenda,* p 125–23.

[86] Ibid, p 130–33.

[87] John Loftus, *The Belarus Secret,* p 136.

[88] Ibid, p 139–41.

[89] Linda Hunt, *Secret Agenda,* p 175–77.

[90] Ibid, p 193.

[91] Ibid, p 184.

[92] Ibid, p 178–79.

[93] Ibid, p 179–80.

[94] Christopher Simpson, *Blowback,* p 210–15.

[95] http://66.102.7.104/search?q=cache:c64K0b_caJ0J:www.bullatomsci.org/pdf/temp/041_004_010.pdf+Karl+Blome+nazi&hl=en&start=5

[96] John Loftus, *The Belarus Secret,* p 88.

[97] Uki Goni, *The Real Odessa* (London, Granta Books, 2002) p 6–7.

[98] John Loftus, Mark Aarons, *Unholy Trinity,* p 37.

[99] Ibid.

[100] Ibid, p 38.

[101] Ibid, p 84.

[102] Christopher Simpson, *Blowback,* p 90–93.

[103] John Loftus, *The Belarus Secret,* p 82.

[104] John Loftus, Mark Aarons, *Unholy Trinity,* p 239.

[105] Vatican Linked to Nazi Gold, ABCNEWS.com.

[106] Christopher Simpson, *Blowback,* p 156–57.

[107] Ibid, p 126.

[108] Ibid, p 127.

[109] http://fraser.stlouisfed.org/publications/ei/1953/download/1334/07-1953.pdf

[110] Christopher Simpson, *Blowback,* p 135-136.

[111] James Bamford, *The Puzzle Place* (New York, Penguin Books, 1982) p 119.

[112] Angus Mackenzie, *Secrets: The CIA's War at Home,* (Berkeley, University of California Press, 1997) p 83.

[113] Christopher Simpson, *Blowback,* p 156–57.

[114] James Bamford, *The Puzzle Place,* p 308–09

[115] Angus Mackenzie, *Secrets: The CIA's War at Home,* p 60–67.

[116] Webster Tarpley and Anton Chaitkin, *George Bush: the Unauthorized Biography* (Joshua Tree, Calif, Progressive Press, 2004) p. 77, resp. http://www.tarpley.net/bush4.htm

[117] Linda Hunt, *Secret Agenda,* p 230–31.

[118] List of unclear authorship posted at a number of sites on the Internet, e.g. http://www.greatdreams.com

[132] http://news.bbc.co.uk/2/hi/europe/2948766.stm

[133] http://www.sfgate.com/cgi-bin/article.cgi?file=/chronicle/archive/2003/11/24 /MNG7U38LD81.DTL

[119] Donald Bain *The CIA's Control of Candy Jones* (Fort Lee, N.J., Barricade, 2002) See also Cathy O'Brien and Mark Phillips, *TRANCE Formation of America: The True Life Story of a CIA Slave* (Reality Marketing, 1995)

[120] John DeCamp, *The Franklin Cover Up* (Lincoln, Neb., AWT, 1996).

[121] Ibid, p 10.

[122] Ibid, p 11.

[123] Ibid, p 12.

[124] Ibid, p 4.

[125] Ibid, p 177.

[126] Ibid, p 326.

[127] Ibid, p 326–27.

[128] Ibid, p 320–22.

[129] Ibid, p 177–78.

[130] Ibid, p 178–79.

[131] Ibid, p 179–80.

[134] William Blum, *Killing Hope: U.S. Military and CIA Intervention Since WWII* (Monroe, Maine, Common Courage Press, 1995) p 64–72

[135] Noam Chomsky, *The Washington Connection and Third World Fascism* (Boston, South End Press, 1979).

[136] Martin Lee, *The Beast Reawakens* p 123–24.

[137] Ibid, p 124–26.

[138] Ibid, p 150.

[139] Ibid, p 184.

[140] Ibid, p 184–85.

[141] Ibid, p 134–36.

[142] http://www.sfgate.com/cgi-bin/article.cgi?file=/chronicle/archive/2003/11/24 /MNG7U38LD81.DTL

[143] William Blum, *Killing Hope,* p 72–83.

[144] http://www.globalexchange.org/campaigns/guatemala/1999/ anzueto0226.html

[145] http://www.igc.apc.org/lawg/soafull.html

[146] http://fhrg.org/trafic.htm

[147] William Blum, *Killing Hope,* p 206.

[148] Ibid, p 207.

[149] Ibid, p 209.

[150] Ibid, p 210.

[151] Ibid, p 210.

[152] http://foia.state.gov/Reports/ChurchReport.asp

[153] http://www.sfbg.com/reality/02.html

[155] http://www.all-natural.com/whiteout.html

[154] http://www.ionet.net/~everett/CIADRUGS.html

[156] http://www.copvcia.com/volii.htm

[157] John Perkins, *Confessions of an Economic Hit Man* (San Francisco, Berrett-Koehler, 2004).

[158] Ibid, p 212.

[159] Ibid, p 141–57.

[160] http://webusers.anet-stl.com/~civil/docs-militarycomplexeisenhower 1961.htm